THE CAROLINA RHETORIC

For English 102

David Fossler/Shutterstock.com

Spring 2019

USC Columbia
The Department of English

Editors:
Sebastian Ivy
Gareth Rees-White

hayden-mcneil
Macmillan Learning

ISBN 978-1-5339-1017-2

Macmillan Learning Curriculum Solutions
14903 Pilot Drive
Plymouth, MI 48170
www.macmillanlearning.com

Fisk 1017-2 W19

Acknowledgements

Alter, Charlotte, "Revenge Porn: How Women Are Fighting Against Revenge Photos" from TIME, June 13, 2017. © 2017 Time Inc. All rights reserved. Reprinted from TIME Magazine and published with permission of Time Inc. Reproduction in any manner in any language in whole or in part without written permission is prohibited.

American Immigration Council, "The Cost of Immigration Enforcement and Border Security." January 25, 2017. https://www.americanimmigrationcouncil.org/research/the-cost-of-immigration-enforcement-and-border-security. Reprinted by permission of the American Immigration Council.

Acknowledgements and copyrights are continued at the back of the book on pages 507–510, which constitute an extension of the copyright page.

TABLE OF CONTENTS

INTRODUCTION

A text is made up of multiple writings, drawn from many cultures and entering into mutual relations of dialogue, parody, contestation.

–Roland Barthes, "The Death of the Author"

Interpretation reveals its complexity when we realize that a new force can only appear and appropriate an object by first of all putting on the mask of the forces which are already in possession of the object.

–Gilles Deleuze, Nietzsche & Philosophy

As students, teachers, recent graduates, or seasoned professionals, we are constantly called upon to compose our ideas. Whether we compose through speech, gesture, art, digital media, or writing—whatever mode we choose situates our thoughts in relation to what others have said. These others to whom we respond may be colleagues, clients, acquaintances, supervisors, team members, half-cousins twice removed, arch-rivals, longstanding friends, or even curious strangers in an elevator. They may be indistinct groups of people we may never meet—or that *particular* relative at Thanksgiving dinner. In other words, while we inhabit the world, we also interact with it: we are constantly reacting and responding to what happens around us. *The Carolina Rhetoric* is designed to aid you in thinking about, researching, and composing the *ways* in which you respond to what happens around you. It encourages you to consider—both carefully and critically—the rhetorical situation surrounding each conversation you enter. In doing so, you'll not only hone your ability to respond to others in a way that is, as Joseph Harris puts it, both "generous and assertive," but you'll also be better equipped to add to conversations and to push them in other, productive, directions.

One of the central goals of *The Carolina Rhetoric* is to offer its users a range of readings, exercises, and activities grounded in the rhetorical tradition. As such, the 2019 edition marks key changes, continuing to refine and tune itself toward an ever-changing audience, even as it models much of its content and structure on the 2018 and 2017 editions, edited by Amber Lee and Ben Harley, respectively.

Part One consists of definitions, exercises, and activities surrounding rhetorical terms as well as supplemental readings chosen to help illustrate important aspects of each chapter, while Part Two is comprised of selected readings on five current, open social debates. Important additions to the 2019 edition offer new perspectives on global and transnational issues: Part One includes revised concept definitions and a new chapter structure, while Part Two has updated over half of its content—content which presents *kairotic* arguments through diverse perspectives. The 2019 *Carolina Rhetoric* considers the ways in which new, overlooked, or underprivileged issues, conversations, and texts have come to light since its previous publication—through the influence of the past, tumultuous year.

The concepts outlined in Part One, then, lay the groundwork for entering discourse in rhetorical study: they provide a map of terms and concepts which help its users navigate other terms and concepts in Part One, as well as the readings in Part Two. In the new edition, Part One is organized to move from analysis to composition, and from the general rhetorical situation to specific arguments. However, it would be a mistake to assume that any portion of *The Carolina Rhetoric* provides a linear, simple blueprint, which, if followed, can be executed to—voilà!—produce a (good) composition. Composing rarely (if ever) happens that way. For example, in English 101, you practiced revision strategies which helped you reassess, recompose, and rewrite your essays in ways which did not always follow traditional "writing process" steps (Invention, Arrangement, Style, Memory, Delivery —or— Prewriting, Drafting, Revising, Editing, Publishing). To use another example, this very introduction comes *first*, yet it was composed *last*, through *many* revisions, *after* the book's contents were confirmed and assembled—because, let's face it, how do you introduce a book when you don't know what the book will contain?

Furthermore, Part One is characterized by many authors. In fact, the differences afforded by multiple authors is part of what makes this book so unique: *The Carolina Rhetoric* is the result of a continuing collaboration between graduate students and faculty members at USC. These scholars have donated their time and expertise to compose the definitions, questions, and exercises in Part One. Their contributions create a collection which highlights a combined perspective in the field broadly writ, yet also features individual specialties in particular practices. Because of such localized and focused attention, *The Carolina Rhetoric* was designed *rhetorically*: it was designed and written *by* USC's First-Year English program to cater *toward* the needs of its students, instructors, and the overall English 102 course design.

Ultimately, *The Carolina Rhetoric* asks you to reassess *how* you can be an ethical, informed, and invested reader and composer, while also situating each argument in a larger context (one you may not even originally recognize) and creating connections to other ways of thinking (connections which may seem, at the outset, tenuous). The concepts, habits, and theories included in this book help to offer this opportunity: they provide methods of interacting with other arguments in ways you are not used to or haven't considered. They offer ways of making arguments across other arguments, connections across other connections.

Such vast diversity of reading—from the definitions of rhetorical concepts in Part One to the differing styles and content matter of Part Two—can certainly be disorienting. However, it is important to be introduced to a variety of ideas, ways of writing, and genres—that is, as many as this genre of a physical book might allow. (For example, one of the genre constraints of this reader is that we can't include videos, GIFs, or moving images—nor can we include outside smelling, tasting, sonic, or tactile content beyond the pages.) Additionally, some of the included texts have been translated into English from other languages, while others have a markedly non-academic style: these differences may challenge you because they aren't, perhaps, what you're used to encountering in a reader. Furthermore, other works may be excerpts from longer pieces. While we would have liked to keep every piece fully intact, doing so would have made the size and cost of this book unreasonable—it is already long enough. Nonetheless, you are encouraged to research the concepts, arguments, authors, full texts, and lines of thought you come across in this book—and sometimes that might involve reading the entirety of a text beyond what has been excerpted here.

The 2019 edition of *The Carolina Rhetoric* continues lines set forth in English 101: it offers ways of entering conversations, and, furthermore, pushes its readers to consider the rhetorical and ethical implications of *how* such conversations are taken up, circulated, and dispersed. In other words, while English 101 provided ways of engaging with the content, with the *what* of a text through Close Reading, and then, asking *why* of these texts through Coming to Terms, English 102 continues this trajectory by asking *how*. *How* do ideas connect, make sense, persuade, dissuade, solve problems, wreak havoc, or make *happen*? Where Part One approaches these questions theoretically, through rhetorical concepts and analysis, Part Two is more concrete—offering you specific examples of conversations and arguments current to our society. This difference is essential: the boundaries between parts, units, concepts, theories, arguments, and styles is porous, and exploring that porosity is part of what we seek to do both as academics, and as people inhabiting and interacting with the world. Theory and practice are inevitably intertwined, and we encourage you to explore this interconnection. Although its structure is limited by its own genre, *The Carolina Rhetoric* nevertheless encourages its users not to be limited by its organization, but to follow connections—no matter how tenuous—whenever they spark curiosity.

—Amber Lee, with Sebastian Ivy

PART ONE

UNIT 1

ANALYZING SITUATIONS

CHAPTER 1

Conditions of Possibility

Rhetoric happens in specific situations—there is no standard individual rhetorical situation. As such, developing rhetorical awareness and an ability to compose rhetorically begins with your ability to analyze these situations. If you are not aware of the situation surrounding a particular debate, then your response is in many ways a shot in the dark. However, simply understanding a situation is not always enough to be able to intervene in it—this book is designed to provide you with rhetorical tools for composing interventions into these situations. More specifically, rhetoric is concerned with interventions that have the ability to create some kind of practical change in these situations. Rhetoric, then, has what we call **conditions of possibility**: certain qualities of a situation that allow for change by rhetorical means.

Before we proceed to exploring some of the most important aspects of situations and methods for analyzing them, then, this chapter addresses four concepts—argument, argumentation, ethics, and bias—that help to outline the conditions of possibility for rhetoric to work effectively. As you learn the conditions for each of these concepts, it is important to remember that they are not hard and fast rules. Rather, they are what is called an **ideal case**—the kind of perfect situation that rarely happens in the real world. Ideal cases are common heuristics, or strategies, for understanding the largest variables in a situation. For instance, in trigonometry, the formula that helps you calculate the various sides of a triangle is accurate in an ideal or perfect situation. In the real world, triangles are never perfect—but the formula will still provide a close result. Similarly, when you examine the conditions of possibility for rhetoric in a specific situation, each situation will vary from the ideal—but understanding how they vary is an important aspect of rhetorical analysis.

As you read about and work with these concepts, also pay attention to the ways that they interact—far from being isolated things, each is closely related to the others. Ask yourself, for instance, how bias can interact with argumentation, or how argumentation and ethics are related to each other; the more familiar you become with these relationships, the more easily you will be able to analyze situations.

Argument

It conjures up many different scenes, and happens in many different situations: heated political debate over holidays, friendly antagonism over the best restaurants, courtroom dramas, controversy over current events. The ancient Greeks of Athens positioned **argument** at the core of democratic government, and it is still an important cornerstone of contemporary American society. Argument, unsurprisingly, is also a complicated topic—it has perhaps as many different definitions as it has scenes, situations, and historical moments. How we define arguments has a direct influence on what kind of argument we expect to have. As such, it is necessary to begin a course on argument with a more specific sense of the topic under discussion.

This book will discuss a number of different ways to think about argument, many of which are complementary and can work together, and some of which are more contradictory; as you will learn, different situations often call for different approaches to argument. However, all of the approaches discussed here have at least one thing in common: an understanding of what argument is *not*. Argument is *not* simply contradicting another person, group, or idea. While gainsaying can and does happen in the course of argument (see, for a humorously exaggerated example of this, Monty Python's "Argument Clinic" linked at the end of this chapter), it acts as a dead end, where no progress can be made. The flip side of this negative definition of argument is an important positive definition. Argument, as it is treated here, is concerned with some kind of practical outcome for particular people—to put it in terms you will discuss in Chapter 2, argument always has both **stakes** and **stakeholders**.

These two points—that argument is not gainsaying and that it is concerned with the practical—apply to argument in the general sense. Before we continue, it is important to note the distinction between this general sense of argument and the specific sense of *an* argument. In the general sense, you might think of argument as a particular kind of conversation—the conversation with your friends in which you eventually decide where to go to dinner, for instance. In the specific sense, *an* argument refers to a particular kind of statement: "we should go to 'Restaurant X,' because it's close and has both carnivorous and vegan options." At the end of this Unit, in Chapter 3, page 32, you will learn a robust method for analyzing specific arguments called **the Toulmin model**. For now, however, we can say that at its simplest, *an* argument has at least two parts: a claim ("we should go to 'Restaurant X'"), and some kind of support for that claim ("because it's close and has both options"). Thus, you can think of the general argument as a conversation (where to eat?) that consists of a series of specific arguments for different positions ("Restaurant X, Y, or Z," "because A, B, or C"), oriented toward a particular practical outcome (full bellies).

This basic structure of specific arguments is particularly important because it allows us to discuss the difference between an argument and an opinion. As you discussed in your English 101 course, an opinion is a statement or claim presented without support, based on an assumption, a personal experience, or perhaps a general public sentiment. Just as an analysis is different from an opinion, an opinion is different from an argument. An argument must be supported by some kind of fact or knowledge. If you or another party to the argument cannot articulate this support, the claim is simply an opinion that can't function within the guidelines of **argumentation**.

Argumentation

Where **argument** refers to particular, concrete things (conversations and state-ments), **argumentation** generally refers to theories that guide and describe how those concrete arguments work—or why they don't. To this end, argumentation theory addresses logical fallacies, the relationship between claims and supports, and how to evaluate arguments. Just like argument, argumentation is a particu-larly complex and diverse topic; in one way or another, every chapter and every concept in this book is an aspect of argumentation. First, though, we need to outline one of the most fundamental and important aspects of argumentation: its conditions of possibility.

In order for argumentation to work, certain conditions must be in place. We've already discussed a number of them—the statements need to be arguments rather than opinions, the conversation should not consist of gainsaying, and there must be desired outcomes. These don't, however, exhaust the conditions of possibility for argumentation. In no particular order, you also need to consider:

- An **arguable issue**. One of the easiest ways to tell if the issue or outcome is arguable is to turn it into a question; if this question requires a yes or no answer, it isn't arguable.

- **At least two reasonable positions** on the issue. If there is only one position, there is no possibility of argument.

- Some kind of **common ground** between the different positions of the argu-ment. Without some common ground between the participants, there is no possibility for agreement—a practical outcome is impossible.

- The issue **should not be too polarizing**. In the case of many polarizing issues—abortion, for instance—the participants in an argument will often refuse to recognize possible common ground.

- The issue, however, **should not be trivial**. Another way to say this is that the issue should be important enough that all participants in the argument care about its outcome.

- The specific statements made need to be **arguments, not opinions**. This is because these statements need to be open to discussion, analysis, and evaluation—methods by which arguments move forward.

Inevitably, not every conversation we might call an argument meets these conditions of possibility. However, these criteria are used to describe the optimal conditions for argument to proceed both **ethically** and with the **least possible bias**.

Ethics and Bias

It can seem like the unethical win arguments, their inflammatorily biased opinions igniting their followers. Yet, while it can be tempting to see recent trends and give in to the screaming voices telling you to abandon **ethics**, one way or another, the unethical *always* fail, it can just take time.

Otherwise known as **moral philosophy**, ethics are those principles that govern our day-to-day behavior. While you will later learn about building *ethos* in an argument, for now, turn inwards and ask what your guiding principles are. In other words, what are the principles that you always strive to head towards? These are your core ethical principles and are what you turn towards when interacting with others, even those who disagree with your views. Ethics, in short, are what prevent us from simply punching those we harbor abhorrence for.

Your ethics evolve with each and every interaction you have: what was a simple black and white situation reveals itself to be a world of grey. Indeed, by being aware of your rhetorical situation, you can understand how each of these interactions shapes your worldview. To ignore the opinions of others because they are different from yours is as unethical as forcing your own opinion onto others: ethical rhetoric is all about engaging in conversation. In other words, an ethical argument looks towards any and all viewpoints before making claims.

When reading an author you disagree with, ask: what is their ethical viewpoint? What guiding principles dictate how *they* are approaching the discussion, and how are your principles affecting how *you* approach them? In other words, what **biases** are at play? An argument should never be a case of "us" vs. "them"; just because something disagrees with your personal ethics does not mean it is inherently wrong, as your biases may distract you from deeper truths.

Despite being a term that is thrown around negatively—"the argument was clearly biased, so can be ignored"—**bias** is perfectly natural. Indeed, the word originally came from knitting, describing the way cloth naturally falls on a divide. In short, everyone you know is biased: your parents, friends, co-workers, and—yes—yourself. Your bias is simply the way in which you personally lean. As such, you are biased towards everything in life: your interests, your work, your lifestyle, your fashion choices. You *can* be biased on political issues, but you could also be biased towards wearing red shirts over blue, listening to heavy metal over jazz, or watching *Star Wars* over *Star Trek*. Everything about you is influenced by your biases, and your bias is influenced by everything: the political views of your parents, the news media you imbibe, your friendship circles, even the most recent film you watched or book you read. This is *not* to say that you should ignore your inherent biases.

Have you ever begun a research project, only to find that all sources agree with you? *This* is **confirmation bias**: only reading sources that support a preconceived thesis, avoiding those that disagree with your **ethical principles**. It is why we all have to read widely before formulating an argument: if we only read sources that agree with our point of view (even if this is a subconscious decision), it is impossible to give the other side a chance, leading to an unethical argument. Whenever entering an argument, read widely before coming to a stance.

Another issue can arise when you don't realize—or, perhaps, want to recognize—that your sources *are and will always be* biased. This is especially problematic if you have spent your life watching or reading specific news sources: it can be easy to adopt that worldview. A useful tool to identify where your preferred media leans is Vanessa Otero's "What Makes a News Source 'Good'?" which can be found here: https://www.adfontesmedia.com/the-chart-second-edition/. If you typically only read sources that lean left, you should balance them out with additional sources that lean right, and vice versa. You also *need* to supplement your news choices with non-partisan sources: these are those sources that explicitly work to *not* offer bias in one direction or another. While it is important to note that it is impossible to report "facts" in a truly non-biased way, sources like *Politifact* are still extremely helpful to find your own position on a subject: once you have taken away the intentionally biased voices telling you *where* you *should* stand on an issue, and are left with as central a view as possible, you can find your true stance within the rhetorical parameters offered by the facts.

Lean so far in one direction that you lose sight of both the other "side," and your personal ethics, and you become prejudiced. When you meet those who are biased to this point—and you *will*—your weapon is consideration. Do not fight irrationally biased claims with anger: fight them with clearly stated facts that cannot be disputed; fight them with the rhetorical awareness you are currently developing, and just maybe they will begin to see just how prejudiced they have become. In other words, stay true to your **ethics**.

Discussion Questions

1. Is it possible to take an opinion and evolve it into an argument? Practice! Each of you will write down a non-offensive personal opinion, and as a group we will try to turn it into an arguable statement.

2. Turn to a reading of your choice in Part Two, Unit One. As a class, we will walk through this article and identify where and when it hits the conditions needed to be considered an argument. What can we do if we find an article that doesn't hit these conditions?

3. Should influential public figures (think: politicians) have to outwardly discuss and/or defend their personal ethics and biases before adopting their podium of power? How might they be able to identify what their personal biases are?

4. Think about news sources: in what ways do the biases of production companies change the way the news is reported? Can you think of specific examples of when news-bias completely changed your view of a subject? Otero's chart may be helpful here. Consider either:

    a. Take the major news networks (Fox, CNN, MSNBC, BBC, Al Jazeera, etc.), and place them on a bias chart: left, bi-partisan, and right leaning.

        Or

    b. Take the major social media news sources (Facebook and Twitter), and place the trending stories on a bias chart: left, bi-partisan, and right leaning.

5. Does knowing the personal ethics of a friend change your opinion of them? What if you find out they fall on the other side of a particularly close issue to you? How do you reconcile this?

Exercises

1. Watch Monty Python's "Argumentation Clinic." With a partner, bullet point a new script that turns this gainsaying into a legitimate argument.

2. Pick any text from Part Two, Unit One. Highlight any areas where the author offers an opinion instead of an argument, then re-write these statements argumentatively.

3. Consider your own personal ethics, and draw up a list of five ethical principles you hold dear. Take a particularly strong item from this list and write a paragraph explaining just *why* you feel this way about the issue. Now, turn things around: write a second paragraph arguing for why you should, perhaps, see things differently. What common ground can be found between these?

4. Take today's other reading(s). In your group, work through paragraph by paragraph, listing out all the biases, placing them into two categories: implicit (unspoken) and explicit (spoken). Once you've finished, use this information

to write a short profile of the author: what can you *now* learn about them that you could not before?

5. Choose a *kairotic* topic. Find an article discussing said topic from a news source that leans in one direction, and note the biases. Now, find an article discussing the same topic but from the other "side": how different is the "take"?

Supplemental Readings

FactCheck.org's "How to Spot Fake News"
Eugene Kiely and Lori Robertson

Fake news is nothing new. But bogus stories can reach more people more quickly via social media than what good old-fashioned viral emails could accomplish in years past.

Concern about the phenomenon led Facebook and Google to announce that they'll crack down on fake news sites, restricting their ability to garner ad revenue. Perhaps that could dissipate the amount of malarkey online, though news consumers themselves are the best defense against the spread of misinformation.

Not all of the misinformation being passed along online is complete fiction, though some of it is. Snopes.com has been exposing false viral claims since the mid 1990s, whether that's fabricated messages, distortions containing bits of truth and everything in between. Founder David Mikkelson warned in a Nov. 17 article not to lump everything into the "fake news" category. "The fictions and fabrications that comprise fake news are but a subset of the larger *bad news* phenomenon, which also encompasses many forms of shoddy, unresearched, error-filled, and deliberately misleading reporting that do a disservice to everyone," he wrote.

A lot of these viral claims aren't "news" at all, but fiction, satire and efforts to fool readers into thinking they're for real.

We've long encouraged readers to be skeptical of viral claims, and make good use of the delete key when a chain email hits their inboxes. In December 2007, we launched our Ask FactCheck feature, where we answer readers' questions, the vast majority of which concern viral emails, social media memes and the like. Our first story was about a made-up email that claimed then-House Speaker Nancy Pelosi wanted to put a "windfall" tax on all stock profits of 100 percent and give the money to, the email claimed, "the 12 Million Illegal Immigrants and other unemployed minorities." We called it "a malicious fabrication"—that's "fake news" in today's parlance.

In 2008, we tried to get readers to rid their inboxes of this kind of garbage. We described a list of red flags—we called them Key Characteristics of Bogusness—that were clear tip-offs that a chain email wasn't legitimate. Among them: an anonymous author; excessive exclamation points, capital letters and misspellings; entreaties that "This is NOT a hoax!"; and links to sourcing that does not support or completely contradicts the claims being made.

Those all still hold true, but fake stories—as in, completely made-up "news"— has grown more sophisticated, often presented on a site designed to look (sort of) like a legitimate news organization. Still, we find it's easy to figure out what's real and what's imaginary if you're armed with some critical thinking and fact-checking tools of the trade.

Here's our advice on how to spot a fake:

Consider the source. In recent months, we've fact-checked fake news from abcnews.com.co (not the actual URL for ABC News), WTOE 5 News (whose "about" page says it's "a fantasy news website"), and the Boston Tribune (whose "contact us" page lists only a gmail address). Earlier this year, we debunked the claim that the Obamas were buying a vacation home in Dubai, a made-up missive that came from WhatDoesItMean.com, which describes itself as "One Of The Top Ranked Websites In The World for New World Order, Conspiracy Theories and Alternative News" and further says on its site that most of what it publishes is fiction.

Clearly, some of these sites do provide a "fantasy news" or satire warning, like WTOE 5, which published the bogus headline, "Pope Francis Shocks World, Endorses Donald Trump for President, Releases Statement." Others aren't so upfront, like the Boston Tribune, which doesn't provide any information on its mission, staff members or physical location—further signs that maybe this site isn't a legitimate news organization. The site, in fact, changed its name from Associated Media Coverage, after its work had been debunked by fact-checking organizations.

Snopes.com, which has been writing about viral claims and online rumors since the mid-1990s, maintains a list of known fake news websites, several of which have emerged in the past two years.

Read beyond the headline. If a provocative headline drew your attention, read a little further before you decide to pass along the shocking information. Even in legitimate news stories, the headline doesn't always tell the whole story. But fake news, particularly efforts to be satirical, can include several revealing signs in the text. That abcnews.com.co story that we checked, headlined "Obama Signs Executive Order Banning The Pledge Of Allegiance In Schools Nationwide," went on to quote "Fappy the Anti-Masturbation Dolphin." We have to assume that the many readers who asked us whether this viral rumor was true hadn't read the full story.

Check the author. Another tell-tale sign of a fake story is often the byline. The pledge of allegiance story on abcnews.com.co was supposedly written by "Jimmy Rustling." Who is he? Well, his author page claims he is a "doctor" who won "fourteen Peabody awards and a handful of Pulitzer Prizes." Pretty impressive, if true. But it's not. No one by the name of "Rustling" has won a Pulitzer or Peabody award. The photo accompanying Rustling's bio is also displayed on another bogus story on a different site, but this time under the byline "Darius Rubics." The Dubai story was written by "Sorcha Faal, and as reported to her Western Subscribers." The Pope Francis story has no byline at all.

What's the support? Many times these bogus stories will cite official—or official-sounding—sources, but once you look into it, the source doesn't back up the claim. For instance, the Boston Tribune site wrongly claimed that President

Obama's mother-in-law was going to get a lifetime government pension for having babysat her granddaughters in the White House, citing "the Civil Service Retirement Act" and providing a link. But the link to a government benefits website doesn't support the claim at all.

The banning-the-pledge story cites the number of an actual executive order—you can look it up. It doesn't have anything to do with the Pledge of Allegiance.

Another viral claim we checked a year ago was a graphic purporting to show crime statistics on the percentage of whites killed by blacks and other murder statistics by race. Then-presidential candidate Donald Trump retweeted it, telling Fox News commentator Bill O'Reilly that it came "from sources that are very credible." But almost every figure in the image was wrong—FBI crime data is publicly available—and the supposed source given for the data, "Crime Statistics Bureau–San Francisco," doesn't exist.

Recently, we've received several questions about a fake news story on the admittedly satirical site Nevada County Scooper, which wrote that Vice President-elect Mike Pence, in a "surprise announcement," credited gay conversion therapy for saving his marriage. Clearly such a "surprise announcement" would garner media coverage beyond a website you've never heard of. In fact, if you Google this, the first link that comes up is a Snopes.com article revealing that this is fake news.

Check the date. Some false stories aren't completely fake, but rather distortions of real events. These mendacious claims can take a legitimate news story and twist what it says—or even claim that something that happened long ago is related to current events.

Since Trump was elected president, we've received many inquiries from readers wanting to know whether Ford had moved car production from Mexico to Ohio, because of Trump's election. Readers cited various blog items that quoted from and linked to a CNN Money article titled "Ford shifts truck production from Mexico to Ohio." But that story is from August 2015, clearly not evidence of Ford making any move due to the outcome of the election. (A reminder again to check the support for these claims.)

One deceptive website didn't credit CNN, but instead took CNN's 2015 story and slapped a new headline and publication date on it, claiming, "Since Donald Trump Won The Presidency ... Ford Shifts Truck Production From Mexico To Ohio." Not only is that a bogus headline, but the deception involves copyright infringement.

If this Ford story sounds familiar, that's because the CNN article has been distorted before.

In October 2015, Trump wrongly boasted that Ford had changed its plans to build new plants in Mexico, and instead would build a plant in Ohio. Trump took credit for Ford's alleged change of heart and tweeted a link to a story on a blog called Prntly.com, which cited the CNN Money story. But Ford hadn't changed its plans at all, and Trump deserved no credit.

In fact, the CNN article was about the transfer of some pickup assembly work from Mexico to Ohio, a move that was announced by Ford in March 2014. The plans for new plants in Mexico were still on, Ford said. "Ford has not spoken with Mr. Trump, nor have we made any changes to our plans," Ford said in a statement.

Is this some kind of joke? Remember, there is such thing as satire. Normally, it's clearly labeled as such, and sometimes it's even funny. Andy Borowitz has been writing a satirical news column, the Borowitz Report, since 2001, and it has appeared in the *New Yorker* since 2012. But not everyone gets the jokes. We've fielded several questions on whether Borowitz's work is true.

Among the headlines our readers have flagged: "Putin Appears with Trump in Flurry of Swing-State Rallies" and "Trump Threatens to Skip Remaining Debates If Hillary Is There." When we told readers these were satirical columns, some indicated that they suspected the details were far-fetched but wanted to be sure.

And then there's the more debatable forms of satire, designed to pull one over on the reader. That "Fappy the Anti-Masturbation Dolphin" story? That's the work of online hoaxer Paul Horner, whose "greatest coup," as described by the *Washington Post* in 2014, was when Fox News mentioned, as fact, a fake piece titled, "Obama uses own money to open Muslim museum amid government shutdown." Horner told the *Post* after the election that he was concerned his hoaxes aimed at Trump supporters may have helped the campaign.

The posts by Horner and others—whether termed satire or simply "fake news"—are designed to encourage clicks, and generate money for the creator through ad revenue. Horner told the *Washington Post* he makes a living off his posts. Asked why his material gets so many views, Horner responded, "They just keep passing stuff around. Nobody fact-checks anything anymore."

Check your biases. We know this is difficult. Confirmation bias leads people to put more stock in information that confirms their beliefs and discount information that doesn't. But the next time you're automatically appalled at some Facebook post concerning, say, a politician you oppose, take a moment to check it out.

Try this simple test: What other stories have been posted to the "news" website that is the source of the story that just popped up in your Facebook feed? You may be predisposed to believe that Obama bought a house in Dubai, but how about a story on the same site that carries this headline: "Antarctica 'Guardians' Retaliate Against America With Massive New Zealand Earthquake." That, too, was written by the prolific "Sorcha Faal, and as reported to her Western Subscribers."

We're encouraged by some of the responses we get from readers, who—like the ones uncertain of Borowitz's columns—express doubt in the outrageous, and just want to be sure their skepticism is justified. But we are equally discouraged when we see debunked claims gain new life.

We've seen the resurgence of a fake quote from Donald Trump since the election—a viral image that circulated last year claims Trump told *People* magazine in 1998: "If I were to run, I'd run as a Republican. They're the dumbest group of voters in the country. They believe anything on Fox News. I could lie and they'd still eat it up. I bet my numbers would be terrific." We found no such quote in *People*'s archives from 1998, or any other year. And a public relations representative for the magazine confirmed that. *People*'s Julie Farin told us in an email last year: "We combed through every Trump story in our archive. We couldn't find anything remotely like this quote—and no interview at all in 1998."

Comedian Amy Schumer may have contributed to the revival of this fake meme. She put it on Instagram, adding at the end of a lengthy message, "Yes this quote is fake but it doesn't matter."

Consult the experts. We know you're busy, and some of this debunking takes time. But we get paid to do this kind of work. Between FactCheck.org, Snopes.com, the *Washington Post* Fact Checker and PolitiFact.com, it's likely at least one has already fact-checked the latest viral claim to pop up in your news feed.

FactCheck.org was among a network of independent fact-checkers who signed an open letter to Facebook's Mark Zuckerberg suggesting that Facebook "start an open conversation on the principles that could underpin a more accurate news ecosystem on its News Feed." We hope that conversation happens, but news readers themselves remain the first line of defense against fake news.

On our Viral Spiral page, we list some of the claims we get asked about the most; all of our Ask FactChecks can be found here. And if you encounter a new claim you'd like us to investigate, email us at editor@factcheck.org.

Argument Clinic
Monty Python Sketch Comedy Troupe

https://youtu.be/XNkjDuSVXiE

The Rhetorical Situation[1]

About 2,500 years ago, the ancient Greek thinker Aristotle defined rhetoric as "the ability to see in each case the available means of persuasion." For Aristotle, rhetorical principles and techniques helped citizens defend themselves and accuse others in law courts, advocate for and against policy in the Assembly, and praise or blame each other on ritual occasions, like a eulogy at a funeral. While initially designed specifically for oral arguments, we can use these ancient rhetorical principles in many different media besides speeches, as they provide a useful foundation for rhetorical analysis and composition.

While writing and rhetoric have changed in the millennia since Aristotle's time, his work can still teach us useful strategies of persuasion. While Aristotle's definition is not the first, only, or best, it does provide a very important idea: **the rhetorical situation**. The rhetorical situation asserts that language does not exist in a vacuum, as "any given case" can vary widely from any other. Simply, we do not talk to everyone about the same things in the same ways (e.g., talking about weekend plans is very different if we are talking with friends, classmates, teachers, or parents). We already change our language implicitly, but reflecting on these choices actively and critically makes us much more effective in our compositions and argumentation. Therefore, we must consider the four primary elements of any given rhetorical situation: the **rhetor** is the one making the message, the **audience** is whomever receives the message, the **text** is the message itself, and the **purpose** is the goal the rhetor hopes to achieve with the message.

Different texts work differently on different audiences; what persuades one audience at one time could fail miserably with the next audience, and what is persuasive coming from one person may not be persuasive coming from another. That is, what can be considered "good writing" or "effective rhetoric" depends on who the rhetor is, what they are writing about, and to whom they are writing. To be effective therefore requires many questions on the part of the rhetor.

1. This chapter introduction is adapted from material originally written by Trevor Meyer.

Before you enter a rhetorical situation, some questions to consider include: Who is the intended audience? What does the audience care about or want? How does the audience perceive you? How do you perceive them? What are you trying to achieve? How are you relating your purpose? What kinds of texts work for that purpose? For that audience? For you as a rhetor?

Paying close attention to these details and thinking deeply about them will help you shape your texts to the situations that call for them. However, remember that what is persuasive in one case may not be persuasive in another. This is a problem that opens up many philosophical questions.

Exigence[2]

In order to help analyze how what is persuasive changes from case to case, the American rhetorician Lloyd Bitzer argued that the concept **exigence**, "an imperfection marked by urgency" and "a thing which is other than it should be," is an important analytical category. You can think of exigence as any event, condition, incident, etc., that requires a response. Bitzer elaborated that "an exigence is rhetorical when it is capable of positive modification and when positive modification requires discourse or can be assisted by discourse." In this way, we can consider an exigence rhetorical when it is possible to influence it through the use of language. Any time when a speaker is able to influence the course of events through rhetorical means, we can say that he or she is responding to a rhetorical exigence. For example, a commencement speech is based on the exigence of students graduating, a political speech shortly before a politician is about to resign from office is based on the need for an explanation, and an acceptance speech after a person receives an award is based on expressing thanks and honoring those who helped that person to succeed. Each of these examples is brought about by a specific event and the speech itself attempts to make an impact on future actions—a student's comportment to their new vocation, how the public understands a politician's legacy, or maintaining comradery among friends, family, and colleagues.

According to Bitzer, exigence not only determines what a rhetor will say but also "specifies the audience to be addressed and the change to be effected." In other words, the exigence determines the kind of audience the rhetor will address. Not all events or incidents are relevant to a large audience. Political speeches, for example, are sometimes only broadcast in the country, state, city, or town where they are relevant. In such a case, public availability of the speech could be limited to just one radio station in one town. However, the President of the United States condemning an act of terrorism will likely be featured in the news around the world. A terrorist attack may not initially seem like a rhetorical exigence, but a speech after such an attack does demonstrate compassion to the families of

2. This section is adapted from material originally written by Andreas Herzog.

the victims and a resolve to respond to the perpetrators. In this way, the speech will create action in the world. Often in such a speech the President will address various specific audiences—community leaders, citizens, Congress, etc.—and ask them to take specific actions—remain calm, remain hopeful, pass a certain bill, etc. In this way, we can see that all situations are to some extent rhetorical, even if the rhetorical response does not have an immediate effect in the world.

Not all rhetoricians agree with Bitzer or his ideas about exigence. Famously, Richard Vatz argued "meaning is not intrinsic in events, facts, people or 'situations,' nor are facts 'publicly observable.'" For Vatz, situations do not have meaning in and of themselves; rather, meaning is constructed through individual interpretation of events. In a linguistic sense, the rhetor herself creates the exigence to which she responds. Instead of a problem in the world forcing a rhetor to speak and determining what she should say, the rhetor creates reasons for speaking by interpreting the world in a particular way. This understanding of exigence is different from Bitzer's because it considers that different people can interpret reality differently, that there are no such things as "problems" beyond the ones people construct, and that rhetors can use language to affect the way others understand reality. In this understanding of exigence, the rhetor frames actual events in the world as problems so that she can make her arguments; whether or not these events are actually problems is not certain.

Kairos[3]

One of the implications of Vatz's re-theorization of exigence is that it demonstrates the importance of **kairos** for any rhetorical situation. The Greek word *kairos* is one of several words the Greeks had to refer to time. Specifically, *kairos* expresses the sense of time as *timing*; the quality of time that makes certain moments ideal for certain actions. *Kairos*, then, is the time in which elements come together to create opportunity. However, not everyone agrees as to when something is *kairotic*. For example, consider the public dialog that occurs whenever a mass shooting makes national news. Often, there is a debate as to when exactly it is appropriate to have discussions about public policy as it pertains to relevant topics such as mental health and gun control. Immediately following such a tragedy, are people too emotionally distraught to engage in a productive discourse? Is immediately having these conversations too disrespectful to the victims? Or, for fear of losing public concern and media coverage, is the best time the soonest and most emotionally ripe moment? All situations have a *kairotic* moment, the difficult part is identifying when it is, and who it best serves.

When considering how to intervene in a rhetorical situation, we have to think about how to utilize the most appropriate language at the most appropriate time. Have you ever sat in class and wanted to say something but didn't, soon feeling

---

3. This section is adapted from material originally written by Adam Padgett.

your ideal moment drift by along with your opportunity to make an important point? Sure, you could speak up later, but your message would certainly lose some of the rhetorical punch it otherwise would have had. This, then, is your *kairotic* moment passing you by. Life is full of these moments, rhetorical or not, where timing seems crucial.

Since ancient Greece, *kairos* has been closely associated with sport because it combines timing with skill, knowledge, instinct, movement, and awareness. In baseball, for instance, the batter has at least three pitches to hit the ball. If the batter swings too early or too late, he'll miss, earning a strike. Of course, he could abstain from swinging altogether. So, how does the batter know when to swing and when not to swing? For one, it has to do with common sense and deductive reasoning. But it also has to do with the athlete's prior experience, the batter's ability to recognize a bad pitch, and the ability to know when a pitch is worth hitting. The batter often has many opportunities to connect with the baseball but is looking for the best moment—not necessarily the only moment—to swing. But it is not only the batter who needs to consider *kairos*. The pitcher pays attention to other players on the field, weather conditions, his own energy levels, previous plays, the catcher's signals, and a myriad of other factors to know when, how, and where to throw the ball. All of the stakeholders in the game—players, coaches, fans, etc.—are concerned with *kairos*.

Successful rhetoric is a balancing act among all the elements involved in a situation (rhetor, audience, topic, exigence, *kairos*, etc.); attention to *kairos* allows the rhetor to take full advantage of a given rhetorical situation. As the adage goes, timing is everything. How might an election year sway legislation? What does arriving late to an interview communicate to an employer? How do you follow up after a first date? In analyzing a rhetorical situation, then, ask how current or upcoming events might inform how an argument is presented. Perhaps your research will reveal something about the history of the topic and how other writers have made use of *kairos* in the past. You also need to ask if the topic is even still relevant, or if the moment of *kairos* has now passed; in other words, consider if the topic is now essentially "done." Moments tend to be fleeting, especially the best or most appropriate ones, and a poor sense of timing runs the risk of dissuading an otherwise persuadable audience.

Stakeholders[4]

Crucial to understanding both exigence and *kairos* is considering who holds a stake in something, who cares about what happens to it. For example, if you buy a new car, you care about its upkeep and maintenance; you invest time, effort, and money into the car. You have, in other words, a stake in it. People with a stake in something are, unsurprisingly, referred to as **stakeholders**. They are people

---

4. This section is adapted from material originally written by Candace Cooper.

who affect or are affected by an issue or object. As a stakeholder in your car, you have the power to affect your car in good and bad ways. You can wash your car regularly, vacuum out the interior once a week, and conduct regular maintenance. Conversely, you can ignore these issues. Either way, you affect your car; perhaps more interestingly, your car also affects you. If your car doesn't start, you're not going anywhere. If your car radio breaks, you have nothing to listen to on your commute. Further, you are not the only one with a stake in your car's ability to function. A brief list of other stakeholders in your car includes mechanics who rely on fixing cars like yours for their livelihood, your friends who may rely on you when they need a ride to school, other drivers on the road who might be harmed if your car malfunctions, and the car manufacturers who would like to eventually sell you a new car.

When it comes to less concrete things like issues, arguments, and debates, the stakes are still important and the stakeholders as tangible. Take for instance the issue of gun rights in the United States. This controversial issue is constantly debated, in part because of mass shootings such as those at the Tree of Life synagogue in Squirrel Hill, PA; Emmanuel African Methodist Episcopal Church in Charleston, SC; Stoneman Douglas High School in Parkland, FL; and the Route 91 Harvest Music Festival in Las Vegas, NV. People with a stake regarding gun rights and gun regulation—those who affect and/or are affected by this issue—include gun owners, law makers, the President of the U.S., gun sellers and manufacturers, etc. Of course, this list does not represent all of the potential stakeholders in this issue, but just some who are immediately affected. When thinking about an issue, it can be helpful to list both who the stakeholders are and what positions they hold; doing so will help you get an idea of the whole situation. Considering the variety of stakeholder positions present in an issue will enable you to present a more complete and informed picture of the issue at hand, which will vastly improve the effectiveness of any argument you create.

When you are writing, one of the stakeholders is always you; you are invested in what you're saying and how you're saying it. Having a strong stake in an issue can make what one writes a bit biased, so it is important to consider taking other positions seriously when doing research in order to make an informed argument. In addition, understanding the stakeholders can help you determine both your addressed and invoked audience. Ask yourself, who is affected by this issue? Who has the power to affect this issue? How do these stakeholders affect my view or argument about this issue? Am I a stakeholder, and if so, how will that affect my writing on this issue? Once you have answered these questions, you will have a good place to start in terms of the direction you want to take your argument, as well as in terms of how you will organize and compose your thoughts on that particular issue. Keep stakeholders in mind throughout the writing process because what you write and how you write it can make a difference to them.

Discussion Questions

1. Earlier we suggest that "all situations are rhetorical to some extent." Do you agree? In groups, a) brainstorm some texts that don't fit the above understanding of the rhetorical situation, and ask what they are used for; and b) brainstorm some non-rhetorical exigences.

2. Since we change our language use based on audience, purpose, and context, can we ever actually be honest? If so, what does *honest* mean within the context of rhetoric? If not, why do we value honesty in our society? What is *truth* anyway?

3. Think of a moment in history (recent or distant) where the timing of a major issue was especially important. Make reference to a specific moment or event that propagated a particular action such as passing of legislation, actions of war, political/social movements, etc. Think of famous speeches with timing that was especially apropos. What made the timing for that issue so key?

4. Can a rhetor create *kairos*? Like with exigence, can a rhetor use the world around her to manufacture *kairos* and make others see her argument as timely, whether or not it objectively is? Try to consider ways in which a rhetor might do that.

5. As a class we will come up with a particularly controversial topic. Half of the class will brainstorm a list of stakeholders interested in keeping the status quo; the other half will draft a list of stakeholders interested in making change. Is it possible to place members of both lists in productive conversation with each other, or does that require us to change how we consider the entire topic?

6. Consider Childish Gambino's "This Is America," printed on page 26. What exigence does he respond to, and how well did he manage the *kairos* of the situation? Who are the stakeholders in this issue? As a class, discuss a response to "This Is America" in terms of its rhetorical situation.

Exercises

1. Read an essay from Part Two, Unit One and then draw a map of the rhetorical situation of which it is a part. Identify not only the rhetor, audience, text, and purpose, but also other actors, media, messages, and background information that you think are important. Consider who holds a stake in the piece. Try to make your map so detailed that someone with no knowledge of the topic could understand the rhetorical situation and the argument being made. Finally, identify the author's exigence: is their argument an effective response to this initial situation?

2. Take the following argument: "free speech is a cornerstone of this country and must be protected at all costs." Compose three short essays (500 words) that each make this argument but in response to completely different exigences. Afterwards, get into groups and discuss how changing the exigences changed the effectiveness of the argument.

3. Write down a moment that was *kairotic* last week, last month, last year, and last decade. Are any of these elements still as relevant now as they were then? Pick the event which seems least relevant now and write a short argument making the case that it is still *kairotic*. Discuss each as a class.

4. In a group, collectively compose both an email and a tweet to your ENGL 102 professor. In each, you will ask for an extension on your next paper, an extra credit opportunity, or forgiveness of an absence due to extenuating circumstances. Your choice. After you have collectively composed this email and crafted it as persuasively as possible, look over the course syllabus. Choose a specific date you would hypothetically deliver this email. Why did you choose that particular date? What role did *kairos* play in that decision? Would there have been a time too early? Or a time too late? Explain. We will regroup and rank the effectiveness of each tweet and email around the room to ask the question: what makes one time-sensitive request more effective than another?

5. Choose one of the various monuments on the USC campus or the Statehouse grounds. Conduct some quick, online research and familiarize yourself with the history of the monument and the person/group/event for which it was erected. What rhetorical purpose does the monument serve? In what way, do you think, did *kairos* influence the construction of these monuments? Would these buildings or monuments be erected today? If so, would they look the same or different? What events, ideologies, or beliefs would change how the monument would look if built today?

6. Make a list of all of the issues/ideas you have a stake in. Make sure to choose not only political issues but also more mundane issues. Choose the issue/idea you find most interesting and write a brief paragraph on why this issue/idea matters to you and what your stake is in it. Then, write three tweet-length statements (280 characters) that take the position of another stakeholder in the issue. Finally, turn to a peer, share your paragraphs with each other, and brainstorm ways to negotiate the needs of the different stakeholders.

Supplemental Reading

Use the following URL, or look up the video for Childish Gambino's "This Is America," and analyze it with a critical eye for the concepts discussed in this chapter. What is the **rhetorical situation** in which this song and video were composed? What **exigence** is it responding to? Who are the **stakeholders**, and what are the **stakes** of this composition? How does the particular moment—its *kairos*—condition the purpose and argumentative function of "This Is America"? Use the lyrics below to help you in your analysis.

https://youtu.be/VYOjWnS4cMY

"This Is America"
Childish Gambino

Yeah, yeah, yeah, yeah, yeah
Yeah, yeah, yeah, go, go away
Yeah, yeah, yeah, yeah, yeah
Yeah, yeah, yeah, go, go away
Yeah, yeah, yeah, yeah, yeah
Yeah, yeah, yeah, go, go away
Yeah, yeah, yeah, yeah, yeah
Yeah, yeah, yeah, go, go away

We just wanna party
Party just for you
We just want the money
Money just for you
I know you wanna party
Party just for me
Girl, you got me dancin' (yeah, girl, you got me dancin')
Dance and shake the frame
We just wanna party (yeah)
Party just for you (yeah)
We just want the money (yeah)
Money just for you (you)
I know you wanna party (yeah)
Party just for me (yeah)
Girl, you got me dancin' (yeah, girl, you got me dancin')
Dance and shake the frame (you)

This is America
Don't catch you slippin' up
Don't catch you slippin' up
Look what I'm whippin' up

This is America (woo)
Don't catch you slippin' up
Don't catch you slippin' up
Look what I'm whippin' up

This is America (skrrt, skrrt, woo)
Don't catch you slippin' up (ayy)
Look at how I'm livin' now
Police be trippin' now (woo)
Yeah, this is America (woo, ayy)
Guns in my area (word, my area)
I got the strap (ayy, ayy)
I gotta carry 'em
Yeah, yeah, I'ma go into this (ugh)
Yeah, yeah, this is guerilla (woo)
Yeah, yeah, I'ma go get the bag
Yeah, yeah, or I'ma get the pad
Yeah, yeah, I'm so cold like yeah (yeah)
I'm so dope like yeah (woo)
We gon' blow like yeah (straight up, uh)

Ooh-ooh-ooh-ooh-ooh, tell somebody
You go tell somebody
Grandma told me
Get your money, black man (get your money)
Get your money, black man (get your money)
Get your money, black man (get your, black man)
Get your money, black man (get your, black man)
Black man

This is America (woo, ayy)
Don't catch you slippin' up (woo, woo, don't catch you
slippin', now)
Don't catch you slippin' up (ayy, woah)
Look what I'm whippin' up (Slime!)
This is America (yeah, yeah)
Don't catch you slippin' up (woah, ayy)
Don't catch you slippin' up (ayy, woo)
Look what I'm whippin' up (ayy)

Look how I'm geekin' out (hey)
I'm so fitted (I'm so fitted, woo)
I'm on Gucci (I'm on Gucci)

I'm so pretty (yeah, yeah)
I'm gon' get it (ayy, I'm gon' get it)
Watch me move (blaow)
This a celly (ha)
That's a tool (yeah)
On my Kodak (woo, Black)
Ooh, know that (yeah, know that, hold on)
Get it (get it, get it)
Ooh, work it (21)
Hunnid bands, hunnid bands, hunnid bands (hunnid bands)
Contraband, contraband, contraband (contraband)
I got the plug on Oaxaca (woah)
They gonna find you like blocka (blaow)

Ooh-ooh-ooh-ooh-ooh, tell somebody
America, I just checked my following list and
You go tell somebody
You mothafuckas owe me
Grandma told me
Get your money, black man (black man)
Get your money, black man (black man)
Get your money, black man (black man)
Get your money, black man (black man)
Black man (one, two, three, get down)

Ooh-ooh-ooh-ooh-ooh, tell somebody
You go tell somebody
Grandma told me, "Get your money," black man
Get your money, black man (black man)
Get your money, black man (black man)
Get your money, black man (black man)
Black man

You just a black man in this world
You just a barcode, ayy
You just a black man in this world
Drivin' expensive foreigns, ayy
You just a big dawg, yeah
I kenneled him in the backyard
No proper life to a dog
For a big dog

CHAPTER 3

Situations and Arguments

The first two chapters in this unit have introduced you to the outlines of rhetorical situations—their conditions of possibility and some of the major players that are involved in any argumentative situation. Now that these outlines are in place, this final chapter of the unit provides you with two methods for analyzing these situations in more detail: **stasis theory** and **the Toulmin model.**

Stasis theory provides you with a method for analyzing how debates function and important *types* of arguments that are commonly found in debates, regardless of topic. Having a grasp of the exigence, timing, stakes, stakeholders, and the conditions of argumentation present in the debate are integral for this theory to work effectively; they allow you to situate the stasis questions in their context and identify why particular types of arguments are important.

The Toulmin model, on the other hand, is a method for examining how specific arguments work; it will introduce you to a much more fine-grained system of analysis than the two-part definition of argument given in Chapter 1 (page 6). Combined with stasis theory and the other aspects of rhetorical situations, the Toulmin model will allow you to delve into specific debates with precision. Further, it sets the stage for the work you will do throughout the rest of this book and course—first by analyzing and cataloging specific arguments, and then in creating your own rhetorical intervention.

Stasis[1]

The word **stasis** comes from the ancient Greek word for *stoppage* or *standing*. Both meanings are relevant for our purposes, but we'll start with *stoppage*. In this understanding, stasis functions as the agreed upon topic of discussion, the limits of an argument.

When speaking and writing, rhetors generally make one overarching claim—in academic writing we call this a thesis. To support this thesis, a rhetor will make

---

1. This section is adapted from material originally written by Mark Schaukowitch.

a series of smaller claims throughout the argument. We can refer to these various small claims as a set of stases. They function by providing the limits to a debate or topic of conversation. They limit the field in which the conversation is taking place. Stases function as the borders of an argument. Speakers/authors and audiences/readers are discouraged from moving beyond the well confined space of debate, though often they do so anyway in order to press their opinions, values, or beliefs.

> *Ex: If a speaker were to claim, "Illegal immigration on the southern US border is a problem. I will build a wall, and make Mexico pay for it," then someone else may counter by saying, "No. Mexico will not pay for a wall." It would be less appropriate for someone to counter with, "Mexico has the largest population of whale sharks off its borders, and a wall will hurt them."*

In the above argument the problem isn't the arguments themselves, but that the second responder is not participating in the same argument as the initial speaker. Whale sharks may be important, but they have little to do with the act of building a wall or who pays for it. In other words, the whale sharks are part of a different argument outside the limits defined by the speaker. However, it is a rare occasion in which an argument never shifts, and there can be good reasons for changing these limits; perhaps to question the building of a wall at all, and thus side-step the question of who pays.

To determine the topic of debate in ways that would make it productive and help rhetors to determine precisely about what it is they disagree, ancient rhetoricians developed four questions that would help debaters identify the main point at issue:

1. **Fact**—The question of fact is the first to consider. It asks whether something happened or if something exists. Keep in mind that facts are not self-explanatory. Facts are historical and change over time. For a long time, it was a fact that the earth was flat, but the fact eventually changed due to overwhelming evidence to the contrary. When a rhetorician says *fact*, then, what they mean is a frequently repeated idea that is understood by a culture or group to be true.

   > *Ex: Will a wall destroy ecosystems?*

2. **Definition**—The question of definition asks about the exact meaning of a term in a particular situation. Definitions are based on agreement between two parties as to what the facts of the situation are. Definition builds on the first stasis question by interrogating how we categorize specific actions.

   > *Ex: A wall will definitely affect ecosystems, but what is the difference between destroying, hurting, and affecting?*

3. **Quality**—The question of quality examines whether an action or situation, once properly defined, is good/bad, productive/unproductive, moral/immoral, etc.

Ex: A wall will definitely destroy ecosystems, but will it improve border control enough to justify this destruction?

4. **Policy**—The question of policy asks what should be done about the situation at hand. We may say not only that certain actions need to be taken but also that certain actors need to take them.

    Ex: The destruction a wall will create is not justified by border control. What, then, should we do about our borders?

Ancient rhetoricians used the stases as an exercise to determine the main point of dispute between two parties, and you too can work through these questions as a brainstorming strategy to determine where any disagreements may lie between you and the texts with which you disagree. You can also use these questions as a framework for organizing your argument. This is where stasis's second meaning of *standing* is useful.

Using the stases—starting with fact and ending with policy—the rhetor invents the ground on which their argument stands. In modern composition these questions are usually worded as claims that need to be evidenced. This creates a specific problem for the rhetor because if any of these layers is not solid, the following layers will lack stability. Still, if you use all the stases, you do not need to deal with them all equally. It is up to the rhetor, after deeply researching the rhetorical situation and its various components, to determine where in an argument interventions need to be made.

> *Ex: If you were writing a paper on whether or not Run DMC should have been admitted into the Rock & Roll Hall of Fame, you may choose to briefly discuss the facts of the situation, while focusing mainly on the definition of rock and roll and the qualities of Run DMC's music that would determine whether or not it is part of the genre; then, you may choose to only briefly discuss what should be done about the situation and by whom. In this case, the intervention is mostly one of definition and quality, but all of the stases are represented.*

Finally, knowing that most arguments either implicitly or explicitly follow stasis theory can accelerate your research because if you know the stases and their order, you can locate the claims that are relevant to your project much faster. Many contemporary compositions follow Cicero's original modes of interrogation, though they are worded as claims, not questions. Authors will often begin by stating the facts of their rhetorical situation and citing the sources that verify those facts. Then, authors will define any ambiguous terms or uncertain aspects of those facts as they pertain to the specific situation. Then, they will explain why these facts are good/bad, problematic/unproblematic, reassuring/concerning, etc. Finally, they present a proposal as to what should be done about the situation and by whom.

The Toulmin Model[2]

While **stasis theory** is helpful in understanding how a debate functions and providing a method for categorizing certain kinds of claims, it does little to help us understand how specific arguments actually work. Thus, British philosopher Stephen Toulmin developed his model of argumentation in the twentieth century after realizing that **syllogisms** (page 92) failed to accurately represent arguments as they took place in the world. Instead of focusing on formal validity, the goal of **the Toulmin model** was to illustrate how arguments *move* at a micro-level and how each action in an argument serves to constrain and extend the argument in a particular direction. In doing so, this model comes closer to capturing the ways people in everyday situations make arguments. For this reason, the Toulmin model is an excellent analytical tool that allows both audiences and rhetors to understand how a particular argument works, how each part of an argument functions, and what an argument's strengths and weaknesses are.

Toulmin's model begins by identifying the three basic components of an argument: the **claim**, the **data**, and the **warrant**.

> **Claim**—a conclusion, or thesis, a rhetor seeks to establish as accepted knowledge, course of action, or value
>
> **Data**—also known as evidence, is the facts, statistics, examples, or expert testimony upon which the claim is based
>
> **Warrant**—a hypothetical statement that bridges the data and claim

Toulmin argued that it is not enough when arguing to simply make a claim and provide evidence for it; rather, an additional step is necessary for audiences to make the jump from evidence to claim. This extra step is the warrant. Warrants explain how the data is connected to the claim. They are usually very simple statements, and in many cases they are not explicitly expressed by rhetors because the audience's cultural practices and values often allow them to infer the connection between claim/data on their own. What information can be considered warranted will, therefore, change depending on the cultural context of your audience: even seemingly simple notions such as what primary colors "mean" will change.

Rhetors aware of their audience's values and prejudices need not make their warrants explicit because the audience has the knowledge to infer what they mean. Identifying these moments was key for Toulmin because warrants expose cultural values and open space for deliberation of their merit. This isn't just an important tool for your own composition: identifying warranted information in other texts is a crucial step toward rhetorical analysis, as what is not said is often as valuable for consideration as what is. To put the first three steps together and see how an argument moves, let us consider a recent argument demanding free college:

---

2. This section is adapted from material originally written by Kimberly Overmier.

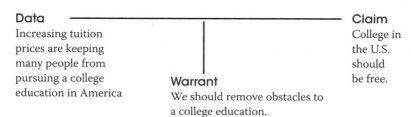

Data ——————————————————————— **Claim**

Data	Claim
Increasing tuition prices are keeping many people from pursuing a college education in America	College in the U.S. should be free.

Warrant
We should remove obstacles to a college education.

The argument seems simple enough, but analyzing it can be difficult when the warrant is hidden. When "we should remove obstacles to a college education" is not stated, it is difficult to critique it. In other words, if warrants are not stated, then the underlying assumption and values they represent will often be passively accepted, misinterpreted, or confused. By identifying the warrant, one opens up the space for informed debate and disagreement about the values it presupposes. Stating the warrant allows the assumption of the argument to be investigated—to have its quality, relevance, and validity critiqued.

Besides allowing us to critique the assumptions that underlie many arguments, the Toulmin model also acknowledges the conversational nature of argument by mapping the series of moves speakers often make after laying out their claim; these moves serve to strategically anticipate and address opposition to the rhetor's claim. Toulmin identifies three such moves: the **backing**, the **rebuttal**, and the **qualifier**.

- **Backing**—additional evidence provided to support the warrant.

- **Rebuttal**—anticipation of potential refutations of the argument by acknowledging what weaknesses/conditions the argument possesses.

- **Qualifier**—tells audiences how certain or strong the argument is by using words such as *mostly, absolutely, possibly*, etc.

When this additional set of moves is added to the first set, it is easy to see how the Toulmin model maps all the moves a rhetor typically makes in a single argument.

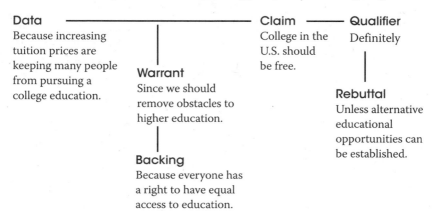

Data ——————————————— **Claim** ——— **Qualifier**

Because increasing tuition prices are keeping many people from pursuing a college education.

Claim
College in the U.S. should be free.

Qualifier
Definitely

Warrant
Since we should remove obstacles to higher education.

Backing
Because everyone has a right to have equal access to education.

Rebuttal
Unless alternative educational opportunities can be established.

Remember, the Toulmin model maps arguments at the micro-level; it demonstrates how, though a rhetor often has an overarching claim that directs her work, the argument she provides is made up of a series of minor claims, data, and warrants. When reading and listening to arguments, try to keep track of how each argumentation chain works to move the audience to the thesis of the piece.

When attempting to apply the Toulmin model to a rhetorical act, there are a series of steps you use:

1. **Identify the claim or thesis**. Understanding where the rhetor wants the argument to go will help you start identifying the directions she has available to get there.

2. **Identify the data, or evidence, the rhetor deploys to support her thesis**. Are there statistics, expert testimony, or facts being used? If so, where does each piece of information come from and is it both sufficient and relevant to her claim?

3. **After looking at the claim and data presented, look for a justification or explanation of why the evidence is applicable to the claim, keeping in mind that the rhetor may not have provided an explanation.** The warrant is in many cases implied. If that is the case, then think about what value or action you have to accept in order to follow the evidence to the claim. (This is in many cases the hardest thing to identify in arguments.)

4. **Once you have identified the first three steps of the Toulmin model, look to see if the rhetor offers backing, or additional evidence, to support her warrant.** Especially if the warrant is not a widely held cultural value, but rather something contested, the rhetor will more than likely try to support why she made that particular "jump" of reasoning.

5. **Next, see if the author addresses any weaknesses her argument may have by limiting the scope of her argument in a rebuttal.** Rebuttals help demonstrate the rhetor's cognizance of the rhetorical situation.

6. **Finally, look to see if the rhetor qualifies the strength of her argument.** Often, rhetors include a word or phrase in their claim that softens or boosts its force or an assertion that tells audiences how much trust they should put in the claim.

Discussion Questions

1. Read through one of the essays in Part Two, Unit One. As a class, identify the different stases the author uses. Does any particular stasis feature more prominently than the others? Are all the stases represented?

2. A rancher in Nevada states: "The US federal government should not own any ranching land. All federal land should be privately held." Based on these two claims answer the following:

    a. On what type of stasis is each sentence based?

    b. What is the general quality of the US federal government that is being implied, and how can you tell?

    c. Based on the general qualities derived from the last question, how might the US federal government be loosely defined?

    d. Based on that definition, what is the assumed fact that the rancher must make of the federal government, which may or may not be true, in order to arrive at his statement?

3. Was Toulmin successful at capturing how arguments at the micro-level move and function with this model? Consider a recent discussion, debate, or argument you had with a friend before you answer the question.

4. What do you think is the usefulness of this model—analysis, invention, arrangement? What challenges do you foresee with using it? What benefits do you think will come from using it?

5. As a class we will pick a *kairotic* topic (i.e., one that has dominated the news cycle this week). First, we will take this topic through stasis to see if it is possible to get both "sides" to agree on a way forward; next, we will apply Toulmin to the debate to identify what each "side's" stance says about them.

6. In what ways might the Toulmin model be helpful in understanding the stasis of a debate? Vice versa? As a class, discuss some strategies for using these two models together.

Exercises

1. Watch the following debate: http://www.intelligencesquaredus.org/debates/free-speech-threatened-campus. At the end of each speech, as a class identify the different stases the speaker used and in what order.

2. Choose one of the articles you have found this semester through your own research and are planning on using in your ILP #2; preferably, choose an article with which you disagree. Then, go through the stasis questions with the article, writing down short versions of the article's answers (e.g., What does the article say the facts are; how does the article define the important words?). Next, go through the responses to the questions you derived from the article and ask yourself if you agree with the answers; if you disagree, write down your position (e.g., What do you think the facts are; how would you define the important words?). Finally, ask if working through this exercise

helped you to clarify why you disagree with your counter-source, and how this helps you prepare your ILP assignment.

3. Consider your own identity. Make a claim to fact based on your identity. Then, develop a paragraph that further refines that claim using sub-claims of definition, values, and policy.

4. Go online and find the poster for a film released in the current six-month window (i.e., it could have been released three months ago, or maybe will be released in the next three months). First, break down the claim: how is the film being sold to its audience? Next, break down all warranted information: what type of audience is this film being advertised towards? What genre is it? What can you implicitly know about the film even if you haven't seen it? Finally, run the argument being made by the poster through stasis: does it actually work? In other words, can an act of propaganda (which all advertising is, to some extent) fulfill the requirements of an argument?

5. As a class, we will choose one paragraph from an essay in Part Two for analysis. In small groups, work through the following questions and be prepared to discuss your findings with the class: a) map the argument using the Toulmin model (note: there are multiple possible maps); b) what about the argument is strong/weak and why?; and c) how could you counter the author's position, or how could you improve their argument?

Supplemental Readings

Why Every American Should Look at "Blue Feed, Red Feed"— and Why the Nation Needs Someone to Build a Better Version
Rich Gordon

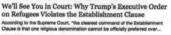

An example of what you might have seen today on Blue Feed, Red Feed

Eight months ago, the Wall Street Journal built a remarkable news application, Blue Feed, Red Feed, which displays—side by side—a selection of Facebook posts from liberal and conservative news sources. Whatever your political persuasion, I don't think you can understand the first week of the Donald Trump administration without taking a look.

I say this as someone whose Facebook feed is dominated by my liberal friends, whose unhappiness with Trump and his policies has been conveyed with anger, tears and in many cases, participation in marches and airport protests. What I've seen in my Facebook feed—stories about airport chaos and protests over the weekend—suggested to me that even if you were in favor of the new immigration restrictions, a reasonable person could be critical of how the decision was made and implemented.

Then I read what the president had to say: "…we were totally prepared," he said. "It's working out very nicely. You see it at the airports, you see it all over."

Add that quote to last week's comments from advisor Kellyanne Conway about "alternative facts" and advisor Steve Bannon's declaration of war on the mainstream media, and something became clear to me for the first time:

Trump is governing as if the only input and feedback he gets come from his political base.

That observation may not be surprising, especially given the president's known tendency to bask in the support of his campaign audiences. It may not even be true. But it's clear from comments over the past week that a lot of people, regardless of political persuasion, are surprised that Trump is doing exactly what he said he would on the campaign trail, and wasting no time in doing so. That has not been typical for incoming presidents, who have often walked back their more controversial statements upon winning the election, and who tried to build support by reaching out to political opponents.

The realization that Trump is behaving differently is what led me back to Blue Feed, Red Feed. I think it's currently the best place for anyone—left, right or center—to see our nation's political polarization in stark relief.

For instance, at 12:50pm Central time today, here were two posts near the top of BFRF if you chose the "Executive Order" view:

The difference couldn't be more stark. On the left, the ACLU says it's clear that the immigration order is unconstitutional. On the right, a "former terrorist prosecutor" says it's totally legal.

There's nothing new about the fact that our nation is polarized politically, or that liberals and conservatives are gravitating to different sources of news. What's new is that it's now so easy for any American using Facebook (or Twitter) to avoid seeing political perspectives that conflict with his or her own preconceptions.

We need to assume that the president and his advisors are among those living in a political bubble in which they are hearing nothing but applause for what they are doing.

If you make that assumption, everything that the new administration is doing makes sense—while, if you are opposed to these actions, you wonder how Trump and his allies can ignore what seem to be obvious missteps.

That's why I love BFRF. It makes clear that when it comes to many issues, there are two wildly different interpretations of reality. If you're pro-Trump or anti-Trump, you will gain a deeper understanding of your political opposites. If you—like me—believe that we need to find common ground and tackle our nation's problems together, BFRF will make clear how hard that's going to be. And you might even learn something from the posts in the other column.

There are some other people who have an even deeper need to spend time with BFRF: namely, people who have the authority to make decisions to implement or block the White House's actions. That includes Congress, the courts and anyone in the executive branch who is charged with implementing policies drawn up by the new administration. Not to mention the opponents of these policies, who need to understand how they are perceived by people outside their own respective political bubbles.

• • •

Still, it's important to recognize the flaws of BFRF, and to build a better version.

The feeds in BFRF are not real Facebook feeds. No real person sees either the left side or the right side of BFRF. As the site itself explains, the blue and red feeds are collected from Facebook pages that were identified by Facebook researchers in a scientifically designed study whose goal was to understand how users interact with socially shared news.

The posts you see in BFRF come from people the researchers determined were "very liberal" or "very conservative" based on self-described political leanings. And the developers of BFRF say they removed sources that were shared by lots of people on both sides of the political spectrum.

So BFRF intentionally presents two dramatically skewed views of the world—posts published by Facebook pages whose audiences are most likely to be isolated from the other side's point of view.

BFRF is still illuminating—and highly useful in understanding what's happening in Washington these days—if you accept my premise that President Trump is basing his actions (and reactions) on the sources on the right side of BFRF.

But I am starting to imagine a better version of BFRF, one whose goal isn't just to display stark contrasts, but instead one that might help our nation attack the toxic political polarization that we are seeing all around us.

A better BFRF might include the following:

> Select posts not just based on the known political orientation of specific Facebook pages—but on which posts are getting traction in "blue" and "red" communities.

> Use natural language processing techniques to match posts based on subject matter, so blue and red posts discussing the same subject appear right next to each other.

Generate permalinks for these "purple" matching posts so they can be shared (side by side) as a single post on social media.

Make it possible to choose your topic of interest rather than be limited to the categories currently built in to BFRF:

To begin, click on a topic:

PRESIDENT TRUMP   HILLARY CLINTON   PRESIDENT OBAMA   AFFORDABLE CARE ACT

GUNS   ABORTION   ISIS   EXECUTIVE ORDER

If we had the BFRF I am imagining, it would serve as a fabulous platform for rigorous fact-checking—one that would make it easy for the fact-checkers to call out lies and exaggerations by both the right and the left.

I think this BFRF could help all of us better understand one another. It might even help centrists and reasonable people with political and philosophical differences find common ground.

Blue Feed, Red Feed
John Keegan

http://graphics.wsj.com/blue-feed-red-feed/

ANALYZING ARGUMENTS

CHAPTER 4

Reading for Invention[1]

Invention is the first of the five canons of classical rhetoric; it refers to the process of discovering or creating arguments on a particular topic. This process can refer to both figuring out the position you want to support and/or coming up with the arguments that support that position. In other words, invention can begin when you don't know what you actually think about a topic (am I for or against gay marriage?) or when you know your conclusion but want to figure out good reasons for various audiences to support it (how would I convince my grandparents to agree with me on gay marriage?). The classical tradition offers a number of different strategies for inventing arguments, including stases (questions for identifying disagreement), the inartistic proofs (evidence and examples) and artistic proofs (*ethos/pathos/logos*), and *topoi* (commonplaces)—all of which are discussed in more detail throughout this book.

To get a sense for invention, imagine you have been asked to give a toast at a wedding. You might start the process of writing your speech by thinking about how you want to come across to the audience (funny, irreverent, sincere, romantic, etc.) or by brainstorming the attributes of the couple you want to mention (What are they good at? What are they bad at? etc.). In this case, you invent arguments by first considering your rhetorical situation—an idea that you learned about in Chapter 2.

Determining what you want to write can be difficult, yet many types of writing instruction in the 20th century skipped this step of the writing process. Instructors simply assumed that students knew what they wanted to argue, or would come up with reasons on their own. Such writing instruction therefore focused more on other canons such as arrangement and style. However, the late 20th and early 21st century writing pedagogies are frequently characterized by a revitalized focus on invention and a commitment to training students in the process of discovering and creating persuasive arguments; *The Carolina Rhetoric* is no exception to this

---

1. This chapter introduction is adapted from material originally written by John Muckelbauer.

trend. While you will explore many aspects of invention in the final unit of this book, this chapter focuses on helping you to *discover* arguments about a topic.

Invention as a Research Strategy

In this course so far, you have begun by analyzing rhetorical situations and the conditions of argumentation in both your chosen topic and various others. As you begin to work toward your first major assignment—The Literature Review—you will need to delve further into your topic, expand your research, and you may need to change the strategy with which you work.

As we proceed with research, we often use what might be called a "question and answer" strategy; you start with a question, research for answers, and develop new and more specific questions based on what you have learned so far. This is an important part of the research process. Through the "question and answer" strategy, you flesh out your understanding of the rhetorical situation, learn what exigences might be involved, and learn what makes the topic timely or not. It allows you to determine whether or not the debate meets the conditions of possibility for argumentation, and can introduce you to the biases at play. As important as this strategy is for good research, however, it shouldn't be the only one you use. Given what you learned in the last chapter about the **stases** and **the Toulmin model**, you now have the knowledge you need to start using a different strategy to create an invention database.

The purpose of this invention database is to compile as many different arguments within a debate as you possibly can: claims, data, warrants, backings, qualifiers, rebuttals, in as many combinations as you can find. In order to do this, you should shift your strategy from searching for answers to attempting to find arguments that you haven't seen yet.

One useful way to engage this strategy is to work through each of the stases. For each stasis, keep a log of all the different arguments you come across. Continue to do this work until you reach a **saturation point**: the point where each new argument you encounter is already present in your log. Be careful, however, when you decide that two arguments are the same.

This is where your knowledge of **the Toulmin model** becomes important. For each argument you log, be sure to analyze it for all of its parts—you'll have to use your judgement to decide when a different warrant, qualifier, or other part of the model makes a similar claim a different argument.

The last important part of your invention database is to pay attention to the **audiences** of the arguments that you analyze and log—a topic you will explore further in the next section. As your database develops, you will start noticing that certain claims, warrants, data, and the like are often associated with different kinds of audiences. Further, while you won't always have access to this kind of information, be sure to note how audiences react to these arguments, if you can.

Audience[2]

When writing anything—even something as trivial as a grocery list, an email, or a text message—an **audience** is involved. In order to help us analyze arguments, Lisa Ede and Andrea Lunsford have argued that in any rhetorical situation, there are two types of audiences to be considered: **audience addressed** and **audience invoked**.

Audience addressed refers to the actual physical audience in the world to whom a rhetor is trying to communicate. It is the people gathered to hear a speech, driving past a billboard, or purchasing a book. To persuade this audience, a rhetor should research their attitudes, beliefs, values, reading habits, media consumption, and preconceived notions of the issues being discussed. Of course, the rhetor cannot know everything about every audience member, but research can help her to connect with a majority of her audience.

Audience invoked, on the other hand, refers to the audience that the rhetor invents for her text. Rhetors bring about these audiences through composition. The goal is for the rhetor to create an ideal subject for her argument, and through her language get her addressed audience to understand themselves that way. The rhetor creates a way for her audience to perceive themselves.

Considering both your addressed audience and your invoked audience is vital to composing an effective essay. Ask yourself who needs to hear your message and who would be sympathetic to it. For example, if you are writing about the need to institute a needle exchange program in Austin, IN, you may need to address the city's principled and stubborn city council members; however, you may want to invoke an audience that is pragmatic and willing to set aside their disdain for enabling drug users in order to stop a serious HIV outbreak. The goal in this case is to get your addressed audience to see themselves as your invoked audience—to see themselves not as stubborn and principled but as reasonable and pragmatic. This strategy can be very persuasive if done with a light touch; going too far with it can come across as pandering, naïve, or insulting.

Many rhetoricians believe that the addressed audience is the most important aspect of the rhetorical situation because they are the ones who ultimately judge the effectiveness of an argument. For this reason, such rhetoricians suggest that rhetors dedicate much time and effort to researching their audiences. However, a broader version of audience complicates this idea because rhetors are often read by audiences they did not intend or anticipate. For example, a scholarly essay about the impact global warming has on coral reefs would likely be intended

---

2. This section adapted from material originally written by Candace Cooper.

for an audience of scientists—the author's peers who read the journal in which the article is published; however, you may end up using that article if you write an essay on coral reefs. In this situation, you would become part of the article's audience, even though the writer of the piece did not write it with you in mind.

In the digital age, it is increasingly likely that anything you write will be found by unintended audiences; consider all the times politicians have said something in "closed events" only to have their messages recorded and distributed to much larger audiences. Because of the ability for anything and everything to be shared and recorded, the digital age makes it vital for us to think deeply about what we write. In our contemporary cultural moment it is important for rhetors to consider their intended audiences and their invoked audiences, but they should also be aware that they can never know the vastness of their possible audiences.

Discussion Questions

1. In a rhetorical situation, audience consideration is very important. However, it shouldn't always be the rhetorical element with the most focus when writing a paper: depending on the situation, other elements could require more attention. What are some other elements in a rhetorical situation that could sometimes be just as, if not more, important than audience? What is an example of such a situation?

2. When writing an essay for class, do you ever consider an audience other than the person who will be grading it? Think about the essay you plan to write for this course, and consider who might be your audience outside of your instructor. How will you consider the audience's needs/expectations in your paper? What kind of audience would you want to invoke your instructor to be? Now consider how your paper changes if this alternate audience is your focus: how does your approach to your topic change if you are specifically writing toward peers, members of your field, or members of the wider public?

3. Think of one of your personal favorite texts—poem, essay, song, etc. What is the person/audience that the writer is invoking you to be? When you engage with that text do you see yourself as that type of person? What strategies does the author use to make you understand yourself that way? Be as specific as possible.

4. As a class, we will pick a debate topic: this can be anything, as long as it has current relevance. Half the class will represent the addressed audience in this topic, and the other half will represent the invented audience. Is it actually possible to have a debate like this, or does the act of invention occur on such an unconscious level that drawing stark attention to it creates a sense of unreality?

Exercises

1. Find an article in Part Two, Unit Two of this textbook, and determine who the intended audience is. For whom is the author writing? How can you tell? Are there particular phrases that identify or allude to certain people or groups? Can you point out certain instances of the audience being addressed and the audience being invoked? If so, what are the differences between the two? Write a 5–7 sentence long paragraph that analyzes the audience of the article you found.

2. Create a list of the types of composing/writing that you do in a normal week during the semester (this may include class work, emails, to do lists, etc.). In small groups, discuss the types of composing you came up with. Identify both who is the addressed audience and the invoked audience for each type of writing.

3. Think about an embarrassing situation/moment in your life. It could be from a long time ago, or it could be from yesterday. Write a short letter to your best friend recounting this incident. Then, write a short letter to your mom/dad/guardian recounting that same incident. When you're done, ask yourself what changes you made when writing about the same incident to your mom/dad/guardian and consider why you made them. Next, turn to a peer and discuss your changes with each other. Are they similar? Why did you feel the need to make changes when the audience changed?

4. As a class we will pick a general, overarching topic. We will then split into groups, each of whom are looking for a specific type of source that addresses this topic: a song, a photo, an advertisement OR a film poster, a popular press article, and an academic article. After identifying who both the invoked and addressed audiences for your specific artifact are, we will regroup and try to discern which is the most effective piece of rhetoric.

Supplemental Reading

On Stereotypes
Mahzarin R. Banaji and Anthony G. Greenwald

Categories

The recognized starting point for modern scientific understanding of stereotypes is Gordon Allport's 1954 book *The Nature of Prejudice*. Allport wrote: "The human mind must think with the aid of categories.... Once formed, categories are the basis for normal prejudgment. We cannot possibly avoid this process. Orderly living depends on it."[3]

The term *Homo categoricus* acknowledges the scientific impact of Allport's view of the importance of mental categories. A category is a collection of things having enough in common so that it is convenient to treat them as kin. The similarity among category members does not need to be great. The category of *car* includes things as different as toy cars, cable cars, and railroad cars. But the use of categories has a powerful effect on our behavior—as a quick look at a situation involving some subordinate categories within the *car* category will make clear: If you are driving on a highway and closing rapidly on a fast-moving car in front of you, your own speed in the next few seconds will be drastically different if you categorize that speeding vehicle as *police car* rather than as *sports car*. Another example: You will act very differently toward small white crystals that you categorize as *sugar* than toward ones you categorize as *salt*, even though you can't visibly tell one from the other in a spoon.

The categories that we use for people also affect our behavior in very clear ways. For example:

■ In a department store to make a purchase, you readily surrender your credit card to a total stranger whom you categorize as a *salesclerk*. You trust this stranger to be a typical member of the salesclerk category—that is, someone who will not surreptitiously record your account information and then sell it to an identity thief.

■ Entering a medical clinic, you assume the obedient role of *patient* (another category). Even though you may never have seen any of the medical staff before, you unquestioningly follow the instructions of people who are dressed in ways that lead you to categorize them as *doctor* or *nurse*. Having so categorized them, you then proceed to trust them with your life—not to mention your willingness to strip naked in their presence.

■ Driving on highways, you stay in your proper lane, you obey the traffic lights, and (a remarkably high percentage of the time) you stop at the stop signs. Without giving it a moment's thought, you behave as a member of the category *driver* and trust that others whom you categorize as drivers will be good members of that category and will act likewise.

Consider the alternatives. You might request a criminal-record check for all salesclerks. You might ask for the diplomas and current certifications of all the medical personnel you encounter. And you might refuse to venture out driving, for fear of being crushed under the wheels of other vehicles. If you did actually behave in so cautious a fashion, however, you yourself might be classified as paranoid or agoraphobic (two more categories), as a consequence of which you would experience inconveniences far greater than those you risk just by trusting others to be good members of their categories. Yes, there are tales of salesclerks who engage in identity theft, stories of medical impostors, and news reports of accidents caused by inebriated, incompetent, and sleepy drivers. It is remarkable that, for almost all of us, knowing that these possibilities exist does not stop us from shopping, getting medical help, or driving. Categories are not only extremely convenient—they are essential in permitting us to get about the business of our lives.

A Mind Built to Use Categories

To show how, as Allport put it, "orderly living" depends on the use of categories, we shall describe four of the many feats that our minds perform with the aid of categories. Each of these is carried out so effortlessly that, even while doing them, we remain entirely unaware of the mental virtuosity that they draw upon.

Feat 1: Multidimensional Categories—A Snap!

Can you make sense of this string of sixteen words?

1991 Subaru Legacy 4-door sedan with 4-cylinder engine, front-wheel drive, and automatic transmission.

Possibly you understood it in no more than the few seconds it took to read it. Next question: Would you have known that the string identified something quite different if it included "station wagon with standard transmission" in place of "sedan with automatic transmission"? If you can answer yes to both questions, you can regard yourself as the proud owner of a seven-dimensional category structure for automobiles. The seven dimensions are the seven columns of Table 1.

The sixteen-word Subaru description is one of thousands of distinct automobile categories that can be formed by stringing together identifiers from the seven columns of the table. The ability to conjure up pictures of a great many distinct automobile categories is one of two important characteristics of Feat 1. The second is the ease and automaticity with which your mind regularly makes use of this seven-dimensional structure.

Because some people are not so familiar with automobiles, not everyone can rapidly decode the sixteen words that describe the 1991 Subaru. If the Subaru example did not work for you, hold on for a moment—the much larger number of groups categorized in Feat 2 should establish the point.

Table 1. Seven-Dimensional Automobile Category Generator

Model	Year	Body Type	Engine Size	Power Source	Transmission	Drive
Ford Taurus	1990	Hatchback	4-cylinder	Diesel	Manual 4-speed	Front wheel
Cadillac Seville	1991	Station wagon	6-cylinder	Electric	Manual 5-speed	Rear wheel
VW Jetta	1992	Convertible	8-cylinder	Hybrid	Automatic	4-wheel
. . .	. . .	SUV		Gasoline		
Subaru Legacy	2007	Pickup				
Audi Turbo	2008	2-door sedan				
Toyota Camry	2009	4-door sedan				
Mercedes 550SL	2010	Van				

Feat 2: Millions of Person Categories Creatable on the Fly

Table 2 shows a small part of a six-dimensional structure that generates distinct categories of people by stringing together terms from its six columns. Some of the categories identified by these six-label strings encompass a relatively large number of people. For example, there are many middle-aged, White, male, Christian, Detroit factory workers. At the same time, if you don't live in Detroit, there is a good chance that you may never have met even one such person. Nevertheless, few Americans will have difficulty in forming an immediate mental conception of that factory worker on reading or hearing the six-label description. You may think that you can form an immediate impression of the Detroit factory worker because you've seen or heard or read about people like him in news media (talking about the closing of factories or being on strike, perhaps), in fiction, through friends, and so on.

But in fact, your facility with the six dimensions of Table 2 cannot be explained that simply. Your category-forming capacity is actually great enough to allow you to instantly conceive even a person described by an entirely unfamiliar combination of the six dimensions. For example, try thinking about a Black, Muslim, sixtyish, French, lesbian professor. Most readers of this book are unlikely to know even one person who could be identified by any four of those six identifiers. (Try it!) But that doesn't make it difficult to imagine one. It's almost a certainty that you will easily be able to form a picture in your mind of a person quite unlike anyone you have ever met: A Black, Muslim, sixtyish, French, lesbian professor.

For people who recognize the four sexuality/gender categories in the table, along with five race groups (add Native American to the four shown), plus approximately fifty nationalities or regions, about ten religions, eight age groups, and perhaps fifty occupations, Table 2 will produce a staggeringly large number of person categories—four million. The rapidity with which we can use the six identifiers to arrive at a picture of a category of person, however large (the Detroit factory worker) or small (the French professor) the category, confirms the brain's agility as a maker and user of categories.

Table 2. Six-Dimensional Person Category Generator

Race	Religion	Age	Nationality/ Region	Sex/Gender	Occupation
White	Christian	Young	French	Male	Professor
Asian	Muslim	Middle-aged	Detroit	Female	Homemaker
Black	Jewish ·	Sixtyish	Australian	Gay	Flight attendant
Hispanic	Zoroastrian	Elderly	American	Lesbian	Factory Worker

Feat 3: Leaping beyond the Available Information[4]

How does your brain deal with learning that a person is "American"—for example, "My English professor is American" or "An American passenger was held for questioning" or "The American lottery winner remained anonymous"? Before reading the next paragraph, please humor us by forming a mental image of one of these—say, the anonymous American lottery winner. Try to visualize that person in the process of making a phone call to claim the winnings.

What characteristics does your imagined person have in addition to being American? We suspect that your imagined person is very likely also White, male, and adult. And if your imagined American did have those three added characteristics, very likely they entered your mind without your having to consciously place them there. You can't form a mental image of a person without attributing a male or female gender to that person, and usually a race and an age too. That said, you could—in theory—have imagined a female Hispanic American teenager making the call to collect the lottery winnings. But there's a much higher likelihood that your mind generated the image of a White male adult. The characteristics that you added can be thought of as your default values for the race, gender, and age of a typical American. Why might White, male, and adult be the default characteristics for an otherwise undescribed "American"? Likely it's because those are the characteristics of Americans whom you see, hear, and read about in newspapers, radio, television, and conversation most frequently, no matter whether they are the characteristics of those you meet and talk with most often as you go about your day.

If you are at all skeptical about the idea that in forming these mental pictures we use default characteristics to flesh out and go far beyond the basic information we've been given, then think about it this way: The default attributes that we add are so taken for granted and so automatic that, without thinking about why we do this, we are usually careful to specify a *different* set of attributes when the default ones don't apply. Thus you simply say "American" when you are referring to a White American. But if you're talking about another kind of American, you may instead say "Asian American" or "African American." Similarly, when you refer to a "taxi driver" you are almost certainly referring to a male taxi driver. If not, you may say "lady cab driver."

You can now understand something that might have been puzzling when we described the 1933 Princeton stereotype study.... The students were asked to describe typical characteristics of nationality or race categories that were identified by single words, such as *Americans*, *Germans*, *Chinese*, and *Italians*. The Princeton students almost certainly assumed, without giving it any thought, that when they were asked to choose characteristics typical of Americans, they were expected to provide traits characteristic of White, male, adult Americans. The two traits that they most often selected for Americans, *materialistic* and *ambitious*, are very unlikely to be characteristics that the students would have chosen if they had been asked to describe American women or children.[5]

Feat 4: Cooperative Categorization

People often actively send signals about the categories to which they themselves belong. Thus, on first meeting, we can often read these signals to help us identify a person's occupation. At the service station, we know that the person wearing coveralls is a mechanic, not a customer. In the hospital, the person in the white coat is a nurse or doctor, not a patient. The use of clothing to identify different occupations is just one of many ways in which people routinely help others to easily place them into appropriate categories.

Probably the most common, and arguably the most important, of these cooperative categorization strategies are those that help others to categorize us as male or female. If you are puzzled by this statement, wondering, "Who needs help in classifying people as male or female?" your puzzlement indicates only how unthinkingly—and routinely—almost everyone provides this help.

Although it is not difficult to distinguish male from female using natural body shape and facial features, we nevertheless use a wide variety of additional aids to help the process along. Women typically wear their hair longer than men. Most men and women wear sex-typical clothes that serve to accentuate body shape differences between male and female. Many people wear styles of collars, sleeves, belts, and shoes that are distinctively masculine or feminine. Cosmetics, manicures, jewelry, and gestures add still more markings that advertise—perhaps *flaunt* is the better word—maleness or femaleness. It could be an interesting exercise in economics to calculate the fraction of American wealth spent on clothing, cosmetics, and other accessories that ease the work of categorizing one another as male or female.

Race is another feature that can usually be identified fairly rapidly without help, but it too is a category that people often choose to make, more identifiable by their choice of hairstyle, clothing, speech, gesture, and other signifiers.

Of course, such signifiers can be co-opted by other groups—witness the phenomenon of White suburban teenagers dressing "ghetto" to make a particular impression. This brings us to recognize that the cooperative categorization phenomenon also has its uncooperative variant form, in which we send visual signals for the explicit purpose of *mis*representing a category to which we belong.

The most common form of uncooperative categorization is the effort that many put into projecting the appearance of an age group younger than their own. A great deal of money is made supplying elders with cosmetics, hair dyes, surgery, and drugs designed to erase wrinkles, shore up sagging body parts, disguise hair that is turning gray or white, and replace hair that has disappeared. Given the traits stereotypically associated with old age—being slow, forgetful, hard of hearing, feeble, and so on—it is easy enough to see why elderly people might want to make it appear that they belong to a younger age group!

Less often disguised than age are religion and ethnicity, but they too are the object of uncooperative categorization under certain circumstances. A well-known strategy is to replace an ethnically identifiable name, such as Winona Horowitz, Issur Demsky, Anna Maria Louisa Italiano, or Jacob Cohen, with something less ethnically identifiable—like the names Winona Ryder, Kirk Douglas, Anne Bancroft, and Rodney Dangerfield (as these people are better known). A more recent cultural invention of the uncooperative categorization variety is the "whitening" of résumés submitted by African Americans in applying for jobs. This involves removing mentions of memberships and positions in obviously African American organizations and altering or omitting names of traditionally Black colleges or universities.

Notwithstanding the relative ease of engaging in uncooperative categorization, many members of often-stigmatized ethnic, racial, or sexual orientation categories not only avoid misrepresenting their categories but choose to do quite the opposite, making it easy for others to place them in their often-stigmatized categories. This suggests that the advantages of signaling those identities may often outweigh the disadvantages.

Think, for example, of gays and lesbians. Although they remain stigmatized and disadvantaged in many settings in modern America, many have decided to make their sexual orientation known—at least to other members of their category, and sometimes to the world at large. Such assists to "gaydar" (the ability to assess another's sexual orientation from a distance) make it much easier for gays to identify one another, and—if the signals are not of the secret-handshake type—often for non-gays to do so as well, helping avoid potential embarrassment on both sides.

Of the four feats, cooperative categorization stands apart from the others, being the only one that directly shows the everyday working of stereotypes. When cooperative categorization comes into play, a stereotype operates, interestingly, exactly opposite to the fashion usually expected. Instead of knowing a person's category (for example, female) and expecting a stereotypic trait (for example, long hair), we observe the long hair and infer that the person is female. Another paradox of cooperative categorization is that deliberately displaying a stereotyped characteristic (for example, the male professor's pipe and elbow-patched jacket) can have the possibly unwanted effect of strengthening observers' conception of the stereotype's validity.

The remainder of this chapter will make use of the mental virtuosity of Feats 1, 2, and 3 to decribe further how stereotypes function in our daily lives. We reach a conclusion that should be a surprise to those familiar with existing scientific understanding of stereotypes.

How We Use Stereotypes

Most of us think that the statement *Ducks lay eggs* is quite reasonable. But "Ducks lay eggs" is actually false for a substantial majority of the world's ducks, and not for one but two reasons. First, because fewer female than male ducklings survive the hatching process, more than half the world's ducks are non-egg-laying males.[6] Second, among female ducks, many are too young to be egg layers. Without doubt, egg-laying ducks are a distinct minority. We anticipate your reaction: "In agreeing that 'Ducks lay eggs' was reasonable, I meant only that I knew that *some* ducks lay eggs, not that *all* ducks lay eggs."

Fair enough. But suppose that the statement had been *Dogs wear clothes*. This is certainly true of *some* dogs. Would you have classified that statement as reasonable? Not likely. In our understanding, "Ducks lay eggs" seems more reasonable than "Dogs wear clothes" because most people have a strong *duck = egg layer* association. And unless you have been greatly influenced by William Wegman's photos of Man Ray, Fay Ray, and their successors, you probably do not have a *dog = clothes wearer* association.

The "Ducks lay eggs" example gives a clue to how stereotypes influence our thinking. Just as we may incorrectly assume that a duck seen swimming in a nearby pond can lay eggs, we may—equally unthinkingly—assume that an elderly person we have just met has poor memory. The *old = forgetful* stereotype is valid only to the extent that a greater proportion of elderly than young people have poor memory. Nevertheless, that stereotype may influence your reactions to *all* elderly people, including ones whose memories may be far better than your own.[7]

Here is another illustration of the tendency to think in stereotypes. For each of the five traits listed on the left below, do you see that trait as a better description of the first of the two groups named to the right, or the second?

Table 3.

Trait	Groups
Leadership	Men more than women?
Musical talent	African Americans more than Native Americans?
Legal Expertise	Jews more than Christians?
Math ability	Asians more than Whites?
Criminality	Italians more than Dutch?

Any yes answer suggests that you possess a stereotype that, undoubtedly, many others also have. It's true that possessing these stereotypes doesn't make it inevitable that you will use them when you are making judgments about individual people, or that you will make important decisions based on them. For example, a corporate manager may believe that the *leader* = *male* stereotype is generally valid but may still be able to recognize that a specific woman who has shown outstanding leadership potential would be a good candidate for an executive position. At the same time, the bar she would have to clear might be higher than for men competing for the same position. Similarly, a teacher with a *math* = *male* stereotype may encourage an obviously gifted girl to pursue her studies in math. But this same teacher may also underestimate the math abilities of many other girls, all the while being more ready to recognize the potential of boys and to single them out for extra help and attention.

Does Stereotyping Have a Useful Purpose?

While we may concede Gordon Allport's point that "the human mind must think with the aid of categories," and that, as he said, orderly living is not possible without using categories, we also have to wonder about the ultimate consequences of our category-making and category-using activities. For, as Allport also told us, "Once formed, categories are the basis for normal prejudgment." Another way of saying this is that the categories that our brains form so easily give rise to stereotypes. Thus we associate certain categories with certain prejudged attributes—Africans with having rhythm, Asians with being good at math, women with being inattentive drivers, and so forth.

Indeed, stereotyping by social category is so widely practiced as to deserve recognition as a universal human trait—as implied by the term *Homo categoricus*, which we used as the title for this chapter. Scientists understand universal traits in terms of the idea of adaptiveness or usefulness. Universal traits are generally assumed either to be presently adaptive or to be unfortunate by-products of other presently adaptive characteristics, or perhaps to be troublesome vestiges of previously (but no longer) adaptive characteristics.

The currently dominant explanation for the pervasiveness of stereotyping is of the "unfortunate by-product" type—stereotyping is an unfortunate by-product of the otherwise immensely useful human ability to conceive the world in terms of categories. Many social psychologists see this explanation as plausible, and we are among them.

There is also a theory of the "presently adaptive" type. This theory supposes that many people derive a useful self-esteem boost because stereotypes allow them to see their own group as superior to other groups. Having unfavorable stereotypes of many other groups makes this fairly easy to do. But this theory is less than compelling, in part because humans have so many other ways to boost self-esteem, and in part because it leads to an expectation that is most likely untrue—that those occupying the higher-status roles in their society or possessing the society's default characteristics should engage in more stereotyping than those lower in the hierarchy.

We offer here a new (and admittedly speculative) theory of the benefits of stereotyping that is also of the "presently adaptive" variety: Stereotyping achieves the desirable effect of allowing us to rapidly perceive total strangers as distinctive individuals.

We hope you read that last sentence at least twice, trying to find words that you thought you must have missed on first reading. The assertion "Stereotyping allows us to perceive strangers as distinctive individuals" may seem incomprehensible, even ludicrous, to anyone who thinks of stereotypes as the one-size-fits-all mental boxes into which we force all members of a group, no matter how different from one another they may be. Recall the inspiration for Walter Lippmann's coinage in 1922—the printer's metal plate that produced many identical copies. If stereotypes cause us to view all _____ (you name the group: Cheerleaders, Italians, Muslims, rocket scientists, whatever) as being alike, then it would seem to follow that stereotypes must undermine, rather than facilitate, our ability to perceive strangers as distinct individuals.

We come to our seemingly absurd theory courtesy of the second mental feat of which *Homo categoricus* is capable: The ability to simultaneously use six (possibly more) person identifiers to produce mental images of many distinct categories of people. Applying the stereotypes associated with these six or so identifiers simultaneously produces a result very different from Lippmann's "identical copies."

This will be a good time to recall the Black, Muslim, sixtyish, French, lesbian professor we used to illustrate Feat 2. Each of her six identifiers carries its own set of stereotypic traits. Using one identifier at a time would mean seeing her only with the Black stereotype, or only the Muslim stereotype, or only the stereotype for one of her other four category labels. But processing her six identifiers together, all at once, lets us conceive of a person who is distinctly different from anyone else we know. Maybe they didn't quite break the mold when they made her, but she'll be seen as a distinct individual, someone whom we will not readily confuse with anyone else we know.

To make our paradoxical explanation convincing, it may help if we make clear how easy it is to grasp half a dozen or so person identifiers within a fraction of a second. We do this all the time. Imagine a person who walks past you while you wait to board an airplane. Five identifiers will almost always be immediately available—sex, age, race, height, and weight. Clothing may permit us to add multiple other identifiers, perhaps including income, social class, religion, ethnicity, and occupation. Each of these identifiers has stereotypical traits associated with it. When our minds automatically activate all these stereotypes at once, we get a rich, complex perception of the person, even though the passerby we are contemplating is a total stranger. After no more than a brief glance we should be able to distinguish this passerby from just about everyone else in sight, and quite possibly from everyone else in the airport. This is why we conclude that the mental virtuosity described in Feat 2 allows us to use stereotypes to *perceive strangers as distinctive individuals.*

Who Uses Stereotypes? Who Gets Stereotyped?

It is not possible to be human and to avoid making use of stereotypes. Stereotypes make up a submerged but significant portion of the meaning that we read into words such as *old, female, Asian,* and *Muslim.* These submerged, automatically activated meanings go well beyond dictionary definitions. For example, nowhere in any dictionary of the English language will you find *old* defined as "slow," "forgetful," "hard of hearing," or "feeble," but these are all parts of the stereotype that the category *old* is packaged with. Not having stereotypes to provide meaning to our person categories would be like knowing the words of a language without knowing what they mean. In other words, *everyone uses stereotypes.*

The answer to "Who gets stereotyped?" is less simple. Stereotypes are not distributed equally. If you can be described by the default attributes of your society—the attributes that don't need to be mentioned because they are assumed unless explicitly stated otherwise (see Feat 3)—you will be subject to less stereotyping than others. You won't be stereotyped by the members of your in-group—those who share the default characteristics that you have—and you may be stereotyped little by others. In Japan, young Japanese men are unlikely to be stereotyped. However, in the United States, they are likely to be stereotyped. This is perhaps why those who belong to their society's "default" categories may see stereotyping as less of a problem than others do—they are much less likely to be its victims.

On the other hand, those who lack their society's default characteristics are likely to be stereotyped, and not just by others but by themselves—which can be to their disadvantage. This conclusion has only recently been established in research, and it may be the unkindest cut of all. The stereotypes applied to a group are sometimes self-applied by members of the group to themselves, and in that case the stereotypes may act as self-undermining and self-fulfilling prophecies.

Self-fulfilling prophecies can be beneficial. An own-group stereotype might guide African Americans toward becoming better track athletes, basketball players, or jazz musicians. Asian stereotypes may prompt Asian Americans to work hard in school, win scholarships, and launch themselves into high-paying careers in science, medicine, and engineering.

But when stereotypes are unfavorable, as many are, the forces that cause people to act in ways that conform to the stereotype applied to their own group can have damaging effects. Elders who internalize stereotypes of the elderly are at greater risk of declining health; women who internalize gender stereotypes are at risk of underperforming in math and science; African Americans who internalize stereotypes of their own group are at risk of not living up to their academic potential. It doesn't take the (stereotypical) rocket scientist to understand the potential for harm in stereotypes.[8]

Notes

3. Allport's statement about the importance of categories appears in his *Nature of Prejudice* (Allport, 1954). A collection of modern perspectives on Allport's contributions to understanding stereotypes and prejudice was published in a fiftieth-anniversary celebration of the book (Dovidio, Glick, & Rudman, 2005). A contemporary overview of scientific work on stereotypes is available in a comprehensive text by David Schneider (2004).

4. The label for Feat 3—"leaping beyond the available information"—is borrowed from an influential essay by cognitive psychologist Jerome Bruner, "Going beyond the information given" (Bruner, 1957).

5. The supposition that stereotypes captured by the methods of the 1933 Princeton study consist of traits characteristic of men (not women) of the various national groups was later tested and confirmed in research by social psychologists Alice Eagly and Mary Kite (1987).

6. Many sources report that sex ratios in ducks, estimated by a variety of methods, show that males are in the majority (e.g., Brown, 1982).

7. The use of "Ducks lay eggs" to illustrate the extent to which a statement that properly applies to "some" (ducks in this case) may be inappropriately applied to "most" is borrowed from illustrations used by cognitive psychologist Sam Glucksberg (Khemlani, Glucksberg, & Rubio Fernandez, 2007).

8. The self-fulfilling prophecy aspect of stereotypes about the elderly has been described by Levy (2009). The self-fulfilling aspect of female and African American stereotypes has received attention in a large body of recent research on stereotype threat, especially by Claude Steele and his colleagues (Steele, Spencer, & Aronson, 2002).

References

Allport, G. W. (1954). *The nature of prejudice.* Cambridge, MA: Perseus.

Brown, D. E. (1982). Sex ratios, sexual selection and sexual dimorphism in waterfowl. *American Birds, 36,* 259–260.

Bruner, J. S. (1957). Going beyond the information given. In H. Gruber et al. (eds.), *Contemporary approaches to cognition* (pp. 41–69). Cambridge, MA: Harvard University Press.

Dovidio, J. F., Glick, P., & Rudman, L. A. (eds.) (2005). *On the nature of prejudice: Fifty years after Allport.* Malden, MA: Blackwell.

Eagly, A. H., & Kite, M. E. (1987). Are stereotypes of nationalities applied to both women and men? *Journal of Personality and Social Psychology, 53*, 451–462.

Katz, D., & Braly, K. (1933). Racial stereotypes of one hundred college students. *Journal of Abnormal and Social Psychology, 28*, 280–290.

Khemlani, S., Glucksberg, S., & Rubio Fernandez, P. (2007). Do ducks lay eggs? How people interpret generic assertions. In D. S. McNamara & J. G. Trafton (eds.), *Proceedings of the 29th Annual Cognitive Science Society*, 64–70. Austin, TX: Cognitive Science Society.

Levy, B. (2009). Stereotype embodiment: A psycho-social approach to aging. *Current Directions in Psychological Science, 18*, 332–336.

Lippmann, W. (1922). *Public opinion*. New York: Harcourt, Brace.

Madon, S., et al. (2001). Ethnic and national stereotypes: The Princeton trilogy revisited and revised. *Personality and Social Psychology Bulletin, 27*, 996–1010.

Rice, S. A, (1926). "Stereotypes": A source of error in judging human character. *Journal of Personnel Research, 5*, 267–276.

Schneider, D. J. (2004). *The psychology of stereotypes*. New York: Guilford.

Steele, C. M., Spencer, S. J., & Aronson, J. (2002). Contending with group image: The psychology of stereotype and social identity threat. In M. P. Zanna (ed.), *Advances in experimental social psychology*, vol. 34 (pp. 379–440). San Diego, CA: Academic Press.

CHAPTER 5

Analyzing Structure

While it is an incredibly useful exercise to break down arguments into their constituent parts through the Toulmin model—their claims, warrants, data, backing, qualifiers, and rebuttals—a **composition** consists of much more than these simple parts; most of the arguments we see, hear, read, or otherwise encounter aren't just presented in a logical diagram. Indeed, part of what makes compositions so endlessly readable is this very fact: even when following the same core framework, no two well-thought-out compositions are ever the same. Furthermore, while creating and analyzing these logical diagrams allows us to better situate specific arguments in the context of their rhetorical situation, analyzing the broader aspects of their composition is also necessary and useful.

This chapter, then, introduces you to a number of ways of thinking about the **structure** of a composition as a whole—or what is traditionally called **arrangement** in rhetorical terms. The second canon of rhetoric, arrangement (*Taxis* in Greek and *Dispositio* in Latin) generally refers to the way the different parts of a composition are ordered. Because of the spoken context of the earliest rhetorical practice, arrangement originally concerned ordering the sections of a speech. Like the other canons of rhetoric, however, modern arrangement deals with any type of composition. While this canon may not immediately seem as important as some of the others, like invention, ancient and modern composers know that even an inventive, well written, extensively researched composition can fall flat if it is disorganized or arranged in a confusing way. As you learned in Chapter 2, *kairos* is concerned with thinking about why a particular argument is made at a particular time; similarly, arrangement asks you to consider why a composition is ordered or structured in the way that it is. Successful rhetors arrange their compositions so that they can present their arguments *effectively* to particular audiences, at particular moments, and to create particular outcomes.

While the "standard" academic essay that you may have learned in high school (introduction, opposing views, point one, point two, point three, conclusion) can be an effective arrangement, there are also many other options, and this chapter introduces you to two of them: the classical structure and the Rogerian structure. Arrangement, however, is not just concerned with the ordering of paragraphs; rather, it includes all different levels of a composition. Within paragraphs, arrangement will help you think about the placement of topic sentences, claims, supporting evidence, transitions, and more. At certain points in history, arrangement has even been considered an important part of **style** because it includes the ordering of the parts *within* a sentence—the words, clauses, and phrases that work together to express a particular idea. The knowledge you gain about arrangement here is also applicable to compositions in any number of media and genre; whether you're analyzing fiction, poetry, newspaper articles, text messages, PowerPoint presentations, etc., how a composition is arranged is vital to its effectiveness.

When thinking about and analyzing different arrangements in your research, the most important thing to remember is that structure should be *effective.* More specifically, think about what kind of experience a rhetor wants to orchestrate for her readers through the composition's structure. You already know that in order for an audience to be engaged with an argument, it must be timely, but *kairos* isn't always enough to keep them interested: an effective arrangement is one that keeps the audience engaged all the way to the end. As such, it also helps you to think through argumentative choices. These choices include, among other things, the type of logic or reasoning used, the placement of examples, which sources should go where, and which aspects of an argument are the most important (see Chapter 7). As you explore these different aspects of arrangement, try to identify them in the arguments you have cataloged in your invention database, experiment with them in your own writing, and pay attention to what works best where—each one will have its opportune use!

Classical Arrangement[1]

Perhaps the oldest known model for arrangement in Western history is the one we call **classical arrangement**. The classical model incorporates the six parts of a discourse that ancient rhetoric teachers believed were necessary for persuasion, especially when presenting in front of variegated audiences, whose members may range from mildly skeptical to hostile.

While classical arrangement may seem to be a cookie-cutter way to structure an essay, it is not necessarily a static template—that is, simply filling in the elements does not itself constitute a successful essay. Indeed, to do nothing but follow the structure will often (but, admittedly, not always) lead to a lifeless composition. It's also worth considering that this arrangement does not mirror specific paragraph structure of a paper: in other words, just because it offers a six-part structure

---

1. This section adapted from material originally written by Amber Lee.

does not mean you should just blindly write a six-paragraph essay. However, if you use this overall structure as a general guideline, it can be a useful heuristic for developing effective arguments.

The classical arrangement consists of six parts:

1. **The Introduction (Exordium)** usually begins the essay and should engage the interest of a particular audience and focus that audience's attention on a specific argument. An effective introduction should:

   a. Introduce your topic

   b. State your position on that topic

   c. Establish your credibility to your particular audience

   As you develop your exordium, ask yourself:

   - What, really, is my argument?

   - Who is my particular audience?

   - What image of myself and my stance do I want to project?

2. **The Statement of Facts (Narratio)** follows. It is necessary to provide an exigency for your audience to believe that there really *is* a problem demanding concern, and speakers or writers often combine this step with the introduction. The statement of facts should provide background information necessary to orient your particular audience to the problem and your argument.

   As you develop your narratio, ask yourself:

   - What is the situation to which this argument is responding?

   - What elements of background or context do I need present for this particular audience?

3. **The Division (Partitio)** is, according to the Roman rhetorician Quintilian, the most effective way to continue. The division summarizes the argument(s) you are about to make. Think of it as a plan or map of your argument, which will allow your audience to know in advance where you are headed, even if they do not know the particular proof, or ways in which you will escort them through your argument.

   As you develop your partitio, ask yourself:

   - What is my thesis?

   - Where do I want my argument to end?

   - How do I want to take my audience to this particular end?

4. **The Proof (Confirmatio)** presents the essential claims and evidence that support and substantiate the thesis of your argument. These claims are often

made and evidenced through rhetorical appeals. In other words, the proof provides the answer to "why should anyone agree with me?"

As you develop your confirmatio, ask yourself:

- What proof supports my thesis? *Is my audience likely to respond to this support?*
- What proof would my audience be *least* likely to respond to?
- How can I demonstrate that my proof is valid and applicable to my argument?

5. **The Concession and Refutation (Refutatio)** allow you to acknowledge other viewpoints and appeal to an audience that may be particularly skeptical.

That is, usually you will be making an argument toward an audience who doesn't necessarily agree with your point of view; why would you make an argument to an audience who already agrees with everything you say? Therefore, because both arguments and audiences are multi-faceted, this part of the classical arrangement gives you the chance to address the complexities of your argument and audience while pointing out the shortcomings of other points of view.

As you develop your refutatio, ask yourself:

- What counterarguments or hesitations are my audience likely to harbor?
- How can the weaknesses in my argument be modestly acknowledged without undermining my entire stance?
- What shortcomings in opposing arguments might I highlight?

6. **The Conclusion (Peroratio)** reiterates your argument as forcefully and memorably as possible. This means that, if you want your audience to remember what you have said, simply restating your thesis or repeating your proof isn't enough. Ancient rhetoricians often advocated for using *pathos* heavily in the conclusion to forge an emotional connection between your audience and your argument. Creating this emotional investment provides a different type of force than facts alone and, often, makes your argument more memorable.

As you develop your peroratio, consider:

- What do I want my audience to remember most about my argument?
- Am I simply repeating what I have already said? What are the broader implications of my argument?
- Is my conclusion doing the rest of my paper justice? (That is, is it furthering all of the work I've done by memorably driving home my point?)

Rogerian Arrangement[2]

A **Rogerian argument** is another format writers use to craft effective arguments. It operates on the belief that a writer's presentation of goodwill and her willingness to compromise are sometimes the quickest route to solving a problem or easing a disagreement. Rogerian arguments persuade by highlighting the common ground between opposing positions and using that common ground to work toward a solution to some, if not all, aspects of the issue.

A Rogerian argument often consists of five sections. Keep in mind that, like in classical arrangement, one section does not necessarily equal one paragraph but rather can include as many paragraphs as necessary:

1. **Introduction:** In this section, the writer provides an overview of the problem or topic about which she is arguing. The overview should include any background information an audience needs to understand the depth and complexity of an argument and its rhetorical situation. For example, a writer arguing in favor of the Black Lives Matter movement would likely compose an introduction summarizing the historical and cultural contexts that shaped what she sees as a demand for justice and equality, the contemporary situations that led to the birth and proliferation of the movement, and the types of actions and initiatives in which the organization is involved.

2. **Summary of Opposing Positions:** Here, the writer describes the opposing sides' arguments. The purpose of this section is to inform rather than persuade, so all positions must be presented with as much objectivity as possible. The writer of the Black Lives Matter argument mentioned previously could use this section to define the perspectives contrary to her own—such as people associated with the Blue Lives Matter movement and people who generally disagree with social protest. Not only will fair treatment of different viewpoints help build her credibility as an informed speaker, but also it will serve as a powerful gesture of goodwill and sympathy towards those with whom she disagrees.

3. **Statement of Understanding:** After outlining the argument, the writer establishes common ground between opposing positions by acknowledging aspects of her opponents' beliefs that she considers valid. The writer focusing on the Black Lives Matter movement could ground her argument in how most people invested in this issue—whether for it or against it—believe that nonviolence is the best way to effect change and have a shared dedication to building safer communities. By building her argument on points of agreement, the writer increases the likelihood that her readers will listen to, and thus potentially be persuaded by, her ideas.

4. **Statement of the Writer's Position:** This section allows the writer to present and argue in favor of her position. It includes the evidence (outside sources,

---

2. This section adapted from material originally written by Melody Pritchard.

inductive/deductive reasoning, examples, etc.) needed to establish her points. Although the purpose of this section is to persuade, it should do so with the goal of reconciling with the opposition, not defeating it. Remember, the strength of the Rogerian argument is its ability to connect with the opposition, not to alienate it. During this section the writer should build her argument on the shared values she described in the previous section. The writer focusing on the Black Lives Matter movement, then, would want to reach out to those who are skeptical of the movement and invoke their best natures rather than alienate them by using negative labels or ignoring their concerns.

5. **Conclusion:** Finally, the writer presents a solution that appeals to everyone. An effective conclusion should highlight how accepting the writer's position on the issue-at-hand would benefit all parties, even if total agreement cannot be reached. To draw from the Black Lives Matter example once more, the argument may not fully solve the issues it addresses, but it should suggest ways to move forward and effect mutually beneficial change.

Discussion Questions

1. When would classical arrangement be beneficial to an argument; in other words, what types of arguments would be best articulated through this form of arrangement? Similarly, when would classical arrangement be detrimental to a topic? Now consider these same questions, but from a Rogerian standpoint. Are there topics where neither seem like the "right" fit?

2. How could we mold or play with classical arrangement to make it work differently? In other words, considering the earlier explanation of how classical arrangement works, adapt it for different purposes.

3. While the outline on pages 65–66 illustrates the different components of classical arrangement and their purpose, it does not explain how much space should be dedicated to each section in relation to the entire argument. What sections do you think would take the longest to write and why? Which sections do you think would take the longest to read and why? Ultimately, what section do you think is the most vital for persuasion? How do your answers change when you consider different topics and different audiences?

4. The Rogerian format is based not only on demonstrating the goodwill of the rhetor but also assuming goodwill on the part of those with whom she disagrees. Many people find that difficult. Why is it so hard to see those with whom we disagree on political and social issues as good people? Why is it so much easier to see them as stupid, ignorant, or nefarious? Think of several specific examples to discuss while answering this question.

5. Debate time, with a difference. We will pick a topic: as always, this can be anything, as long as it is *kairotically* relevant. Half the class will outline a response using classical arrangement; the other half will outline a Rogerian

response. Both will, ultimately, present: which, in this case, is more effective? Time permitting, we will then choose a new topic, and the "sides" will flip: Team Classical will now be Team Rogerian, and vice versa.

Exercises

1. Go online and listen to Dr. Martin Luther King Jr.'s speech "I Have a Dream." Outline the classical moves he makes in this speech. Then, in a separate paragraph, answer the following questions: Are his movements all classically arranged? Does he rearrange at all? What might be the purpose for the arrangement he uses?

2. Using a paper you have written in the past (whether for this class, or one previously), outline your arrangement. Is the arrangement working for your purpose and your intended audience? Does this paper more closely fit the Classical or Rogerian guidelines? Rearrange your outline to fit the arrangement style it does not seemingly match: how is it now working differently? Does it even still make the same core argument?

3. While outlining your next paper, first outline it following the classical arrangement structure, then consider:

   a. How is this outline working toward your purpose and intended audience?

   b. Do you think this is a structure that will do your paper justice?

   c. Should any of the arrangement be rearranged in a way that will better serve your argument? Why?

4. Find an article in Part Two, Unit Two of this book. Create a reverse outline of the article to get a clear sense of its arrangement. Consider how effective the author's arrangement is—both its strengths and weaknesses. Then, restructure the argument to follow a Rogerian format. What does this shift in arrangement change? Does it make the argument more or less persuasive? Why?

5. In small groups pick an issue or problem that is highly divisive. Outline the main points of argument for each position and find places of possible consensus. Discuss the areas of agreement between opposing parties and develop a "Statement of Understanding" that meets the goals of the Rogerian format. Make sure your paragraph treats both sides fairly and ethically while finding common ground and pointing towards shared goals.

6. Look at the article you used for your most recent ILP. Does it follow a Rogerian or Classical format? Did the structure in which it was written have any impact on your using it for this project? Now think about the larger research you're working on for our class: is it possible to label each of your sources as either Classical or Rogerian, or are things not as clear as this chapter may initially suggest?

Supplemental Reading

Structural Rhythm
Eric Hayot

I do not think, I should say, that you have to know about your structure before you begin; nor do I think that your writing needs to be fundamentally structure-driven. The Uneven U helps you think about how your writing could or should work; it helps you chunk your own work, so that you can consider the ways you want it to fit together. I often start with a loose structure in mind (certainly with an idea about the number of sections or chapters), but the final structure of a piece only emerges in the process of rewriting and development that happens as my ideas become clear to me. I say all this because I know some people feel oppressed or intimidated by structure, like it means that they have to know everything in advance or that their writing must conform to a rigid set of parameters whose function it is to make them feel inadequate. Please don't take this that way—this is all supposed to help you, to increase your sense that you can control your prose and your writing practice, so that you can be ambitious on its behalf and use it to imagine and write the projects that matter to you.

So.

Structural rhythm: once you start building the book or essay, you will inevitably have to make some decisions about the relation of the parts to the whole. Whether you want long sections or short ones, long chapters or short ones, how the sections will be balanced relative to one another, what types of relations they will have—all these choices determine how structure shapes the overall rhythm of your work. A thirty-page essay can have three sections, or it can have ten; which decision you make will make a big difference to the reader's experience of the work.

Let's look at one very common structure for an academic essay:

Introduction	Section A Usually longer	Section B Usually shorter	Conclusion

In general, but not always, sections A and B will focus on different texts or authors, or they will cover instances within the same text or author; they may also focus on different theoretical problems, partly as a function of the change in text or topic. The second section tends to be shorter partly because some of the preliminary or theoretical work that it needs has been done by the first one.

The structure has a couple major variations. In one you'll find a third section, C, which will either be significantly shorter than A and B or will split the body of the essay evenly with A and B; in another you'll find a shorter A and a longer B. In a third the conclusion contains a third major primary document, which extends that section, allowing it to function as a counterpoint to the work in A and B. And, in a structure more common in book chapters than articles (because it often requires more time), you will start with an introduction, then have a second section (A) that provides background material (and hence also counts as introductory), before moving into the longer section B, which contains the reading and analysis, and finally to a conclusion. In that model B is often split into two major sections, like so:

Introduction	A	B1	B2	Conclusion
3–5 pp	10 pp	10–15 pp	10–20 pp	3–5 pp

...or

Introduction	A	B1	B2	C	Conclusion
1–3 pp	5–8 pp	10 pp	10+ pp	4–6 pp	2 pp, or fold into C

In the second variation, the decision to create a section C will usually stem from some kind of break in the conclusion, after which the conclusion ends up working as a kind of coda. In both cases the A section will actually extend and expand the introductory material, often with historical or theoretical context that sets up the readings in B1 and B2. (I call them B1 and B2 because often book chapters focus on single authors, so the B section therefore considers two movements in a single work, or two works by the same person; for chapters that deal with two authors, you might think of B1 and B2 as B and C [and then section C as D].)

Essays and chapters that follow these structural patterns propose, implicitly or explicitly, a series of relationships among their parts. Essays that have two major sections will have to manage and describe the relationship between A and B (i.e., what does B do that A didn't? what does B add to the analysis in A?), and these in turn can be managed or related to a possible section C. If we structure the sections *oppositionally*, we compose relationships of balanced pairs: A vs. B, then (A/B) vs. C, in which the C section adds nuance to what might otherwise feel like too reductive a binary (this or that...but actually a third way!). Alternatively, we can put sections A, B, and C in a triangular relation. Or, finally, we could structure the sections *developmentally*, giving us something like A + B (that is, the insights in A are tested and improved by the example of B), which gives a preliminary result that is then tested in turn (and boosted, twisted, ironized, or extended) by C.

The point is that there are really only so many ways that two or three things relate to one another, and that you should know which ones you're choosing and why. You want to think about both development and balance. In terms of development: How do the structures organize the reader's experience of the argument? Do they reflect any claims about the actual relationships among your subjects? (Imagine an essay in which the sections on Isherwood and Wilde are oppositional in terms of their relation to the argument, even though they do not together argue that Isherwood and Wilde were somehow opposed; you can also imagine an essay in which the argumentative structure aligns with the representational one.) For balance, consider not only length (long vs. short sections) but also referential weight and discursive type. By "referential weight" I mean the relative importance of your subjects, either relative to the discipline at large or to your project. It's not uncommon in an essay that has two large sections on relatively unknown authors to put a highly canonical figure in section C or in the conclusion, allowing the weight of the famous person to balance our (and rhetorically justify) the inclusion of the other two. If your essay has one very famous subject and one unknown one, you will want to think about which one to discuss first and about section length devoted to each, since an essay mainly about Shakespeare but only a little bit about someone else is not the same as an essay mostly about someone else with a little bit on Shakespeare. As for "discursive type," I refer to the different kinds of functions a section can have—historical background, review of critical debates, theoretical context, close reading. Especially in chapters, where you may end up devoting whole sections to different types of critical discourse, you will want to consider what order to put those in, and to vary the order so that you don't end up with a series of sections all doing the same thing. In articles this is less of a problem since the restriction of twenty-five to thirty-five pages means that most sections will include a number of different types of discourse.

As for books, we're really talking about the balance of chapters to one another. For dissertations and first books, you will almost certainly be doing something that's three to six chapters long, focusing on one or two authors per chapter. With that in mind you need to think about geographic, historical, and thematic balance. Three chapters tend to be balanced around the middle (that is, you usually can't, say, write three chapters that primarily address the years 1830, 1840, and 1950; instead you should probably end up with something like 1830, 1890–1900, 1950). Four chapters must have rough parity, either four ways or two (ex. 1830 and 1840, 1930 and 1940; or 1830, 1880, 1920, 1970). The same rules apply to geography, so that in general you can't do three chapters from one place and one from another.

Some exceptions: some books follow a one/three pattern, where the one will be from another place or from a substantially earlier time than the other three, allowing the author to open the book with a canonical or classic version of a problem. The latter three chapters, grouped thematically or historically, follow with a more recent time or a different place. The crossing of the one to the three thereby splits the book in two—unevenly in terms of page numbers, but evenly from a conceptual point of view. (For example: "Here's how the Greeks handled metaphor; *now* let's see what happens to that problem in the eighteenth century.") Much rarer is the three/one structure, in which the outlier appears last; when outliers appear at the end of books, they almost always do so in conclusions.

All this goes out the window when you have more than four or five chapters. In a book with ten chapters, structure matters less because the relative weight of any given chapter or example diminishes as it participates in a larger whole. Such books will sometimes be attempts to completely cover some topic (a book on the entire canon of Léopold Senghor, for example). More often they are a series of successive, developmentally organized meditations structured by varying degrees of nearly aphoristic intensity, or they are a series of geological "core samples," in which a variety of approaches to a single conceptual problem illuminate and alter it by degrees. Some books with many chapters also divide themselves into units of two or three or more, using these sections to reduce the chaos and returning to themselves the basic decisions involving smaller, more obvious numbers.

Why Are Book Chapters Longer Than Articles?

A comparison of the article and chapter versions of the same piece of work will show that though the chapter includes more information, it rarely includes more argument. Chapters are usually longer than articles (many chapters are forty to sixty pages in manuscript, compared to thirty or so for articles) because they move elements of the iceberg from the footnotes or the deep, unpublished background into the main text. As a result chapters tend to cover more examples than articles, which usually results in the appearance of a third or fourth major section in the latter half of the chapter, there where the article will have closed out its major claims and started moving toward a conclusion.

This relationship may affect your writing practice. It would seem to make sense to do the article before the chapter, since it's shorter (you can imagine laddering up the scale with a project, from conference paper to article to chapter). But in fact that tends not to work for me. Since articles function best if they present a series of strong arguments and their minimum necessary exemplification, it is actually easier (for me) to get to the article from a chapter. By the time I've written the chapter I have a clear sense of the biggest and best arguments, because all the examples and background I've worked through have had their effect on the overall piece. As a result the article that comes from the chapter has a better chance of being the *best* version of the project; if the article comes first, the chapter will suffer because the arguments in the original article will tend to normalize themselves, meaning that the new material will feel extra or tacked-on. That's a bad model for chapter writing, since even if chapters are longer, you still want every piece of them to have a significant and meaningful relation to the conclusions the chapter reaches. Otherwise you're just wasting your reader's time.

Understanding how the arrangement of a book constitutes a fundamental aspect of its logic and its implicit argument will help you in two ways: it will undergird the various decision you make about length, metalanguage, and rhythm, and it will allow you to use those decisions to communicate, implicitly or explicitly, rhythm and pattern to the reader.

• • •

To put some of this information in context, I want to show you some numbers from an analysis my research assistant, Darwin Tsen, did of one hundred recently published books in literature and cultural studies (he looked at ten books each from ten major university presses). The first thing we tried to confirm was my sense that first books tend to have fewer chapters than other books. The sample had 41 first books and 59 non-first books: the first books averaged 5.6 chapters, not counting introductions and conclusions; the others averaged 6.9 apiece. The first books clustered very strongly around five or six chapters, with a small few at three, and some at four or (more rarely) eight. A heavy clustering around five or six chapters was largely true of the non-first books as well, where the mean was dragged upward by a small number of books with nine, ten, or more chapters (including books with fourteen or even twenty). This seems to suggest that the academic norm for all books is for something between three and eight chapters, with a strong central grouping around five or six. These rules seem to loosen for second books and beyond, when the top of the range opens out substantially, even though the central norm remains roughly the same.

The other thing Darwin and I looked at had to do with structural rhythm as it affects the presence of introductions and conclusions. Of the books in the sample, 51 (of 100) had both a labeled introduction and a labeled conclusion; 37 had a labeled introduction only, and folded their conclusive material into a final chapter; six had a labeled conclusion only; and six had neither, folding both introductory and conclusive material into named and numbered chapters. This confirms my general impression that labeled or marked introductions are close to normative (88 of the one hundred books in the sample) and that labeled conclusions are not (57 of one hundred books had them). This general balance of the relationship between introduction (almost necessary) and conclusion (optional) reappears when we note that introductory material took up, on average, 8.8 percent of the available pages of the books in our sample (that is, roughly seventeen pages of a 200-page book), whereas conclusive material took up 3.7 percent (eight pages of a 200-page book). We'll talk about why that is, and how it might affect your own work, in the chapters on introductions and conclusions. For now I simply want you to observe that the pattern exists, and to think about how such a pattern expresses, at a large scale, some general sense of the *rhetoric* of literary and cultural studies as fields, and thus teaches us all, mostly unconsciously, about the nature and modalities of research, scholarship, and argument.

Chronology and Development in Books

One effect of the dominance of historical approaches to literature (in the last couple decades) is that almost all books in literary studies will order their chapters according to the chronological appearance of their primary examples. But that creates a problem: unless the biggest argument of the book itself is about chronological development—in which case it will tell us how what happened in 1055 affected what happened in 1155, which in turn changed 1255, and so on—then the chapters will be ordered according to a logic that does not necessarily match the argumentative or theoretical rhythm of the book itself. If you're comparing, for instance, the interaction between literature and urbanization in ancient Babylon, early modern Chang'an, and Victorian London, you will almost certainly have the chapters in that order, but what you discover will not lead successively via a historical logic from one to the next.

How, then, do you manage the relationship between the order in which things appear to the reader in the book and the order in which they appeared historically? If you're not saying that this relation is the same (first one then the next), then you are faced with a situation in which you are almost obliged—if you want your book to develop and to have a sense of self that exceeds its parts—to choose one of two paths: either shape your argument to the examples, so that the development of your argument actually does parallel (*parallel*, mind you! not reflect!) the chronology of your examples; or, layer over the chapters another, non-ordered logic that happens simultaneously as the chronological, developmental one. Either way you'll probably need some metalanguage to keep the reader settled.

I tried the first of these in *Chinese Dreams*, where, quite explicitly, the lessons learned in the first chapter on Pound became the subject of the chapter on Brecht, and the questions that came out of the work on Brecht opened the chapter on *Tel quel*. In a secondary key, the Brecht chapter began, following Pound, with a discussion of his poetry before passing over, late, to his theater and his politics; and the *Tel quel* chapter then began with politics. In this way the thematic shifts also paralleled, for neatness, the chronologies. I tried the second approach in *The Hypothetical Mandarin*, where the chronological ordering felt genuinely arbitrary, and so as I wrote I had to discover another structure that would supersede it. I ended up organizing the entire book around the structural possibilities of a Greimasian semiotic square. I located the chapters within a simpler version of that square in both the intro and the beginning of the conclusion; on the book's final page I reproduced the square, which then retroactively produced (or reproduced) for the reader the full logic of the book. (As always, I'm not saying that these strategies worked; I'm just saying that they're what I did.)

One final option, which would be a variant on the one I tried in *The Hypothetical Mandarin*, would be to drop the chronological ordering of your examples altogether, subjecting the entire project to the demands of some other pattern or structure that would be its dominant logic. You see something like this in the twenty-one chapters of Daniel Heller-Roazen's *Echolalias: On the Forgetting of Language*, whose ordering logic belongs solely to their appearance in that book or, more arbitrarily, in the alphabetical organization of the chapters in Roland Barthes's *A Lover's Discourse*. Less extravagantly, you can imagine a series of chapters on different affective stances (Sianne Ngai's *Ugly Feelings*) or a sequence like this one, from Laura U. Marks's *Touch: Sensuous Theory and Multisensory Media:* "The Haptic Subject," "Haptics and Erotics," "Olfactory Haptics," and "Haptics and Electronics." None of these imply or require chronology at all.

CHAPTER 6

Analyzing Performance[1]

Like the canon of arrangement, the canon of **style** often gets underestimated and undersold as "mere ornamentation," worthless decoration to be layered on top of the more important ideas or concepts. However, style involves every single aspect of our performance; it is how we connect to audiences through particular choices of words, tone, gestures, and ideas. Style is the glue that connects the other canons to one another. We invent arguments while considering how we want to style ourselves and our beliefs through them. We anticipate delivering claims to certain audiences and we identify with them—just as we help them identify with us—through the values we make apparent through our stylistic decisions.

This doesn't mean that style is all about "pretending" or otherwise acting artificially or inauthentically. Indeed, most audiences can see straight through artifice, and will at best treat your claims with skepticism. Rather, we usually recognize that there are often better (or worse) ways to go about persuading certain audiences. For example, you may face skepticism or resistance if you tell people you're a Gamecocks fan while you're dressed in orange and purple. Or, if you've ever asked family for money, you might have found that certain approaches worked better than others, depending on who you asked (e.g., politeness, forthrightness, compliments made before the request, etc.). Similarly, you probably haven't turned in many assignments for your college classes in neon green, 17-point Comic Sans text printed on cardboard. These decisions may be tactical but they are not disingenuous.

To put it another way, style is a part of everything we do in the world and everyone with whom we communicate. You can't escape style, although there are certainly times when you might not, or definitely do not, know you're infusing certain kinds of style into your words and actions. Part of becoming a more skilled rhetor, then, is recognizing how to employ style more effectively when communicating with others—highlighting or emphasizing those stylistic decisions we think might be

1. This chapter introduction adapted from material originally written by Kevin Brock.

most appropriate and useful while downplaying or avoiding those that might not be so helpful. The Public Turn assignment that we will work on toward the end of the semester is, arguably, your chance to play around with style in a way that the academic institution does not usually allow.

In this section, you'll learn about some concepts that are closely tied to style. It's not accurate to say that they're hierarchically subordinate to style, but it's impossible to consider any of these concepts without keeping style clearly in mind. First, you will read about **voice**, which refers to the means by which authors identify themselves in connection to others and make themselves stand out; attitude, orientation, language choice, and other qualities all contribute to the construction of an effective and recognizable voice.

Then, you will read about **delivery**, which refers to your physical output, be it vocal, written, or something else (an interpretive dance, say, delivers its message and argument silently through movement, or a cake may deliver its concept both visually and through taste and texture). Finally, you will read about **memory**, the canon dedicated to what happens after a performance has been delivered: how will your voice impact the way an audience moves forward? Through these three core concepts, you will gain a sense of how to both analyze the performances you encounter on a daily basis, as well as how to mobilize your own personal style.

Voice

Perhaps the aspect of style you are most familiar with discussing in an English class, analyzing **voice** is central to understanding the performance of an argument. When we talk about voice in rhetoric, we are referring to the way an author expresses his or her attitude towards a *topic* and an *audience*. For instance, let's say a physicist has written a scholarly article in their field, and the article discusses the complexities of string theory in explaining our universe at its earliest stages of development. Their voice might be performed like this:

> String tension **T** is the only dimensionful quantity in string theory, using the parameter called the Regge slope.

What is clear right away is that the voice of the physicist expresses a scholarly attitude towards the topic. It is also clear that the voice assumes the audience understands the highly mathematical language of physics (*"tension T," "dimensionful quantity," "parameter," "Regge slope"*). But what if the physicist were to give a talk about string theory to a class of third graders? To be effective, her voice would have to modulate so that it is much less scholarly and technical, and a bit more entertaining. The physicist might say something like this:

> To understand what string theory is about, imagine the universe full of billions of guitar strings being played at once. Isn't that cool?

Here the physicist's voice shifts to a more engaging, playful attitude towards both the audience and the topic *("imagine the universe," "billions of guitar strings," "Isn't that cool")*. As a result, the physicist's voice may accomplish less technical precision, but it gains more for third grade attention. Now consider if the physicist had switched voices for her audiences. That is, the first quote above is said to the children, and the second quote is written in a scholarly journal. The third graders' reception of the topic would have certainly fallen flat, and no scholarly journal would have published her article.

For voice to be most effective rhetorically, it is important to understand that you must carefully calibrate your attitude towards topic and audience based on your *purpose*. As in the physicist's two hypothetical quotes, one was meant to inform and discuss, the other to entertain and motivate.

Voice can be difficult to control if an author has an inflexible attitude about the topic and audience. Take, for example, a Black Lives Matter activist writing about racial injustice in a conservative newspaper. For the voice of this author, we might assume that the activist is already passionate about the topic and extremely angry towards the audience. The author will have to decide what the purpose is for engaging a conservative audience so as to determine what type of voice to use. For instance, is the purpose to enrage the audience or connect with the audience? In the following two quotes, the first is clearly meant to anger the audience, while the second is meant to find common ground.

> *#1—Until America locks up its murderous cops for destroying our black communities, then blacks will never be free in a land of white terrorism.*

> *#2—As we fight for justice together, let us work to achieve more fairness in how neighborhoods of color are policed, while seeking cooperation and peace between law enforcement and black citizens.*

In this case, you might ask how an author's voice could balance their anger, finding important common ground, and stating their opinion.

Delivery[2]

Delivery, the fifth canon of rhetoric, focuses on the way in which a message is sent, conveyed, or displayed—in this sense, it is different from voice in that voice addresses the rhetor's attitude toward a topic, whereas delivery addresses how an audience experiences the composition—it isn't just about the language used or what is expressed. After all, there are many ways to convey a message without using words, such as wearing black at a funeral to signal mourning or crossing your arms when you feel defensive. In Book Three of his *Rhetoric*, Aristotle describes delivery as having "as much to do with oratory as with the poetry ... It is, essentially, a matter of the right management of the voice to express the

---

2. This section is adapted from material originally written by Ashley Moore Walker.

various emotions—of speaking loudly, softly, or between the two; of high, low, or intermediate pitch; of the various rhythms that suit various subjects."

As explained above, the rhetorical canons were originally used predominantly for the crafting of oral speeches; as such, delivery focused on the speaker's tone of voice, volume, stance, hand gestures, and so on. Today, however, delivery can refer to many different aspects of your message depending on the modes you are working with. For example, when crafting a written piece, your choices of font, paper style, and paragraph breaks can all affect how your message is delivered and what additional or supplemental meaning is carried along with it. When putting together a short film, choices such as music, camera movements, and transitions should be considered. If you create a poster, colors, lines, and images are additional things to think about. All of the possible considerations can be a little overwhelming, but the important thing to remember is to be purposeful in your decisions. Each method of delivery has affordances and constraints, and your goal for any particular piece of writing will help you to narrow down your delivery options; for example, if you want to share your message with a global community, a digital video would afford you the ability to reach many people that may otherwise not see or hear your message if you were limited to your local community. To then offer this same message with subtitles, sign language, or to cut out speech altogether and rely solely on visuals, opens up your audience even further.

If you need some extra help when making decisions about your delivery, practice analyzing some of its aspects:

1. Tone: think about how tone is developed in a variety of mediums, such as writing or movies. For example, you may want to pay attention to how the soundtrack of your favorite movie impacts the thoughts or feelings you experience while you watch the action on screen or examine an advertisement in a magazine for persuasive or emotional appeals. When putting together your own delivery, think about what kind of overall "feel" you want it to have, such as professional, fun, serious, scary, or inspirational, and go from there.

2. Medium: think about the affordances and constraints of different kinds of medium, such as songs, documentaries, pamphlets, posters, performances, and even written academic papers. What does each medium do well in terms of communication? For example, a pamphlet is very portable, so the reader can carry it with him; it also has the ability to carry visual and written information. However, the information needs to be very concise, so you can't include every detail. A documentary can use music, visuals, and speaking to deliver information to the audience, so it can be easy to create an emotional reaction. However, a documentary is a bit less portable than a pamphlet, and you cannot include much written text to get your message across.

Memory[3]

While traditionally considered to be the fourth of the five rhetorical canons, for our purposes it makes sense to think about **memory** last. Why? First, it exceeds rhetoric in the sense that it is a foundation for other disciplines: history, psychology, and, recently, neuroscience, to name a few. As memory is linked to the after effects of a composition, it can be beneficial to think of it as the culminating canon. For Aristotle, memory is usually conceived of as both the *ability* to remember (our brain function of memory) and *what* is remembered (our memories of the past). The ancient focus on memory—Aristotle, it's worth noting, dedicated an entire work to the canon—can be attributed, once more, to the speech-heavy focus of ancient rhetoric. Memory was essential for an effective orator; ancient orators needed to memorize their speeches in order to deliver them to the public. For the Greeks, a strong memory was indicative of intelligence, and relying upon written notes or reminders was not only frowned upon, but it was a sign of a weak mind. Simply put, memory is that much more important when you can't just re-read an article later.

Traditionally, rhetorical memory is valued for three main capacities:

1. It **allows us to remember our argument** as well as **how we want to deliver that argument**. Usually this applies to speeches and other oral communication. Think about speakers you've witnessed (for example, the President of the United States giving a speech, or your teacher delivering a lecture). Are those speakers more powerful if they read verbatim from a script or if they make eye contact with the audience, engaging what they are saying with how they say it in both tone and body language?

2. Our **words themselves being memorable**. That is, in tandem with the other four canons which work together to make our arguments persuasive, memory is what allows the audience the ability to remember (in order to apply) what we have said. That is, there would be little value in being persuasive if our audiences would forget what we persuade them to do.

3. **Memory can act as a storage space** or bank for archiving important information. Classical rhetoricians described this as a treasury through which the orator navigates, saving valuable facts, quotes, or anecdotes for later use.

It is important to note that in these three elements of classical memory, memory operates as a *tool for humans*: that is, memory is a capacity which humans possess (the ability to remember), the thing itself that is remembered, as well as the storage space from which what is remembered is retrieved. The central force surrounding memory in the classical conception, then, is the human. Overall, this understanding has changed very little since its inception and is still the most widely accepted. However, some philosophers have explored memory in

---

3. This section is adapted from material originally written by Amber Lee.

a different way. Friedrich Nietzsche, for example, valorizes forgetting over remembering in claiming that "there could be no happiness, cheerfulness, hope, pride, immediacy, without forgetfulness." Others—such as Henri Bergson and Paul Ricoeur—deviate from the classical understanding of memory by exploring memory's potential for productively functioning **outside human control**. That is, this scholarship attempts to view memory as that which is not *simply* memorization: it explores what is made possible through forgetting, or through *not* remembering.

While these philosophers are perhaps most well-known within rhetorical memory studies itself, more contemporary scholarship (in trauma studies and neurorhetorics, for example) has begun to overlap and develop in tandem with memory studies. And while this cross-pollination and consideration of forgetting has not detracted from the importance of a classical understanding of memory, it has provided alternate and perhaps more productive ways of conceiving memory's rhetorical potential.

That is to say, memorization is certainly a crucial strategy for our education system today: how would you have survived elementary school without remembering the sequence of letters that would allow you to pass spelling tests? Or high school without being able to memorize historical dates or mathematical sequences? However, while this type of memorization is certainly valuable, it is not the only way memory can be productive. In fact, an over-fidelity to memorization can be detrimental to the composition process. For example: in order to analyze another text, event, problem, etc.—we must be able to both consider what we *do* remember (what we think we "know" based on observation) as well as the possibility for alternate solutions—ones that are speculative, or, perhaps, ones which we have forgotten and then, in the process of forgetting, recreate.

Discussion Questions

1. Discuss the importance of voice in your English class—both when you speak and when you write. What changes in voice do you notice in yourself and your peers as you converse, peer edit, and revise? What about when you speak to your teacher instead of a peer? Are these changes due to the topic, the audience, and/or the purpose? Explain your answer and give specific examples.

2. Gauge and discuss how your written voice should usually be expressed in this English class. What aspects of your class should you be considering as you modulate your voice? Explain.

3. Do you have an authentic voice—one that represents your truest self? Can you have multiple authentic voices? Is it possible to have an inauthentic voice? How do you gauge authenticity?

4. How does your delivery of ideas change when you move from writing them down, to saying them out loud? What, then, changes if you deliver your thoughts from your desk, or from the front of the class?

5. In what ways might remembering be valuable for your writing process? Conversely, in what ways might forgetting be valuable for your writing process?

6. It is clear that memory used to be very important for composition, but in contemporary society—with our ability to take notes, save documents, copy and paste information, bookmark websites, and mark e-books—is memory still as valuable? Does memory function differently than it used to?

Exercises

1. Think back to the BLM examples on page 79. Consider how they shift the voice of the activist. How does each indicate the author's attitude towards policing in America (*topic*) and towards law-and-order readers (*audience*)? Next, note the word choices (#1's murderous cops versus #2's law enforcement, for instance). What attitudes does each example express? What role do pronouns play in these examples, and how can you incorporate that into your own writing?

2. Read the following excerpt from the Oscar-winning movie *Norma Rae* and explain how *voice* is used and expressed by the lead character, Norma Rae Webster. Norma Rae was a real-life union organizer in North Carolina. In the film depiction, she is shown fighting for better wages at her hometown textile plant in Roanoke Rapids in the 1970s. Below is part of her speech in which she calls her fellow laborers into a strike for better wages. Be sure to consider *word choice*, *topic*, and *audience* as you describe and explain Norma Rae's *voice*. After you have analyzed the passage, use the internet to find the scene. Watch the clip and consider what else is happening in the scene that makes Norma Rae rhetorically effective. Can we consider these things as voice as well?

   ■ (After pursuing plans to unionize her plant, Norma Rae walks to the middle of the textile plant while being followed by a plant security guard who has been ordered to remove her from the premises. As she turns around, she makes this speech to both the guard and other workers in the plant, and then stands on a table, holding a sign that says, "UNION." Within minutes all the laborers have shut off their textile machines and joined Norma Rae in a strike.)

   NORMA RAE: I'm staying put! Right where I am! It's gonna take you, and the police department, and the fire department, and the National Guard to get me outta here! I'm waitin' for the sheriff to come and take me home! And I ain't gonna budge till he gets here!

3. Compose a short paragraph to deliver orally (to a roommate or friend or class, etc.). Try to memorize the paragraph for its delivery. What do you notice about your composition process (i.e., because you know you will have to memorize this paragraph)? What are some benefits from memorizing your own composition? What are some drawbacks? What about the delivery? In other words, how did your initial intent change in the space between writing and oration?

4. Think about how delivery changes the impact of words. Specifically, think back to Childish Gambino's "This Is America," the lyrics of which can be found at the end of Chapter 2 (page 26). First, read through the lyrics silently and write a short response. Next, listen to the song: how do the added inflections and intonations of speech change your initial response? Finally, watch the video to the song: with the full picture, does Gambino's message change? Does your reception of it differ from when you first "just" read his lyrics?

5. Write down three topics you feel confident discussing on a piece of paper, and exchange topics with a partner. For five minutes, research one of your partner's topics you'd like to know more about and develop three questions for your partner. Ask each other your questions. Neither is allowed to use research materials in answering questions; you must rely on your memories. After exchanging and answering questions, reflect on the process: does your personal memory of the topic effectively compare to brief research?

6. Compare a studio version of a favorite song to a live version. What are the differences and similarities? How does memory play into the performance itself? How does memory play into your experience as an audience member?

Supplemental Readings

Dr. A.D. Carson rapped his dissertation. While he did submit a traditional, written document to Clemson University, the dissertation he defended was in another format. As you watch and listen, think about genre, affordances and constraints, voice, style, and other forms your arguments might take other than a written essay.

"Owning My Masters" Hip-Hop Album
A.D. Carson
http://phd.aydeethegreat.com

Interview with A.D. Carson

https://aydeethegreat.com/wp-content/uploads/2018/06/ADCarson
ComplexLiveInterview.mp4

CRAFTING ARGUMENTS

Methods of Reasoning

If there was only one way to approach an argument, it would be tempting to think that we would get more done: we would, after all, be able to more broadly address our audience, safe in the knowledge that they also followed the one and only way to reason through an issue. Yet, while this may seem good, in practice it would stifle creativity: each and every one of us will approach a problem from a different direction, drawing upon different background experience and other facets that make us individual, to find unique solutions. The same, then, goes for your audience: making assumptions about what type of reasoning an audience is looking for and then blindly following this singular rote path is one of the quickest ways to losing core followers of your argument. Keep things interesting for both your reader and yourself, and work through your core problems in a variety of ways.

This chapter, then, will introduce you to the binaries of reasoning: **induction** and **deduction**. Inductive reasoning begins with empirical data and moves to generalizable claims; deductive reasoning begins with larger claims and moves towards data that helps prove them. As you will read, neither of these forms of reasoning are worthier than the other: they each work more routinely with different audiences or rhetorical situations. Generally, it might be said that scientific papers often follow more inductive paths, while humanities essays are often more deductive. On the surface this assumption is correct. Yet, begin to deeply read the aforementioned scientific report, and instances of deduction soon begin to make themselves clear. Likewise, that deductive humanities paper will often draw upon induction to help prove claims. For example, a paper for this class could explore #livingwhileblack, making a deductive argument about institutionalized racism; each time you draw upon a specific incident in which the hashtag has been employed to move back toward your larger claim, you are then working inductively. The point is that your use of one method of reasoning is only as strong as your balancing of the other.

The following sections will first walk you through core examples of inductive (below) and deductive (page 92) reasoning, before demonstrating just how these can work together (page 94). There are three core benefits to understanding these types of reasoning. First, they help you analyze other rhetors' arguments more deeply, allowing you to ask how these methods of reasoning relate to arrangement (as discussed in Chapter 5: see page 63). Second, they help you more directly appeal to your audience; pay attention to what methods different situations tend to use as you read and research, and you can begin to work these methods into your own composing. Third, they help you personally understand how and why you approach persuasion from a certain position, allowing you to both experiment and further strengthen what you do best. In short, gaining a greater understanding of how both you and your reader react to different reasonings is an important culminating step before you actually write your way into the rhetorical conversation.

Inductive Reasoning[1]

Induction is a species of reasoning that involves making probable generalizations about the future from particular empirical instances or facts from the past. This move from particular to general is also commonly described as an inference from sample to population. Since we, inevitably, have only finite samples and can never be sure of the future, our conclusions are always probabilities rather than certainties.

Within this context, it makes sense to speak of the relative strength of a given inductive argument. For example, consider the following cases:

> *Ex: My roommate never studies and has a 4.0 GPA; therefore, studying is not a necessary part of being a successful student.*

> *Ex: In a survey of one hundred American universities, it was found that students with a 4.0 or higher studied an average amount of 30 hours a week; therefore, putting in lots of hours studying is essential for being a successful student.*

In the first case, while the premise may be true—the author's roommate may, in fact, be excelling in school without studying—the conclusion is not warranted since this is a very limited sample.

In the second case, we can see that a much more extensive sample was taken, making the conclusion much more probable; however, once again, the conclusion is not certain since it is always possible that there is a genius that doesn't need to study.

---

1. This section is adapted from material originally written by David Stubblefield.

While sample size often provides some indication of a good inductive argument, things are not always that simple. Sometimes a particularly significant example can be very persuasive for a specific audience. For example, from the fact that one person was able to hack into a computer system, a group of computer engineers might infer that the computer's security system is not acceptable, despite the minuscule sample size. Likewise, within some communities, a single expert's testimony might be very convincing, as when a world-renowned scholar shares her opinion on a certain matter. In other words, though sample size is certainly something to consider, there are many cases where sample size fails to fully capture the persuasive capacity of an inductive argument.

When thinking about induction, it is important to remember that we make inductive generalizations every day of our lives and would not be able to function effectively without them. Indeed, many of our decisions—from deciding where to eat or what route to take to work—rely on inductive reasoning. But these kinds of generalizations can also go awry.

We may have had our instructors write something like "generalization" on our papers when the inference from particular evidence to general conclusion does not seem warranted. In real life, we are likely to call such hasty generalizations **stereotyping**—remember Banaji and Greenwald's article from Chapter 4 (page 50). For example, we may reason inductively that since the best students we have known in the Mechanical Engineering department are males, women do not make good mechanical engineers. Of course such an erroneous conclusion is not only based on a small sample size but also neglects other factors such as the social emphasis on femininity, sexism in education, discrimination in STEM fields, our evaluative process to determine "best," and noteworthy exceptions to our conclusion. Thus, we can see that inductive arguments cannot only be evaluated in terms of their reasonableness but also in terms of their ethicalness. In the light of such potential for bad or unethical uses of induction, you might ask what constitutes good, effective, and ethical uses of inductive reasoning.

While there is an answer to this question, it is neither simple nor steadfast; rather, like most things in rhetoric, it is complex and contingent. According to *The Stanford Dictionary of Philosophy*, "There is no comprehensive theory of sound induction, no set of agreed upon rules that license good or sound inductive inference, nor is there a serious prospect of such a theory." In the absence of any consensus on this matter, we can think of making good inductive arguments as a situated art form. And while there is no definitive method that can guarantee good inductive arguments, as we analyze and participate in specific rhetorical situations, we learn more about what constitutes a good inductive argument within those situations.

Deductive Reasoning[2]

In many ways the direct opposite of induction, a **deductive argument** is one that relies on general premises thought to be universally true, and through valid forms of reasoning, leads to a conclusion that does not claim to be merely probable, like inductive arguments, but rather certain. You may have encountered deductive arguments in your geometry class when you were asked to prove certain theorems. In these cases, various premises could definitively prove certain conclusions beyond a shadow of a doubt. This is precisely the kind of certainty that deductive arguments attempt to provide.

Perhaps the most common type of deductive argument is called the *syllogism.* A syllogism consists of a general statement called the major premise, a specific statement called the minor premise, and a conclusion.

A famous example of a syllogism can be found below:

> *All men are mortal (Major Premise)*
>
> *Socrates is a man (Minor Premise)*
>
> *Therefore, Socrates is mortal (Conclusion)*

Notice that this argument tries to move to a particular conclusion based on a general, or universal, truth: "All men are mortal." This is the important difference between deductive arguments and inductive arguments. Deductive arguments use general principles to reach conclusions about specific cases, whereas inductive arguments use specific examples to reach a general principle.

While it is certainly important to be able to identify deductive arguments, it is also important to know how to evaluate them. Deductive arguments are evaluated on two criteria: **validity** and **soundness**. To illustrate how this works, let's consider an example. The argument above about Socrates' mortality is an example of a well-known form of deductive argumentation called *Modus Ponens.* As you can see, the form is as follows:

> *All P's are Q*
>
> *S is P*
>
> *Therefore, S is Q*

This is an example of a deductive argument that is valid. An argument is called valid if the form of the argument is such that the conclusion logically follows from the premises. Validity is purely a formal criterion of arguments; it does not establish that the argument is, in fact, true or false. It simply establishes that if the premises do indeed turn out to be true, then the conclusion will be true as well. In other words, the following argument is valid despite its premises being untrue:

---

2. This section is adapted from material originally written by David Stubblefield.

All men are immortal

Socrates is a man

Therefore, Socrates is immortal

This argument is still valid, but it is not *sound*. An argument is called sound when its form is valid and the premises have been found to be true. The soundness of an argument is established by interrogating the premises in terms of their truth or falsehood and determining that the premises are indeed true.

When one reads deductive arguments, often the first task is to establish whether or not the argument is valid, by looking at the form of the argument, and then proceeding to ask whether or not it is sound, by looking at the actual content of premises and interrogating them in terms of their truth and falsehood. Keep in mind that when your instructor reads your paper, she will most likely go through some sort of process like this and will likely attempt to flesh out the argument being made and evaluate it. Sketching the deductive argument that you make or want to make is often a good idea at the invention stage, at the revision stage, or at a conference with your instructor. Remember, however, that these "stages" are never mutually exclusive—reevaluating your argument as you go is a good habit to get into. In other words, just because an argument seemed valid in a proposal doesn't mean it will always stay that way when you start fleshing out your ideas. Getting clear about exactly what you are arguing is an important step in creating a successful composition.

As may be clear at this point, deductive arguments are often attractive: we all would like to be able to prove our conclusions beyond a shadow of a doubt. However, despite this appeal, deductive arguments have their limitations. For example, in everyday affairs, they can sound unnecessarily mechanical or formulaic, since very few people argue this way on a daily basis. For this reason, Aristotle argued that leaving the major premise out often increased the audience's attention, and since the major premise is often something that would be obvious to the audience, there was little risk of confusion. Further, he surmised that the shortened or "truncated" syllogism that resulted from omitting the major premise, which he called the **enthymeme**, forced audiences to supply this major premise, and this action, in turn, psychologically predisposed the audience to accept the truth of the argument. However, even with these advantages, the enthymeme is, in the end, still based on a deductive argument that can, in theory, be made explicit and discussed. Therefore, understanding deduction is an important part of learning to analyze and compose effective arguments.

Finally, it is important to consider where the premises of a deductive argument come from; in the standard form of the syllogism (or in an enthymeme), you have both a specific example (the minor premise) and a general statement or rule (major premise). As you learned in the previous section, general statements are derived from a form of inductive reasoning—they are, therefore, subject to probability, not certainty. Because the truthfulness of the major premise is a question of probability, deductive reasoning does not provide any more certainty than the inductive reasoning that produced the general rule.

Integrating Inductive and Deductive Reasoning

As you see, **inductive** and **deductive** reasoning are two sides of the same coin: they both work towards proving an argumentative point—they just do so in the opposite manner. How, when, and where you use them will change dependent on your topic, audience, and personal preferences. For example, a paper that mainly deals with scientific information will often tend to use more **inductive** reasoning as you gather replicable empirical data; contrarily, work that begins with grandiose emotional appeals may be more **deductive**, as you work to prove your wider point with newly found sources. In short, one is *not* objectively "better" than the other; they just have different uses.

This does *not* mean that the two forms of reasoning are mutually exclusive; deductive and inductive reasoning both make use of general and specific claims. Indeed, stronger arguments will often integrate a combination of both forms: while the larger argument and method of research may be deductive, the rhetor may use inductive reasoning to prove their points. Furthermore, an argument can jump between the two: one sub-topic may be more suited for induction, whereas another may simply work better deductively.

How, then, do you go about integrating these two different but closely related methods? In order to see how this integration works, let's turn towards Constance Steinkuehler and Sean Duncan's "Scientific Habits of Mind in Virtual Worlds," the supplemental text for this chapter. We'll walk through the beginning of this paper together to identify when, and why, the authors switch modes of reasoning.

The text begins **deductively**, as Steinkuehler and Duncan make general claims about their topic. Indeed, it is not uncommon for papers from a multitude of genres to begin this way. Think of the various hooks you have read this semester, whether they constituted singular sentences or entire paragraphs: deductive reasoning offers readers something larger to take hold of, that generally relies upon knowledge that all in that particular field will already possess; in other words, the reader is hooked deductively by seeing a twist on what they already know to be true.

As the paper continues into its literature review ("Leveraging Online Play"), Steinkuehler and Duncan begin to mix their reasonings: each time they refer to litanies of other articles, they **inductively** present work they have researched to prove their **deductive** claim; however, when they draw upon more general knowledge (discussing how MMOs work, for example) to show how these works fit together, they do so **deductively**. Here, then, you can see how these two types of reasoning can work in unison: the greater argument may, indeed, be deductive, but the finding and presentation of facts and figures is almost entirely inductive.

The Research Methods section ("Data Collection and Research Methods") moves deeper into **inductive** reasoning, as the authors spend time showing exactly how their research was collected. For those of you more familiar with scientific research, this section should seem familiar. Yet, while this section *is* indicative of inductive reasoning, the Analytic Codes displayed in Table 1 are ***deductive***. Why? Simply put, here the authors list the information they presumed to find seemingly based on prior knowledge before the research began.

As Steinkuehler and Duncan continue, their work continues to answer deductive claims with inductively produced research. Either as a class, or on your own, continue through the text identifying each time the authors switch styles. While we do not expect you to produce work to this extent—as, for one, the shortness of a singular semester doesn't gift you the time needed for lengthy inductive experiments—we do believe that each you *can* write in this reason-switching style. It keeps your audience interested, it prevents you from relying too heavily on one form of reasoning, and it ensures there is always data to support wider claims.

Discussion Questions

1. Consider how induction works in your own life. For instance, when you decided to attend University of South Carolina, did you conduct a poll of everyone you knew, or did you seek out specific opinions that seemed to matter more than others? Describe what it was that made some voices louder than others. How much evidence did you need before you were comfortable making the decision? Alternatively, was your conclusion to attend USC reached deductively? If so, write out the syllogism.

2. Inductive reasoning can be very persuasive. How do you utilize it without engaging in stereotyping, making hasty generalizations, or choosing poor examples? As a class, develop some specific real-life examples and discuss their reasonableness and ethicalness.

3. Consider your invention database and your analyses of the various arguments' arrangements. What is the relationship between inductive/deductive reasoning and arrangement? Invention?

4. As a class, create a list of true general statements upon which you think everyone would agree and could serve as sound major premises. Then interrogate them to see if they really are certain or not. By what criteria do you judge truth?

5. What type of reasoning do articles in your major lean toward? What do you think this says about the type of logic your field favors? How does this fit in with your personal preferences?

6. As a class, we will decide upon a topic for debate and then split in half: 12 of you will argue for your "side" based solely in deductive reasoning; the other 12 will argue inductively. Does taking this blinkered approach make argumentation easier or harder?

Exercises

1. Using the internet, research different types of inductive fallacies. In a small group, prepare a presentation for your class that names one inductive fallacy, explains it, provides an example of it, and explains what makes it both problematic and persuasive.

2. Use the internet to find other forms of deductive arguments than *Modus Ponens*. Create arguments using these various forms. In small groups discuss these arguments, their validity, and their soundness. What is useful about these forms; what is limiting?

3. Find a deductive argument in Part Two, Unit Three of this book and write it as a syllogism or series of syllogisms. Then write a paragraph explaining both the benefits and limitations of constructing arguments in this manner.

4. Ask yourself the perennial philosophical question: would you rather face a herd of 100 duck-sized horses, or a singular horse-sized duck? Answer the question in the form of a paragraph-long deductive-based argument. Then switch to inductive, answering the same question. Which of these two arguments do you find more persuasive? Why?

5. In your group of three, choose a *kairotic* topic (i.e., one that is in the news this week). Each group member should find a different source that discusses this topic: a news article, a news video, and a satirical cartoon. First analyze the type of reasoning being used in *your* source: is it deductive or inductive? Next argue, to your group, why your source's reasoning is or is not effective: would it be more effective to use different reasoning? Note: it's absolutely fine to rip your source to pieces if you *don't* think it's effective. Finally, as a group, write a paragraph that argues why either a) one source is considerably stronger than the others; or b) why you need all three sources together to understand your topic. If time permits, you will present your findings to the class as a whole.

6. Take your own research project for the semester and write a 250-word abstract for it that is exclusively inductive in nature. Now write another abstract that is exclusively deductive. Is either of these statements more appealing to your sense of your topic, or does staying to one "type" of reasoning feel limited?

Supplemental Reading

Scientific Habits of Mind in Virtual Worlds
Constance Steinkuehler and Sean Duncan

In 1905, at a gathering of the world's greatest minds in the physical sciences, Henri Poincaré reflected on the rapid progress of scientific inquiry and the means through which the scientific community at the turn of the twentieth century and beyond would refine our understanding of the world. In his historical address, Poincaré warned against the seduction of reducing science to a domain of seeming facts, stating, "Science is built up of facts, as a house is built of stones; but an accumulation of facts is no more science than a heap of stones is a house" (1905/2001, p. 141). A century later, his admonition against the framing of science as a "rhetoric of conclusion" (Schwab 1962, p. 24) still holds, with science scholars and educators from Dewey on repeatedly warning us against the teaching of science as only content rather than process. In Dewey's own words, "the future of our civilization depends upon the widening spread and deepening hold of the *scientific habit of mind* [italics added] ... the problem of problems in our education is therefore to discover how to mature and make effective this scientific habit" (1910, p. 127).

In today's world of massive globalization and technological interconnectivity, the need for a scientifically literate citizenry in the United States has only grown more urgent; yet, by some measures, it seems we have done a poor job at fostering the right habits of mind in our schools. Currently only one in five Americans is scientifically literate (Miller 2004), despite mandatory instruction in science. In a recent study of contemporary classroom practice, Chinn and Malhotra (2002) found that standard "inquiry" activities not only failed to engender scientific habits of mind, but in fact actually fostered epistemological beliefs directly *antithetical* to them. Recent assessment of high school laboratory activities by the National Research Council (Singer et al. 2005) reaches similar conclusions: science labs, long heralded as *the* site for engaging students in science practice, fail. Meanwhile, the public seems to grow increasingly hostile to the scientific enterprise (Elsner 2005).

Leveraging Online Play

But, if the inquiry activities used currently in education are unable to foster the right attitudes toward science, what can? Games, potentially. Despite dismissals as "torpid" and inviting "inert reception" (Solomon 2004) in some mainstream press, videogame technologies may be one viable alternative—not to the role of teachers and classrooms in learning science, but rather to textbooks and science labs as educational experiences about the inquiry process. Recent studies indicate that the intellectual activities that constitute successful gameplay are nontrivial, including the construction of new identities (Gee 2003; Steinkuehler 2006b), collaborative problem solving (Squire 2005; Steinkuehler 2006a; cf. Nasir

2005), literacy practices that exceed our national standards (Steinkuehler 2007, 2008a), systemic thinking (Squire 2003), and, as one might expect, computer literacy (Hayes and Games in press; Steinkuehler and Johnson, 2007, unpublished manuscript).

Games, however, are more than just the sum of their intellectual practices (as important as those may be); they are, in fact, *simulated worlds:*

> The first step towards understanding how video games can (and we argue, will) transform education is changing the widely shared perspective that games are "mere entertainment." More than a multi-billion dollar industry, more than a compelling toy for both children and adults, more than a route to computer literacy, video games are important because they let people participate in new worlds. (Shaffer, Squire, Halverson, and Gee 2005, p. 106)

As simulations, games allow "just plain folk" (Lave 1988) to build situated understandings of important phenomena (physical laws, for example) that are instantiated in those worlds amid a culture of intellectual practice that render those phenomena culturally meaningful (Steinkuehler 2006c). Their affordances for learning have not gone unnoticed, and the last two years have witnessed a marked rise in interest across various academies in leveraging game technologies toward educational ends: the Woodrow Wilson Foundation's Serious Games Initiative; the Games, Learning and Society program at the University of Wisconsin-Madison; the Education Arcade project at MIT; the Games for Social Change Movement; and Stanford University's Media X "Gaming To Learn" Workshop, to name a few.

One genre of videogame in particular offers distinctive promise in terms of fostering scientific habits of mind: *massively multiplayer online games.* Massively multiplayer online games (MMOs) are 2- or 3-D graphical, simulated worlds played online that allow individuals to interact, through their digital characters or "avatars," not only with the designed environment in which activities take place, but also with other individuals' avatars as well. For example, five friends or strangers could create an impromptu group and go hunting "boss" dragons in one of the virtual world's more difficult dungeons. Previous ethnography of such online worlds demonstrates their function as naturally occurring learning environments (Steinkuehler 2004, 2005), yet the forms of scientific argumentation, model-based reasoning, and theory-evidence coordination that arise in the context of MMO play warrant further investigation.

In MMOs, individuals collaborate to solve complex problems within the virtual world, such as figuring out what combination of individual skills, proficiencies, and equipment are necessary to conquer an in-game boss dragon in the example above. As part of developing efficient and effective solutions, players are customarily expected to research various game strategies and tactics by consulting on- and offline manuals, databases, and discussions, as well as by using such knowledge as the basis for in-game action. Such research might include, to continue our example, consulting collective online databases about where the boss dragon lives, what its special skills are, and what previous strategies have been successful.

Members of the group then come to the activity well-versed in known research on the problem and enter into collaborative work under the mutual expectation that each will apply known information to solving the problem. Should the solution not prove to be straightforward, the group learns from what fails, discounting some solution paths while raising others. In prior ethnographic work (2005), Steinkuehler found that it was not unusual for players to gather data about a specific monster or challenge in the virtual world in Excel spreadsheets, create models of the data in the form of simple mathematical equations, and then argue about whose model was "better" in terms of prediction and explanatory scope.

Thus, as part of standard gameplay (particularly beyond the beginning levels), individuals share their own hypotheses about what strategies work by proposing models for solutions, justifying their "theories" with evidence (such as tabulated mathematical results aggregated across multiple trials), and debate the merits of conflicting hypotheses. This collaborative construction of knowledge, parallel to what takes place in the scientific community, is not aimless contentious discussion (although there is a bit of that as well), but rather part and parcel of the *collective intelligence* (Levy 1999) amassed through patterned participatory consumption (Jenkins 1992), which is a hallmark of interactive "entertainment" media such as games.

Innovative projects such as Harvard University's *River City* (e.g., Ketelhut 2007; Ketelhut et al. 2007; Nelson et al. 2007) and Indiana University-Bloomington's *Quest Atlantis* (e.g., Barab et al. 2005; Barab et al. 2007) have begun to tackle the complexities of designing MMOs for science learning, offering proof of concept of the argument presented above. Yet, as Lave and Wenger (1991) note, understanding informal contexts for learning is crucial if we are to advance educational theory and practice beyond the contexts we ourselves contrive. Therefore, in order to extend our understanding of the forms of scientific reasoning that emerge as a natural part of gameplay in informal MMOs and the design features that appear to foster them, this paper presents an examination of discussions on the official online forum for the commercial MMO *World of Warcraft*.

In this investigation, we analyzed a random sample of nearly 2,000 discussion posts in which participants discuss various game-related topics. Using codes based on national benchmarks for scientific literacy (American Association for the Advancement of Science 1993), Chinn and Malhotra's (2002) theoretical framework for evaluating inquiry tasks, and Kuhn's (1992) epistemological framework, we highlight the scientific habits of mind displayed within the forum discussions and the features of the game—both as designed object and emergent culture—that appear to foster them. This study moves beyond arguments about the *potential* of MMOs for learning by documenting and assessing which *specific* literacy practices emerge within such game-related online communities (and which do not). Based on those findings, we then take a first step toward identifying the characteristics of MMOs that may be enabling such practices to emerge.

Data Collection and Research Methods

Context of the Research and Data Corpus

The context for this investigation is *World of Warcraft* (*WoW*), a successful MMO released in November 2004 and currently boasting the single largest share of the global MMO market with well over ten million subscribers globally (Woodcock 2008). The game is set in a fantasy world in which players of various classes (nine total, at the time of this article's writing) wander the environment hunting, gathering, questing, battling, and crafting in order to strengthen or "level" their character in various ways.

The data analyzed for this particular study consist of threaded discussions that took place early November of 2006 (before the release of the expansion, *World of Warcraft: The Burning Crusade*) on the "priest forum" of the official *World of Warcraft* website (http://forums.worldofwarcraft.com). Although there are a number of relevant online forums to be found, the official website alone featured thirty-one separate forums totaling well over 270,000 separate, active threads. Therefore, we chose to limit our data corpus by selecting a single character class-related forum rather than, say, the guild recruitment or bug report forum. Class-related forums are just like any other discussion forum, except the content is ostensibly focused on class-related topics for discussion. Content is not restricted in any way (other than by the overarching rules of the forums, such as decency), but posters are expected to discuss something related to the respected character class in some way, whether that be anecdotes, strategies, complaints, preferences, or what have you. We pulled a random sample of 1,984 posts across eighty-five threads of 4,656 threads total ($\overline{X} = 23$, $\sigma = 38$ posts per thread), resulting in a confidence level of approximately 91 percent. Data from the discussion forums were saved as text files, extraneous information and HTML markup tags were removed, and descriptive information (such as data on the "level" of each poster) was collected in a separate spreadsheet. The final corpus included discussion posts made by 1,087 unique *WoW* characters.

Method of Analysis

In order to assess the *scientific habits of mind* that characterize (or fail to characterize) the data corpus examined here, we developed a set of codes (following methods outlined in Chi 1997) based in combination on a subset of the AAAS benchmarks for scientific literacy (American Association for the Advancement of Science 1993), Chinn and Malhotra's (2002) theoretical framework for evaluating inquiry tasks, and Kuhn's (1992) framework for categorizing epistemological stances in argumentation. Both the AAAS benchmarks and the Chinn and Malhotra report have been quite influential in science education, with the former serving as the basis of the National Research Council's (1996) Science Standards and many state science standards for K–12 education in the United

States. Kuhn's work has also proven quite influential in its own right in research on argumentation in informal scientific reasoning. The codes were selected from these sources based on a combination of a priori assumptions about the forms of scientific reasoning such spaces ought to generate (e.g., understanding systems and feedback among components of a system), previous games related literature (Gee 2003; Squire 2003, 2005; Steinkuehler 2004, 2005, 2006a, 2006b, 2006c), and a pilot study conducted in preparation for this investigation (Steinkuehler and Chmiel 2006).

Our goal was to focus on scientific reasoning as "the building of houses" rather than the "collection of stones," per the vision of science practice articulated by Poincaré (1905/2001) and science education forwarded by Dewey (1910) and Schwab (1962). Therefore, important aspects to scientific understanding that are specific to *content knowledge* rather than practice per se (e.g. an understanding of natural forces) are notably absent. However, given the focus of our interests (scientific practices rather than content) and the nature of the phenomenon under investigation (a simulated world that makes no claims of correspondence with the natural one), such omission was justified. Table 1 includes the full set of eighteen codes and their definitions.

Together, the coding set addresses aspects of scientific thinking as seen through three major groups of codes: scientific discursive practices (including social knowledge construction), systems- and model-based reasoning, and tacit epistemologies. The scientific discursive practices codes each addressed a different aspect of argumentation, discourse, and the use of evidence or other resources in the formulation of an argument. The systems- and model-based reasoning codes each addressed a different aspect of scientific thinking, cutting across specific scientific domains, including reasoning using systems and models; understanding feedback, prediction and testing; and the use of mathematics to investigate the problem under discussion. Finally, the tacit epistemology codes addressed the implicit conception of knowledge employed by an author in a given post—that knowledge is objective and absolute, or that it is subjective and nothing is certain, or that knowledge is shaped through evaluation and argument. Four raters, each of whom had at least 4 months of experience as participant observer within the game, coded the data; four-way interrater reliability, calculated on a subset of roughly 10% of the corpus, was 92%.

In addition, a second set of codes were developed in order to characterize the *WoW*-specific content discussed in each post. Two raters, both with over a year of participant-observer experience within the game, coded the data; two-way interrater reliability, calculated again on roughly 10% of the corpus, was 93%. Additionally, for each poster, we collected virtual "demographic" information—including character level, race, class, guild status, and player-vs.-player rank—in addition to the total number of occurrences of each scientific reasoning and content code their posts received and the total number of posts per individual made.

Table 1. The Full Set of Analytic Codes Used to Assess Scientific Habits of Mind

Scientific discursive practices	
Social knowledge construction	Scientists construct knowledge in collaborative groups; students do not (AAAS.D.12.6 & 1.A. 12.2; Chinn and Malhotra 2002)
Build on others' ideas	Participate in group discussions on scientific topics by restating or summarizing accurately what others have said, asking for clarification or elaboration (AAAS)
Use of counterarguments	Suggest alternative claims or arguments, criticize arguments in which data, explanations, or conclusions are represented as the only ones worth consideration with no mention of other possibilities, suggest alternative trade-offs in decisions and designs, criticize designs in which major trade-offs are not acknowledged (AAAS.I2.E)
Uses data/evidence	Use data or evidence in making arguments and claims (AAAS)
Alternative explanations of data	No matter how well one theory fits observations, a new theory might fit them just as well or better, or might fit a wider range of observations. In science, the testing, revising, and occasional discarding of theories, new and old, never ends. This ongoing process leads to an increasingly better understanding of how things work in the world but not to absolute truth (AAAS.1.A.12.3, AAAS.12.A.8.3)
References outside resources	References outside resources in making arguments and claims (e.g., other threads or stickies, online articles, databases) (AAAS12.D.8.3/Chinn and Malhotra 2002)
Systems- and model-based reasoning	
Systems-based reasoning	Reasons about some phenomenon or problem in terms of a system—a collection of components and processes that interact in some way (i.e., have relationships to one another of some form). Defined systems have boundaries, subsystems, relation to other systems, and inputs & outputs (AAAS.11.A)
Understanding feedback	Thinking about things as systems means looking for how its components relate to each other. Output from one part of a system can function as input to other parts of a system. A change in one component's state can result in changes in another component's state. This includes relationships among components within a system or between systems (AAAS. 11.A.8.2)
Model-based reasoning	Model-based reasoning involves the envision of a principle-based mechanism with interacting components that represents the operation of a system within the natural (virtual) world. A model may concretize phenomena that are not directly observable (Mayer 1992; AAAS.11.B)
Model testing and prediction	The usefulness of a model can be tested by comparing its predictions to actual observations in the real world. But a close match does not necessarily mean that the model is the only "true" model or the only one that would work (AAAS.11.B. 12.2)
Mathematical modeling	The basic idea of mathematical modeling is to find a mathematical relationship (e.g., algebraic equation, relationship between two quantities, etc.) that behaves in the same ways as the objects or processes under investigation. A mathematical model may give insight about how something really works or may fit observations very well without any intuitive meaning (AAAS.11.B.12.1)
Mathematical computation	Explicitly gives some form of mathematical calculation in their argument or thesis that is not given by the game itself (e.g., not merely the DPS listed on a weapon). For example, demonstrates how an algebraic equation (a mathematical model) can be solved for (or predict) the relative trade-off between two variables, or compares two groups using their mean, median, variance, standard deviation, etc. (AAAS.12.B)
Not relevant to sci reason	Social banter, non science related topics, etc.
Uncodable	Cannot tell if it is science related or not
Tacit epistemologies	
Absolutist	Knowledge is objective, certain, and simply accumulates (Kuhn 1992)
Relativist	Knowledge is subjective, dictated only by personal tastes and wishes of the knower. Nothing is certain, all opinions are of equal validity, and even experts disagree (Kuhn 1992)
Evaluative	Knowledge is an open-ended process of evaluation and argument (Kuhn 1992)
Uncodable	Cannot tell what epistemology the poster tacitly holds

Findings

The results from this analysis are presented in Figure 1, which shows the percentage of posts that exhibit each code we focused on for analysis. Here, we see the saturation of key characteristics of scientific reasoning skills and dispositions across the sample. Several interesting patterns emerge from this analysis.

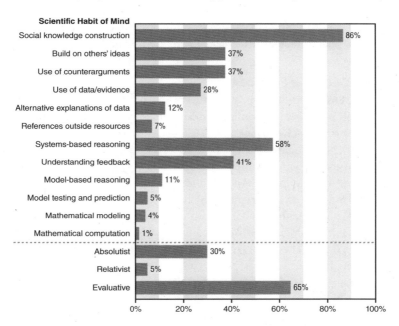

Figure 1. Proportion of posts within the data corpus that exhibit each scientific habit of mind and tacit epistemology under examination.

Social Knowledge Construction

The first and most obvious pattern is the large proportion of productive discussion found on the boards: We found that 86% of the *WoW* discussion forums consisted of talk that could be considered "social knowledge construction"—meaning, the collective development of understanding, often through joint problems solving and argumentation. In other words, in the overwhelming majority of forum talk, participants were solving problems through discussion, knowledge sharing, and debate through threads that began with posts such as "I notice that high level priests carry around a great deal of potions...Which potions do you carry around constantly and why?" (post #3357.0) Only 8% of the discussion posts were mere social banter (the remaining 6% were uncodable with this coding scheme)—perhaps a surprising result for those who presume that discussions around videogames are a "torpid" waste of time.

One of our initial hypotheses was that only the more experienced *WoW* players would engage in higher order intellectual work on the discussion forums. In fact, we found no relationship between a given poster's character level (which represents their experience with the game) and the quality or quantity of the attributes for which we coded, other than a very mild and negative correlation ($r = -0.08$) between author's character level and social banter. Thus, while we cannot disprove the notion that only the "hardcore" gamers engage in the forms of informal science literacy investigated here, we find no evidence that such is indeed the case.

Scientific Discursive Practices

Of the 86% of the forum posts that were not social banter or simply uncodable, roughly one-third (37%) built on ideas that previous posters had raised; for example, by stating "Given your advice, I've spec'd out the following talents ..." (post #4109.29). Roughly another third (37%) used counterarguments against previous posters' ideas; for example, stating "The real question is 'Are Holy or Disc priests going to kill as much?' And the answer is no. Shadow has more offensive utility, which is just as important as the increase in damage..." (post #2143.5). That *WoW* players either elaborated on or disagreed with previous people's comments in the context of a forum should come as no surprise given the "collectively intelligent" (Levy 1999) nature of many such communities. However, it is interesting that forms of *scientific* argumentation were also prevalent within this informal context, given previous findings indicating that such practices do not come naturally and are difficult to foster (Kuhn 1992; Osborne et al. 2004).

As another illustration of scientific argumentation, in 28% of the posts made individuals used data or evidence of some form in order to warrant their claims. For example, in a thread discussing priest healing strategies, one poster argues for his strategy by stating, "my +355 healing allows me to use Heal4 [spell] to hit around 1k+ every time, ignoring crits [critical hits]. That's good enough to spam [cast repeatedly] for most battles while throwing in a Fheal [flash heal] now and then" (post #3247.20). In another 12%, individuals challenge one another's hypotheses by providing alternative explanations of evidence used to support those suppositions with statements such as the following:

> The calculations correctly show that mind flay [spell] receives just as much +damage percentage as mind blast. However mind blast has a 1.5 second cast time, and mind flay has a 3 second cast time. And therefore mind flay receives half the dps [damage per second] boost it should. (post #2609.43)

And in 7% of the posts, participants cited a variety of information resources beyond the current discussion thread itself (see Table 2). For example, one poster: recommended a particular character configuration (i.e. "talent build," discussed below) over another with the statement "I would be more inclined to go with a build similar to: http://www.wowhead.com/?talent=bVMhzZZxOgtczR if you would like to go Shadow [one particular form of character specialization]" (post #3374.9).

What did the typical "social knowledge construction" discussion thread containing "scientific discursive practices" look like? As the example in Figure 2 illustrates, most such discussions began with an initial question about a given mechanic in the game or game-playing strategy, often coupled with the proposal of some theory. A second poster would typically then elaborate in answering the question or responding to the proposed theory, at times using data from the game to warrant the claims made. The response would then be discussed and debated by a larger group. Often a second, alternative hypothesis or explanation would eventually be offered (or, more rarely, the interpretation of the data used in the first explanation was reinterpreted), followed by an additional round of discussion and debate, and so on. Occasionally, confirming or disconfirming claims or evidence from other resources, such as collaborative online manuals to the game (e.g., WoWWiki, http://wowwiki.com) or other archived discussions on this or other forums, would be introduced into the discussion. In some threads, a comparison or synthesis of the two or more explanations would culminate the discussion; in others, the conversation simply petered out as though the participants had accepted the most recently posted theory or explanation as the preferred one or had perhaps tired of the topic and moved on.

Table 2. Types of Outside Resources Referenced by Forum Poster Within the Sample

	Outside Resources Referenced
Talent calculators/builds	Links to an official or unofficial tools for calculating talent point allocations
Personal talent builds	Links to a player's specific talent build
WoW databases and Wikis	Links to information on publicly accessible WoW databases and Wikis created by WoW players themselves
Official blizzard documents	Links to official information published by Blizzard
Other **WoW** forums	Links to other discussions in the WoW forums (beyond current forum)
Personal websites	Links to a player's personal website or other online material

post #	social knowledge construction	build on others' ideas	use of counterarguments	use of data / evidence	alternative explanations of data	references outside resources	systems-based reasoning	understanding feedback	model-based reasoning	model testing and prediction	mathematical modeling	mathematical computation	absolutist	relativist	evaluative
0 Poses question: group healing strategy (A) or (B)?	•			•			•	•	•						•
1 Advocates (B) & gives strategy (C)	•				•		•	•							•
2 Compares (A) & (B) on use conditions, advocates (A)	•													•	
3 Critiques (A) & (B), advocates (C), raise issue (X)	•	•	•				•	•							•
4 Elaborates (X)	•	•		•			•	•							•
5 Elaborates (X)	•	•			•		•	•					•		
6 Argues (A) > (B)	•	•	•				•	•							•
7 Elaborates (X)	•	•					•	•					•		
8 Elaborates (A) > (B) but dependent on conditions	•	•					•	•						•	
9 Argues (A) = (B) under the right conditions for each	•	•	•		•		•	•						•	
10 Counterargues (B) > (A)	•	•	•	•			•	•					•		
11 Elaborates counterargument (B) > (A)	•	•	•	•			•	•		•	•		•		
12 Details scenario with (B) strategy & issue (X)	•			•			•	•	•						•
13 Details scenario with both (A) & (B) strategies	•			•	•		•	•	•						•
14 Details scenario with (A) strategy & new issue (Y)	•	•													•
15 Challenges detail of scenario with (A)	•	•													
16 Argues (A) > (B)	•			•	•		•	•							•
17 Argues (B) > (A) & details issue (X)	•		•	•	•		•	•	•				•		
18 Elaborates (A) > (B)	•	•					•								
19 Counterargues (B) > (A)	•	•													•
20 Argues (B) > (A)	•			•			•	•							•
21 Compares (A) & (B) on use conditions, advocates (A)	•		•	•	•		•	•							•
22 Original poster acknowledges discussion	•														•
23 Argues both (A) & (B) strategies	•						•	•							•
24 Argues (A) > (B)	•			•									•		
25 Counterargues (B) > (A)	•		•	•											•
26 Argues (A) = (B) under right conditions based on (X)	•	•	•	•	•		•	•	•					•	•
27 Details scenario w/ (A) & (B) & (C) strategies given (X)	•	•					•	•	•						•
28 Argues (A) > (B)	•			•	•										•
29 Argues (A) = (B) under right conditions based on (X)	•				•		•	•	•						•
30 Elaborates detail of scenario with (A) & (B) & (C)	•						•	•							•
31 Counterargues (B) > (A)	•	•	•				•	•	•	•					•
32 Argues (B) > (A)	•				•		•	•							•
33 Challenges initial characterization of (B)	•												•		
34 Argues (A) > (B) & raises issue (X)	•			•	•		•	•	•				•		
35 Argues (A) > (B)	•			•	•						•	•	•		
36 Details scenario with both (A) & (B) strategies	•			•	•		•	•	•						•

A = spam PoH   B = Holy Nova   C = renew   X = FR gear   Y = FR pots

Figure 2. An example "social knowledge" construction thread (#329) of thirty-six posts detailed in terms of both the augmentative moves made within each and the codes applied to them.

System- and Model-Based Reasoning

Over half (58%) of the *WoW* forum posts evinced *systems-based reasoning,* the majority of which also demonstrate an understanding of feedback among components of the system. For example, participants discussed the game in terms of components and processes that interact in ways such that changes in one impact cause changes in another, as in the following post:

> By choosing a slower spell [variable one] and the lowest rank [variable two] you can live comfortably with (or your tank can live with, in our case), you are still making the most of your mana [variable three], given your gear [variable four]. (post #3247.12)

Roughly one tenth of the forum posts illustrated *model-based reasoning*—essentially, using some form of model to understand a given system under consideration—with about half of those (5% of posts total) including some comparison between the model's predictions and actual observations of the phenomenon it is intended to capture or explain in some way. One example of such discussion focused on a phenomenon called "scaling." Imagine that, for a level 2 priest, a given spell does ten damage; when the priest reaches to level 20, that ten damage accomplishes much less because the level 20 priest is now fighting much harder monsters. In order to balance ability with challenge, *WoW* makes higher level, stronger spells available as one's character level increases. In place of a spell that does ten damage would be a spell that does one hundred damage, for example, so that the ability to do damage to monsters using a given spell "scales" as character level increases. Scaling is not the same for every spell or character class, and one way that designers "balance" their game mechanics is to monitor and tweak scaling. In the following excerpt, a participant proposes one particular model of how the in-game scaling mechanics work and considers that model's predictions given changes in input:

> If mind flay [priest spell] actually got the full scaling of a 3 second cast spell, then by combining mind flay with both dots [priest damage over time spells] and all available talents [point system for specializing character types] to improve those, you would actually see a shadow priest's scaling maxing out at a little under 80% of what a fire mage's scaling would max out at with 40 fire and nothing more. (post #2609.51)

Thus, posters orient toward the usefulness of a model in terms if its ability (or inability) to make predictions that match actual observations. Slightly less than half of those models (4% of posts total) were explicitly mathematical, and only 1% of the total forum posts included actual computations as well. An example illustrating both is the following post excerpt raising issues about the balance of priest versus mage abilities:

By intuition, you should notice a problem ...

but I'll give you the numbers anyways

For Mindflay, SW:P, and presumpably VT [3 priest spells]:

Damage = (base_spell_damage + modifier * damage_
gear) * darkness * weaving * shadowform * misery

For Frostbolt [mage spell]

Average Damage = (base_spell_damage + (modifier + empowered frost)
* damage_gear) * (1 * (1 − critrate − winter's chill − empowered frost) +
(1.5 + ice shards) * (critrate + winter's chill + empowered frost)) * piercing
ice

mindflay = (426 + 0.45 * dam) * 1.1 * 1.15 * 1.15 * 1.05

650.7 + 0.687 * dam

frostbolt = (530 + (0.814 + 0.10)*dam) * ((1 − crit − 0.10 − 0.05) +
(1.5 + 0.5) * (crit + 0.10 + 0.05)) * 1.06

(530 + 0.914 * dam) * ((0.85 − crit) + 2 * (crit + 0.15)) * 1.06

0.968 * (dam + 579.7) * (crit + 1.15)

Please notice the 0.687 versus the 0.968. That's the scaling factor. (post
#2609.18)

In this example, the author makes an argument about the relative scaling of priest skills compared to mage skills based on a thoroughly mathematical argument, using computation as a form of evidence for the points made. His conclusion—that the scaling factor of each class type (0.687 and 0.968 respectfully) is unequal—is his climactic justification for the initial claim that the two character classes are not balanced.

What did a typical "systems- and model-based reasoning" forum post discussion thread look like? Figure 3 shows the analysis of one post-containing relevant codes.

Typically, such posts would occur in context of broader "social knowledge construction" threads (described above). In order to make an argument for one particular hypothesis or solution for some in-game system, the poster would often present a model to explain the system as evidence for their claim. In some rare cases, that model would be mathematical in nature, and fidelity between the model's prediction and actual in-game observations would function as evidence of its explanatory power. More frequently, evidence would include direct observations taken in-game and references to outside resources such as collective data sets, heuristics in the form of online database backed websites, or fan-created user manuals and guides. Generally speaking, the proportion of model-based reasoning, model testing and prediction, use of mathematics, and explicit computation (11%, 5%, 4%, 1%, respectively) were rather low; however, the sophistication of arguments that leverage such models warrants consideration. For example, Figure 4 shows the model linked in the post detailed in Figure 3.

social knowledge construction	The unfortunate fact is that there is no shadow nuke [prior topic] … and no shadow nuke which benefits from reduced casting time. All other casters (including holy priests) have a nuke which benefits from reduced casting time: bane, improved fireball, improved frostbolt, divine fury,
uses data/evidence	improved wrath. I have put together **my own spreadsheet** which goes into more detail and takes into account exactly what happens to **spells**
systems based reasoning	**with regard to talents** and gives a column at the end expressing **each**
understanding feedback	**spell's total scaling with respect to +dmg [damage] applied per**
	second (i.e. how much your gear actually improves your dps):
model based reasoning	http://geocities.com/[omitted].htm ⎯⎯⎯⎯▶
mathematical modeling	
mathematical computation	
	If I got anything wrong feel free to email me at [omitted]@gmail.com but if you read up at
references outside resources	**wowwiki.com** and check out the **coefficients**
evaluative epistemology	**used in the theorycraft mod** you'll find that I'm consistent with respect to them.
	You see there at the end - if you add flay and swp together you see that shadow is at 31%, where fire mages are around 48%. I have done some preliminary numbers for the expansion and shadow only improves to
model testing & prediction	35% as fire mages jump way up to 60%. **If flay were empowered to the point that it recieved 65% of +dmg then shadow would be up around 45% dps scaling.** That would be quite respectible considering that a shadow priest can swp/flay for nearly 2 minutes without interruption where other classes would peter out in a minute or less except for their mana recovery abilities. Without empowered scaling shadow priests will languish at under 50% of the endgame dps of mages and warlocks. (post #2609.6)

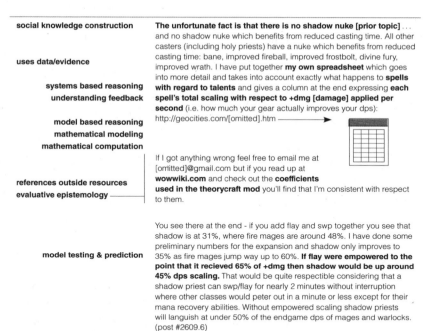

Figure 3. Analysis of an individual post exemplifying system- and model-based reasoning.

Tacit Epistemologies

We chose to examine the dispositions toward knowledge exhibited in the data corpus because previous pilot work indicated that, while we may find informal science reasoning and argumentation in *WoW* forum discussions, it may also be the case that the stance authors in such contexts take toward their claims is appropriate for *reverse engineering,* but inappropriate for *scientific inquiry* (Steinkuehler and Chmiel 2006). An "absolutist" epistemology, for example, might serve someone well when operating in a virtual world where there really is a single algorithm (or set of algorithms) underlying a given phenomenon and success is only a matter of finding them. However, such an absolutist approach does not serve someone well for understanding science in the real world. Instead, in science, an evaluative disposition is most appropriate, one that treats knowledge as an open-ended process of evaluation and argument of hypotheses about whether and how "algorithms" govern natural phenomena.

The epistemology tacitly displayed in 27% of the data corpus was too ambiguous to code. Of the remaining data corpus that could be coded for epistemological disposition, we found that 65% of the forum posts displayed an evaluative epistemology through rhetorical moves that treat knowledge as an open-ended process of evaluation and argument such as "Shadow Affinity [priest talent] and

Constants: Crit Rate = 5%

Solo Caster Classes at Level 60

Class	Spec	Spell (+ talent conditions)	Spell Damage Scale (Cast Time / 3.5)	Damage Talents (per talents)	Target Debuffs (per abilities)	Damage Scale (talents * debuffs)	Spell Damage Total Scale (scale * talents * debuffs)	Crit Bonus (per talents no benefit for dots)	Crit Rate Bonus (per talents benefit for dots)	Crit Rate Scale (total scale * crit bonus)	Damage Interval (limited by dots)	Cast Interval (limited by cooldowns)	Cast Time	Casts Per Interval	DPS Scale (total scale / dmg interval)	Time Ratio (dmg interval / cast interval / casts)	Max Crit DPS (crit interval / dmg interval / dots)	Modified Crit Rate (crit rate + crit rate bonus)	TOTAL DPS SCALE (dps * (1 - crit rate) + crit dps * crit rate)	Notes
Priest	Shadow	Mind Flay	45.7%	125%	115%	144%	65.7%	100%	0%	65.7%	3	3	3 Channel	1	21.90%	100.00%	21.90%	5.00%	21.90%	Channeled
		SWP	133.3%	125%	115%	144%	191.7%	100%	0%	191.7%	18	18	1.5	1	10.65%	100.00%	10.65%	5.00%	10.65%	
		Mind Blast	42.9%	125%	115%	144%	61.6%	150%	0%	92.4%	1.5	5.5	1.5	1	41.07%	27.27%	61.61%	5.00%	42.10%	Cooldown
	Disc/Holy	Smite	71.4%	115%	100%	115%	82.1%	150%	15%	123.2%	2	2	2	1	41.07%	100.00%	61.61%	20.00%	45.18%	
		Holy Fire	75.0%	115%	100%	115%	86.3%	150%	15%	129.4%	3	3	3	1	28.75%	100.00%	43.13%	20.00%	31.63%	
		Holy Fire Dot	25.0%	115%	100%	115%	28.8%	100%	15%	28.8%	10	10	3	1	2.88%	100.00%	2.88%	20.00%	2.88%	Dot
		SWP	100.0%	105%	100%	105%	105.0%	100%	0%	105.0%	18	18	1.5	1	5.83%	100.00%	5.83%	5.00%	5.83%	
		PI + Smite	71.4%	135%	100%	135%	96.4%	150%	15%	144.6%	2	180	2	6	48.21%	6.67%	72.32%	20.00%	53.04%	Cooldown
		PI + Holy Fire	75.0%	135%	100%	135%	101.3%	150%	15%	151.9%	3	180	3	5	33.75%	8.33%	50.63%	20.00%	37.13%	
		PI Holy Fire Dot	25.0%	135%	100%	135%	33.8%	100%	15%	33.8%	10	180	3	2	3.38%	11.11%	3.38%	20.00%	3.38%	Dot + Cooldown
Warlock	SM/Ruin	Shadowbolt	85.7%	110%	110%	121%	103.7%	200%	5%	207.4%	2.5	2.5	2.5	1	41.49%	100.00%	82.97%	10.00%	45.63%	
		Corruption	100.0%	110%	110%	121%	121.0%	100%	0%	121.0%	18	18	1.5	1	6.72%	100.00%	6.72%	5.00%	6.72%	
		Curse of Agony	100.0%	110%	110%	121%	121.0%	100%	0%	121.0%	24	24	1.5	1	5.04%	100.00%	5.04%	5.00%	5.04%	Improved CoA does not apply to gear
		Shadowburn	42.9%	110%	110%	121%	51.9%	200%	5%	103.7%	1.5	10	1	1	34.57%	15.00%	69.14%	10.00%	38.03%	
		Improved Shadowbolt	85.7%	110%	132%	145%	124.5%	200%	5%	248.9%	2.5	2.5	2.5	1	49.78%	100.00%	99.57%	10.00%	54.76%	Luck
	SM/DS	Shadowbolt	100.0%	125%	110%	138%	137.5%	150%	0%	206.3%	3	3	3	1	45.83%	100.00%	68.75%	5.00%	46.98%	
		Corruption	100.0%	125%	110%	138%	137.5%	100%	0%	137.5%	18	18	1.5	1	7.64%	100.00%	7.64%	5.00%	7.64%	
		Curse of Agony	100.0%	131%	110%	144%	144.1%	100%	0%	144.1%	24	24	1.5	1	6.00%	100.00%	6.00%	5.00%	6.00%	
	Ember/DS	Soul Fire	100.0%	125%	110%	138%	137.5%	200%	5%	275.0%	6	6	6	1	22.92%	100.00%	45.83%	10.00%	25.21%	Reagent
		Searing Pain	42.9%	125%	110%	138%	58.9%	200%	15%	117.9%	1.5	1.5	1.5	1	39.29%	100.00%	78.57%	20.00%	47.14%	
		Immolate	19.8%	150%	110%	165%	32.7%	200%	0%	65.3%	1.5	1.5	1.5	1	21.78%	100.00%	43.56%	10.00%	23.96%	
		Immolate Dot	65.3%	125%	110%	138%	89.8%	100%	5%	89.8%	15	15	15	1	5.99%	100.00%	5.99%	10.00%	5.99%	Dot
	MD/Ruin	Shadowbolt	85.7%	110%	110%	127%	108.4%	200%	5%	216.9%	2.5	2.5	2.5	1	43.37%	100.00%	86.74%	10.00%	47.71%	
		Corruption	100.0%	115%	110%	127%	126.5%	100%	0%	126.5%	18	18	1.5	1	7.03%	100.00%	7.03%	5.00%	7.03%	
		Curse of Agony	100.0%	115%	110%	127%	126.5%	100%	0%	126.5%	24	24	1.5	1	5.27%	100.00%	5.27%	5.00%	5.27%	Improved CoA does not apply to gear
		Shadowburn	42.9%	115%	110%	127%	54.2%	200%	5%	108.4%	1.5	10	1	1	36.14%	15.00%	72.29%	10.00%	39.76%	
		Improved Shadowbolt	85.7%	115%	115%	132%	130.1%	200%	5%	260.2%	2.5	2.5	2.5	1	52.05%	100.00%	104.09%	10.00%	57.25%	Luck
Mage	Frost	Frostbolt	81.4%	106%	100%	106%	86.3%	200%	10%	172.6%	2.5	2.5	2.5	1	34.53%	100.00%	69.05%	15.00%	39.70%	winter's chill for all ice
		Frozen + Frostbolt	81.4%	106%	100%	106%	86.3%	200%	60%	172.6%	2.5	2.5	2.5	1	34.53%	100.00%	69.05%	65.00%	56.97%	Frozen target
	AP/Frost	Frostbolt	81.4%	109%	100%	109%	88.8%	200%	63%	177.5%	2.5	2.5	2.5	1	35.50%	100.00%	71.01%	68.00%	38.34%	
		Frozen + Frostbolt	81.4%	109%	100%	109%	88.8%	200%	3%	177.5%	2.5	2.5	2.5	1	35.50%	100.00%	71.01%	8.00%	59.64%	Frozen target
		AP + Frostbolt	81.4%	139%	100%	139%	113.2%	200%	63%	226.4%	2.5	180	2.5	5	45.27%	6.94%	90.55%	68.00%	48.90%	Cooldown
		AP + Frozen Frostbolt	81.4%	139%	100%	139%	113.2%	200%	3%	226.4%	2.5	180	2.5	5	45.27%	6.94%	90.55%	8.00%	76.06%	Cooldown + Frozen target
	Fire	Fireball	100.0%	110%	115%	127%	126.5%	219%	6%	277.0%	3	3	3	1	42.17%	100.00%	92.35%	11.00%	47.69%	imp scorch for all fire mage
		Fire Blast	42.9%	115%	115%	127%	54.2%	219%	10%	118.7%	1.5	8	1.5	1	36.14%	18.75%	79.15%	15.00%	42.59%	imp ignite is 150% + 150% * 40% * debuffs
		Scorch	42.9%	115%	115%	127%	54.2%	219%	10%	118.7%	1.5	1.5	1.5	1	36.14%	100.00%	79.15%	15.00%	42.59%	
	AP/Fire	Fireball	100.0%	103%	115%	118%	118.5%	219%	6%	259.4%	3	3	3	1	39.48%	100.00%	86.47%	11.00%	44.65%	
		Scorch	42.9%	103%	115%	118%	50.8%	219%	6%	111.2%	1.5	1.5	1.5	1	33.84%	100.00%	74.12%	11.00%	38.27%	
		AP + Fireball	100.0%	133%	115%	153%	153.0%	219%	6%	335.0%	3	180	3	4	50.98%	6.67%	111.65%	11.00%	57.66%	Cooldown
Druid	Balance	Moonfire	20.0%	110%	100%	110%	22.0%	200%	13%	44.0%	1.5	3	1.5	1	14.67%	100.00%	29.33%	18.00%	17.31%	Dot, imp MF doesn't apply to gear
		Moonfire	57.1%	110%	100%	110%	62.9%	100%	13%	62.9%	12	12	12	1	5.24%	100.00%	5.24%	18.00%	5.24%	
		Wrath	57.1%	110%	100%	110%	62.9%	200%	3%	125.7%	1.5	1.5	1.5	1	41.90%	100.00%	83.81%	8.00%	45.26%	
		Starfire	100.0%	110%	100%	110%	110.0%	200%	3%	220.0%	3	3	3	1	36.67%	100.00%	73.33%	8.00%	39.60%	
Shaman	Elemental	Lightning Bolt	85.7%	105%	100%	105%	90.0%	200%	10%	180.0%	2	2	2	1	45.00%	100.00%	90.00%	15.00%	51.75%	
		Chain Lightning	71.4%	105%	100%	105%	75.0%	200%	10%	150.0%	1.5	6	1.5	1	50.00%	25.00%	100.00%	15.00%	57.50%	Cooldown

Figure 4. An example model of an in-game phenomenon called scaling (Basic n.d.) that illustrates the complexity of the models sometimes discussed.

Silent Resolve [priest talent]: Do they stack? If so, why would a shadow priest need a 45% reduction in threat?" (post #1937.0). Thirty percent displayed an absolutist epistemology, treating knowledge as objective, certain, and simply accumulative through statements such as: "There is a basic strategy for any one class vs any other class and whoever carries out that strategy most successfully will win" (post #415.92) [even though no such basic strategy exists]. Another 5% displayed a relativist epistemology, treating claims about the world as subjective and "to each his own" (post #215.58). Thus, the majority of posts that could be coded in terms of the attitude toward knowledge held fell into the "evaluative" category, which is consistent with scientific inquiry and inconsistent with reverse engineering. We discuss these findings in greater depth below.

Game Specific Content

What specific content areas of the game elicit these forms of informal science literacy practice? Examining the relationships among our scientific habits of mind codes (see Table 1) and our *WoW* content codes (Table 3), we found that the only moderately strong and non-obvious relationship between the two was between systems-based reasoning (and its concomitant "understanding feedback") and discussion of the priest "talent tree" ($r = 0.48$ and 0.42, respectively), shown in Figure 5, whereby players allocate "talent points" toward customizing the functions and abilities of their online character or "avatar."

In working through this system, participants are faced with the challenge of finding the best-fit solution to a problem of limited resources (talent points) for distribution across multiple variables, each with their own mathematical relationship to underlying avatar characteristics (e.g., hit points, mana points, regeneration speed). Because *WoW* is a complex system with no single obvious solution, a significant amount of time on the priest discussion boards is spent assessing how choices in one area of the talent tree affect outcomes elsewhere and debating which point allocations are best given various play styles and goals. Many of the examples used throughout this paper are a testament to the intellectual labor spent on just this one game-related content area.

Table 3. A Second Set of Codes Used to Describe the Game-Related Content of the Post

World of Warcraft *Content Codes*		
Guilds	Items, equipment, supplies	PvP content, battlegrounds
Quests, instances, raids	Talent trees, spells, abilities	Collaborative play
Other classes (than priests)	Addons, macros	Patches, expansions
Factions (horde vs. alliance)	*WoW* forums, trolling	Class/profession guides, how-to's
Reputation/experience grinding, leveling	Null/social banter	Uncodable

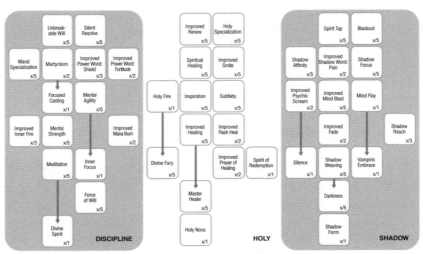

Figure 5. The *World of Warcraft* "talent tree" for the priest class (at the time of data collection), which enables players to customize their avatars.

Discussion and Implications

Our goal has been to provide empirical evidence to substantiate claims of the potential of MMOs as sites fostering learning, especially informal science literacy. Given the overall representativeness of our sample (confidence level of 91%), we are in a good position to make reasonably strong claims. Overwhelmingly, game related forums like the one examined here are rich sites for social knowledge construction. That game communities engage in productive forms of discussion and problem solving is not surprising; that such an overwhelming majority of their conversation (86%) is dedicated to such labor *is* surprising. Discursive practices include argument, counterargument, and the use of evidence to warrant one's claims. In such contexts, much of the conversation focuses on puzzling through complex systems within the virtual world and the relationships among components within those systems. At times, that inquiry includes the proposal of explanatory models of how the system under scrutiny functions. On rare occasions, posts debate the merits of their models in terms of their predictive power. On even rarer occasions still, those models take the form of mathematical equations whose computations are done explicitly and publicly.

The findings on tacit epistemology displayed throughout the discussions were also a surprise. Contrary to our initial hypotheses, the pre-dominant epistemological disposition exhibited in the forum posts was "evaluative" and therefore appropriate to science. Such findings are quite encouraging. In an earlier study of argumentative reasoning in everyday contexts that examined Americans across gender, age, class, and educational level (Kuhn 1992), only 15% of those interviewed held an evaluative epistemology, 50% held an absolutist epistemology, and

35% held a relativist epistemology. In this earlier study, argumentative ability did not differ systematically as a function of gender or age but it did differ systematically in terms of level of education. Kuhn therefore concluded that classrooms are one promising context for the development of such skills. However, she also points out the limitations of teacher led dialogues, crediting the positive impact education has on such attributes to the "social environment of peers" that school, as a byproduct, enables rather than teacher led formal dialogues per se:

> ... does school experience in fact offer the opportunity for the kinds of exchange of ideas and argumentative discourse that would enhance development of argumentative thinking? In one sense, the answer is yes; in another sense it is no. The answer is yes in the sense that from the earliest years, schooling provides a social environment of peers. In the informal social interaction that is a major part of school experience, ideas are tested and inevitably challenged; thus social experience serves as the natural challenge to individual thought. In a second deeper sense, however, the answer is no; schools do not provide this opportunity, or at least do not provide it optimally. Even in the best schools, what may appear to be genuine group debates about an issue are usually heavily controlled by the teacher ... [who] already possesses the understanding of an issue that he or she wishes students to attain ... Most often missing, even in the best of such "discovery-based" pedagogies, is genuine, open debate of complex, unanswered questions. (Kuhn 1992, pp. 175–176).

While Kuhn does not advocate the use of informal social dialogue necessarily either (in her own words, they "only occasionally leads [sic] students to think explicitly about their ideas—to reflect on their own thought" p. 175), these data suggest their efficacy, at least under certain conditions. In the context of game related forums, informal social dialogues are indeed "genuine, open debate of complex, unanswered questions" and therefore may very well lead participants toward a more reflective stance toward knowledge ultimately. Such a hypothesis is certainly worth future consideration in studies that follow. Of course, one could also argue that game forums (like the one studied here) tend to attract individuals with a more nuanced stance toward knowledge rather than fostering such a stance themselves. Regardless, we can at least say that the cultural norms that emerge in this part of *WoW* fandom preference an evaluative epistemology and that this preferencing of an evaluative disposition varies significantly from the disposition preferenced by other cultural norms, including but certainly not limited to the typical cultural norms of an American classroom.

In addition to providing empirical evidence to substantiate the potential of such play contexts for informal science literacy learning, this study sheds some curious light on the nature of collective intelligence (Levy 1999). Discussion environments such as these are best characterized as *collective* rather than *collaborative*. It could have easily been the case that a handful of verbose posters engage in extended dialogue with each other, making it a highly collaborative (albeit small) community of exceptional minds who happen to make their cognition public. This, however, was not at all the pattern we found. Rather, as Figure 6 shows, the relationship between length of discussion thread and number of players contributing to it is strongly linear.

In such contexts, solutions developed by one person are referenced, debated, and built upon by masses of other participants, not merely a handful of designated experts. Thus, a large number of posters each make one or two contributions to the discussion, with the solution to the problem or answer to the inquiry emerging as a result of swarms of thinkers, not a lonely few.

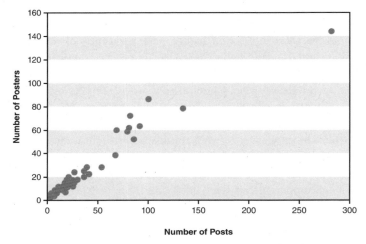

Figure 6. Scatter plot of number of posts by number of unique posters for each thread in the data corpus.

Such findings are useful in that they enable us to more accurately characterize virtual worlds as learning contexts that stretch across both intra-game and extra-game spaces. As our study shows, forms of inquiry within play contexts such as these are *authentic* although *synthetic:* even though the worlds themselves are fantasy, the knowledge building communities around them are quite real. And, it is their designed nature that makes these communities so lively. For they were designed such that particular user-controlled configurations (e.g., how one builds her talent tree) has powerful and important implications for the success of one's game play. In fact, in these synthetic worlds designers can manipulate these dynamics so that they are most likely to breed rich conversations as users struggle with the most appropriate configurations.

What, then, are the implications for science education and future research? There are several. First, the veritable firewall against games and gaming culture within schools might erode. While virtual worlds may seem "torpid" (Solomon

2004) to a non-gaming older generation, empirical analysis of what game communities do and value indicates that this interactive medium might well be a worthy vehicle of learning for those who value intellectual and academic play. In a school system sometimes sidetracked by testing regimes that pressure teachers and students to focus on only a narrow range of topics, popular culture contexts such as these might be a nice complement to classrooms, augmenting classroom instruction by situating informal science literacy in popular culture context.

Second, we should ask ourselves how these practices are distributed across various groups by demographic variables known to be important, such as age, education level, and income. Demonstrating that game communities such as those in *WoW* engage in important forms of science literacy again raises the specter of a new form of digital divide—one not between the have and have-nots, but between the do and do-nots. We need to think deeply about what people are doing with the technologies that are becoming so ubiquitous and engaging. As educators, we have a responsibility to better understand what these different forms of technology afford and communicate this to the public more broadly.

Third and finally, we should actively seek out ways to build *bridging third spaces* (Steinkuehler 2008b) between school and home that incubate forms of academic play such as those studied here. In so doing, we might address both growing digital divides at once. We can ameliorate the generational divide by educating the keepers of the canon as to the genuine merit of games and gaming cultures, and we can close the access gap by providing rich intellectual play spaces in technically and cognitively sophisticated environments to kids and young adults who might not otherwise happen upon them. As Dewey himself once argued, good education, effective and life-enhancing education, represents life "as real and vital to the child as that which he carries on in the home, in the neighborhood, or on the play-ground" (1897).

References

American Association for the Advancement of Science (1993) Benchmarks for science literacy. Oxford University Press, New York

Barab S, Árcici A, Jackson C (2005) Eat your vegetables and do your homework: a design-based investigation of enjoyment and meaning in learning. Educ Technol 45(1):15–21

Barab SA, Sadler T, Heiselt C, Hickey D, Zuiker S (2007) Relating narrative, inquiry, and inscriptions: a framework for socio-scientific inquiry. J Sci Educ Technol 16(1):59–82. doi: 10.1007/s10956-006-9033-3

Basic (n.d.) Scaling model. Retrieved November 1, 2007 from http://geocities.com/karlthepagan/wow/damage_scale.htm

Chi MTH (1997) Quantifying qualitative analyses of verbal data: a practical guide. J Learn Sci 6(3):271–315. doi:10.1207/s15327809jls0603_1

Chinn CA, Malhotra B (2002) Epistemologically authentic inquiry in schools: a theoretical framework for evaluating inquiry tasks. Sci Educ 86(2):175–218. doi:10.1002/sce.10001

Dewey J (1897) My pedagogic creed. Sch J 14(3):77–80

Dewey J (1910) Science as subject matter and as method. Science 31(787):121–127. doi:10.1126/science.31.787.121

Elsner A (2005) Is US becoming hostile to science? CNN.com. Retrieved October 31, 2005 from http://www.cnn.com/2005/TECH/science/10/28/science.debate.reut

Friedman TL (2005) The world is flat. Farrar, Straus, and Giroux, New York

Gee JP (2003) What video games have to teach us about learning and literacy. Palgrave, New York

Hayes E Games I Learning through game design: a review of current software & research. Games Cult (in press)

Jenkins H III (1992) Textual poachers: television fans & participatory culture. Routledge, New York

Ketelhut DJ (2007) The impact of student self-efficacy on scientific inquiry skills: an exploratory investigation in River City, a multiuser virtual environment. J Sci Educ Technol 16(1):99–111. doi: 10.1007/s10956-006-9038-y

Ketelhut DJ, Dede C, Clarke J, Nelson B, Bowman C (2007) Studying situated learning in a multi-user virtual environment. In: Baker E, Dickieson J, Wulfeck W, O'Neil H (eds), Assessment of problem solving using simulations. Lawrence Erlbaum Associates, Mahwah, NJ

Kuhn D (1992) Thinking as argument. Harv Educ Rev 62(2):155–178

Lave J (1988) Cognition in practice. Cambridge University Press, Cambridge UK

Lave J, Wenger E (1991) Situated learning. Cambridge University Press, Cambridge

Levy P (1999) Collective intelligence. (Robert Bononno, trans.). Perseus Books, Cambridge MA

Mayer RE (1992) Thinking, problem solving, cognition, 2nd edn. WH Freeman, New York

Miller JD (2004) Public understanding of, and attitudes toward, scientific research: what we know and what we need to know. Public Underst Sci 13(3):273–294. doi:10.1177/0963662504044908

Nasir NS (2005) Individual cognitive structuring and the sociocultural context: strategy shifts in the game of dominoes. J Learn Sci 14(1):5–34. doi:10.1207/s15327809jls1401_2

National Research Council (1996) National science education standards. National Academy Press, Washington DC

Nelson B, Ketelhut DJ, Clarke J, Dieterle E, Dede C, Erlandson B (2007) Robust design strategies for scaling educational innovations: The River City MUVE case study. In: Shelton BE, Wiley DA (eds) The design and use of simulation computer games in education. Sense Press, Rotterdam, The Netherlands

Osborne J, Erduren S, Simon S (2004) Enhancing the quality of argumentation in school science. J Res Sci Teach 41(10):994–1020. doi:10.1002/tea.20035

Poincaré H (2001) Science and hypothesis. In: Gould SJ (ed) The value of science: essential writings of Henri Poincaré. The Modern Library, New York, pp 7–180 (Original work published 1905)

Schwab JJ (1962) The teaching of science as enquiry. Harvard University Press, Cambridge MA

Shaffer DW, Squire KD, Halverson R, Gee JP (2005) Video games and the future of learning. Phi Delta Kappan 87(2):105–111

Singer SR, Hilton M, Schweingruber HA (2005) America's lab report: investigations in high school science. The National Academy Press, Washington DC

Solomon A (2004, July 10) The closing of the American book. The New York Times p. A17

Squire K (2003) Replaying history: learning world history through playing Civilization III. Unpublished dissertation. Indiana University, Bloomington IN

Squire KD (2005) Educating the fighter. Horizon 13(2):75–88. doi: 10.1108/10748120510608106

Steinkuehler CA (2004) Learning in massively multiplayer online games. In: Kafai YB, Sandoval WA, Enyedy N, Nixon AS, Herrera F (eds) Proceedings of the sixth ICLS. Erlbaum, Mahwah, NJ, pp 521–528

Steinkuehler CA (2005) Cognition and learning in massively multiplayer online games: a critical approach. Unpublished dissertation. University of Wisconsin, Madison WI

Steinkuehler C (2006a) The mangle of play. Games Cult 1(3):1–14

Steinkuehler CA (2006b) Massively multiplayer online videogaming as participation in a Discourse. Mind Cult Act 13(1):38–52. doi: 10.1207/s15327884mca1301_4

Steinkuehler CA (2006c) Why game (culture) studies now? Games Cult 1(1):1–6

Steinkuehler C, Chmiel M (2006) Fostering scientific habits of mind in the context of online play. In: Barab SA, Hay KE, Songer NB, Hickey DT (eds) Proceedings of the international conference of the learning sciences. Erlbuam, Mahwah NJ, pp 723–729

Steinkuehler C (2007) Massively multiplayer online gaming as a constellation of literacy practices. eLearning 4(3):297–318

Steinkuehler CA (2008a) Cognition and literacy in massively multiplayer online games. In: Coiro J, Knobel M, Lankshear C, Leu D (eds) Handbook of research on new literacies. Erlbaum, Mahwah NJ, pp 611–634

Steinkuehler C (2008b) Massively multiplayer online games as an educational technology: an outline for research. Educ Technol 48(1):10–21

Woodcock BS (2008) An analysis of MMOG subscription growth 23.0. Retrieved April 21, 2008 from http://www.mmogchart.com

Crafting Rhetorical Proofs

In the last chapter, you learned about the different directions that reasoning can take—here, you will learn about rhetorical proofs, or different categories of reasoning that can help you think through the types of evidence you might use. Rhetorical proofs are, perhaps, the aspect of rhetoric that you were most famil- iar with before beginning this class: they are the appeals to **ethos** (page 120), **logos** (page 121), and **pathos** (page 122); they are the aspect of our subject that most generally gets thrown and analyzed around in the media. Think, say, of the number of times you have heard a news reporter speak of a subject's poor *ethos*, or someone's argument has been attacked due to a lack of logic; more pointedly, think of the emotional manipulation that has defined the past two election cycles. In short, rhetorical proofs are as vital to understand as they are dangerous to employ: when misused they can be nothing short of manipulative, drawing audiences in with poorly (or, sometimes, deviously) thought out fallacies. In short, the rhetorical proofs transcend the rhetorical situation of this classroom, the university, or even your current lives: they affect every single interaction you have with the world, and the greater a grasp you can have on them, the stronger a contributor to societal conversations you become.

Why, though, is it so important to understand these appeals? Well, it goes both ways. To take *pathos*, if you do not know how to appeal to your audiences' emo- tions, they will not connect with your topic; if you do not know how to recognize how another rhetor is manipulating *your* emotions, you may not know when you are, indeed, being manipulated. Similarly, you need to know how to best prove ethical credibility to an audience, but it is also vital to know whether or not a fellow rhetor is ethically composing. In short, it is just as important to ask how another speaker is employing the proofs as it is to ask how *you* will use them in your composition.

The Appeals[1]

As you begin to think about the rhetorical situation in which you compose, it is time to properly consider the two modes through which rhetors can act persuasively, which Aristotle referred to as the **artistic and inartistic appeals**. This is not "artistic" in the usual sense of the term, but closer to what you understand as "artificial." Artistic appeals are those *made* by the rhetor in the text, while inartistic are those *found* and brought into the text.

Artistic Appeals

Beyond considering the specific situation, there are specific ways that rhetor, audience, purpose, and text affect the way we persuade and are persuaded; these are famously known as the artistic (*entechnic*) appeals: *ethos, logos,* and *pathos.* Traditionally, *ethos* is appeal to credibility, *logos* is appeal to logic, and *pathos* is appeal to emotion. Often, *ethos, logos,* and *pathos* are understood as discrete and mutually exclusive parts, but they are far subtler than that.

We can better understand the artistic appeals as types of *motivation*, and Aristotle's frame as one of the first attempts at psychology: literally "studies of the soul." We are persuadable because we believe, we think, and we feel. A good piece of rhetoric makes the audience *believe, think,* and *feel* all at once. The appeals are like instruments in a symphony, members of a sports team, or spices in a meal: only when they work together do they really work well. Still, there is an ease in looking at them each individually.

1. ***Ethos*** is the credibility of the rhetor as they present themselves in the text. To do so, rhetors must demonstrate virtue, goodwill, and practical wisdom. When these elements are combined together, we have an effective *ethos*, a rhetor who is <u>a good person who cares about the audience and knows what they are doing</u>.

    a. **Virtue** (*arête*): a "good person" performs and embodies qualities that are valued by the audience. These can vary and even contradict, making this quite difficult. How partisan politicians describe the "other side" is a prime example of how virtue can be vice, depending on the audience. Tolerance for one audience is weakness to another, so too with passionate/hateful, principled/stubborn, humorous/cruel, etc. <u>We do not believe those we perceive to be "bad people."</u>

    b. **Good will** (*eunoia*): caring about the audience is not just being nice (or not being mean), but rather relating that you as a rhetor have their interests in mind. Even in situations with a hostile audience, demonstrating that you want the best for them, rather than self-promotion, is necessary to be effective. <u>We do not believe those we perceive not to care about us.</u>

---

1. This section is adapted from material originally written by Trevor Meyer.

c.   **Practical wisdom** (*phronesis*): effective rhetors have a solid and detailed understanding of the topic at hand, the assumptions of their argument, and the consequences of their proposals. You do not have to know everything, but knowing what you know and what you do not is vital. <u>We do not believe those we perceive not to know what they're doing.</u>

2.   *Logos*: While formal logic is mathematical in rigor, most of our arguments are judged by less rigid standards, such as whether or not they are "reasonable" or "probable." This standard is generally sufficient. You must have a thorough and defensible line of reasoning, but it does not *necessarily* have to be formally logical. To be effective rhetorically, <u>a text has to make minimal sense with reasonable reasons.</u>

   a.   The **syllogism**, as discussed in the previous chapter, is an important basic logical form consisting of premises and a conclusion that is judged by its validity and soundness. An argument is **valid** if the conclusion *necessarily* follows from the premises, regardless of the truth of the premises. However, if a valid argument also has true premises, it is **sound**. <u>It is important to differentiate truth and logic, but even more important to use them together.</u>

   b.   **Enthymemes**, unlike the syllogisms, skip a premise—the one that "goes without saying" or "most people know to be true." These kinds of *commonplaces* are both widespread and various, so <u>knowing what premises your audience already accepts and those your argument relies on are very important</u> for effective *logos*.

      When the premise it omitted, it's up to the audience to supply it and it is this audience participation, even if unconscious, that makes enthymemes so powerful. The audience helps create the argument, sometimes without realizing it. Because the commonplace is unstated, you need to be especially reflective about the validity of your enthymemes, because what people assume to be true can very often be false.

   c.   The **example** is another important part of rhetorical reasoning; an effective example can be a story, image, chart, or an outside source cited and quoted. Since lots of reasoning and argumentation can be abstract, presenting clear and concrete examples is vital. Be critical and reflective in what examples you use and how you use them because <u>evidence is not self-evident.</u>

   d.   While premises can change, the logical process operates on the level of necessity. If a conclusion does not *necessarily* follow from the premises, it is a **logical fallacy**. However, because rhetoric does not rely strictly on necessity, fallacious arguments are common and even usefully persuasive. Fallacies are persuasive because a certainly reasonable and common justification for doing something is not always logical. Consider the following examples of fallacious arguments:

This car is the best because it's the most popular model (ad populum)

He is wrong about immigration policy because he is a racist (ad hominem)

He's right about my illness because he's a doctor (ad verecundiam)

3. ***Pathos*** is the most challenging, most powerful, and most dangerous of the appeals, and it is increasingly being wielded as a force in politics. Making the audience feel things can be manipulative; however, if an audience doesn't feel, then believing and thinking will never turn into action; <u>*pathos* concerns the bodily affect of the audience</u>. Consider the following types of *pathos*, but remember feeling is complex, intertwined, and messy. It may be confusing, but feelings so often are.

   a. **Emotions** are the most intellectual of the pathetic appeals; they are the feelings that are later named as anger, happiness, sadness, and all the nuances, degrees, and combinations of them. While Aristotle outlines some and psychologists like Robert Plutchik have developed more complex schemes, there is no definitive guide to emotions. Therefore, try to think about <u>specific kinds, intensities, and targets of feelings, rather than simply "good" or "bad."</u>

   b. **Bodily desire** is the most base of *pathos*; some even consider emotions and values to be illusions to hide from our desirous, bodily being. This can be desire for food and water, safety and security, sex and reproduction, adrenaline, or even just <u>"gut feeling."</u> Advertising relies heavily on this type of *pathos*, and it is best to avoid it unless you are very specific, critical, and reflective about it.

   c. **Moral values** are different from emotions and desires, but no less strongly felt. Whether they come from a particular creed, culture, or "common sense," feelings about right and wrong are especially powerful. However, since these are deeply involved in people's ideas of identity, do not assume that your values are the right or only ones; instead, try to find commonality with your audience. <u>No one believes a villain, but patronizing isn't effective either.</u>

Inartistic Appeals

Inartistic (*atechnic*) appeals are the counterpoint to artistic appeals, and refer to anything found outside and brought into the text (i.e., finding, analyzing, and integrating outside research and previous arguments on the subject). Even though each text is contextual, context is never isolated either, so you will have to use the resources and arguments that came before you to make your own arguments recognizable, coherent, and effective. Consider the following as some types of evidence you might use:

- **Anecdotal evidence** is any story or narrative presented from your own or another's experience. Be careful because singular experiences may not resonate with general cases.

- **Testimonial evidence** is using the words of another, usually in direct quote or paraphrase. Generally, you'll want to find established authorities on the subject and think deeply about what gives them that authority.

- **Numerical evidence** is using specific statistics, measurements, dates, and times that have been established as true. However, while "numbers don't lie," people with numbers often do. Numerical evidence must be made to support your claims, which requires reflective framing and explanation.

- **Graphical evidence** is any image, chart, or diagram through which you illustrate your claim. Because we generally believe what we see, images can be very powerful, but they are subject to the same framing, explanation, and scrutiny as other types of evidence.

Getting a hold on the appeals may seem difficult; this is because it is. Practice—and the failure that comes along with it—is crucial to working out exactly how you should best appeal to an audience. This, at least partially, is why we continuously redraft and revise papers. The beauty of the appeals is that how you employ them—and how they act upon you—will change as your own rhetorical situation changes. These are tools that will help you succeed not only in this class, but in your further university career, and in all future endeavors.

Topoi[2]

Knowing how you will use proofs in your work is often directly tied to the **topoi** (Greek for "places") you are speaking toward. The seven basic types of argument discussed in this section are, generally, found in almost all argumentation—indeed, most compositions mesh and combine *topoi* in order to be effective. The *topoi* are similar in some ways to stasis theory, which we discussed in Chapter 3 (page 29), but in your composition the *topoi* provide a more fine-grained strategy for constructing your arguments. Thus, you might use a strategy that first asks what stasis you are addressing. Then, you use the *topoi* to invent claims that help you establish your point, and finally you ask which appeals will provide you with the strongest evidence for your claim. In rhetoric, the *topoi* provide places in the mind or mental shortcuts for accessing information helpful in developing an argument. Aristotle divides the *topoi* into two categories: common places (general) and special places (specific). The common *topoi* can be used to analyze or to invent any argument, whereas the special *topoi* are used to discover

---

2. This section is adapted from material originally written by John Bailes.

knowledge for experts (such as engineers, lawyers, or physicians). Although Aristotle listed many common *topoi*, here are seven particularly useful ones to help on your path to discovery. Each of these seven *topoi* serve as questions that will prompt you to discover and examine key information that can then be used to develop a claim. The following examples use the *topoi* to ask questions about chess; these questions help us to identify key information, which then makes it possible to make a claim about the game:

1. **Topic of Definition**—To what group does it belong? How does it fit into this group? What are the group's characteristics?

   - *Key information*: Chess is a two-player board game that has a long history as being highly challenging. It requires complex logical strategies and tactics when playing. The objective is to "checkmate" the opponent's king.

   - *Claim*: Chess is the most challenging board game for the mind, requiring a player to use complex logical strategies and tactics in outthinking and outmaneuvering an opponent.

2. **Topic of Division**—What parts make up this thing or idea? How do they relate to one another?

   - *Key information*: Chess has six types of pieces that are placed on the board. Each player begins with eight pawns, two knights, two bishops, two rooks, a queen, and a king. The pieces may also be put in order of importance from weakest to strongest. Although the king is the most important piece, the most powerful is the queen.

   - *Claim*: Chess pieces have retained the hierarchical order of a medieval society, which demonstrates the values represented in the game.

3. **Topic of Similarity/Difference**—How is it similar to other things? How is it different from those same things? To what can we compare and contrast it?

   - *Key information*: Chess uses the same 64-checkered board as checkers. But the two games have different pieces, different rules about movement, and different objectives.

   - *Claim*: Chess demands more thought, intelligence, and cunning than checkers.

4. **Topic of Degree**—In what way is it *more* or *less* than similar things? Is there abundance of it? Is there scarcity?

   - *Key information*: Across the world chess has different degrees of popularity. Chess has been highly popular in Russia and Eastern Europe over the past century, producing most of the world champions. In Europe, chess has been more popular than in the United States, which prefers board games like Monopoly instead.

- *Claim*: If chess had the same popularity in the United States that it does in Russia, then Americans might produce more world chess champions.

5. **Topic of Cause/Effect**—What causes it to exist? What causes it to behave a certain way? What effects does it cause? What consequences?

- *Key information*: The earliest origin for chess is as a strategic military game in ancient Persia. The game's pieces were based on army divisions. As the game developed, it kept its combative play while adding more sophistication over the years.

- *Claim*: The militaristic culture of ancient Persia shaped the combat-oriented rules of chess.

6. **Topic of Negation**—If it or a part of it is negated, what happens?

- *Key information*: In chess, clocks are used to intensify play by creating time constraints that pressure players to move quickly. When chess clocks are removed, the game can move at a leisurely pace.

- *Claim*: Without chess clocks to keep time, some New York City street hustlers would be less effective at luring bystanders into betting on "speed chess" matches and pocketing easy cash.

7. **Topic of Substitution**—If it or part of it is replaced by something else, what is significant?

- *Key information*: If we substituted checker pieces for chess pieces, the pieces would be indistinguishable.

- *Claim*: Unlike other games with pieces as markers, chess marshals pieces that have special significance and power because of their shapes and sizes. The variety of pieces is one of the things that makes the game so unique.

Discussion Questions

1. What kind of appeal is the most persuasive? Why? Does this change based upon audience and subject?

2. Imagine you are writing your paper. All scholarly sources seem to support your counter more than your own argument, despite your own strong personal beliefs that your chosen "side" is where you want to argue from. How can the appeals work to help you still make your argument? Is it possible to argue against overwhelming *logos* or *ethos* just because you bring a lot of *pathos* to the table? Once you've thought through these questions, consider

the following: why could *pathos* be considered the most dangerous of the appeals to abuse? In other words, how is it that *pathos* can be manipulative?

3. As we see above, "logic" is a much more specific term than we might commonly understand. Except for cases of formal logic above, what do people commonly mean when they call something "logical," or reject something as "illogical"? Furthermore, what does such labeling try to do? What does calling something "logical" make us think about it?

4. Aristotle himself was very distrustful of pathetic appeals to emotion since they could lead people to be persuaded against their own interests or promote harmful ideas and policies. Does emotion have to be suppressed, controlled, or directed? If so, which, and why? Are some feelings inherently destructive or inherently beneficial?

5. Debate time! Today the class will split in three, once we have decided upon a *kairotic* topic: 1/3 of you will argue based solely in *ethos*, 1/3 in *logos*, and 1/3 in *pathos*. Is one team's argument more persuasive than another? If time permits, we will rotate so each team gets a chance at arguing from the standpoint of each appeal.

6. Look back at the chess examples of *topoi*: for each, discuss which stasis the claim might respond to in a debate. Then, discuss how you might use the different artistic and inartistic appeals to help support those claims.

Exercises

1. In a short writing assignment, outline what values you think define a *good person* (aka, someone with a strong *ethos*), and explain how such a person can perform these values in their writing. Then, with a partner, compare your values and discuss how they are similar, whether they're different, and why you chose the values you did. If you both define "good person" differently, does this mean you both conceive of *ethos* differently?

2. Find an article from Part Two, Unit Three. In a group, break the article down by appeals. Identify each use of *ethos*, *pathos*, and *logos*, and any uses of inartistic proofs. Does one appeal occur more frequently than the others? If so, why?

3. Using the seven common *topoi* above, find arguments for the list below. Use a different topos OR a different mix of *topoi* for each argument. Be sure to compose your statements as argumentative.

   - Choose a sport (football, hockey, rugby, soccer, etc.) to invent arguments about.

   - Choose a geographical location (Florida everglades, Rocky Mountains, Sahara Desert, etc.) to invent arguments about.

- Choose a hobby (scrapbooking, knitting, stamp collecting, etc.) to invent arguments about.

- Choose an economic issue (higher minimum wage, college tuition, national debt, etc.) to invent arguments about.

- Choose a digital issue (social media, texting, gaming, etc.) to invent arguments about.

4. Using the internet, search Aristotle's common *topoi*. List at least five other common *topoi* you discover. Be sure these five are not the seven mentioned above. Then, explain how these other five *topoi* might be effective for inventing arguments. Provide some examples.

5. Considering the extremely different world we now inhabit compared to Aristotle, are there any arguments that suggest we should add new *topoi*?

Supplemental Reading

Countering
Joseph Harris

Palin: Oh look, this isn't an argument.

Cleese: Yes it is.

Palin: No it isn't. It's just contradiction.

Cleese: No it isn't.

Palin: It is!

Cleese: It is not.

Palin: Look, you just contradicted me.

Cleese: I did not.

Palin: Oh you did!

Cleese: No, no, no.

Palin: You did just then.

Cleese: Nonsense!

Palin: Oh, this is futile!

Cleese: No it isn't.

Palin: I came here for a good argument.

Cleese: No you didn't; you came here for an argument.

Palin: An argument isn't just contradiction.

Cleese: It can be.

Palin: No it can't. An argument is a connected series of statements intended to establish a proposition.

Cleese: No it isn't.

Palin: Yes it is! It's not just contradiction.

Cleese: Look, if I argue with you, I must take up a contrary position.

Palin: Yes, but that's not just saying, "No it isn't."

Cleese: Yes it is!

Palin: No it isn't! Argument is an intellectual process. Contradiction is just the automatic gainsaying of any statement the other person makes.

(short pause)

Cleese: No it isn't.

—*Monty Python, "Argument Clinic"*

Always, no sometimes, think it's me
But you know I know when it's a dream
I think I know I mean a "Yes" but it's all wrong
That is I think I disagree.

    —*John Lennon and Paul McCartney, "Strawberry Fields Forever"*

I recall writing an essay in graduate school in which I did everything I could to rebut the views of a certain scholar. I was determined to prove my opponent wrong, and I seized upon every gap, contradiction, or misstep that I could find in his text in order to do so. After reading my essay, my professor evidently agreed that I had won the imaginary debate I had set up, since he made no effort to find fault with my argument or examples. But rather than congratulating me, as I had expected and hoped, he asked instead: "Why are you spending so much time discussing the work of somebody you seem to think isn't very bright?"

I often think back to that moment when I find myself locked in argument with a text that I am trying to write about. The question I've learned to ask myself at such times is: What do I hope will result from pursuing this disagreement? If the answer is simply that I think I can prove that the text I am reading has certain shortcomings or limits, then I try to set aside the temptation to argue. All texts have their moments of blindness. Simply to note them is to do little. But if I can use certain problems in a text as a springboard to get at something I couldn't otherwise say, to develop a line of thinking of my own, then I try to note those problems in a way that allows me to quickly move on to my own counterproposals or ideas.

Or, to put this another way, the aim of academic writing should not be simply to prove how smart you are but to add to what can be said about a subject. To do so, you may sometimes need to identify the weaknesses or limits of other writings, but that shouldn't be the sole point of your writing. Critique needs to lead to alternatives. Correcting the ideas of another writer may seem an intuitive way of rewriting their work—you identify what they've gotten wrong and then you show them how to get it right—but the sort of countering I want to talk about in this chapter differs from such verbal swordplay. As I use the term, to *counter* is not to nullify but to suggest a different way of thinking. Its defining phrases are *On the other hand* … and *Yes, but* … (In contrast, the defining phrase of forwarding is *Yes, and* …) Countering looks at other views and texts not as wrong but as *partial*—in the sense of being both interested and incomplete. In countering you bring a different set of interests to bear upon a subject, look to notice what others have not. Your aim is not to refute what has been said before, to bring the discussion to an end, but to respond to prior views in ways that move the conversation in new directions.

Projects

The Tone of Countering

Find two texts that counter the work of other writers but that strike you as doing so with differing degrees of civility. That is, see if you can locate one text whose writer articulates her or his differences with other intellectuals clearly but with a sense of restraint or good humor, and another whose writer seems more overly antagonistic toward the work he is responding to. Try to point to specific moments or moves in the two texts that help account for their differences in tone.

This is not to suggest that academic writers disagree with one another in especially muted or polite ways. On the contrary, they often state their differences in quite clear and forceful terms. But what distinguishes the practice of countering is that it pushes beyond mere disagreement. Popular debates tend to begin with their conclusions. That is, a speaker is identified from the start as holding a specific, already formulated position—as being for or against capital punishment or tax cuts or gay marriage or whatever—and then everything she or he goes on to say is understood as either defending that position or attacking the opposing view. But the aim of countering is to open up new lines of inquiry. The questions to ask of a writer countering another text thus have less to do with decorum than use. If all you really want to do is to show how someone else is wrong, then it doesn't much matter how politely you phrase your criticisms. But if it is clear that your own writing in some real sense depends upon the text you are countering, that your own position has evolved in response to its ideas and phrasings, then your readers (if not always the author of the text you are discussing) are more likely to see your criticisms of it as fair and useful.

Since the aim of countering is to develop a new line of thinking in response to the limits of other texts, it almost always involves a close attention to the specifics of their structure and phrasing. In countering the work of another writer, then, you usually need first to come to terms with his or her project, to offer a sense of its aims and strengths. To identify what a text fails to do, you need to be clear about what it achieves—or at least what it attempts. Otherwise your criticisms will seem flippant or unearned. But even the most civil of criticisms can sting. There is an unavoidable adversarial edge to countering, as you seek less to connect your views with those of the texts you are reading than to separate them. Forwarding aligns; countering individuates. I see three main ways of creating this sort of critical distance:

- *Arguing the other side:* Showing the usefulness of a term or idea that a writer has criticized or noting problems with one that she or he has argued for.

- *Uncovering values:* Surfacing a word or concept for analysis that a text has left undefined or unexamined.

- *Dissenting:* Identifying a shared line of thought on an issue in order to note its limits.

All three of these moves can be easier to make with force than grace. It is hard to differ in a pleasing or civil way. The only real way to do so, it seems to me, is to show as clearly as you can how noting the limits of a text has led you to a new line of work or inquiry. In that sense, the key moment in a counterstatement is when it stops, when a writer turns from the text he is reading in order to offer a proposal of his own. Let me turn to a number of examples of how writers can set up such points of divergence, of new lines of thought emerging from old ones.

Arguing the Other Side

In his celebrated series of essays on *Ways of Seeing,* John Berger shows how we can look at oil paintings in ways that focus not only on their artistic form or technique but also on the content of their images—that is, on the people and things that these paintings represent. Berger argues that an exclusive attention to form obscures much of what paintings can tell us about how people lived in the past, not only in terms of their material surroundings but also their social relationships—how they wished to be seen by others and how others actually viewed them. This view puts him at odds with many art historians and critics. For instance, in discussing how women are portrayed in oil paintings, Berger takes on the work of Kenneth Clark, a distinguished writer on the history of art.

We can now begin to see the difference between nakedness and nudity in the European tradition. In his book on *The Nude* Kenneth Clark maintains that to be naked is simply to be without clothes, whereas the nude is a form of art. According to him, the nude is not the starting point of a way of a painting, but a way of seeing which the painting achieves. To some degree, this is true—although the way of seeing "a nude" is not necessarily confined to art: there are also nude photographs, nude poses, nude gestures. What is true is that the nude is always conventionalized—and the authority for its conventions derives from a certain tradition of art.

What do these conventions mean? What does a nude signify? It is not sufficient to answer these questions merely in terms of the art-form, for it is quite clear that the nude also relates to lived sexuality.

To be naked is to be oneself.

To be nude is to be seen naked by others and yet not recognized for oneself. A naked body has to be seen as an object in order to become a nude. (The sight of it as an object stimulates the use of it as an object.) Nakedness reveals itself. Nudity is placed on display.

To be naked is to be without disguise.

To be on display is to have the surfaces of one's own skin, the hairs of one's own body, turned into a disguise which, in that situation, can never be discarded. The nude is condemned to never being naked. Nudity is a form of dress.

Intertexts

John Berger, *Ways of Seeing*, (New York: Penguin, 1977), 53–54. This book was based on a series of programs broadcast on the BBC and has been reprinted over twenty times.

Berger is responding to Kenneth Clark, *The Nude* (Princeton: Princeton University Press, 1972).

Projects
Reading Visual Culture
Read through the essays in *Ways of Seeing* with the aim of better understanding how Berger makes use of visual texts in his writing. How useful are the terms I offer in this book in accounting for how he cites, describes, and comments on the images in his book? How might you draw on his work to revise and expand the vocabulary of rewriting that I propose here?

I need to note that in simply quoting Berger's prose here I am slighting one of the most remarkable aspects of *Ways of Seeing*, which is his interspersing of images throughout his text not simply to illustrate but to advance his thinking. (In this instance the first paragraph I've quoted is framed, top and bottom, by images of Eastern erotica and by softcore photos of nude models from a men's magazine.) But my interest here centers on how Berger inverts Clark's distinction between the naked and the nude. He begins by rehearsing what Clark has to say about their differences: "to be naked is simply to be without clothes, whereas the nude is a form of art." He then grudgingly admits that there is something to this distinction, at least in the sense that the nude is always a conventionalized way of seeing. But he then quickly raises some points that Clark doesn't consider—that the conventions of the nude are not confined to the higher realms of art but are also part of the vernacular of erotica, of "nude photographs, nude poses, nude gestures," and, more important, that nakedness and nudity refer not just to painting but to the lived experiences of individuals. And in life rather than art, Berger argues, nakedness has a value that nudity does not. To be naked is to be at home in your own skin; to be nude is to pose for the gaze of another.

Berger thus offers here an unusually clear illustration of *arguing the other side*—attaching a positive value to something another writer denigrates or a negative value to what another writer applauds. In this case, Kenneth Clark sees the nude as an artistic achievement and nakedness as merely banal, while for Berger nakedness represents authentic sexuality and the nude its conventionalized packaging. The values attached to the two terms are flipped. But note how Berger suggests that Clark is not so much wrong as incomplete, unaware of the full implications of the distinction he is making. He agrees with Clark that the nude is a conventionalized form of seeing, but he also counters that what may sometimes be good for art is not always good for living. His critique thus does not simply cancel out what Clark has to say but rather adds to the ways we can think about the ways bodies are represented in art.

Uncovering Values

In a way, Clark does Berger a favor in so clearly opposing the naked and the nude—since Berger is then able to use Clark's own terms of analysis in countering his work. He simply needs to flip the terms of a distinction that Clark has already made for him. But you will often find that you need to *uncover* a term of value that a text has obscured or repressed before you can question it. For instance, in her book on the masculine *ethos* of cyberculture, *Cracking the Gender Code*, Melanie Stewart Millar looks at the image of the digital generation offered by the cover of *Wired* magazine.

It is useful to once again compare *Wired* with a more familiar and ubiquitous magazine genre, the women's fashion magazine.

According to Ellen McCracken's useful study of the genre, the cover model on a so-called women's magazine represents a "window to the future self," a symbol of what the reader can achieve by consuming the magazine's content. The cover of *Wired* magazine serves an analogous function as both the window to the individual reader's future and to a more generalized future world. The cover does more than simply catch the eye of the casual passerby. *Wired*'s cover graphic, which most often depicts a celebrity of the digital generation, challenges the (presumed) male reader to emulate the achievements of the cover "model," who is almost always a white male. Just as the cover model of *Cosmopolitan* comes to signify the "Cosmo girl," and all the values endorsed by the magazine, so the figure on *Wired* magazine represents elite members of the digital generation. And, like the model on the cover of a fashion magazine, the image on *Wired*'s cover plays on the vulnerabilities of its intended readers in order to draw them in. Female readers of fashion magazines find themselves drawn to the unrealistic, fantastic images of the current feminine ideal and the attendant promises of happiness and regeneration; so the digital generation sees on the cover of *Wired* magazine a graphic representation of all that they (apparently) want to be. While the fashion magazine promises to replace anxiety and emptiness with the adulation that cosmetic beauty provides, *Wired* promises to replace a sense of lack of control or fear of emasculation with a reinvigorated form of masculine privilege in a digital world.

Intertexts

Melanie Stewart Millar, *Cracking the Gender Code: Who Rules the Wired World?* (Toronto: Sumach Press, 1998), 114–15.

Millar refers to Ellen McCracken, *Decoding Women's Magazines* (New York: St. Martin's 1993).

Projects

Extending Millar

In countering *Wired*, Millar borrows an idea from Ellen McCracken's *Decoding Women's Magazines*—that of the magazine cover as a "window to the future self." Locate a copy of McCracken's book to see how she develops this approach. What are the strengths of this mode of reading? What are its limits? Are there things that the covers of popular magazines do besides present an idealized image of themselves to their readers? That is, how might you extend or counter Millar's and McCracken's view of how magazine covers seduce prospective readers?

Millar plays here with a distinction found not so much *in* the text of *Wired* as *around* it. It is as if she is reading *Wired* not in isolation but as it sits on a newsstand or supermarket rack, next to magazines whose covers feature, in one sense, the very same thing, the cover model as future self, and in another sense, something quite different: *women*. In showing how the "Wired man" is similar in many ways to the "Cosmo girl," she raises questions about why, in each case, the self of the future seems governed by stereotypes of the present. She uncovers a male/female binary underlying the cover images of *Wired* that associates technical progress with masculine sexuality. Unlike Berger, she does not argue for the devalued term in this binary; there is no case made here for the "Wired girl." Her aim is rather to call into question *Wired*'s implicit (and perhaps unconscious) linking of technology, power, and sexuality.

Millar's stance toward *Wired* is more unremittingly hostile than Berger's toward Clark. But while she is critical of the sexual politics of *Wired*, she acknowledges the power of its response to the "sense of lack of control or fear of emasculation" felt by its readers. She reads the cover of *Wired* as a sign of a larger problem in our culture in which technology is offered as an easy solution to anxieties whose actual sources are personal and political. In that sense she uses her critique of *Wired* to begin to develop new ways of thinking about the appeals and perils of digital culture.

Projects

Countering and Agonism

Perhaps the clearest place to see intellectual work at its most adversarial or antagonistic is in the "Letters to the Editor" or the "Comments and Response" sections of magazines and journals, since this is a site where writers often directly confront each other over the meaning or intent of their work—correcting inaccuracies, protesting misinterpretations, arguing politics, contesting reviews and uses of their writing.

Find an exchange between two writers in a "Letters" or "Response" section. (You will probably also want to look up the book, article, or review that prompted their interchange of views.) Read their letters in light of what I have said here about countering the work of others. To what degree do you see them employing the moves—reversing and uncovering terms of value, disputing consensus positions—that I discuss here? In what ways does their exchange or argument draw on different strategies and modes of response? What do you find interesting about their exchange? What, if anything, do you find troubling?

Our texts always say more than we mean. As writers we participate in the discourses of our culture in ways we can never fully control, and may not always be aware of. Rather, the values and attitudes of our society are often insinuated in the very metaphors and turns of phrase, examples and images, stories and characters, that we are given to work with in writing. And so while I doubt that the designers of *Wired* consciously intended to reinforce the masculine *ethos* of our culture, any more than the creators of the Dodge ad that Todd Gitlin talks about did, or than Sigmund Freud did in developing his theories of psychoanalysis—this doesn't mean that you can't look for signs of how their texts were (in part) shaped by the gendered attitudes of that culture. This is a frequent move in countering, the *uncovering* of values that, without being stated openly, undergird a text and influence what it says.

Such values are sometimes stated outright, at other times repressed, and at still others only hazily conceived. They often turn out to be connected to deep cultural beliefs about gender, race, sexuality, social class, and religion. But countering is not an exercise in political correctness; it is a move to examine what a text (or set of texts) leaves unmarked or unquestioned, to highlight the unseen. Noticing what is absent, what a certain text or approach fails to consider, is not an easy task, but it is a key move in writing criticism. One way of uncovering the values that drive a text is to ask what it appears *not* to find interesting. And so, for instance, John Berger reclaims the value of nakedness, which for Kenneth Clark seemed merely the mundane raw material of the nude; Carol Gilligan explores what Freud simply left unstudied as the "dark continent" of women's psychological development; and Melanie Stewart Millar reveals the "Cosmo girl" as the anxious alter ego of the "Wired man." Each critic illustrates how learning to notice what a text leaves unasked, or takes for granted, can offer you a powerful way of not only countering but also building upon its ideas.

Dissenting

As you will have noticed by this point, countering draws on many of the skills involved in coming to terms with texts that I discussed in chapter 1. You need to be able to represent the project of another writer, to identify key words and concepts from his text, to suggest its possible uses and strengths—so you can then pivot and show what the text leaves undone or how its terms might serve a different set of aims and interests. This move is made even more complex when your aim is to counter not just the work of a single writer but to dissent from a view shared by a number of thinkers. In such cases you need first to show that a certain consensus exists, so you can then define your position against it. Like a fruit cart on the set of a chase scene in a movie, you build it in order to knock it over.

One quick way of defining a shared approach to an issue is to list some of the key words in its vocabulary or to catalogue some of its central concepts. Recall, for instance, how Marjorie Garber deftly assembled shared definitions for "genius" from seemingly disparate authors. But while such an approach works well when you are trying to identify a loose *cluster* of concerns, you are likely to find at other times that you need to counter something more like a shared *line* of thought. What you need to do in such cases is to show how this line proceeds from one point to the next, to restate the key moves or logic of the argument in your own words—and then to offer examples of writers making these same moves. You are then in a position to counter the line of thinking you have defined.

There is a kind of template for many academic essays in which a writer says something like this: *Until now, writers on this subject have disagreed on points* a, b, *and* c. *However, underlying this disagreement, there is a consensus of views on point* d. *In this essay, I will show why point* d *is wrong.* Such a countering of an accepted position, of the common ground on which other disagreements rest, is shown brilliantly by the philosopher and critic Alexander Nehamas in his essay "Serious Watching." In this piece Nehamas takes on the view held by many academics and intellectuals (like Neil Postman) that television is somehow an inferior medium to print. Here is how Nehamas sets up his argument:

> The common criticisms of television, though they are united in their disdain for the medium, come from various directions and have differing points. Wayne Booth, for example, expresses a relatively traditional preference for primarily linguistic over mainly visual works:
>
>> The video arts tell us precisely what we should see, but their resources are thin and cumbersome for stimulating our moral and philosophical range.

A related criticism is made by John Cawelti, whose celebrated study of the arts of popular culture, particularly of formulaic literature, has led him to conclude that

> formulaic works necessarily stress intense and immediate kinds of excitement and gratification as opposed to the more complete and ambiguous analyses of character and motivation that characterize mimetic literature.

He also considers that a "major characteristic of formulaic literature is the dominant influence of the goals of escape and entertainment." The contrast here is one between the straightforward, action-oriented, and entertaining popular works which by and large belong to popular culture—works which include the products of television—and the ambiguous, innovative, psychologically motivated and edifying works of high art.

Finally, Catherine Belsey, who has approached the study of literature from a Marxist point of view, following the work of Louis Althusser, draws a contrast between "classic realism, still the dominant popular mode in literature, film, and television" which is characterized by "illusionism, narrative which leads to closure and a hierarchy of texts which establishes the 'truth' of the story" with what she calls "the interrogative text" ... It would be easy to cite many other similar passages, but the main themes of the attack against television, to which those other passages would provide only variations, are all sounded by these three authors: (1) given its formulaic nature, television drama is simple and action-oriented; it makes few demands of its audience and offers them quick and shallow gratification; (2) given its visual, nonlinguistic character, it is unsuited for providing psychological and philosophical depth; and (3) given its realist tendencies, it fails to make its own fictional nature one of its themes ... These reasons are taken to show that television does not deserve serious critical attention—or that, if it does, it should only be criticized on ideological grounds.

And yet there are reasons to be suspicious of this view, which can all be based on a serious look, for example, at *St. Elsewhere*—a television drama that appears straightforward, action-oriented, and realistic.

Nehamas then goes on to offer a close reading of the 1980s series *St. Elsewhere*, a program that blended the conventions of realistic drama and ironic farce in ways that many viewers found alternately moving and hilarious. Nehamas argues that such programs demonstrate that television can well repay "serious watching," that psychological depth and artistic innovation are not solely the properties of the medium of print. What interests me here, though, is how hard

Nehamas works to show that he is not arguing against a straw man, but that there is in fact a widespread "disdain" toward TV shared by most intellectuals.

Intertexts

Alexander Nehamas, "Serious Watching," *South Atlantic Quarterly* 89 (Winter 1990); reprinted in Joseph Harris, Jay Rosen, and Gary Calpas, eds., *Media Journal: Reading and Writing about Popular Culture*, 2nd ed. (Boston: Allyn & Bacon, 1999), 320–36.

In the interest of concision, I have edited the passages Nehamas quotes, along with some of his own prose. The critics he cites are:

Wayne Booth, "The Company We Keep: Self-Making in Imaginative Art," *Daedalus* 111 (Fall 1982).

John Cawelti, *Adventure, Mystery, and Romance* (Chicago: University of Chicago Press, 1976).

Catherine Belsey, *Critical Practice* (London: Verso, 1980).

Nehamas's argument is unusually complex and involved—in large part because he is dealing with not one but several writers. In grouping and responding to the critics of TV, Nehamas makes a number of moves that are worth noting and imitating. First, he offers a diverse set of figures who endorse a negative view of TV—citing a traditional humanist, a writer on popular culture, and a Marxist critic (all of whom he is careful to identify as such). These are not the sorts of thinkers whom you might expect to agree on many issues, and so when Nehamas can show each of them expressing the same attitude of impatience with the seemingly formulaic nature of TV, then his claim that this is a common view seems reasonable. (And while there is of course no magic number of examples needed to prove such a case, three seems just enough to quickly suggest a trend.) Second, Nehamas quotes from these critics in a way that allows him to associate the stance he is describing with a series of key opposing terms: Television is thin, formulaic, escapist, illusionist; high art is philosophical, complex, interrogative. He is then able to echo these terms and values in his own summary of the antitelevision position (in the next-to-last paragraph). Finally, this groundwork allows him, much like Berger, to argue the other side, to use the words of Booth, Cawelti, Belsey, et al. in pointing out the problems of their position. You can see the beginnings of this reversal in the last paragraph I've quoted, in which Nehamas tells us that he will now turn to look seriously at a television text that "*appears* straightforward, action-oriented, and realistic" (my emphasis). It will probably not surprise you to learn that he reads *St. Elsewhere* instead as complex, absorbed in the intricacies of character, and reflective about its status as a fiction—as possessing, that is, all of the qualities of art as Booth, Cawelti, and Belsey define it. I say this not to suggest that the rest of his essay is routine but to point out how powerfully Nehamas's own position evolves in response to theirs. In rereading *St. Elsewhere*, Nehamas rewrites their stance on the boundaries between art and popular entertainment.

Civility

I have struggled in this chapter to define countering as a practice that differs from the sort of argument whose goal is simply to vanquish your opponent. I've suggested that coming to terms with another text is a necessary prelude to countering it, and have tried to show how the aim of countering should not be simply to note the gaps or limits of another text but to use that critique to develop a position of your own. And I have identified three tactics for doing so: *arguing the other side, uncovering values,* and *dissenting.* But even if you keep your focus as a writer less on the problems of a text than on the work you want to do with it, you still can't counter without disagreeing. There is a necessary agonism—a staking out of positions and differences—to much intellectual work. But behind texts and ideas lie people, and you want to be able to disagree about points of view without alienating persons who hold them. I'd like to conclude this chapter, then, with some thoughts on the art of honest yet civil disagreement.

- *Focus on positions more than phrasings:* You need to attend to a writer's particular use of words in order to precisely note and counter the limits of his or her work. However, an unremitting focus on the wording of a text can often seem more hostile than scrupulous. The novelist Mary McCarthy is said to have remarked of her political and intellectual rival Lillian Hellman, "Every word she writes is a lie, including *and* and *the.*" The comment tells us far more about McCarthy than Hellman. You don't want to seem preoccupied with niceties of phrasing, with refuting every step or move made by a writer, as though nothing she might ever do could possibly please you. Your job is not to correct the infelicities of a text but to respond to and rework the position it puts forward. If you describe that position as mean-spirited or flimsy, as riddled with unfortunate phrasings and lying *ands* and *thes*, you are also likely to raise questions about your own motives in responding to it (as I learned back in grad school). But if you represent that position as a serious one, then your response is likely to seem the same as well. And so, in countering another writer, restate her or his project in clear and generous terms, quote just enough of her or his text to set up your response to it, and then move as quickly as you can from its language to your own.

- *Don't guess at intent:* It's tempting to imagine that people who disagree with you do so for sinister reasons. Maybe the guys at *Wired* did really just want, in the end, to be cooler than the jocks, to invent a new and improved form of machismo. Or maybe the critics of TV really are just a bunch of snobs who refuse to like anything that ordinary people enjoy. Or maybe not. We'll never know, and in any case, it doesn't much matter. If the new image of manhood now has as much to do with technical prowess as muscle, then jokes about cyber-geeks miss the mark. If television really is incapable of conveying psychological nuance, then the snobs are right. In countering you need to respond to the position taken, not to the person taking it. Assume that other writers say what they have to say not out of an overweening desire for status or power, or because their thinking has been molded by their profession or class or gender, but because they genuinely find certain ideas compelling and useful. And then explain why you don't. Notice, for instance, how John Berger says very little about Kenneth Clark himself, but rather restates the distinction he draws between the naked and the nude, points out what that contrast accomplishes, and then turns it on its head, arguing for the value of nakedness. He offers a critique without picking a fight. This isn't to say that all aspects of the personal can be removed from intellectual disagreement. But what most often sparks anger is the questioning not of ideas but of motives.

■ *Be careful with modifiers:* Don't use adjectives and adverbs to do your dirty work, to hint at a negative attitude toward a text or writer that you are reluctant to state more openly. What may seem throwaway terms can subtly but powerfully color an account of another writer's work: *clearly, simply, wholly, indeed, in fact, quite,* and so on. If it is *quite clear,* for instance, that there is a problem with a certain point of view, then it can seem as if it must have taken a willful obtuseness for other writers to have missed it. Be cautious, too, with terms of faint praise. I once read a response to an essay I had written that at various points described my work as "well-intentioned," "sincere," "reasonable," and "earnest" (although also, of course, completely mistaken; these are all terms invariably followed by a *but*). Now it's one thing to be called wrong, but being cast as a well-meaning but bumbling do-gooder struck me as an unkind—even if unintended—cut. Neither was it flattering to realize that the writer had evidently felt it necessary to assure readers that my approach in fact was not conniving, insincere, unreasonable, and duplicitous. The point is that small modifiers can play large roles in how your work gets read. You want the force of what you have to say to reside in your nouns and verbs, not in your descriptors. State both the strengths and limits of other positions as plainly as you can; in most cases, you will simply want to say that there are problems with a certain view, not that it is either "clearly mistaken" or "sincere but misguided."

■ *Stress what you bring to the discussion:* The point of countering is to push knowledge forward. In the end, the readers of your text want to know what *you* have to tell them about the subject or issue at hand. I've suggested in this chapter that there are three steps to countering: coming to terms with another point of view, noting its limits, and constructing your own position in response. The emphasis of your writing should fall on that third step.

An essay needs to be something more than simply a critique of the work of someone else. You need to have a point of your own to make, and you need to give yourself space to make it. While I don't want to reduce the notion of emphasis to a simple counting of lines or paragraphs, there's almost surely something wrong, for instance, with a six-page essay that consists of five pages of critique and only one of new thinking. The most civil way to counter another writer is to show how your response to her work opens up new forms of talk about her (and your) subject.

Intertexts

McCarthy's notorious comment was made on the PBS *Dick Cavett Show* on October 18, 1979. Her words precipitated an almost total collapse in civil discourse, as Hellman responded with a suit for libel that came to a close only with her death a few years later. Cavett recounts the whole sad incident in "Lillian, Mary, and Me," in the December 16, 2002, issue of the *New Yorker*.

• • •

Some readers of this book have argued that the view I offer here of countering is idealized—that the goal of much academic writing really is to demonstrate a mastery over your materials and your rivals, to stake out a position and to defend it against attack. And, certainly, there is plenty of evidence for such a view. For instance, in *You Just Don't Understand*, her study of differing conversational styles, Deborah Tannen suggests that it is the pleasure that intellectuals take in the exchange of opposing views, in the give-and-take of open debate, that most distinguishes (and sometimes isolates) them from the rest of the culture. And in *Clueless in Academe*, itself an engaging brief for the life of the mind, Gerald Graff suggests that how to engage in a good argument is precisely what many university students (whose writing he feels is more likely to suffer from blandness than contentiousness) most need to learn. And I perhaps ought to acknowledge that I have not often been faulted myself for a reluctance to say what I think. But to admit that academic writing can often be adversarial is not to say that such writing is always *at its best* adversarial. I'm all for energetic and sharp prose that clarifies where a writer stands. But the sort of academic argument I most admire doesn't look all that much like argument in the familiar sense—since it aims less to offer reasons *behind* competing positions than to suggest what such differences might point *toward*. And so, for instance, in the passage I quote above, the point that Alexander Nehamas makes is not simply that he disagrees with the academic critics of television. Rather, he uses his differences with those writers to set up his own more appreciative reading of *St. Elsewhere* and popular culture. The critics of TV remain present in his prose even as he moves past them. That's the sort of intellectual work I'm trying to teach toward (and that I imagine Tannen and Graff teach as well). In arguing for civility, then, I'm not pressing for a mere politeness, but for a style of countering that doesn't stop at disagreement but instead pushes on for something more—that rewrites the work of others in order to say something new.

Intertexts

Gerald Graff, *Clueless in Academe: How Schooling Obscures the Life of the Mind* (New Haven: Yale University Press, 2003).

Deborah Tannen, *You Just Don't Understand: Women and Men in Conversation* (New York: Morrow, 1990).

Projects

Skepticism and Civility

Go back through an essay you are currently working on and reread those passages where you deal with other texts. Make some notes regarding the stance or attitude you take toward their authors' work:

What *use* do you make of the texts you cite? (You can either draw on the terms of this book or invent your own.) How do these texts contribute to your own line of thinking? What phrases in your writing mark out this use?

How would you describe your *attitude* toward the texts and writers you deal with? Angry? Superior? Respectful? Generous? Doubtful? Admiring? Noncommittal? What particular words or phrasings in your text suggest this stance? Ask yourself if your prose conveys the attitude toward these other texts and writers that you want it to.

Use your notes to consider how you might change or refine your use of other texts in your essay. The point here is to think about how you want to approach these texts on both *intellectual* and *stylistic* levels. There is no formula for how to do so. You can counter work that you respect and draw insights from texts that you find problematic. You can seem too aggressive, but you can also seem too dutiful. It's up to you to decide both what uses you want to make of other writers and how you want to be seen as approaching them.

CHAPTER 9

From Proof to Composition

You explored a topic. You asked how to reason through it. You questioned which proofs would be more effective and where to utilize them. Now remains the task of composing your argument. There is an argument to be made that this is, surprisingly, the simplest stage of the creative process: you have all your various pieces waiting for you, and you just need to put them together; you just need to compose.

This chapter first introduces you to the conventions of different **genres** (page 144); even if dealing with the exact same topic and using the exact same sources, a piece of academic writing, satire, or journalism will follow entirety different conventions. As such, understanding the conventions—why they exist, how to write within them, and how to challenge them—of your chosen genre of persuasion is as important as understanding your chosen topic: an excellently thought out argument can fizzle and die if not applied to the correct genre.

Once you understand your genre, your next task as a compositionist is to consider and question aspects of **design** (page 145). How you design a composition can largely depend on who you are composing for. Think back to the rhetorical situation: your audience often dictates the form your work takes, and the form will then dictate design. While questions of design become visually more apparent when you focus on compositions that do not simply rely upon written language to persuade an audience (so, in our class, the culminating Public Turn project), do not be mistaken into forgetting that they are *always* present, even when it does not appear so.

Finally, this chapter asks you to think about the **opportunities and constraints** (page 148) afforded during the composition process. How you view these potential challenges and what opportunities are presented to you will differ with each and every step of your composition; the important thing to remember is to always keep an open mind, and go where the composing takes you. In other words, don't ignore a constraint because it's inconvenient, and don't bypass an opportunity because it wasn't part of your original plan. As you find yourself deeper and deeper into your project, just remember that you have the tools, you have the material, you now just need to put it all together.

Genre Conventions

Science Fiction, Action, Romantic Comedy, Drama. These categories of movies—or **genres**—are pervasive in popular culture and make regular appearances in our everyday conversations. Similarly, the idea of musical genres is so commonplace in twenty-first-century American society that you will more than likely be familiar with at least a few *sub-genres*, like Gangsta Rap or Indie Rock. While these everyday uses of genre are probably familiar to you, you may not have heard the term used in reference to literature or academic writing. In fact, genre ("a kind" in French) is applicable to any compositional endeavor—including English essays, lab reports, and even business presentations. As such, understanding how genres work is important for developing your skill in composing.

When we think of different genres of movies or music, we usually think of certain characteristics that the genre tends to include. For instance, Science Fiction movies may concern time travel, and many Country songs include references to pick-up trucks. In an academic context, we call these tendencies **conventions** of the genre. When reading (or viewing or listening to) a composition, **genre conventions** help the reader understand what an author is trying to do, as well as the context in which they are composing. In an academic essay, one genre convention is to place the thesis statement at the beginning or end of the introduction; it helps readers to understand the purpose of the essay. In fact, because this is expected, placing your thesis statement somewhere else runs the risk of confusing your reader and making your arguments less effective. These conventions are what allow your audience to recognize your arguments, so in a certain sense, the genre conventions actually help you to *create* your composition. That said, it is important to remember that genre conventions are not hard-and-fast; they are not rules, just generally accepted patterns. In other words, not all compositions in a genre will use every convention. Some Science Fiction doesn't use time travel at all; instead, it may rely on futuristic or seemingly impossible technology. In the same way, not every country song includes pick-up trucks but they are still identifiably country because of their instrumentation. Most compositions, no matter their medium, will use enough conventions that the reader can easily identify their genre.

While categorizing a composition is often an easy task, composers also experiment with conventions, sometimes using multiple genres to create new (and strange) effects. Because of this experimentation, genre conventions are constantly changing. Think of Pop music from the 1980s—one of its conventions was the heavy use of synthesized instruments. But as music preferences changed—as hip hop, rap, grunge, and even punk music became more mainstream—Pop music changed as well (or it wouldn't be popular anymore). For Pop composers who were trying to evolve their genre, one of the most effective tactics was to incorporate aspects of other genres; they used more hip-hop beats, the overdriven guitar of grunge, and different vocal techniques to keep up with their audience. When we get to the twenty-first century, then, we recognize the Pop genre by a vastly different set of conventions, and 80s Pop often feels dated (at least until it becomes fashionable again, as genre is recursive). Academic writing has developed in similar ways. For instance, because the internet is such a ubiquitous resource, academic citation practices have had to adapt, incorporating URLs, online databases, and social media sources. Further, with the development of online journals, scholars can now publish articles as web pages, which use a set of conventions quite different from traditional academic journals. Paying attention to these changes, and especially the different tactics composers use to address them, is an effective strategy for gaining insight into their work. In your own compositions, too, being aware of how you are using genre conventions—conforming to them, ignoring them, resisting them, or helping them grow—is an invaluable tool for crafting your arguments and creating a relationship with your audience.

Design[1]

Design draws our attention specifically toward the relationship between audience and author. This relationship requires that we consider and make rhetorical choices when it comes to how our argument is designed for delivery. Depending upon our audience, we select what we say and how we say it as well as how we organize an argument. Often we think of design in terms of style in that it adds or ornaments an author's message, but design is much more than ornamentation; it is choosing from various rhetorical tropes and schemes (our rhetorical toolbox, if you will) and arranging, adjusting, and tinkering with those tools to create the most suitable argument for the intended audience. Traditionally viewed as being linguistic in nature, the analysis of style becomes insufficient when dealing with multimodal forms of communication. The New London Group and others in multimodal or visual rhetoric study, such as Gunther Kress, also find this deficiency and hold that multimodal forms of communication characteristically combine two or more modes to try and create more complex, holistic, and moving arguments. Therefore, relying on linguistic analysis alone limits argument examination. Design helps us here as we can examine rhetorical choices in our argument that are not just linguistic; i.e., music layered over images in a Power-Point presentation or gestures synchronized with the spoken words of a speech require choices. What kind of music do we select? Which images convey what we

---

1. This section is adapted from material originally written by Kelly Wheeler.

Some Elements of Design

Table 1. Modes of Meaning

Linguistic Design	Audio Design	Gestural Design	Visual Design	Spatial Design
Delivery ■ Intonation ■ Stress ■ Rhythm ■ Speed ■ Accent Vocabulary and Metaphor Transitivity ■ Types of process of participants in the clause ■ Positioning Information Structures ■ Clauses ■ Sentences Local Coherence Relations ■ Cohesion between clauses ■ Logical relations between clauses Global Coherence ■ Overall organizational properties of texts (e.g., genres)	■ Music ■ Sound Effects ■ Noises ■ Ambient Noises ■ Silence ■ Volume ■ Pitch ■ Tone ■ Rhythm	■ Behavior ■ Physicality ■ Gesture ■ Sensuality ■ Kinesics ■ Proximics ■ Patterns	■ Colors ■ Contrast ■ Complementary ■ Saliency ■ Perspective ■ Framing ■ Distance ■ Angle ■ Vectors ■ Foregrounding and Backgrounding ■ Scale ■ Layout ■ Balance ■ Symbols ■ Still versus Moving Image ■ Camera movement ■ Subject movement ■ Screen format	■ Ecosystem and Geographic Meanings ■ Architectonic Meanings ■ Layout ■ Proximity ■ Direction ■ Place Identity ■ Navigability

Opportunities and Constraints[2]

Imagine you walk into your English classroom for the first time, and your instructor hands you a full outline of a paper, including a thesis statement, point-by-point paragraph breakdown, and a bibliography of sources. Not only must you adhere to standard requirements such as page or word count, but you must also use exactly this thesis statement, exactly these supporting paragraphs in exactly this order, and exactly this set of sources and no others. It's hard to imagine an assignment that affords fewer **opportunities** than the one described above. In such a scenario, most people will produce a paper that is uninteresting to read and downright torturous to write. However, it would be equally problematic if you came in the first day of class and your instructor simply said, "Write." Your response might be, "Write? About what? For how long? Can I write down my grocery list? How would you even grade my grocery list?" In other words, in the absence of any **constraints**, most of us would immediately ask for some; after all, an infinite number of choices can make it very difficult to choose.

Whether we're aware of it or not, we negotiate opportunities and constraints each time we sit down to write. Some are *situated*, while others are *generated*. *Situated* means that they preexist your own writing choices. For instance, perhaps the assignment sheet asks for an essay, thereby constraining you from writing a poem. On the other hand, *generated* means that the choices you make while writing generate new opportunities and constraints that didn't exist before. For instance, you may decide to include a personal anecdote in your essay, which affords you the opportunity to humanize your issue; however, if you've chosen to construct an overtly formal *ethos*, it may constrain you from relying too heavily on this kind of emotional argument. In an English class, many of the "dos and don'ts" that seem to be rules of writing are actually the opportunities and constraints afforded by the medium/genre of a written academic essay—in other words, they can and do change when your argument takes another form. In a way, then, this is what your final assignment—The Public Turn—both offers and asks of you: a space wherein you can break the typical constraints of an academic paper, and invent new opportunities for your argument by way of a genre and/or modal shift.

For example, a written academic essay constrains you to an academic audience of some kind and affords you the opportunity to cite an in-depth sociological study on the relationship between violence at home and violence at school in order to support your proposal for counselling as a deterrent to bullying. If you choose to reimagine this argument as an interpretive dance, you are no longer constrained to an academic audience, and you also no longer have the opportunity to describe the compelling study that was so convincing to you. Now, you are constrained from using words and are afforded the opportunity to visibly demonstrate the visceral impact that violence can have on real human bodies and minds. Neither

---

2. This section is adapted from material originally written by Alana Hatley.

medium is "freer" or "more confining" than the other; instead, each medium affords *different* kinds of opportunities and constraints.

It's important to remember, too, that "opportunities and constraints" is not simply synonymous with "possibilities and impossibilities." It's perfectly *possible* to video yourself slowly turning the pages of a paper you've written so that the watcher can read it, but doing so doesn't really take advantage of any particular *opportunity* offered by the medium of video. Likewise, it's not *impossible* to include large chunks of text within an image collage, but breaking the *constraint* of using only images would defeat the purpose of choosing to do an image collage in the first place.

As you practice thinking about opportunities and constraints, you will begin to notice that the same thing can be thought of as both an opportunity and a constraint, depending on your perspective. Having a required number of sources in an academic essay is both an opportunity and a constraint, in that it allows you to weave many voices together into a rich conversation while simultaneously curbing either your impulse to describe only your own position or from throwing in so many voices that your paper is no longer your own. Rethinking your argument as a puppet show affords you the opportunity to bring your message straight to the kids, while simultaneously constraining you to simplify your message so that it both appeals to and makes sense to children—a notoriously difficult-to-please audience.

Thinking about opportunities and constraints is useful throughout the composing process, from invention all the way through to re-envisioning. The worst position to find yourself in as a writer is not knowing what to do next; considering opportunities and constraints shifts the question from "What do I do next?" to the much more productive and answerable question, "What do I *get* to do next?"

Discussion Questions

1. How does the use of genre conventions change the legitimacy of a composition? As an example, the movie *Shaun of the Dead* is marketed as a romantic comedy, with zombies. Does this mixture of three different genres affect the movie's legitimacy as an artifact of any stand-alone genre (for example, the Zombie Film)?

2. Consider genres of music. Other than musical tastes, what are some of the factors that can influence the way genre conventions change? Are some of these more powerful than others?

3. What are all of the conventions of the academic research essay? Do these conventions change due to academic sub-genres? Can you think of any examples?

4. Consider the opportunities and constraints afforded to you as a college student. What do you get to do now that you couldn't before (or won't be

able to do later)? What is harder for you to do now that was easier before (or will be easier later)? How might you separate these opportunities and constraints into the categories of *situated* and *generated*?

5. Think about how design affects your everyday life. Specifically, consider the products you use on a daily basis: how does their design affect how you interact with the world and with others? Does this design create any constraints on your life? What about opportunities?

6. Reflect on the process of composing your Researched Argumentative Essay. How did design decisions affect your final work? What are some situated and generated opportunities that stand out in your memory of that process, and how did you take advantage of them? What about situated and generated constraints? How did you use these to your advantage?

Exercises

1. Choose your favorite genre and list out as many of its conventions as you can. If you were to compose your own genre piece, which of these would you use? Leave out? Why?

2. Take a piece that you've read for this course and pretend that you're going to "translate" it into another genre. In order to do this, what conventions of the new genre will you use? How do the new conventions change the original piece? Keep in mind genre transcends medium, so it is possible to have a hip-hop essay or a science fiction album.

3. You have had something taken and will stop at nothing to get it back. In groups, write short plot summaries that apply this sentence to three of the following genres: rom-com, action, adventure, biopic, horror, comedy, musical, animated, anime, documentary, drama, thriller, family, or any other you can think of.

4. Find a celebrity that frequently uses at least two different social media platforms: Facebook and Twitter, Twitter and Instagram, etc. Analyze some of their more recent posts on both platforms. What seems to be the reason they choose one platform over the other? In other words, if they post different kinds of things to different platforms, each platform must be offering them some opportunities and constraints that the other platforms don't offer. How might you articulate these differences?

5. Choose an essay from Part Two, Unit Three of this book, and analyze it from a) a genre perspective; and b) a design standpoint. How did the author rise to their various constraints, and did they make the most of their opportunities?

6. As a way to begin choosing the medium and/or genre you will be using for your Public Turn assignment, look back at your Researched Argumentative Essay. Make a list of the situated and generated constraints that you would

like the opportunity to redirect. (For instance, maybe you were aware that an academic essay would probably not reach a particular audience that you would like to include in the conversation, or maybe you had trouble making your project sound as fun as you know it can be.) Then, make a list of the media and/or genres that might afford you the opportunities to achieve those goals. Finally, for each of the media and/or genres you have in this second list, what *new* situated constraints would you encounter if you were to choose that option? Write out as many as you can foresee.

Supplemental Reading

Shitty First Drafts
Anne Lamott

Now, practically even better news than that of short assignments is the idea of shitty first drafts. All good writers write them. This is how they end up with good second drafts and terrific third drafts. People tend to look at successful writers who are getting their books published and maybe even doing well financially and think that they sit down at their desks every morning feeling like a million dollars, feeling great about who they are and how much talent they have and what a great story they have to tell; that they take in a few deep breaths, push back their sleeves, roll their necks a few times to get all the cricks out, and dive in, typing fully formed passages as fast as a court reporter. But this is just the fantasy of the uninitiated. I know some very great writers, writers you love who write beautifully and have made a great deal of money, and not one of them sits down routinely feeling wildly enthusiastic and confident. Not one of them writes elegant first drafts. All right, one of them does, but we do not like her very much. We do not think that she has a rich inner life or that God likes her or can even stand her. (Although when I mentioned this to my priest friend Tom, he said you can safely assume you've created God in your own image when it turns out that God hates all the same people you do.)

Very few writers really know what they are doing until they've done it. Nor do they go about their business feeling dewy and thrilled. They do not type a few stiff warm-up sentences and then find themselves bounding along like huskies across the snow. One writer I know tells me that he sits down every morning and says to himself nicely, "It's not like you don't have a choice, because you do—you can either type, or kill yourself." We all often feel like we are pulling teeth, even those writers whose prose ends up being the most natural and fluid. The right words and sentences just do not come pouring out like ticker tape most of the time. Now, Muriel Spark is said to have felt that she was taking dictation from God every morning—sitting there, one supposes, plugged into a Dictaphone, typing away, humming. But this is a very hostile and aggressive position. One might hope for bad things to rain down on a person like this.

For me and most of the other writers I know, writing is not rapturous. In fact, the only way I can get anything written at all is to write really, really shitty first drafts.

The first draft is the child's draft, where you let it all pour out and then let it romp all over the place, knowing that no one is going to see it and that you can shape it later. You just let this childlike part of you channel whatever voices and visions come through and onto the page. If one of the characters wants to say, "Well, so what, Mr. Poopy Pants?," you let her. No one is going to see it. If the kid wants to get into really sentimental, weepy, emotional territory, you let him.

Just get it all down on paper because there may be something great in those six crazy pages that you would never have gotten to by more rational, grown-up means. There may be something in the very last line of the very last paragraph on page six that you just love, that is so beautiful or wild that you now know what you're supposed to be writing about, more or less, or in what direction you might go—but there was no way to get to this without first getting through the first five and a half pages.

I used to write food reviews for *California* magazine before it folded. (My writing food reviews had nothing to do with the magazine folding, although every single review did cause a couple of canceled subscriptions. Some readers took umbrage at my comparing mounds of vegetable puree with various ex-presidents' brains.) These reviews always took two days to write. First I'd go to a restaurant several times with a few opinionated, articulate friends in tow. I'd sit there writing down everything anyone said that was at all interesting or funny. Then on the following Monday I'd sit down at my desk with my notes and try to write the review. Even after I'd been doing this for years, panic would set in. I'd try to write a lead, but instead I'd write a couple of dreadful sentences, XX them out, try again, XX everything out, and then feel despair and worry settle on my chest like an x-ray apron. It's over, I'd think calmly. I'm not going to be able to get the magic to work this time. I'm ruined. I'm through. I'm toast. Maybe, I'd think, I can get my old job back as a clerk-typist. But probably not. I'd get up and study my teeth in the mirror for a while. Then I'd stop, remember to breathe, make a few phone calls, hit the kitchen and chow down. Eventually I'd go back and sit down at my desk, and sigh for the next ten minutes. Finally I would pick up my one-inch picture frame, stare into it as if for the answer, and every time the answer would come: all I had to do was to write a really shitty first draft of, say, the opening paragraph. And no one was going to see it.

So I'd start writing without reining myself in. It was almost just typing, just making my fingers move. And the writing would be terrible. I'd write a lead paragraph that was a whole page, even though the entire review could only be three pages long, and then I'd start writing up descriptions of the food, one dish at a time, bird by bird, and the critics would be sitting on my shoulders, commenting like cartoon characters. They'd be pretending to snore, or rolling their eyes at my overwrought descriptions, no matter how hard I tried to tone those descriptions down, no matter how conscious I was of what a friend said to me gently in my early days of restaurant reviewing. "Annie," she said, "it is just a piece of *chicken*. It is just a bit of *cake*."

But because by then I had been writing for so long, I would eventually let myself trust the process—sort of, more or less. I'd write a first draft that was maybe twice as long as it should be, with a self-indulgent and boring beginning, stupefying descriptions of the meal, lots of quotes from my black-humored friends that made them sound more like the Manson girls than food lovers, and no ending to speak of. The whole thing would be so long and incoherent and hideous that for the rest of the day I'd obsess about getting creamed by a car before I could write a decent second draft. I'd worry that people would read what I'd written and believe that the accident had really been a suicide, that I had panicked because my talent was waning and my mind was shot.

The next day, I'd sit down, go through it all with a colored pen, take out everything I possibly could, find a new lead somewhere on the second page, figure out a kicky place to end it, and then write a second draft. It always turned out fine, sometimes even funny and weird and helpful. I'd go over it one more time and mail it in.

Then, a month later, when it was time for another review, the whole process would start again, complete with the fears that people would find my first draft before I could rewrite it.

Almost all good writing begins with terrible first efforts. You need to start somewhere. Start by getting something—anything—down on paper. A friend of mine says that the first draft is the down draft—you just get it down. The second draft is the up draft—you fix it up. You try to say what you have to say more accurately. And the third draft is the dental draft, where you check every tooth, to see if it's loose or cramped or decayed, or even, God help us, healthy.

Reading Issues

The Carolina Rhetoric for English 102 is designed to do two things: introduce you to the major concepts involved in rhetorical composition and argumentation, and provide you with a range of readings in and around rhetorical issues in contemporary society. Part Two of this book, then, focuses on five contemporary problems: border control, privacy and cyber-security, healthcare, gentrification, and cultural representation. Each of these problems has been chosen because they are examples of *open* issues—debates within twenty-first-century American (and often global) society that have not already been resolved. In other words, each of these issues is open for debate. As such, you should read these texts as you would any position within an argument—they don't have all the answers, but they highlight specific aspects of the issues and make their arguments for specific reasons.

For most of the issues addressed in Part Two, there are nine different texts presented across the three units. In keeping with the idea of presenting *open* debates, these nine texts present many different perspectives and avenues for approaching the debates in question. However, there are inevitably many more voices in a debate than can be represented in nine texts—don't make the mistake of thinking that these readings include (or try to include) everything that is important about these topics. Rather, they are organized along the pattern established by the units of Part One. The first unit, then, is oriented toward rhetorical situations. The second unit, toward specific arguments. The third unit, toward particular appeals, methods of reasoning, or genres. You should think of these readings as opportunities to practice using the concepts you learn in Part One in the context of vibrant, relevant issues.

PART TWO

READING SITUATIONS

For each of the five issues presented, the readings in this unit are selected because they provide general introductions to the rhetorical situations of the debates. These introductions may take the form of important theoretical background, concrete problems that are associated with these debates, important questions posed by them, conversational interviews with individuals highly familiar with the issues, or—as in the case of George Yancy's "Dear White America"—open letters closely tied to the issue in question.

While every text will give insight into the rhetorical situations surrounding a debate, these texts are chosen because they provide particularly broad or important information about them; as you read them, pay careful attention to how they inform you about the **exigence, *kairos*, stakes, stakeholders, biases, and conditions of argumentation** in each debate. What **ethical** issues are at play? Consider how they help you think about the important **stases** involved. Remember, too, that no single text will give you all the relevant information; develop your sense of the rhetorical situation by compiling this information from each of the three readings.

Border Control

How Immigrants Become "Other"
Marcelo M. Suárez-Orozco and Carola Suárez-Orozco

Unauthorized Immigration

No human being can be "illegal." While there are illegal actions—running a red light or crossing an international border without the required authorization, one action should not come to define a person's existence. The terms *illegal*, *criminal*, and *alien*, often uttered in the same breath, conjure up unsavory associations.[1] Unsettling and distancing ways to label people, they have contributed to the creation of our very own caste of untouchables.

In many cases, "illegal status," or what we prefer to term unauthorized status, may not be voluntary. We prefer this term to *undocumented immigrant* as many have documents or could have documents but often find themselves in a limbo state pending a formal legal outcome.

In the mid-1990s, Sonia Martinez, mother of four children, all under the age of ten, became a young widow when her husband was stricken with cancer. With a limited education and no means to support her family on a rancho in rural southern Mexico, she reluctantly left her children behind in the care of her mother and crossed the border without papers. The week after arriving Sonia took up a job as a live-in housekeeper and nanny in the Southwest. Every month she faithfully sent money home to her family. She called them every week. Each time she called, they had less and less to say to her. Lovingly, she selected presents for each of her children over the course of the year. By Christmas she would make the pilgrimage back to her rancho to see her children and, Santa-like, shower them with American gifts. But the sweet visits home were always too short and she would soon have to face the dangerous and expensive crossing back to California, relying on the help of treacherous *coyotes* (smugglers) she hired each time. After September 11, as border controls tightened, she no longer dared to make the trek back and forth. She has stayed behind the trapdoor on this side of the border and has not seen her children since then.[2]

Sonia found herself a young widow and in a post–NAFTA [North Atlantic Free Trade Agreement] Mexican economy with promised jobs that simply never materialized and in an unforgiving economy for poorly educated, unskilled, rural workers. Plentiful jobs in the Southwest economy in the mid-1990s, relatively comfortable working conditions as a live-in housekeeper and nanny in a middle-class neighborhood, and an extremely advantageous wage differential proved

---

1. Santa Ana, O. (2002). *Brown tide rising: Metaphoric representations of Latinos in contemporary public discourse.* Austin: University of Texas Press. [All notes are the Suárez-Orozcos', except 13.]

2. Note that we have used a pseudonym; this case is from IS @ NYU data—see http://steinhardt.nyu.edu/scmsAdmin/media/users/ef58/metrocenter/Online_Supplemental_Notes.pdf.

irresistible. Although not raising her children came at a high emotional cost, the ability to support them was its own reward.

In 1998, Hurricane Mitch devastated Honduras, leaving little in the way of work opportunities. Like many others, Gustavo Jimenez made his way north, dangerously riding atop trains through Central America and Mexico and then crossed with a hired *coyote* into Texas. He worked a series of odd jobs but found it difficult to find steady work. Then, yet another hurricane changed his fate. When Katrina devastated New Orleans in 2005, ample work opportunities opened—dirty work in horrific conditions were hard to fill over the long haul of the cleanup and reconstruction. Mr. Jimenez quickly found work: "Who but us migrants would do these hard jobs without ever taking a break? We worked day and night in jobs Americans would never do, so that the Gulf could be rebuilt." But he found that he would be treated with disdain. It left him mystified. On one hand, "I know that by coming here illegally I am breaking the law," but he added, "I did not come to steal from anyone. I put my all in the jobs I take. And I don't see any of the Americans wanting to do this work."[3] Gustavo's story is both old and new. Unauthorized immigrants have always been called upon to do the jobs on the dark side of the American economy. The post-Katrina cleanup is a fitting example. Adding insult to injury, these workers are the target of disdain and disparagement. The stigma of the work gets attached to them—as if those doing dirty, demanding, and dangerous jobs themselves by mimesis become dirty, despised, and dispensable.

Hervé Fonkou Takoulo is a college-educated professional with a knack for stock trading in his spare time. Mr. Takoulo arrived in the United States in 1998 on a valid visa from the troubled African nation of Cameroon. He took to New York like a duck to water. He graduated with an engineering degree from the State University of New York and married a U.S. citizen hailing from California. She was the vice president of a Manhattan media advertising company. The bi-racial professional couple was ecstatic when President Obama spoke of his dual African and American roots. Takoulo's wife, Caroline Jamieson, "recalled that she cried when Mr. Obama said during a 2008 campaign speech, 'With a mother from Kansas and a father from Kenya'—I said, 'Oh, Hervé, even the alliteration is right—with a mother from California and a father from Cameroon, our child could do the same!'" She cried again but for a very different reason when the letter she wrote to President Obama resulted in her husband's arrest. The letter to the president "explained that Ms. Jamieson, 42, had filed a petition seeking a green card for her husband on the basis of their 2005 marriage. But before they met, Mr. Takoulo, who first arrived in the country on a temporary business visa, had applied for political asylum and had been denied it by an immigration judge in Baltimore, who ordered him deported." Surely, this president with his extensive

---

3. Gustavo's quotes are to be found in Orner, P. (Ed.). (2008). *Underground America: Narratives of undocumented lives.* San Francisco, CA: McSweeney's.

personal experience in Africa would understand that Cameroon had a horrendous record of human rights abuses. Instead of the hoped-for presidential reprieve, the asylum seeking Obamista was met by two immigration agents, "in front of the couple's East Village apartment building. He says one agent asked him, 'Did you write a letter to President Obama?' When he acknowledged that his wife had, he was handcuffed and sent to an immigration jail in New Jersey for deportation."[4]

When she was four, Marieli's father was assassinated in front of his wife and children. Left as a widow responsible for her family, Marieli's mother reluctantly left Guatemala for the United States, as she put it, "in order to be able to feed my family." Once in California, she applied for asylum status and waited patiently for her papers to be processed. The unforgiving bureaucratic labyrinth took six years and a small fortune to complete. Only then could she begin the process of applying to reunite with her children. In the meantime, the grandmother, who had been raising the children in her absence, died. With no one to care for them and after having patiently waited for years, Marieli's mother made the drastic choice of having her children make the crossing without papers. Finally, at age eleven, after having spent more than half her childhood away from her mother, Marieli arrived in northern California after being smuggled into the country by *coyotes*. Recognizing she "owed everything" to her mother but at the same time angry she had been left behind for so long, the reunification with the mother she barely knew was a rocky and bittersweet one. Marieli is now an unauthorized immigrant waiting in limbo.

The Reagan-inspired U.S. wars of proxy in El Salvador, Guatemala, and Nicaragua of the 1980s resulted in systematic killings—largely of noncombatant civilians, massive displacements of people, and the beginning of an international exodus of biblical proportions not only to the United States but also to neighboring Latin American countries. The U.S. invasion of Iraq has made Iraqis top the list of formally admitted refugees in the United States in 2009. While those escaping our foreign policy debacles often make it through the legal maze, thousands of others fall through every year.

The cases reveal how war and conflict drive human migration. But the heart also plays an unanticipated but powerful role. Work, war, and love are behind almost every migrant journey—authorized or unauthorized.

Many come here fully aware that they will be breaking a law by crossing without the proper documents, but in other cases accidents, misunderstandings, and an unforgiving bureaucracy can turn good faith errors into labyrinths without exit.

During his tour of duty in Iraq, Lt. Kenneth Tenebro "harbored a fear he did not share with anyone in the military. Lieutenant Tenebro worried that his wife, Wilma, back home in New York with their infant daughter, would be deported. Wilma, who like her husband was born in the Philippines, is an

---

4. Bernstein, N. (2010, June 18). Plea to Obama led to an immigrant's arrest. *New York Times*.

illegal immigrant.... That was our fear all the time." When he called home, "She often cried about it.... Like, hey, what's going to happen? Where will I leave our daughter?" The Tenebros' story, like many others, began as a love story and an overstayed visa. They met several years ago while Wilma was on vacation in New York at the end of a job as a housekeeper on a cruise ship. Love kept her from returning to the Philippines, and ultimately she overstayed her visa. Today, the lieutenant and the wife face an unhappy choice: "Wilma is snagged on a statute, notorious among immigration lawyers, that makes it virtually impossible for her to become a legal resident without first leaving the United States and staying away for 10 years." Lt. Tenebro is not alone—thousands of U.S. soldiers facing dangerous tours of duty have the additional burden of worrying that loved ones close to them will be deported.[5]

Combined, these testimonies embody the varieties of unauthorized journeys into the United States. Synergetic "push" and "pull" factors coalesce, luring immigrants away from familiar but relatively scarce surroundings to an alluring unknown. Immigrant optimism springs eternal. While some fly in with documents and visas and simply overstay, more immigrants come undetected through the southern border. Often they hire dangerous *coyotes* (typically from Mexico or Central America) or *snakeheads* (working from as far away as China, India, or Russia). Immigrants pay a very high price for these unauthorized journeys. While the crossing from Mexico to the United States can run approximately $3,000, the costs of longer passages are substantially higher, running up to an exorbitant $30,000 per journey. Those who arrive under the long shadow of transnational smuggling syndicates often face a period of protracted indentured servitude, as they must pay back exorbitant crossing fees. Whether the journey begins in Fujian, China, or Puebla, Mexico, tough border controls have made the crossing more dangerous than ever before—on average more than a person a day dies at the southern border attempting to cross.

The Children of Unauthorized Immigrants

Unauthorized immigrants are neither from Mars nor Venus. The majority have roots in American society. While some are married to U.S. citizens, others partner with migrants already here. Nearly half of unauthorized immigrants live in households with a partner and children. The vast majority of these children—79 percent—are U.S. citizens by birth.[6] The number of U.S.-born children in mixed-status families has expanded rapidly from 2.7 million in 2003 to 4 million in 2008.[7] Adding the 1.1 million unauthorized children living in the United

5. Preston, J. (2010, May 8). Worried about deploying with family in limbo. *New York Times.*

6. Passel, J. S., & Taylor, P. (2010). Unauthorized immigrants and their U.S.-born children. Washington, DC: Pew Research Center. Retrieved from pewhispanic.org/reports /report.php?ReportID=125.

7. Ibid.

States (like Marieli) means that there are 5.1 million children currently living in "mixed-status" homes.[8]

Nowhere is the story of the unauthorized immigration more dystopic than for the children who grow up in the shadows of the law. On an unbearable steamy afternoon in July 2010, Carola Suárez-Orozco found herself in a somber congressional chamber testifying on behalf of the American Psychological Association in front of an ad hoc committee of the United States House of Representatives headed by Arizona's Congressman Raúl Grijalva (D-Tucson). At her side were two children—precocious, overly serious. A congressional photographer afterward whispered to Carola that in over twenty years on the job he had never seen such young children testify before the U.S. Congress.

Eleven-year-old Mathew Parea was poised and collected as he spoke in the august chamber. At a tender age, he had already been active in social justice causes for several years including a four-day fast honoring the patron saint of migrant workers, César Chávez. Mathew spoke on behalf of thousands of children of migrant families. His steady voice was riveting: "I am here to tell you about my fears growing up in Arizona. Children want to be with their parents because we know that our parents love us. The laws in Arizona are just unjust and make me fear for my family. I am always worried when my family leaves the house that something might happen to them. I think about it when my dad goes to work that he might not come back or when I go to school that there might not be someone to pick me up when I get out."[9]

Heidi Portugal physically appeared younger than twelve, yet she carried herself in an unsettling serious manner. Her story embodies the immigrant dream turned nightmare: "At only 10 years of age I had a sad awakening the day of February 11th. When I woke up, I found out that my mother had been arrested.... My biggest preoccupation was my two little brothers and sister. What was going to happen to them? And what about my little brother that my mother was breast feeding?" She went on to explain how as the eldest sister, she took on the responsibility of caring for her younger siblings, how her mother was deported, and how she has never seen her mother again. She went on, "Before, I would admire all uniformed people that protect our country ... [but they] took away the most precious thing that children can have, our mother. With one hit, they took away my smile and my happiness."[10]

---

8. Ibid.

9. See Testimony of Carola Suárez-Orozco before the United States House of Representatives, www.apa.org/about/gr/issues/cyf/immigration-enforcement.aspx.

10. Ibid.

Mathew and Heidi are part of an estimated one hundred thousand citizen[11] children whose parents have been deported. They face an impossible choice no child should have to make—staying in the United States with relatives or going with their parents to a country they do not know. These youngsters are a caste of orphans of the state, citizen children who day in and day out lose "the right to have rights"[12]—for them the protections of the Fourteenth Amendment[13] are an elusive mirage. Children whose parents are detained and/or deported by Immigration and Customs Enforcement exhibit multiple behavioral changes in the aftermath of parental detention, including anxiety, frequent crying, changes in eating and sleeping patterns, withdrawal, and anger. Such behavioral changes were documented for both short-term after the arrest as well as in the long-term at a nine-month follow-up.[14]

They also experience dramatic increases in housing instability and food insecurity—both important dimensions of basic developmental well-being. Such insecurities, while heightened for children whose parents are detained, is ongoing for children growing up in mixed-status households. These insecurities exist even though unauthorized immigrants have very high levels of employment; among men, fully 94 percent are active in the labor force (a rate substantially higher than for U.S.-born citizens—83 percent and legal immigrants—85 percent). At the same time, more than 30 percent of children growing up in unauthorized households live below the poverty line. Harvard psychologist Hiro Yoshikawa, in his detailed study of infants and their families, documents the range of penalties American-born preschool children of unauthorized parents face. First, the children's housing and economic situation was often quite fragile. Second, unauthorized parents were less likely to take advantage of a range of benefits to which their citizen children are entitled (like Temporary Assistance to Needy Families, Head Start, the Women, Infants and Children Nutritional Program, Medicaid, and others). Lastly, they had less access to extended social networks that can provide information, babysit, or lend money in a crisis.[15]

While the majority of children of unauthorized immigrants are citizen children (4 million), there are some 1.1 million children who just like Marieli have no papers. Many arrive when they are very young, others in their teen years. These children grow up in America, attending American schools, making American friends, learning English, and developing an emerging American identity. Every year approximately 65,000 young people graduate from high schools without the requisite papers either to go on to college or to legally enter the work force.

---

11. Ibid.

12. Arendt, H. (1966). *The origins of totalitarianism*. New York: Harcourt.

13. **the Fourteenth Amendment:** Provides equal protection and due process under the law. [Eds.]

14. Chaudry, A., Pedroza, J., Castañeda, R. M., Santos, R., & Scott, M. M. (2010). *Facing our future: Children in the aftermath of immigration enforcement*. Washington, DC: Urban Institute.

15. Yoshikawa, H. (2011). *Immigrants raising citizens: Undocumented parents and their young children*. New York: Russell Sage Foundation.

Unauthorized immigrants live in a parallel universe. Their lives are shaped by forces and habits that are unimaginable to many American citizens. Work and fear are the two constants. They lead to routines, where the fear of apprehension and deportation is an ever-present shadow in their lives. Dropping off a child to school, a casual trip to the supermarket, a train or bus ride, expose them to the threat of apprehension, deportation, and the pain of being separated from their loved ones.

Mass unauthorized immigration has become a social phenomenon with deep structural roots in American institutions. The responsibility must be shared beyond the immigrants themselves to the businesses that thrive on their labor, the middle-class families who rely on them for housekeeping, babysitting, landscaping, and other amenities, consumers who have come to expect their affordable produce and rapid delivery services, and all citizens who have consciously or unconsciously enabled a dysfunctional system to flourish. Above all the political class shares the bulk of the responsibility by oscillating between denial, grand-standing, and hysterical scapegoating. They have brought us demagogic, unworkable, and self-defeating policy proposals.

Broken Lines

Outcry over our broken immigration system is focused on the borderline. Frustrated and fearful, Americans ask, "Why won't these illegals get in line like everybody else?" On the surface that is a perfectly reasonable question.

The reality, however, is that there is no orderly line to join. The terrorist attacks of September 11 threw sand in an already rusty machinery of legal immigration. In countless U.S. consulates and embassies the world over and in U.S. Citizenship and Immigration Services offices all over the country, millions wait in interminable queues. New security considerations brought an already inefficient system to a near standstill.

There are nearly 3.5 million immediate family members of U.S. citizens and permanent lawful immigrants waiting overseas for their visas.[16] In U.S. consulates in Mexico alone, approximately a quarter of a million spouses and minor children of U.S. citizens and permanent lawful residents wait to legally join their immediate relatives north of the border. In the Philippines, approximately 70,000 spouses and minor children are in the same situation. The average wait in line for these countries is from four to six years for spouses and under-age children. If you are a U.S. citizen and your sister is in the Philippines, you will have to wait twenty years before she can join you. If you are a U.S. citizen and would like to sponsor your unmarried adult child in Mexico, you will wait sixteen years and spend considerable resources.

---

16. Anderson, S. (2010). Family immigration: The long wait to immigrate. Arlington, VA: National Foundation for American Policy. Retrieved from www.nfap.com/.

The visa allocation system for work permits is no more functional.[17] The annual quota for work visas is 140,000 per year; as this includes spouses and children, the actual number of workers is much lower. There is no systematic queue for low-skilled workers. There are a million people waiting in Mexico alone in any given year.[18] As Roxanna Bacon, the chief counsel for the United States Citizenship and Immigration Services in Washington, D.C., succinctly stated, "Our housing industry, our service industry, our gardening, landscape industry, you name it—it's been dependent for decades on Mexican labor. None of these people qualify for an employment-based visa. So when the hate mongers say, 'Why can't they wait in line? Can't they get a visa?'—there aren't any visas to get! There is no line to wait in! And that's why everyone who knows this area of law says without comprehensive immigration reform you really aren't going to solve any of these pop-up issues."[19]

Reasonable voices have been driven off stage, while demagogic venting, grandstanding, and obfuscation saturate the airwaves, the print media, the Internet, and town halls throughout the nation. Rather than offering new solutions, an amalgamation of cultural xenophobes and economic nativists has joined together to fuel the fire. Xenophobes see mass immigration, especially from Latin America, as a growing menace to the pristine tapestry of American culture that would be stained by new arrivals from the "Brown" continent. Economic nativists wring their hands: immigration presents unfair competition for ever-scarcer jobs as well as putting downward pressure on wages. For them, immigration has come to embody the globalization in all its pathologies. Immigrants are tangible representations of enormous and amorphous problems—the globalization of terror, the outsourcing of jobs, and the discomfort of being surrounded by strangers (dis)figuring the social sphere with exotic languages, cultural habits, and uncanny ways.

References

Anderson, S. (2009). *Employment-based green card projections point to decade-long waits.* Arlington, VA: National Foundation for American Policy. Retrieved from www.nfap.com/.

Anderson, S. (2010). *Family immigration: The long wait to immigrate.* Arlington, VA: National Foundation for American Policy. Retrieved from www.nfap.com/.

Arendt, H. (1966), *The origins of totalitarianism.* New York: Harcourt.

Bernstein, N. (2006, May 22). 100 years in the back door, out the front. *New York Times.* Retrieved on July 31, 2011 from www.nytimes.com/learning/teachers/featured_articles/20060522monday.html?scp=10&sq=Ari%20Zolberg&st=cse.

---

17. Anderson, S. (2009). *Employment-based green card projections point to decade-long waits.* Arlington, VA: National Foundation for American Policy. Retrieved from www.nfap.com/.

18. U.S. State Department (2009). Annual report on immigrant visa applicants in the family sponsored and employment based preferences registered at the National Visa Center as of November 1. Annual Report on Immigrant Visas. Washington, DC: U.S. State Department.

19. Bacon, R. (2010, May 22). One border, many sides. *New York Times.* Retrieved on 22 February 2012 from www.nytimes.com/2010/05/23/opinion/23deavere-smith.html?sc =8&sq-Deveare-Smith&st=cse&pagewanted=1.

Bernstein, N. (2010, June 18). Plea to Obama led to an immigrant's arrest. *New York Times*.

Chaudry, A., Pedroza, J., Castañeda, R. M., Santos, R., & Scott, M. M. (2010). *Facing our future: Children in the aftermath of immigration enforcement*. Washington, DC: Urban Institute.

Orner, P. (Ed.). (2008). *Underground America: Narratives of undocumented lives*. San Francisco, CA: McSweeney's.

Passel, J. S., & Taylor, P. (2010). Unauthorized immigrants and their U.S.-born children. Washington, DC: Pew Research Center. Retrieved from pewhispanic.org/reports/report.php?ReportID=125.

Preston, J. (2010, May 8). Worried about deploying with family in limbo. *New York Times*.

Santa Ana, O. (2002). *Brown tide rising: Metaphoric representations of Latinos in contemporary public discourse*. Austin: University of Texas Press.

The Politics of Fear
Al Gore

Fear is the most powerful enemy of reason. Both fear and reason are essential to human survival, but the relationship between them is unbalanced. Reason may sometimes dissipate fear, but fear frequently shuts down reason. As Edmund Burke wrote in England twenty years before the American Revolution, "No passion so effectually robs the mind of all its powers of acting and reasoning as fear."

Our Founders had a healthy respect for the threat fear poses to reason. They knew that, under the right circumstances, fear can trigger the temptation to surrender freedom to a demagogue promising strength and security in return. They worried that when fear displaces reason, the result is often irrational hatred and division. As Justice Louis D. Brandeis later wrote: "Men feared witches and burnt women."

Understanding this unequal relationship between fear and reason was crucial to the design of American self-government.

Our Founders rejected direct democracy because of concerns that fear might overwhelm reflective thought. But they counted heavily on the ability of a "well-informed citizenry" to reason together in ways that would minimize the destructive impact of illusory, exaggerated, or excessive fears. "When a man seriously reflects on the precariousness of human affairs, he will become convinced that it is infinitely wiser and safer to form a constitution of our own in a cool deliberate manner, while we have it in our power," wrote Thomas Paine in his legendary pamphlet *Common Sense*, specifically warning that the Founders should not take the risk of waiting until some fear seized the public imagination, in which event their reasoning processes would be hampered.

Nations succeed or fail and define their essential character by the way they challenge the unknown and cope with fear. And much depends on the quality of their leadership. If leaders exploit public fears to herd people in directions they might not otherwise choose, then fear itself can quickly become a self-perpetuating and freewheeling force that drains national will and weakens national character, diverting attention from real threats deserving of healthy and appropriate fear and sowing confusion about the essential choices that every nation must constantly make about its future.

Leadership means inspiring us to manage through our fears. Demagoguery means exploiting our fears for political gain. There is a crucial difference.

Fear and anxiety have always been a part of life and always will be. Fear is ubiquitous and universal in every human society. It is a normal part of the human condition. And it has always been an enemy of reason. The Roman philosopher and rhetoric teacher Lactantius wrote, "Where fear is present, wisdom cannot be."

We have always defined progress by our success in managing through our fears. Christopher Columbus, Meriwether Lewis and William Clark, Susan B. Anthony, and Neil Armstrong all found success by challenging the unknown and overcoming fear with courage and a sense of proportion that helped them overcome legitimate fears without being distracted by distorted and illusory fears.

The Founders of our country faced dire threats. If they failed in their endeavors, they would have been hanged as traitors. The very existence of our country was at risk. Yet in the teeth of those dangers, they insisted on establishing the freedoms that became the Bill of Rights. Are members of Congress today in more danger than were their predecessors when the British army marched on the Capitol?

Are the dangers we now face so much greater than those that led Franklin Delano Roosevelt to famously remind us that the only thing we have to fear is fear itself? Is America in more danger now than when we faced worldwide fascism on the march—when our fathers fought and won a world war on two fronts simultaneously?

Is the world more dangerous than when we faced an ideological enemy with thousands of missiles poised to annihilate our country at a moment's notice? Fifty years ago, when the nuclear arms race with the Soviet Union was raising tensions in the world and McCarthyism was threatening our liberties at home, President Dwight Eisenhower belatedly said, "Any who act as if freedom's defenses are to be found in suppression and suspicion and fear confess a doctrine that is alien to America." Edward R. Murrow, whose courageous journalism was assaulted by Senator Joseph McCarthy, declared, "We will not be driven by fear into an age of unreason."

It is simply an insult to those who came before us and sacrificed so much on our behalf to imply that we have more to be fearful of than they did. In spite of the dangers they confronted, they faithfully protected our freedoms. It is up to us to do the same.

Yet something is palpably different today. Why in the early years of the twenty-first century are we so much more vulnerable to the politics of fear? There have always been leaders willing to fan public anxieties in order to present themselves as the protectors of the fearful. Demagogues have always promised security in return for the surrender of freedom. Why do we seem to be responding differently today?

The single most surprising new element in America's national conversation is the prominence and intensity of constant fear. Moreover, there is an uncharacteristic and persistent confusion about the sources of that fear; we seem to be having unusual difficulty in distinguishing between illusory threats and legitimate ones.

It is a serious indictment of the present quality of our political discourse that almost three-quarters of all Americans were so easily led to believe that Saddam Hussein was personally responsible for the attacks of September 11, 2001, and that so many Americans *still* believe that most of the hijackers on September 11 were Iraqis. And it is an indictment of the way our democracy is currently operating that more than 40 percent were so easily convinced that Iraq did in fact have nuclear weapons, even after the most important evidence presented—classified documents that depicted an attempt by Saddam Hussein's regime to purchase yellowcake uranium from the country of Niger—was revealed to have been forged.

Clearly, the current administration has misused fear to manipulate the political process, and I will return to this issue later in this chapter. But I think a far more important question is: How could our nation have become so uncharacteristically vulnerable to such an effective use of fear to manipulate our politics?

A free press is supposed to function as our democracy's immune system against such gross errors of fact and understanding. As Thomas Jefferson once said, "Error of opinion may be tolerated where reason is left free to combat it." So what happened? Why does our immune system no longer operate as it once did? For one thing, there's been a dramatic change in the nature of what philosopher Jürgen Habermas has described as "the structure of the public forum." As I described in the introduction, the public sphere is simply no longer as open to the vigorous and free exchange of ideas from individuals as it was when America was founded.

When errors of fact and judgment are no longer caught and neutralized by the nation's immune system, it is time to examine the problem and to work toward good health in our political discourse. In order to do this, we need to start paying more attention to new discoveries about the way fear affects the thinking process. And, in fact, recent advances in neuroscience offer new and interesting insights into the nature of fear.

For most of the last century, the human brain was studied almost exclusively in the context of accidents and unusual head injuries. Doctors would note the part of the brain taken out by the injury and then, after careful observation of strange behaviors, would slowly determine what functions had been controlled by the injured part. But now scientists are able to observe healthy brains in normal operation, measuring current, blood flow, and chemical activity that indicate which part of the brain is most active at a particular time.

New technologies in any field can have a revolutionizing impact. When Galileo used new and more powerful telescopes to study the heavens in greater detail, he was able to see the movements of the planets around the sun and the movements of Jupiter's moons around Jupiter in order to describe in compelling detail the comprehensive new model of the solar system first proposed by Copernicus. It was the new technology itself that empowered Galileo to describe a reality that was impossible to perceive so clearly until the new technology of the telescope made it possible.

In almost exactly the same way, the new technology called "functional magnetic resonance imaging," or FMRI, has revolutionized the ability of neuroscientists to look inside the operations of a living human brain and observe which regions of the brain are being used at which times and in response to which stimuli. Just as Galileo could suddenly see the moons of Jupiter, neuroscientists are now able for the first time to see the proper relationships among areas of the brain such as the amygdala and the hippocampus and the neocortex, to name only a few.

An entirely new understanding of the brain is coming forth, and one of the areas that has been richest in discoveries has to do with how we as human beings function in relation to fear. The implications for democracy are profound.

In a democracy, the common (if usually unstated) assumption is that citizens operate as rational human beings, reasoning their way through the problems presented to them as if every question could be analyzed rationally and debated fairly until there is a well-reasoned collective conclusion. But the new research demonstrates that, of course, this is not the way it works at all.

One of the world's leading neuroscientists, Dr. Vilayanur S. Ramachandran, has written, "Our mental life is governed mainly by a cauldron of emotions, motives and desires which we are barely conscious of, and what we call our conscious life is usually an elaborate post hoc rationalization of things we really do for other reasons."

There are other mental structures that govern feelings and emotions, and these structures have a greater impact on decision making than logic and reason. Moreover, emotions have much more power to affect reason than reason does to affect emotions—particularly the emotion of fear.

A scientist at Stony Brook University, Charles Taber, went so far as to say, "The Enlightenment model of dispassionate reason as the duty of citizenship is empirically bankrupt."

In the words of New York University neuroscientist Joseph LeDoux, author of *The Emotional Brain*, "Connections from the emotional systems to the cognitive systems are stronger than connections from the cognitive systems to the emotional systems." Our capacity for fear is "hardwired" in the brain as an ancient strategy that gives us the ability to respond instantly when survival may be at stake. But fear is not the only arousing emotion that is "hardwired" to quickly activate responses. The amygdala, for example, is almost certainly involved in speeding other responses important to our species's survival, such as the urge to reproduce. (It may be partly for that reason that sexual titillation along with fear is also a staple ingredient of modern television programming.) By contrast, reason is centered in parts of the brain that have most recently evolved and depends upon more subtle processes that give us the ability to discern the emergence of threats before they become immediate and to distinguish between legitimate threats and illusory ones.

Neurologists and brain researchers describe how disturbing images go straight to a part of the brain that is not mediated by language or reasoned analysis. There are actually two parallel pathways from the visual centers to the rest of the brain, and one of them serves as a crude but instantaneous warning system. (Evolution often forces a tradeoff between speed and accuracy.) Moreover, whatever the cause of the fear, the phenomenon itself is difficult to turn off once it's turned on.

Psychologists have studied the way we make decisions in the presence of great uncertainty and have found that we develop shortcuts—called "heuristics"—to help us make important choices. And one of the most important shortcuts that we use is called "the affect heuristic." We often make snap judgments based principally on our emotional reactions rather than considering all options rationally and making choices carefully.

This shortcut is actually a useful trait. It allows us to make quicker decisions, and it helps us avoid dangerous situations. However, our use of emotions to make decisions can also cloud judgment. When an emotional reaction like fear is especially strong, it can completely overwhelm our reasoning process.

Moreover, just as fear can interfere with reason in the presence of an imminent threat, it can also exercise the same power over reason in the realms of memory. We mistakenly assume that memory is the exclusive province of reason, but in fact those regions of the brain that give us our capacity for fear have their own memory circuits. Over the course of our lives, we emotionally tag traumatic experiences as memories that are especially accessible to recall—either consciously or unconsciously—and they are constantly being retrieved to guide us in new situations, especially when a rapid response is required.

Most of us are familiar with the phenomenon of post-traumatic stress disorder (PTSD), which is common to rape victims, child abuse victims, and combat veterans, among others. Normally, when an experience is translated into memory, it's given a sort of "time tag," a mechanism that gives us the ability when we recall those experiences to sense how long ago the events we recall occurred and a rough understanding of their temporal sequence. You can sense that the remembered experience was before this and after that. Or that it was ten weeks ago or eleven weeks ago.

However, when traumatic events—those involving anxiety or pain—are stored in memory, the process is different. All bets are off. The amygdala is activated, and that memory is coded and stored differently. In effect, the "time tag" is removed—so that when the traumatic experiences are later recalled, they feel "present." And the memory has the ability to activate the fear response in the present moment—even though the trauma being remembered was a long time ago—because the intensity of the memory causes part of the brain to react as if the trauma were happening again right now. PTSD is the constant intrusion into the mind of traumatic memories and a reexperiencing of the events as if the event had just happened. As Dr. Ramachandran has pointed out, it is this preoccupation with the trauma that can be so disabling.

Even if we know intellectually that the events were long ago, the specialized and robust memory circuits in the fear centers of the brain reexperience the traumatic events when they are remembered and drive the same kinds of responses—such as a faster heartbeat and increased feelings of fear—that would be driven if the experiences were actually occurring at the time.

Structural similarities between previous experiences and subsequent ones can cause the fear centers of the brain to pull memories forward and force them into the present moment. If a subsequent experience is even superficially similar to a traumatic memory, it can wield incredible power over emotions and can trigger the same fear responses evoked by the original trauma.

Moreover, reasoned analysis of the superficial nature of these structural similarities has very little influence over the fear center of the brain and seldom dissipates the power of the fearful memory. Yet the fear center has incredible influence over the reasoning process and also over the way memories are shaped. As UCLA research psychologist Dr. Michael Fanselow describes, "The available evidence suggests the amygdala learns and stores information about fear-arousing events *but also modulates* storage of other types of information *in different brain regions*" (emphasis added).

When human beings developed a higher order of thinking, we gained an advantage in being able to anticipate emerging threats. We gained the ability to conceptualize threats instead of just perceiving them. But we also gained the ability to conceptualize *imaginary* threats. And when groups of people are persuaded to conceptualize these imaginary threats, they can activate the fear response as powerfully as would *real* threats.

This ability to conceive of something that activates the amygdala and starts the fear response is particularly significant because of another important and closely related phenomenon, called "vicarious traumatization." If someone, such as a family member or an individual with whom we identify has experienced trauma, that person's feelings can be communicated to us even though we didn't directly experience the traumatic event.

Recent research proves that the telling of traumatic stories to those who feel linked by identity to the victims of trauma—whether the shared identity is ethnic, religious, historical, cultural, linguistic, tribal, or nationalistic—can actually produce emotional and physical responses in the listener similar to those experienced by the victims.

Indeed, physiologists have recently discovered a new class of neurons, called "mirror neurons," that create a powerful physical capacity for empathy. Dr. Ramachandran described the startling significance of this new finding to me:

> It has long been known that neurons in this region (a part of the brain called the anterior cingulate that receives a major input from the amygdala) fire when you poke the patient to cause pain—so they were called "pain sensing neurons" on the assumption that they alert the organism to potential danger—leading to avoidance. But researchers in Toronto found that in human patients some of these cells responded not only when the patient himself was poked with a needle—as expected—but

also fired equally when the patient watched *another* patient being poked. These neurons (mirror neurons) were dissolving the barrier between the "self" and others—showing that our brains are actually "wired up" for empathy and compassion. Notice that one isn't being metaphorical in saying this; the neurons in question simply can't tell if you or the other person is being poked. It's as if the mirror neurons were doing a virtual reality simulation of what's going on in the other person's brain—thereby almost "feeling" the other's pain. (I call them Dalai Lama cells.)

Therapists first discovered the powerful phenomenon of vicarious traumatization well before the discovery of the mirror neurons that explain how it works. Dr. I. Lisa McCann and Dr. Laurie Ann Pearlman offer the original definition of vicarious traumatization as "the enduring psychological consequences for therapists of exposure to the traumatic experience of victim clients. Persons who work with victims may experience profound psychological effects, effects that can be disruptive and painful for the helper and persist for months or years after work with traumatized persons."

Throughout the world, stories about past traumas and tragedies are passed down from one generation to the next. Long before television added new punch and power to the ability of storytellers to elicit emotional responses, vivid verbal descriptions of traumas physically suffered by others evoked extremely powerful reactions—even centuries after the original traumas occurred.

In the early summer of 2001, Tipper and I went to Greece. While we were there, the pope made a historic visit to Greece, and was met with thousands of angry demonstrators holding signs, yelling epithets. I looked into what was going on. They were angry about something that had happened eight hundred years ago: The Fourth Crusade had stopped off in Constantinople, sacked the city, and weakened it for the later overthrow by the Turks. And they're angry today, eight hundred years later.

To take a second example, Slobodan Milošević, in the early summer of 1989, went to the plains of Kosovo on the six-hundredth anniversary of the battle that defeated the Serbian Empire in its heyday. Government spokesmen said a million and a half people came. Western estimates said a million people came, covering the hillsides to listen to him speak. In his speech, Milošević revivified the battle of six hundred years earlier. And in the years that followed that collective retraumatization, a brutal campaign of violent expulsion began against the Croats and the Bosnians and the Kosovars at least in part because there was a vicarious experience of a trauma six centuries earlier that activated in the physical bodies of the individuals present, in this generation a response as if they were reliving that fear of so long ago.

If you look at the conflicts on the Indian subcontinent, in Sri Lanka, in Africa, in Northern Ireland, in the Middle East—indeed, in almost every conflict zone in the entire world—you will find an element of amygdala politics based on vicarious traumatization, feeding off memories of past tragedies. In each case, there is a political process that attempts to solve these conflicts through reasoned discourse. But such a response is insufficient to dissipate the continuing power of the reawakened and revivified traumatic memories. We need new mechanisms, like the Truth and Reconciliation Commission in South Africa—or mechanisms not yet invented—to deal with the role of collective vicarious traumatic memory in driving long-running conflicts.

The principal way we now tell stories in our culture is over television. As I noted, forty years have passed since the majority of Americans adopted television as their primary source of information. As we've seen, its dominance has become so extensive that the average American spends two-thirds of his or her "discretionary time" (time other than working, sleeping, and commuting) watching television. And virtually all significant political communication now takes place within the confines of flickering thirty-second television advertisements.

Research shows that television can produce "vicarious traumatization" for millions. Survey findings after the attacks of September 11 showed that people who had frequently watched television exhibited more symptoms of traumatization than less frequent TV viewers. One analyst of this study said of respondents describing their reactions to 9/11, "Those who watched the most television reported the most stress."

The physical effects of watching trauma on television—the rise in blood pressure and heart rate—are the same as if an individual has actually experienced the traumatic event directly. Moreover, it has been documented that television can create false memories that are just as powerful as normal memories. When recalled, television-created memories have the same control over the emotional system as do real memories.

And the consequences are predictable. People who watch television news routinely have the impression that the cities where they live are far more dangerous than they really are. Researchers have also found that even when statistics measuring specific crimes actually show steady decreases, the measured fear of those same crimes goes up as television portrayal of those crimes goes up. And the portrayal of crime often increases because consultants for television station owners have advised their clients that viewership increases when violent crime leads newscasts. This phenomenon has reshaped local television news.

Many of the national morning programs now lead with crime and murders, and we'll watch them for hours because they are so compelling. The visual imagery on television can activate parts of the brain involved in emotions in a way that reading about the same event cannot.

Television's ability to evoke the fear response is especially significant because Americans spend so much of their lives watching TV. An important explanation for why we spend so much time motionless in front of the screen is that television constantly triggers the "orienting response" in our brains.

As I noted in the introduction, the purpose of the orienting response is to immediately establish in the present moment whether or not fear is appropriate by determining whether or not the sudden movement that has attracted attention is evidence of a legitimate threat. (The orienting response also serves to immediately focus attention on potential prey or on individuals of the opposite sex.) When there is a sudden movement in our field of vision, somewhere deep below the conscious brain a message is sent: *LOOK!* So we do. When our ancestors saw the leaves move, their emotional response was different from and more subtle than fear. The response might be described as "Red Alert! Pay attention!"

Now, television commercials and many action sequences on television routinely activate that orienting reflex once per second. And since we in this country, on average, watch television more than four and a half hours per day, those circuits of the brain are constantly being activated.

The constant and repetitive triggering of the orienting response induces a quasi-hypnotic state. It partially immobilizes viewers and creates an addiction to the constant stimulation of two areas of the brain: the amygdala and the hippocampus (part of the brain's memory and contextualizing system). It's almost as though we have a "receptor" for television in our brains.

When I was a boy growing up on our family farm in the summers, I learned how to hypnotize chickens. You hold the chicken down and then circle your finger around its head, making sure that its eyes trace your hand movement. After a sufficient number of circles, the chicken will become entranced and completely immobile. There's a lot you can do with a hypnotized chicken. You can use it as a paperweight, or you can use it as a doorstop, and either way, the chicken will sit there motionless, staring blankly. (What you can't do is use it as a football. Something about being thrown through the air seemed to wake that chicken right up.)

It turns out that the immobility response in animals is an area that has received some scholarly attention, and here is one thing the scientists have found: The immobility response is *strongly* influenced by fear. A fear stimulus causes the chicken's amygdala to signal the release of neurochemicals, and controlled experiments show that they make immobility much more likely.

No, I'm not saying that television viewers are like hypnotized chickens. But there may be some lessons for us larger-brained humans in the experiences of barnyard hens. I remember times in my youth when I spent hours in front of a TV without noticing how much time had passed. My own experience tells me that extended television watching can be mind numbing.

That is one of the reasons why I feel so passionately about connecting the television medium to the Internet and opening it up to the creativity and talent of individuals. I believe it is extremely important to pay considerably more attention to the quality and integrity of television programming made by citizens. That is also one of the reasons I am concerned about the potential for exploitation of the television medium by those who seek to use it to manipulate public opinion in ways that bypass reason and logic.

Television's quasi-hypnotic effect is one reason that the political economy supported by the television industry is as different from the vibrant politics of America's first century as those politics were different from the feudalism that thrived on the ignorance of the masses of people in the Dark Ages.

Our systematic exposure to fear and other arousal stimuli on television can be exploited by the clever public relations specialist, advertiser, or politician. Barry Glassner, a professor of sociology at the University of Southern California, argues that there are three techniques that together make up "fearmongering": repetition, making the irregular seem regular, and misdirection. By using these narrative tools, anyone with a loud platform can ratchet up public anxieties and fears, distorting public discourse and reason.

There are, of course, many historical examples of vivid imagery producing vicarious traumatization that has been used for positive purposes. For example, the images of civil rights protesters being threatened with snarling dogs and being brutalized with fire hoses helped mobilize ordinary Americans to become part of a broader movement for social justice. In my own experience, I have learned that visual images—pictures, graphs, cartoons, and computer models—communicate information about the climate crisis at a level deeper than words alone could convey. Similarly, the horrifying pictures that came back to us from both Vietnam and the Iraq war helped facilitate shifts in public sentiment against failing wars that needed to end.

Even though logic and reason have played more prominent roles in the medium of print, they can also be used along with images to powerful and positive effect in the television medium. In fact, visual images of suffering are significant precisely because they can help generate empathy and goodwill. The horrifying pictures from inside Abu Ghraib prison communicated the essence of the wrongdoing there far more powerfully than any words could have. Even so, when such strong feelings are manipulated, the possibility for abuse becomes considerable.

It is well documented that humans are especially fearful of threats that can be easily pictured or imagined. For example, one study found that people are willing to spend significantly more for flight insurance that covers "death from 'terrorist acts'" than for flight insurance that covers "death from 'all possible causes.'" Now, logically, flight insurance for death by any cause would cover terrorism in addition to a number of other potential problems. But something about the buzzword *terrorism* creates a vivid impression that generates excessive fear.

The flight insurance example highlights another psychological phenomenon that is important to understanding how fear influences our thinking: "probability neglect." Social scientists have found that when confronted with either an enormous threat or a huge reward, people tend to focus on the magnitude of the consequence and ignore the probability.

Consider how the Bush administration has used some of the techniques identified by Professor Glassner. Repeating the same threat over and over again, misdirecting attention (from al Qaeda to Saddam Hussein), and using vivid imagery (a "mushroom cloud over an American city").

September 11 had a profound impact on all of us. But after initially responding in an entirely appropriate way, the administration began to heighten and distort public fear of terrorism to create a political case for attacking Iraq. Despite the absence of proof, Iraq was said to be working hand in hand with al-Qaeda and to be on the verge of a nuclear weapons capability. Defeating Saddam was conflated with bringing war to the terrorists, even though it really meant diverting attention and resources from those who actually attacked us.

When the president of the United States stood before the people of this nation and invited us to "imagine" a terrorist attack with a nuclear weapon, he was referring to terrorists who actually had no connection to Iraq. But because our nation had been subjected to the horrors of 9/11, when our president said "imagine with me this new fear," it was easy enough to bypass the reasoning process that might otherwise have led people to ask, "Wait a minute, Mr. President, where's your evidence?"

Even if you believe that Iraq might have posed a threat to us, I hope you will agree that our nation would have benefited from a full and thorough debate about the wisdom of invading that country. Had we weighed the potential benefits of an invasion against the potential risks, perhaps we could have prevented some of the tragic events now unfolding there.

Terrorism relies on the stimulation of fear for political ends. Indeed, its specific goal is to distort the political reality of a nation by creating fear in the general population that is hugely disproportionate to the actual danger that the terrorists are capable of posing. Ironically, President Bush's response to the terrorist attack of September 11 was, in effect, to further distort America's political reality by creating a new fear of Iraq that was hugely disproportionate to the actual danger Iraq was capable of posing. That is one of the reasons it was so troubling to so many when in 2004 the widely respected arms expert David Kay concluded a lengthy, extensive investigation into the administration's claim that Iraq posed an enormous threat because it had weapons of mass destruction with the words *We were all wrong.*

As we now know, of course, there was absolutely no connection between Osama bin Laden and Saddam Hussein. In spite of that fact, President Bush actually said to the nation at a time of greatly enhanced vulnerability to the fear of attack, "You can't distinguish between al-Qaeda and Saddam."

History will surely judge America's decision to invade and occupy a fragile and unstable nation that did not attack us and posed no threat to us as a decision that was not only tragic but absurd. Saddam Hussein was a brutal dictator, to be sure, but not one who posed an imminent danger to us. It is a decision that could have been made only at a moment in time when reason was playing a sharply diminished role in our national deliberations.

Thomas Jefferson would have recognized the linkage between absurd tragedy and the absence of reason. As he wrote to James Smith in 1822, "Man, once surrendering his reason, has no remaining guard against absurdities the most monstrous, and like a ship without rudder, is the sport of every wind."

I spoke at the Iowa Democratic Convention in the fall of 2001. Earlier in August, I had prepared a very different kind of speech. But in the aftermath of this tragedy, I proudly, with complete and total sincerity, stood before the Democrats of Iowa and said, "George W. Bush is my president, and I will follow him, as will we all, in this time of crisis." I was one of millions who felt that same sentiment and gave the president my total trust, asking him to lead us wisely and well. But he redirected the focus of America's revenge onto Iraq, a nation that had nothing whatsoever to do with September 11.

The fear campaign aimed at selling the Iraq war was timed precisely for the kickoff of the 2002 midterm election. The president's chief of staff explained the timing as a marketing decision. It was timed, Andrew Card said, for the post–Labor Day advertising period because that's when advertising campaigns for "new products," as he referred to it, are normally launched. The implication of his metaphor was that the old product—the war against Osama bin Laden—had lost some of its pizzazz. And in the immediate run-up to the election campaign of 2002, a new product—the war against Iraq—was being launched. For everything there is a season, particularly for the politics of fear.

The president went to war verbally against terrorists in virtually every campaign speech and fund-raising dinner for his political party. It was his main political theme. Democratic candidates like Senator Max Cleland in Georgia, a triple-amputee Vietnam vet, were labeled unpatriotic for voting counter to the White House's wishes on obscure amendments to the homeland security bill.

And when Tom DeLay, the former Republican leader in the House of Representatives, was embroiled in an effort to pick up more congressional seats in Texas by forcing a highly unusual redistricting vote in the state senate, he was able to track down Democratic legislators who fled the state to prevent a quorum—and thus prevent the vote—by enlisting the help of President Bush's new Department of Homeland Security. As many as thirteen employees of the Federal Aviation Administration conducted an eight-hour search, joined by at least one FBI agent (though several other agents who were asked to help refused to do so). DeLay was admonished by the House Ethics Committee but refused to acknowledge any wrongdoing.

By locating the Democrats quickly with the technology put in place for tracking terrorists, the Republicans were able to succeed in focusing public pressure on the weakest of the senators and forced passage of their new political redistricting plan. Thanks in part to the efforts of three different federal agencies,

Bush and DeLay were able to celebrate the gain of up to seven new Republican congressional seats.

This persistent effort to politicize the war in Iraq and the war against terrorism for partisan advantage is obviously harmful to the prospects for bipartisan support of the nation's security policies. By sharp contrast, consider the different approach that was taken by Prime Minister Winston Churchill during the terrible days of October 1943 when, in the midst of World War II, he faced a controversy with the potential to divide his bipartisan coalition. He said,

> What holds us together is the prosecution of the war. No ... man has been asked to give up his convictions. That would be indecent and improper. We are held together by something outside, which rivets our attention. The principle that we work on is, "Everything for the war, whether controversial or not, and nothing controversial that is not bona fide for the war." That is our position. We must also be careful that a pretext is not made of war needs to introduce far-reaching social or political changes by a side wind.

What Churchill warned against is exactly what the Bush administration has attempted to do, using the war against terrorism for partisan advantage and introducing far-reaching changes in social policy in order to consolidate its political power.

On many other issues as well, it is now clear that the Bush administration has resorted to the language and politics of fear in order to short-circuit debate and drive the public agenda without regard to the evidence, the facts, or the public interest. As I will discuss later in chapter 5, the administration has not hesitated to use fear of terrorism to attack measures in place for a generation to prevent a repetition of Cold War abuses of authority by the FBI and the intelligence community. Fear of terrorism has also conveniently distracted the American people from pesky domestic issues such as the economy, which was beginning to seriously worry the White House in the summer of 2002.

Rather than leading with a call to courage, this administration has chosen to lead by inciting fear. In the 2006 election campaign, Bush was even more explicit, saying that "if Democrats win, the terrorists win."

There is legitimate fear, of course, and a legitimate and responsible way to address it. But fear of death rouses us like no other. It is unconscionable to use forged documents and false arguments to generate such panic by convincing Americans that terrorists are going to detonate nuclear weapons in cities where they live.

When physical survival is connected to a conjured fear, that fear has a qualitatively different aspect. All fears should be talked about and can be talked about in a responsible way if they're real and if they're dealt with in a way that has integrity. But the intentional creation of false fears for political purposes is harmful to our democracy.

Of course, the use of fear as a political tool is not new. American history is rife with examples, "Remember the *Maine*" and the Gulf of Tonkin Resolution to mention only two. I personally recall the way President Richard Nixon used the fear of violent crime in the midterm elections of 1970.

It was a campaign I saw firsthand. My father, who was the bravest politician I have ever known, was slandered as unpatriotic because he opposed the Vietnam War; he was accused of being an atheist because he opposed a constitutional amendment to foster government-sponsored prayer in the public schools.

I was in the military at the time, on my way to Vietnam as an army journalist in an engineering battalion. I was on leave the week of the election. Law and order, court-ordered busing, a campaign of fear emphasizing crime—these were the other big issues that year. It was a sleazy campaign by Nixon, one that is now regarded by political historians as a watershed, marking a sharp decline in the tone of our national discourse.

In many ways, George W. Bush reminds me more of Nixon than of any other president. Like Bush, Nixon subordinated virtually every principle to his hunger for reelection. He instituted wage and price controls with as little regard for his conservative principles as President Bush has shown in piling up trillions of dollars of debt.

After the oil embargo of 1973, Nixon secretly threatened a military invasion of the Middle Eastern oil fields. Now Bush has actually done it, keeping his true intentions secret, as Nixon did. After he was driven from office in disgrace, Nixon confided to one of his regular interlocutors: "People react to fear, not love. They don't teach that in Sunday school, but it's true."

Speaking on national television the night before that 1970 election, Senator Ed Muskie of Maine addressed the real choice confronting the voters: "There are only two kinds of politics. They're not radical and reactionary or conservative and liberal or even Democratic and Republican. There are only the politics of fear and the politics of trust. One says you are encircled by monstrous dangers. Give us power over your freedom so we may protect you. The other says the world is a baffling and hazardous place, but it can be shaped to the will of men.

"Cast your vote," he concluded, "for trust in the ancient traditions of this home for freedom."

The next day, my father was defeated—defeated by the politics of fear. But his courage in standing for principle made me so proud and inspired me. I really felt that he had won something more important than an election. In his speech that night, he stood the old segregationist slogan on its head and defiantly promised, "The truth shall rise again." I wasn't the only person who heard that promise, nor was I the only one for whom that hope still rings loud and true.

But before such a hope can be realized, we need to understand the implications of fear's new prominence in our democracy. In the following chapter, I will explore why, in an atmosphere of constant fear, the public is more likely to discard reason and turn to leaders who demonstrate dogmatic faith in ideological viewpoints. These new demagogues don't actually offer greater security from danger, but their simplistic and frequently vitriolic beliefs and statements can provide comfort to a fearful society.

Unfortunately, the rise of these leaders serves only to exacerbate the decline of reason and further jeopardize our democracy.

Trade-Offs Between Civil Liberties and National Security: A Discrete Choice Experiment

Eric Andrew Finkelstein, Carol Mansfield, Dallas Wood,
Brent Rowe, Junxing Chay, and Semra Ozdemir

We explore differences in perception of national security policies between self-identified liberals, moderates, and conservatives from a national sample of U.S. adults. Using a discrete choice experiment, we also quantify each group's willingness to trade off select policies in exchange for reduced risk of a 9/11-style terrorist attack. Relative to other groups, liberals are more likely to view such policies as ineffective and susceptible to government abuse. They also perceive a lower threat of terrorism. All groups are willing to make trade-offs between civil liberties and risk of a terrorist attack. However, loss of civil liberties affects liberals more than conservatives. (JEL D61, H41, H56)

Abbreviations

DCE: Discrete Choice Experiment
DHS: Department of Homeland Security
KN: Knowledge Networks
RUM: Random Utility Model

I. Introduction

The September 11th, 2001, terrorist attacks shocked the nation and the world, inflicting emotional and financial costs that would be impossible to fully enumerate. In an effort to prevent future attacks, in October 2001, President George W. Bush signed the USA Patriot Act into law. At that time, both liberals and conservatives overwhelmingly supported this law (it passed the Senate 98 to 1) which made it easier for government agencies to clandestinely gather intelligence, monitor and regulate financial transactions, and broadened the discretion of law enforcement and immigration authorities to detain, perhaps indefinitely, and/or deport immigrants suspected of terrorism-related acts, among other provisions. Major provisions of the law have been extended since 2001, once in 2005 by President Bush and again in 2011 by President Obama in the National Defense Authorization Act. This is despite growing concern that several aspects of the Act severely impinge upon civil liberties (Coghlan 2011; Kain 2011; Ramasastry 2005).

Beyond the Patriot Act, in 2003 then Defense Secretary Donald Rumsfeld approved the use of "enhanced interrogation techniques," including water boarding, where water is poured over the head of a captive to simulate the sensation of drowning (Greenberg, Rosenberg, and de Vouge 2008). These techniques became the subject of much public debate in the late 2000s. This debate subsided in 2009 when President Obama issued an executive order barring the CIA from using water boarding or similar interrogation techniques (Isikoff 2009).

Other policies, such as enhanced screening at airports, are seen both as an invasion of privacy and an inconvenience, and, not surprisingly, public support is mixed for these as well (Cohen and Halsey 2010). The June 2013 leak surrounding the National Security Agency's secret surveillance programs, which involved tracking citizens' phone calls and internet activity, reinvigorated public debate concerning how much leeway the government should have in its fight against terrorism. When it comes to these programs, reaction again is mixed; a Pew Research Center (2013) poll fielded within a month after the leak found that 51% of Americans view the programs as unacceptable. Putting legal issues aside, what these examples reveal is that, in an effort to reduce the risk of terrorist attacks, policymakers are faced with the delicate task of increasing the security of the nation without overly impinging on civil liberties or imposing an undue burden on the public.

Viscusi and Zeckhauser (2003) present a theoretical model depicting trade-offs between civil liberties and security. They present a series of indifference curves with varying levels of utility where individuals are indifferent between given bundles of civil liberties and security. They further assume that individuals have a perceived frontier (similar to a production possibilities frontier) that traces out the maximum perceived level of security associated with any given level of civil liberties. Optimality occurs at the tangency point: when individuals reach the highest possible indifference curve that does not extend beyond the perceived frontier.

Consistent with this model, a number of published studies have shown that Americans recognize and are willing to accept trade-offs between civil liberties and terrorism risk reduction (Davis and Silver 2004; Garcia and Geva 2014; Mondak and Hurwitz 2012). Other studies show that individuals are willing to accept other types of inconveniences, such as longer waiting times at airports (Smith, Mansfield, and Clayton 2009; Viscusi and Zeckhauser 2003), and are willing to pay higher taxes (Smith, Mansfield, and Clayton 2009) to reduce terrorism risk. However, these studies do not quantify the reduction in civil liberties and/or personal freedoms that individuals would be willing to accept in exchange for reduced risk of a terrorist attack nor do they explore results separately by political ideology.

Whereas the theoretical model suggests that all individuals are willing to make trade-offs between civil liberties and security, the optimal level of each varies by political ideology. For example, if liberals, on average, place a greater emphasis on civil liberties than do conservatives, then for a liberal to be indifferent to a reduction in civil liberties, they must be compensated with greater improvements in security than what a conservative would require. Second, if liberals perceive a greater likelihood that the government would abuse security policies, they would again require more effective policies before they would willingly accept them. Finally, if liberals view the likelihood of future attacks as lower, this would alter their perceived trade-off curve and optimality would occur at a greater level of civil liberties.

Using data from a national survey of U.S. adults, we explore beliefs about homeland security policies and quantify the extent to which individuals are willing to trade off civil liberties in exchange for increased security. We then test whether the estimates vary by political affiliation. Specifically, we hypothesize that liberals, compared to moderates and then conservatives (1) believe the threat of a terrorist attack to be lower, (2) believe that national security policies are more likely to be abused by government officials, and (3) believe that such policies are less likely to be effective. With regards to policy preferences, we hypothesize that, *ceteris paribus*, liberals place more weight on protecting civil liberties than do moderates or conservatives and thus would be willing to accept greater risk of terrorist attacks. We test this hypothesis using data collected from a stated-preference discrete choice experiment (DCE) survey that quantifies individuals' willingness to trade off select features of homeland security policies in exchange for risk of a 9/11 style terrorist attack. The nonmarket nature of terrorism risk and homeland security policies makes DCE an effective tool to quantify differences in strength of preferences. Given the abstract nature of the policies, we do not view the specific dollar amounts calculated as precise estimates of willingness to pay, but rather as a way to quantify trade-offs across multiple attributes and provide insights into the public's preferences about homeland security policies. In addition to exploring the factors driving differences in preferences between political groups, we also investigate the welfare consequences of adopting different homeland security policies.

The remainder of the paper proceeds as follows. Section II describes the survey design and methods for analysis. Section III presents select survey results, including results of the DCE analyses. Section IV concludes with a discussion of policy implications.

II. Methods

A. Data Collection

To measure the risk and welfare trade-offs with select homeland security policies, we conducted a web-based survey administered to the online Knowledge Networks (KN) panel in November and December 2010.[1] Our sample consisted of individuals who are over the age of 18 and reside within the United States.

The survey consisted of five sections. The first section included questions on security-related behaviors. Respondents were asked about their perceptions

---

1. KN (now GfK) maintains a web-based panel of U.S. households that were originally recruited through random-digit dialing; more recently KN has begun using address-based sampling to recruit the panel (for more information on KN, see http://www.knowledgenetworks.com). If the household does not have a computer, KN provides the household with a computer and internet access. If the household does have a computer, KN pays for internet access. In return, the households agree to take a specific number of surveys. KN controls the number of survey invitations panel members receive. Samples for specific surveys are drawn from the panel using probability methods.

of airline travel and their travel habits, as this is the context in which most U.S. citizens are directly affected by counterterrorism policies. Questions on library, internet, and telephone use were also included as were perceptions about past terrorist events.

The second and third sections focused on introducing respondents to five counterterrorism policy levers: government access to personal information; racial or ethnic profiling; confinement of suspected terrorists; harsh methods of interrogation; and increasing taxes to fund counterterrorism efforts.

Respondents were given a short description of each of the five policy options (Table A1) and made familiar with the range of levels of these options to be used in the DCE section of the survey. A further set of questions about these options yielded data on the perceived effectiveness of these policies, the potential for abuse, and the level of support. Questions on terrorism outcomes, including an estimate of the number of deaths in the United States from terrorism over the next 10 years were also included.

The final section of the survey, after the DCE questions, collected information about opinions and personal characteristics, including demographics and political leanings (liberal, moderate, or conservative). To ascertain political leaning, the survey contained a question from the American National Election Survey: "When it comes to politics, do you usually think of yourself as: extremely liberal; liberal; slightly liberal; moderate or middle of the road; slightly conservative; conservative; or extremely conservative?" We combined the first and last three categories to represent liberals and conservatives, respectively, and left moderates to include those respondents who selected the middle category.

The fourth section of the survey was the DCE section. DCE is a type of stated-preference survey (Hensher, Rose, and Greene 2005). Goods, services, or policies are defined by a set of attributes. Respondents evaluate a series of tasks that require them to choose amongst these goods, services, or policies and their choices reveal the rate at which they are willing to trade off attributes and attribute levels against each other. DCE has been widely used in consumer product marketing and also to evaluate health, environmental, and transportation programs and policies. In recent years, this method has been used to evaluate the social welfare implications of government homeland security policies (Smith, Mansfield, and Clayton 2009). The nonmarket nature of many of the costs and benefits associated with homeland security policies makes stated-preference surveys one of the few appropriate methods to evaluate public preferences (Kanninen 2007).

Attributes and levels for the policy options were determined by consulting the literature, through a series of one-on-one interviews, and through feedback from social scientists at the Human Factors Division (now called the Resilient Systems Division) of the Department of Homeland Security.[2] Levels were further

---

2. The final choices for the survey questions were made by the authors and do not reflect the opinions of the Department of Homeland Security.

refined via analysis of results from two pilot studies. All attributes and levels are given in Table 1. The National Security Outcome is defined as "the chance that a major terrorist attack occurs on U.S. soil that kills 3,000 individuals over the next 10 years." For each policy option considered, respondents were told to assume that the outcomes were accurate predictions made by a panel of experts.

Prior to beginning the DCE questions, respondents were shown text that encouraged them to answer the DCE questions assuming these were real choices. The purpose of this text, referred to as "cheap talk" was to mitigate the problem of hypothetical bias that can occur in stated-preference surveys (Özdemir, Johnson, and Hauber 2009). Respondents were also told to assume that there were no legal barriers to implementing the policy choices and to assume that only tax increases could be used to pay for these policies. Table 2 provides the full set of text presented to participants prior to the start of the DCE section.

Table 1. Attributes and Levels

Attributes	Levels
Increasing your taxes to fund efforts to prevent terrorism	$500 over the next 10 years or $50 per year on average $1,500 over the next 10 years or $150 per year on average $3,000 over the next 10 years or $300 per year on average $7,000 over the next 10 years or $700 per year on average
Government access to personal information	Never allowed Allowed but only with a judge's permission Allowed if suspected of terrorist activity but without a judge's permission Always allowed
Using race, ethnicity, or country of citizenship to identify potential terrorists	Never allowed Allowed based on country of citizenship only Always allowed
Jailing suspected terrorists without trial	Less than 6 months 6 months to 2 years 2–7 years Indefinite (no limit)
Using harsh methods to question suspected terrorists	Never allowed in any case Allowed, but only after approval from a responsible official (like a judge) and to prevent a possible imminent attack Allowed, but only after approval from a responsible official (like a judge) regardless of whether an attack is imminent Allowed whenever the questioner thinks it might be effective in gathering information that will help in the fight against terrorism
National security outcomes	0.0% chance of an attack will occur 0.1% chance of an attack that will kill 3000 people 1.0% chance of an attack that will kill 3000 people 5.0% chance of an attack that will kill 3000 people 7.0% chance of an attack that will kill 3000 people

Table 2. Introductory Text for Stated-Preference Questions

In the next set of questions, imagine that the U.S. government is proposing different policy options for combating terrorism and you are being asked to choose between each option. These options are created from a mix of the different security strategies we have asked you to think about earlier in the survey. Below each policy option, we list the expected probability that a terrorist attack will kill 3,000 individuals on U.S. soil if the option is chosen.

Please respond to each of these questions. We understand that choosing between each policy option may not be easy, but your results will be of value in determining how U.S. residents respond to various trade-offs related to homeland security.

Consider each choice carefully and as though they are real choices. Think carefully about the benefits and costs of each option. How would you feel if the policy option you chose were implemented by the government?

Assume all the strategies we ask you to consider are legal. It is possible that some options will contain strategies that are not allowed under current U.S. law. For the purpose of this survey, please ignore this fact and assume all strategies are legal when selecting which option you prefer.

Assume only tax increases can be used to pay for the policies. We understand that many respondents might prefer that other government programs be cut in order to pay for these policies. However, for the purposes of this survey we are interested in your willingness to pay for increased security with your own tax dollars. So, for simplicity, please assume that these tax increases are necessary to pay for the policies.

The DCE section required respondents to choose between two hypothetical homeland security policies with varying levels of the key policy options and the outcome variable. A sample task for the survey is presented in Figure 1. The experimental design was generated by Sawtooth Choice Based Conjoint software, which uses an iterative algorithm to produce a design that is statistically efficient, minimizes level overlap, and ensures level balance (Zwerina, Huber, and Kuhfeld 1996). The design for the survey produced 25 versions of four choice tasks. Respondents were randomly assigned to one of these versions.

	Option A	Option B
Increase in your taxes to fund efforts to prevent terrorism over the next 10 years	$500 over the next 10 years ($50/year on average)	$3000 over the next 10 years ($300/year on average)
Government access to personal information	Allowed, but only with a judge's permission	Allowed, but only with a judge's permission
Using race, ethnicity, or country of citizenship to identify potential terrorists	Not allowed	Not allowed
Jailing suspected terrorists without trial	Less than 6 months	Less than 6 months
Using harsh methods to question suspected terrorists	Allowed, but only with approval from responsible official to prevent imminent attack	Allowed, but only with approval from responsible official to prevent imminent attack

National Security Outcomes

Chance that 3000 deaths from terrorism will occur on U.S. soil over the next 10 years	Chances are 70 out of 1000 (7%)	Chances are 10 out of 1000 (1%)
If these were your only two options, which would you choose?		

©Hayden-McNeil, LLC

Figure 1. Example Conjoint Task

In addition to the four choice tasks from the experimental design, each respondent was given three more choice tasks which were the same for all respondents to ensure data quality and check the reliability of the data. First, a warmup choice task was included where only two attributes were allowed to differ—taxes and terrorism risk (Figure A1). Data collected from this question were excluded from the analysis below but this simplified choice task served as a practice question so that quality of responses to subsequent questions would be improved. Second, a choice task was included where one option was clearly better than the other to test whether respondents were paying careful attention to the choice tasks (Figure A2). Specifically, Option B had lower taxes and lower risk of terrorist attack than Option A. The levels of the other attributes were the same between the two options as preferences differ for these attributes. Lastly, a holdout task was included to test the predictive validity of our data analysis. The attribute levels of this task were so that they overlapped well with the levels presented in the other choice tasks and so that neither option dominated the other (Figure A3).

The holdout task was used to test the out-of-sample prediction performance of the econometric model. Specifically, the model was estimated using only the answers to the four choice tasks generated from an experimental design. The results of the model were then used to predict how respondents would answer the hold-out choice task. These predictions were then compared to the actual choices of respondents to evaluate how well the model performs. If the model accurately predicts respondent's choices, this lends additional credibility to the results.

1. How effective do you believe using harsh and painful methods to question a suspected terrorist is for gaining information and reducing terrorist threats?
   - ☐ Very effective
   - ☐ Somewhat effective
   - ☐ Somewhat ineffective
   - ☐ Very ineffective

2. How likely do you think it is that if U.S. government officials were allowed to use harsh and painful methods when questioning suspected terrorists, this policy would be abused by government officials?
   - ☐ Very likely
   - ☐ Somewhat likely
   - ☐ Somewhat unlikely
   - ☐ Very unlikely

Figure 2. Example Questions—Harsh Methods

B. Data Analysis

In the theoretical model discussed in Section II, an individual's policy choices depend on their perceived risk of terrorism for any given level of civil liberties, perceived effectiveness of counterterrorism policies, perceived likelihood of abuse, and relative preferences for both goods. We use the data collected in the 2010 survey to investigate how liberals, moderates, and conservatives differ in their perceptions of each of these factors. We hypothesize that liberals, compared to moderates or conservatives, are more likely to believe that counterterrorism policies are unlikely to be effective and also more likely to believe that these policies would be abused by government. To test these hypotheses, we first examined the percent of each group selecting different response categories. We then estimated logistic regression models where the dependent variable was based on (1) a question that asked respondents to evaluate the effectiveness of each counterterrorism policy and (2) a question concerning how likely it is that the policy would be abused by government officials. For example, Figure 2 contains the questions pertaining to harsh methods for interrogation.

We collapsed responses for each question into dichotomous variables (effective or not effective, likely or unlikely) and estimated the odds of (1) effectiveness and (2) likelihood of abuse as a function of self-described political leaning (liberal, moderate, or conservative). Each regression included dummy variables for political leaning (with liberals as the omitted reference category). Covariates in both sets of regressions included age, gender, race, education, whether or not the respondent has a household income of over $35,000, and employment status.

We also estimated the perceived risk of a terrorist attack using data collected from two questions. The first question asked respondents what they thought the likelihood was of a terrorist attack killing at least 3,000 people in the next 10 years. The second question asked respondents to predict the number of expected deaths from terrorism over this same time period. We fitted Generalized Linear Models to determine the association between the expected risk of a terrorist attack and the expected number of deaths from terrorism as a function of political leanings using the same covariates as described above. For expected risk, we specified the Binomial family with a logit link, for the expected number of deaths we specified the Negative Binomial family with a log link. We hypothesized that liberals will predict the least number of deaths from terrorism, followed by moderates and conservatives.

C. Methods for Measuring Differences in Policy Preferences: Results of the DCE

In addition to differences in perceived policy constraints, our theoretical discussion also revealed that policy choices can be driven by differences in preferences over the importance of protecting civil liberties. To measure differences in policy preferences, we analyzed responses to the DCE tasks using a random utility model (RUM; Hensher, Rose, and Greene 2005). For each policy option j, the total utility (u_j) is determined by the observable component of utility (v_j) and a random error term (ε_j) representing the component of utility which is unobservable:

$$u_j = v_j + \varepsilon_j$$

Assuming participants are rational, respondents will choose the option that gives them the highest expected utility. Given this framework, the probability that option j will be chosen over option k is $\Pr(u_j > u_k) = \Pr(\varepsilon_k - \varepsilon_j < v_j - v_k)$. The random error terms are assumed to be independently and identically distributed extreme value. We use the mixed logit model (Train 2003) to account for possible heterogeneity in preferences:

$$v_{ij} = \beta'_i x_j + \gamma_{p(i)} t_j + \delta_{p(i)} r_j$$
$$\beta_{ik} \sim N(\beta_{p(i)k}, \sigma_k)$$

The observable component of utility (v_{ij}) of an individual i for policy j is approximated by a linear combination of the civil liberties attributes ($\mathbf{x}_j$), increase in taxes (t_j) and the risk of a major terrorist attack (r_j) over the next 10 years. The contribution of policy features to v_{ij} is weighted by random individual-specific preference weights (β_i), while the contribution of tax increases and risk of major terrorist attack are weighted by fixed affiliation-specific preference weights $(\gamma_{p(i)}$ and $\delta_{p(i)})$. Each kth element in β_i is independently and identically distributed normal with affiliation-specific mean $\beta_{p(i)k}$ and standard deviation σ_k. Tax and national security outcome attributes were coded as continuous variables whereas the other attributes were effects coded. Effects coding allows for comparisons of relative preferences of attribute levels. The model was estimated over the whole sample, with interaction terms between all attribute levels and political affiliation.

D. Net Welfare Change Calculations

The welfare gain or loss for a given change in a policy is the amount of money (or, in this case, increase in taxes) that would leave a respondent indifferent between a new policy and an existing one. If we assume x_1 to represent the vector of attribute levels of civil liberties for a new policy while x_0 to represent the same for an existing policy, then the change in welfare for a given change in attribute levels is the level of increase in taxes (t^*) which satisfies the following equation:

$$v_{i1} = \beta_i'x_1 + \gamma_{p(i)}t^* + \delta_{p(i)}r_1 = \beta_i'x_0 + \delta_{p(i)}r_0 = v_{i0}$$

Hence the welfare change is given as $t^* = \beta_i'(x_1 - x_0) / \gamma_{p(i)}$. We estimated the change in welfare for each political group following a shift from their least to most preferred level of a given civil liberty attribute, and also following a shift from a common baseline policy to policies with different levels of restrictions on civil liberties.

Similarly, the maximum acceptable risk of a terrorist attack for a given change in attribute-levels is given as $r^* = \beta_i'(x_1 - x_0) / \delta_{p(i)}$. We also estimated the maximum acceptable risk of a terrorist attack that each political group is willing to accept to transition from their most to their least preferred level, and also to transition from a common baseline policy to policies with different levels of restrictions on civil liberties.

III. Results

A. Sample Characteristics

Of 973 individuals who were invited to take this survey, 782 individuals responded; yielding a completion rate of 80%. However, 53 individuals who did not respond to the DCE choice tasks and 78 individuals who failed the consistency test—as discussed below—were excluded from the analysis; leaving the final sample size to 652.

Table 3 presents descriptive statistics for respondents of the survey as compared to the 2010 U.S. Census. Although KN's panel is designed to be representative of the U.S. adult population, unweighted, individual samples are not guaranteed to match the U.S. population. Compared to the 2010 U.S.

Census, our sample is 12 years older and differs along several other dimensions, although in many cases the magnitude of the differences is small. In particular, the distribution of political affiliation in the sample is not significantly different from census (p = 0.9407). Also income differences across political groups were insignificant (p = 0.1424).

Table 3. Descriptive Statistics

	Survey Sample	Census
Sample size	652	
General demographics[a]		
Age (median)	49*	36
Female	47%	51%
Income (above $35,000)[b]	58%*	66%
College graduate or some college	60%*	55%
Race, ethnicity, nationality[a]		
Non-white	23%	26%
U.S. citizen	97%*	93%
Employment status[c]		
Employed	57%	58%
Unemployed	9%*	6%
Not in labor force	34%	35%
Political beliefs[d]		
Liberal	28%	29%
Moderate	32%	29%
Conservative	40%	43%

[a]General demographic and race/ethnicity/nationality data were obtained from the American Community Survey (2011) as national averages for 2005–2009.

[b]Approximately 10% of respondents refused to provide information about their income.

[c]Employment status data were obtained from U.S. Bureau of Labor Statistics (BLS) (2010) and reflect annual U.S. estimates for 2010.

[d]Data regarding U.S. political beliefs were obtained from the American National Election Survey (ANES) Guide to Public Opinion and Electoral Behavior (2009) and reflect 2008 estimates.

*Estimates are significantly different from census data estimates at the 5% level.

Table 4 reports the percentage of respondents who believe the different countermeasures would be effective, stratified by political affiliation.[3] Consistent with our hypotheses, in each case liberals were least likely to believe these strategies would be effective, followed by moderates and then conservatives. All three groups believed that allowing government greater access to personal information would be an effective counterterrorism policy, with effectiveness ranging from 79% for liberals to roughly 87% for moderates and conservatives. Liberals were more suspicious of the effectiveness of racial profiling and harsh methods of interrogation, with only 51% believing these to be effective policies. That figure climbed to over 70% for moderates and over 83% for conservatives.

---

3. The effectiveness question was not asked for jailing suspected terrorists without trial.

Although all three groups believed the threat of government abuse of these policies is high, as expected, liberals reported the highest likelihood of abuse, with values ranging from 89% for jailing suspected terrorists without trial to 93% for allowing greater access to personal information. Although percentages were lower, conservatives also recognized the high potential for abuse, with estimates ranging from 68% for jailing without trial to 89% for greater access to personal information. Moderates were generally somewhere in between.

The three groups also differed greatly on the perceived threat of a terrorist attack over the next 10 years. Whereas only 20% of liberals believed there would be a major terrorist attack on U.S. soil over the next 10 years, this figure was 26% for moderates and 34% for conservatives. Liberals also believed the attack was likely to be less severe. They predicted mean deaths from such an attack of 1,100, whereas moderates predicted over 13,000 deaths and conservatives predicted over 42,000. These differences, in addition to differences in perceived effectiveness and likelihood of abuse, were likely to drive differences in preferences for select counterterrorism measures.

Table 5 presents results of the logistic regressions that explore whether or not the differences by political affiliation remain after controlling for other covariates. Differences in perceived effectiveness of greater access to personal information were not significantly different across the three groups after taking differences in sociodemographics into account. Those over age 50, blacks, and the "other" race category were more likely to perceive this measure to be effective. For racial profiling and harsh methods of interrogation, even after controlling for differences in sociodemographics, liberals remained less likely to believe these measures to be effective, followed by moderates and then conservatives, and in each case, the magnitude of the differences was large. Those over age 50 and those from higher income households were more likely to believe racial profiling to be effective. As compared to whites, blacks also were more likely to believe harsh methods of interrogation to be effective. Few other variables were predictive across the different policy options.

Table 6 presents logistic regression results for the likelihood of abuse for each of the four counterterrorism policies. Results were generally consistent with the unadjusted results of Table 4 with liberals much more likely to believe these policies would be abused by government, followed by moderates and then conservatives. Those over age 50 reported a statistically significant lower likelihood of abuse for access to personal information and harsh methods of interrogation. Those from higher income households also reported lower likelihoods of abuse, with differences statistically significant for racial profiling and harsh methods of interrogation. As with the results for effectiveness of these policies, few other variables were predictive.

Table 4. Perception of Counterterrorism Policies and Risk of Terrorist Attack by Political Affiliation

	Political Affiliation		
Perception of Counterterrorism Policies and Perceived Risk of Terrorist Attack	Liberals (n = 182)	Moderates (n = 209)	Conservatives (n = 261)
% who believe counterterrorism policy to be effective (SE)			
Access to personal information	79.3% (4.0%)	87.0% (2.7%)	87.8% (2.1%)
Racial profiling	51.8% (4.8%)	70.9% (3.7%)	87.9% (2.2%)
Harsh methods	51.4% (4.8%)	71.3% (3.9%)	82.8% (2.8%)
% who believe policy will likely be abused by the government (SE)			
Access to personal information	93.4% (1.9%)	86.1% (2.8%)	89.1% (2.5%)
Racial profiling	89.0% (2.3%)	81.4% (3.1%)	70.3% (3.6%)
Harsh methods	92.8% (1.9%)	80.1% (3.5%)	71.7% (3.5%)
Jailing	88.7% (3.0%)	73.4% (3.8%)	67.9% (3.5%)
Perceived threat of terrorist attack over the next 10 years			
Mean likelihood of an attack (SE)	20.0% (2.0%)	25.7% (2.1%)	33.8% (2.2%)
Mean deaths in thousands (SE)	1.1 (0.1)	13.1 (9.6)	42.5 (31.7)

Table 5. Logit Model of Association between Perceived Effectiveness of Counterterrorism Policies and Political Affiliation after Controlling for Covariates

Variables	Odds Ratio (SE)		
	Access to Personal Information	Racial Profiling	Harsh Methods
Liberal	Reference		
Moderate	1.690 (0.610)	1.889* (0.524)	2.979* (0.854)
Conservative	1.561 (0.518)	6.225* (1.929)	4.903* (1.457)
Age under 50	Reference		
Age over 50	2.036* (0.600)	2.099* (0.647)	1.144 (0.306)
Male	Reference		
Female	1.101 (0.313)	1.307 (0.319)	1.075 (0.253)
Income under $35,000	Reference		
Income over $35,000	1.109 (0.357)	1.739* (0.479)	1.296 (0.362)
High school diploma or lower	Reference		
College graduate or some college	0.605 (0.190)	0.309* (0.088)	1.034 (0.267)
White	Reference		
Black	4.341* (2.650)	0.749 (0.291)	2.278* (0.981)
Asian	0.938 (0.646)	0.833 (0.482)	0.629 (0.368)
Other	1.251* (0.779)	0.878 (0.375)	0.696 (0.322)
Employed	Reference		
Unemployed	0.810 (0.416)	1.047 (0.425)	2.098 (1.016)
Not in labor force	1.147 (0.378)	0.788 (0.246)	0.923 (0.271)
Constant	3.772* (1.646)	1.603 (0.584)	0.728 (0.287)

$^*p < 0.05$.

Table 6. Logit Model of Association between Perceived Likelihood of Abuse of Counterterrorism Policies and Political Affiliation after Controlling for Covariates

| Variables | Odds Ratio (SE) | | | |
	Access to Personal Information	Racial Profiling	Harsh Methods	Jailing
Liberal	Reference			
Moderate	0.334* (0.145)	0.612 (0.204)	0.311* (0.119)	0.366* (0.136)
Conservative	0.402 (0.199)	0.298* (0.102)	0.169* (0.062)	0.256* (0.091)
Age under 50	Reference			
Age over 50	0.461* (0.159)	1.084 (0.295)	0.558* (0.155)	0.677 (0.175)
Male	Reference			
Female	0.644 (0.220)	0.763 (0.196)	1.229 (0.335)	1.076 (0.248)
Income under $35,000	Reference			
Income over $35,000	0.762 (0.304)	0.476* (0.142)	0.409* (0.129)	0.791 (0.248)
High school diploma or lower	Reference			
College graduate or some college	0.899 (0.327)	1.603 (0.437)	1.010 (0.291)	0.906 (0.243)
White	Reference			
Black	0.471 (0.315)	0.966 (0.501)	1.125 (0.665)	1.247 (0.568)
Asian	1.468 (1.128)	4.111 (2.997)	0.711 (0.645)	16.936* (18.151)
Other	0.179* (0.079)	0.979 (0.471)	0.663 (0.316)	0.746 (0.321)
Employed	Reference			
Unemployed	1.102 (0.765)	0.863 (0.402)	2.348 (1.509)	1.515 (0.732)
Not in labor force	0.999 (0.356)	0.825 (0.258)	1.099 (0.319)	1.204 (0.348)
Constant	55.705* (31.956)	11.067* (4.606)	28.522* (11.981)	9.579* (4.831)

*$p < 0.05$.

Table 7 presents regression adjusted results for the expected number of deaths from terrorism over the next 10 years and the expected risk of a terrorist attack that kills more than 3,000 people. For expected number of deaths from terrorism, the ordering is similar to that reported in Table 4 but smaller in magnitude. This results because other variables that differed across the three groups also influenced this prediction. *Ceteris paribus*, older adults, those with higher income, and the "other" race category also reported higher predictions, whereas females, those with greater levels of education, and blacks reported lower estimates. Results are similar for predictions of expected risk of a terrorist attack, although differences between liberals and moderates were not statistically significant nor were the racial differences or differences in education and income levels.

B. Results on Data Validity

In the choice task where we tested attention, 78 individuals failed to choose the better option. We dropped these respondents from the analysis, as we believe that these respondents were not paying close attention to the attributes and levels or they did not understand the task they were given. The results from the hold-out task analysis show that the predicted uptake for Option A is 60% and it is 40% for Option B; the actual choice of Option A is 59% and it is 41% for Option B. These results indicate that when predicting out-of-sample choices, the RUM model performs well.

C. DCE Results—Measuring Differences in Policy Preferences

Table 7. Generalized Linear Model of Association between Expected Number of Deaths from Terrorism Over the Next 10 Years and Political Affiliation after Controlling for Covariates

Variables	Log of Expected Number of Deaths (SE)	Logit of Expected Risk of a Terrorist Attack (SE)
Liberal	Reference	Reference
Moderate	1.093* (0.362)	0.244 (0.168)
Conservative	1.230* (0.241)	0.690* (0.158)
Age under 50	Reference	Reference
Age over 50	1.107* (0.372)	0.394* (0.145)
Male	Reference	Reference
Female	−0.516* (0.259)	−0.293* (0.131)
Income under $35,000	Reference	Reference
Income over $35,000	0.867* (0.303)	0.087 (0.146)
High school diploma or lower	Reference	Reference
College graduate or some college	−0.728* (0.317)	−0.274 (0.139)
White	Reference	Reference
Black	−1.046* (0.333)	−0.136 (0.238)
Asian	0.127 (0.544)	0.666 (0.486)
Other	2.749* (0.767)	−0.151 (0.269)
Employed	Reference	Reference
Unemployed	−0.147 (0.423)	−0.319 (0.223)
Not in labor force	−0.109 (0.375)	−0.139 (0.156)
Constant	6.972* (0.339)	−1.204* (0.196)

*$p < 0.05$.

Mixed logit results from the DCE data are shown in Table A2 and graphically in Figure 3. In Table A2, the first three columns show the estimated mean preference weights for each attribute level, conditional on political affiliation. Reference levels are fixed at zero and attribute levels associated with larger values indicate greater preferences. The last column of Table A2 reports standard deviations of the preferences weights, which were assumed to be uniform across political affiliations. The standard deviations were significant for "always allowing government access to personal information" and for "2 to 7 years of jailing suspected terrorists without trial." Hence, these variables had the highest taste heterogeneity.

Figure 3 conveys the regression coefficients rescaled, via a positive affine transformation, such that the sum of the coefficients within an attribute is set to 5 (as opposed to 0 due to effects coding) and the scale ranges between 0 and 10. Since utility functions are unique up to a positive affine transformation, the rescaled coefficients represent the same preferences as in Table A2. Figure 3 provides a visual representation of the optimal policy for each political affiliation but also makes clear that there is considerable uncertainty around the estimates.

The figure reveals that all three groups showed a strong aversion for always allowing government access to personal information. Liberals and moderaters did not have strong preferences over racial profiling, whereas conservatives were opposed to never allowing profiling. Neither moderates nor conservatives had strong preferences in terms of duration of jailing suspected terrorists without a trial, whereas liberals were against holding them indefinitely.

The most striking difference was that in preferences for the use of harsh methods for interrogation. Liberals and moderates had strong preferences against these methods being always allowed but were indifferent over the levels for the remaining categories. Conservatives, however, were opposed to never allowing harsh methods, but differences across the remaining categories were not statistically significant.

Table 8 presents the maximum risk of a terrorist attack that each political group would willingly accept for a shift from the most restrictive set of policies to less restrictive policies. Liberals were willing to accept an 18% (95% C.I. 12%–24%) and 19% (95% C.I. 12%–25%) greater risk in the next 10 years for a shift from the "most restrictive" to the "less restrictive" and from the "most restrictive" to the "least restrictive" policies, respectively, whereas moderates were willing to accept an 11% (95% C.I. 7%–14%) and 9% (95% C.I. 5%–13%) greater risk for the same shift in policy. Conservatives were willing to accept a 6% (95% C.I. 2%–9%) greater terrorist risk for a shift from the "most restrictive" to the "less restrictive" policy; however, they were not willing to accept any increase in risk for a shift to the "least restrictive" policy. The differences in willingness to accept risk between liberals and conservatives for transition to both sets of policies were statistically significant.

Figure 3. Preferences by Political Affiliation

Table 8 also presents the welfare change for each group for a shift from the most restrictive but lowest risk (0.1%) of terrorist attack scenario to the least restrictive policy with highest risk of terrorist attack (7%). Liberals have a welfare gain of $1,333 (95% C.I. $594–$2,073) in the next 10 years, whereas moderates' welfare gain was not significant. Conservatives, however, because they prefer more restrictive policies, had a welfare loss of $590 (95% C.I. $219–$960). The overall welfare change would be a (nonsignificant) gain of $175 (95% C.I. −$96 to $447) per capita for the society.

IV. Discussion

The September 11th and more recent terror attacks have highlighted the vulnerability of nations to terrorism. To reduce the likelihood of these acts, governments can utilize a variety of policy options. However, an overriding theme of nearly all of these policies is that they come at a cost, both monetarily and in terms of an infringement on civil liberties, privacy, and personal freedoms. Prior to enactment of new homeland security policies, governments would benefit from a better understanding of the trade-offs the public is willing to make and how these trade-offs vary based on their perceptions of the level of threat, the effectiveness of the policies, and their trust in the government.

Table 8.

Group	Average Willingness to Accept Risk of Terrorist Attack Over the Next 10 Years in Order to Transit from the "Most Restrictive" Set of Policies to the "Less Restrictive" and the "Least Restrictive" Policies, Holding Tax Constant	
	Most Restrictive to Less Restrictive	Most Restrictive to Least Restrictive
Liberal	17.6% [11.6%; 23.6%]*	18.8% [12.1%; 25.4%]*
Moderate	10.6% [7.0%; 14.1%]*	9.1% [5.4%; 12.8%]*
Conservative	5.5% [1.8%; 9.3%]*	−0.2% [−3.9%; 3.6%]

Group	Average Willingness to Pay over the Next 10 Years in Order to Transit from the "Most Restrictive but Least Risky" Set of Policies to the "Least Restrictive but Most Risky" Set of Policies
	Most Restrictive to Least Restrictive
Liberal	$1,333 [$594; $2,073]*
Moderate	$188 [−$117; $493]
Conservative	−$590 [−$960; −$219]*

Note: 95% confidence intervals in square brackets.
*$p < 0.05$.

This study used a stated-preference DCE method to identify the preferred homeland security policies out of a set of predefined options, while recognizing that the individual impact of a given policy differs based on a variety of factors, including an individual's political views. Results suggest that self-identified liberals place a higher weight on policies that provide more protection of civil liberties/personal freedoms than self-identified conservatives or moderates. Liberals, for instance, were willing to accept higher terrorist risk to protect civil liberties than moderates and conservatives, and liberals had the strongest preferences, as measured by willingness to pay, for policies that placed the least restrictions on personal freedom and privacy. However, conservatives had stronger preferences for policies that allowed discretion in applying policies that might infringe on privacy and personal freedoms. These differences may reflect the greater trust conservatives have that the government will not abuse their power, rather than that conservatives value the protection of civil liberties less.

It should be noted that although this study is the first to quantify maximum acceptable terrorist risk and welfare changes separately by political affiliation for select homeland security policies, there is a significant political science literature related to the impact of political ideology on normative preferences. For example, Jenkins-Smith and Herron (2009) showed that preferences for the optimal balance between liberty and security were systematically influenced by political beliefs. As with our findings, liberals preferred the normative balance to be weighted toward liberty over security. However, conservatives preferred an emphasis on security over liberty. Other authors have found similar effects of ideology and partisanship in trade-offs between civil liberties and security (Davis 2007; Davis and Silver 2004); however, none have shown that liberals were willing to accept larger risks for less restrictive policies.

More recent studies show that the public is more likely to support counter-terror policies at the expense of restricted civil liberties if they perceive a greater threat of terrorism, perceive these policies to be effective at preventing such acts, and have high trust in the government (Garcia and Geva 2014; Van Es 2012). We found a similar pattern in our results: compared to liberals, conservatives perceive the threat of terrorism to be higher, perceive counterterrorism policies to be more effective, and have more trust in the government not to abuse policies. In fact, we find that beliefs about nearly every aspect of homeland security policy, ranging from likelihood of attack to perceived effectiveness to potential for abuse, differed by political affiliation. These differences likely drive the decision to align with a particular political group (i.e., they are endogenous). As such, it is not surprising that once political affiliation was included in the regression analyses, few other variables were predictive. The finding that blacks did not find racial profiling to be an effective measure is consistent with that reported by Viscusi and Zeckhauser (2003, 2005).

These results should be interpreted in light of several limitations. First, respondents were asked about the likelihood of 3,000 deaths in the next 10 years, which may prime and possibly influence their response to the open-ended question about the expected number of deaths over the next 10 years. This may be why the open-ended questions reported by Viscusi and Zeckhauser (2003, 2005) for the expected number of deaths in the next 12 months generated higher estimates than the ones reported in this paper. Second, although we presented a specific national security outcome for each policy, each respondent has their own opinion about the likelihood of terrorist acts, which influences their support for specific options. It is possible that in answering the questions, respondents relied on their own beliefs, in addition to the specified outcome, when choosing their preferred option. To the extent that respondents recoded the attribute levels to match their own beliefs, the respondents were evaluating different scenarios, which affect the comparisons of willingness to pay across groups. Third, although this study targeted a nationally representative sample, the sample used in our study differed from the averages from the Census data in some dimensions, so the results may not generalize to the population at large. For example, the mean age of the sample data is 12 years older than the U.S. Census data. Age over 50 years is associated with a great likelihood of self-identifying as conservative and was a significant predictor of opinions about the likelihood of abuse and effectiveness of different policies. Fourth, as with any stated-preference survey, respondents were asked to consider hypothetical policy options with hypothetical tax implications and effectiveness; alternately, if they were asked to vote on specific policies or if they believed their results would be used to set policy, they might provide different responses. In addition, our results are not applicable if the benefits of actual policies differed greatly from the range of estimates presented here.

Fifth, in some cases, differences across political groups were not statistically significant. For many comparisons, statistical significance likely would have been achieved with asking more DCE trade-off questions to each respondent, but we were limited in the number of questions possible given concerns of excess participant burden. DCE questions are not easy to answer and there is an inherent trade-off between breadth and depth when administering participant surveys. We chose to cover several domains in this survey, but recognize this as a limitation for making comparisons across political groups in the DCE section. Finally, public support for a particular counterterrorism policy will fluctuate over time and may vary for reasons beyond those included in the DCE section.

Despite these limitations, this study adds to the growing body of research on the attitudes and opinions of the American public toward homeland security policies. The study demonstrates the potential for stated-preference surveys to provide information on how people trade off the multiple dimensions of policies against each other, which can provide greater understanding of public preferences than surveys that ask about each issue separately.

Appendix A: Description of Attributes

Table A1. Counterterrorism Policy Options

Strategy	Short Description in Survey
Increasing taxes to fund efforts to prevent terrorism	The Department of Homeland Security (DHS) is one of several U.S. government agencies that work to reduce the risk of terrorist attacks on U.S. soil. It has been estimated that the average U.S. taxpayer spends roughly $200 to fund DHS each year. Of course, the specific amount an individual pays in taxes will depend on his/her income but $200 per year is an average across all taxpayers. One strategy that a government could take that might lower the threat of a terrorist attack is to increase taxes to fund additional efforts to prevent terrorism.
	Later in the survey, we will ask you to choose between options that increase *your* taxes by different amounts to fund government efforts to prevent terrorism. Under each option, the amount your taxes will increase ranges between:
	$500 over the next 10 years ($50 per year on average)
	$1,500 over the next 10 years ($150 per year on average)
	$3,000 over the next 10 years ($300 per year on average)
	$7,000 over the next 10 years ($700 per year on average)
Increasing government access to personal information	One strategy that governments could take that might lower the threat of a terrorist attack is to give government agencies more access to individuals' personal information, such as library records, e-mail messages, Web site use, and telephone calls.
	Later, we will ask you to choose between options that differ in terms of when the U.S. federal government is allowed to see the personal information of its citizens. Under each option, the level of government access to personal information will range between:
	Never allowed
	Allowed but only with a judge's permission
	Allowed if suspected of terrorist activity but without a judge's permission
	Always allowed
Using race, ethnicity, or country of citizenship to identify potential terrorists	One strategy that governments could take that might lower the threat of a terrorist attack is to identify potential terrorist suspects for investigation based on a person's race, ethnicity (where their family came from), or their country of citizenship.
	Later in the survey, we will ask you to choose between options that differ in terms of whether race, ethnic group, or country of citizenship can be used to identify potential terrorist suspects for investigation. Under each option, the use of race, ethnic group, or country of citizenship to identify potential terrorists will be either:
	Never allowed
	Allowed based on country of citizenship only
	Always allowed
Jailing suspected terrorists without trial	Another strategy that governments could take that might lower the threat of a terrorist attack is to keep suspected terrorists in jail for extended periods of time without a trial.
	Later, we will ask you to choose between options that differ in terms of how long people may be held *without a trial*. Under each option, the length of time a suspected terrorist can be jailed without a trial will range between:
	Less than 6 months
	6 months to 2 years
	2–7 years
	Indefinite (no limit)
Using harsh methods to question suspected terrorists	Another strategy that governments could take that might lower the threat of a terrorist attack is to use harsh and painful methods when questioning suspected terrorists to obtain information that might otherwise not be revealed.
	Later in the survey, we will ask you to choose between options that differ in terms of when harsh and painful methods can be used to question suspected terrorists. Under each option, the circumstances of when harsh and painful methods can be used to question suspected terrorists will range between:
	Never allowed in any case
	Allowed, but only after approval from a responsible official (like a judge) *and* to prevent a possible imminent attack
	Allowed, but only after approval from a responsible official (like a judge) regardless of whether an attack is imminent
	Allowed whenever the questioner thinks it might be effective in gathering information that will help in the fight against terrorism

Appendix B: Additional Tables and Figures

Table A2. Mixed Logit Coefficient Estimates by Political Affiliation

Variables	Mean (SE) Liberal (n = 182)	Moderate (n = 209)	Conservative (n = 261)	Standard Deviation (SE)
Tax[a]	−0.606* (0.124)	−1.043* (0.134)	−0.789 *(0.103)	NA[b]
National security outcome[a]	−0.136* (0.020)	−0.180* (0.021)	−0.132* (0.017)	NA[b]
Government access to personal information				
Never allowed		Reference[c]		
Allowed but only with a judge's permission	0.199* (0.097)	0.211* (0.097)	0.144 (0.078)	0.004 (0.220)
Allowed if suspected of terrorist activity but without a judge's permission	0.066 (0.102)	0.139 (0.095)	0.027 (0.081)	0.222 (0.196)
Always allowed	−0.469* (0.107)	−0.463* (0.101)	−0.222* (0.081)	0.305* (0.138)
Using race, ethnicity, or country of citizenship to identify potential terrorists				
Never allowed		Reference[c]		
Allowed based on country of citizenship only	0.067 (0.076)	−0.044 (0.072)	0.091 (0.061)	0.003 (0.237)
Always allowed	−0.129 (0.077)	−0.051 (0.077)	0.064 (0.062)	0.177 (0.148)
Jailing suspected terrorists without trial				
Less than 6 months		Reference[c]		
6 months to 2 years	0.198* (0.098)	0.129 (0.096)	0.105 (0.080)	0.000 (0.128)
2–7 years	0.024 (0.103)	0.047 (0.100)	−0.022 (0.081)	0.344* (0.131)
Indefinite (no limit)	−0.428* (0.103)	−0.189* (0.093)	−0.121 (0.078)	0.011 (0.187)
Using harsh methods to question suspected terrorists				
Never allowed		Reference[c]		
Allowed, but only with approval from responsible official to prevent imminent attack	0.152 (0.101)	0.062 (0.096)	0.197* (0.079)	0.001 (0.139)
Allowed, but only with approval from responsible official regardless of whether an attack is imminent	0.199* (0.096)	0.347* (0.095)	0.085 (0.077)	0.058 (0.380)
Always allowed	−0.702* (0.117)	−0.558* (0.113)	−0.022 (0.082)	0.220 (0.209)
Log Likelihood				−1531.43

[a] Coded as a linear term.

[b] Nonrandom coefficients.

[c] Value of reference category is the negative of the sum of the remaining categories.

*$p < 0.05$; tests whether the coefficient is significantly different than zero.

Government Policy Options to Improve Security

	Option A	Option B
Increase in your taxes to fund efforts to prevent terrorism over the next 10 years	$500 over the next 10 years ($50/year on average)	$3000 over the next 10 years ($300/year on average)
Government access to personal information	Allowed, but only with a judge's permission	Allowed, but only with a judge's permission
Using race, ethnicity, or country of citizenship to identify potential terrorists	Not allowed	Not allowed
Jailing suspected terrorists without trial	Less than 6 months	Less than 6 months
Using harsh methods to question suspected terrorists	Allowed, but only with approval from responsible official to prevent imminent attack	Allowed, but only with approval from responsible official to prevent imminent attack

National Security Outcomes

Chance that 3000 deaths from terrorism will occur on U.S. soil over the next 10 years	Chances are 70 out of 1000 (7%)	Chances are 10 out of 1000 (1%)
If these were your only two options, which would you choose?		

Figure A1. Warm-Up Choice Task

Government Policy Options to Improve Security

	Option A	Option B
Increase in your taxes to fund efforts to prevent terrorism over the next 10 years	$3000 over the next 10 years ($300/year on average)	$500 over the next 10 years ($50/year on average)
Government access to personal information	Allowed, but only with a judge's permission	Allowed, but only with a judge's permission
Using race, ethnicity, or country of citizenship to identify potential terrorists	Not allowed	Not allowed
Jailing suspected terrorists without trial	Less than 6 months	Less than 6 months
Using harsh methods to question suspected terrorists	Allowed, but only with approval from responsible official to prevent imminent attack	Allowed, but only with approval from responsible official to prevent imminent attack

National Security Outcomes

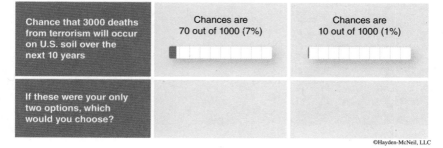

	Option A	Option B
Chance that 3000 deaths from terrorism will occur on U.S. soil over the next 10 years	Chances are 70 out of 1000 (7%)	Chances are 10 out of 1000 (1%)
If these were your only two options, which would you choose?		

Figure A2. Choice Task for Consistency Test

Government Strategies to Improve Security

	Option A	Option B
Increase in your taxes to fund efforts to prevent terrorism over the next 10 years	$7000 over the next 10 years ($700/year on average)	$1500 over the next 10 years ($150/year on average)
Government access to personal information	Allowed if suspected of terrorist activity, but without a judge's permission	Never allowed
Using race, ethnicity, or country of citizenship to identify potential terrorists	Allowed based on country of citizenship only	Never allowed
Jailing suspected terrorists without trial	Less than 6 months	6 months to 2 years
Using harsh methods to question suspected terrorists	Allowed, but only with approval from responsible official to prevent imminent attack	Never allowed

National Security Outcomes

Chance that 3000 deaths from terrorism will occur on U.S. soil over the next 10 years	Chances are 1 out of 1000 (0.1%)	Chances are 70 out of 1000 (7%)
If these were your only two options, which would you choose?		

©Hayden-McNeil, LLC

Figure A3. Hold-Out Task for Out-of-Sample Prediction

References

American Community Survey. "ACS Public Use Microdata Sample (Pums) 2005–2009 5-Year." 2011. Accessed August 13, 2013. http://factfinder2.census.gov/faces/tableservices/jsf/pages/productview.xhtml?pid=ACS_11_5YR_DP02&prodType=table.

Coghlan, J. "Patriot Act: A Civil Liberties Breach or a Foreign Policy Necessity?" *Foreign Policy Journal*, June 17, 2011. Accessed August 7, 2013. http://www.foreignpolicyjournal.com/2011/06/17/patriot-act-a-civil-liberties-breach-or-a-foreign-policy-necessity/.

Cohen, J., and A. Halsey. "Poll: Nearly Two-Thirds of Americans Support Full-Body Scanners at Airports." *Washington Post*, November 23, 2010.

Davis, D.W. *Negative Liberty: Public Opinion and the Terrorist Attacks on America*. New York: Russell Sage Foundation Publications, 2007.

Davis, D. W., and B. D. Silver. "Civil Liberties vs. Security: Public Opinion in the Context of the Terrorist Attacks on America." *American Journal of Political Science*, 48(1), 2004, 28–46.

Ellsberg, D. "Classic and Current Notions of 'Measurable Utility'." *The Economic Journal*, 64(255), 1954, 528–56.

Garcia, B. E., and N. Geva. "Security Versus Liberty in the Context of Counterterrorism: An Experimental Approach." *Terrorism and Political Violence*, 28(1), 2014, 30–48.

Greenberg, J. C., H. L. Rosenberg, and A. de Vouge. "Sources: Top Bush Advisors Approved 'Enhanced Interrogation'." *ABC News*, April 9, 2008.

Hensher, D. A., J. M. Rose, and W. H. Greene. *Applied Choice Analysis: A Primer*. Cambridge/New York: Cambridge University Press, 2005.

Isikoff, M. "Obama's Order Ends Bush-Era Interrogation Tactics." *Newsweek*, January 21, 2009. Accessed May 5, 2015. http://www.newsweek.com/obamas-order-ends-bush-era-interrogation-tactics-77965.

Jenkins-Smith, H. C., and K. G. Herron. "Rock and a Hard Place: Public Willingness to Trade Civil Rights and Liberties for Greater Security." *Politics & Policy*, 37(5), 2009, 1095–129.

Kain, E. "The National Defense Authorization Act Is the Greatest Threat to Civil Liberties Americans Face." *Forbes.com*, May 12, 2011.

Kanninen, B. J. *Valuing Environmental Amenities Using Stated Choice Studies: A Common Sense Approach to Theory and Practice*, Vol. 8. Berlin: Springer, 2007.

Mondak, J. J., and J. Hurwitz. "Examining the Terror Exception Terrorism and Commitments to Civil Liberties." *Public Opinion Quarterly*, 76(2), 2012, 193–213.

Özdemir, S., F. R. Johnson, and A. B. Hauber. "Hypothetical Bias, Cheap Talk, and Stated Willingness to Pay for Health Care." *Journal of Health Economics*, 28(4), 2009, 894–901.

Pew Research Center. *Majority Views NSA Phone Tracking as Acceptable Anti-Terror Tactic: Public Says Investigate Terrorism, Even if It Intrudes on Privacy*. Washington, DC: Pew Research Center, 2013.

Ramasastry, A. "Reform the Patriot Act to Ensure Civil Liberties." *CNN*, April 20, 2005.

Smith, V. K., C. Mansfield, and L. Clayton. "Valuing a Homeland Security Policy: Countermeasures for the Threats from Shoulder Mounted Missiles." *Journal of Risk and Uncertainty*, 38(3), 2009, 215–43.

Train, K. *Discrete Choice Methods with Simulation*. Cambridge: Cambridge University Press, 2003.

U.S. Bureau of Labor Statistics (BLS). "Current Population Study." 2010. Accessed August 13, 2013. http://www.bls.gov/cps/.

Van Es, R. "Public Opinions on Security and Civil Liberties in America after the Terrorist Attacks of September 11, 2001." *Social Cosmos*, 3(1), 2012, 118–23.

Viscusi, W. K., and R. J. Zeckhauser. "Sacrificing Civil Liberties to Reduce Terrorism Risks." *Journal of Risk and Uncertainty*, 26(2), 2003, 99–120.

———. "Recollection Bias and the Combat of Terrorism." *Journal of Legal Studies*, 34(1), 2005, 27–55.

Zwerina, K., J. Huber, and W. F. Kuhfeld. *A General Method for Constructing Efficient Choice Designs*. Durham, NC: Fuqua School of Business, Duke University, 1996.

Privacy and Cyber-Security

Compromising Over Technology, Security, and Privacy
Gus Hosein

The post-Snowden debates have often referred to an alleged trade-off between human rights and security that digital citizens need to negotiate, and to a balance that needs to be struck by policy makers. In this brief commentary, Gus Hosein problematizes the often uncritical discussion over an alleged balance between rights and security by addressing the recent conflict between Apple and the FBI over the encryption of mobile phones. He argues that an increase in privacy will also enhance the security of digital citizens.

How do we balance the need to secure society with the individual's right to privacy? Debates on surveillance and ubiquitous data monitoring by intelligence agencies often boil down to this question. It sounds logical and it allows us to reduce a complex technological issue to a widely understandable social concern. However, as I will argue, this is not a helpful way of approaching one of the key debates of our times.

To imagine a balance is to imagine that there are only two entities. Yet to limit our thinking to either the protection of privacy in the modern era, or the maintenance of a secure society, is a simplification that is inadequate for understanding the complex interplay between security and privacy. *Complex* here means that a far wider range of issues need to be considered than just the individual's demand for privacy and society's need to protect itself and its citizenry. Technology is one such, particularly elusive, issue.

The latest high-profile example of the interplay between security and privacy is the Apple and FBI court case from February 2016. In this case, the FBI asked the court to demand that Apple assist the FBI to gain access to the work phone of one of the San Bernardino attackers.[1] The device was secured by Apple's operating system, which included encryption that made the data inaccessible to the FBI. The FBI argued that Apple needed to compromise and build a system that allowed for government access to this one phone. This led to discussion in the United States and beyond about the balance between security and privacy, focused on issues of encryption. In March 2016, the U.S. attorney general stated that she supported "strong encryption," but not "warrant-proof encryption" (Geller, 2016). President Obama explained his position as follows:

> We recognize that just like all of our other rights, freedom of speech, freedom of religion, etc., that there are going to be some constraints imposed to ensure we are safe.

---

1. In December 2015, two attackers killed and seriously injured several dozen people at a San Bernardino County Department of Public Health training event and Christmas party.

I am of the view that there are very real reasons why we want to make sure the government cannot just wily-nilly [sic] get into everyone's iPhones or smartphones that are full of very personal information or very personal data.

We also want really strong encryption ... [though] there has to be some concession to the need to be able to get to that information somehow.

I suspect the answer will come down to how can we make sure the encryption is as strong as possible, the key is as strong as possible, it's accessible by the smallest number of people possible, for a subset of issues that we agree are important. (quoted in Constine, 2016, paras. 12–15)

His take appears nuanced, and the attorney general's distinction sounds logical. Both suggest that some form of political compromise is possible: Access could be given to phones belonging to a small number of reasonably targeted individuals, but not to the general public. Both point to a necessary balance—an equilibrium that involves taking a bit from one side (privacy) to give it to the other (security). This narrative presents a solution, as it states that compromise is possible and reasonable. And it is convenient because it simplifies complex problems.

Complicating Compromise

However, once we start dealing with technology, this act of compromise becomes far less clear. The specific characteristics, challenges, and opportunities of technology make the distinction between strong and warrant-proof encryption equivalent to supporting drinkable water, but not clean water. On the surface, the distinction may sound logical, but if we look at the details, it becomes more difficult.

To better understand this conundrum, we may turn toward the voices of experts. These "epistemic communities" have proven influential in challenging technology and science policy debates: In environmental debates, they are climate scientists; in food safety, they are biologists and agriculture experts. They may disagree among themselves on specifics, but on most matters, there is a common understanding.

In this current debate around privacy and security, and many related debates in our field, the experts are security researchers. They analyze the complications and risks of security, and the vast majority agree on the core issues. These include a widespread consensus that compromising encryption inevitably results in undermining the security of communication systems, and thus the security and privacy of Internet users. A number of seminal reports over the past 20 years have consistently explained and reaffirmed this position (Abelson et al., 1997; Abelson et al., 2015). Security experts typically accept that it is possible to build a "warrant-friendly" encryption system but warn that this would create significant risks that are deemed unacceptable to this expert community. According to them, the only safe encryption system is one that is likely to be described as "warrant-proof."

That coherence within the epistemic community is not shared by governments. As we know, not least, from the Snowden leaks, governments have significant surveillance interests, and they argue for "concessions" (as in the quote from President Obama) to encryption and Internet security. Yet, at the same time, former NSA directors have proclaimed that strong encryption is essential (Franceschi-Bicchierai, 2015). The FBI even once had content on their website advising smartphone users to encrypt their devices (Pagliery, 2016).

Although this dissonance seems confusing, it is sensible. A department of defense or national defense agency of any given country should resist another country's warrant-friendly encryption being forced on their own citizens because they would know that their citizens and government officials are subject to foreign attack and therefore need the strongest forms of protection. Law enforcement officials who want to see a reduction in phone thefts and identity fraud would welcome stronger locks and the use of encryption. At the same time, this may not be in the interest of the national security agent who wants to know what a foreign terrorist is doing and the law enforcement officials who investigate child porn, drugs, and gang activity.

What emerges from this perspective is that a distinction of security versus privacy is inadequate and simplistic. We can fight a war of rhetoric on the simple balance of those two entities, which is typically reflected in front pages and un-nuanced court cases. Or we can seek to introduce new voices and narratives and show how complex and fascinating this problem is. Then we may come to some resolution.

Does It Move?

As executive director of an organization campaigning on civil liberties, it is easy to extol the virtues of these alternative voices because, in this debate, those voices endorse my worldview. But at the moment, at least on digital security, they have the more profound arguments than the mere balancing of the goods of state security and user privacy.

We need to understand the social issues around us (laws, practices, cultures) as both movable and immovable, just as the technological issues around us (mathematics, security engineering, physics of materials, biology of DNA) are sometimes immovable and sometimes quite movable. In highly emotive debates about state power, national security, and the rule of law, the fact that these issues are mobile dynamics is sometimes forgotten.

For instance, for years we asked companies to include encryption in their products, but their engineers and business teams said it would be too expensive and users did not demand it. Those were supposedly the scientific realities. Yet we have managed to change their minds, to some extent, although government abuses and security failures also helped along the way. Now, as a result of our work (a bit) and the work of Edward Snowden (mostly), the articulations of the companies' engineers, and now some CEOs, are very different: Security has become a part of privacy.

The Apple v. FBI fight has demonstrated this. At long last, after years of civil libertarians saying so, Apple says that building strong security into their products is essential. Experts have found their voices and articulated a similar concern. The U.S. government argued in the court case that Apple should build a mechanism so that it could get access to the iPhone, to undo the security. It argued that this would only be used in this particular case and was not a substantial demand for such a rich company.

Experts varied in their opinions on this specific point, and Apple raised many security contentions. My own organization contributed to the debate by stating in our amicus brief that the international precedent is too great. Others spoke out on the political and legal implications. But everyone agreed on the fundamental premise—even the attorney general and the president of the United States have now said it: Building strong security into our systems is essential.

The FBI almost stands alone in saying that there is no risk in building a single solution to compromise the security of a single phone. And when you start including in the balance the importance of the security measures in the phone, the value of digital security to our economy, how global commerce and social infrastructure relies on this security, and how Apple operates in many different markets and under different legal regimes, the problem becomes too complex to point to a simple balance.

A compromise here is not easy nor necessarily desirable. I relish this complexity. Now we only hope that courts everywhere will also relish it. Our legislatures, we hope, shall too. And so must the public.

References

Abelson, H., Anderson, R., Bellovin, S. M., Benaloh, J., Blaze, M., Diffie, W., ... Schneier, B. (1997). *The risks of key recovery, key escrow, and trusted third-party encryption.* Retrieved from https://www.schneier.com/cryptography/archives/1997/04/the_risks_of_key_rec.html

Abelson, H., Anderson, R., Bellovin, S. M., Benaloh, J., Blaze, M., Diffie, W., ... Weitzner, D. J. (2015). Keys under doormats: Mandating insecurity by requiring government access to all data and communications. *Journal of Cybersecurity, 1*(1), 69–79. Retrieved from http://cybersecurity.oxfordjournals.org/content/early/2015/11/17/cybsec.tyv009.full?ijkey=mjwJomF75oqYdwm&keytype=ref

Constine, J. (2016, March 11). What Obama said about encryption and tech's double-edged sword at SXSW. *Tech Crunch.* Retrieved from https://techcrunch.com/2016/03/11/obama-sxsw/

Franceschi-Bicchierai, L. (2015, October 6). Former NSA chief: I "would not support" encryption backdoors. *Motherboard.* Retrieved from http://motherboard.vice.com/read/former-nsa-chief-strongly-disagrees-with-current-nsa-chief-on-encryption

Geller, E. (2016, March 9). U.S. attorney general defends fight against Apple over terrorist's iPhone. *The Daily Dot.* Retrieved from http://www.dailydot.com/layer8/apple-doj-encryption-loretta-lynch-senate-judiciary-hearing/

Pagliery, J. (2016, January 13). Ex-NSA boss says FBI director is wrong on encryption. *CNN.* Retrieved from http://money.cnn.com/2016/01/13/technology/nsa-michael-hayden-encryption/

Why Protecting Privacy Is a Losing Game Today—
And How to Change the Game
Cameron F. Kerry

Introduction: Game Change?

There is a classic episode of the show "I Love Lucy" in which Lucy goes to work wrapping candies on an assembly line. The line keeps speeding up with the candies coming closer together and, as they keep getting farther and farther behind, Lucy and her sidekick Ethel scramble harder and harder to keep up. "I think we're fighting a losing game," Lucy says.

This is where we are with data privacy in America today. More and more data about each of us is being generated faster and faster from more and more devices, and we can't keep up. It's a losing game both for individuals and for our legal system. If we don't change the rules of the game soon, it will turn into a losing game for our economy and society.

The Cambridge Analytica drama has been the latest in a series of eruptions that have caught peoples' attention in ways that a steady stream of data breaches and misuses of data have not.

The first of these shocks was the Snowden revelations in 2013. These made for long-running and headline-grabbing stories that shined light on the amount of information about us that can end up in unexpected places. The disclosures also raised awareness of how much can be learned from such data ("we kill people based on metadata," former NSA and CIA Director Michael Hayden said).

The aftershocks were felt not only by the government, but also by American companies, especially those whose names and logos showed up in Snowden news stories. They faced suspicion from customers at home and market resistance from customers overseas. To rebuild trust, they pushed to disclose more about the volume of surveillance demands and for changes in surveillance laws. Apple, Microsoft, and Yahoo all engaged in public legal battles with the U.S. government.

Then came last year's Equifax breach that compromised identity information of almost 146 million Americans. It was not bigger than some of the lengthy roster of data breaches that preceded it, but it hit harder because it rippled through the financial system and affected individual consumers who never did business with Equifax directly but nevertheless had to deal with the impact of its credit scores on economic life. For these people, the breach was another demonstration of how much important data about them moves around without their control, but with an impact on their lives.

Now the Cambridge Analytica stories have unleashed even more intense public attention, complete with live network TV cut-ins to Mark Zuckerberg's congressional testimony. Not only were many of the people whose data was collected surprised that a company they never heard of got so much personal information, but the Cambridge Analytica story touches on all the controversies roiling around the role of social media in the cataclysm of the 2016 presidential election. Facebook estimates that Cambridge Analytica was able to leverage its "academic" research into data on some 87 million Americans (while before the 2016 election Cambridge Analytica's CEO Alexander Nix boasted of having profiles with 5,000 data points on 220 million Americans). With over two billion Facebook users worldwide, a lot of people have a stake in this issue and, like the Snowden stories, it is getting intense attention around the globe, as demonstrated by Mark Zuckerberg taking his legislative testimony on the road to the European Parliament.

The Snowden stories forced substantive changes to surveillance with enactment of U.S. legislation curtailing telephone metadata collection and increased transparency and safeguards in intelligence collection. Will all the hearings and public attention on Equifax and Cambridge Analytica bring analogous changes to the commercial sector in America?

I certainly hope so. I led the Obama administration task force that developed the "Consumer Privacy Bill of Rights" issued by the White House in 2012 with support from both businesses and privacy advocates, and then drafted legislation to put this bill of rights into law. The legislative proposal issued after I left the government did not get much traction, so this initiative remains unfinished business.

The Cambridge Analytica stories have spawned fresh calls for some federal privacy legislation from members of Congress in both parties, editorial boards, and commentators. With their marquee Zuckerberg hearings behind them, senators and congressmen are moving on to think about what do next. Some have already introduced bills and others are thinking about what privacy proposals might look like. The op-eds and Twitter threads on what to do have flowed. Various groups in Washington have been convening to develop proposals for legislation.

This time, proposals may land on more fertile ground. The chair of the Senate Commerce Committee, John Thune (R-SD) said "many of my colleagues on both sides of the aisle have been willing to defer to tech companies' efforts to regulate themselves, but this may be changing." A number of companies have been increasingly open to a discussion of a basic federal privacy law. Most notably, Zuckerberg told CNN "I'm not sure we shouldn't be regulated," and Apple's Tim Cook expressed his emphatic belief that self-regulation is no longer viable.

This is not just about damage control or accommodation to "techlash" and consumer frustration. For a while now, events have been changing the way that business interests view the prospect of federal privacy legislation. An increasing spread of state legislation on net neutrality, drones, educational technology, license plate readers, and other subjects and, especially broad new legislation in California pre-empting a ballot initiative, have made the possibility of a single set of federal rules across all 50 states look attractive. For multinational companies that have spent two years gearing up for compliance with the new data protection law that has now taken effect in the EU, dealing with a comprehensive U.S. law no longer looks as daunting. And more companies are seeing value in a common baseline that can provide people with reassurance about how their data is handled and protected against outliers and outlaws.

This change in the corporate sector opens the possibility that these interests can converge with those of privacy advocates in comprehensive federal legislation that provides effective protections for consumers. Trade-offs to get consistent federal rules that preempt some strong state laws and remedies will be difficult, but with a strong enough federal baseline, action can be achievable.

How Current Law Is Falling Behind

Snowden, Equifax, and Cambridge Analytica provide three conspicuous reasons to take action. There are really quintillions of reasons. That's how fast IBM estimates we are generating digital information, *quintillions* of bytes of data every day—a number followed by 30 zeros. This explosion is generated by the doubling of computer processing power every 18–24 months that has driven growth in information technology throughout the computer age, now compounded by the billions of devices that collect and transmit data, storage devices and data centers that make it cheaper and easier to keep the data from these devices, greater bandwidth to move that data faster, and more powerful and sophisticated software to extract information from this mass of data. All this is both enabled and magnified by the singularity of network effects—the value that is added by being connected to others in a network—in ways we are still learning.

This information Big Bang is doubling the volume of digital information in the world every two years. The data explosion that has put privacy and security in the spotlight will accelerate. Futurists and business forecasters debate just how many tens of billions of devices will be connected in the coming decades, but the order of magnitude is unmistakable—and staggering in its impact on the quantity and speed of bits of information moving around the globe. The pace of change is dizzying, and it will get even faster—far more dizzying than Lucy's assembly line.

Most recent proposals for privacy legislation aim at slices of the issues this explosion presents. The Equifax breach produced legislation aimed at data brokers. Responses to the role of Facebook and Twitter in public debate have focused on political ad disclosure, what to do about bots, or limits to online tracking for ads. Most state legislation has targeted specific topics like use of data from ed-tech products, access to social media accounts by employers, and privacy protections from drones and license-plate readers. Facebook's simplification and expansion of its privacy controls and recent federal privacy bills in reaction to events focus on increasing transparency and consumer choice. So does the newly enacted California Privacy Act.

Measures like these double down on the existing American privacy regime. The trouble is, this system cannot keep pace with the explosion of digital information, and the pervasiveness of this information has undermined key premises of these laws in ways that are increasingly glaring. Our current laws were designed to address collection and storage of structured data by government, business, and other organizations and are busting at the seams in a world where we are all connected and constantly sharing. It is time for a more comprehensive and ambitious approach. We need to think bigger, or we will continue to play a losing game.

Our existing laws developed as a series of responses to specific concerns, a checkerboard of federal and state laws, common law jurisprudence, and public and private enforcement that has built up over more than a century. It began with the famous Harvard Law Review article by (later) Justice Louis Brandeis and his law partner Samuel Warren in 1890 that provided a foundation for case law and state statutes for much of the 20th Century, much of which addressed the impact of mass media on individuals who wanted, as Warren and Brandeis put it, "to be let alone." The advent of mainframe computers saw the first data privacy laws adopted in 1974 to address the power of information in the hands of big institutions like banks and government: the federal Fair Credit Reporting Act that gives us access to information on credit reports and the Privacy Act that governs federal agencies. Today, our checkerboard of privacy and data security laws covers data that concerns people the most. These include health data, genetic information, student records and information pertaining to children in general, financial information, and electronic communications (with differing rules for telecommunications carriers, cable providers, and emails).

Outside of these specific sectors is not a completely lawless zone. With Alabama adopting a law last April, all 50 states now have laws requiring notification of data breaches (with variations in who has to be notified, how quickly, and in what circumstances). By making organizations focus on personal data and how they protect it, reinforced by exposure to public and private enforcement litigation, these laws have had a significant impact on privacy and security practices. In addition, since 2003, the Federal Trade Commission—under both Republican and Democratic majorities—has used its enforcement authority to regulate unfair and deceptive commercial practices and to police unreasonable privacy and information security practices. This enforcement, mirrored by many state attorneys general, has relied primarily on deceptiveness, based on failures to live up to privacy policies and other privacy promises.

These levers of enforcement in specific cases, as well as public exposure, can be powerful tools to protect privacy. But, in a world of technology that operates on a massive scale moving fast and doing things because one can, reacting to particular abuses after-the-fact does not provide enough guardrails.

As the data universe keeps expanding, more and more of it falls outside the various specific laws on the books. This includes most of the data we generate through such widespread uses as web searches, social media, e-commerce, and smartphone apps. The changes come faster than legislation or regulatory rules can adapt, and they erase the sectoral boundaries that have defined our privacy laws. Take my smart watch, for one example: data it generates about my heart rate and activity is covered by the Health Insurance Portability and Accountability Act (HIPAA) if it is shared with my doctor, but not when it goes to fitness apps like Strava (where I can compare my performance with my peers). Either way, it is the same data, just as sensitive to me and just as much of a risk in the wrong hands.

It makes little sense that protection of data should depend entirely on who happens to hold it. This arbitrariness will spread as more and more connected devices are embedded in everything from clothing to cars to home appliances to street furniture. Add to that striking changes in patterns of business integration and innovation—traditional telephone providers like Verizon and AT&T are entering entertainment, while startups launch into the provinces of financial institutions like currency trading and credit and all kinds of enterprises compete for space in the autonomous vehicle ecosystem—and the sectoral boundaries that have defined U.S. privacy protection cease to make any sense.

Putting so much data into so many hands also is changing the nature of information that is protected as private. To most people, "personal information" means information like social security numbers, account numbers, and other information that is unique to them. U.S. privacy laws reflect this conception by aiming at "personally identifiable information," but data scientists have repeatedly demonstrated that this focus can be too narrow. The aggregation and correlation of data from various sources make it increasingly possible to link supposedly anonymous information to specific individuals and to infer characteristics and information about them. The result is that today, a widening range of data has the potential to be personal information, i.e., to identify us uniquely. Few laws or regulations address this new reality.

Nowadays, almost every aspect of our lives is in the hands of some third party somewhere. This challenges judgments about "expectations of privacy" that have been a major premise for defining the scope of privacy protection. These judgments present binary choices: if private information is somehow public or in the hands of a third party, people often are deemed to have no expectation of privacy. This is particularly true when it comes to government access to information—emails, for example, are nominally less protected under our laws once they have been stored 180 days or more, and articles and activities in plain sight are considered categorically available to government authorities. But the concept also gets applied to commercial data in terms and conditions of service and to scraping of information on public websites, for two examples.

As more devices and sensors are deployed in the environments we pass through as we carry on our days, privacy will become impossible if we are deemed to have surrendered our privacy simply by going about the world or sharing it with any other person. Plenty of people have said privacy is dead, starting most famously with Sun Microsystems' Scott McNealy back in the 20th century ("you have zero privacy ... get over it") and echoed by a chorus of despairing writers since then. Without normative rules to provide a more constant anchor than shifting expectations, true privacy actually could be dead or dying. The Supreme Court may have something to say on the subject in we will need a broader set of norms to protect privacy in settings that have been considered public. Privacy can endure, but it needs a more enduring foundation.

The Supreme Court in its recent *Carpenter* decision recognized how constant streams of data about us change the ways that privacy should be protected. In holding that enforcement acquisition of cell phone location records requires a warrant, the Court considered the "detailed, encyclopedic, and effortlessly compiled" information available from cell service location records and "the seismic shifts in digital technology" that made these records available, and concluded that people do not necessarily surrender privacy interests to collect data they generate or by engaging in behavior that can be observed publicly. While there was disagreement among Justices as to the sources of privacy norms, two of the dissenters, Justice Alito and Gorsuch, pointed to "expectations of privacy" as vulnerable because they can erode or be defined away.

How this landmark privacy decision affects a wide variety of digital evidence will play out in criminal cases and not in the commercial sector. Nonetheless, the opinions in the case point to a need for a broader set of norms to protect privacy in settings that have been thought to make information public. Privacy can endure, but it needs a more enduring foundation.

Our existing laws also rely heavily on notice and consent—the privacy notices and privacy policies that we encounter online or receive from credit card companies and medical providers, and the boxes we check or forms we sign. These declarations are what provide the basis for the FTC to find deceptive practices and acts when companies fail to do what they said. This system follows the model of informed consent in medical care and human subject research, where consent is often asked for in person, and was imported into internet privacy in the 1990s. The notion of U.S. policy then was to foster growth of the internet by avoiding regulation and promoting a "market resolution" in which individuals would be informed about what data is collected and how it would be processed, and could make choices on this basis.

Maybe informed consent was practical two decades ago, but it is a fantasy today. In a constant stream of online interactions, especially on the small screens that now account for the majority of usage, it is unrealistic to read through privacy policies. And people simply don't.

It is not simply that any particular privacy policies "suck," as Senator John Kennedy (R-LA) put it in the Facebook hearings. Zeynep Tufecki is right that these disclosures are obscure and complex. Some forms of notice are necessary and attention to user experience can help, but the problem will persist no matter how well designed disclosures are. I can attest that writing a simple privacy policy is challenging, because these documents are legally enforceable and need to explain a variety of data uses; you can be simple and say too little or you can be complete but too complex. These notices have some useful function as a statement of policy against which regulators, journalists, privacy advocates, and even companies themselves can measure performance, but they are functionally useless for most people, and we rely on them to do too much.

At the end of the day, it is simply too much to read through even the plainest English privacy notice, and being familiar with the terms and conditions or privacy settings for all the services we use is out of the question. The recent flood of emails about privacy policies and consent forms we have gotten with the coming of the EU General Data Protection Regulation have offered new controls over what data is collected or information communicated, but how much have they really added to people's understanding? Wall Street Journal reporter Joanna Stern attempted to analyze all the ones she received (enough paper printed out to stretch more than the length of a football field), but resorted to scanning for a few specific issues. In today's world of constant connections, solutions that focus on increasing transparency and consumer choice are an incomplete response to current privacy challenges.

Moreover, individual choice becomes utterly meaningless as increasingly automated data collection leaves no opportunity for any real notice, much less individual consent. We don't get asked for consent to the terms of surveillance cameras on the streets or "beacons" in stores that pick up cell phone identifiers, and house guests aren't generally asked if they agree to homeowners' smart speakers picking up their speech. At best, a sign may be posted somewhere announcing that these devices are in place. As devices and sensors increasingly are deployed throughout the environments we pass through, some after-the-fact access and control can play a role, but old-fashioned notice and choice become impossible.

Ultimately, the familiar approaches ask too much of individual consumers. As the President's Council of Advisers on Science and Technology Policy found in a 2014 report on big data, "the conceptual problem with notice and choice is that it fundamentally places the burden of privacy protection on the individual," resulting in an unequal bargain, "a kind of market failure."

This is an impossible burden that creates an enormous disparity of information between the individual and the companies they deal with. As Frank Pasquale ardently dissects in his "Black Box Society," we know very little about how the businesses that collect our data operate. There is no practical way even a reasonably sophisticated person can get arms around the data that they generate and what that data says about them. After all, making sense of the expanding data universe is what data scientists do. Post-docs and Ph.D.s at MIT (where I am a visiting scholar at the Media Lab) as well as tens of thousands of data researchers like them in academia and business are constantly discovering new information that can be learned from data about people and new ways that businesses can—or do—use that information. How can the rest of us who are far from being data scientists hope to keep up?

As a result, the businesses that use the data know far more than we do about what our data consists of and what their algorithms say about us. Add this vast gulf in knowledge and power to the absence of any real give-and-take in our constant exchanges of information, and you have businesses able by and large to set the terms on which they collect and share this data.

This is not a "market resolution" that works. The Pew Research Center has tracked online trust and attitudes toward the internet and companies online. When Pew probed with surveys and focus groups in 2016, it found that "while many Americans are willing to share personal information in exchange for tangible benefits, they are often cautious about disclosing their information and frequently unhappy about what happens to that information once companies have collected it." Many people are "uncertain, resigned, and annoyed." There is a growing body of survey research in the same vein. Uncertainty, resignation, and annoyance hardly make a recipe for a healthy and sustainable marketplace, for trusted brands, or for consent of the governed.

Consider the example of the journalist Julia Angwin. She spent a year trying to live without leaving digital traces, which she described in her book "Dragnet Nation." Among other things, she avoided paying by credit card and established a fake identity to get a card for when she couldn't avoid using one; searched hard to find encrypted cloud services for most email; adopted burner phones that she turned off when not in use and used very little; and opted for paid subscription services in place of ad-supported ones. More than a practical guide to protecting one's data privacy, her year of living anonymously was an extended piece of performance art demonstrating how much digital surveillance reveals about our lives and how hard it is to avoid. The average person should not have to go to such obsessive lengths to ensure that their identities or other information they want to keep private stays private. We need a fair game.

Shaping Laws Capable of Keeping Up

As policymakers consider how the rules might change, the Consumer Privacy Bill of Rights we developed in the Obama administration has taken on new life as a model. *The Los Angeles Times*, *The Economist*, and *The New York Times* all pointed to this bill of rights in urging Congress to act on comprehensive privacy legislation, and the latter said "there is no need to start from scratch .." Our 2012 proposal needs adapting to changes in technology and politics, but it provides a starting point for today's policy discussion because of the wide input it got and the widely accepted principles it drew on.

The bill of rights articulated seven basic principles that should be legally enforceable by the Federal Trade Commission: individual control, transparency, respect for the context in which the data was obtained, access and accuracy, focused collection, security, and accountability. These broad principles are rooted in longstanding and globally-accepted "fair information practices principles." To reflect today's world of billions of devices interconnected through networks everywhere, though, they are intended to move away from static privacy notices and consent forms to a more dynamic framework, less focused on collection and process and more on how people are protected in the ways their data is handled. Not a checklist, but a toolbox. This principles-based approach was meant to be interpreted and fleshed out through codes of conduct and case-by-case FTC enforcement—iterative evolution, much the way both common law and information technology developed.

The other comprehensive model that is getting attention is the EU's newly effective General Data Protection Regulation. For those in the privacy world, this has been the dominant issue ever since it was approved two years ago, but even so, it was striking to hear "the GDPR" tossed around as a running topic of congressional questions for Mark Zuckerberg. The imminence of this law, its application to Facebook and many other American multinational companies, and its contrast with U.S. law made GDPR a hot topic. It has many people wondering why the U.S. does not have a similar law, and some saying the U.S. should follow the EU model.

I dealt with the EU law since it was in draft form while I led U.S. government engagement with the EU on privacy issues alongside developing our own proposal. Its interaction with U.S. law and commerce has been part of my life as an official, a writer and speaker on privacy issues, and a lawyer ever since. There's a lot of good in it, but it is not the right model for America.

What is good about the EU law? First of all, it is a law—one set of rules that applies to all personal data across the EU. Its focus on individual data rights in theory puts human beings at the center of privacy practices, and the process of complying with its detailed requirements has forced companies to take a close look at what data they are collecting, what they use it for, and how they keep it and share it—which has proved to be no small task. Although the EU regulation is rigid in numerous respects, it can be more subtle than is apparent at first glance. Most notably, its requirement that consent be explicit and freely given is often presented in summary reports as prohibiting collecting any personal data without consent; in fact, the regulation allows other grounds for collecting data and one effect of the strict definition of consent is to put more emphasis on these other grounds. How some of these subtleties play out will depend on how 40 different regulators across the EU apply the law, though. European advocacy groups were already pursuing claims against "*les GAFAM*" (Google, Amazon, Facebook, Apple, Microsoft) as the regulation went into effect.

The EU law has its origins in the same fair information practice principles as the Consumer Privacy Bill of Rights. But the EU law takes a much more prescriptive and process-oriented approach, spelling out how companies must manage privacy and keep records and including a "right to be forgotten" and other requirements hard to square with our First Amendment. Perhaps more significantly, it may not prove adaptable to artificial intelligence and new technologies like autonomous vehicles that need to aggregate masses of data for machine learning and smart infrastructure. Strict limits on the purposes of data use and retention may inhibit analytical leaps and beneficial new uses of information. A rule requiring human explanation of significant algorithmic decisions will shed light on algorithms and help prevent unfair discrimination but also may curb development of artificial intelligence. These provisions reflect a distrust of technology that is not universal in Europe but is a strong undercurrent of its political culture.

We need an American answer—a more common law approach adaptable to changes in technology—to enable data-driven knowledge and innovation while laying out guardrails to protect privacy. The Consumer Privacy Bill of Rights offers a blueprint for such an approach.

Sure, it needs work, but that's what the give-and-take of legislating is about. Its language on transparency came out sounding too much like notice-and-consent, for example. Its proposal for fleshing out the application of the bill of rights had a mixed record of consensus results in trial efforts led by the Commerce Department.

It also got some important things right. In particular, the "respect for context" principle is an important conceptual leap. It says that a people "have a right to expect that companies will collect, use, and disclose personal data in ways that are consistent with the context in which consumers provide the data." This breaks from the formalities of privacy notices, consent boxes, and structured data and focuses instead on respect for the individual. Its emphasis on the interactions between an individual and a company and circumstances of the data collection and use derives from the insight of information technology thinker Helen Nissenbaum. To assess privacy interests, "it is crucial to know the context—who is gathering the information, who is analyzing it, who is disseminating and to whom, the nature of the information, the relationships among the various parties, and even larger institutional and social circumstances."

Context is complicated—our draft legislation listed 11 different non-exclusive factors to assess context. But that is in practice the way we share information and form expectations about how that information will be handled and about our trust in the handler. We bare our souls and our bodies to complete strangers to get medical care, with the understanding that this information will be handled with great care and shared with strangers only to the extent needed to provide care. We share location information with ride-sharing and navigation apps with the understanding that it enables them to function, but Waze ran into resistance when that functionality required a location setting of "always on." Danny Weitzner, co-architect of the Privacy Bill of Rights, recently discussed how the respect for context principle "would have prohibited [Cambridge Analytica] from unilaterally repurposing research data for political purposes" because it establishes a right "not to be surprised by how one's personal data issued." The Supreme Court's *Carpenter* decision opens up expectations of privacy in information held by third parties to variations based on the context.

The Consumer Privacy Bill of Rights does not provide any detailed prescription as to how the context principle and other principles should apply in particular circumstances. Instead, the proposal left such application to case-by-case adjudication by the FTC and development of best practices, standards, and codes of conduct by organizations outside of government, with incentives to vet these with the FTC or to use internal review boards similar to those used for human subject research in academic and medical settings. This approach was based on the belief that the pace of technological change and the enormous variety of circumstances involved need more adaptive decisionmaking than current approaches to legislation and government regulations allow. It may be that baseline legislation will need more robust mandates for standards than the Consumer Privacy Bill of Rights contemplated, but any such mandates should be consistent with the deeply embedded preference for voluntary, collaboratively developed, and consensus-based standards that has been a hallmark of U.S. standards development.

In hindsight, the proposal could use a lodestar to guide the application of its principles—a simple golden rule for privacy: that companies should put the interests of the people whom data is about ahead of their own. In some measure, such a general rule would bring privacy protection back to first principles: some of the sources of law that Louis Brandeis and Samuel Warren referred to in their famous law review article were cases in which the receipt of confidential information or trade secrets led to judicial imposition of a trust or duty of confidentiality. Acting as a trustee carries the obligation to act in the interests of the beneficiaries and to avoid self-dealing.

A Golden Rule of Privacy that incorporates a similar obligation for one entrusted with personal information draws on several similar strands of the privacy debate. Privacy policies often express companies' intention to be "good stewards of data;" the good steward also is supposed to act in the interests of the principal and avoid self-dealing. A more contemporary law review parallel is Yale law professor Jack Balkin's concept of "information fiduciaries," which got some attention during the Zuckerberg hearing when Senator Brian Schatz (D-HI) asked Zuckerberg to comment on it. The Golden Rule of Privacy would import the essential duty without importing fiduciary law wholesale. It also resonates with principles of "respect for the individual," "beneficence," and "justice" in ethical standards for human subject research that influence emerging ethical frameworks for privacy and data use. Another thread came in Justice Gorsuch's *Carpenter* dissent defending property law as a basis for privacy interests: he suggested that entrusting someone with digital information may be a modern equivalent of a "bailment" under classic property law, which imposes duties on the bailee. And it bears some resemblance to the GDPR concept of "legitimate interest," which permits the processing of personal data based on a legitimate interest of the processor, provided that this interest is not outweighed by the rights and interests of the subject of the data.

The fundamental need for baseline privacy legislation in America is to ensure that individuals can trust that data about them will be used, stored, and shared in ways that are consistent with their interests and the circumstances in which it was collected. This should hold regardless of how the data is collected, who receives it, or the uses it is put to. If it is personal data, it should have enduring protection.

Such trust is an essential building block of a sustainable digital world. It is what enables the sharing of data for socially or economically beneficial uses without putting human beings at risk. By now, it should be clear that trust is betrayed too often, whether by intentional actors like Cambridge Analytica or Russian "Fancy Bears," or by bros in cubes inculcated with an imperative to "deploy or die."

Trust needs a stronger foundation that provides people with consistent assurance that data about them will be handled fairly and consistently with their interests. Baseline principles would provide a guide to all businesses and guard against overreach, outliers, and outlaws. They would also tell the world that American companies are bound by a widely-accepted set of privacy principles and build a foundation for privacy and security practices that evolve with technology.

Resigned but discontented consumers are saying to each other, "I think we're playing a losing game." If the rules don't change, they may quit playing.

Cyber Espionage and Electronic Surveillance: Beyond the Media Coverage
William C. Banks[1]

Introduction

In the twenty-first century it seems that everyone is eavesdropping on everyone else—governments and companies, militaries, law enforcement and intelligence agencies, hackers, criminals, and terrorists. State-sponsored and private cyber espionage and criminal and foreign-intelligence surveillance have ramped up in part because the national security threat environment is ever more complicated and multifaceted, and the ability to meet it is increasingly dependent on good intelligence, in real time. However, surveillance and espionage have also increased because the Internet and cyber technology so readily enable exploitation of intellectual property and other commercially valuable information. Among its many attributes, the Internet has introduced new dynamics to the age-old tensions between security and liberty. The Internet expands our freedom to communicate at the same time it makes us less secure. It expands our online vulnerabilities while it lowers the visibility of intrusions. The Internet provides new means for enabling privacy intrusions and causing national security and economic harm even as it provides governments with ever more sophisticated tools to keep tabs on bad actors. Yet in the cat and mouse game between the government agents and suspected terrorists and criminals, ever newer devices and encryption programs ratchet up privacy protections in ways that may prevent government access to those devices and their contents. These devices and programs, in turn, may enable cyber theft or even destructive terrorist attacks.

Espionage and intelligence collection are part of the national security apparatus of every state. Cyber espionage involves deliberate activities to penetrate computer systems or networks used by an adversary for obtaining information resident on or transiting through these systems or networks. A pertinent subset is economic espionage, where a state attempts to acquire secrets held by foreign companies. Of course, states conducted economic espionage before the Internet, but the availability of cyber exploitation rapidly and significantly expanded the activity.[2]

Electronic surveillance intercepts communications between two or more parties. The intercepts can give insight into what is said, planned, and anticipated by adversaries. Because such vast quantities of communications now travel through the Internet, more than humans can comprehend in their raw form, surveillance often leads to processing and exploitation through algorithms or

---

1. Board of Advisers Distinguished Professor, Syracuse University College of Law; Director, Institute for National Security and Counterterrorism.

2. Gerald O'Hara, *Cyber-Espionage: A Growing Threat to the American Economy*, 19 COMMLAW CONSPECTUS: J. COMM. L. & POL'Y 241, 241–42 (2010).

other search methods that can query large amounts of collected data in pursuit of more specific intelligence objectives.[3]

Traditional state-sponsored surveillance and espionage have been transformed into high-tech and high-stakes enterprises. Some of the cyber activity is electronic surveillance for foreign intelligence purposes, mimics traditional spying, and services a range of what most of us would concede are legitimate national security objectives—anticipating terrorist attacks, learning about the foreign policy plans of adversaries, and gaining advantage in foreign relations negotiations.[4] However, a good deal of the cyber sleuthing involves economic matters, sometimes extending to include intellectual property theft, and is undertaken by states or their proxies to secure comparative economic advantage in trade negotiations, other deals, or for particular companies.[5]

I. Economic Cyber Espionage

Governments and their agents have been exploiting Internet connectivity by penetrating the electronic networks of foreign companies for nearly a quarter century.[6] Until 2010, companies chose to ignore the problem, more or less.[7] Then Google publicly claimed that China had stolen source code and used it to spy and to penetrate other companies' networks.[8] At about the same time, major economic espionage was carried out against large western oil companies and traced to a site in China, and another theft lifted security key tokens, which in turn led to the penetration of other firms, including defense contractors in the United States.[9]

In May of 2014, the FBI issued "Most Wanted" posters for five Chinese nationals, members of the Peoples' Liberation Army.[10] In *United States v. Wang*, the five were indicted by a federal grand jury for breaking into computer systems of American companies and stealing trade secrets for the benefit of Chinese companies.[11] Although there was no chance that the United States would obtain jurisdiction over the accused so that they could be tried, the indictments may have

---

3. *See* Joe Pappalardo, *NSA Data Mining: How It Works*, POPULAR MECHANICS (Sept. 11, 2013), http://www.popularmechanics.com/military/a9465/nsa-data-mining-how-it-works-15910146/.

4. Heather Kelly, *NSA Chief: Snooping Is Crucial to Fighting Terrorism*, CNN (Aug. 1, 2013, 10:35 AM), http://www.cnn.com/2013/07/31/tech/web/nsa-alexander-black-hat/; David E. Sanger, *U.S. Cyberattacks Target ISIS in a New Line of Combat*, N.Y. TIMES (Apr. 24, 2016), http://www.nytimes.com/2016/04/25/us/politics/us-directs-cyberweapons-at-isis-for-first-time.html.

5. *See infra* notes 6–10 and accompanying text.

6. Joel Brenner, *The New Industrial Espionage*, 10 AM. INT., Winter 2015, at 28, 28–29, http://www.the-american-interest.com/2014/12/10/the-new-industrial-espionage/.

7. *Id.* at 30.

8. Andrew Jacobs & Miguel Helft, *Google, Citing Attack, Threatens to Exit China*, N.Y. TIMES (Jan. 12, 2010), http://www.nytimes.com/2010/01/13/world/asia/13beijing.html.

9. Nathan Hodge & Adam Entous, *Oil Firms Hit by Hackers from China, Report Says*, WALL ST. J. (Feb. 10, 2011, 12:01 AM), http://www.wsj.com/articles/SB10001424052748703716904576134661115188 64; Elinor Mills, *China Linked to New Breaches Tied to RSA*, CNET (June 6, 2011, 4:00 AM), https://www.cnet.com/news/china-linked-to-new-breaches-tied-to-rsa/.

10. *Cyber's Most Wanted*, FBI, https://www.fbi.gov/wanted/cyber (last visited Apr. 25, 2016).

11. Indictment, United States v. Wang, Criminal No. 14-118 (W.D. Pa. May 1, 2014), https://www.justice.gov/iso/opa/resources/5122014519132358461949.pdf.

been intended to incentivize negotiations with the Chinese on corporate spying. At first, the Chinese responded by complaining about U.S. hypocrisy and double standards.[12] The Chinese asserted that American authorities have conducted large-scale, organized cyber-espionage activities against government officials, companies, and individuals, in China and many other states.[13] The distinction that our government draws between spying for national security purposes and not spying on companies to give a competitive edge to one's own businesses is not recognized as valid by China, and they point out that our definition of national security includes obtaining advantages in trade negotiations and for other international economic purposes, including enforcing sanctions regimes and detecting bribery.[14]

Then, in 2015, some seemingly remarkable things happened. Following the indictment of the Chinese hackers and an executive order promulgated by President Barack Obama that authorized sanctions against malicious hackers,[15] the United States and China reached an agreement on a range of cybersecurity matters.[16] In addition to cooperation on law enforcement matters in cyberspace, China reversed its prominent policy position and committed not to engage in commercially-motivated cyber espionage.[17] The agreement also includes implementation and compliance provisions, the violation of which could lead to sanctions under the Obama administration executive order.[18]

Although the 2014 indictments had been dismissed as meaningless by many, the Chinese appear not to have understood their lack of practical significance and instead viewed them more like sanctions.[19] The PLA unit also may have felt exposed and diminished in its prestige after the indictments.[20] Meanwhile, news reports indicate that China began to dismantle its economic espionage network and started to crack down on PLA hackers who were moonlighting on the side and selling information to Chinese companies that was not central to the PLA

---

12. Jonathan Kaiman, *China Reacts Furiously to US Cyber-Espionage Charges*, GUARDIAN (May 20, 2014, 8:31 AM), https://www.theguardian.com/world/2014/may/20/china-reacts-furiously-us-cyber-espionage-charges.

13. David E. Sanger, *With Spy Charges, U.S. Draws a Line that Few Others Recognize*, N.Y. TIMES (May 19, 2014), http://www.nytimes.com/2014/05/20/us/us-treads-fine-line-in-fighting-chinese-espionage.html.

14. *Id.*

15. Exec. Order No. 13,694, 80 Fed. Reg. 18,077 (Apr. 2, 2015).

16. JOHN W. ROLLINS, CONG. RESEARCH SERV., IN10376, U.S.–CHINA CYBER AGREEMENT (2015), https://www.fas.org/sgp/crs/row/IN10376.pdf.

17. *Id.*

18. *Id.*

19. Ellen Nakashima, *Following U.S. Indictments, China Shifts Commercial Hacking Away from Military to Civilian Agency*, WASH. POST (Nov. 30, 2015), https://www.washingtonpost.com/world/national-security/following-us-indictments-chinese-military-scaled-back-hacks-on-american-industry/2015/11/30/fcdb097a-9450-11e5-b5e4-279b4501e8a6_story.html.

20. *Id.*

national security mission.[21] A few weeks after the U.S.–China agreement was reached, similar agreements were reached between China and the United Kingdom and China and Germany.[22]

II. Surveillance

Meanwhile, governments are not the only participants in the cybersleuthing. The Islamic State (ISIS) has broadened its recruitment and appeal, focusing in part on young, tech-savvy persons living far from the battlefields of Syria and Iraq.[23] In October 2015, the United States arrested Kosovar Ardit Ferizi while he was living in Malaysia and charged him with providing material support to terrorism by hacking a U.S. government database and stealing personal information on more than 1350 military and civilian government personnel.[24] Ferizi allegedly passed the information to an operative of ISIS.[25]

The ISIS Cyber Caliphate hacking unit seized control of U.S. Central Command Twitter and YouTube feeds early in 2015, using them to post propaganda videos and personal information on top military officials.[26] The hackers seized more than 54,000 Twitter accounts for the same objectives again late in 2015.[27] Even terrorists who seek visible, kinetic effects from their attacks—and are thus less likely to engage in malware insertion and other disruptive, but not destructive, cyber attacks—increasingly rely on digital protections (encryption) to assure the secrecy of their communications.[28] Most notably, ISIS has demonstrated a sophisticated understanding of methods for shielding its communications from electronic surveillance by intelligence agencies. Security companies have described a manual released by an ISIS operative urging its followers to use fake phone numbers to set up an encrypted chat system that will shield ISIS

---

21. *Id.*

22. Rowena Mason, *Xi Jinping State Visit: UK and China Sign Cybersecurity Pact*, GUARDIAN (Oct. 21, 2015, 12:13 PM), http://www.theguardian.com/politics/2015/oct/21/uk-china-cybersecurity-pact-xi-jinping-david-cameron; Stefan Nicola, *China Working to Halt Commercial Cyberwar in Deal with Germany*, BLOOMBERG TECH. (Oct. 29, 2015, 8:31 AM), http://www.bloomberg.com/news/articles/2015-10-29/china-working-to-halt-commercial-cyberwar-in-deal-with-germany.

23. Maeghin Alarid, *Recruitment and Radicalization: The Role of Social Media and New Technology*, *in* IMPUNITY: COUNTERING ILLICIT POWER IN WAR AND TRANSITION 313, 322 (Michelle Hughes & Michael Miklaucic eds., 2016).

24. Joe Davidson, *ISIS Threatens Feds, Military After Theft of Personal Data*, WASH. POST (Jan. 31, 2016), https://www.washingtonpost.com/news/federal-eye/wp/2016/01/31/isis-threatens-feds-military-after-theft-of-personal-data/.

25. *Id.*

26. CNN Staff, *CENTCOM Twitter Account Hacked, Suspended*, CNN POLITICS (Jan. 12, 2015, 5:43 PM), http://www.cnn.com/2015/01/12/politics/centcom-twitter-hacked-suspended/.

27. Jigmey Bhutia, *Isis 'Cyber Caliphate' Hacks More than 54,000 Twitter Accounts*, INT'L BUS. TIMES (Nov. 9, 2015, 9:10 AM), http://www.ibtimes.co.uk/isis-cyber-caliphate-hacks-more-54000-twitter-accounts-1527821.

28. Kate O'Keeffe, *American ISIS Recruits Down, but Encryption Is Helping Terrorists' Online Efforts, Says FBI Director*, WALL ST. J. (May 11, 2016, 8:54 PM), http://www.wsj.com/articles/american-isis-recruits-down-but-encryption-is-helping-terrorists-online-efforts-says-fbi-director-1463007527?mg=id-wsj.

communications from intelligence surveillance and avoid revealing personal information.[29]

For the most part, international law has been a bystander to this entire fabric of stealth, deception, and greed. The individual strands of this story are bound together by a unique set of oppositional forces and compelling needs for action.

- The costs of economic cyber espionage are staggeringly high and will continue to rise unless something is done.[30]

- The Snowden leaks have sewn distrust among citizens and between allied governments, each doubting the veracity of the United States and other nations' intelligence collection practices.[31]

- Intelligence collection incidentally but persistently invades citizens' liberties in collecting beyond the reasonable needs of government.[32]

- Yet continuing terrorist attacks in a wide range of locations reinforces the need for the most effective means of electronic surveillance of potential terrorist activities.[33]

- Traditional espionage is now scapegoated in ways that harm allied relationships and impose costs on intelligence collection.

If we do not act to put a stopper in these escalating crises of costs and confidence soon, the security and integrity of the Internet may be up for grabs. Not to mention the efficacy of intelligence collection by electronic means.

III. The Limited Role of International Law

Cyberspace remains a netherworld for intelligence activities—whatever surveillance or cyber spying a government does outside its own national borders is, in most circumstances, an international law free-for-all. Decades of state practice tell us that surveillance or espionage may be conducted across borders without violating sovereignty.[34] Examples of presumably permissible behavior include collecting the contents of electronic communications or metadata about them; watching government computer systems, including SCADA systems, through cyber penetration; exfiltration of government data, including military or other national security secrets; and denial of service penetrations that decrease the bandwidth for government web sites. Disruptive cyber activities that are not

---

29. Kim Zetter, *Security Manual Reveals the OPSEC Advice ISIS Gives Recruits*, WIRED (Nov. 19, 2015, 4:45 PM), http://www.wired.com/2015/11/isis-opsec-encryption-manuals-reveal-terrorist-group-security-protocols/.

30. *See infra* note 54 and accompanying text.

31. Alan Travis, *Snowden Leak: Governments' Hostile Reaction Fuelled Public's Distrust of Spies*, GUARDIAN (June 15, 2015, 11:19 AM), https://www.theguardian.com/world/2015/jun/15/snowden-files-us-uk-government-hostile-reaction-distrust-spies.

32. *See infra* notes 46–50 and accompanying text.

33. *See* Kelly, *supra* note 4; Sanger, *supra* note 3

34. Glenn Sulmasy & John Yoo, *Counterintuitive: Intelligence Operations and International Law*, 28 MICH. J. INT'L L. 625, 626, 628 (2007).

destructive or coercive in some way apparently do not violate international law. The line between permitted espionage and unlawful cyber intrusions is far from clear.

One response to the increasing concerns about online theft of intellectual property and complaints of invasions of privacy has been for more governments around the world to enact or at least talk about data-localization laws. Such laws, already in place in authoritarian states such as Russia, China, and Iran, typically enforce limitations for all citizen data and the infrastructure that supports it.[35] China strictly vets companies selling Internet technology and services in China.[36] Now-democratic states such as Brazil, India, and Germany are contemplating data-localization. Brazil plans to stop using Microsoft Outlook for e-mail, and Germany has unhooked from Verizon and signed on with Deutsche Telekom.[37] There is talk among our European allies about creating a European Internet.[38]

To what extent does the uniqueness of the cyber domain make cyber espionage and foreign intelligence surveillance legally distinct? On the one hand, the fact that no person has to cross a border to accomplish the espionage or surveillance probably does not matter, legally. Remoteness is just a means of collection. On the other hand, attribution, knowing who stole your secrets, is a serious technical problem and makes controlling cyber exploitation more difficult than keeping tabs on traditional spying. In addition, in the cyber world distinguishing exploitation from a cyber attack (an intrusion designed to disrupt or destroy systems or data) can be difficult. The malware that exploits a computer to retrieve its data may be indistinguishable at first from malware that will destroy the computer hard drive. Thus, the exploited state may be hard-pressed deciding how to prepare and respond.

States have historically tolerated traditional espionage because they all do it and gain from it.[39] Domestic laws proscribe spying for those that are caught. Most espionage disputes are resolved through diplomacy, and in extreme cases, states send the spies home. In cyber espionage, the status quo favors sophisticated countries with the finances and technological capabilities to extract the intelligence. But the status quo is changing rapidly. Cyberspace reduces the power differentials among actors. Powerful states have more cyber resources but also

---

35. Anupam Chander & Uyên P. Lê, *Data Nationalism*, 64 EMORY L.J. 677, 686–88, 701–02, 735–36 (2015).

36. Paul Mozur, *New Rules in China Upset Western Tech Companies*, N.Y. TIMES (Jan. 28, 2015), http://www.nytimes.com/2015/01/29/technology/in-china-new-cybersecurity-rules-perturb-western-tech-companies.html?_r=0.

37. Anton Troianovski & Danny Yadron, *German Government Ends Verizon Contract*, WALL ST. J. (June 26, 2014, 2:54 PM), http://www.wsj.com/articles/german-government-ends-verizon-contract-1403802226; *see also Brazil to Create Its Own Email System After Protesting U.S. Spying*, UPI.COM (Oct. 14, 2013, 5:12 PM), http://www.upi.com/Science_News/Technology/2013/10/14/Brazil-to-create-its-own-email-system-after-protesting-US-spying/69911381785172/.

38. Sam Ball, *Plans to Stop US Spying with European Internet*, FRANCE 24, http://www.france24.com/en/20140217-european-internet-plans-nsa-spying (last updated Feb. 18, 2014).

39. *See* Sulmasy & Yoo, *supra* note 34, at 626–29.

more government and private-sector vulnerabilities. The advantage increasingly lies with state-sponsored and non-state hackers—the offense, not the defense—and the costs of cyber exploitation of security and proprietary data are forcing states to look for ways to curb the espionage.

To date, efforts to anchor the law of cyber espionage or foreign-intelligence surveillance in international law have developed in three mostly nascent directions. One potential pathway is the conventional and customary norm of non-intervention, a corollary to state sovereignty. The principle of nonintervention is reflected in Article 2(4) of the U.N. Charter and its prohibition of "the threat or use of force against the territorial integrity or political independence of any state."[40] In theory at least, nonintervention is broader than use of force and the Charter. As the International Court of Justice stated in *Nicaragua v. United States*,[41] wrongful intervention involves "methods of coercion,"[42] and the United States engaged in wrongful intervention even though it did not use force in Nicaragua. Should nonintervention take on new meaning in the twenty-first century based on the expanding cornucopia of technical means for crossing sovereign borders without human intervention? Apart from the technical means, does the contemporary use of state-supported espionage to steal trade secrets and intellectual property constitute intervention? Is a breach of the norm measured by the impact of the intervention, whether virtual or physical? Certainly cyber surveillance or espionage targeting government activities interferes with the internal affairs of the victim state.

However, the legislative history of the Charter and later commentary confirm that "force" in Article 2(4) does not include economic or political pressure.[43] Thus, under the Charter, espionage does not constitute an internationally wrongful act triggering state responsibility under international law. (If a state is responsible for an unlawful act, the victim state is entitled to reparation, and a state may take any responsive actions that neither amount to a use of force nor breach a treaty or customary law obligation. Or it may take countermeasures.)[44] Cyber exploitation directed at financial targets, for example, could cause economic loss, panic in the streets, and a loss of public confidence in the state. Yet if there is no physical damage or loss of life, the Charter suggests that the norm of nonintervention has not been violated.

---

40. U.N. Charter art. 2, ¶ 4.

41. Military and Paramilitary Activities in and Against Nicaragua (Nicar. v. U.S.), Judgment, 1986 I.C.J. Rep. 14 (June 27).

42. *Id.* at ¶ 205.

43. Matthew C. Waxman, *Cyber-Attacks and the Use of Force: Back to the Future of Article 2(4)*, 36 YALE J. INT'L L. 421, 422 (2011).

44. Michael N. Schmitt, *"Below the Threshold" Cyber Operations: The Countermeasures Response Option and International Law*, 54 VA. J. INT'L L. 697, 703 (2014).

Some scholars have argued in the alternative that cyber espionage is a lawful precursor to a state's exercise of its U.N. Charter Article 51 self-defense rights.[45] Preparing for and anticipating an armed attack is critically important in the modern world, the argument goes. If not affirmatively allowed as an adjunct to Article 51, others maintain that espionage has been recognized by widespread state practice and thus is supported by a norm of customary international law.

From the human rights perspective, electronic surveillance could be seen to violate the International Covenant on Civil and Political Rights (ICCPR), Article 17(1), which protects against "arbitrary or unlawful interference with ... privacy."[46] The reach and application of the ICCPR and a similar provision in the European Convention on Human Rights[47] (ECHR) outside any state's territory are unsettled, although there is support for the view that the protection extends to foreign nationals outside the territory of the state party in the context of electronic surveillance or cyber intrusions. The U.N. Special Rapporteur wrote that Article 17 protects against "mass surveillance of the Internet," and that bulk surveillance must be justified following a proportionality analysis that accounts for "systematic interference with the Internet privacy rights of a potentially unlimited number of innocent people located in any part of the world."[48] The Rapporteur finds bulk collection "indiscriminately corrosive of online privacy" and threatening to the core of Article 17 privacy.[49] (Jurisdictional issues cloud whether any court or treaty body would apply human rights law to surveillance or cyber spying.) Cases are pending now in the European Court of Human Rights alleging privacy violations due to the U.K. Government Communications Headquarters's cooperation with the National Security Agency in collecting upstream contents and bulk data.[50]

An unusual alignment of interests between some powerful governments (victims of cyber exploitation and overbroad surveillance), ordinary citizens, and major corporations and their clients present what may be a propitious time for forging new international law in these areas. Governments, citizens, and influential opinion makers learned a great deal about foreign intelligence surveillance from the Snowden leaks. And the governments most affected by the

---

45. Ashley Deeks, *An International Legal Framework for Surveillance*, 55 VA. J. INT'L L. 291, 302 (2015); see also U.N. Charter art. 51 ("Nothing in the present Charter shall impair the inherent right of individual or collective self-defense...").

46. International Covenant on Civil and Political Rights art. 17, ¶ 1, Dec. 19, 1966, 999 U.N.T.S. 171.

47. Convention for the Protection of Human Rights and Fundamental Freedoms art. 8, Nov. 4, 1950, 213 U.N.T.S. 221.

48. U.N. Secretary-General, *Report of the Special Rapporteur on the Promotion and Protection of Human Rights and Fundamental Freedoms While Countering Terrorism*, ¶ 59, U.N. Doc. A/69/397 (Sept. 23, 2014).

49. *Id.*

50. *See, e.g.*, Applicant's Reply, 10 Human Rights Orgs. v. United Kingdom, App. No. 24960/15 (2016), https://www.documentcloud.org/documents/3115985-APPLICANTS-REPLY-to-GOVT-OBSER VATIONS-PDF.html; Ryan Gallagher, *Europe's Top Human Rights Court Will Consider Legality of Surveillance Exposed by Edward Snowden*, INTERCEPT (Oct. 3, 2016), https://theintercept.com/2016/09/30/echr-nsa-gchq-snowden-surveillance-privacy/.

Snowden leaks are some of the same ones most victimized by cyber espionage of one sort or another.

The United States has already begun to limit their surveillance activities in response to political pressure, not least from the heads of state whose conversations were recorded.[51] Meanwhile, litigation in European and U.S. courts and a resolution by the U.N. General Assembly addressing the right of privacy in the digital era[52] sow the seeds of a rights-based reorientation of international law. Perhaps most important, the economic impacts of cyber espionage and foreign surveillance are considerable. On the surveillance side of things, Internet service providers and social media companies in the United States are losing contracts and clients in many places, and the data-localization laws and other steps taken by some states to insulate "their" piece of the Internet threaten to further constrain the global economy.[53] As for cyber espionage, the estimated $300–600 billion annual price tag[54] is illustrative of the costs imposed by theft of IP and trade secrets, along with other valuable government and private sector information.

States could agree to distinguish national-security espionage from all other forms, and tolerate only the former. After all, keeping a nation safe is a high and noble objective, and intelligence can directly serve that end. The trick is to thoughtfully limit that power to collect intelligence only where it is necessary to safeguard national-security interests, and then to be sure that the intelligence function is subject to effective oversight. All other forms of espionage could be treated as theft, and rules forbidding that activity could be enforced in the private, commercial realm. It remains difficult in some instances to distinguish national-security espionage from other spying. Developing customary international law is a slow, lengthy process, but it could begin in just this way. If a sufficient number of other states sign on, new international norms may be made. A similar process could lead to developing international law on surveillance, perhaps starting with agreements[55] among the Five Eyes—the English speaking democracies.

Similarly, states could agree that international law forbids spying by a state for the direct benefit of a private company. Governments can and have at times established rules of the road for limiting espionage and created incentives for

---

51. Presidential Policy Directive PPD-28: Directive on Signals Intelligence Activities, 2014 DAILY COMP. PRES. DOC. 31 (Jan. 17, 2014); REVIEW GROUP ON INTELLIGENCE AND COMMC'NS TECHS., LIBERTY AND SECURITY IN A CHANGING WORLD: REPORT AND RECOMMENDATIONS OF THE PRESIDENT'S REVIEW GROUP ON INTELLIGENCE AND COMMUNICATIONS TECHNOLOGIES 20 (2013), https://www.whitehouse.gov/sites/default/files/docs/2013-12-12_rg_final_report.pdf (suggesting steps to place certain allied leaders' private communications off-limits for the NSA).

52. Human Rights Council, Rep. of the Office of the U.N. High Comm'r for Human Rights, The Right to Privacy in the Digital Age, U.N. Doc. A/HRC/27/37 (June 30, 2014).

53. Claire Cain Miller, *Revelations of N.S.A. Spying Cost U.S. Tech Companies*, N.Y. TIMES, (Mar. 21, 2014), http://www.nytimes.com/2014/03/22/business/fallout-from-snowden-hurting-bottom-line-of-tech-companies.html.

54. Ellen Nakashima & Andrea Peterson, *Report: Cybercrime and Espionage Costs $445 Billion Annually*, WASH. POST (June 9, 2014), https://www.washingtonpost.com/world/national-security/report-cybercrime-and-espionage-costs-445-billion-annually/2014/06/08/8995291c-ecce-11e3-9f5c-9075d5508f0a_story.html (CSIS places the figure at $375–$575 billion).

cooperation. The 2015 U.S.–China agreement is exemplary.[55] The new approaches are necessary because the model response to conventional espionage—arrest their spies, expel diplomats, and the like—does not work when the cyber theft is accomplished remotely by unnamed agents. Trade sanctions, tariffs, and diplomatic pressures are often effective tools.

Another method of influencing international law could be to adapt domestic laws to international law. Domestic regulation of cyber espionage in the United States has been provided by the Economic Espionage Act (EEA), which proscribes the possession, collection, duplication, transfer, or sale of trade secrets for the benefit of a foreign nation or any of its agents.[56] The Justice Department is expressly given extraterritorial enforcement authority.[57] Amendments to the EEA in 2012 and 2013 increased the criminal penalties and the breadth of coverage for stealing trade secrets to benefit a foreign government.[58] New amendments have been recommended that would provide a private right of action for those who hold trade secrets that have been subject to theft.[59] In addition, the Computer Fraud and Abuse Act (CFAA) prohibits intentionally causing damage through a computer code or program to any computer connected to the Internet.[60] Although not written with espionage in mind, the CFAA could be used to counter cyber exploitation. These domestic laws could provide foundational concepts for developing international agreements and, eventually, international law.

The benefits of augmenting international law with domestically grown mechanisms are numerous, but ultimately, customary international law needs an international platform. For example, in the intellectual property realm, customary international law could incorporate intellectual property theft proscriptions from the World Trade Organization (WTO) and the related Trade Related Aspects of Intellectual Property Rights agreement.[61] An advantage is the use of a respected international forum, where nations such as China could also seek relief from cyber exploitation (by the United States). A drawback is that WTO agreements presently require meeting obligations only within the member's territory.[62] The structure of the agreements could be changed, if they could figure out how to prove responsibility for a state's actions outside its territory.

In an effort to distinguish espionage while applying domestic legal structures, states could determine that disruptive cyber actions should be treated differently

---

55. See supra notes 16–22 and accompanying text.

56. 18 U.S.C. § 1831 (2012).

57. 18 U.S.C. § 1836 (2012).

58. Id.

59. Dennis Crouch, *Defend Trade Secret Act Moving Forward*, PATENTLY-O (Apr. 5, 2016), http://patentlyo.com/patent/2016/04/secret-moving-forward.html.

60. 18 U.S.C. § 1030 (2012).

61. Agreement on Trade-Related Aspects of Intellectual Property Rights, Apr. 15, 1994, 1869 U.N.T.S. 299.

62. *See, e.g., id.* art. 1, ¶ 1.

than espionage. Such agreements could be grafted onto the Cybercrime Convention.[63] The Cybercrime Convention commits states to enact domestic laws criminalizing cyber theft.[64] Of course, the Cybercrime Convention could be amended to make unlawful espionage that steals trade secrets or other proprietary information for the benefit of domestic firms. The domestic laws required by the Convention are largely ineffective against state-sponsored theft because of the difficulties of obtaining jurisdiction of accused cyber criminals and because of diplomatic immunities. The domestic laws are difficult to enforce anyway because of attribution problems. There are no enforceable international law violations recognized by the treaty. As it now stands, the Cybercrime Convention includes no universal definition of cybercrime, for example.[65] Does cybercrime include theft for espionage purposes? The Convention has demonstrated that problems of cyber espionage cannot be addressed as a traditional crime problem because a large portion of what is criminal is state-tolerated or state-supported. Nor are Mutual Legal Assistance Treaties useful where the crimes are politically motivated and state sponsored.

Furthermore, distinguishing between cyber espionage and disruptive cyber activity could encourage states to come to agreements upon some off-limits parts of cyber. For example, agreements not to disrupt nuclear installations or other critical infrastructure would be beneficial to all sides. Abolishing spying on these systems goes hand in hand with limiting disruption. Once the infrastructure is off-limits for attack, there is no legitimate reason to illicitly obtain information about that system.

Conclusions

The confluence of interests between victims of overbroad surveillance and cyber espionage presents an opportunity to begin developing new norms and eventual international law that could bring more rationality, predictability, and privacy protections to the cyber domain. The costs of cyber espionage are real, and the threats and vulnerabilities will increase with the progression of technology. Companies and governments are underprepared for the level of cyber espionage they are facing. Solutions vary, but they all share the common foundation of increased international cooperation and the development of a customary international legal framework that everyone understands.

Meanwhile, blowback from the Snowden leaks has generated sufficient political pressure to cause some changes to surveillance authorities. As those reforms develop and privacy claims are litigated in international fora and European courts, it is likely that new international law will emerge, too, perhaps in tandem with reforms to the limits on cyber espionage.

---

63. Convention on Cybercrime, Nov. 23, 2001, 2296 U.N.T.S. 167.
64. *Id.* art. 2.
65. *Id.* art. 1.

Healthcare

Why Our Health Care Costs So Much—
and Why Fixes Aren't Likely
Paul Sisson

Practically everyone knows health care in the United States is expensive—the most expensive in the world by seemingly every measure. But judging by the raging debate over the Affordable Care Act, few really understand why.

At the moment, the GOP-led push in Congress and the White House to overhaul Obamacare is focusing on premiums and deductibles, coverage rates and co-pays. Yet they are just the mechanisms of paying for a system that continues to consume a larger percentage of the nation's gross domestic product than in any other highly industrialized country. For example, a study from the Commonwealth Fund, a nonpartisan health-care think tank, said the United States spent $9,086 per person in 2013 on medical expenses—$2,761 more than Switzerland, the next-highest spender on the list of 13 wealthy nations.

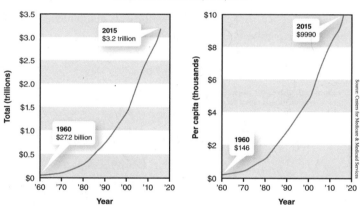

National Health Expenditures

Despite this big spending gap, the United States' overall life expectancy was only 78.8 years in 2013, the lowest among its peers. It also had the highest infant mortality rate and obesity rate in the group, according to the study.

So if Americans are not getting better results, then why is our health care so costly? The experts give resoundingly similar conclusions.

"When you do the research, you realize it's really not because we're using more care. It is that we have these higher prices that we don't see in other countries," said David Squires, a senior researcher at the Commonwealth Fund.

"The biggest reason is that we have higher prices for health-care services in the U.S. than other countries have," said Cynthia Cox, associate director of the Program for the Study of Health Reform and Private Insurance at the nonpartisan Kaiser Family Foundation.

"We pay our doctors more, we pay our hospitals more, we pay more for our drugs," said Geoffrey Joyce, a health-care economist with the Schaeffer Center for Health Policy and Economics at the University of Southern California.

The Commonwealth study found that among industrialized nations, there were significant pricing differences for many medical procedures. An MRI scan in the U.S. cost $1,145 on average in 2013, compared with $138 in Switzerland, $350 in Australia and $461 in the Netherlands. An appendectomy cost $6,645 in New Zealand and $13,910 in America.

The U.S. has experimented with many ways to reduce skyrocketing medical costs, including moving to the health management organization model—HMOS—in the 1980s and '90s and, more recently under Obamacare, to systems that allow health providers to keep part of the money they save as long as the quality of patient care remains high.

There are recent signs that some of these efforts are bearing fruit. After decades of steady increases, the amount of GDP consumed by health-care services has flattened in recent years.

However, American drug companies, health providers and patients themselves are still largely unwilling to give up control over myriad medical choices—a relinquishment that has been crucial for governments in other countries to hold down costs more effectively.

Health-care specialists cite several key reasons why Americans are shelling out more money for what's often less quality:

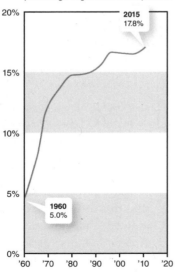

Share of U.S. GDP over time
National health expenditures as a percentage of gross domestic product

2015 — 17.8%
1960 — 5.0%

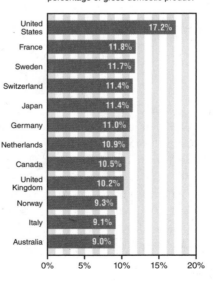

Share of GDP for selected countries
National health expenditures as a percentage of gross domestic product

Country	%
United States	17.2%
France	11.8%
Sweden	11.7%
Switzerland	11.4%
Japan	11.4%
Germany	11.0%
Netherlands	10.9%
Canada	10.5%
United Kingdom	10.2%
Norway	9.3%
Italy	9.1%
Australia	9.0%

Price Variations

Need a knee replacement? That will cost you a different price depending on where you go in the United States.

A California website shows that hospitals in San Diego County charged anywhere from $52,010 to $98,327 for the procedure in 2014, but that's just the list price. Each hospital brokers its own deal with each insurance company. The public never really gets a full picture of what insurance companies pay behind the scenes, though the amount of information available is gradually increasing.

Medicare, on the other hand, has a much more standardized pricing structure that attempts to pay based on a person's severity of illness, the cost of living in each geographic location and other factors.

America's system of variable and relatively opaque pricing does not exist in other countries, said Squires at the Commonwealth Fund. Government-run "single payer" systems, even those with several insurance companies participating, get much more involved in setting prices for everything from prescription drugs to individual medical procedures.

"In other countries that have more centralized prices, those sorts of price disparities don't really occur," Squires said.

Such systems also wield much greater control over what kinds of medical procedures, medications and therapies are available to consumers. They conduct cost-effectiveness reviews to decide if a given service is worth the investment of limited health-care dollars, said Cox at the Kaiser Family Foundation.

The United States has resisted all attempts to adopt a similar approach.

For example: The Affordable Care Act originally called for a panel to conduct effectiveness research, but that provision was quickly scrapped when some legislators said cost-benefit analyses would result in "death panels" that denied care to people whose lives were not deemed valuable enough to justify the medical expense.

Meanwhile, many free-market thinkers such as Dr. Michael Accad, a San Francisco cardiologist who runs a blog called Alert & Oriented, believe excessive regulation is to blame. They note that consumers, if given enough accurate pricing information, are capable of finding the best combination of price and quality. They said insurance coverage—with its complicated mix of premiums, co-pays, deductibles and co-insurance—only drives up costs by obscuring the true pricing dynamics.

"When health insurance pays for medical care, the demand for health-care services, medical technology, drugs and so forth is bound to go up, and this naturally pushes prices up by the law of supply and demand," Accad said.

Like some physicians, he treats only cash-paying patients and posts his prices on his website for everyone to see.

Prescription Drugs

Studies have repeatedly made it clear that Americans pay more for prescription drugs than people in other countries.

The International Federation of Health Plans compiles an annual list of drug prices by country. According to that comparison in 2015, the rheumatoid arthritis drug Humira cost $2,515 to $2,996 in the U.S., $1,362 in the United Kingdom and $552 in South Africa. The painkiller OxyContin cost an average of $265 in the U.S. that year, versus $95 in Switzerland.

"Pharmaceutical prices are very easy to compare, and we can see very clearly that we pay two, three or even four times as much, in many cases, for the exact same pill," Cox said.

Countries with centralized health systems have an advantage in this regard as well, she noted. They are able to negotiate for an entire nation all at once, in contrast to individual insurance companies or government programs working out their own narrower deals.

"We have more of a fractured purchasing system, and as a result, we don't have the same negotiating power," Cox said.

Here again, Accad sees the current health insurance system, which offers prepaid drug benefits rolled up in the premiums that consumers pay, as the real problem. Just as the market has convinced some doctors to offer their services on a cash-only basis, some consumers are buying their medications on the Internet from sellers in countries charging lower prices.

"Things are so bad that the market is finding ways to circumvent the (U.S.) system and get people what they need at a price they can afford," Accad said.

Technology

American health care generally uses more high-tech devices than other well-off countries' medical systems.

The Commonwealth Fund's report said the United States has 35.5 MRI machines and 43.5 CT X-ray scanners per one million residents. Among the 13 other industrialized nations analyzed, the median numbers were 11.4 MRI machines and 17.6 CT scanners. Only Japan showed a greater investment in these two technologies.

In addition, Americans underwent more scans with such machinery than in most other industrialized countries. And yet their medical outcomes were not superior to those of people in those other nations.

Likewise, studies have shown that within the U.S., hospitals that order noticeably more scans generally do not have better patient results than hospitals that prescribe fewer scans.

Joyce, the USC health-care economist, said technology is a major driver of medical-pricing inflation in the United States. He described an interplay between technology and insurance that, over time, has driven up premiums as never-ending demand for the latest gadgets continues.

On one hand, this pattern creates an incentive to invent and bring new technologies to market. "Clearly, technology wouldn't be developed at the pace and wouldn't be able to command the price if insurance costs were not increasing to meet those prices," Joyce said.

But a lack of centralized pricing control in the U.S. means that access to new technologies is rationed with the pocketbook instead.

"Everybody rations access to these technologies. In European countries, they do it on the supply side by deciding what they're going to buy and how much. In the U.S., we typically ration based on income and ability to pay," Joyce said.

Doctors' Compensation

A major focus of health reform in the United States has been changing the financial incentives for doctors, and many health-care economists said this push has helped contribute to the recent plateau in America's overall health-care costs.

Joyce said provisions in the Affordable Care Act that compelled both health providers and insurance companies to concentrate on the financial value of care, rather than pure volume of care, have made a significant difference.

"The (Great Recession) did contribute some to the plateau we're seeing in the growth of health care costs, but moving away from the fee-for-service model of incentives is a big deal. We have a long way to go still, but I think you can say it has helped," he said.

In the past, insurance companies and government programs paid per medical procedure, which encouraged doctors to do more procedures so they could collect more money. Now, the strategy is to increasingly pay one flat fee for an overall case—say, all services related to a brain surgery, from preparation work before the operation to post-surgical radiation and physical therapy.

Experts have said the traditional compensation approach also has contributed to physicians ordering more tests, scans and other unnecessary services to shield themselves from complaints of malpractice. The concept, often called "defensive medicine," holds that doctors are less exposed to lawsuits if they can show that they had provided a lot of care to a patient.

Waste and Fraud

A 2012 report from the Institute of Medicine estimated that the U.S. health system wastes about $750 billion per year.

Unnecessary services made up the largest category of waste. Other major segments were excess administrative costs and an over-abundance of efforts to document care given to patients.

Fraud—even though it tends to grab the public's attention because of high-profile prosecutions of such criminals—was one of the least significant categories of waste, according to the institute.

The Affordable Care Act has had mixed results in reducing these costs.

A massive move toward computerized record-keeping for medical centers was supposed to achieve greater efficiency and thus lower expenses, but that campaign remains fragmented, said Cox at the Kaiser Family Foundation. For instance, systems designed and installed by different vendors still don't communicate with each other as they should.

$3.2 Trillion total spent on health care in 2015

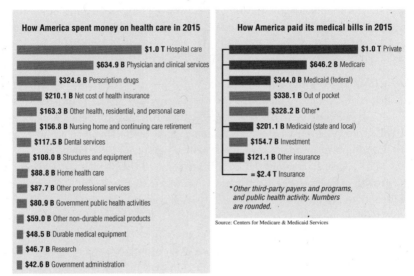

How America spent money on health care in 2015

- **$1.0 T** Hospital care
- **$634.9 B** Physician and clinical services
- **$324.6 B** Perscription drugs
- **$210.1 B** Net cost of health insurance
- **$163.3 B** Other health, residential, and personal care
- **$156.8 B** Nursing home and continuing care retirement
- **$117.5 B** Dental services
- **$108.0 B** Structures and equipment
- **$88.8 B** Home health care
- **$87.7 B** Other professional services
- **$80.9 B** Government public health activities
- **$59.0 B** Other non-durable medical products
- **$48.5 B** Durable medical equipment
- **$46.7 B** Research
- **$42.6 B** Government administration

How America paid its medical bills in 2015

- **$1.0 T** Private
- **$646.2 B** Medicare
- **$344.0 B** Medicaid (federal)
- **$338.1 B** Out of pocket
- **$328.2 B** Other*
- **$201.1 B** Medicaid (state and local)
- **$154.7 B** Investment
- **$121.1 B** Other insurance
- **= $2.4 T** Insurance

*Other third-party payers and programs, and public health activity. Numbers are rounded.

Source: Centers for Medicare & Medicaid Services

British Health Care: Free for Citizens, Low-Priced for Visitors. Is That the Whole Story?

Frances Stead Sellers

I didn't expect to be billed. I thought that emergency care in the Britain's National Health Service was free, particularly for a British citizen like me.

But after falling off a horse when I was on vacation there last September and landing in the hospital under the care of a "polytrauma" team, I got a call. It was from Jacqueline Bishop, the hospital's Overseas Visitors Coordinator. She told me that the NHS is a residence—not citizenship—based system and that since I live in the United States, I'd be treated like any other foreign visitor: I would have to pay full freight.

With visions of U.S. health-care dollars dancing in my head, I lost a little sleep that night. I thought about the bills from the orthopedic surgeon (for my broken pelvis and ribs) and the charges from the general surgeon (for my punctured lung); I imagined the costs of the CT scans and bedpans, of the blood thinners and painkillers and of the nurse's hasty consultation with a doctor in the middle of one night when my blood pressure plunged, and I panicked. And I felt a wave of relief that the team had decided to treat my injuries "conservatively"; I would be spared the expense (and pain!) of surgery.

When the bill arrived, I was in for another surprise. It was a "package" deal comprising just six items, and it didn't separate the hospital from the physician fees. There were no charges for the army of attentive doctors and nurses who met me in the ER, nor for the monitoring, blood tests and drips there. But from the moment I was admitted on a Wednesday morning until the following Saturday, when I was discharged to recuperate with relatives, the bill came to 3,464 pounds.

Or $5,572.54.

Talk about sticker shock. That would have covered little more than one day's stay in a U.S. hospital, which a 2012 report by the International Federation of Health Plans put at $4,287. That allows for an array of hospital charges such as labs and imaging but not, of course, physician fees. (The IFHP based its number on the average negotiated amount actually paid by U.S. insurers, not the far higher prices that providers typically charge.)

Britain, like other industrialized countries, spends far less on health care than the United States. A 2012 analysis of care in 13 countries showed that "health care spending in the U.S. dwarfs that found in any other industrialized country." (It's 9.3 percent of GDP in Britain, for example, compared with 17.9 percent here.) "Higher prices" and "greater use of more expensive medical technology" are key factors in that spending, according to the analysis, which was authored by David Squires of the Commonwealth Fund, a New York-based group that supports independent health-care research.

Underlying it all is a philosophical difference, explains Uwe Reinhardt, an expert on health-care economics at Princeton University.

"Unlike England, that has a budget, we don't have any of that" in the United States, he says. "It's absolutely honorable here for everyone in the chain to try to extract as much money as they can from the economy, and that adds up—the drug companies and the medical device makers and then the hospital, which makes the biggest markup it can. Rehab, home health care, you name it. That becomes a cost to you."

Those factors would have made my treatment several times more expensive in the United States, Reinhardt and other experts say.

Take my CT scans. Tom Sackville, chief executive of the IFHP, the global network of health insurers, views scanning as a good illustration of pricing differences.

"For the same machinery in a similar facility with the same level of staffing—assistants, nurses and so on—there are very different costs." According to IFHP data, a pelvic CT scan, for example, costs $175 in the NHS, while the average price paid to a U.S. hospital is $567—and many insurers shell out far more.

Not that Sackville, a former Conservative government health minister, is a fan of Britain's taxpayer-funded system. "It's a classic rationed system," he says, "with delays and waiting lists." Those are well-publicized criticisms of the cash-strapped NHS, which prioritizes care according to medical urgency and sometimes fails to meet guidelines for acceptable waiting times for non-urgent care (no more than 18 weeks from a primary-care referral until hospital care begins).

As a patient with potentially life-threatening injuries, I experienced none of those problems. But I did wonder where the NHS was saving money that might have been spent on me if a horse had bucked me off in rural Virginia rather than in rural England—and what effect that could have had on my treatment.

In the Royal Sussex County Hospital, I shared a bay in the trauma ward with four other women. One night, when beds in the men's bay were in short supply, a nurse asked if a man could join us. Nobody objected, so he was wheeled in behind a heavy screen to give us (and him) some privacy.

Would that have happened in America? I doubt it. Did it affect my care? I don't think so. The other patients were a more or less welcome distraction, though the nights were noisy.

More important, I didn't really understand who was in charge of my care. The Royal Sussex County is a teaching hospital, where doctors did their morning rounds with teams of junior doctors and medical students. On the few occasions I had a question, the nurses seemed to turn to a different doctor every time. My discharge papers were signed by a physician I don't even remember having met. The whole approach left me unclear about who the point person was if anything went wrong.

But when I returned to the States, I heard similar concerns. "That is why 'hospitalists' were invented," a former Post health reporter told me, referring to the physicians who specialize in coordinating patients' hospital care.

And despite my initial relief at having avoided surgery, I continue to wonder whether anything more should have been done. Six months on, one bone in my pelvis hasn't fully healed. It still hurts.

Several British doctors suggested that if my accident had happened in America I would likely have had surgery to insert screws and plates and fix my fractures. In the U.S. fee-for-service system, the argument goes, doctors have an incentive to treat what their salaried British counterparts believed would heal with time (and without the risks of cutting me open). As a 2011 report comparing health systems put it, the United States "does a lot of elective surgery—the sort of activities where it is not always clearcut about whether a particular intervention is necessary or not."

One British friend, a surgeon, thought I could find a range of legitimate opinions, which is pretty much what I learned from Greg M. Osgood, who took over my care when I returned to this country. He's an orthopedic trauma surgeon at Johns Hopkins Hospital (where, incidentally, technicians have taken three X-rays of my pelvis from three different angles on each outpatient visit, as opposed to the single X-ray taken at each follow-up visit in Britain).

My case lay in a "gray area," Osgood said. "Pelvises like to heal," he told me. "They have a good blood supply." And for the one bone that continued to cause discomfort, he recommended ultrasound to hasten healing rather than a trip to the OR.

And the multiple X-rays? Higher cost, more radiation, yes. But they offer a more complete view of the pelvic ring, and doctors here don't want to risk missing a thing. "A large part of what U.S. doctors do is medical-legal," said Hopkins chief orthopedic resident Savyasachi Thakkar, alluding to the costs of medical liability, which are far higher here than in Britain where the NHS also administers the legal aspects of medical practice.

Both doctors exemplify the sort of individualized attention that a place such as Hopkins stakes its reputation on. As Sackville put it, "About half the population in America get the best treatment in the world." With a steady income and good health insurance, I suspect I'm lucky enough to be in that half. I get very good treatment.

But I am hard-pressed to see how I would have been better off here than in Britain. And a comparative study of how seven countries' health systems function ranks the United States below Britain—in fact, last—"on dimensions of access, patient safety, coordination, efficiency, and equity."

As it turned out, I needn't have wasted a minute worrying about the bills I was running up in Britain. My husband confirmed very quickly with our U.S. health insurance company that it covered treatment overseas.

But the possibility of foreigners' freeloading on the NHS has become politically contentious. "What we have is a free National Health Service," Prime Minister David Cameron said last year, "not a free *inter*national health service." While I waited in England for my lung to heal enough for travel, I'd hear echoes of that sentiment on the nightly news, as a vitriolic debate evolved over whether the problem was real or a reflection of the Conservative government's anti-immigrant stance.

Once back in the States, I got another surprise: a letter from the Royal Sussex County Hospital saying my bill hadn't been paid, along with a note saying that failure to pay could result in "a future immigration application to enter or remain in the UK being denied."

What followed was the flurry of phone calls and e-mails familiar to any American who has haggled with a health insurance company.

First, the copies of the forms I e-mailed in were deemed illegible.

Then, in early February, I found out that my claim had been denied by my insurer, on the grounds that the British hospital did not get pre-authorization for admitting me—a step that nobody had told us was necessary.

I appealed, and was told it might take 60 days for the appeal to be considered.

Worrying about what might happen when I next tried to enter Britain—even with a British passport—I appealed the appeals process and asked for it to be expedited.

In mid-March, payment finally came through—and I contacted Bishop back in Sussex to let her know. She has become something of an expert on overseas patients and has been invited to speak before a parliamentary committee.

Unless they ask for private care, overseas visitors are treated clinically just like NHS patients, Bishop explained. But while legal residents receive free care, people like me are asked to pay the NHS package rate for procedures that is set by the government. It's a fairly straightforward process, and Bishop handles overseas visitor billing for the Royal Sussex County and five other sites, which have about 780 inpatient beds. Billing for private care can get more complicated.

In the United States, billing is a business unto itself. "A typical academic health center will have 300 to 400 billing clerks," Reinhardt reckons. "And each will have his counterpart in the insurance industry. To handle the billing of one hospital, you need 800 people. That would be unthinkable in England." Johns Hopkins Medicine has more than 500 billing clerks across its six hospitals.

How my $5,572.54 British bill might have ballooned here, not only because of "higher prices" and "greater use of more expensive medical technology," but if it had been caught up in the administrative quagmire of U.S. billing—costs that Reinhardt estimates account for a quarter of U.S. health spending.

Being badly hurt does funny things; it makes you selfish, turns your focus inward. But as visions of those U.S. health-care dollars spiraled upward in my head, I realized how fortunate I was to have received the care that Britain provides for all its people and how lucky I am to be in what Sackville described as the half of the American population that gets the best treatment in the world.

Because ultimately there's the rub.

What about the other half?

Minding Ps and Qs: The Political and Policy Questions Framing Health Care Spending
William M. Sage

Within five years of Medicare's enactment in 1965, liberal social activists Barbara and John Ehrenreich conjured a new demon—the "medical-industrial complex"—which they associated with large, profit-seeking entities that were supplanting individual physicians, acquiring political influence, and plundering public funds.[1] The choice of words, of course, echoed those of conservative President Dwight Eisenhower, who in his televised Farewell Address three days before leaving office in 1961 had warned the nation of a "military-industrial complex." If one edits Eisenhower's original text to substitute "healthcare" for "military," parallels emerge between the American public's fear of Communist invasion or thermonuclear war and its fear of disease or death in their potential for serious economic mischief.

> Our healthcare must be mighty, ready for instant action.... Until the latest of our social welfare laws, the United States had no healthcare industry.... But now we can no longer risk emergency improvisation of national healthcare; we have been compelled to create a permanent healthcare industry of vast proportions. Added to this, fourteen and a half million men and women are directly engaged in the healthcare establishment. We annually spend on healthcare security more than the net income of all United States corporations.

> This conjunction of an immense healthcare establishment and a large healthcare industry is new in the American experience. The total influence—economic, political, even spiritual—is felt in every city, every State house, every office of the Federal government. We recognize the imperative need for this development. Yet we must not fail to comprehend its grave implications.

> In the councils of government, we must guard against the acquisition of unwarranted influence, whether sought or unsought, by the healthcare-industrial complex.... Only an alert and knowledgeable citizenry can compel the proper meshing of the huge industrial and healthcare machinery with our non-health care methods and goals, so that security and liberty may prosper together.[2]

This "healthcare-industrial complex" has prospered beyond expectation, with spending exceeding $3 trillion and accounting for nearly 18% of GDP and approximately 10% of employment by 2014.[3] Measured against other developed countries or against "best practice" guidelines, health care in the U.S. costs far more than it should for the benefits it provides. At the same time, the health of the American public lags those same benchmarks, particularly in terms of obesity, physical inactivity, and the associated burden of chronic disease. I have often described these as the challenges of the ballpoint pen and the drive-through French fry—two similarly shaped objects that represent in turn the inefficiency of fragmented care based on "doctor's orders" and the poor lifestyle choices of the American public. Solve either of these problems and the cost curve will begin to bend; solve both and health care expenditures should become sustainable for a nation as wealthy as ours.

Collectively, health care spending was long viewed as the acceptable price of scientific progress given our national wealth. Roughly two decades ago, however, the governmental contribution to rising medical costs began to force budgetary tradeoffs for scarce tax dollars and add unacceptably to public debt—often because organized health care interests could extract sizeable rents through aggressive lobbying. More recently, analysts have suggested that continued cost growth in employment-based coverage is crowding out cash raises in the private sector and decreasing standards of living for American workers.

The cost problem is even more disturbing at a personal level. Illness is (very) unevenly distributed, and severe illness can be impoverishing because it simultaneously imposes expense and diminishes earning capacity. Even with "Obamacare," coverage is not universal. Prices for recommended care are very high, and cheaper alternatives are seldom available. Paying for a single high-cost diagnostic test or meeting the annual cost-sharing obligations under a basic health insurance policy can be crippling. Our poorer citizens enjoy less welfare support generally than in other countries, and health disparities favoring the rich and white are large and growing.[4] And it is even harder for individuals than for society as a whole to decide that "enough" health care has been received, especially for potentially serious medical conditions.

Health care spending is about science and ethics, markets and government, freedom and community. Whether one is an Ehrenreich or an Eisenhower, *these are inherently political conversations*. None are easy to sidestep, and few ever end. But they do *change*, and tracing the evolution of political conversations about health care spending and their relationship to the formation of policy is a valuable exercise. Minding the Ps of politics and policy in each of the conceptual-temporal phases discussed below enables one to identify the Qs—the key questions that must be confronted going forward to achieve substantial, sustained improvement in the affordability of the U.S. health care system.

What follows is a retelling of the recent history of health spending and health policy. Although cost concerns in health care long predate the events described,[5] by the late 1980s the unique upward trajectory of post-Medicare U.S. health care spending had been established, recessions and tax cuts were eroding federal and state budgets, and efforts to harness market forces to serve policy goals were accelerating. From the initial writings on "managed competition" by Enthoven and Kronick, through the failed Clinton health reform effort in the early 1990s, to the passage of the Affordable Care Act in 2010, the policy narrative of health spending acquired a superficial consistency.[6]

On closer examination, however, it becomes apparent that the cost problem has been repeatedly reframed in political discourse even during this relatively brief period. The clearest transition has been from a narrative centered on rationing necessary care to one committed to reducing wasteful care—although the role of accumulated health law and professional self-regulation in perpetuating waste remains largely unrecognized and the recently articulated commitment to population health seems an imperfect proxy for explicitly developing social solidarity with respect to health and health care in the United States.

Phase I Cost Control: "The Best Health Care in the World"

When an economic downturn in the early 1990s threatened jobs and the health insurance that stable employment confers, universal coverage re-entered the national policy agenda for the first time in a generation. The obstacle was cost: in harm to business (if mandated of private employers) or in higher taxes or ballooning deficits (if publicly financed), with the third-party presidential candidate Ross Perot bringing the arcana of government borrowing into mainstream consciousness. Health care had reached 12%(!) of US GDP by 1990, and serious commentators wondered how much more we could afford.

Progress

Could the expected cost of universal coverage be reduced? Not without jeopardizing the quality of care, answered the cognoscenti, because—as virtually every American politician routinely declared—health care in the United States was "the best in the world." Correspondingly, the prevailing health policy narrative of the time declared that new technology, much of it scientifically miraculous, was the principal driver of high health care spending. America's decision to prioritize "supply"—to develop new treatments, train specialized physicians to administer them, and proliferate acute care hospitals where patients could receive them—made expanding "access" an expensive proposition.[7] Physicians, moreover, seemed able to "induce" demand for their services almost at will, so that each new graduate joining the medical workforce added cost to the system rather than making it more competitive, as basic economics would predict.[8]

Power

There were supplementary explanations for high and rising spending. Medicare's deference to physicians and lack of structural safeguards against cost overruns had bred an unholy alliance between America's seniors—active, single-issue voters with considerable political influence—and an array of special interest providers seeking to do business with government on terms favorable to them.[9] Passage of the Medicare Catastrophic Coverage Act of 1988, a modest attempt to place Medicare on a sounder actuarial footing by raising premiums for higher-income seniors, provoked such a strong backlash that Congress was forced to repeal it before its effective date. This sent a shockwave through the Beltway that discouraged policy innovation, and made Medicare into an untouchable "third rail" for the health reform debate that followed.

Profiteers

If physicians are assumed to provide scientifically optimal medicine, any unnecessary cost must come from elsewhere. A series of allegations therefore targeted forces external, or at least tangential, to the doctor-patient relationship. Chief among them was "defensive medicine," a loosely defined, imperfectly quantified belief that physicians fearing malpractice lawsuits routinely performed expensive tests and procedures of little clinical benefit.[10] Absent an acute crisis in the availability (mid-1970s) or affordability (mid-1980s) of physicians' malpractice insurance, reducing costly defensive medicine became the principal argument in favor of tort reform. In addition to greedy trial lawyers, common villains in the profiteering narrative included pharmaceutical and health insurance companies—large corporate entities that lacked the individuality, local connections, and familiar ethics of physicians and charitable hospitals.

Paperwork

The predations of the accused profiteers fed a general belief that "waste, fraud, and abuse"—again loosely defined but excluding bona fide clinical activities—was a major drain on health care coffers.[11] The political consensus to eliminate it through stricter oversight resulted in a general bureaucratic escalation. More regulation on the payer side required greater investment in both compliance and evasion on the provider side, a pattern that was most pronounced in government reimbursement programs but that was replicated by private insurers seeking to reduce their claims payouts—which in turn provoked public concern over both profits and high administrative costs crowding out payment for necessary medical services (the poorly named "medical loss ratio").

This "Phase I" conceptualization of the health care cost problem had its intellectual apotheosis in a 1994 book by Dr. William Kissick.[12] Portraying health policy as an "iron triangle" of cost, access, and quality, Kissick argued that society's "finite resources" could never meet its "infinite demand" for medical care. Although Kissick's cost dilemma was largely a testament to medicine's success, his formulation was unappealing to both politicians and physicians. For government to solve the health care cost problem, it had to reach a definitive political settlement regarding limits that had failed in the 1970s under the rubric "health planning," and was patently unachievable in the 1990s.[13] For the profession to solve the cost problem, it had to endorse forms of rationing that ran contrary to established ethics and threatened to drain patient care of its greatest satisfactions, both psychic and material.[14]

Only one U.S. state confronted the purported cost drivers of health care head-on. Through an explicit, highly visible process that included both clinical-technical expertise and democratic participation, the Oregon Health Plan (OHP) broadened Medicaid to a larger group of beneficiaries but guaranteed coverage only for condition-specific treatments meeting cost-effectiveness standards.[15] Rationing health care patient-by-patient was a radical reconceptualization of health insurance, though the approach suffered by accepting reported costs as real costs, not questioning the organization or efficiency of care delivery, and failing to invest in health at the population level.

OHP's reception in Washington, D.C., was hostile, with the first Bush administration denying a Medicaid waiver on Americans with Disabilities Act grounds, but likely viewing any formalized process of health care rationing as defeatist and un-American. Oregon itself struggled with the harshness of the priorities its analysis had generated, and by the time OHP received a waiver from the Clinton administration, much of its prioritization process had been eviscerated, and what little data-driven rationing remained was supplanted shortly thereafter by moving Medicaid beneficiaries into private managed care.[16]

Dissonance between policy rationale and political reality also plagued the unsuccessful effort to expand coverage nationally in 1993–94. The Clinton administration's political advisers led it down the path of "managed competition," mandating coverage through employers that would be provided by private health plans competing on cost and quality in a structured marketplace.[17] While managed competition has much to commend it, and had formed the backbone of the embryonic coverage expansion that President Nixon did not remain in office long enough to gestate, it was at odds with the administrative cost critique emphasized by President Clinton's health reform czar, Ira Magaziner. If administrative expense and profiteering were the major sources of excess spending, a single-payer plan would have been a more suitable policy prescription. But a centrist Democrat following a dozen years of Republican rule could not easily embrace "socialized medicine," particularly when balanced budgets had acquired political salience. Nor would the Clinton White House consider rationing care using explicit controls on coverage. Prominent bioethicists drawn to the reform effort by the perceived necessity of ethically allocating scarce medical resources were soon diverted to other tasks.

Phase II Cost Control: The Kaiser Fallacy

In the 1990s and 2000s, the United States tried to contain health care costs using private "managed care." The poster child for managed care has always been Kaiser Permanente, a group-model HMO with a 75-year history that—most everyone agrees—delivers excellent health care to its members. It is only a slight exaggeration to say that President Nixon signed the HMO Act of 1973 to help Kaiser-like organizations overcome the AMA's longstanding opposition to prepaid practice, and that proponents of managed competition in the 1980s imagined a world of competing Kaisers. But the factors that made Kaiser successful were not generally understood 20 years ago, especially in the Beltway, and were hard to replicate outside of California using private physician practices and community hospitals.

Even more importantly, policymakers turned to managed care without reframing the cost problem they were trying to solve. Although the shift hinted at the importance of "delivery system reform" to cost control, many viewed the failure of the Clinton administration's effort primarily as confirming the weakness of government as a limiting force. Handicapped by politics and by legal requirements of due process, it could not exclude greedy or incompetent providers, it could not resist special interests, and it could not ration care. Perhaps, they thought, private health plans looking out for their own financial interests would be better at saying, "No!"[18]

Patchwork

Organized systems of care such as Kaiser seemed uniquely able to streamline the delivery of care without sacrificing quality and safety. Health services research begun in the 1970s had revealed substantial, unexpected geographic variation in medical treatment that was not associated with either greater needs or superior outcomes.[19] "Best practices" were seldom available, and clear advances in medical knowledge took years to diffuse into communities and alter the habits of local physicians. "Fragmentation" was also structural: most physicians continued to work in undercapitalized solo or small-group practices; hospitals competed for physician referrals by amassing expensive technologies with little attention to their necessity; and the results of care were essentially unmeasurable.[20] Kaiser's physicians and hospitals, by contrast, were dedicated to their members, coordinated care among themselves, avoided duplication, followed standardized guidelines, and could be held accountable for both costs and outcomes as a unit.

Prepaid Care

The core logic of the HMO approach involved a convergence of coverage and care at the health plan level, with plans receiving an annual "capitated" premium (i.e., a per enrollee payment) and taking responsibility for providing necessary care to a defined population of members. State Medicaid programs, and to some degree Medicare, pursued similar strategies as the private sector, anticipating that it would be easier to deal with a small number of competing health plans than legions of individual providers.

In Kaiser itself, physicians are salaried and the organization tracks member health and health care rather than processing claims to "reimburse" itemized services. Kaiser even assumes liability at the health plan level for malpractice claims against its affiliated physicians. In this way, patients enjoy one-stop shopping while the worst impulses of providers to over-treat, and of insurers to undertreat, are counterbalanced. In return for these benefits, members of Kaiser-like managed care organizations give up their right to coverage of services from unaffiliated physicians and hospitals. Services received within the organization, however, are covered on very favorable terms, with low deductibles and co-payments.

Prevention

The managed care era brought the potential cost-savings of preventive care into serious policy debate. Preventive care is undervalued by physicians and hospitals, who are more likely to be called on when serious illnesses arise and who are better paid to respond to them. As the term implies, "health maintenance organizations" are intended to prevent disease as well as treat it. Because members receive care exclusively from the HMO over a period of years, the theory goes, the HMO has a financial incentive to invest in prevention, including regular screening, early diagnosis, and prompt treatment. Preventive care is also usually free to members so that they will access it routinely.

Purchasers

Managed care was supposed to control cost in part because purchasers would become as organized as integrated insurer-providers. For this reason, the Clinton health reform had created "health alliances" (originally called "health insurance purchasing cooperatives") that were the policy progenitors of the ACA's insurance exchanges. Pooled purchasing, the advantages of which had already been demonstrated by large employers, saved money by creating more stable risk pools, generating economies of scale in enrollment and administration, and conferring greater bargaining power on the buyer. The cost disadvantages of employer purchasing were that it attenuated the connection between available coverage and individual preferences, and that it added a large taxpayer subsidy to health care that further reduced price consciousness.

The managed care experiment failed. Competing Kaisers never materialized. In retrospect, it was asking too much.[21] Closed-panel HMOs prosper in a few parts of the country where both patients and physicians are acculturated to them. Moreover, they require massive capital investment. Physicians in private practice elsewhere were not about to migrate en masse to corporate entities whose facilities were unbuilt and whose businesses were untested. The flawed alternative was to assemble "virtual" HMOs by contract, leaving physicians and hospitals as structurally fragmented as before but relying on financial incentives to break providers of their profligate habits. And interposing "gatekeeper" physicians and preauthorization requirements between patients and the specialized care they were accustomed to receiving. Making things worse, the insurers and intermediaries who stepped forward to serve the market were often new, for-profit entities with ambitious executives and strict earnings targets. Given the high level of annual churn in enrollment, long-term investment in health proved unprofitable, and public confidence in quality and trustworthiness evaporated.

The backlash came quickly.[22] Faced with employee unrest (and buoyed by a sound economy), private employers retreated as active purchasers while politicians, encouraged by lobbyists protecting provider interests, seized on the shift in public opinion. Nearly all states passed "patient protection" acts. Congress was more restrained, but one high-profile law it enacted—the "Newborns' and Mothers' Health Protection Act of 1996"—made abundantly clear from its title and content (guaranteeing generous private coverage for post-delivery hospitalization) that even transparent, scientifically reasonable measures limiting care for generally healthy and economically secure individuals were politically unacceptable.[23] Private rationing would be no easier than public rationing.

When the dust settled on "Phase II," little progress had been made, and cost growth—which had briefly stalled—accelerated again. Streamlined organizations like Kaiser remained rare, with most managed care gravitating to large Blue Cross plans that contracted unselectively (and sometimes unaggressively) with every hospital and nearly every physician. Under these conditions, premiums for prevention-oriented HMO-style products became unaffordable, and—boosted by the rising political fortunes of conservative Republicans who blamed costs on moral hazard and the welfare state—health insurance coverage itself became seen as the problem rather than the solution.

The result was a far less transparent shift of financial responsibility from insurers and employers to insured workers and patients in the form of high deductibles and co-insurance. This movement (ironically called "consumer-directed care") was billed as cultivating savvy buyers who had "skin in the game," but served mainly to conceal continued growth in health care costs by moving it from visible premiums to less visible individual and family debt. By the time this was generally known, a national economic collapse unrelated to health care had intervened, and a new Democratic administration took over—promising universal health coverage as a prerequisite to financial security and opportunity.

Phase III Cost Control: Information, Incentives, and Value

The Patient Protection and Affordable Care Act of 2010 (ACA) was an ambitious and risky endeavor. It attempted to expand health coverage to nearly all citizens, but not saddle the country with even more debt than existing entitlement programs—notably Medicare—had already created. It maintained many of the premises of 1990s-style managed competition, yet never spoke the words "managed care" above a whisper. Most importantly, it simultaneously engaged all three parts of the health reform puzzle—health insurance, health care delivery, and the underlying health of individuals and communities.

Skeptics immediately labeled it a giveaway to a few and a takeaway from the rest, and whether the ACA can credibly offer something to everyone remains an open question. But there were reasons beyond overconfidence why universalizing an already-too-costly health care system was the majority's political choice. These included three related beliefs, each backed by research: that the insured were already paying a lot for the uninsured, that these shifted expenditures were made greater (and their benefits diminished) by lack of attention to "social determinants" of health, and that perverse incentives and lack of information made the existing health care system massively wasteful. Rhetoric regarding the "best health care in the world" receded; "delivery system reform" became a consensus objective.[24]

Productivity

By 2010, the intellectual mantle of health care cost control had passed from the Kissicks of the post-Medicare generation, alighted briefly on conservative theorists of health savings accounts, and wrapped itself firmly around the Institute for Healthcare Improvement (IHI) and its founder, pediatrician and former Harvard Community Health Plan quality leader Don Berwick. Examining quality, management, and the rise in chronic disease, IHI distilled its reform goals into a "Triple Aim": improving the patient experience of care, improving the health of populations, and reducing per capita costs.[25]

This "value-based" analysis was bolstered by authoritative reports from the Institute of Medicine and others that demonstrated major safety lapses, a "quality chasm," and nearly a trillion dollars in annual waste.[26] In asserting that the component parts of the Triple Aim are simultaneously achievable, Berwick's formulation had an immediate advantage over Kissick's. Instead of requiring a definitive political settlement regarding limits on resource use (e.g., the ACA's apocryphal "death panels"), the Triple Aim called only for iterative, incremental improvements—hard tradeoffs being premature when so many mutually beneficial efficiency gains are possible.[27]

Processing

A clear divergence between health care and ostensibly efficient industries is the latter's much greater use of 21st century information and communications technologies. To its proponents, Health IT can facilitate coordination of care using Electronic Health Records and Health Information Exchanges; communicate information that is more timely and accurate; offer alerts to improve safety and decision support to boost quality; expand access to services through inexpensive telehealth modalities; and measure processes and results to enable efficient production, informed consumer choice, and public accountability. The George W. Bush administration created the Office of National Coordinator for Health IT by executive order in 2004, and its funding increased substantially under HITECH (part of the American Recovery and Reinvestment Act) and the ACA. Early supply-side assistance to developers of platforms and software eventually gave way to a demand-side "pull strategy" with financial incentives for "meaningful use" by hospitals and physicians, but overall enthusiasm has remained strong.

Payment

Fee-for-service medicine can be blamed for many perversities in the existing health care system. Procedures are overused. Physicians neglect simple preventive measures in favor of complex therapeutic ones. Because health professionals and health facilities bill separately, production is uncoordinated.

Avoiding complications reduces profit rather than raising it. Defensive medicine enhances revenue without adding value. Maximizing "reimbursement" adds to administrative overhead and increases the potential for fraud. For these reasons, "alternative payment systems" and "risk-based contracting" are universally praised, if incompletely specified, by the current generation of policymakers.[28] Depending on the size and nature of the organization receiving it, "value-based" payment can include care bundles or episodes, "reference pricing," and various forms of "shared savings" ranging from modest bonuses for efficient performance to globally capitated payments that place providers at full financial risk.[29]

Performance

"Accountable care" has replaced "managed care" in the cost-control lexicon. Quality assessment before the 1990s was largely an academic exercise, and entered the policy mainstream only when the public began to doubt the loyalty and competence of physicians who seemed increasingly in thrall to managed care organizations. But one cannot pay for value unless one can measure it, and avoiding another backlash requires an information-rich environment for both patients and providers. Performance metrics, therefore, have proliferated in the post-ACA health care system. New metrics range across care processes, clinical outcomes, patient experiences, and population health improvement, and are adaptable to both traditional settings and new delivery models such as accountable care organizations and patient-centered medical homes.[30] Nearly half the states have also put in place All-Payer Claims Databases to facilitate quality measurement and empower both consumers and regulators, although the states' power to mandate reporting by self-insured ERISA plans was recently limited by the Supreme Court.[31]

Prices

High service and input prices contribute significantly to overall U.S. health care spending.[32] Patients seldom know the price or quality of their care in advance of receiving it. Policies to make quality more transparent to consumers began in the 1990s to help monitor the cost-cutting activities of managed care organizations. Making price more transparent began in the 2000s, in part to facilitate prudent purchasing in high-deductible health plans. Still, recent analyses have exposed hospital pricing that continues to be both exorbitant and arbitrary.[33] Pharmaceutical prices are also notably higher in the U.S. than abroad; sharp increases in prices for established drugs as well as new biological entities have renewed interest in government negotiating or controlling prices. Corporate consolidation amplifies these pricing concerns—large hospitals can gain market power or dominant hospitals and dominant insurers can lock out competitors for their mutual benefit—which may require stronger antitrust enforcement to prevent.[34] More generally, arbitrary and variable pricing suggests that many health care providers do not understand their own cost structures, which bodes poorly for improving productive efficiency.

Populations

The chronic disease burden associated with poor nutrition, insufficient physical activity, and other lifestyle factors, combined with overall population aging, threatens a substantial increase in health care spending.[35] Health care and public health—historically related fields that drifted apart in the 20th century—have been brought together again by a series of challenges such as AIDS/HIV, tobacco control, biopreparedness, pandemic influenza, substance abuse, environmental exposures, and child and adult obesity. Drawing on research mapping the social determinants of health and documenting disparities that unfairly burden low-income and minority populations, the ACA has accelerated the coalescence of individual and population health management. ACA-related population health initiatives include accountable care organizations, community workforce investments, and hospital-generated community health needs assessments.

Although the Triple Aim reflects a profound rethinking of health policy, it is too soon to tell whether the payment reform and information exchange that embody "Phase III" cost control will prove effective remedies for waste and inefficiency. A welcome post-ACA dip in health care spending may have been only transitory, and early returns on accountable care organizations and bundled payment programs are mixed.[36] Incentives and information may bring people to the table and begin conversations, but may not change behavior. Recognized problems include overshoot in the number and complexity of accountability metrics and "meaningful use" standards, difficulties attributing outcomes when several providers share responsibility for a given patient's care, rewarding inefficient providers for improvement rather than efficient providers for achievement, and limitations associated with using claims data rather than clinical data to monitor and improve performance.[37]

The role of government in fostering efficiency is also unsettled. The current generation of reforms is more market-oriented than collective, with President Obama tending to equate the interests of "consumers" with those of "the American public."[38] This bias has already endangered the ACA's "Cadillac tax" on very expensive employee health benefits, a reform widely supported by health policy experts but lacking the social solidarity needed to justify it politically. Dislodging long-standing industry practices also seems to require a top-down approach in many instances, particularly through Medicare policy. However, lack of attention to why the health care system is so *persistently* inefficient, notably its accretion of self-protective professional regulation at the state as well as the federal level, decreases the likelihood that missteps in the reform process will be self-correcting.

Looking Ahead to Phase IV: Revisiting Law and Culture

A truism of management consulting is that "culture eats strategy for breakfast."[39] Three cultures are relevant to health care: professional, personal, and political. Engaging these cultures is likely to lie at the heart of any successful effort to reconcile health care spending with other critical uses of public and private resources.

At the professional level, changing the culture is made easier by a new generation of *practitioners*, who are more diverse in their professional skills and training, and more willing than their predecessors to embrace clinical redesign and population health management.[40] However, it also will be necessary to reexamine and begin to unwind a century of regulatory and self-regulatory *protectionism* that constitutes the deep legal architecture of the health care system, and that may largely be responsible for its inefficiency.[41]

At the personal level, genuine *participation* by individuals in setting health goals, exploring medical and non-medical options, and managing health-related decisions is indispensable to obtaining better value from the health care system. For situations in which a market framework is appropriate, health care *products* must be available that meet individuals' needs, are sold on a fully assembled basis, and include warranties for basic quality and safety like other complex consumer goods.[42]

At the political level, promoting health and providing health care must become expressions of *patriotism* in America, as they are elsewhere in the world.[43] In particular, the crippling multi-generational effects of endemic poverty on education and health, and therefore on economic and social opportunity, can no longer be ignored.[44] This collective commitment is necessary not only to salvage scarce financial resources from low-value health care uses—only some of which constitute pure "waste"—but also to identify higher value social uses and channel saved resources toward them.

In other words, health care cost control depends critically on resurgent belief, both medical and social, in compassion and community as well as clinical capability and consumerism. It cannot be coincidental that both Don Berwick and Avedis Donabedian, luminaries of health care quality improvement, came late in their careers to emphasize personal service and social consciousness over technical achievement. Berwick's view, recently stated, is that "[w]ithout a new moral ethos, there will be no winners."[45] Donabedian, in an interview conducted shortly before his death, put it even more directly: "The secret of quality is love."[46]

References

1. B. Ehrenreich, *The American Health Empire: Power, Profits, and Politics* (New York: Random House, 1970).
2. Eisenhower's Farewell Address to the Nation, Jan. 17, 1961, *available at* <http://mcadams.posc.mu.edu/ike.htm> (last visited November 30, 2016).

3. A. B. Martin, M. Hartman, J. Benson, and A. Catlin, "National Health Spending in 2014: Faster Growth Driven by Coverage Expansion and Prescription Drug Spending," *Health Affairs* (Millwood) 35, no. 1 (2016): 150–160.

4. R. Chetty, M. Stepner, S. Abraham, S. Lin, B. Scuderi, N. Turner, A. Bergeron, and D. Cutler, "The Association between Income and Life Expectancy in the United States, 2001–2014," *JAMA* 315, no. 16 (2016): 1750–1766.

5. P. Starr, *The Social Transformation of American Medicine* (New York: Basic Books, 1982): at 261 (discussing the Committee on the Costs of Medical Care, which was convened in 1926 by fifteen economists, physicians, and public health specialists); D. Blumenthal and J. A. Morone, *The Heart of Power: Health and Politics in the Oval Office* (Berkeley: University of California Press 2009).

6. A. Enthoven and R. Kronick, "A ConsumerChoice Health Plan for the 1990s: Universal Health Insurance in a System Designed to Promote Quality and Economy," *New England Journal of Medicine* 320, no. 1 (1989): 29–35 (First of Two Parts) and *New England Journal of Medicine* 320, no. 2 (1989): 94–100 (Second of Two Parts).

7. L. R. Jacobs, "Politics of America's Supply State: Health Reform and Technology," *Health Affairs* 14, no. 2 (1995): 143–157.

8. Graduate Medical Education National Advisory Committee (GMENAC), Report to the Secretary on Physician Manpower (Sept. 1981).

9. B. C. Vladeck, "The Political Economy of Medicare," *Health Affairs* 18, no. 1 (1999): 22–36.

10. D. M. Studdert, M. M. Mello, W. M. Sage, C. M. Des Roches, J. J. Peugh, K. Zapert, and T. A. Brennan, "Defensive Medicine among High-Risk Specialist Physicians during a Malpractice Crisis," *JAMA* 293, no. 21 (2005): 2609–2617.

11. J. F. Blumstein, "The Fraud and Abuse Statute in an Evolving Health Care Marketplace: Life in the Health Care Speakeasy," *American Journal of Law & Medicine* 22, nos. 2–3 (1996): 205–231.

12. W. Kissick, *Medicine's Dilemmas: Infinite Needs Versus Finite Resources* (New Haven, Yale University Press, 1994).

13. J. A. Califano, *America's Health Care Revolution: Who Lives? Who Dies? Who Pays?* (New York: Simon & Schuster, 1986).

14. J. P. Kassirer, Editorial, "Managing Care—Should We Adopt a New Ethic?" *New England Journal of Medicine* 339, no. 6 (1998): 397–398, at 398 (concluding that physicians should not "capitulate to an ethic of the group rather than the individual").

15. J. F. Blumstein, "The Oregon Experiment: The Role of Cost-Benefit Analysis in the Allocation of Medicaid Funds," *Social Science & Medicine* 45, no. 4 (1997): 545–554.

16. J. Oberlander et al., "Rationing Medical Care: Rhetoric and Reality in the Oregon Health Plan," *Canadian Medical Association Journal* 164, no. 11 (2001): 1583–1587.

17. P. Starr and W. A. Zelman, "A Bridge to Compromise: Competition under a Budget," *Health Affairs* 12, no. Supp. 1 (1993): 7–23.

18. *Cf.* E. McCaughey, "No Exit," *New Republic*, February 7, 1994, *available at* <http://www.newrepublic.com/article/healthcare/no-exit> (equating rationing under the Clinton reform with private managed care) (last visited September 9, 2016).

19. The Dartmouth Atlas of Healthcare, "Understanding of the Efficiency and Effectiveness of the Health Care System (2015)," *available at* <http://www.dartmouthatlas.org> (last visited September 9, 2016).

20. See E. Elhauge, "Why We Should Care about Health Care Fragmentation and How to Fix It," in E. Elhauge, ed., *The Fragmentation of U.S. Health Care: Causes and Solutions* (New York: Oxford University Press, 2010): 1–20, at 5.

21. R. A. Berenson, "Beyond Competition," *Health Affairs* 16, no. 2 (1997): 171–180, at 176 ("The alignment between health plans and providers envisioned in managed competition is virtually impossible.").

22. R. J. Blendon et al., "Understanding the Managed Care Backlash," *Health Affairs* 17, no. 4 (1998): 80–94, at 94 (examining the depth and breadth of the public backlash against managed care and the underlying causes).

23. D. A. Hyman, "What Lessons Should We Learn from Drive-Through Deliveries?" *Pediatrics* 107, no. 2 (2001): 406–407.

24. W. M. Sage, "Legislating Delivery System Reform: A 30,000-Foot View of the 800-Pound Gorilla," *Health Affairs* 26, no. 6 (2007): 1553–1556.

25. Institute for Healthcare Improvement, "IHI Triple Aim Initiative (2015)," *available at* <http://www.ihi.org/Engage/Initiatives/TripleAim/pages/default.aspx> (last visited September 9, 2016).

26. Institute of Medicine, *Crossing the Quality Chasm: A New Health System for the 21st Century* (2001): at 83; Institute of Medicine, *To Err Is Human: Building a Safer Health System* (1997): at 37; Institute of Medicine, *Best Care at Lower Cost: The Path to Continuously Learning Health Care in America* (2012).

27. M. E. Porter and E. O. Teisberg, *Redefining Health Care: Creating Value-Based Competition on Results* (Boston: Harvard Business Review Press, 2006); M. E. Porter and T. H. Lee, "The Strategy That Will Fix Health Care," *Harvard Business Review* 91, no. 10 (2013): 50–70.

28. U.S. Department of Health and Human Services, *Better, Smarter, Healthier: In Historic Announcement, HHS Sets Clear Goals and Timeline for Shifting Medicare Reimbursements from Volume to Value*, Press Release, January 26, 2015, *available at* <http://www.hhs.gov/news/press/2015pres/01/20150126a.html> (last visited September 9, 2016); B. Wynne, "May the Era of Medicare's Doc Fix (1997–2015) Rest in Peace. Now What?" *Health Affairs Blog*, April 14, 2015, *available at* <http://healthaffairs.org/blog/2015/04/14/may-the-era-of-medicares-doc-fix-1997-2015-rest-in-peace-now-what> (last visited September 9, 2016).

29. S. Delbanco, "The Payment Reform Landscape: Bundled Payment," *Health Affairs Blog*, July 2, 2014, *available at* <http://healthaffairs.org/blog/2014/07/02/the-payment-reform-landscape-bundled-payment> (last visited September 9, 2016); R. E. Mechanic, "Mandatory Medicare Bundled Payment—Is It Ready for Prime Time?" *New England Journal of Medicine* 373, no. 14 (2015): 1291–1293; S. A. Farmer et al., "Breaking Down Medicare's Bold New Proposal to Transform Hip and Knee Replacements," Brookings, August 11, 2015, *available at* <http://www.brookings.edu/blogs/health360/posts/2015/08/joint-replacement-model-care> (last visited September 9, 2016).

30. S. M. Shortell and L. P. Casalino, "Health Care Reform Requires Accountable Care Systems," *JAMA* 300, no. 1 (2008): 95–97; H. H. Luft, "Becoming Accountable—Opportunities and Obstacles for ACOs," *New England Journal of Medicine* 363, no. 15 (2010): 1389–1391.

31. *Gobeille v. Liberty Mutual Ins. Co.*, 577 US _ (2016).

32. G. F. Anderson et al., "It's the Prices, Stupid: Why the United States Is So Different from Other Countries," *Health Affairs* 22, no. 3 (2003): 89–105.

33. S. Brill, "Bitter Pill: Why Medical Bills Are Killing Us," *Time*, March 4, 2013, *available at* <http://time.com/198/bitter-pill-why-medical-bills-are-killing-us/> (last visited September 12, 2016); E. Rosenthal, "The Odd Math of Medical Tests: One Scan, Two Prices, Both High," *New York Times*, December 15, 2014, *available at* <http://www.nytimes.com/2014/12/16/health/the-odd-math-of-medical-tests-one-echocardiogram-two-prices-both-high.html> (last visited September 12, 2016); E. Fuse-Brown, "Irrational Hospital Pricing," *Houston Journal of Health Law & Policy* 14, no. 1 (2014): 11–58.

34. W. B. Vogt and R. Town, Robert Wood Johnson Foundation, *How Has Hospital Consolidation Affected the Price and Quality of Hospital Care?* (2006): at 11–12.

35. D. N. Lakdawalla, D. P. Goldman, and B. Shang, "The Health and Cost Consequences of Obesity among the Future Elderly," *Health Affairs* published online, September 26, 2005, *available at* <http://content.healthaffairs.org/content/early/2005/09/26/hlthaff.w5.r30.citation> (last visited September 12, 2016).

36. M. Susan Ridgely et al., "Bundled Payment Fails to Gain a Foothold in California: The Experience of the IHA Bundled Payment Demonstration," *Health Affairs* 33, no. 8 (2014): 1345–1352, at 1352.

37. D. M. Berwick, "Era 3 for Medicine and Health Care," *JAMA* 315, no. 13 (2016): 1329–1330.

38. President Barack Obama, Remarks in the Rose Garden of the White House on the Supreme Court's Decision in King v. Burwell (June 25, 2015).

39. Source unknown, *but cf.* E. Schein, *Organizational Culture and Leadership* (San Francisco: Jossey-Bass, 1985).

40. Institute of Medicine, *The Future of Nursing: Leading Change, Advancing Health* (Oct. 5, 2011), *available at* <http://www.nap.edu/read/12956/chapter/1> (last visited September 12, 2016); T. Kelley, "Young Docs: The New Blood That Health Care Needs," *Managed Care*, February 2016, *available at* <http://www.managedcaremag.com/archives/2016/2/young-docs-new-blood-health-care-needs> (last visited September 12, 2016).

41. W. M. Sage, "Relating Health Law to Health Policy: A Frictional Account," in I. G. Cohen, A. Hoffman, and W. M. Sage, eds., *Oxford Handbook of U.S. Healthcare Law* (New York: Oxford University Press, 2016).

42. W. M. Sage, "Assembled Products: The Key to More Effective Competition and Antitrust Oversight in Health Care," *Cornell Law Review* 101, no. 3 (2016): 609–700.

43. W. M. Sage, "Why the Affordable Care Act Needs a Better Name: 'Americare,'" *Health Affairs* 29, no. 8 (2010): 1496–1497; W. M. Sage, "Solidarity," in T. H. Murray and M. Crowley, eds., *Connecting American Values with American Health Care Reform* (Garrison, NY: The Hastings Center, 2009): at 10.

44. R. Cooper, *Poverty and the Myths of Health Care Reform* (Baltimore: Johns Hopkins University Press, 2016).

45. D. M. Berwick, "Era 3 for Medicine and Health Care," *JAMA* 315, no. 13 (2016): 1329–1330.

46. F. Mullan, "A Founder of Quality Assessment Encounters a Troubled System Firsthand," *Health Affairs* 20, no. 1 (2001): 137–141.

Gentrification

The Monthly Interview: A Conversation with Christopher B. Leinberger

The Editors of *Washington Monthly*

Among liberals, few topics are as hotly debated as gentrification. The issue is often presented in moralistic terms: privileged white people are pushing poor black and Hispanic people out of their neighborhoods.

The truth is a little more complicated. Booms in places like New York City and Washington, D.C., have both positive and negative effects—including for the poor. They have revitalized previously dangerous and economically depressed neighborhoods, bringing better jobs, safer streets, and, for homeowners, rising property values. The rapid pace of change and rising rents also raise the danger, however, of too many spoils going to the white and wealthy, leaving the poor and minorities behind.

Chris Leinberger, a real estate developer and chair of the Center for Real Estate and Urban Analysis at the George Washington University School of Business, spoke with the *Washington Monthly* at the Wharf, the new waterfront development in Southwest D.C., about the underlying policy choices that have led to urban housing unaffordability, and how to change those policies to make sure urban renewal doesn't just benefit the rich.

(This interview has been edited and condensed.)

WM: What do you worry about with these booming towns, like D.C.—who is potentially getting hurt by development?

CL: The folks who get hurt the most are existing renters. They'll not only see their rents go up; they'll be moved out completely, if their building gets rehabbed.

Now, a development like [the Wharf], of course, nobody was living here, so there's no displacement, which happens quite a bit in our formerly abandoned cities.

WM: So maybe a better example of this in D.C. would be a neighborhood like Shaw or Williamsburg in New York?

CL: Exactly. But the interesting thing is, Federal Reserve research shows that neighborhoods which are gentrifying (a) make up a very small fraction of city neighborhoods—as in 5 percent—and (b) actually have less movement than poor neighborhoods do. The primary reason is that people will try their hardest just to stay there, because it's getting better. All of a sudden you have options like a supermarket, and crime is going down, and there are more public amenities. You would want to stay if at all possible. In a poor neighborhood, there's much more spin.

WM: You're saying the research on gentrification shows that some of our concern about the victims of gentrification may be misplaced?

CL: If it's a moderate to poor neighborhood, the people who have lived in the neighborhood for decades and own their own house will have a much larger net worth than if gentrification didn't happen. It may be what pays for their retirement.

WM: But in an urban area, isn't there usually a very high proportion of people who rent and don't own?

CL: Suburbs are 75–25 ownership versus rental, urban areas will be closer to 50–50. In New York City, it's closer to 33 percent ownership and 67 percent renter—which is why I mentioned that the main concern is for renters. But the other key point is that those low-income households—and I'm talking about households earning less than 50 percent of the metropolitan area median income—are far better off living in a revitalized, walkable urban place. Yes, the housing prices may be higher as a percentage of their household income, but the transportation costs are much lower, and transportation is the second-highest household spending category. That offsets those higher housing prices. And they have accessibility to three, four, five times more jobs than they would have if they were in a low-income drivable suburb.

WM: But even if there's less individual displacement than people think, over time a certain class of people is going to be priced out of moving into that neighborhood, right?

CL: Yes. When you combine the pent-up demand for this kind of place—walkable urban, safe, lots of exciting things happening—with the fact that there's not enough land that's zoned for that kind of activity to take place, the land that is zoned for it gets bid up to ridiculous levels. And that's the major reason for gentrification and making mixed-income development hard to do.

WM: You used the term "walkable urban." What does that mean?

CL: There are two ways to build a metropolitan region. One is "drivable suburban," which is very low-density development that segregates land by type of use, meaning offices are separate from residential is separate from retail, and so on. It relies on one transportation system: cars and trucks. The other way is "walkable urban," which is much more dense, mixed use, and historically more mixed income. We built only walkable urban cities for the 7,000 to 8,000 years we've been building cities, until drivable suburban was introduced in the mid-twentieth century.

WM: And much of what we think of as "cities" in the United States, or metropolitan areas, counts as drivable suburban, right?

CL: Yes. The metropolitan Washington region is only 2 percent walkable urban land; the other 98 percent is low-density drivable suburban. The most important criterion in building walkable urban is higher density, but the other issue is, do you have multiple transportation options to get to work, shopping, school, so you're not just forced to use the car?

WM: And your argument is that we have too many places where you have to drive everywhere, and not enough of the other kind—walkable urban. And that this is what makes walkable urban so expensive.

CL: Right. It is almost entirely the high land price in walkable urban places that causes gentrification. Increase the land in metro Washington that's zoned for walkable urban development from 2 percent to 4 percent, and most of this price premium goes away.

WM: How do you know there's unmet demand for walkable urban? Because you might think, well, if people want it, then the market will supply it.

CL: One way is by doing consumer research. Depending on the poll, somewhere between 35 and 50 percent of us want to live and work in walkable urban areas. Whereas only 5 to 20 percent actually can, depending on the metro area. So there's a gap, known as pent-up demand.

WM: How did we end up in the situation where there's not enough walkable urban?

CL: Zoning. It's illegal to build walkable urban development in 98 percent of metropolitan Washington, and that's why the market cannot supply enough—and what the market does deliver is at a high price. It's not just D.C., of course. We put in place zoning in the 1940s, '50s, '60s, that mandated a separation of land uses. You could not have retail underneath rental apartments. That was illegal. It is illegal to have auxiliary housing units in a single-family neighborhood, sometimes called "granny flats," which is a great form of affordable housing. And 95 to 98 percent of the metropolitan zoning in this country is the same way. It's been in place for half a century, or more, and it's a bitch to change.

WM: And is the key problem that it suppresses density, or that it rules out mixed use?

CL: Both. It's a web of restrictions that makes walkable urban development impossible: height limits, restrictions on mixed use, setbacks. And it also demands a very high amount of parking. The only way to meet those high parking ratios is to build low density with surface parking lots.

WM: What are some problems with this, besides the effect on rental prices?

CL: Number one, drivable suburban development is the U.S.'s biggest contributor to climate change. The built environment—our buildings and the transportation system we use to move between them—represents about 73 percent of greenhouse gas emissions in this country. You move a household from Potomac or McLean [D.C. suburbs] to Dupont [a D.C. urban neighborhood], you're going to cut your greenhouse gas emissions by 50 to 80 percent.

WM: So how do we go about fixing this market inefficiency?

CL: It's a very simple thing conceptually: allow for more walkable urban land. The reason we are only building luxury walkable urban right now is because each unit has to justify between $300,000 and $1 million, maybe more, of land value. And that's stupid. We have an artificial constraint on the market. As I mentioned, if you make 4 percent of the land walkable urban, the affordability problem gets a lot easier to solve.

WM: I think a lot of people would be skeptical that the kind of development we're sitting in now is going to help with housing affordability.

CL: Additional supply, even just at the top of the market, does mean rents will begin to fall. But it's too slow. The better way is to build middle-income housing, which we know how to do. This is not rocket science. You don't have to have gold-plated faucets. But you need land that costs $50,000 to $100,000 per unit, not $300,000 per unit.

WM: So how do we break this resistance that we find in zoning laws all over the country, making land artificially scarce?

CL: The main keepers of the status quo are neighborhood organizations—the "not in my backyard" people. It's actually rational. If building more supply makes housing prices go down, then the existing homeowners have something to lose. Also, existing homeowners are afraid this might bring "undesirables" to their neighborhood. And it's very easy to stop things. Saying no to something is a whole lot easier than building something.

WM: Thinking about some of the older neighborhoods in D.C.—those row houses have a lot of charm to them. And if someone wanted to come in and knock them down and build higher-density housing, that might have good secondary consequences, but folks might also say they like the way the neighborhood looks now.

CL: We don't have to knock down anything. Again, 2 percent of the total land in the D.C. metro area is walkable urban. There is plenty of unused land, especially in the suburbs. The urbanization of the suburbs is where much of this market demand is being satisfied, though it requires great effort to change zoning.

WM: What about transportation?

CL: Transportation drives development. A good example here is the Purple Line. [The Purple Line is a new rail line that will allow travel between D.C. suburbs without having to go in and out of the city center.] It will drive more development around those suburban stations, but only within walking distance. So now all of a sudden you can live in, say, New Carrollton [a Maryland suburb]. You'll at least be able to get rid of one car in your household, which greatly increases your mortgage capacity. The average American family spends 18 percent of their household income on transportation, almost all for cars. Dropping one car out of a household budget on average increases the mortgage capacity by $150,000.

WM: But if you put mass transit into a poor or working-class neighborhood, won't that bring in a flood of wealthier people and more upscale development and the people who were living there before won't benefit as much?

CL: The key is for the new transit to go hand in hand with new high-density housing. New transit won't drive up land prices if we add more housing at the same time. Generally speaking, these walkable urban places see an explosion in population density. As an example, if an existing neighborhood had 50 percent of the housing occupied by lower-income households, the new development of market rate housing at a higher density might reduce the low-income household percentage to, say, 20 percent without people actually getting displaced.

WM: When most people think about urban development, they think "urban," so they're going to picture stuff in the city center. We're talking a lot about the metro area. So what role do the suburbs play?

CL: A minimum of 50 percent of the demand for walkable urban will be satisfied in the suburbs—places like Silver Spring, Maryland, or Evanston, Illinois. We built the bulk of existing walkable urbanism before 1930. In 1930, we had forty million households in this country, twenty-two million of which were in our metropolitan areas. So those twenty-two million units, whether they be flats or townhouses or single-family homes in tight densities, they're the heart of the walkable urban stock that we have. Well, today we have 123 million household units in metropolitan areas. So a very small percentage of the total housing stock is walkable urban, and it's all the old stuff, the focus of gentrification.

WM: What role does federal policy play in helping fix this?

CL: The biggest way the federal government can help is by making its balance sheet available to local governments. Places like Los Angeles, Washington, Denver are in a mad rush to build more rail transit. In Los Angeles, they voted last November to tax themselves an additional $120 billion to build rail transit. The feds should be loaning money up front to municipalities and states to build mass transit, repaid by the local tax funds it generates. That would allow these places to get moving right now and pay the money back using the local tax obligations.

WM: If we were to get this right, what would happen to the people who are currently living in drivable suburbs who don't intend to move?

CL: Those property values, based on the market right now, are flat or going down. Many are still under water from the 2008 housing debacle, where the bulk of lost value was in drivable suburban housing. Our big social challenge is that a lot of drivable suburban places, particularly in low-income suburbs, are where the next slums will be.

WM: And this is related to what people worry about when it comes to gentrification: residents being pushed from the convenient neighborhood closer to the city center, being pushed out to places that are less convenient.

CL: One thing we have not discussed is that we need to have a very aggressive affordable housing program at the walkable urban place level. That's another part of the answer.

WM: What would that look like?

CL: This would be part of the work of the "place manager." Right now, just as we have growth of neighborhood groups, we have growth of place management in this country. It tends to take the form of business or community improvement districts. The government passes legislation that allows property owners to come together and form these districts through voluntary taxes. So the property owners say, for example, "We're going to increase our taxes and provide services to this 300-acre place in downtown D.C. It's going to be cleaner, it's going to be safer, we're going to put flowers out, we're going to run festivals and promote economic development."

Going forward, place managers need to be responsible not just for economic development, but also for social equity and for providing the affordable housing. So people who work in downtown D.C. can also live in downtown D.C., if they so choose.

WM: But how do you force a business improvement district to make sure there's enough affordable housing?

CL: Every few years, a business improvement district or community improvement district has to go back to the city council to be reauthorized. So it would be very simple: the city council says, "In addition to the economic development work that you're doing, you also have to take on affordable housing."

WM: What is the purpose of devolving the responsibility over affordable housing from the city-wide level to this more micro level?

CL: Because the cities have generally failed to provide enough affordable housing. Not all—New York City has built a remarkable amount of affordable housing that works as well as anyplace. But after fifty years of relying on the feds and the cities to provide affordable housing, there's just not enough of it—and what does exist is usually pretty bad. But place management organizations have proven themselves to be effective, and they are closest to the issue.

WM: In other words, given their success at economic development, why not entrust them with this other difficult task?

CL: Exactly. And I'm not going to guarantee that they're going to succeed. But I was involved personally with, in essence, a place manager, which was the University of California at Irvine. Irvine, one of the largest universities in the country, was having a massive affordable housing problem for faculty and staff. We came up with an idea to set up a nonprofit development corporation and transfer some of the university land to it. We borrowed $2 million of working capital from the UC Board of Regents, which was paid back within three years. We built 1,500 housing units, most of them for sale. We sold them to the faculty and staff at 60 percent of market price. Today the price is still 60 percent of market because we set up resale controls. Households can't sell at the market rate and have a windfall profit, because it would deprive the next generation of affordable housing. And it worked.

The Criminalization of Gentrifying Neighborhoods
Abdallah Fayyad

In the early hours of Labor Day, Brooklynites woke up to the sound of steel-pan bands drumming along Flatbush Avenue, as hundreds of thousands of people gathered to celebrate J'ouvert, a roisterous Caribbean festival that commemorates emancipation from slavery. But having been marred by gang violence in recent years, this J'ouvert was markedly different, as *The New York Times* described. The event, which derives its name from a Creole term for "daybreak," was heavily staffed by the New York City Police Department. Floodlights and security checkpoints were scattered along the parade route, and many revelers were piqued by what they saw as excessive police presence—an overwhelming show of force in response to a comparatively small number of bad actors.

"There's a criminalization of our neighborhood," Imani Henry, the president of the police-accountability group Equality for Flatbush, told me recently. After the NYPD declined Henry's public-information request about security ahead of and during the festival, citing safety concerns, his group decided to sue for it. (The NYPD did not respond to a request for comment.)

Henry believes the stepped-up law enforcement at J'ouvert is part of a larger pattern of increased police surveillance in gentrifying areas. The lawsuit—which has since made its way to the New York Supreme Court—argues that the NYPD recently increased "broken windows"-style arrests in Flatbush and East Flatbush, and claims that these "police actions have coincided with increased gentrification."

That claim is not just speculative. Over the past two decades, gentrification has become a norm in major American cities. The typical example is a formerly low-income neighborhood where longtime residents and businesses are displaced by white-collar workers and overpriced coffeehouses. But the conventional wisdom that image reflects—that gentrification is a result of an economic restructuring—often leaves out a critical side effect that disproportionately affects communities of color: criminalization.

When low-income neighborhoods see an influx of higher-income residents, social dynamics and expectations change. One of those expectations has to do with the perception of safety and public order, and the role of the state in providing it. The theory goes that as demographics shift, activity that was previously considered normal becomes suspicious, and newcomers—many of whom are white—are more inclined to get law enforcement involved. Loitering, people hanging out in the street, and noise violations often get reported, especially in racially diverse neighborhoods.

"There's some evidence that 311 and 911 calls are increasing in gentrifying areas," Harvard sociology professor Robert Sampson told me. And "that makes for a potentially explosive atmosphere with regard to the police," he added.

By degrees, long-term residents begin to find themselves tangled up in the criminal-justice system for so-called "quality of life" crimes as 311 and 911 calls draw police to neighborhoods where they didn't necessarily enforce nuisance laws before. As Paul Butler, a former federal prosecutor in Washington, D.C., describes it, misdemeanor arrests are more reflective of police presence than the total number of infractions committed in an area. "It's not a question of how many people are committing the crime—it's a question of where the police are directing their law-enforcement resources," Butler said. "Because wherever they direct the resources, they can find the crime."

In 2013, the city of San Francisco launched Open311, a mobile app that allows residents to easily report public disorder like loitering, dirty sidewalks, or vandalism by snapping a photo and sending their location. The app can feel altruistic; residents, for example, are able to report the whereabouts of homeless people who seem to be in need of assistance. But some worry that the dispatches can result in unnecessary citations or harassment. And while broken-windows policing remains controversial, a 2015 poll suggested that it's still largely accepted by the general public, so when people see something, they're likely to say something. After the app launched, 311 calls increased throughout the city, and one study showed that gentrifying neighborhoods saw a disproportionate spike.

Butler, who recently wrote the book *Chokehold: Policing Black Men*, believes that this is a result of newcomers refusing to assimilate to longstanding neighborhood norms. "Culturally, I think the way that a lot of African American and Latino people experience gentrification is as a form of colonization," he said. "The gentrifiers are not wanting to share—they're wanting to take over." One of the tools they can use to take over public spaces, he argues, is law enforcement.

Butler's home of Washington, where he's a law professor at Georgetown University, provides an illustrative example. On most Sunday afternoons, a performance group hosts a drum circle in Malcolm X Park, whose official name is Meridian Hill. The tradition dates back to 1965—shortly after Malcolm X was assassinated—and was intended to celebrate black liberation. While the drumbeats can still be heard today, the ritual was called into question when the surrounding neighborhood began to change in the late 1990s. New arrivals living in the blocks surrounding the park repeatedly complained about the noise until the police imposed and enforced a curfew on the drummers.

But increased police presence in gentrifying neighborhoods is not merely the result of new residents calling for service; police departments sometimes proactively deploy officers in areas that see bars and other alcohol-serving outlets pop up, as they tend to do in gentrifying neighborhoods. After conducting an analysis on economic development in 2013, for example, the D.C. Metropolitan Police Department established its nightlife unit, which deploys officers to areas with budding or resuscitated nightlife scenes. "If you're bringing in more bars, there's going to be drunk people congregating in the street, so you need police to tamp that down," Sampson said. "But that may lead to potential confrontations."

Officers can find themselves in altercations with both bar goers and longtime residents of the area.

Cathy Lanier, who was the police chief in Washington from 2007 to 2016, told me that when a neighborhood's population and economy begin to change, certain problems are bound to arise. "You're going to have traffic issues, you're going to have parking issues, and you're going to have everything that comes along with a rapidly developing community," she said. "So you want to have that police presence there, and establish community engagement long before the change so you can work with long-term residents to help them through the transition." Zero-tolerance enforcement, she said, can be avoided if the police are proactive in creating a safe and orderly environment in advance of any major economic disruptions.

Still, residents can feel overwhelmed by a sudden increase in security, which is not always confined to public law enforcement. Sampson said private security and third-party police contribute to a sense of over-surveillance. "In a kind of rough neighborhood that's about to flip, there may be demand on the part of new residents for safety that goes beyond what the police can provide, which means more eyes on the street on the part of private police," he said.

While low-income and minority neighborhoods are often subject to heavy police patrol regardless of their development status, gentrification and aggressive policing are two sides of the same coin and tend to reinforce one another. "The concern when there are misdemeanor offenses is that neighborhoods seem unsafe or disorderly and that decreases their attractiveness for gentrification," Butler said. "So in a number of cities, people have observed that enforcement of low-level offenses against black and brown people increases when neighborhoods are prime for gentrification."

A top concern in communities of color is that greater police presence amplifies the risk of police misconduct and violence. In 2014, when San Francisco native Alejandro Nieto was fatally shot by four police officers responding to a 911 call, many residents believed the incident wouldn't have occurred had his neighborhood not gentrified. Nieto was accused of behaving suspiciously in a place where he'd lived his entire life, and it was a new resident who'd made the 911 call. After he had a brief altercation with a neighborhood dog, Nieto, who worked as a bouncer, was anxiously pacing with his hand on his Taser, according to the passerby who reported him. Police said that when they arrived, he pointed his Taser at them, which they mistook for a gun.

Gentrification and police violence don't necessarily have a causal relationship. But stepped-up law enforcement does create conditions for more potential misconduct. That'd be true in any neighborhood that suddenly saw an influx of police—it's a simple matter of numbers. "If you're ticketing more people or patrolling more often, you're stopping more people to ask questions on the street," Sampson said. "Now, that's different than pulling a gun and shooting someone, or beating someone up, but the more stop-and-frisks and the more interactions you have, then probabilistically, you're increasing the risk for police brutality. So it's sort of a sequence or cycle."

Butler offered the example of Eric Garner, who first drew police officers' attention because he was selling loosies, or individual cigarettes, in Tompkinsville Park on Staten Island, a widespread practice since New York City began to sharply raise taxes on tobacco products in 2006. The surrounding neighborhoods had experienced some economic development, and calls reporting misdemeanor offenses were increasing. After a landlord made a 311 complaint regarding illegal drug and cigarette sales taking place outside his apartment building, officers began to closely monitor the area. Several months later, when Garner was confronted by police as he attempted to break up a street fight, an officer moved to arrest him for having previously sold loosies. The arrest went awry—and subsequently drew national attention—when Garner died after an officer put him in a chokehold.

"Before there was this effort to gentrify the neighborhood around the [Staten Island] ferry, I think it's fair to say that it hadn't received much attention from the police," Butler said. "And you can imagine that of all the crimes police have to worry about, selling loosie cigarettes shouldn't be a priority."

Gentrification also has long-lasting impacts on the criminal-justice system that go far beyond police surveillance. As cities become whiter, so do juries. In Washington, for example, it's not unusual to have a predominantly white, if not all-white, jury in a predominantly black city. "Jurors often have different life experiences based on their race. And so if the defense is 'the police lied' or 'the police planted evidence,' that's something that an African American or a Latino juror might well believe or find credible," Butler said. "A white person might find that hard to believe based on that person's experience with the police."

The public debate over how to best deal with gentrification often brushes over these tensions, focusing solely on the economic impacts. There are some who argue gentrification is a natural part of urban development, while others say local governments should do more to regulate housing markets. But there's one question cities haven't really reckoned with as they evaluate changing neighborhoods: Are they prepared to decriminalize them?

U.S. Cities Gentrifying the Fastest—You'll Never Guess No. 1
Yuqing Pan

It's the hottest of hot-button urban housing issues. In fact the *g-word*—gentrification—can be looked upon as a virtual catchall for *all* of the high-decibel talking points about American cities flung about during the endless campaign season of 2016—crime, poverty, upward mobility, urban renewal, and economic opportunity.

But here's what it really comes down to: poor or working-class families in growing cities being pushed out of their neighborhoods after better-off outsiders move in and substantially drive up the cost of living.

It's a transformative force that is sweeping through some cities like an economic tsunami. It affects lives and fundamentally alters neighborhoods. On the flip side, long-term residents can benefit, too—particularly homeowners.

Back in the 1980s, Charleston, SC, resident Joseph Watson saw his friends moving out of his depressed Eastside neighborhood because of the lack of opportunity.

"They couldn't afford to hold onto their properties, and there wasn't [enough] employment," says Watson, 67, owner of Mary's Sweet Shop, which his mother opened in 1968. Local businesses and hotels preferred to hire college graduates, who were few on the ground in Eastside.

But today, it's a different story. With many neighborhoods in Charleston undergoing gentrification, developers see Eastside as a newly desirable location.

"People come to me daily and ask me if I want to sell my house," Watson says. Some longtime residents are again moving away, but this time it's because of the rising prices. And yet for those sticking around, the neighborhood is safer and awash with new retailers, services—and gigs.

"It's coming back to what it was when I was a little child growing up," Watson says. "You have people from all over the world living in the neighborhood," he says. And "there are [new] opportunities for jobs."

The Good News and the Bad News

Welcome to the complicated push-pull of modern urban gentrification.

"It's a trade-off," says **David Fiorenza**, an urban economics professor at Villanova University.

"Whole communities can be displaced," he says. "But people [also] can benefit from it, because home values and business values go up … and eventually, there will be more jobs and better schools." If they can afford to remain nearby, that is.

We decided to dive into the heart of the matter by deploying the realtor.com® data team to find the fastest gentrifying cities in the country.

So we looked at cities whose population was 50,000 or more between 2000 and 2015. Then we took a look at the U.S. Census Tracts—that's data-speak for neighborhoods of 1,200 to 8,000 people. We focused on lower-income areas with home values that had the potential for gentrification (excluding wealthier communities that had already arrived). Then we compared home values as well as residents' income and education levels in the years from 2000 to 2015, to assess which cities were seeing the biggest turnaround. (Want specifics on our methodology? Check 'em out at the end of the article).

1. Charleston, SC

Gentrification potential achieved: 62.5%

Median home price increase, 2000 to 2015: $152,100 to $270,000 (+77.5%)

The issue of gentrification exploded in Charleston in 2001, when Shoreview Apartments, a large, low-income housing project downtown, was razed to the ground to make way for an upscale community of single-family homes. Other neighborhoods that had long been solidly African-American working class also saw a shift toward white, middle-class families. Since 1990, Charleston's black population has declined from 42% to 23%, according to the Census Bureau.

2. Asheville, NC

Gentrification potential achieved: 50%

Median home price increase, 2000 to 2015: $125,000 to $235,000 (+88%)

Back in 2000, Rolling Stone called Asheville "America's new freak capital," attracting an eclectic population of hippies, artists, and musicians. Today, tourists flock to its craft beer breweries, and gated golf communities sell homes for prices as high as $6.5 million—but the quirky, creative characters who once defined the city are vanishing.

Vincent's Ear, an iconic dive bar where the White Stripes played before they became famous, has been replaced by a high-priced eatery. In the River Arts District, which a city report describes as being "in the middle phase of gentrification," two dozen artists were displaced in 2014, when their buildings were ordered to close because of fire hazards. The site is currently being renovated, and the hope is that some units will be affordable for artists, according to photographer **Jeremy Russell**, one of those who were kicked out.

But the newly upscale neighborhood isn't for everyone. "Some artists definitely moved away [from Asheville] ... those who are more progressive, and pushing the boundaries," Russell says.

3. Washington, DC

Gentrification potential achieved: 39.4%

Median home price increase, 2000 to 2015: $159,900 to $525,000 (+228.3%)

At the beginning of this century, DC Mayor Anthony Williams had ambitious plans to revitalize the city's depressed neighborhoods. Today, the Navy Yard (home of the Nationals' new ballpark), NoMa, and Columbia Heights have shed their dingy image and become the new "it" neighborhoods.

"There are a lot more things to do—restaurants, bars, shopping like Best Buy and Target. It's very convenient," says **Andrew Wiseman**, a resident of Columbia Heights since 2007 who runs the blog New Columbia Heights. However, he adds, "the reactions to the changes are really mixed. Families that have been here for generations don't like it. Local retailers are being pushed out, corner stores are closing."

4. Portland, OR

Gentrification potential achieved: 33.9%

Median home price increase, 2000 to 2015: $148,000 to $340,000 (+129.7%)

Hmmm... could the trendsetting Portland *really* have achieved only 33.9% of its gentrification potential? Well, yes, since our analysis starts with 2000, and the poster child for the modern hipster movement was ahead of the curve.

"Gentrification in Portland is not a new phenomenon," says **Katrina Holland**, executive director of Community Alliance of Tenants in Portland. "Since the 1960s and '70s, there has been serial displacement of the African-American community. Now it's the first time that white, middle-class families are also being priced out."

Perhaps that's why lots of "urban pioneers" are ditching Portland for places like Detroit, in search of a cheaper cultural scene.

5. Denver, CO

Gentrification potential achieved: 32.8%

Median home price increase, 2000 to 2015: $162,000 to $316,000 (+95.1%)

We've noted it before: The Denver market is *hot*. Scalding, in fact. The booming tech industry, outdoor lifestyle, and more recently, Colorado's legalization of marijuana have drawn transplants and starry-eyed developers to the city.

The North Denver neighborhoods of Globeville and Elyria-Swansea are going through significant changes. Depending which day you visit the area, it either smells of legal weed—due to a high concentration of marijuana businesses—or dog food from the nearby Purina factory. But three multibillion-dollar developments have lifted property values by 60% from 2013 to 2015, and residents saw their property taxes increase by as much as $600, according to **Stephen Moore**, policy director for FRESC, a nonprofit organization working with low-income communities.

"Many of our historical black and Hispanic communities are being destroyed explicitly by gentrification," Moore says. "We are not against investment in those communities, we *want* that. But we'd like to see more policies that protect the people that live there now, and help them stay."

6. Nashville, TN

Gentrification potential achieved: 27.6%

Median home price increase, 2000 to 2015: $118,400 to $205,000 (+73.1%)

Every day, the Nashville metro gains 71 to 100 people. The city's entertainment and health care industries bring in a steady flow of wealthy transplants. East Nashville, where the city's musicians and artists have long resided, was on the frontline of gentrification.

"The most significant change in the last 10 years was the influx of builders, because the houses here were old and cheap," says Realtor **Cindy Evans** of RE/MAX Choice Properties, who moved to East Nashville in 1980. "After the commercial areas were built, young professionals moved in—for the amenities more than the housing."

But since the urban core is still relatively inexpensive, Nashville is experiencing intense speculation by developers and investors.

7. Sacramento, CA

Gentrification potential achieved: 26.5%

Median home price increase, 2000 to 2015: $127,500 to $255,000 (+100%)

Thanks to decades of urban redevelopment and to its affordable real estate, Sacramento—just a couple of hours east of San Francisco—is seeing an influx of young professionals and well-off empty-nesters. Midtown, a former hard-knock neighborhood, has been taken over by stylish white-linen restaurants and pricey new condos.

The latest wave of gentrification has also hit Oak Park, a historically black neighborhood where **Patti Miller**, owner of Patris Studio Gallery, moved 20 years ago.

"It was a ghetto, and rent was really cheap," Miller says, adding that artists, because they often can't afford much, "are usually dealing with the grittier side of a city."

In the past decade, the rents got higher and Miller's artist friends began to leave—for Oregon, Arizona, and even South America. Miller nearly lost her gallery to developers in September. And what's in Oak Park today? Trendy locales like "holistic spa" Capitol Floats, where customers spend $65 for an hour of relaxing in lukewarm saltwater.

8. Jersey City, NJ

Gentrification potential achieved: 24.5%

Median home price increase, 2000 to 2015: $142,000 to $380,000 (+167.6%)

It wasn't long ago that downtown Jersey City was more of a punch line than a destination stop, typified by vacant lots and abandoned tenements. Now, its falling crime rate has made it safer for families, and new condos are going up at a rapid clip.

With Manhattan just over the river, Jersey City offers a relatively easy commute and more affordable homes than the fast-track meccas of gentrification nearby, like the more desirable parts of Brooklyn.

The housing market is also driven by wealthy foreign buyers, says **Saquib Rahim**, a sales associate from Coldwell Banker. "In the rental market, New Jersey has rent control, so renters are protected from huge rent increases. But local businesses are being priced out, for sure."

9. Long Beach, CA

Gentrification potential achieved: 22.4%

Median home price increase from 2000 to 2015: $179,000 to $455,000 (up 154.2%)

In downtown Long Beach, developers are turning all kinds of buildings—even a former department store—into high-end condos. The previous industrial hub with rundown buildings is now a residential community, with amenities like boutiques, craft breweries, and restaurants.

The average rent downtown is now $2,645, according to Rent Jungle. Who's paying those prices? A 2016 report by the Downtown Long Beach Alliance showed that the largest number of downtown residents were "metro renters"—young, educated singles who love the arts and spend money on the newest technology.

"Millennials are moving in for walkability and bikeability—there are custom bike lanes and bike-share stations," says Realtor **Jason Patterson** from RE/MAX College Park Realty, who represents a waterfront condo building selling for $729,500 a unit.

10. Austin, TX

Gentrification potential achieved: 22.2%

Median home price increase from 2000 to 2015: $152,600 to $299,300 (96.1%)

Many residents tout the unofficial motto, "Keep Austin Weird," but they may be fighting a losing battle. Condos and upper-income apartments are popping up everywhere, driving up rents and home prices as developers cash in on the city's trendiness.

For years, East Austin residents have decried gentrification. In 2006, a local nonprofit had about 250 people on a waiting list for affordable housing, but that number had risen to 700 by 2015. The previously forgotten neighborhood with a largely African-American and Latino population began to get attention in the early 2000s. As Austin's population grew, people from outside the community were drawn to the low rents of the area close to downtown. The result was a wave of new developments, and now East Austin is rebuilding a fancier, more congested version of itself.

*Our methodology considered a Census Tract **eligible for gentrification** if it had a population of more than 500 people, and both median household income* *and median home value fell within the bottom 40th percentile of all tracts within its metro in 2000.*

*Of those eligible tracts, a tract was further considered **gentrified** if it had experienced a significant increase in median income, median home value, and educational attainment between 2000 and 2015.*

The ranking is based on the share of gentrified tracts out of a city's total eligible tracts. The final list included only cities that had more than five gentrified tracts.

Data were collected from the realtor.com sales database, American Community Survey, and the US2010 project of Brown University's Russell Sage Foundation. We consulted research methodology from a 2005 Columbia University study and a 2015 Governing magazine report.

Cultural Representation

Marvel Ain't Foolin' Nobody
Tirhakah Love

Hashtag this: Portrait of a seemingly-liberal but comically ignorant conglomerate of anti-heroes talking out the side of their collective necks. Through hip-hop variant covers, recruiting a cohort of beloved writers and creatives representing a multiplicity of experiences, and a forthcoming all-black, comic-based film, Marvel has demonstrated that it's at least concerned with its marketability to the historically marginalized—and it has to be.

If the critical and commercial success of representational casting in Hollywood is any indication, there's a large swath of young kaleidoscopic consumers clamoring—and willing to pay for—realistic portrayals of their experiences in the superpowered worlds of comic books. But for all the ostensibly diverse-conscious motives, Marvel is known to step in its own shit every once in awhile, because the company doesn't quite understand how to enact substantial, sustainable representation.

In the last year alone, Marvel has repeatedly stepped into a trap they set for themselves. The outrage around the sexualized images of Riri Williams in *The Invincible Iron Man* should have been enough of a warning. Before her debut, the 16-year-old black girl genius who plays the new Iron Man was subject to some bizarre white male fetishization, which happens pretty often in comics, though it's underreported. Adding last year's tone deaf decision for a black Spider-Man, Miles Morales, to admonish a fan for celebrating Morales's ethnicity, and/or recklessly defending those obtuse choices, simply doubled down on bad PR in a calendar year. But lo and behold, the latest public gaffe: Marvel's VP of Sales, David Gabriel, claimed in an interview that Marvel's emphasis on non-traditional (non-white, non-male, non-heterosexual) narratives are the reason the company's sales dipped in 2016.

This belief isn't just shortsighted. As many have noted, it's also inaccurate. If Gabriel looked at recent sales charts, he'd see that nontraditional stories—Ta-Nehisi Coates and Brian Stelfreeze's *Black Panther* run and Jane Foster's ongoing stint as the Norse god in *The Mighty Thor*—were the highest-selling comic books in 2016.

Editor-in-Chief Axel Alonso later tried to save face by telling fans not to worry about their beloved diverse heroes, but the whole affair was a harrowing reminder of how much whiteness covets the minority experience without having to engage, critique, or celebrate the spirit of that experience. What should've been a unique opportunity to praise the commercial success of diverse titles like *Black Panther*, *Ms. Marvel*, or Miles Morales as Spider-Man became misguided scapegoating of already marginalized voices.

Underneath its colorful veneer, Marvel is still a company tending towards antiquated sensibilities. That dissonance between the characters that the corporation creates and the target audience grounds Gabriel's small-minded statement and legitimizes Marvel faking the funk.

Let's be clear, corporations commodifying the call for more diverse properties for profit isn't new, and it probably isn't changing anytime soon. What's annoying is this idea that white corporate creatives should be given a pat on the back for fetishizing this body, this experience, and this reality. Gabriel and Alonso speak as if creating characters who accurately represent their reading audience is a risk. They simply cannot think of this skin of mine outside of its implied political resourcefulness and the inevitable discourses it evokes out of those who encounter it in fear or intrigue.

When Gabriel foolishly cited retailers' qualms surrounding comics with non-white, non-male, and queer heroes as the reason behind Marvel's shitty financial year, he painfully reinstated the idea of liberal "diversity" as a service to a larger political agenda—and not a recognition of the inherent power of comics that reflect their readership. On the contrary, books bottoming out in sales, like *International Iron Man* and *All-New Hawkeye*, mirrored the old, stale guard they targeted.

Despite all the hand-wringing over the place of these comics, it's clear that audiences are down with the brown, the black, and the other—if these stories are written in a way that feels real, inasmuch as a hero comic can be. The common denominator in Marvel's successful diversity work is the inclusion of their targeted audience within the auspices of the writers' room.

G. Willow Wilson's work on *Ms. Marvel*, for example, is soaring digitally, even though it's penned by a white woman who, despite being a recent convert, is still under the guidance of Sana Amanat, whose presence as both creator and editor ensures accuracy. Wilson's penchant for gravid dialogue and Amanat's corrective lens coalesce for an awesome, relatable character in Kamala Khan.

Coates's successful run on *Black Panther* predestined the *World of Wakanda* spin-off series, which features a revolving cast of popular black writers, starting with Roxane Gay's 5-issue run and followed up by *NY Mag* writer Rembert Browne.

Gay's story, which contextualizes the events leading up to the Wakandan Civil War in the main plot, is centered around the love, fearlessness, and honor of two queer black women—and personal bodyguards to T'Challa—who revolted after years of negligence via the royal patriarchy. Their stories are about black people, yes, but they are not caught up in the pretension of a tokenized character like similar comics written by white men. When I crack open something like *Black Panther* or *World of Wakanda*, it's a relief because I'm not beaten over the head with their blackness. The characters can just *be* in a way that no doubt references both mainland African and Black culture with an insight that feels real. They can exist in this world because they are written by black people who do not feel the need to reassert their blackness. That freedom is sorely lacking in the majority of "diversity" comics.

Marvel fans aren't just down, they are in fact so desperate for representation that when Marvel disregards their proven model of success to stick a white creative team behind POC books, like on many of Bendis's books, they still sell. Diversity and discourse go hand in hand, and in our media-based world, they're increasingly rubbing shoulders with dollars and cents. Now, corporate marketing teams and representatives that do or say utterly dumb shit in the name of "sparking a conversation" are seen as well-meaning and, in some cases, even edgy, or progressive. The inherent problem with framing diversity in this way is that it sterilizes what should be meaningful entry points for new comic readers through tepid attempts by white men to tell stories using the narrow, stereotypical motifs of black, brown, and queer life.

Miles Morales's Spider-Man, as written by Bendis, suffers from the gap in experience, and the ripples can be felt in the vastly more popular Marvel Cinematic Universe. Not only is Miles's story penned by Bendis, a white man with no lived experience of the mixed-race culture of Puerto Rico, but it's also difficult to tell how significant Morales is as a character, because Peter Parker—who is supposed to be dead—is still living his fullest life out here. While Morales's story has become a bit more nuanced following the merging of the Ultimate and Earth-616 worlds during the *Secret Wars* event, Morales admonishing a fan for celebrating the teen hero's black-Hispanic heritage remains a sore spot. Coming to terms with nationality and heritage is a phase many children of immigrants go through (and grow out of), but it's such an out-of-character response that it feels, problematically, meta; it's a fourth wall break from a writer who's tired of having the race conversation, despite writing a character who will always have to have it.

To add a bit of insult to injury, the latest repackaging of Peter Parker's Spider-Man in the Marvel Cinematic Universe—the upcoming film *Spider-Man: Homecoming*—features some plot elements from Morales's story. His friendship with Ganke Lee and a relationship with Katie Bishop, who looks a lot like Zendaya in the film, raises an important question: Why is Miles Morales's story good enough to cast a white boy and call him Peter but not good enough to get its own direct live-action adaptation?

Marvel's faux-progressive chickens are coming home to roost, and the company will need to rationalize why they still choose to create barriers between marginalized voices and the writers' room they crave access to.

To be black and a comic fan is to know that even the most productive minds can't imagine you whole. It is to be reminded that however they covet our bodies and our culture, our souls; our particular perspective is still insignificant, if not functioning to service their preexisting worldviews. To be black and a comic fan means you hardly get to engage in a black story that simply is—rather than some pet project for a self-styled white knight with a kingdom of profit margins to maintain. Imagine the wide wealth of experiences that could be imbued within Marvel's pages if the company used diversity consciousness less like a trendy universe shakeup and more like the lens through which the company can speak back to and celebrate their readership.

From *Gender Trouble*
Judith Butler

1. Subjects of Sex/Gender/Desire

One is not born a woman, but rather becomes one.

—*Simone de Beauvoir*

Strictly speaking, 'women' cannot be said to exist.

—*Julia Kristeva*

Woman does not have a sex.

—*Luce Irigaray*

The deployment of sexuality . . . established this notion of sex.

—*Michel Foucault*

The category of sex is the political category that founds society as heterosexual.

—*Monique Wittig*

i. 'Women' as the Subject of Feminism

For the most part, feminist theory has assumed that there is some existing identity, understood through the category of women, who not only initiates feminist interests and goals within discourse, but constitutes the subject for whom political representation is pursued. But *politics* and *representation* are controversial terms. On the one hand, *representation* serves as the operative term within a political process that seeks to extend visibility and legitimacy to women as political subjects; on the other hand, representation is the normative function of a language which is said either to reveal or to distort what is assumed to be true about the category of women. For feminist theory, the development of a language that fully or adequately represents women has seemed necessary to foster the political visibility of women. This has seemed obviously important considering the pervasive cultural condition in which women's lives were either misrepresented or not represented at all.

Recently, this prevailing conception of the relation between feminist theory and politics has come under challenge from within feminist discourse. The very subject of women is no longer understood in stable or abiding terms. There is a great deal of material that not only questions the viability of 'the subject' as the ultimate candidate for representation or, indeed, liberation, but there is very little agreement after all on what it is that constitutes, or ought to constitute, the category of women. The domains of political and linguistic 'representation' set out in advance the criterion by which subjects themselves are formed, with the result that representation is extended only to what can be acknowledged as a subject. In other words, the qualifications for being a subject must first be met before representation can be extended.

Foucault points out that juridical systems of power *produce* the subjects they subsequently come to represent.[1] Juridical notions of power appear to regulate political life in purely negative terms—that is, through the limitation, prohibition, regulation, control and even 'protection' of individuals related to that political structure through the contingent and retractable operation of choice. But the subjects regulated by such structures are, by virtue of being subjected to them, formed, defined, and reproduced in accordance with the requirements of those structures. If this analysis is right, then the juridical formation of language and politics that represents women as 'the subject' of feminism is itself a discursive formation and effect of a given version of representational politics. And the feminist subject turns out to be discursively constituted by the very political system that is supposed to facilitate its emancipation. This becomes politically problematic if that system can be shown to produce gendered subjects along a differential axis of domination or to produce subjects who are presumed to be masculine. In such cases, an uncritical appeal to such a system for the emancipation of 'women' will be clearly self-defeating.

The question of 'the subject' is crucial for politics, and for feminist politics in particular, because juridical subjects are invariably produced through certain exclusionary practices that do not 'show' once the juridical structure of politics has been established. In other words, the political construction of the subject proceeds with certain legitimating and exclusionary aims, and these political operations are effectively concealed and naturalized by a political analysis that takes juridical structures as their foundation. Juridical power inevitably 'produces' what it claims merely to represent; hence, politics must be concerned with this dual function of power: the juridical and the productive. In effect, the law produces and then conceals the notion of 'a subject before the law'[2] in order to invoke that discursive formation as a naturalized foundational premise that subsequently legitimates that law's own regulatory hegemony. It is not enough to inquire into how women might become more fully represented in language and politics. Feminist critique ought also to understand how the category of 'women,' the subject of feminism, is produced and restrained by the very structures of power through which emancipation is sought.

Indeed, the question of women as the subject of feminism raises the possibility that there may not be a subject who stands 'before' the law, awaiting representation in or by the law. Perhaps the subject, as well as the invocation of a temporal 'before,' is constituted by the law as the fictive foundation of its own claim to legitimacy. The prevailing assumption of the ontological integrity of the subject before the law might be understood as the contemporary trace of the state of nature hypothesis, that foundationalist fable constitutive of the juridical structures of classical liberalism. The performative invocation of a nonhistorical 'before' becomes the foundational premise that guarantees a presocial ontology of persons who freely consent to be governed and, thereby, constitute the legitimacy of the social contract.

Apart from the foundationalist fictions that support the notion of the subject, however, there is the political problem that feminism encounters in the assumption that the term *women* denotes a common identity. Rather than a stable signifier that commands the assent of those whom it purports to describe and represent, *women*, even in the plural, has become a troublesome term, a site of contest, a cause for anxiety. As Denise Riley's title suggests, *Am I That Name?* is a question produced by the very possibility of the name's multiple significations.[3] If one 'is' a woman, that is surely not all one is; the term fails to be exhaustive, not because a pregendered 'person' transcends the specific paraphernalia of its gender, but because gender is not always constituted coherently or consistently in different historical contexts, and because gender intersects with racial, class, ethnic, sexual, and regional modalities of discursively constituted identities. As a result, it becomes impossible to separate out 'gender' from the political and cultural intersections in which it is invariably produced and maintained.

The political assumption that there must be a universal basis for feminism, one which must be found in an identity assumed to exist cross-culturally, often accompanies the notion that the oppression of women has some singular form discernible in the universal or hegemonic structure of patriarchy or masculine domination. The notion of a universal patriarchy has been widely criticized in recent years for its failure to account for the workings of gender oppression in the concrete cultural contexts in which it exists. Where those various contexts have been consulted within such theories, it has been to find 'examples' or 'illustrations' of a universal principle that is assumed from the start. That form of feminist theorizing has come under criticism for its efforts to colonize and appropriate non-Western cultures to support highly Western notions of oppression, but because they tend as well to construct a 'Third World' or even an 'Orient' in which gender oppression is subtly explained as symptomatic of an essential, non-Western barbarism. The urgency of feminism to establish a universal status for patriarchy in order to strengthen the appearance of feminism's own claims to be representative has occasionally motivated the shortcut to a categorical or fictive universality of the structure of domination, held to produce women's common subjugated experience.

Although the claim of universal patriarchy no longer enjoys the kind of credibility it once did, the notion of a generally shared conception of 'women,' the corollary to that framework, has been much more difficult to displace. Certainly, there have been plenty of debates: Is there some commonality among 'women' that preexists their oppression, or do 'women' have a bond by virtue of their oppression alone? Is there a specificity to women's cultures that is independent of their subordination by hegemonic, masculinist cultures? Are the specificity and integrity of women's cultural or linguistic practices always specified against and, hence, within the terms of some more dominant cultural formation? If there is a region of the 'specifically feminine', one that is both differentiated from the masculine as such and recognizable in its difference by an unmarked and, hence, presumed universality of 'women'? The masculine/feminine binary constitutes not only the exclusive framework in which that specificity can be recognized, but in every other way the 'specificity' of the feminine is once again fully decontextualized and separated off analytically and politically from the constitution of class, race, ethnicity, and other axes of power relations that both constitute 'identity' and make the singular notion of identity a misnomer.[4]

My suggestion is that the presumed universality and unity of the subject of feminism is effectively undermined by the constraints of the representational discourse in which it functions. Indeed, the premature insistence on a stable subject of feminism, understood as a seamless category of women, inevitably generates multiple refusals to accept the category. These domains of exclusion reveal the coercive and regulatory consequences of that construction, even when the construction has been elaborated for emancipatory purposes. Indeed, the fragmentation within feminism and the paradoxical opposition to feminism from 'women' whom feminism claims to represent suggest the necessary limits of identity politics. The suggestion that feminism can seek wider representation for a subject that it itself constructs has the ironic consequence that feminist goals risk failure by refusing to take account of the constitutive powers of their own representational claims. This problem is not ameliorated through an appeal to the category of women for merely 'strategic' purposes, for strategies always have meanings that exceed the purposes for which they are intended. In this case, exclusion itself might qualify as such an unintended yet consequential meaning. By conforming to a requirement of representational politics that feminism articulate a stable subject, feminism thus opens itself to charges of gross misrepresentation.

Obviously, the political task is not to refuse representational politics—as if we could. The juridical structures of language and politics constitute the contemporary field of power; hence, there is no position outside this field, but only a critical genealogy of its own legitimating practices. As such, the critical point of departure is *the historical present*, as Marx put it. And the task is to formulate within this constituted frame a critique of the categories of identity that contemporary juridical structures engender, naturalize, and immobilize.

Perhaps there is an opportunity at this juncture of cultural politics, a period that some would call 'postfeminist', to reflect from within a feminist perspective on the injunction to construct a subject of feminism. Within feminist political practice, a radical rethinking of the ontological constructions of identity appears to be necessary in order to formulate a representational politics that might revive feminism on other grounds. On the other hand, it may be time to entertain a radical critique that seeks to free feminist theory from the necessity of having to construct a single or abiding ground which is invariably contested by those identity positions or anti-identity positions that it invariably excludes. Do the exclusionary practices that ground feminist theory in a notion of 'women' as subject paradoxically undercut feminist goals to extend its claims to 'representation'?[5]

Perhaps the problem is even more serious. Is the construction of the category of women as a coherent and stable subject an unwitting regulation and reification of gender relations? And is not such a reification precisely contrary to feminist aims? To what extent does the category of women achieve stability and coherence only in the context of the heterosexual matrix?[6] If a stable notion of gender no longer proves to be the foundational premise of feminist politics, perhaps a new sort of feminist politics is now desirable to contest the very reifications of gender and identity, one that will take the variable construction of identity as both a methodological and normative prerequisite, if not a political goal.

To trace the political operations that produce and conceal what qualifies as the juridical subject of feminism is precisely the task of a *feminist genealogy* of the category of women. In the course of this effort to question 'women' as the subject of feminism, the unproblematic invocation of that category may prove to *preclude* the possibility of feminism as a representational politics. What sense does it make to extend representation to subjects who are constructed through the exclusion of those who fail to conform to unspoken normative requirements of the subject? What relations of domination and exclusion are inadvertently sustained when representation becomes the sole focus of politics? The identity of the feminist subject ought not to be the foundation of feminist politics, if the formation of the subject takes place within a field of power regularly buried through the assertion of that foundation. Perhaps, paradoxically, 'representation' will be shown to make sense for feminism only when the subject of 'women' is nowhere presumed.

Notes

1. See Michel Foucault, 'Right of Death and Power over Life', in *The History of Sexuality, Volume I, An Introduction*, trans. Robert Hurley (New York: Vintage, 1980), originally published as *Histoire de la sexualité 1: La volonté de savoir* (Paris: Gallimard, 1978). In that final chapter, Foucault discusses the relation between the juridical and productive law. His notion of the productivity of the law is clearly derived from Nietzsche, although not identical with Nietzsche's will-to-power. The use of Foucault's notion of productive power is not meant as a simple-minded 'application' of Foucault to gender issues. As I show in chapter 3, section ii, 'Foucault, Herculine, and the Politics of Sexual Discontinuity', the consideration of sexual difference within the terms of Foucault's own work reveals central contradictions in his theory. His view of the body also comes under criticism in the final chapter.

2. References throughout this work to a subject before the law are extrapolations of Derrida's reading of Kafka's parable 'Before the Law', in *Kafka and the Contemporary Critical Performance: Centenary Readings*, ed. Alan Udoff (Bloomington: Indiana University Press, 1987).

3. See Denise Riley, *Am I That Name?: Feminism and the Category of 'Women' in History* (New York: Macmillan, 1988).

4. See Sandra Harding, 'The Instability of the Analytical Categories of Feminist Theory,' in *Sex and Scientific Inquiry*, eds. Sandra Harding and Jean F. O'Barr (Chicago: University of Chicago Press, 1987), pp. 283-302.

5. I am reminded of the ambiguity inherent in Nancy Cott's title, *The Grounding of Modern Feminism* (New Haven: Yale University Press, 1987). She argues that the early twentieth-century U.S. feminist movement sought to 'ground' itself in a program that eventually 'grounded' that movement. Her historical thesis implicitly raises the question of whether uncritically accepted foundations operate like the 'return of the repressed'; based on exclusionary practices, the stable political identities that found political movements may invariably become threatened by the very instability that the foundationalist move creates.

6. I use the term *heterosexual matrix* throughout the text to designate that grid of cultural intelligibility through which bodies, genders, and desires are naturalized. I am drawing from Monique Wittig's notion of the 'heterosexual contract' and, to a lesser extent, on Adrienne Rich's notion of 'compulsory heterosexuality' to characterize a hegemonic discursive/epistemic model of gender intelligibility that assumes that for bodies to cohere and make sense there must be a stable sex expressed through a stable gender (masculine expresses male, feminine expresses female) that is oppositionally and hierarchically defined through the compulsory practice of heterosexuality.

Dear White America

George Yancy

In 2015, I conducted a series of 19 interviews with philosophers and public intellectuals on the issue of race. My aim was to engage, in this very public space, with the often unnamed elephant in the room.

These discussions helped me, and I hope many of our readers, to better understand how race continues to function in painful ways within our country. That was one part of a gift that I wanted to give to readers of The Stone, the larger philosophical community, and the world.

The interviewees themselves—bell hooks, Cornel West, Judith Butler, Peter Singer, David H. Kim, Molefi Kete Asante among them—came from a variety of racial backgrounds, and their concerns and positions were even more diverse. But on the whole I came to see these interviews as linked by a common thread: They were messages to white America—because they often directly expressed the experience of those who live and have lived as people of color in a white-run world, and that is something no white person could ever truly know firsthand.

That is how I want to deliver my own message now.

• • •

Dear White America,

I have a weighty request. As you read this letter, I want you to listen with love, a sort of love that demands that you look at parts of yourself that might cause pain and terror, as James Baldwin would say. Did you hear that? You may have missed it. I repeat: *I want you to listen with love.* Well, at least try.

We don't talk much about the urgency of love these days, especially within the public sphere. Much of our discourse these days is about revenge, name calling, hate, and divisiveness. I have yet to hear it from our presidential hopefuls, or our political pundits. I don't mean the Hollywood type of love, but the scary kind, the kind that risks not being reciprocated, the kind that refuses to flee in the face of danger. To make it a bit easier for you, I've decided to model, as best as I can, what I'm asking of you. Let me demonstrate the vulnerability that I wish you to show. As a child of Socrates, James Baldwin and Audre Lorde, let me speak the truth, refuse to err on the side of caution.

This letter is a gift for you. Bear in mind, though, that some gifts can be heavy to bear. You don't have to accept it; there is no obligation. I give it freely, believing that many of you will throw the gift back in my face, saying that I wrongly accuse you, that I am too sensitive, that I'm a race hustler, and that I blame white people (you) for everything.

I have read many of your comments. I have even received some hate mail. In this letter, I ask you to look deep, to look into your souls with silence, to quiet that voice that will speak to you of your white "innocence." So, as you read this letter, take a deep breath. Make a space for my voice in the deepest part of your psyche. Try to listen, to practice being silent. There are times when you must quiet your own voice to hear from or about those who suffer in ways that you do not.

What if I told you that I'm sexist? Well, I am. Yes. I said it and I mean just that. I have watched my male students squirm in their seats when I've asked them to identify and talk about their sexism. There are few men, I suspect, who would say that they are sexists, and even fewer would admit that their sexism actually oppresses women. Certainly not publicly, as I've just done. No taking it back now.

To make things worse, I'm an academic, a philosopher. I'm supposed to be one of the "enlightened" ones. Surely, we are beyond being sexists. Some, who may genuinely care about my career, will say that I'm being too risky, that I am jeopardizing my academic livelihood. Some might even say that as a black male, who has already been stereotyped as a "crotch-grabbing, sexual fiend," that I'm at risk of reinforcing that stereotype. (Let's be real, that racist stereotype has been around for centuries; it is already part of white America's imaginary landscape.)

Yet, I refuse to remain a prisoner of the lies that we men like to tell ourselves—that we are beyond the messiness of sexism and male patriarchy, that we don't oppress women. Let me clarify. This doesn't mean that I intentionally hate women or that I desire to oppress them. It means that despite my best intentions, I perpetuate sexism every day of my life. Please don't take this as a confession for which I'm seeking forgiveness. Confessions can be easy, especially when we know that forgiveness is immediately forthcoming.

As a sexist, I have failed women. I have failed to speak out when I should have. I have failed to engage critically and extensively their pain and suffering in my writing. I have failed to transcend the rigidity of gender roles in my own life. I have failed to challenge those poisonous assumptions that women are "inferior" to men or to speak out loudly in the company of male philosophers who believe that feminist philosophy is just a nonphilosophical fad. I have been complicit with, and have allowed myself to be seduced by, a country that makes billions of dollars from sexually objectifying women, from pornography, commercials, video games, to Hollywood movies. I am not innocent.

I have been fed a poisonous diet of images that fragment women into mere body parts. I have also been complicit with a dominant male narrative that says that women enjoy being treated like sexual toys. In our collective male imagination, women are "things" to be used for our visual and physical titillation. And even as I know how poisonous and false these sexist assumptions are, I am often ambushed by my own hidden sexism. I continue to see women through the male gaze that belies my best intentions not to sexually objectify them. Our collective male erotic feelings and fantasies are complicit in the degradation of women. And we must be mindful that not all women endure sexual degradation in the same way.

I recognize how my being a sexist has a differential impact on black women and women of color who are not only victims of racism, but also sexism, *my sexism*. For example, black women and women of color not only suffer from sexual objectification, but the ways in which they are objectified is linked to how they are racially depicted, some as "exotic" and others as "hyper-sexual." You see, the complicity, the responsibility, the pain that I cause runs deep. And, get this. I refuse to seek shelter; I refuse to live a lie. So, every day of my life I fight against the dominant male narrative, choosing to see women as subjects, not objects. But even as I fight, there are moments of failure. Just because I fight against sexism does not give me clean hands, as it were, at the end of the day; I continue to falter, and I continue to oppress. And even though the ways in which I oppress women is unintentional, this does not free me of being responsible.

If you are white, and you are reading this letter, I ask that you don't run to seek shelter from your own racism. Don't hide from your responsibility. Rather, begin, right now, to practice being vulnerable. Being neither a "good" white person nor a liberal white person will get you off the proverbial hook. I consider myself to be a decent human being. Yet, I'm sexist. Take another deep breath. I ask that you try to be "un-sutured." If that term brings to mind a state of pain, open flesh, it is meant to do so. After all, it is painful to let go of your "white innocence," to use this letter as a mirror, one that refuses to show you what you want to see, one that demands that you look at the lies that you tell yourself so that you don't feel the weight of responsibility for those who live under the yoke of whiteness, your whiteness.

I can see your anger. I can see that this letter is being misunderstood. This letter is not asking you to feel bad about yourself, to wallow in guilt. That is too easy. I'm asking for you to tarry, to linger, with the ways in which you perpetuate a racist society, the ways in which you are racist. I'm now daring you to face a racist history which, paraphrasing Baldwin, has placed you where you are and that has formed your own racism. Again, in the spirit of Baldwin, I am asking you to enter into battle with your white self. I'm asking that you open yourself up; to speak to, to admit to, the racist poison that is inside of you.

Again, take a deep breath. Don't tell me about how many black friends you have. Don't tell me that you are married to someone of color. Don't tell me that you voted for Obama. Don't tell me that *I'm* the racist. Don't tell me that you don't see color. Don't tell me that I'm blaming whites for everything. To do so is to hide yet again. You may have never used the N-word in your life, you may hate the K.K.K., but that does not mean that you don't harbor racism and benefit from racism. After all, you are part of a system that allows you to walk into stores where you are not followed, where you get to go for a bank loan and your skin does not count against you, where you don't need to engage in "the talk" that black people and people of color must tell their children when they are confronted by white police officers.

As you reap comfort from being white, we suffer for being black and people of color. But your comfort is linked to our pain and suffering. Just as my comfort in being male is linked to the suffering of women, which makes me sexist, so, too, you are racist. That is the gift that I want you to accept, to embrace. It is a form of knowledge that is taboo. Imagine the impact that the acceptance of this gift might have on you and the world.

Take another deep breath. I know that there are those who will write to me in the comment section with boiling anger, sarcasm, disbelief, denial. There are those who will say, "Yancy is just an angry black man." There are others who will say, "Why isn't Yancy telling black people to be honest about the violence in their own black neighborhoods?" Or, "How can Yancy say that all white people are racists?" If you are saying these things, then you've already failed to listen. I come with a gift. You're already rejecting the gift that I have to offer. This letter is about *you*. Don't change the conversation. I assure you that so many black people suffering from poverty and joblessness, which is linked to high levels of crime, are painfully aware of the existential toll that they have had to face because they are black and, as Baldwin adds, *"for no other reason."*

Some of your white brothers and sisters have made this leap. The legal scholar Stephanie M. Wildman, has written, "I simply believe that no matter how hard I work at not being racist, I still am. Because part of racism is systemic, I benefit from the privilege that I am struggling to see." And the journalism professor Robert Jensen: "I like to think I have changed, even though I routinely trip over the lingering effects of that internalized racism and the institutional racism around me. Every time I walk into a store at the same time as a black man and the security guard follows him and leaves me alone to shop, I am benefiting from white privilege."

What I'm asking is that you first accept the racism within yourself, accept all of the truth about what it means for you to be white in a society that was created for you. I'm asking for you to trace the binds that tie you to forms of domination that you would rather not see. When you walk into the world, you can walk with assurance; you have already signed a contract, so to speak, that guarantees you a certain form of social safety.

Baldwin argues for a form of love that is "a state of being, or state of grace—not in the infantile American sense of being made happy but in the tough and universal sense of quest and daring and growth." Most of my days, I'm engaged in a personal and societal battle against sexism. So many times, I fail. And so many times, I'm complicit. But I refuse to hide behind that mirror that lies to me about my "non-sexist nobility." Baldwin says, "Love takes off the masks that we fear we cannot live without and know we cannot live within." In my heart, I'm done with the mask of sexism, though I'm tempted every day to wear it. And, there are times when it still gets the better of me.

White America, are you prepared to be at war with yourself, your white identity, your white power, your white privilege? Are you prepared to show me a white self that love has unmasked? I'm asking for love in return for a gift; in fact, I'm hoping that this gift might help you to see yourself in ways that you have not seen before. Of course, the history of white supremacy in America belies this gesture of black gift-giving, this gesture of non-sentimental love. Martin Luther King Jr. was murdered even as he loved.

Perhaps the language of this letter will encourage a split—not a split between black and white, but a fissure in your understanding, a space for loving a Trayvon Martin, Eric Garner, Tamir Rice, Aiyana Jones, Sandra Bland, Laquan McDonald and others. I'm suggesting a form of love that enables you to see the role that you play (even despite your anti-racist actions) in a *system* that continues to value black lives on the cheap.

Take one more deep breath. I have another gift.

If you have young children, before you fall off to sleep tonight, I want you to hold your child. Touch your child's face. Smell your child's hair. Count the fingers on your child's hand. See the miracle that is your child. And then, with as much vision as you can muster, I want you to imagine that your child is black.

In peace,
George Yancy

UNIT 2

READING ARGUMENTS

As compared to those in Unit 1, the readings in Unit 2 present more specific arguments on each of the five issues. As you read these texts, practice your skills at analyzing arguments—map them out using the **Toulmin Model**, and catalog these arguments in an invention database. Consider how the **arrangement** of each argument is tied to its **audience**, and pay attention to how the **performance** or **style** of each argument affects it.

Border Control

Why Europe Could Melt Down Over a Simple Question of Borders

Max Fisher

The European Union has always been sold, to its citizens, on a practical basis: Cheaper products. Easier travel. Prosperity and security.

But its founding leaders had something larger in mind. They conceived it as a radical experiment to transcend the nation-state, whose core ideas of race-based identity and zero-sum competition had brought disaster twice in the space of a generation.

France's foreign minister, announcing the bloc's precursor in 1949, called it "a great experiment" that would put "an end to war" and guarantee "an eternal peace."

Norway's foreign minister, Halvard M. Lange, compared Europe at that moment to the early American colonies: separate blocs that, in time, would cast off their autonomy and identities to form a unified nation. Much as Virginians and Pennsylvanians had become Americans, Germans and Frenchmen would become Europeans—if they could be persuaded.

"The keen feeling of national identity must be considered a real barrier to European integration," Mr. Lange wrote in an essay that became a foundational European Union text.

But instead of overcoming that barrier, European leaders pretended it didn't exist. More damning, they entirely avoided mentioning what Europeans would need to give up: a degree of their deeply felt national identities and hard-won national sovereignty.

Now, as Europeans struggle with the social and political strains set off by migration from poor and war-torn nations outside the bloc, some are clamoring to preserve what they feel they never consented to surrender. Their fight with European leaders is exploding over an issue that, perhaps more than any other, exposes the contradiction between the dream of the European Union and the reality of European nations: borders.

Establishment European leaders insist on open borders within the bloc. Free movement is meant to transcend cultural barriers, integrate economies and lubricate the single market. But a growing number of European voters want to sharply limit the arrival of refugees in their countries, which would require closing the borders.

This might seem like a straightforward matter of reconciling internal rules with public demand on the relatively narrow issue of refugees, who are no longer even arriving in great numbers.

But there is a reason that it has brought Europe to the brink, with its most important leader, Chancellor Angela Merkel of Germany, warning of disaster and at risk of losing power. The borders question is really a question of whether Europe can move past traditional notions of the nation-state. And that is a question that Europeans have avoided confronting, much less answering, for over half a century.

Backpedaling on Open Borders

In 2015, at the height of the refugee crisis, Ms. Merkel warned that if European countries did not "fairly" share the burden, then opportunistic leaders could exploit the issue to dismantle Europe's freedom of internal movement. "It won't be the Europe we want," she said.

Three years later, Ms. Merkel has become the leader she warned about. To save her governing coalition in Berlin and bleed off populist sentiment, she has proposed imposing controls at the Austrian border to block refugees.

Most refugees arrive in Italy, Greece or Spain and are meant to remain there while waiting for asylum. In practice, though, many head north.

But how to pick out refugees from dozens of open roads and rail lines that connect Germany with Austria?

One option is to screen selectively for possible refugees; in essence, racial profiling. No one is sure how this would work. Spotters on border watchtowers with binoculars? Random pullovers? Any scheme seems likely to miss most refugees while harassing enough dark-skinned non-refugees to guarantee a backlash.

The other option is to set up checkpoints and screen everyone, making travel from Austria to Germany far more difficult, likely hurting both economies. In either scheme, Ms. Merkel's plan calls for camps along the border to hold refugees seeking to cross.

As Ms. Merkel warned three years ago, this could break the European Union as we know it. It would tacitly encourage other countries to harden their own borders, if only to protect from becoming holding pens for stricter nations like Germany.

Should enough borders harden, refugees could end up stuck in Italy, Greece and Spain—an outcome Ms. Merkel has also warned could doom the bloc by encouraging those countries to leave.

Shutting down internal movement would withdraw some of the union's most popular perks—ease of travel for work, vacation or family—and undercut trade and labor transfers, weakening the single market economy.

It might seem strange, then, that such a policy could be seen as indulging public demand. The fact that its ramifications would go so far beyond refugees, whose arrivals are anyway down sharply, suggests that public demand is about more than anti-refugee sentiment.

Perhaps the drive to restore European borders is, on some level, about borders themselves. Maybe when populists talk about restoring sovereignty and national identity, it's not just a euphemism for anti-refugee sentiment (although such sentiment is indeed rife). Maybe they mean it.

The Impulse to Close Ranks

Traveling Germany with a colleague to report on the populist wave sweeping Europe, we heard the same concerns over and over. Vanishing borders. Lost identity. A distrusted establishment. Sovereignty surrendered to the European Union. Too many migrants.

Populist supporters would often bring up refugees as a focal point and physical manifestation of larger, more abstract fears. They would often say, as one woman told me outside a rally for the Alternative for Germany, a rising populist party, that they feared their national identity was being erased.

"Germany needs a positive relationship with our identity," Björn Höcke, a leading far-right figure in the party, told my colleague. "The foundation of our unity is identity."

Allowing in refugees, even in very large numbers, does not mean Germany will no longer be Germany, of course. But this slight cultural change is one component of a larger European project that has required giving up, even if only by degrees, core conceits of a fully sovereign nation-state.

National policy is suborned, on some issues, to the vetoes and powers of the larger union. That includes control over borders, which are partially open to refugees but fully open to other Europeans.

Though the backlash has focused on refugees, who tend to present as more obviously foreign, studies suggest that it is also driven by resentment toward European migrants.

Traveling recently through Yorkshire, a postindustrial swath of northern England, I heard complaints that began about refugees but shifted quickly to Polish workers, who have arrived in much greater numbers. Some spoke ominously, if implausibly, of towns where Polish was more commonly heard than English.

It is not easy for Europeans to abandon the old-style national identity, rooted in race and language, that has caused them such trouble. The human desire for a strong group identity—and for perceived homogeneity within that group—runs deep.

Germany for the Germans, Catalonia for the Catalans. A country of people who look like me, speak my language and share my heritage. These nationalist impulses, however dangerous, emerge from basic human instinct. It makes us feel safe; losing it makes us feel threatened. It is reinforced in our popular culture and built into the international order.

New Orders, Old Instincts

European leaders hoped they could rein in those impulses long enough to transform Europe from the top down, but the financial crisis of 2008 came when their project was only half completed. That led to the crisis in the euro, which revealed political fault lines the leadership had long denied or wished away.

The financial crisis and an accompanying outburst in Islamic terrorism also provided a threat. When people feel under threat, research shows, they seek a strong identity that will make them feel part of a powerful group.

For that, many Europeans turned to their national identity: British, French, German. But the more people embraced their national identities, the more they came to oppose the European Union, studies found—and the more they came to distrust anyone within their borders who they saw as an outsider.

European leaders, unable to square their project's ambition of transcending nationalism with this reality of rising nationalism, have tried to have it both ways. Ms. Merkel has sought to save Europe's border-free zone by imposing one hard border.

Sebastian Kurz, the Austrian chancellor, has called for ever-harder "external" borders, which refers to those separating the European Union from the outside world, in order to keep internal borders open.

This might work if refugee arrivals were the root issue. But it would not resolve the contradiction between the European Union as an experiment in overcoming nationalism versus the politics of the moment, in which publics are demanding more nationalism.

That resurgence starts with borders. But Hungary's trajectory suggests it might not end there. The country's nationalist government, after erecting fences and setting up refugee camps, has seen hardening xenophobia and rising support for tilting toward authoritarianism.

As the euro crisis showed, even pro-union leaders could never bring themselves to fully abandon the old nationalism. They are elected by their fellow nationals, after all, so naturally put them first. Their first loyalty is to their country. When that comes into conflict with the rest of the union, as it has on the issue of refugees, it's little wonder that national self-interest wins.

Working with Mexico Is the Key to Strong American Border Security

Henry Cisneros and Carlos Gutierrez

The recent decision by the Trump administration to step back from separating families detained at the border offers an opportunity to reflect on what immigration enforcement policies make the most sense going forward. Separating families is not the path forward, nor is it something that Americans, who prize their family values, will tolerate.

As a country of laws, the United States needs to make sure that potential immigrants enter the country through legal channels, while respecting the rights of those who seek legal protection. How do we strengthen border security while staying committed to due process and family values? Sensible options exist, and we should act on them.

First, we should increase investment in the asylum system at the border to make certain that legitimate claims can be heard and decided expeditiously. Before 2014, most attempted border crossers were economic migrants, overwhelmingly from Mexico. Today, U.S.-Mexico border apprehensions are at the lowest level in 46 years, primarily due to broad improvements in the Mexican economy, education, and healthcare systems that have made it more attractive to stay in Mexico.

Most border detainees today are from Central America. The number of Hondurans, El Salvadorans, and Guatemalans attempting to cross the border jumped dramatically five years ago. While it has declined slightly, the number still remains high. This rise in the flow of Central Americans presents a different set of challenges because many are not purely economic migrants. Most are fleeing a toxic mix of poverty and violence in the region, and many hold legitimate grounds for asylum.

Democrats and Republicans should be able to agree that a significant investment in asylum officers and immigration judges to speed up processing at the border makes sense. More timely decision-making would likely help deter those without a substantiated case and provide a fairer process for those who deserve protection.

Speeding up asylum would also shorten the time people need to be in detention. However, it is important to note that proven alternatives to detention are potentially a far better option, especially for families. Those awaiting hearings could be released with their location monitored through a case management system that the Department of Homeland Security has already tested and found extremely effective.

Another strategic option is for the U.S. government to view Mexico as an ally rather than an adversary at the border. Mexico has deported far more Central Americans than the United States in recent years, a major reason that unauthorized immigration flows remain quite low at the southern border. Thus,

Mexico acts essentially as a buffer to stop potential illegal crossers before they reach the United States.

The Mexican government now faces strains on its own asylum system and capacity issues in its immigration detention centers. Following the Mexican election yesterday, there is a risk that a new government will decide it has no incentive to continue to collaborate with the United States on slowing migration flows from Central America, especially in light of the tense relations it has with the Trump administration.

The time is ripe for more creative cooperation with Mexico around dealing with Central American migrants, as part of our own national interest. The U.S. government could help Mexico improve both its enforcement capacities and its asylum system. We are still far from the day when most Central American migrants would choose to stay in Mexico, but much can be done to address legitimate asylum claims before migrants ever reach the U.S. border and help Mexico welcome those Central Americans who would prefer to stay in that country rather than continue northward.

Finally, and perhaps most importantly, any border solution must address the root causes of migration. Today, the vast majority of those trying to get into the United States through the southern border are from three Central American countries that face enduring poverty and endemic violence. Both the Obama and Trump administrations have endorsed efforts to invest in economic development and build rule of law in these countries, working hand in hand with the Mexican government.

Yet, these efforts appear to be flagging, with little high-level attention from Congress or the administration. The solution to staunching the flow of Central Americans desperate to leave their countries requires commitment by the United States, together with Mexico, to help these countries build more stable societies and economies.

As a country of laws, the United States has a vested interest in guaranteeing that its immigration laws are respected, but must do so with respect for due process and the family values that underpin our national identity. We will be stronger and more successful if we undertake these efforts in partnership with our southern neighbor. This approach should appeal to all Americans, regardless of their political persuasion.

Privacy and Cyber-Security

Why Have We Given Up Our Privacy to Facebook and Other Sites So Willingly?

Alex Hern

Facebook is on the ropes. A week of revelations about Cambridge Analytica's use of data gleaned from the social network has left the world demanding answers. The company can't seem to decide: is it outraged that it was taken advantage of by an unscrupulous actor, or relieved that this is just normal use of tools that it made widely available for almost five years? Should Mark Zuckerberg come out front and centre leading the response, or should he hide in a cupboard until it all blows over?

Faced with its first true crisis, the company is paralysed with fear. And that paralysis is, remarkably quickly, leading people to reassess their relationship with the site as a whole. The teens got there first, really. Facebook usage among younger people has been declining for years, in the face of competition from upstart rivals such as Snapchat, internal disruption from Facebook-owned Instagram, and a general sense that Facebook is full of old people and parents. But the backlash isn't a generational thing any more. We're all losing control of our data, both online and off, and we're starting to kick back.

Not only is the burgeoning #deletefacebook movement picking up steam (although it will take a few weeks before hard numbers are available about how many have followed through on their words), but people are also beginning to look up, as if from a daydream, to ask: how exactly did we end up in this situation? Why did we give up our privacy so willingly? And how can we get it back?

The 50m profiles harvested from Facebook by a Cambridge Analytica partner under the guise of research are a huge data store, but they pale in comparison with the amount of information the company holds on its own users. At the same time that Facebook turned off the spigot that had been used to pump industrial quantities of data off its platform, the company opened up a second set of floodgates: the Facebook Audience Network, which allows third parties to track, profile and advertise to Facebook users wherever they find them on the internet.

Facebook isn't really a social network. It's barely even an advertising company. It's a data analytics firm, which manages to use its position as the middleman for a vast proportion of all human communication to find out everything there is to know about its users.

Just as Cambridge Analytica claimed enormous powers of perception with a scant selection of personal information, Facebook also boasts to advertisers about how much it knows about its users—and how effective it can be at influencing their minds: it cites a games company that "made video adverts to match different gamer styles" for a "63% increase in purchase intent"; a clothes retailer that achieved "a dramatic increase in sales" with "richly personalised ads"; and a mobile network that scored "a major boost in awareness and purchase intent" by focusing on users with families. (Facebook used to have a similar page on which it showed off to politicians about how effective it was at swinging elections, but it quietly removed that in February.)

If you think you're a passive user of Facebook, minimising the data you provide to the site or refraining from oversharing details of your life, you have probably underestimated the scope of its reach. Facebook doesn't just learn from the pictures you post, and the comments you leave: the site learns from which posts you read and which you don't; it learns from when you stop scrolling down your feed and how long it takes you to restart; it learns from your browsing on other websites that have nothing to do with Facebook itself; and it even learns from the messages you type out then delete before sending (the company published an academic paper on this "self-censorship" back in 2013).

This data life isn't limited to Facebook. Google, famously, is in the same basic business, although the company is a bit more transparent about it (for a shock, try going to the "My Activity" and "Location History" pages to be vividly reminded that Google is tracking everything). And Amazon is building a modern surveillance panopticon, replete with an always-on microphone for your kitchen and a jaunty camera for your bedroom, purely to sell you more stuff.

Avoiding the big players doesn't help much. Large data brokers such as Experian and Equifax exist to collate information about everyone, whether or not they're online. The security services continue to build their own surveillance databases, with powers strengthened in the UK through the recent Investigatory Powers Act. Even going to church now comes with the potential for a dose of surveillance: the Church of England has authorised the roll-out of 14,000 contactless card readers, to let parishioners give without carrying cash. Is it time to say goodbye to the anonymity of the collection plate, and hope you're one of the more generous donors?

Richard Stallman has been warning of this state of affairs since before Zuckerberg even touched his first computer. The veteran computer scientist, creator of the GNU operating system and leader of the Free Software Movement, warns that "the only database that is not dangerous is the one that is never collected."

"There is a limit on the level of surveillance that democracy can co-exist with, and we're far above that," he tells me on the phone from the Massachusetts Institute of Technology. "We suffer more surveillance than the inhabitants of the Soviet Union, and we need to push it way down.

"Any database of personal data will be misused, if a misuse can be imagined by humans. It can be misused by the organisation that collects the data. In many cases, the purpose of collecting it *is* to misuse it, as in the case of Facebook, but also in the case of Amazon, Google to some extent, and thousands of smaller companies as well.

"It can also be misused by rogue employees of the company and it can also be stolen by some third party and misused. There'd be no danger of data breaches if a database doesn't exist. And, finally, it can be taken by the state and misused."

Stallman has little sympathy for those who choose to use such services. "They're foolish," he says, when I ask him why he thinks data harvesting is tacitly accepted by so many people. "They're accustomed to a certain kind of convenience ... they choose to ignore that it might be dangerous."

I'm less certain that there's a choice being made at all, though. Yes, people may regularly be accepting terms and conditions that require them to give up their data, but that doesn't mean they read them. I should know: I have. A few years ago, I decided to read, in full, the small print for every single product or service I used. I read almost 150,000 words of legalese—three-quarters of Moby Dick—in less than a week, from the 21,000 words required to turn off the alarm on my iPhone on a Monday morning to the 4,000 words required to browse BuzzFeed in my lunch break.

The experience was gruesome. Legal documents are not written to be read by humans, and certainly not to be read back-to-back in a harrowing marathon of End-User Licence Agreements. But I did learn one thing, which is that the modern notion of consent upon which the entire data edifice is built has the shakiest of foundations.

Lukasz Olejnik, an independent security and privacy researcher, agrees: "Years ago, people and organisations used to shift the blame on the users, even in public. This blaming is unfortunate, because expecting users to be subject-matter experts and versed in the obscure technical aspects is misguided.

"Blaming users is an oversimplification, as most do not understand the true implications when data are shared—they cannot. You can't expect people to fully appreciate the amount of information extracted from aggregated datasets. That said, you can't expect users to know what is really happening with their data if it's not clearly communicated in an informed consent prompt, which should in some cases include also the consequences of hitting 'I agree.'"

He adds that at many organisations, privacy was not being taken seriously, "except when there was a need to include the phrase 'We take the privacy of our users very seriously' following a data breach."

It doesn't have to be like this. Doctors are required to demonstrate not just consent, but informed consent, from patients: the latter have to understand what they are agreeing to, or the agreement is moot. After years of mis-selling scandals, the same principle is slowly making its way to the financial industry. Logging in to check an ISA, you may be confronted with a 12-point questionnaire designed to check you understand the risks and are happy for the investment to continue.

Yet online, the biggest companies in the world base their businesses around users hitting "I agree" on a dialogue box on a website once, a decade ago, and then never being told what their agreement entails, nor being offered any way to retract their consent and take back control of the information they gave up.

Change is coming. In the EU, the General Data Protection Regulation— GDPR—overhauls a continent's worth of rules around a clear principle that the only person who can ever own an individual's data is that individual. Olejnik describes the law as a "good starter," but notes that even it will still need to be "reviewed and updated on a regular basis."

Stallman wants to go one step further. "I recommend a law prohibiting any system that collects data," he says, "no matter who runs it, whether it's a company, some non-profit organisation, or a public agency, whatever, that they are not allowed to collect data unless they can justify it as absolutely necessary for the function to be done."

It would be a huge step, and one that is unlikely to come without a radical change in how the public views mass data collection. But he has hope, and rejects the label of a Cassandra, doomed with accurate predictions that will always be ignored.

"I don't know the future, because the future depends on you, so I'm going to try my damn best," he says. "I'm a pessimist by nature. But just because things look dim, is no reason to give up. And that's what I've been saying for many, many years."

Quantum Computing Is the Next Big Security Risk
Will Hurd

The 20th century gave birth to the Nuclear Age as the power of the atom was harnessed and unleashed. Today, we are on the cusp of an equally momentous and irrevocable breakthrough: the advent of computers that draw their computational capability from quantum mechanics.

The potential benefits of mastering quantum computing, from advances in cancer research to unlocking the mysteries of the universe, are limitless.

But that same computing power can be used to unlock different kinds of secrets—from your personal financial or health records, to corporate research projects and classified government intelligence.

It's more than just theoretical: An algorithm formulated by mathematician Peter Shor demonstrates that quantum computers are able to factor large numbers more efficiently than classical computers. Large-number factoring is the foundation of today's encryption standards.

The impact of quantum on our national defense will be tremendous. The question is whether the United States and its allies will be ready.

The consequences of mastering quantum computing, while not as visual or visceral as a mushroom cloud, are no less significant than those faced by the scientists who lit up the New Mexico sky with the detonation at the Trinity test site 72 years ago. In the same way that atomic weaponry symbolized power throughout the Cold War, quantum capability is likely to define hegemony in today's increasingly digital, interconnected global economy.

Unlike traditional computers, which process information in binary bits, quantum computers exploit the ability of quantum bits (qubits) to exist in multiple states simultaneously. This allows them to perform incredibly complex calculations at speeds unimaginable today and solve certain classes of problems that are beyond the grasp of today's most advanced super computers.

Today, quantum computers are beginning to move out of research labs in search of broader investment and applications. In October, Google announced that by the end of this year it expects to achieve quantum supremacy—the point at which a quantum computer can outperform a classical computer.

Because nations around the world, including China, are investing heavily in research and development, the world is likely less than a decade away from the day when a nation-state could use quantum computers to render many of today's most sophisticated encryption systems useless.

From academics to the National Security Agency, there is widespread agreement that quantum computers will rock current security protocols that protect global financial markets and the inner workings of government.

Already, intelligence agencies around the world are archiving intercepted communications transmitted with encryption that's currently all but unbreakable, in the hopes that in the future computing advances will turn what's gibberish now into potentially valuable intelligence. Rogue states may also be able to leverage the power of quantum to attack the banking and financial systems at the heart of western capitalism.

Everyone has seen the damage individual hackers can do when they infiltrate a system. Imagine a nation-state intercepting the encrypted financial data that flows across the globe and being able to read it as easily as you are reading this. Quantum computers are so big and expensive that—outside of global technology companies and well-funded research universities—most will be owned and maintained by nation-states. That means the first quantum attacks are likely to be organized by countries hostile to the US and our allies. Rogue states could read military communiques the way the United States and its allies did after cracking the Nazi Enigma codes.

In short, quantum computing presents both an unprecedented opportunity and a serious threat. The United States must lead this transition, in collaboration with its allies around the world. Whether lawmakers want to think of it as a new Manhattan Project or a race to the moon, the US cannot abdicate leadership in scientific discovery or international security.

The window is closing, fast. It took more than five years and nearly half a trillion dollars for companies and governments to prepare for Y2K, which resulted in a non-event for most people. But, the US is not ready for what experts call Y2Q (Years to Quantum), and the time to prepare is now. Even in a pre-quantum era, the need for quantum-safe encryption is real. Banks, government agencies, insurers, hospitals, utilities, and airlines all need to be thinking now about how to implement security and encryption that will withstand a quantum attack.

On complex, large-scale networks, it can take years to roll out even a relatively straightforward update. Quantum-safe encryption relies on mathematical approaches that even quantum computers have difficulty solving. The challenge is ensuring that every point through which data flows, and even the data itself, is wrapped in quantum-safe security.

Private sector research and development are happening in pockets across North America and among the US's allies. Google and IBM both have well-publicized programs to build viable quantum computers. At the same time, though, the US and its allies must take practical steps to prepare for the quantum threat. The National Institute of Standards and Technology is working to evaluate quantum-safe cryptographic candidate algorithms. Other organizations like the European Telecommunications Standards Institute and the United Nations' International Telecommunications Union are working to ensure our standards for connecting systems continue to evolve to be quantum safe. Companies like ISARA are among a small cadre of cryptographers and programmers building quantum-safe security solutions to help high-risk industries and organizations begin protecting themselves.

It's these kinds of efforts that the US and its allies must collaborate on to align the goals of scientific discovery, technological advancement, and national security. As companies build powerful quantum machines, leaders must simultaneously understand the risks those machines pose and the counter-measures required. Executives in every industry need to understand the implications that quantum computing will have on their legacy systems, and take steps to be ready. At a minimum, that means retrofitting their networks, computers, and applications with encryption that can withstand a quantum attack.

Nowhere is it more vital to begin preparations than with the vast network of governmental systems that do everything from processing Social Security checks to analyzing vast amounts of electronic intelligence.

Whether it was the discovery of fission or the launch of Sputnik, the United States has responded to scientific challenges of the past century with resolve and determination. The US must do the same with quantum computing.

The Wellness Epidemic

Amy Larocca

Why are so many privileged people feeling so sick? Luckily, there's no shortage of cures.

When Gwyneth Paltrow first launched Goop in 2008, it was a great place to find out where to eat the best tapas in Barcelona. It was straight-up celebrity-lifestyle voyeurism, and Paltrow, with her long blonde hair and aura of complete self-satisfaction, was irresistible. There's the expression "living your best life," and then there is Paltrow: best life manifest.

But then Goop's focus started to shift. Paltrow began to describe in detail her exercise regimen with her trainer Tracy Anderson, who believes one should work out two hours a day, six days a week. Then she began providing information on a cleanse she does each January. The mission became less about revealing the trappings of the good life and more about the notion that the really good life is internal. Rich and beautiful people don't just go to nicer places, their organs work better. They even know how to breathe better, with more oxygen per ounce. They're not afraid to try fecal transplants, with really top-notch, vegan-only feces. Goop became less about hotels and restaurants and more about chakras and thyroids, with the implication that maybe what's actually standing between you and your inner Gwyneth is some mysterious virus that your overextended, pharmaceutically corrupt doctor is too narrow-minded to address.

Goop began publishing long interviews with doctors, healers, and shamans. One of its most-shared pieces is an interview with Oscar Serrallach, an Australian doctor, about "postnatal depletion," which suggested that women live in a depleted state for up to ten years after the birth of a child. Among the contributing factors: overwhelming stress, nutrient-poor food, and "electrosmog." While Goop had traditionally done well selling products related to its content (spiralizers blew up after Paltrow's recipe for "zucchini cacio e pepe" went live), what could it sell a woman who's just received medical confirmation that the negative feelings simmering in her gut are not just in her mind? How about vitamins? Goop Wellness now offers four vitamin "protocols" (*protocols* and *practice* are words you'll encounter a lot in this world) based on four common complaints: The Mother Load addresses postnatal depletion; High School Genes is for women who find it harder to lose weight as they age (i.e., all women); Why Am I So Effing Tired? is for the pernicious fatigue faced by do-it-all women; and Balls in the Air is similar, only more for the chronically stressed.

"It's been overwhelming," says Ashley Lewis, senior director of wellness at Goop. "We sold over $100,000 worth of vitamins on day one, and that trajectory has just continued."

Wellness is a very broad idea, which is no small part of its marketing appeal. On the most basic level, it's about making a conscious effort to attain health in both body and mind, to strive for unity and balance. And it's not a new idea either. Homeopathy, which uses natural substances to promote the body's ability to self-heal, was popularized in Germany in the late-18th century, and 50 years later, the YMCA set its mission as caring for the body, mind, and spirit. Dan Rather did a *60 Minutes* segment on wellness in 1979, but it was approached more as a fringe phenomenon. "*Wellness,*" he said, "that's not a word you hear every day."

Diets, exercise, and various versions of self-care have been around forever: Antecedents are found at an Austrian spa still famous for its enemas and in 1970s L.A., where wheatgrass was just as popular as cocaine. The seeds were in the Jane Fonda workout and the Scarsdale diet, in the EST movement and the yoga craze that brought us Lululemon. In 1978, this magazine ran a cover story on "The Physical Elite," the new class of people who had quit smoking and devoted themselves to working out. Some were known to make odd food demands, like requesting that an entire onion be concealed in an omelet.

Four decades later, wellness is not only a word you hear every day; it's a global industry worth billions—one that includes wellness tourism, alternative medicine, and anti-aging treatments. The competition for a hunk of that market is intense: In Manhattan, two for-profit meditation studios are vying to become the SoulCycle of meditation, and Saks Fifth Avenue has temporarily converted its second floor into a "Wellery," where you can experience aroma and light therapy in a glass booth filled with salt, or get plugged into a meditation app during a manicure. Every giant corporation has a wellness program: yoga at Goldman Sachs, communal sleep logs at JPMorgan Chase. A new magazine has debuted out on Long Island this summer, *Hamptons Purist.* ("Look around the city," says its editor, Cristina Greeven, who came up with the idea on a surfboard in Costa Rica: "It used to be a butcher, a baker, and a hardware store. Now it's SoulCycle, Juice Press, and a meditation place.") It will have to compete with the Goop magazine, to be edited by Paltrow and published by Condé Nast, which this spring also announced the launch of Condé Nast Pharma, a division that offers "brand-safe" wellness-based content to pharmaceutical advertisers. The advertising giant Saatchi & Saatchi has its own wellness division, capitalizing on "women's unmet wellness needs" in the marketplace.

Wellness is used to sell hotel rooms ("Stay well at Westin Hotels & Resorts, a place where together, we can rise") and condos (Leonardo DiCaprio just sold his "wellness" condo, but Deepak Chopra still has one at the same address), and it has become a political movement, too. "Radical Self Care" seeks to heal wounds both recent (Trump) and systemic (trauma as a result of one's race or gender), using the words of the poet Audre Lorde as a rallying cry: "Caring for myself is not self-indulgence. It is self-preservation, and that is an act of political warfare."

It can be easy to be cynical about wellness, about the $66 jade eggs that Gwyneth Paltrow suggests inserting in your "yoni." There's something grotesque about this industry's emerging at the moment when the most basic health care is still being denied to so many in America and is at risk of being snatched away from millions more. But what's perhaps most striking about wellness's ascendancy is that it's happening because, in our increasingly bifurcated world, even those who *do* have access to pretty good (and sometimes quite excellent, if quite expensive) traditional health care are left feeling, nonetheless, incredibly unwell.

I was in the elevator of a Park Avenue apartment building on my way to a lunch celebrating the launch of a blog when I ran into Kerrilynn Pamer, whom I knew as the owner of Castor & Pollux, a clothing store in the West Village. Beautiful and tall, she was wearing a long white dress and had a mellow, happy smile. She had closed Castor & Pollux, she explained, and reopened it as a natural-beauty store called CAP Beauty two years ago. "With fashion, there was often a sense of lack," she said. "It was always, 'I don't fit into that,' or, 'I don't have the wallet,' or, 'I don't have the life to wear it.' It all just led to a sense of people being left out."

Pamer had long been interested in wellness. "I didn't really embrace it," she said, "but I felt bad all the time. I went to the doctor for an annual physical and just said that I was tired. I wasn't aging how I wanted to. I wasn't feeling how I wanted to feel in my body."

The doctor called after her appointment and said, "'I don't know how you're walking around right now. You're not retaining anything.' I just thought, *This is the norm. I live in New York, I'm getting older, I have a business.* But he said, 'No, you have celiac disease.' I gave up gluten, and it was just like, *boom*." Pamer started analyzing everything she was eating, then everything she was putting on her skin. "It all comes from a place of diagnosis." She and her business partner Cindy DiPrima are part of "a very solution-oriented group of people. I want to make myself feel better and then I want everyone to feel good." Pamer invited me to come see the store. "We've laid down some rose quartz beneath the floorboards, and the vibrations are great."

I went a week later. It was a rainy day, and the shop was friendly: all brass fixtures and raw snacks from Amanda Chantal Bacon's Moon Juice line. The vibrations seemed good! I was led into a back room where I had a facial from an especially warm, kind woman named Crystal. A lot of the products she used had an earthy, sometimes rank smell—like very, very ripe fruit on the verge of crossing over—but otherwise it was pretty standard as facials go. Crystal never scolded me or criticized my skin, which was nice, as that, too, is often standard as facials go. A few days later, I got an email recommending a new "protocol" for my skin. The protocol involved nine products, and if I bought all of them (there were links), it would cost close to $1,000. I panicked for a moment: *But I need this! Clearly I am poisoning myself with the drugstore moisturizer my dermatologist recommends!* I started to click on the links: Maybe I'd just buy a few, maybe just the $40 probiotic mist to balance and restore my facial microbiome. *Don't my children deserve a nontoxic mother, don't I deserve a nontoxic self?* But I didn't get far: Almost all of it was sold out.

Spend a little time in the wellness world, and it seems like everyone has an official diagnosis. "I think for women in general there's the expectation that of course you feel like shit—of course!" says Elise Loehnen, the head of content at Goop. "For the most part, people are finding more and more that everyone they know is kind of sick. Their friend's son might have autism or bad digestion. People are self-identifying as sick much, much more. There are concerns about our food supply, about the rampant use of glycosate. Food used to grow in many feet of loamy soil! I think we're just depleted. I think there's a vitamin-D deficiency because we don't go outside, and when we do, we're always wearing sunscreen. We're out of touch with the Earth in general, and I just don't think this is the way we were intended to live."

I, too, know women with celiac disease, maybe-kind-of-celiac disease, and a million different autoimmune diseases with long, complicated names that affect their skin and their gut. It's hard not to wonder what's going on sometimes, if we are all being poisoned somehow, if our bodies and minds are in revolt against this highly processed, digitized life, or if some of the ailments being named and treated would have been quietly borne—for better or worse—in other generations. Are the University of Chicago medical school's estimates about celiac disease (one percent of the U.S. population) outdated, or are we being overdiagnosed? Anxiety levels have shot up in this country, and though illness can of course be both a source and symptom of stress, the body is also one zone where, however futilely, we may see a chance to reexert control.

Online, there's a community known as the "spoonies" that might be described as both the fringe and core of the wellness world. Spoonies take their name from Spoon Theory, an idea proposed by a woman named Christine Miserandino who was diagnosed with a chain of illnesses including chronic-fatigue syndrome before landing with a diagnosis of lupus. For years, she was embarrassed and suffered silently, endlessly having to explain her behavior (her blog is called butyoudontlooksick.com). Her theory is simple: When you are healthy, you have a never-ending supply of renewable energy. When you live with chronic illness or pain, your energy capacity is finite and you must constantly be measuring it out, via spoons, negotiating how they might be spent. Taking a shower costs a spoon, but, then, sometimes, so does just getting out of bed. If you choose to cook a healthy dinner at night, that might cost you so many spoons that you won't be able to do the dishes. And so on. Miserandino gained a following, and there is now a robust online group of self-identified spoonies who come together to discuss their daily struggles, to share treatments and theories, to discuss what it means to live with chronic pain of the physical and mental variety. "We always have to look out for the spoonies," says Carolyn Kylstra, the editor-in-chief of *Self.* "They are really at the heart of all of this."

There's a whole world of doctors frustrated with the wellness movement, with what they see as the shady, shallow science behind it, and they too are vocal. Just get Timothy Caulfield, a health and law expert at the University of Alberta and author of *Is Gwyneth Paltrow Wrong About Everything?*, started on the topic of detoxifying one's body. "It's completely ridiculous from a scientific perspective on every level," he's said. "The idea that we need to detoxify our bodies—we have organs that do it ... There's no evidence that we have these evil toxins in our cells that are making us put on weight, that give us fatigue. But it plays to our intuition in a very powerful way."

Jennifer Gunter, an OB/GYN and pain-medicine physician in Toronto, writes a frank and often funny blog that often takes on Paltrow and Goop. One post reads: "Your goopshit bothers me because it affects my patients. They read your crackpot theories and they stop eating tomatoes (side note, if tomatoes are toxic why do Italians have a longer life expectancy than Americans?) or haven't had a slice of bread for two years, they spend money on organic tampons they don't need, they ask for unindicated testing for adrenal fatigue (and often pay a lot via co-payments or paying out of pocket), or they obsess that they have systemic Candida (they don't). I have a son with thyroid disease and I worry that in a few years he might read the kind of batshit crazy thyroid theories you promote and wonder if he should stop his medication and try to cure the chronic EBV that he doesn't have. I also worry that science will have to spend more and more resources disproving snake oil as opposed to testing real hypotheses. I worry that you make people worry and that you are lowering the world's medical IQ."

The criticism doesn't faze Goop. "Our job is to be skeptical of the status quo ... to offer open-minded alternatives," Goop said in a statement, insisting, "Our content isn't meant to instill fear ... We want to give people the tools to have some autonomy over their health."

And then there are the physicians in the middle, "functional medicine" doctors like Frank Lipman. They are credentialed M.D.'s who prescribe antibiotics, but are just as likely to prescribe massage, a walk in a forest, or an overhaul of your diet and exercise regimens. Lipman has been in private practice for 30 years, but it was during a residency at a Bronx hospital that he noticed higher success rates among addicts treated with acupuncture and decided to find a way to merge Western medical practice with alternative practices. Lipman tells me that he believes the capacity to forgive can have tremendous health benefits, but when I tell him my hay fever is driving me nuts, he says, with a shrug, "My wife really likes Claritin."

Among the New Guard is Dr. Robin Berzin, who has a degree from Columbia Medical School, trained at Mount Sinai, and is also a certified yoga and meditation teacher. She heads up Parsley Health, a boutique medical practice. For $150 a month, members get five visits with their doctor a year, plus 24 sessions with a health coach whose job it is to make sure they implement the doctor's recommendations (you can do these meetings via video, if you'd like). "Look," she says one day in her office, which occupies a big percentage of a WeWork near Union Square (the new functional medicine is, aesthetically at least, far less Orientalist—far fewer mandalas and Ganesh statues), "people don't feel good, and they're looking for solutions, and they're getting a lot of bad advice. They're downing juices that are just as bad as soda." Berzin's mission is to reduce medications, to get to the root cause of common complaints that she sees as utterly fixable, complaints of PMS, IBS, insomnia, eczema. "In service of technology, we are chronically stressed, exhausted, and on drugs: anti-anxiety drugs. 'Wired and tired' is the way many people describe feeling to me," she says. A lot of her patients are young. "Millennials are more interested in quality of life. They expect to feel better."

After a meeting with Berzin, I submit to the Parsley screening. I fill out paperwork for 30 minutes one night, describing the ear infections I had as a kid, the fact that I was delivered naturally but bottle fed. Parsley suggests an intense blood screening, so I fast one morning and visit a lab near my house. A kind technician with a long ponytail looks at the forms: "Parsley Health!" she says, and laughs a bit. "They look for everything. Not everybody looks for everything." She shrugs, filling vial after vial, 14 in all.

My test results were posted on Parsley's portal a week later: high cholesterol, which I've known forever, and a name for the dust-mite and hay-fever allergies I've also had forever. Berzin had recommended giving up wheat and gluten, but my blood work indicates no allergic response to either. She says I am like only 5 percent of her patients—what she would call an "optimizer"—in that I don't suffer from chronic illness or pain, like the many women she sees with polycystic-ovary syndrome. Nonetheless, she has some tweaks for me: She recommends changing my exercise schedule and that I learn to meditate—Parsley members are given a free Headspace membership. She also recommends a vitamin regimen: a B-complex in the mornings, magnesium to help me find the solid, black sleep I used to get in my 20s. She recommends nettles for allergy season but also acknowledges that they don't knock out symptoms 100 percent of the time. "Look," she says, "we're not going to reiki an infection away."

One of the things that's difficult to reconcile in the wellness world is that creeping paranoia is welcome—*what* are you eating? *What* are you putting on your skin?—yet there's an untroubled faith in so much of the cure. A loaf of bread may be considered toxic, but a willingness to plunge into the largely unregulated world of vitamins and supplements is a given. My lovely, thorough, and smart GP says every year at my annual checkup: Please tell me you're not taking any supplements. At best, she says, you're doing no harm, you're just giving yourself some very expensive pee.

A lot of the wellness movement addresses aspects of our lives previously considered basic and fundamental, like breathing or sleep. This spring, Arianna Huffington celebrated the tenth anniversary of what she calls her "great blessing." On April 6, 2007, Huffington collapsed and broke her cheekbone. After a journey through many traditional medical disciplines, her diagnosis was just burnout—no cancer, no stroke, no sneaky diabetes. She was just very, very tired. "I was just literally burning the candle at both ends," she says now. "And what I find interesting is that if you had asked me that morning, 'How are you, Arianna?,' I would have said, 'Fine,' because it was normal running on empty. Think about how aware we are of how much battery remains on our smartphone, but we don't have that same awareness about ourselves." Huffington wrote a book about just how important sleep is, offering a prescription (the rhythms of which will be familiar to anyone who has recently sleep-trained a baby: a totally routinized wind-down time including warm baths, soft lights, and a blackout shade). Later, she left the Huffington Post and started Thrive Global, an organization dedicated to wellness. Thrive publishes a blog, organizes wellness programs for companies like Uber, and sells products on its website, like the wooden Thrive phone bed, which comes with a set of tiny satin sheets for your iPhone to sleep on. "You know, there is something so satisfying...," Huffington explains one day in her crowded Soho office as she tucks her phone in beneath a satin sheet. "We're going to launch one that looks like a little race car." She smiles and fusses with her iPhone's pillow. "After all, you have to teach children to tuck their phones in, too."

One of Thrive's first clients was JPMorgan Chase, which worked with the company on a 28-day wellness challenge for its more than 300,000 employees. Wellness, Thrive promises, does wonders for the corporate bottom line. "This is not for people who want to chill out under the mango tree," says Huffington. "Those people are fine. They don't need us. This is for people who want to get things done, who want to achieve."

And if we need to relearn how to sleep, wellness also seeks to transform our relationship to exercise. The SoulCycle classes I take vary little in content from the spinning class I took at Crunch 15 years ago: There are the same funny little jumps, the same sprints and hills, and, sometimes, there's even the same Madonna songs. But the teacher at Crunch used to shout things about bathing-suit season and bingo wings: We all knew what we were doing there. At SoulCycle, the ethos is unrecognizable. The lights are off, the candles burn, and the wall is covered in words like ROCK STAR and WARRIOR. Lately, I've noticed lots of women wearing T-shirts to class that say SPIRITUAL GANGSTER on them.

"Who in here has cried at SoulCycle?" an instructor asked one morning, and more than half the hands went up. "Close your eyes and think about who you love, what you're doing this for. Where is your compassion, where is your kindness, what are you riding toward?"

The Class by Taryn Toomey, which takes place in a millennial-pink studio in Tribeca, is the wellness class to beat. Toomey started her career in retail at Ralph Lauren and was soon working her way up. "But I was just feeling just … *Why am I unhappy? Everything on paper looks really good*," she explains. She began teaching friends a mix of yoga and dance and cathartic shouting in the basement common room of her Tribeca condo. A lot of celebrities started coming—Naomi Watts, Christy Turlington—which is solid gold in the fitness world, and last year, Toomey was able to open a studio. "I think we're all up against all this feedback from the outside world," she says one afternoon before class. "It's all this social media, it's all *How do I compare myself*, it's all this illusion people are creating for themselves about how perfect things are. Or aren't. Or they're using it as a platform to shame or hate. I think wellness is a movement, and all these different types of practices are about stretching your mindfulness and your consciousness, and it has become so necessary. I think we're really scared and confused and we're looking for community." Against a wall are products for sale: more of the Moon Juice snacks and dusts, some essential oils that Toomey rubs into my hand. She closes her eyes and inhales loudly: "Now," she says, "now you smell like love."

When Toomey walks into a classroom, she starts to shout: *"Get out of the fucking mirror. Get out of the Mother. Fucking. Mirror and get into your fucking. Physical. Body!"* Her students beat their fists on their thighs and moan. They wiggle and quake and wail—a bunch of Maori warriors descended on a Southern Baptist revival tent, except that it's all women, almost entirely white women, and they're all wearing sports bras. Everyone gets really sweaty (the room is not ventilated) doing jumping jacks and burpees and sit-ups, with the occasional downward dog thrown in. What's remarkable about all of it is Toomey, who talks in her low, gravelly voice into her headset the entire time, a chanting monologue of self-help and advice and encouragement: "Say good-bye to your stories," she says. "Don't blame and shame. Community. Unity. You, you, you," she chants. She never once mentions body parts, and I find myself embarrassed for thinking, while doing kicks I remember from a Tae Bo class a hundred years ago, *Oh, this one's good for the butt.* When it's all over, Toomey starts winding her monologue down. No more shouting, no more "fucks." The mirror is too fogged up to see anything, anyway. Toomey invites the room to clutch their chests (on hers is a crystal necklace she designed, a variety of which are on sale for $400 to $10,800 in the lobby. "It helps ground you," she explains). "Oh, hi," she says softly. "Oh, hi, my dear heart. There you are. It's me. I'm sorry."

Meditation, that centuries-old practice, is to this movement what jogging was to 1978's "physical elite." The core protocol—and a growth opportunity. Right now, there are two major competitors in the New York "meditation studio" arena. One, Inscape, is the brainchild of Khajak Keledjian, who made his fortune with Intermix, which curated outfits by high-end designers into looks that could work on the Jitney or at Marquee. He sold the chain to the Gap, and, as often happens with very successful people, was inundated with questions about how he pulled it off. His answer was meditation. He'd learned from a friend who ran a hedge fund about the benefits of looking inward. "Self-care is a new dimension for luxury," Keledjian tells me. "Instead of being human beings, we have become human doings. I've worked enough on people's outsides. Now I'm helping people's insides. And I'm working just as hard. Just more mindfully."

Ellie Burrows of Inscape's competitor Mndfl was a junior film executive depressed that she didn't seem to love work the way her colleagues did. She went on an odyssey of the eat-pray-love variety, and when she returned to New York, she began volunteering at the Institute for Compassionate Leadership, which was run by Lodro Rinzler, who'd been raised a Shambhala Buddhist on the Upper East Side ("Probably wasn't the only reason I was shoved into lockers as a kid, but it was up there") and had written a number of books, including *The Buddha Walks Into a Bar*.

They had this idea and, through family and friends, were able to raise capital to open three studios in New York. "We didn't do a seed round. We did a love round," Burrows says one afternoon. She is wrapped in scarves and lots of delicate gold jewelry in the lobby of the Mndfl studio on 8th Street. NO TECH, says a sign, BUT WE UNDERSTAND IF YOU *NEED* TO INSTA THE PLANT WALL.

"We've seen this affect our lives firsthand," she says. "We'd like to be in service to others, and that was ultimately very inspiring for the people who decided to invest: They did it from a place of service."

In the calm skylit back room at Mndfl, a 30-minute meditation class is being led by Kevin Townley, a blond-haired sometimes actor with horn-rim glasses and an unusually sweet face. "You're standing on a bridge," he incants, "and your thoughts are flowing by. You just let them go, you observe them." One man breathes loudly through his nose; otherwise, the room is silent, but for the occasional readjustment, sniffle, clearing of the throat. At the close of class, Townley opens the floor to questions.

"I haven't been able to come much lately," says a man in the front row. He is dressed in khaki pants and a gingham shirt—his physical being is resolutely mainstream. "I'm wondering about what to do with what I've learned when I can't make it here. Because some of the stuff I've realized, when I'm meditating, well … it's not all good." Townley nods empathically. He knows. There is no guarantee that all this looking will yield beauty or peace. There's the possibility of uncovering suffering, of uncovering pain. Pain, after all, is still life. As is dissatisfaction, and nights of terrible sleep, and joint troubles. As is growing old. We find cures, only to chase new ones.

"I'm not sure where to put my anger," he says. "And then I can't make it here, and it's just there. And I'm stuck."

The Road to Medicare for Everyone
Jacob S. Hacker

Yesterday, Democratic Senators Jeff Merkley of Oregon and Chris Murphy of Connecticut introduced the Choose Medicare Act, which would enable Americans not already eligible for Medicare or Medicaid to purchase Medicare as their insurer, and enable employers to purchase Medicare for their employees. Americans of all ages would thereby be able to purchase a plan that allows no discrimination based on pre-existing conditions. The bill would provide more generous tax credits and eligibility thresholds than those currently in the ACA, and it insures coverage for all reproductive services. It improves the existing Medicare system (and hence, for seniors already covered) by allowing Medicare to negotiate prices for prescription drugs and setting an out-of-pocket maximum for medical services. And—by establishing in essence a public option—it could drive down private insurance premiums by creating genuine competition.

The bill's senate co-sponsors include California's Kamala Harris, New Jersey's Cory Booker, Wisconsin's Tammy Baldwin, Hawaii's Brian Schatz, New Hampshire's Jean Shaheen, New Mexico's Martin Heinrich, Connecticut's Richard Blumenthal, New Mexico's Tom Udall, and New York's Kirsten Gillibrand.

Merkley and a number of the bill's co-sponsors are also co-sponsors of Vermont Senator Bernie Sanders's Medicare for All bill. By placing Medicare in competition with private insurance, the bill, if enacted, could help legitimize the idea and reality of a government health plan (although, of course, it is already legitimate, and wildly popular, as a plan for those over 65). In that sense, it might well become a steppingstone to Medicare for All.

In a number of ways, the bill introduced yesterday follows the plan outlined by Yale political science professor Jacob Hacker in the Winter 2018 issue of the Prospect—*and not just in adopting his name for the plan, Medicare Part E (for Everyone). Hacker's is a more comprehensive proposal, automatically enrolling all workers and their families either in Medicare Part E (partly funded by employers) or requiring their employers to provide comparable coverage. Nonetheless, the new bill improves upon the public option provision (for which Hacker was also the primary intellectual author) that almost made it into the ACA.*

To provide context and background for the basic ideas behind Merkley-Murphy bill, if not all its particulars, we are reposting Hacker's article, below.

—Harold Meyerson

For the first time since the passage of the Affordable Care Act in 2010, Democrats are debating the next big steps in federal health policy. What they're beginning to see is a path toward universal health care that looks very different from that embarked on seven years ago. This path depends on Medicare rather than the expansion of private insurance. And for those most eager to take this route, it depends on achieving something that has proven impossible in the past: replacing the patchwork quilt of American health insurance, including the employment-based health plans that cover more than 150 million people, with a single government insurance program.

In a way that wasn't true during the last fight—indeed, because of the last fight and its legacies—a growing share of those on the left are making the case that the United States is finally ready for Medicare for All. Is it? And if not, is there another way to achieve the goal it embodies—affordable health care as a basic right?

Lessons of the Past

These are questions I've struggled with for a long time. As a health policy expert, I'm one of the many social scientists and historians who've sought to understand why the American framework of health insurance looks so different from the systems found in other nations. Why do we spend roughly twice as much per person as any other nation while leaving tens of millions of people without insurance and many times more with inadequate protection—all with worse health outcomes?

The basic answer is simple: Americans are distrustful of government, and America's fragmented political institutions make transformative policies hard to enact, especially when they're opposed by powerful interest groups. Even at the height of the Great Depression, with overwhelming Democratic majorities in Congress, FDR decided not to include health insurance in the Social Security Act of 1935, because he feared the opposition of physicians would kill the whole bill.

FDR's decision turned out to be fateful. With America's entry into World War II, the nation's agenda shifted away from domestic affairs. Unions, corporations, and private insurers stepped into the breach—thanks in part to favorable tax laws and federal support for collective bargaining—and by the 1950s, the majority of working-age Americans got health benefits at work. By the time advocates of government insurance finally had another bite at the apple after LBJ's landslide election in 1964, they had strategically retreated to the goal of covering those left out of the employment-based system: the elderly and the poor. The result was Medicare and Medicaid—the biggest step toward universal health care until the passage of the Affordable Care Act.

The system was a mess, but it was also a minefield. You had a huge insurance industry, allied with a range of profitable sectors that benefited from its open checkbook, from drug manufacturers to medical device makers to highly paid specialists. You had excessive costs that government could finance only with hefty taxes. Most important, for every unfortunate American who fell through the cracks, you had eight or nine more who had benefits at work or through Medicare or Medicaid. To make matters worse, most of these eight or nine had no idea how much their health benefits really cost, because the expense was hidden in their pay packages or spread across all taxpayers.

It would be hard to design a less welcoming context for single-payer. Enacting a universal program meant taking on a lobbying juggernaut to impose taxes on people generally suspicious of government, most of whom were insulated from the true costs of their care. Our unique health-financing system was a reflection of our unique political hurdles. But increasingly it was the system itself that posed the biggest hurdle of all.

There's a lesson in this history: The struggle over health care has always been about politics as much as policy. The evidence that the American model is inferior is overwhelming, and many policies would make it better. The challenge is figuring out how to overcome the political barriers to pursuing those policies—not only to get them passed, but to ensure that they foster the political conditions for continuing improvement.

In the 2000s, I began to write about this challenge, too, drafting a proposal for expanded coverage that contributed to the development of what would be called the "public option." The idea was to let Americans who didn't have coverage at work or through existing public programs buy into a Medicare-like national health plan. Thanks to the work of advocacy organizations, such as Health Care for America Now!, the public option eventually made its way into the reform plans of all the leading Democratic candidates for president in 2008—including Barack Obama.

The public option was the main addition by left-of-center thinkers to reform blueprints based on the bipartisan law passed in Massachusetts in 2006. That law, which became the template for the Affordable Care Act, sought to expand private insurance to those who lacked it while trying not to disrupt employment-based plans. It did so by creating a new regulated market for individually purchased private plans (called "marketplaces"). These regulated plans weren't allowed to discriminate against the less-healthy, and there was new government assistance to help poorer people pay for them. In turn, citizens would be required to show proof of coverage (a.k.a. the individual mandate).

The idea of the public option was to give people who bought insurance through the new marketplaces the choice of a public plan that used Medicare's payment rates to hold down prices. The aim was to guarantee good backup insurance, especially in the many parts of the nation where there are not many competing insurers, while simultaneously putting pressure on insurance companies to bring down their own costs.

Needless to say, those companies were not fans, and they hammered the public option relentlessly. Critics on the right described it as a backdoor route to single-payer, despite the fact that it would be available only to those who were buying coverage through the exchanges. In the end, the public option died a death of a thousand cuts. A pared-back version that lacked the ability to use Medicare's rates did make it through the House. But it was eventually stripped from the final bill at the insistence of Senator Joe Lieberman of insurance-rich Connecticut (my home state). Since the bill needed the support of all 60 of the Senate's Democrats to overcome a GOP filibuster, the public option was dead. It was a painful reminder of just how difficult the politics of government insurance could be.

Republican Destruction, Democratic Resistance

Many progressives rallied to the public option back in 2009. Yet they are now setting their sights much higher. The threat posed by unified Republican control has galvanized Democratic voters and activists, especially the party's progressive wing. Many have spent the past year in the political trenches fighting to preserve the Affordable Care Act in the face of the GOP's relentless assault. Now, energized and mobilized, they have turned that passion toward their own party, pressing candidates and public officials to adopt much bolder positions. In progressive circles, "I support single-payer" is fast becoming a required declaration of a politician's seriousness about health care.

The most visible sign of the shift is the single-payer plan introduced by Senator Bernie Sanders in September. In 2013, a similar bill introduced by the Vermont senator attracted not a single co-sponsor. His most recent has 16—a third of the Senate Democratic caucus. Moreover, they include all of the party's most-mentioned presidential contenders, including Cory Booker of New Jersey, Kirsten Gillibrand of New York, Kamala Harris of California, and Elizabeth Warren of Massachusetts. Sanders lost the Democratic Party's nomination in 2016, but he is defining its health-care vision for 2020.

The increasing boldness of the Democratic left reflects more than political calculations. It also reflects serious shortcomings of the Massachusetts-inspired approach. The individual marketplaces, in particular, have failed to live up to expectations. Their enrollment of around 12 million is approximately half what the nonpartisan Congressional Budget Office projected when the law passed. Those who've enrolled have also been less healthy than expected, sharply driving up premiums (though, thanks to government assistance, few pay the full tab, and premiums are roughly in line with initial CBO projections despite these increases). And many of the ACA marketplaces have had trouble getting private insurers to offer plans at all.

One consequence of all this is that most of the coverage gains under the law have come not from private plans offered in the marketplaces, but from Medicaid, the government program for low-income Americans that was expanded under the law. Indeed, Medicaid enrollment has so exceeded expectations that the CBO's overall projections for increased coverage have largely panned out despite the disappointing individual marketplace numbers. In an outcome that Medicare's designers never foresaw, Medicaid (the program for low-income Americans) is now larger than Medicare (the program for the permanently disabled and those over the age of 65), with almost 75 million enrollees, including those covered by the Children's Health Insurance Program (CHIP).

Of course, the ACA's travails reflect in part the ceaseless Republican attacks. In addition to the 19 Republican-controlled states that continue to refuse to expand Medicaid, many conservative states worked actively to undermine establishment of and enrollment in the individual marketplaces. Congressional Republicans couldn't repeal the law outright so long as President Obama held the veto pen. (Not for want of trying: They voted more than 50 times to kill it.) But they sued the president to stop subsidy payments for private plans, failed to appropriate funds to boost marketplace enrollment, and generally tried to turn their warnings about the ACA's imminent collapse into a self-fulfilling critique. Republicans have also dragged their feet on re-authorizing CHIP, which once enjoyed broad bipartisan support.

Even with a willing ally in President Trump, Republicans' repeal ambitions have continued to fall short. But the president who had promised on the campaign trail to provide "insurance for everyone" has done almost everything within his power to undermine the ACA, and congressional Republicans have shown no sign they're letting up. Witness their willingness to add repeal of the individual mandate to their big Senate tax bill, which was being reconciled with the House version at the time this article went to press.

In short, many of the problems with the Affordable Care Act are a product of Republican sabotage. But there's another reason Democrats are gravitating away from the approach enacted in 2014. Those once skeptical of the public option now seem willing to embrace it, and many on the party's left want to go much further. Those more progressive Democrats generally saw mandated private insurance as a second-best route to expanded coverage and political accommodation—one that had a chance of winning some Republican support, if not at the outset, at least down the road. But if the expansion is lackluster and the political accommodation nonexistent, why cling to the second best?

To a degree that seemed impossible even a year ago, then, the discussion within the party has come to encompass a whole range of ideas for expanding Medicare, not just the public option. These range from voluntary buy-ins for workers and employers, to lowering the Medicare eligibility age from 65 to 55 or 50, or all the way to Medicare for All.

Indeed, to those pressing for single-payer, the public option is small bore. It would provide a backup in parts of the nation at risk of having no private plans, and bring some sanity to health-care prices for those it covered. But it would only be relevant to the limited slice of the population getting coverage through the exchanges. Something much bigger is needed, Medicare for All enthusiasts argue, to rally the sustained enthusiasm of grassroots activists and progressive leaders and truly achieve transformative change.

They might be surprised to know I agree. The case for single-payer is much stronger than it was during the strait-jacketed debate of 2009. The question is whether it's strong enough, and if not, what might be able to deliver on its promise.

Is It Time for Single-Payer?

What is the case for single-payer? The term itself dates back at least to the 1980s, when a small group of Massachusetts doctors founded Physicians for a National Health Program and began calling for a "single payer" to replace all private insurance and public programs. Unlike reformers in the 1940s and 1950s, they looked not to Social Security for inspiration, but to the universal health systems found abroad, especially that of Canada—which consolidated a system of universal government insurance (at the provincial level) in the 1970s.

Today, single-payer is generally a synonym for Medicare, not the Canadian system. But the emphasis on foreign experience remains. Introducing his plan, Senator Sanders declared it would "end the international disgrace of the United States, our great nation, being the only major country on earth not to guarantee health care to all of our people."

In fact, most major countries on earth don't have single-payer. They have multiple payers, but all the payers pay the same negotiated health-care prices and play by the same strict rules to ensure more or less equal treatment of all subscribers—rich and poor, well and sick, young and old. Even Medicare isn't really single-payer: A component of Medicare called "Medicare Advantage" allows beneficiaries to enroll in private plans that meet strict standards, and roughly a third of Medicare beneficiaries are in such plans.

The defining feature of the systems found in other rich democracies isn't the way payments are channeled. It's who's covered and how medical prices are set. First, these systems are universal. The government guarantees all citizens coverage and then figures out how to pay for it. Only in the United States is the responsibility to get and pay for coverage largely left up to individuals and their employers, leaving tens of millions to fall through the cracks. The ACA dramatically improved things, but roughly 30 million Americans still remain uninsured and the number appears to be rising again.

Second, these systems use government's bargaining power to restrain health-care costs. In recent years, as Paul Starr discusses elsewhere in this issue, a consensus has formed among health-care experts that the major reason why U.S. spending is so high is that we pay such high prices for medical goods and services and prescription drugs. When a nation's leaders commit themselves to providing insurance to everyone, they become much more aware of bill-padding and price-gouging. They also discover that government has a unique capacity to do something about it: It can require that providers charge uniform prices.

Medicare doesn't cover the entire population, but it's evolved in the same direction. At first, it paid whatever health-care providers demanded, and costs soared. Since the 1980s, however, it's increasingly improved its ways of paying for care, and costs have risen significantly more slowly than in the private sector.

My Yale colleague Zack Cooper, a health economist, has gained access to the claims records of some of the biggest commercial insurers. What he's found is that the prices they pay are much higher than Medicare's. They also vary enormously across providers. Moreover, the gap between Medicare and private insurance has been growing, as doctors and hospitals increasingly consolidate into large medical systems demanding premium prices. In recent years, Medicare's overall tab has risen with the retirement of the baby-boom generation. Yet its spending per enrollee, which is what really matters, has been essentially flat, rising less quickly than either economic growth or inflation.

The experience of Medicare turns on its head the thinking behind the Republican repeal drive. According to many conservative critics of the ACA, patients should be left to pay for most care directly, so they have an incentive to shop wisely. But patients want and need insurance, especially for the big-ticket items that account for most health spending. And they need the expertise of providers to know what to shop for, especially when they're sick or injured. So insurance is going to pay for a lot of care, and providers are going to make most of the decisions that determine how that money is spent. This means, in turn, that someone has to put limits on what providers charge. The only institution that has the proven ability to do that is the government.

In short, Medicare for All isn't just a good slogan—and certainly a much better slogan than single-payer. It's a policy grounded in evidence about what works both here and abroad. It's also insanely popular, seen across the partisan divide as a vital part of the American social contract. Even voters who hate Obamacare love Medicare.

Medicare is also simple—or at least a lot more simple than the Affordable Care Act or the complex tweaks to it now being debated. Everyone pays in during their working lives, and everyone is covered at age 65 (or if they're permanently disabled). And unlike private plans, Medicare doesn't limit which doctors and hospitals patients can see: Virtually all accept its payments. It limits what prices those providers can charge.

The message that's being sent by Medicare for All enthusiasts is that the days of technocracy and triangulation are over. Stop offering Rube Goldberg contraptions that Americans will barely understand and activists won't rally behind. Stop trying to fill the gaps in a flawed system and smuggle in cost-control through the back door. Just say everyone is covered by Medicare, period. After all, Republicans are certain to call anything that Democrats try to do a "government takeover." So why not embrace the epithet and offer voters a takeover they seem to like: Medicare?

It's a powerful message, and it counsels a bold path. Unfortunately, that path is far more daunting than many embarking on it seem to understand.

Political Reality Bites

Our nation's distinctive policy trajectory has left us with a fragmented and exorbitantly expensive system. At the same time, however, that system all but guarantees that every reasonably well-insured group—whether workers with employee health plans or beneficiaries of Medicare—will be distrustful of change and hyper-sensitive to new costs, even if those costs merely replace hidden charges they're now paying.

Remember: More than 150 million Americans are covered by employment-based health plans. These plans have become less common, more expensive, and more restrictive. Still, we're talking half the population, and people with workplace coverage are generally satisfied (though beneficiaries of Medicare are even happier). Replacing these plans with Medicare would be a huge lift. Even the extremely modest dislocations caused by the ACA precipitated a bipartisan scramble to ensure people could keep their current plans, however ill-designed or inadequate.

Financing this transition would also be a formidable challenge. We don't know exactly how much Medicare for All would cost, but independent analysts who looked at Sanders's 2016 campaign proposal estimated it would require new federal spending on the order of $2.5 trillion a year. Sanders's campaign said the total would be closer to $1.5 trillion a year. Yet whatever the exact number, we're talking about a historic tax increase: $1.4 trillion represents around 8 percent of our economy. By way of comparison, the 1942 tax hike to fund World War II amounted to 5 percent of GDP. The 1993 tax hike under President Bill Clinton that Republicans (falsely) claimed was the "largest in history" equaled just over half a percent of GDP.

Financing is always the hardest part of health reform. In recent years, Vermont and California have each flirted with statewide single-payer—only to founder when the scope of required taxes became clear. Vermont and California are not the federal government, with its much greater revenues and power. But the federal government isn't Vermont or California, either, with Democrats holding unchallenged control.

Now, it's important to note these taxes would replace private sources of financing. Alas, however, most well-insured Americans have no idea how much they're now paying. What they see is their portion of the premium and their out-of-pocket spending. What they're *actually* paying is much greater. It includes the lower wages they receive because they get health benefits instead of cash, as well as the higher taxes they pay on everything else because of the lower revenues that government receives because it doesn't tax their medical benefits as pay.

Our system is almost perfectly designed to hide the true costs of health care. Indeed, it would be hard for a system with such outrageous costs to survive if this were not so. Donald Trump lamented earlier this year: "Nobody knew health care could be so complicated." But complexity isn't randomness. Much of what makes health care so complicated reflects the preferences of those who benefit from a lack of transparency: drug companies, highly paid specialists, medical device manufacturers, commercial insurers, and so on. Yet the cure offered by Medicare for All—immediately bringing all these costs into the open—could very well kill the patient. Those with good coverage would suddenly face a steep tax bill for something they mistakenly believed they were getting on the cheap.

To be sure, Medicare for All would generate big savings, and not only because it pays doctors and hospitals less than private insurers do. Medicare's administrative costs are a tiny fraction of commercial plans'. Nor does it have to earn profits or pay high CEO salaries.

But extending Medicare to the whole population would involve new spending as well as new savings—not only to cover those currently uninsured, but also to raise payment levels for the 70 million-plus Americans covered by Medicaid, a notorious under-payer that makes Medicare look lavish. Moreover, single-payer advocates want to upgrade Medicare as well as expand it. Sanders's new bill offers extremely broad protections, including dental and vision benefits, with no out-of-pocket costs. That's much more than what's now offered by Medicare—or Canada, for that matter—and would likely raise spending a lot.

BUT DOESN'T MEDICARE FOR ALL at least make sense as an aspiration? Shouldn't advocates start with their strongest proposal, rather than compromise even before the debate begins? It's one thing to aim for revolutionary change—any campaign for social transformation should have a vision that extends beyond the immediate fight. It's quite another to put forth a concrete plan to achieve that change, only to find you've divided your supporters, galvanized your opponents, and frightened everyone else.

Here it's worth noting another perverse feature of our system: It enriches a whole set of deep-pocketed stakeholders willing to spend whatever it takes to block changes that threaten them. Any political liabilities of a plan will be found and ruthlessly exploited. That has been the story of every health-care debate our nation has had, including the failure of the Clinton health plan back in 1994. When President Clinton described his plan before a joint session of Congress, it commanded majority support among voters. But after a few months of GOP and industry attacks, its poll numbers were in the basement. By the time Democrats gave up on trying to pass it, a majority in favor of congressional action had turned into a majority afraid of it.

Medicare for All is much simpler than the Clinton plan was, and it builds on a popular program. But it still has vulnerabilities that opponents will ruthlessly exploit. In polls, support for single-payer declines substantially when these vulnerabilities—higher taxes, a greater government role—are mentioned even innocuously. The longtime reform advocate Richard Kirsch, who headed Health Care for America Now! during the struggle to pass the ACA, puts it this way: "The solution is the problem." When public attention shifts from problems to solutions, every bit of rhetorical ammunition will be used to demonize the solution. And overcoming this initial impression can be close to impossible. In politics, opponents don't have to offer an alternative. They can just destroy yours.

Even candidates could put themselves at risk. Fast-forward to the 2020 campaign. The Democratic nominee has electrified the convention by promising to enact a Medicare for All bill. The campaign releases a detailed blueprint. The GOP and a vast assemblage of deep-pocketed organizations respond by hammering Democrats for wanting to raise taxes steeply while taking away Americans' health care. It's hard to see how the candidate—or the cause of Medicare for All—wouldn't be hurt.

Republicans just learned what happens when you make a health-care promise that turns out to be unpopular beyond your base. Democrats should not make the same mistake.

Medicare Part E

But Democrats should not make the opposite mistake either. A proposal must have a realistic path to enactment. But it also has to be ambitious enough to inspire supporters, and compelling and understandable enough to convince others to become supporters. It has to be grounded in policies that are popular and known to work—policies that can actually reach universal coverage and restrain health-care prices.

Perhaps most important, it has to be able to command support not just before it passes, but also afterward. If the troubled saga of the exchanges tells us anything, it's that even the most technically sound policy will fall short if it does not generate and sustain pressure for continuing expansion and improvement. Successful policies do not just reflect the politically possible; they reshape it.

I've already said I don't think the public option is robust enough to create such pressure, even though it would do much good. As a rallying cry, "Make Medicare available to the 12 million people buying insurance through the ACA marketplaces!" leaves much to be desired. Instead, the message should be at once simpler and bolder: "Make Medicare available to *everyone.*" All Americans should be guaranteed good coverage under Medicare if they don't receive it from their employer or Medicaid.

To achieve this goal, a new part of Medicare would need to be created for those not already covered by the program. I've been calling this new component "Medicare Part E" (for "everyone")—a term that's been used before by Johns Hopkins's Gerard Anderson and others. Medicare Part E would cover the broad range of benefits covered by Medicare Parts A (hospital coverage), B (coverage of physicians' and other bills), and D (drug coverage).

The central feature of Medicare Part E is guaranteed insurance. All Americans would be presumed to be covered. They would not need to go through complicated eligibility processes or hunt down coverage that qualified for public support or even re-enroll on an annual basis. Once someone was in Part E, they would remain in Part E unless and until they were enrolled in a qualified alternative—whether an employment-based health plan with good benefits or a high-quality state Medicaid program.

Thus, the centerpiece of Medicare Part E is the same as that of single-payer: a guarantee that Medicare is there for everyone. Unlike single-payer, however, Medicare Part E seeks to improve employers' role rather than replace it. It does so by establishing new standards for employment-based plans and requiring that all employers contribute to Medicare if they do not provide insurance directly to their employees.

In this respect, Medicare Part E builds on the ACA's requirement that large employers provide coverage or pay a penalty. Under the 2010 law, companies with more than 50 full-time workers are already required to pay a penalty if they don't offer insurance and their workers get subsidized ACA marketplace coverage. The penalty, however, is modest compared with the cost of health benefits, and there's no guarantee workers whose employers pay it actually get marketplace coverage.

Democrats knew this was a problem back in 2010. In fact, they tried to fix it: The House version of the Affordable Care Act required that employers that didn't insure their workers not only pay a fee, but also provide the federal government with the information to enroll those workers in health coverage though the marketplaces. Like the public option, however, this provision was dropped in the Senate.

It should be resurrected. Under the proposal I'm describing, employers would either provide insurance that was at least as generous as Medicare Part E's or they would contribute to the cost of Medicare Part E, which would automatically enroll their workers. Because the contribution requirement is central to signing people up, it should cover the entire workforce—including independent contractors and other self-employed workers (who would pay the contribution directly, as they do Medicare and Social Security taxes). But the level of contribution should vary with wages. That's how the House bill worked: The contribution would have risen from nothing for the lowest-wage firms up to 8 percent of payroll for the highest-wage firms.

Health policy wonks call this "play or pay." Employers would either play by offering qualified coverage to their workers (and their workers' families) or pay the federal government to cover their workers (and their workers' families) through Medicare Part E. Under this system, everyone who worked or lived in a family with a worker—including the self-employed—would be automatically covered. Those without any tie to the workforce could be signed up when they received other public benefits or filed their taxes or sought care without insurance. But just as important as signing people up is making sure they remain signed up. Once people were enrolled in Medicare Part E, they would remain enrolled for as long as they didn't have verified alternative insurance.

What about those eligible for Medicaid? I was once highly skeptical of retaining Medicaid as a separate federal-state program. But Medicaid has evolved tremendously in the past half-century—from a marginal program of welfare medicine into the nation's largest insurer. And it has proved more politically resilient than many experts, including me, expected. Nonetheless, it remains highly variable in quality and breadth across the states, is facing severe political and fiscal pressures, and pays doctors and hospitals so little that many providers refuse to accept it. The biggest problem is the continuing unwillingness of many

Republican-controlled states to expand their programs. But there are also millions of Americans who are eligible for Medicaid, but who fall through its cracks, deterred by complex and burdensome eligibility rules and the stigma that still attaches to the program.

Medicare for All has a straightforward answer to these problems: fold Medicaid into Medicare. And, indeed, under my proposal Medicaid could be replaced with Medicare Part E, with wraparound benefits for those previously eligible for Medicaid to ensure they continue to receive as broad benefits as in the past. But total nationalization of Medicaid would be both costly and disruptive, and it may not be necessary to achieve the objective of ensuring that state programs are high-quality and that no one falls through their cracks.

Instead, the federal government could assume much of the responsibility of enrolling people into state Medicaid programs. When someone receives insurance through Medicare Part E—whether through the workplace or through other outreach and enrollment efforts—the federal government would check to see if they qualified for Medicaid and, if so, transfer their coverage to the states. States, in turn, would be required to tell Medicare Part E whenever someone's Medicaid coverage lapsed for whatever reason, so they could be covered by the federal government instead. Finally, the federal government could put up new funding to bring Medicaid's payment levels closer to Medicare's—as it did in the initial years of the Affordable Care Act.

These simple steps could all but eliminate the most serious problem with Medicaid today: that millions who are eligible never receive its protections. Indeed, they could complete Medicaid's historical transformation from a complex, stigmatizing program that many health-care providers shun into a system of easily accessible coverage with payment levels high enough to attract broad provider participation.

Equality *and* Efficiency

In short, opening up Medicare to everyone would deliver what's most inspiring about single-payer—health care as a basic right of citizenship. Yet it wouldn't require replacing employment-based health insurance in one fell swoop. That's because a large share of employers now providing health benefits would likely continue to do so.

After all, the penalty in the ACA is modest compared with the cost of benefits, but most larger employers still offer health insurance. Some might feel less compunction about paying the fee if it were a contribution rather than a penalty. Some might not want to upgrade their plans to match Medicare Part E. But previous estimates of play-or-pay plans suggest that at any contribution rate close to the House plan's, most employers providing coverage would continue providing coverage.

Medicare Part E would also begin to deliver on Medicare for All's second promise—lower prices. For one, more people would be covered by Medicare, which would mean more services financed at Medicare rates. For another, private plans would face competitive pressure to demand better prices so their customers wouldn't switch to Part E.

At the same time, Medicare should be allowed to bargain for lower prescription drug prices as do other rich nations. Americans pay far higher prices for drugs than do citizens abroad, despite the fact that much of the investment in new drug development begins in U.S. federal R&D spending. The Medicare Part D benefit enacted in 2003 by President George W. Bush and a Republican congressional majority explicitly barred Medicare from providing drug coverage directly (it vested this responsibility in regulated private plans)—precisely because drug manufacturers knew they would be required to bring down their prices if it did. Drug coverage should be part of the basic Medicare package, for young and old alike.

Private insurance plans that participate in Medicare Advantage should also be required to offer coverage to both old and young. Medicare patients like these options, and younger Americans will want them, too. No less important, private insurers are deeply invested in Medicare Advantage. Ensuring they would still have a role—especially when it is lessened in other parts of the market—would reduce their inevitable opposition.

So too, of course, would ensuring that large employers still have the option and incentive to provide private coverage. (Most large employers pay medical claims directly—a practice known as "self-insurance"—but they often contract with large insurers to manage the benefits). Indeed, this system might even be more attractive than the ACA to the largest insurers, which have not shown much interest in the ACA marketplaces.

Many policy experts are critical of Medicare Advantage, because private plans have tended to skim off the healthiest Medicare patients. But the program was improved by the ACA, which reduced the payments to health plans to better reflect the actual cost of providing benefits to enrollees. Moreover, the playing field between Medicare and private plans would be even more level if Medicare could provide drug coverage directly. Today, only Medicare Advantage plans are allowed to cover prescription medicine alongside other services, which is one big reason beneficiaries enroll in them. Sweeten traditional Medicare, and private plans will lose this unfair advantage.

According to recent studies, the most efficient Medicare Advantage plans are already delivering Medicare's core benefits for less than Medicare can. This is, in large part, because these plans operate in a market in which their main competitor is Medicare, with its relatively low rates. Thus, they can pay rates close to Medicare's, and still get providers to participate in their networks. (This, by the way, is one reason why privatizing Medicare would be a disaster; without the bargaining clout of the traditional program, private plans would be paying the exorbitant prices they pay in the rest of the market.)

Medicare Part E could even give private plans additional leverage over providers. This idea is counterintuitive—wouldn't a bigger public program just shift costs onto the private sector?—but it's borne out in the experience of Medicare Advantage. And if Medicare covered more Americans younger than 65, this dynamic could play out in the rest of the market, too. After all, even the most consolidated and costly provider systems accept Medicare rates for older patients. Once Medicare Part E entered the mix, these lower rates would be paid on behalf of many younger Americans, too. For providers, the alternative to private payments would increasingly be Medicare rates for younger as well as older patients. As a result, private plans would be able to lower what they paid for nonelderly patients and still attract providers.

Of course, even with these savings, Medicare Part E would require additional financing beyond the employer contributions. For starters, those enrolled in Medicare Part E should have to pay an additional premium beyond the payroll-based contributions made by employers (or by self-employed workers). As in Medicare Part B, these premiums should cover only a modest fraction of the total cost of Medicare Part E, and they should vary by income, with lower-income enrollees paying a minimal amount. (For workers, these premiums should be automatically deducted from pay.) The exact premium would depend on the precise benefits covered, as well as the employer contribution rate. But the full charge for higher-income enrollees would likely be in the range of $300 per month for family coverage. This estimate is based on a 2008 analysis conducted by the Lewin Group—an independent consulting firm with expertise in micro-simulation modeling of health-care plans.

To be sure, other sources of financing would also be needed. The improved benefits for current Medicare beneficiaries could be financed, in part, by increasing the Medicare tax paid by workers (which the ACA applied, for the first time, to capital as well as labor income). There is also a strong argument for bridging some of the remaining funding gap with relatively progressive tax sources, such as an income-tax surcharge on extremely high-income households. Still, because most Americans who receive employment-based insurance will continue to do so, the new costs are much more modest than those for single-payer. In its 2008 analysis, Lewin estimated that 99.6 percent of Americans would be covered and that the proposal would lower national health spending and require modest new federal spending. Over time, it was projected to produce enormous savings for employers, households, states, and the federal government.

Daring—and Doable

Medicare Part E is an ambitious proposal, and I'm under no illusion about how difficult it will be to enact. Obviously, any significant expansion of Medicare is a non-starter so long as Republicans control Washington, but Democrats are not unified, either. The Affordable Care Act was the product of a debate within the party that began well before President Obama's election. The next big steps toward universal insurance will require a similar conversation and convergence.

It will also require tough thinking about how to build support for these steps over time, something Democrats haven't exactly excelled at. So far, the ACA has failed to generate the kind of middle-class buy-in that has made Medicare so popular and resilient. To the contrary, many Americans—including those covered by Medicare—ended up seeing the law as a threat to their benefits, despite the many ways in which it improved Medicare and private plans. Indeed, over three election cycles from 2010 to 2014, Republicans peeled off the votes of older Americans by frightening them into believing that the ACA would cut their benefits—or worse (remember "death panels"?).

Thus, advocates will need to prominently improve Medicare for the elderly and disabled even as they open up the program to the rest of Americans. The two most important upgrades are long overdue: a cap on out-of-pocket costs, which Medicare inexplicably lacks, and a direct prescription drug benefit. No less important, these upgrades need to be coupled with ongoing strengthening of the ACA standards for employment-based health plans as well, so workers covered by their employers rather than Medicare don't feel they're getting a raw deal.

Even with these boxes checked, the battle will be intense. Providers, drug manufacturers, and insurers will vigorously fight any plan that threatens their profits and privileges. Every interest group will have a pet demand: Big commercial insurers will want new Medicare enrollees to get access to private health plans through Medicare Advantage; drug manufacturers will inevitably try to limit the scope of federal bargaining for better prices; providers will want a premium over Medicare rates. No country has gotten to universal health insurance without making concessions to industry stakeholders. (Asked how he overcame doctors' resistance, the architect of the British National Health Service replied that he "stuffed their mouths with gold.") But every step toward a bigger Medicare program increases government's capacity to resist such special pleading in the future.

How big a step will be possible if Democrats regain unified control of Washington? It's hard to know and will depend on whether they can come together around a common vision, as they did in the late 2000s. But one of the virtues of Medicare Part E is that its core components could be pursued sequentially if they couldn't be enacted all at once. Medicare could be upgraded, and Part E could be added to the exchanges. Employers could be given the option of buying into Medicare Part E to cover their workers; at the same time, the standards for private employment-based plans could be raised. Then, the penalty under the ACA could be transformed into a contribution requirement—first for larger employers, then for all employers. Each of these steps would be popular, do much good, and create momentum for further action.

Even Medicare for All purists understand a staged approach might be necessary. Buried in the back of Sanders's new bill, for example, are provisions that are supposed to go into effect during the law's first four years, before the complete replacement of private insurance. These include an expansion of Medicare's benefits, coverage under Medicare for everyone up to age 18, and measures to allow people older than 35 to buy into Medicare. These provisions reflect the idea that an expanded Medicare program may have to be achieved in steps. The problem, however, is that last great leap: the replacement of all employment-based coverage with Medicare overnight. The big steps implied by Medicare Part E will get us to guaranteed universal coverage. Unless we can jump across that last political divide, Sanders's big steps will not.

Other proposals on the table—such as lowering the Medicare eligibility age to 55 or 50—might also stall out. The question to ask is whether an expansion will increase or decrease the pressure for more. Those who designed Medicare thought it would be a stepping stone to universal insurance. But because it basically took the most sympathetic group out of the employment-based system, it never moved much beyond its original beneficiaries. (Indeed, those beneficiaries have resisted coverage expansions they see as hurting their coverage.) The same thing might happen if Medicare were expanded to 55- to 65-year-olds: a bigger Medicare program but not affordable health care as a right.

Fortunately, Democrats will be able to move forward even if they don't have the 60 Senate votes they momentarily had in 2009. That's because many of the changes I've discussed—improved Medicare benefits, stricter rules for employment-based plans, even the establishment of Medicare Part E—could be achieved through the so-called reconciliation process. As Republicans have learned, it's difficult (though hardly impossible) to use this process to roll back the ACA's regulations. But advocates of expanded coverage want to build on these rules, not gut them. Nothing is simple when it comes to budget procedures, but many of the big steps toward Medicare Part E should be possible through the budget process, meaning they need just 50 votes in the Senate.

THE BIG UNANSWERED QUESTION is whether those now demanding single-payer will fight for these changes, even if they fall short of Medicare for All. Every social movement in our nation's past has featured tensions between pragmatists and purists. These fissures can be painful, but they can also be productive. The Social Security Act passed only because powerful grassroots forces were pressing for more.

The passion of those who resist half-measures is essential. But passion should not blind us to political risks. The test of seriousness should not be whether politicians say, "I support single-payer," but whether they are willing to support policies that will truly achieve its goals: health care as a right, at a cost our nation can afford.

Top 2018 Challenges

Jeffrey Bendix, Rose Schneider Krivich, Keith L. Martin, Chris Mazzolini, and Todd Shryock

Many physicians are relieved to see 2017 come to an end.

From day one of his administration, President Donald J. Trump has pledged to repeal and replace the Affordable Care Act, an effort that gained and lost steam repeatedly. Efforts to chip away parts of the law continue both inside and outside of Congress. The Medicare Access and CHIP Reauthorization Act (MACRA), moved from acronym to reality as physicians began reporting data in hopes of avoiding reimbursement cuts, or receiving financial bonuses in 2019. And that's what happened just in Washington, D.C.

On the front lines of healthcare, physicians continued to find themselves stuck in the middle. They are torn between patients and paperwork for their time. They are caught in between payers and patient requests. And with their career, many want to remain dedicated to medicine while fighting against the forces that further divide their time and attention.

For the fifth consecutive year, *Medical Economics* reveals its list of obstacles physicians say they face next year and, more importantly, how to overcome them. As we've done before, we asked readers to tell us what challenges they face each day and where they needed solutions.

Here are their responses, starting with the biggest challenge of the coming year.

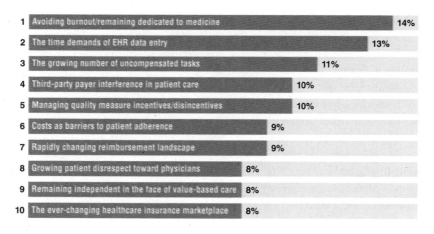

1	Avoiding burnout/remaining dedicated to medicine	14%
2	The time demands of EHR data entry	13%
3	The growing number of uncompensated tasks	11%
4	Third-party payer interference in patient care	10%
5	Managing quality measure incentives/disincentives	10%
6	Costs as barriers to patient adherence	9%
7	Rapidly changing reimbursement landscape	9%
8	Growing patient disrespect toward physicians	8%
9	Remaining independent in the face of value-based care	8%
10	The ever-changing healthcare insurance marketplace	8%

Figure 1. For our 5th annual issue exploring the top challenges facing doctors in the New Year, *Medical Economics* polled our physician readers on what issues keep them awake at night.

1. Avoiding Burnout/Remaining Dedicated to Medicine

For primary care physician Dan Diamond, MD, the signs of his looming burnout were evident.

"I was waking up as tired as when I went to bed and I was going to bed incredibly tired," he says. "I had intense physical and emotional exhaustion and doubted whether I was actually making a difference in medicine for such incredible sacrifices."

But something happened to Diamond after Hurricane Katrina in 2005. He served as director of the mass casualty triage unit at the New Orleans Convention Center. Surrounded by disease and death, he had a personal and professional epiphany.

"What got my attention were the people that in spite of losing everything, did not become victims," he says. "Instead they became unstoppable and I wanted to become unstoppable myself."

Today, Diamond deploys to sites of international disasters with Medical Teams International and consults with healthcare professionals on how to overcome burnout, build stronger teams and transform their organizations.

He is the first to acknowledge that the medical environment in the U.S. is "brutal" right now, between increasing regulations, physicians being tethered to their electronic health records and payers bringing productivity to a halt with prior authorizations and other requirements. Over time, those who went into medicine wanting to give back can get weighed down and this leads directly to burnout.

"I don't think we can change whole organizations and cultures, without starting on individual mindset," Diamond says.

He encourages physicians to remember their passion for medicine and not let the challenges of the day—from a busy waiting room to cranky patients to dealing with payer rules—slowly drag them down.

Instead, he wants physicians to become "empowered givers," focusing not on themselves, but rather their medical practice team and their patients first. By shifting attention to the team and its performance, the work becomes more manageable and care improves.

"As empowered givers, physicians can work to make the members of their team successful," he says. "And then rally the team to look at the teams around them in [their medical] sphere of influence and do what we can to make the other team successful. I don't see how we can go forward as a profession any other way."

Three Key Symptoms of Burnout

1. **Emotional exhaustion**

   Waking up just as tired as when a physician goes to bed.

2. **Detachment from patients and staff**

   People in the exam room become "the hip in room three," not patients physicians care about.

3. **A sense of being ineffective**

At the end of a long day, physicians doubt they made a difference.

2. The Time Demands of EHR Data Entry

Health information technology tools such as electronic health records (EHRs) have the potential to significantly improve care delivery and patient outcomes. However, physicians who have adopted EHRs continue to struggle to effectively use these systems because of the difficulty of dividing their time between the patient and the computer.

The average physician spends 30% to 50% of a patient encounter looking directly at the EHR, with the majority of that time spent typing in an office layout that does not allow the patient to remain engaged through screen sharing, according to 2013 research from the *Journal of General Practice*.

Thus the question has become: How can physicians find a balance between EHRs and satisfactory patient engagement? One solution is to use scribes, as Jerry Hizon, MD, told *Medical Economics* earlier this year.

"The key to a good EHR is the minimal touching of keys," says Hizon, the owner of Motion Sports MD, a primary care practice in Murrieta, California.

Hizon says the scribe's responsibilities are to update the patient's medical records since his or her last encounter and determine the purpose for the patient's visit.

After presenting the information to the physician, the scribe transcribes the physician-patient encounter through a combination of free typing and completion of premade templates. The scribe also documents all procedures performed in the office, new imaging and/or laboratory results and any notes from outside physicians.

Melissa Lucarelli, MD, a solo primary care physician in Randolph, Wisconsin and *Medical Economics* Editorial Advisory Board member says that before entering the exam room she:

- Studies the patient's data and history to make sure she has the basic knowledge she needs to avoid relying on the computer;

- Copies and pastes the patient's history in her EHR to get a head start on the note before seeing the patient; and

- Uses laptops on carts, which lets her position herself to look the patient in the eye regardless of the layout of the exam room.

"Ideally, your EHR would become invisible, but what I've set for myself as the sort of gold standard for the computer in the room, is to make it as unobtrusive as a paper chart," says Lucarelli.

3. The Growing Number of Uncompensated Tasks

Doctors are spending too much time during their day on uncompensated tasks. As much as 20% of the workday is spent grinding through tasks such as prior authorizations, EHR data entry and nonclinical paperwork. This busywork costs physicians at least $50,000 in lost revenue annually, says Joseph Valenti, MD, a board member of the Physicians Foundation, a nonprofit group that advocates for practicing physicians.

It's impossible to entirely eliminate uncompensated tasks from the daily schedule, but practices can minimize the disruptions they cause and redirect physician efforts toward revenue-generating work. Consider these solutions to common problems related to uncompensated care.

Problem: Non-clinical tasks

Solution: Physicians should avoid tasks that do not require a medical license. Physicians who find themselves performing non-clinical tasks, such as answering phones, should delegate these to non-clinical staff members. "What we've found is that physicians who are better at delegating unlicensed tasks to others are the ones who tend to have the highest net incomes," says Keith C. Borglum, CHBC, a healthcare consultant.

Problem: EHR documentation

Solution: Nitin Damle, MD, an internist at a small practice in Rhode Island, takes notes on a paper form during a patient encounter. Staff members enter the notes in the EHR afterwards. This adds to overhead costs as it requires additional staff, but Borglum argues that it can increase revenue by freeing up physicians to see more patients.

Problem: Family conferences

Solution: Physicians often spend uncompensated time addressing requests and questions from family members. Jeffrey Kagan, MD, an internal medicine physician and member of the *Medical Economics* Editorial Advisory Board, says it's important to do this, but taking phone calls and responding to emails may not be the most efficient method. At his Newington, Connecticut-based practice, he asks families to accompany the patient to appointments. When the patient is present, he can bill for the time he spends talking with family members.

4. Third-Party Payer Interference in Patient Care

David Belk, MD, who runs a solo internal medicine practice in the San Francisco Bay area, understands the frustration many doctors feel when insurance companies tell them how to practice medicine and require prior authorizations.

When a patient shows symptoms of diverticulitis, for example, he wants to order a CT scan, but it requires a prior authorization. "I don't get paid extra for the scan, so why does a nurse from an insurance company have to sign off on that? How is that about saving money?" he told *Medical Economics* earlier this year.

Physicians are increasingly baffled by payers' use of prior authorizations for what they say are often routine, low-cost treatments or for drugs that have already proven effective for years at treating a patient.

Interference from insurance companies costs practices time and money. Here are five ways to be more efficient when dealing with prior auths.

1. Document the Details

Brief practice staff members on the importance of thorough documenting of symptoms and prior treatment measures. Payers need to see everything that's been done for a patient and details of all the symptoms. The more they know, the less likely they are to challenge a doctor's decision—or waste time by asking for details they should already have.

2. Know Prior Auth Medications

Create a list of medications that commonly trigger prior authorizations, either in the EHR or on paper. Note which medications are on a payer's formulary and keep that list updated. If physicians check the list before prescribing, many prior auths can be avoided.

3. Loop in the Staff

Physicians are often focused solely on delivering the best care and not what payers are pushing back against. Encourage nurses and practice staff to keep all providers informed when prior authorization issues arise and to point out any tests or medications that continually create difficulties with payers.

4. Work with Payers

Many prior authorizations may be unavoidable, but practices can still save time by finding out how payers prefer prior authorization communication and what details they are looking for.

Track the types of care for which payments are being denied. Are there recurring administrative errors that can be corrected? When a prior auth goes well, have the staff note how the information was delivered and to whom and use that same approach for future requests. Is one staffer getting approval for a particular treatment that gets denied when others request it? Examine the differences between approvals and denials for the same treatment.

5. Share the Criteria

Once the payer criteria for prior authorizations is known, keep it handy so physicians in the practice know what kind of information to include in the request to better the chances of success. If possible, assign a staffer to particular payers so they are familiar with the requests and the rules for prior authorizations. These connections can lead to smoother approvals in the future.

5. Managing Quality Measure Incentives/Disincentives

The Centers for Medicare & Medicaid Services (CMS) recently released its final rule governing its Medicare Quality Payment Program in 2018.

While the final rule did not deviate significantly from the proposed rule released in June, there was a major change for those eligible for participation in the Merit-based Incentive Payment System (MIPS)— beginning in 2018 the cost category, based on claims data, becomes 10% of eligible physicians' final MIPS score.

This represents a major change from the proposed rule, which kept it at 0% next year. CMS will calculate cost through Medicare Spending per Beneficiary (MSPB) and total per capita cost measures for 2018—carryovers from the Value Modifier program.

The change will affect physicians—who already report struggling with managing quality measures and the incentives and disincentives that come with it—in a major way.

"Physicians are supplying data, but it stops there," Owen Dahl, MBA, FACHE, a practice consultant, tells *Medical Economics*. Getting little direction from CMS "is a universal frustration for all offices I talk with."

So, what can physicians do to make quality measure reporting easier?

Focus on What You Do Well

Because physicians and practices are allowed to pick the measures used to evaluate them, they should examine the menu and figure out where they might do well, says Cristina Boccuti, MA, MPP, associate director of the program on Medicare policy at the Kaiser Family Foundation.

Consider Areas of Improvement

Eric Schneider, MD, FACP, formerly a practicing internist and now a senior vice president for policy and research at The Commonwealth Fund, advises physicians to think about the selection of measures where there is room for improvement over time.

Think About Type of Clinical Care

By selecting measures that accurately reflect the types of clinical care they most commonly provide, physicians will have sample sizes large enough to be statistically significant, Schneider says.

Range of Quality Measures Does Matter

According to Harold Miller, president and chief executive officer of the Center for Healthcare Quality and Payment Reform, physicians should ensure that the range of quality measures they choose is broad. The proposed list of quality measures "doesn't even come close to being able to address the various types of patient conditions and the different needs of patients," he says. "You wind up with a lot of those measures being designed for patients with only one health problem and don't work well for those with multiple health problems."

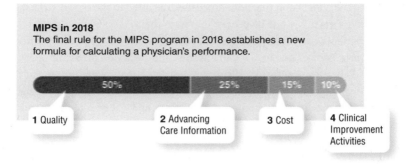

MIPS in 2018
The final rule for the MIPS program in 2018 establishes a new formula for calculating a physician's performance.

50%   25%   15%   10%

1 Quality   **2** Advancing Care Information   **3** Cost   **4** Clinical Improvement Activities

Figure 2. The final rule for the MIPS program in 2018 establishes a new formula for calculating a physician's performance.

6. Costs as Barriers to Patient Adherence

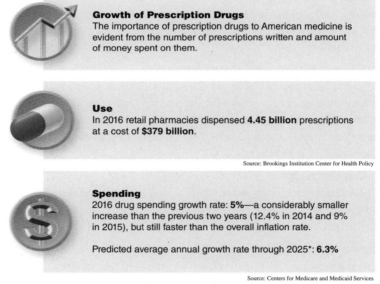

Growth of Prescription Drugs
The importance of prescription drugs to American medicine is evident from the number of prescriptions written and amount of money spent on them.

Use
In 2016 retail pharmacies dispensed **4.45 billion** prescriptions at a cost of **$379 billion**.

Source: Brookings Institution Center for Health Policy

Spending
2016 drug spending growth rate: **5%**—a considerably smaller increase than the previous two years (12.4% in 2014 and 9% in 2015), but still faster than the overall inflation rate.

Predicted average annual growth rate through 2025*: **6.3%**

Source: Centers for Medicare and Medicaid Services

Figure 3.

Getting patients to adhere to a medication regimen has been a long-standing challenge for doctors. But the ever-rising costs of prescription drugs, combined with the greater share of those costs falling on patients in the forms of deductibles and copays, are making the task even harder.

The reasons for the increases in prescription drug prices, whether brand-name or generic, are a matter of debate. But the impact on patients is not. Studies from a wide variety of governmental, professional and nonprofit organizations all point to the conclusion that adherence is closely tied to the cost of drugs, and what patients must pay out-of-pocket to obtain them.

"All patients care about the cost [of prescriptions], even patients who are wealthy," says Damon Raskin, MD, an internist and addiction medicine specialist in Pacific Palisades, California. "Especially older patients who are on multiple medications. It's a big chunk each month depending on what they're taking."

Doctors who have confronted the problem and experts recommend the following:

Address the Issue Head-On

"If adherence is detected to be a problem for a patient, one of the questions that's often asked now is, 'Are you having trouble affording your medications?'" says former practicing internist Eric Schneider, MD, FACP, now with The Commonwealth Fund.

Prescribe Generics Whenever Possible

While prices for generic drugs have also been rising, in most cases they're still substantially below their brand name equivalents. So except in cases where a generic is ineffective or contraindicated, they are powerful tools for overcoming financial barriers to adherence.

Help Patients Find Financial Assistance

Provide information about the financial assistance programs most major pharmaceutical companies now offer. Patients who meet the income criteria can get free or deeply discounted copays. Nonprofit and government organizations in many communities also provide help to patients who can't afford needed medications.

Turn to Technology

Make sure patients know about the numerous apps and websites, such as GoodRx and OneRx,that enable comparison shopping for copays and/or provide access to discounts for certain medications.

Partner with Pharmacists

As the professionals actually dispensing the medications doctors prescribe, pharmacists can help battle high drug costs. Some large, multispecialty practices employ their own pharmacists who work directly with patients to find the most cost-effective medications for treating their diseases or conditions. Joe Moose, Pharm D., co-owner of a North Carolina-based chain of independent pharmacies, notes that the typical patient in that state sees a pharmacist 10 times more often than a primary care provider in the course of a year. "That means we have 10 times more opportunities to reinforce the care plan. That's the real way you save on drug costs," Moose says. He suggests making pharmacists part of the care team by sharing patient treatment plans with them whenever possible.

7.The Rapidly Changing Reimbursement Landscape

After years of discussion, the shift from rewarding volume to value took formative steps this year, but there is uncertainty that it is moving at the pace set by federal officials.

In 2015, the U.S. Department of Health and Human Services (HHS), announced that it would tie 30% of all Medicare fee-for-service payments to quality or value through alternative payment models (APMs) by 2016 and 50% by 2018. These APMs include accountable care organizations and bundled payment arrangements among physicians.

Furthermore, HHS said it would tie 85% of all Medicare fee-for-service payments to quality or value by 2016 and 90% by 2018. A Centers for Medicare & Medicaid Services (CMS) spokesperson told *Medical Economics* via email it could tie 31.2% of fee-for-service payments to APMs in 2016 based on reconciled claims data. This result would be updated with quarterly data from 2016 as part of the next CMS budget in 2019, the spokesperson said, so it will still not have final data for some time.

Regarding the 85% projection, however, CMS says it would not comment on that goal at this time.

The spokesperson says that under a value-based system it is not CMS who should define value.

"CMS should equip patients with the information they need so they can choose the providers that they feel deliver high value," the email states. "Patients must have the tools and incentives to seek value and quality as they shop for services—the competitive pressure that results will drive the system towards efficiency."

The statement also says that "getting the move to value-based care right" requires giving clinicians flexibility on process and then holding them accountable for a small set of meaningful outcome measures. This ties to CMS' recent "meaningful measures" initiative, its pledge to physicians to streamline quality measures and reduce regulatory burden.

CMS says the new approach to quality measurement will assess only core challenges to providing high-quality care and improving patient outcomes. It will achieve this primarily through a re-focused CMS Innovation Center, which will lead efforts to promote greater flexibility and patient engagement.

Tips to Survive Value-Based Reimbursement

Randy Buchnowski, an executive with healthcare firm Halley Consulting Group, recommends practices heed the following advice to survive and thrive under value-based payments:

Realize you may already be there. Many practices are either already participating in CMS' initiatives that were precursors for MACRA (i.e. Meaningful Use and the Physician Quality Reporting System). In addition, simple changes like extending access hours to see patients can count toward quality metrics.

Get informed. CMS has included lots of education on value-based reimbursement on its website (qpp.cms.gov/), including access to live webinars to ask questions affecting specific practices.

Be agile and adaptable. The future health of a practice will be determined by its ability to adapt and change. Value-based care is a good start.

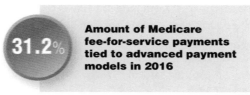

31.2%

Amount of Medicare fee-for-service payments tied to advanced payment models in 2016

Source: CMS

8. Growing Patient Disrespect toward Physicians

The doctor-patient relationship has changed in recent years. Whereas patients used to follow their doctor's advice without question, thanks to the internet and social media patients today often come to the examining room convinced they know what ails them and what should be done about it. Meanwhile, doctors are able to spend less time with patients and thus can't get to know them as well as they used to.

Gail Gazelle, MD, FACP, an executive coach for physicians and physician leaders and author of *"How to Build Your Resilient Self,"* discusses how these trends erode patient respect for physicians and the medical profession, and how doctors can respond.

Medical Economics: Do patients respect doctors as much as they used to?

Gail Gazelle: I think a lot has changed. We can all get vast amounts of information about anything. So that divide between physicians and patients has really shifted. There's an attitude of, 'How do you know you're right, doctor?' People can doubt the wisdom of the medical field.

In addition, society has changed. With all our electronic devices, we don't relate to one another with the same compassion that we might have in the past. And with the corporatization of medicine, doctors have much less time with patients than they used to and many more distractions.

ME: How does all this play out in the context of the one-on-one encounter between the patient and the doctor?

GG: What doctors talk about is the erosion of respect. Part of that's on the patient's side, but I think a great deal of it is doctors don't feel respected by their employer. The doctor in private practice had a lot of autonomy. Now the doctor has become just another employee, and they're not used to that. So the doctor enters the exam room feeling kind of resentful of all the pressures and not valued.

ME: Anger can sometimes be the product of discovering how much of a bill you owe. That's different than no longer taking the doctor's word as gospel, or respect. Is there anything doctors can do about those?

GG: I think what's critical for both the doctor and the patient is basic human respect and compassion. So it behooves the doctor who encounters a hostile patient to realize it's nothing personal. They need to check that personal reaction and ask, 'What's actually going on with this individual that they're reacting to me in this way?' Because when we do that, we come to a more compassionate place and have more clarity about what's going on, what we have to accomplish in the medical encounter.

ME: Which can be hard to do sometimes, when it's late in the day, and the doctor has had to deal with lots of other hassles?

GG: Of course it's hard to do, but at the end of that long day the doctor will feel a lot better about herself or himself if they have responded this way than if they've gotten irritable. What's going to make you hold your head a little higher at the end of the day? Aligning actions with our personal values, which for most doctors is caring for patients.

I'm a believer in the power of awareness and shared humanity of any endeavor. And the more we align with that I think we actually build pathways to mutual respect. We all want to be acknowledged and valued and have our basic human dignity appreciated. The more we can treat one another from that perspective I think a lot of these problems will resolve themselves.

9. Remaining Independent in a Time of Value-Based Care Initiatives

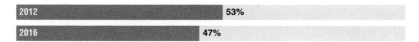

Figure 4. Physicians with ownership stake in practice

The ranks of independent primary care practices continue to dwindle. A report from the American Medical Association shows that the percentage of physicians with an ownership stake in their practice declined from 53% in 2012 to 47% in 2016. The rising cost of compliance with government reporting and changing reimbursement models has forced many doctors to either join larger physician groups or sell their practice to a hospital.

Here are three strategies experts recommend to help physicians remain independent.

1. Change the Practice Model

If insurance reimbursements are declining and compliance costs are up, do away with both problems by contracting directly with patients via a direct primary care (DPC) model. Patients pay a flat monthly fee to the doctor in exchange for expedited access. By eliminating much of the documentation, billing and coding, doctors are able to spend more time with patients.

2. Join an ACO or Become a PCMH

ACOs and patient-centered medical homes (PCMHs) are models that take a team approach to coordinating care across providers. The benefit to the physician is that patients receive better care, while many of the costs of compliance are shared across the group. Both ACOs and PCMHs may be eligible for additional payment bonuses from government and private payers, depending on their structure.

For Lerla Joseph, MD, a primary care physician in Richmond, Virginia, participating in an accountable care organization (ACO) was a way to stay independent and handle increasing government regulations. "As a small practice, we've been challenged by many things in terms of electronic health records (EHRs), regulations and managing quality metrics," Joseph told *Medical Economics* earlier this year. Although doctors in her area were increasingly deciding to become employees of hospitals or large groups, she had no interest in leaving private practice, because she felt she could better serve her community by remaining independent.

3. Add Ancillary Services

If reimbursement from standard medical care isn't providing enough revenue to survive, consider adding ancillary services to boost the bottom line.

In-house labs, echocardiography, X-rays, mammography, aesthetics and dietary assistance are all potential moneymakers, but experts warn to study the numbers carefully before making a commitment. Insurance reimbursement may not cover the full cost to provide a service, and patient demand may not be as high as projected.

But if the patient population is right and the service is carefully studied before buying anything, ancillary services can add much-needed revenue that allows a practice to remain independent.

10. The Ever-Changing Healthcare Insurance Marketplace

The year 2017 was one of great uncertainty in healthcare policy, and next year appears murky as well. President Donald Trump and Republicans in Congress made multiple efforts to "repeal and replace" the Affordable Care Act (ACA), failing each time. Meanwhile, Republican leaders have discussed Medicare and Medicaid reform, including per capita limits and block grants to the states, which if enacted could have significant ramifications for physicians and patients.

Medical Economics spoke with Robert Berenson, MD, an internist and fellow at the Urban Institute, about the coming healthcare policy challenges for physicians. Here is his advice for physicians.

Physicians Should Not Dwell Too Much on ACA Exchange Turbulence.

Physicians who see patients with insurance bought on the exchanges must be vigilant in monitoring changes to the ACA. Yet Berenson cautions physicians not to get overwhelmed by that and to focus on other areas, such as Medicare and Medicaid.

Only 4% to 5% of patients insured in America have coverage through the exchanges, Berenson says. "The Republicans have a major stake in exaggerating the problems of Obamacare," he says. "They imply that it's affecting all healthcare when it's not. Now, if you are a doctor caring for marketplace patients it is going to affect you. I'm not minimizing it, but I just think the politics of it overwhelm the reality of it."

Required to Participate in MACRA? If Not, Don't Worry Too Much About It.

As many as 134,000 physicians and 926,000 providers will be exempt from the Merit-based Incentive Payment System (MIPS), according to the final MACRA rule released in November. Since the exemptions exclude most small practices, this will leave almost exclusively large groups in the program, who will have to decide whether they want to attempt to earn a financial bonus through MIPS or shift to the Alternative Payment Model (APM) track, Berenson says.

"MIPS may not be applying to anyone anymore," he says. "I've argued for three years that it was bad legislation. CMS is working very hard, correctly, to nullify the impact of MIPS."

Physicians should find out now whether they are eligible for MIPS exemption. Physicians or groups with $90,000 or less in Medicare Part B charges or 200 or fewer Part B patients will not be required to participate in quality metric reporting.

Medicare and Medicaid Reform Attempts Are Coming.

The 2018 budget resolution passed by Congress to pave the road for Republican tax cut efforts included roughly $1.5 trillion worth of cuts to Medicare and Medicaid. Berenson says physicians tracking healthcare policy should watch for efforts to introduce premium support concepts into Medicare and block-granting and per-capita caps in Medicaid.

These programs are vital to patients, Berenson says. While he believes Republicans would be politically foolish to attempt these reforms, all indications are that House Speaker Paul Ryan and Republican congressional leadership plan to explore this, and that President Trump won't stop them despite his assurances to protect the entitlement programs.

"I think that's alive and will be part of this going forward," Berenson says. "How do you cut $1 trillion from Medicaid without moving to fundamental restructuring? That's the same issue with cutting $500 billion from Medicare."

Market Consolidation Isn't Going Away—and Many Physicians Want It.

The past year featured two failed mergers by four major payers in an attempt to gain market dominance. News in November that CVS wants to purchase Aetna shows that the payer market is still ripe for a shakeup.

Meanwhile, providers continue to integrate into larger groups, even while data suggest that smaller independent practices provide better care and value, Berenson says. "We are going to have more and more vertical integration, less because they are going to be more efficient and lower costs and more because physicians want to be employed," Berenson says. "They want shift work."

This trend is discouraging for national healthcare outcomes because there's growing evidence that small practices provide better care, Berenson says. "Docs in small practices know their patients and they don't have all these barriers to communicating with them. And so they have better performance, yet that's who we're putting out of business."

Chicago: The Vertical Farm
Jennifer Cockrall-King

The line of the buildings stood clear-cut and black against the sky; here and there out of the mass rose the great chimneys, with the river of smoke streaming away to the end of the world.

—Upton Sinclair, *The Jungle (1906)*

Dickson Despommier's *The Vertical Farm: Feeding the World in the 21st Century* arrived in late 2010 to as much promotion and anticipation as a book gets these days.[1] Well before the book's publication, Despommier appeared as a guest on the *Colbert Report*, the culturally influential satirical news program on U.S. specialty channel Comedy Central. Musician and activist Sting blurbed the book's cover. Majora Carter, a MacArthur "genius" fellow, contributed the foreword. And the *Economist* appointed Despommier "the father of vertical farming" in its magazine pages. Articles about vertical farming were seemingly everywhere at once. According to the media, the year 2010 was the year of the vertical farm—essentially a skyscraper layered with pigs, fish, arugula, tomatoes, and lettuce. There was just one problem. No one had yet built one.

Sure, there were a number of architectural renderings on paper just waiting for a visionary developer or a wealthy billionaire looking for a legacy project. Despommier's book features images of the 30-story verdant spiraling staircase that American architect Blake Kurasek envisioned as his 2008 graduate thesis project at the University of Illinois at Urbana-Champaign.[2] It also includes the drawing for the Dragonfly vertical farm concept, an elaborate 132-floor wing-shaped "metabolic farm for urban agriculture" designed for the New York City skyline by Belgian architect Vincent Callebaut.[3] These visions were (and still are) undeniably intellectually interesting and aesthetically impressive, as are those of Despommier and fellow professor Eric Ellingsen's own glass pyramidal farm.[4] Ellingsen's work was designed with Abu Dhabi in mind, as it is likely the only city with the money to build such structures for food production. These vertical farms, however, would likely come with a $100 million price tag or more—perhaps just one of the reasons they remain more science fiction than food-growing reality.

A few years ago, not many outside academia had heard the term "vertical farm," but the concept has been around since the Hanging Gardens of Babylon, with its mythical living walls of cascading greenery. With traditional farming being so land-, water-, labor-, and fuel-intensive, it was a logical leap to transform the two-dimensional nature of farming by shrinking its footprint radically and adding a third dimension: height. A farm built as a high-rise, with different crops or livestock layered on every floor, could conceivably allow large-scale food production right into the middle of any space-starved urban setting.

The vertical farming school of thought has led to some provocative designs. MVRDV, a Dutch design firm, proposed Pig City in 2001, an open-air 40-story farm that would house 15 million pigs and produce enough organic pork for half a million people and endless amounts of manure for biogas.[5] It earned the vertical farm an early nickname of "sky-scraper." Other open-air vertical-farming concepts emerged soon after on architects' drawing boards in Toronto, Vancouver, Paris, and Chicago, but none were actually built.

The most recent wave of vertical-farming ideas is especially focused on "closed-loop systems." (Think a traditional mixed farm, sliced into layers, stacked vertically, and hermetically sealed under glass.) Livestock waste is intensively recycled as plant fertilizer; freshwater fish grow in tanks and produce nutrient-rich water for salad crops; water loss due to evaporation is minimized; and the whims of Mother Nature no longer interrupt the 24/7, 365-day-a-year indoor growing system. Hungry deer, grasshoppers, and other pests wouldn't devastate crops. Climate wouldn't matter—nor would climate change, droughts, or mid-crop hailstorms.

For some, this will be the only way to feed our growing cities in scenarios of nine billion people living in the megacities of the very near future. For others, it's putting the cart before the horse. Vertical-farm designers and architects talk about aeroponics (soilless growing where roots are merely misted with nutrient-dense water), hydroponics (growing plants in nutrient-rich water but without the need for soil), and aquaponics (indoor fish farming tied in with hydroponic techniques to form a self-cleansing and self-fertilizing water-recycling loop) as if we've perfected these techniques. We've been experimenting with them on rather small scales, but large-scale farming is another matter. The technology isn't there yet. Then again, Leonardo da Vinci drew models for helicopters in the fifteenth century.

What will push the technology forward? Maybe a combination of factors that are currently upon us: Climate change, rapid urbanization, the rise in fuel costs of conventional farming and transportation, and population growth may finally stretch our current food resources to the limits.

Time will tell if these models, or versions of them, will become viable as the technology catches up to the visions of the future of urban farming. For that to happen, however, a lot of ground will have to be covered. Specifically, there will have to be a significant leap in construction and indoor growing technology, especially for the fanciful vertical-farm skyscrapers in Despommier's book to leap from page into being.

Just when I thought the vertical farm was decades away from becoming a reality and that we'd continue to imagine elaborate futuristic scenarios that seemed to completely ignore that agriculture is a marginal business, I learned of Chicago industrial developer John Edel and the new urban reuse project he's calling The Plant. It lacked the ego-driven designs of the other vertical farms that were languishing on paper, and its modesty and practicality made the idea of an indoor multistory farm seem feasible. It was enough to make me want to take a look for myself. After all, if Edel could accomplish even a modest version of a vertical farm, it would be urban-agriculture history in the making. I made plans to visit Chicago to see The Plant in its early stages of becoming the world's first, albeit four-story, vertical farm.[6]

The Plant, Chicago

As Blake Davis took off his dust mask and slapped puffs of concrete off his hands, he joked, "Clearly, as you can see, I'm a college professor."[7] Davis, a burly Chicagoan with a crew cut and a constant grin, teaches urban agriculture at the Illinois Institute of Technology. The day I met him, however, he was putting some skills to use from his preprofessorial days. His worn Carhartt work jacket and overalls were covered in fine concrete dust from jackhammering concrete floors rotten with moisture. By afternoon, he'd be wielding a plasma torch—like a welding torch, but it cuts through stainless steel, slicing panels of it out of meat smokers for food-safe countertops and other novel reuses. Chicago had "literally, millions of square feet" of vacant, often abandoned, industrial space "right in the city," Davis said. "It costs too much to tear down."

Davis was just one of several members of Edel's team of highly skilled, sustainability-minded volunteers determined to strip the former 1925-built, 93,500-square-foot (8,700-square-meter) meatpacking plant back to its outer red-brick shell and put as much of the recycled materials back into use to create a working model for a vertical farm.

While other entrepreneurs might be tight-lipped about their prototype projects—vertical farms are the current holy grail of urban agriculture, and there will likely be significant amounts of money for those who can deliver workable models—Edel instead cleared a few hours to show me around his "fixer-upper." He let me roam at will to chat with people like Davis, Alex Poltorak (another volunteer with engineering credentials), and Audrey Thibault (an industrial designer who, as her jobs kept leaving for China, figured that she "just wanted to be part of something awesome" like The Plant).[8]

It's an experiment in motion with two rather ambitious purposes. If Edel and his team can figure out the right models and mix of elements that actually work synergistically,[*] they will have built a viable physical and economic model for a vertical farm. Edel also intends that The Plant will serve as an open-source laboratory and catalyst for industrial reuse in a city that has no shortage of ready-built shells just waiting for a reason to remain standing.

Chicago's Stockyards

In 1878, Gustavus Swift built the first refrigerated railcar, which quickly allowed the meatpacking industry to concentrate in Chicago, scale up to incredible

---

[*]synergistically: In a cooperative, mutually beneficial way.

efficiencies, and go on to dominate the national market. By the turn of the 1900s, the Union Stockyards covered 435 acres (176 hectares) and became known as "the hog butcher to the world." If that was a slight exaggeration, it was at least the butcher that fed America. Eighty-two percent of the meat consumed in the United States at the time came from the Union Stockyards. It achieved huge efficiencies of scale that had never been attempted in livestock agriculture before. Historic photos show aerial views of the 40 acres (16 hectares) of cattle and hog pens; what would now be referred to as a Concentrated Animal Feedlot Operation (CAFO).

The industrialized meat trade came with significant hidden costs then as it does now. The poverty, squalor, and brutal working (and living) conditions experienced by workers in the meatpacking industry were immortalized in Upton Sinclair's 1906 novel *The Jungle*. Waves of cheap, nonunionized immigrant and "underclass" labor allowed for the innovation of assembly-line slaughtering, butchering, and processing of the carcasses.[9]

The Back of the Yards neighborhood came to life as a bedroom community, if you will, for the waves of immigrants who cut and packed meat, and for the various businesses—tanneries, soap manufacturers, and instrument-string makers, for example—that surrounded the meatpacking industry on the south and west boundary of the Union Stockyards. By the 1950s, however, meatpacking was headed west, closer to the herds and where land was cheaper. The stockyards officially closed in 1971, and the only relic from that era is a giant limestone entrance arch. Back of the Yards transitioned somewhat into an industrial park. But over the years, the massive infrastructure had a dwindling reason to exist. And when industry leaves, as it did in this part of Chicago, infrastructure is left to crumble and decay. The scale of the surplus in Chicago has generally led to blight.

Much of what I saw as I left Chicago's vibrant skyscrapers and downtown core known as the Loop and made my way to the city's historic stockyards and Back of the Yards' district was heading in the direction of decay and blight. There were too many gaps in the residential streets where houses should otherwise be standing together. There were too many rusted padlocks on gates and chain-link fences encircling trucking depots, warehouses, and factories of indeterminate purposes. The businesses that remained were the signposts of a neighborhood in decline: fast-food joints, liquor stores, and convenience stores with bars on the windows.

The red-brick Peer Foods building, built in 1925 and added to over the years, was a holdout; the family-owned specialty smoked-and-cured-meat company had stayed in business in the Back of the Yards until 2007.

At the time, Edel was in negotiations with the city to buy a six-hundred-thousand-square-foot World War I armory turned vacant Chicago Board of Education building. Faced with a $12 million demolition price tag, the city seemed prepared to sell it for $1.[10]

Edel already had a bit of local reputation for industrial building rehab. He had left a lucrative broadcast television design job that involved too much computer-assisted drawing and modeling to instead scratch an itch for preserving historic buildings by finding low-cost creative uses for them and reusing the materials that were simply lying around inside most of them.

In 2002, he bought a 1910 paint factory that had been officially unoccupied since the 1960s and had since become a derelict, bike-gang-ridden building with shot-out windows. (The building, in Edel's words, had been colonized by "lots of tough guys" with names like Googs, Mack, Santa Claus, the Boob, and Cowboy. There were "lots of guns, lots of knives," involved in the "informal economy" that had taken over the building.) Edel completely reformed the 24,000-square-foot (2,230-square-meter) building, putting his industrial design training, a tremendous amount of personal and volunteer sweat equity, and innate scavenger mentality into play. Useful industrial machines, like a giant, old air compressor that was left behind, were put back into service to run the air chisels used to poke holes in brick walls and the jackhammer used to remove unwanted concrete. Scrap sheet metal was refashioned to create such items as a new entrance awning, and former machine-tool parts and pipes found lying around became an art-school-esque stairway banister. Edel planted a living green roof with thousands of heat-and drought-tolerant sedum (a succulent plant that needs little irrigation) to mitigate storm water runoff and installed cisterns to catch rainwater for reuse in the building. (Seen from above, or on Google Earth, the thousands of sedum create a red-and-green pattern of Edel's daughter's smiling face.)

Edel did it all on a shoestring budget, and 95 percent of the existing derelict structure was repurposed. The building is now home to Bubbly Dynamics, though its official name is the Chicago Sustainable Manufacturing Center.[11] Bubbly Dynamics now runs at 100 percent occupancy and is a magnet for the niche boutique manufacturing and sustainable technologies entrepreneurs in Chicago. It is home to 35 permanent salaried jobs, which include a co-op of five custom-bicycle-frame builders, a fabric-print-screening outfit, and a tutoring program for at-risk children. It's full and extremely efficient, and it turns a profit for Edel, the landlord. It was all the proof he needed to confirm his gut feeling that no building is so derelict that it can't be saved and made profitable.

After the success of Bubbly Dynamics, Edel's next idea was to turn another hopeless case of a building into a zero-waste organic food-producing building in Chicago. He thought he'd found it with the Board of Education building. Edel wanted to create a net-zero building that combined some select food-manufacturing processes with the growing of food.

"Everybody in city government, except one alderman, was in support of it. Instead, he wanted to tear down the 'orange-rated' historical building we were trying to acquire and have a Walmart. That was *his* dream," Edel recounted.[12]

(Orange-rated is a Chicago urban-planning term that means that the building was one step below landmark protection status.)

One alderman's Walmart dream was enough to stall the process for two years, but during that time, Edel continued to plan an ambitious new life for the 600,000-square-foot (55,741-square-meter) space, using his team and networks of like-minded, hands-on experts who had gravitated to Edel and Bubbly Dynamics. That's when and how Davis fell into Edel's orbit. Davis was looking for urban-agriculture projects for his students, and Edel's business models included lots of volunteer hours and "open-source expertise." While Edel worked on acquiring space, Davis and his students began working on a symbiotic aquaponics/hydroponics system integrating fish production with a plant-growing system in the basement of Bubbly Dynamics.

Though the one-dollar price tag of the Board of Education building was attractive, the negotiations with the city were dragging on. Edel decided that ultimately it wasn't worth the wait, given all the existing inventory of available buildings in Chicago. He found a former meat slaughtering, smoking, and processing plant that was in relatively good shape. It had been built in 1925 but over the years had been upgraded and expanded. And it had sat empty for only four years, so there hadn't been time for too much to deteriorate. Most importantly, it was built for food production, which would save Edel an enormous amount of time and money because it was already up to code for many food-related commercial purposes.

Edel closed on the old Peer Foods Building on July 1, 2010, for $5.50 per square foot. What sounds like a real estate bargain, however, amounted to a $525,000 purchase that would test even Edel's resourcefulness. But Edel seems just as capable of attracting paying tenants as he is overqualified volunteers. There's already a list of entrepreneurs who have signed up for space at The Plant, which will move businesses in as its space is completed.

Touring the Plant

I wasn't prepared for how shockingly cold (and dark) it would be inside The Plant on the early January day I had arranged to visit.[13] It certainly wasn't the natural-light-flooded ethereal skyscraper that the academic vertical-farming camp was known for; it wasn't even the conventional greenhouse structure one associates with a covered growing space. There were high ceilings, which on that particular day actually seemed to trap the chill, making it a few degrees cooler on the inside than it was outdoors.

I had somewhat naively assumed that Edel would have to "work around" the lack of natural light, that it was a problem to be solved. Instead, Edel explained that the thick brick walls and lack of windows was a major benefit of The Plant. What currently functioned as windows—antique glass block—would, however, have to be replaced. ("Glass block neither lets light in, nor does it keep heat in or out," said Edel. As windows, they were useless.) One of the few outside purchases that the building would get was some new windows with high-efficiency glass.

However, high-efficiency glass is very limiting as well, explained Edel, holding up a sample of a high-efficiency window product he had been considering. "See how dark the glass is?" It was a smoky-gray color. High-efficiency glass, by its very nature, blocks those parts of the light spectrum that plants need for growing. And clear glass, which lets more of the light spectrum pass through, allows too much heat transfer. Edel then explained the problem of light units in northern latitudes during the Chicago winter. "In the upper Midwest on a day like today," he snorted, "you'll get no usable light. In an ideal [summer] day, you might get light penetration of about 15 feet.

"That means you'll be growing under artificial lights anyway. And the last thing you want is huge amounts of glass for that heat energy to escape through." Any gains made by electrical savings on using natural light would be negated or completely irrelevant compared to the heating costs escaping out through glass. Besides, a well-insulated brick building such as The Plant will be very effective at trapping heat inside in the winter (the heat from the lights can go a long way toward heating a building if it's well enough insulated, Edel believes) and keeping it cooler in the summer. Heat, as I would learn that day, is as valuable an asset in an ultra-efficient vertical farm in a cold climate as anything else.

But the great advantage, Edel explained, to the cavernous nature of the building is that "you can control the time of day." This gives Edel the ability to "grow at night" when electricity costs are a fraction of what they are during the day when the demand is high. And plants need a period of darkness just like they need a period of light, so you can create night during the day, when energy costs are high. Edel figures he can cut the energy expenses in half by growing during nonpeak hours.

The other advantage, continued Edel, is that "you can create different time zones in various parts of the indoor system. You can flatten your nominal load so that you don't have demand spikes." Electrical utility companies like to charge you at the rate when you are at your peak daily energy consumption rate. By "moving the time of day around" between a few growing zones, again, you can achieve a "flatter," more consistent pattern of consumption and therefore save on utilities. Flattening the demand for electrical consumption will play a huge role in regulating the metabolism of the building as the building starts to produce its own electrical power and heating when the anaerobic digester is built and takes over the energy needs of the tenants and the food-growing spaces.

The one concession Edel has made to a tiny bit of inefficiency will be the "growing lobby." Large windows along the front of the building will let in lots of natural light. "We'll have things like hops and lavender, and probably the finishing tanks for the tilapia where the water is really clean and the fish look pretty."

Heat and light were not the only valuable commodities in the building's equation; oxygen and carbon dioxide also needed to be considered. Nathan Wyse, a fresh-faced twenty-something, came by The Plant that day to talk to Edel. Wyse was a potential tenant who was looking to take his Thrive label of kombucha—a fermented medicinal tea hitting the lucrative mainstream specialty-beverage market these days—to the next business level.

The yeasts used to ferment the sugars in kombucha require oxygen and produce excess carbon dioxide in the fermentation process. Growing plants, handily, love carbon dioxide. According to Edel, plants "do quite well on six times the normal atmospheric carbon dioxide." Wyse asked if Edel could think about how these two gases could be exchanged efficiently between the brewing space and the growing spaces at The Plant.[14] If they could be exchanged, Wyse's aeration of his batches of kombucha would be greatly enhanced. Edel suggested that they could likely pipe excess carbon dioxide into growing areas, while drawing oxygen out (one being a heavier gas than the other) to recirculate it between the kombucha fermentation beds and the growing beds.

"So you've already thought about this?" Wyse asked.

"I just did," said Edel, matter-of-factly.

"OK, well, I'd gladly exchange carbon dioxide for oxygen for better fermentation."

I felt like I'd stepped into the future, where resources like oxygen and carbon dioxide are valued on an open-market trading system. Clearly, a closed-loop system, such as a vertical farm, as Edel conceived it, was so much more than providing artificial light to a few plants and recycling fish waste as plant fertilizer. It was about striking a delicate balance in the building to create a zero-waste ecosystem where "the only thing that will go out is food."

As we climbed the stairs to the second floor, the unmistakable greasy aroma of bacon wrapped itself around me. "The smokers were in use twenty-four-seven right up until the day Peer Foods moved out," confirmed Edel.

Some of the smokers were new: huge stainless steel tanks with what looked like ships' portholes at about five feet high. The stainless steel was valuable, and Edel and crew had already started to hack it into panels for food-grade countertops and tables. Other panels would become the new bathroom stalls.

There were also older cavernous smokers that smelled like they had been used continuously for a century, which was likely not far off. Smoke stains had left huge black licks up the beautiful 1920s glazed-tile walls. I remarked that it was a shame to think that buildings like this were decaying and being torn down due to a lack of knowledge of how to resuscitate existing construction. And yet, city aldermen had dreams of demolition and replacement with Walmarts.

"Building a new building is a really inefficient thing to do!" Edel fired back. "Plants don't care about columns, or taking a freight elevator to get out to a market. Really an existing structure is the best possible situation."[15]

The stainless steel smoke tanks were in the area designated to be the bakery, one of the food-based business incubator areas. Start-ups will be able to rent the space by the hour and still be in a completely 2,000-square-foot (185-square-meter) food-grade shared commercial kitchen, a major economic hurdle for most people getting into the food-production business, given the overhead on commercial space. Tenants can also rent garden plots on the rooftop garden and source other items, like mushrooms, that will be grown in other parts of the building. "There'll be a wood-fired oven in here," enthused Edel. The heat from the bakery will be important to heat the other parts of the building. Because of the original function of the building as a food facility, the floors undulate every few feet where floor drains exist. "How expensive would that have been to put in?"

"All of these rooms were great forests of electrical wires, pipes, and everything else. There was meat-cutting equipment everywhere. We are keeping bits of it and reusing almost everything. The oldest wiring is only 15 years old, fortunately." There was even a beauty to the age-blackened iron rails formerly used to move the carcasses along from one worker to the next. Edel was planning to keep them suspended from the timber supports as a historical memento of the building's past.

"This is the one mess I'm going to keep because it's so out of control," he laughed, pointing toward one particularly absurd tangle of meters, pipes, wiring, gauges, and switches. Edel quipped that this is where his art school education will come into play. A floor-to-ceiling glass wall will be installed and dramatic lighting will be focused on the "industrial found art"—a ready-made point of interest that will be a central art piece on the third floor, visible from the conference room and the incubator office space that will be rented out to small businesses that will use The Plant's commercial baking, brewing, and food-preparation facilities.

The New Chicago Brewing Company has signed on to be a major keystone tenant, and there will even be a homebrew co-op that operates out of The Plant. Not only will brewing produce a lot of heat; it will supply vast amounts of spent brewing mash to compost for the gardens and green house or for the biodigester.

We descended into a dark, cavernous basement for the grand finale. We cautiously picked our way around scrap metal, spools of wiring, and over curbs that were scheduled to be sledge-hammered like we were climbing through the innards of a submarine. Edel pointed out rooms that would soon be filled with mushroom beds. He had secured a former military fighter jet engine that would be put into use for electrical generation once the biodigester was built.

Edel yanked on a solid steel door, and we passed from the submarine scenario into a laboratory-white immense room bathed in a fuchsia light on one side, with gurgling vats of tilapia-filled water on the other. The Plant Vertical Farm wasn't just demolition and future scenarios; there was actual food growing in test systems in this basement room.

"This is Growing System Number One," said Edel as we walked toward the four square plastic 275-gallon (1,000-liter) tubs that were the fish tanks. This was the project that Davis's students were working on, tweaking and perfecting, so that it could be implemented on a larger scale when The Plant ramped up its food ecosystem.

Slivers of fingerling tilapia flashed around the tank, and as soon as they saw us looming over, they made for the surface. "They would eat twenty-four hours a day," said Edel, as the fish poked at the water's surface. There were two more tanks attached to this chain of plastic vats and white plastic PVC pipes, and the nearby pump was noisily forcing water around through the tanks. Sixty market-weight tilapia swirled in the final tank. "You want to control how much you feed them or they'll get too big, too fast. And you also have to balance the amount of food with the amount of plants you are growing." Edel explained that the fish were "on a diet" until they got more plants into the system.

The water from the fish pens flowed into another water-filled tank with run-of-the-mill hardware-store black plastic garden netting for filtering. Edel explained that the netting caused "the richer stuff" to fall to the bottom of the filter tank. When The Plant's biodigester is ready, this solid fish waste will be used to produce methane gas, which will be turned back into heat and electrical energy.

The next tank after the netting had a black plastic honeycomb-like panel—"a $400 mistake," whined Edel. The tank is simply a place to harbor the bacteria that turns the ammonia of the fish waste into the nitrites and nitrates (the nitrogen compounds) that make fantastic plant fertilizer. Instead of the special, expensive plastic comb, Edel proposed that "rocks or old chopped-up plastic bottles" would do just as good a job for a fraction of the price.

The pump then sent the water from the filters into shallow pans where foam rafts studded with tiny plant plugs floated on clear but nitrogen-rich water. Each hole in the raft contained a small plastic basket filled with coconut husk to stabilize the roots of each little seedling of arugula, red lettuce, or whatever the team wants to grow. The coconut husk fiber is nearly indestructible yet is porous enough to not restrict the rooting systems that dangle through the gaps in the baskets and into the water. As the plants take up the nitrogen, they effectively clean the water—as they do in ecosystems in nature—allowing the water to be recycled back into the fish tanks for the waste-fertilizer loop to begin again.

The plants looked very happy and healthy bathed in the fuchsia light of the state-of-the-art LED grow lights. "Plants can't see green," Edel explained, so you only need the red and blue lights. Edel, Davis, and students are testing the LED lights, as they are relative newcomers to the market; but if they work, they'll be much more efficient than other grow lights commonly used. A computer engineer is working out the open-source software and hardware that will move the lights along a variable-height track suspended above the seedlings. The lights move slowly from one end of the beds to the other "so they don't end up growing like this," explained Edel, listing sharply to one side.

I finally asked the big question that seems to be a sticking point where new ideas tend to hit the proverbial brick wall of city bylaws.

"And you're allowed to do all of this?"

Overall, the city has just let Edel and company continue without too much concern. The brewing permit was a hassle, but they got it. "The only other resistance we'd had is from the zoning department that didn't like the idea of fish and aquaculture," said Edel. "Not for any *good* reason, because under the same zoning, you can crush cars, smelt iron, and slaughter cattle. But raising organic fish for some reason is bad. Go figure."

The fish were not yet a particular concern anyhow, as they were part of Davis's students' course work. They were working out the details of this aquaponics-agricultural loop as part of the student curriculum, which involved the microgreens, sprouts, and mushrooms that would soon be tested out at The Plant.

Part of this course work also included marketing plans and economic feasibility studies by students at the Illinois Institute of Technology. When I asked Davis how strong the demand was in Chicago for locally grown food, he replied that even drawing from a radius of 500 miles around the city, there aren't enough farms for the markets and the demand that already exists. And being right in the city will be a huge advantage for restaurants willing to pay a premium for ultra-fresh product. "We're about the only people who can say, 'We'll pick this for you at nine a.m., have it to you by ten, and you can serve it for lunch.' "[16]

The other factor that favors the viability of vertical farming in the city, according to Davis, is that Chicago's public school system now sets aside 20 percent of its school lunch budget for local foods. "Even keeping in mind that they don't actually go to school in the summer when most of the food is produced, it still creates opportunity for us."

Food wholesale produce suppliers have also told Davis that they'll take everything The Plant can produce. So whether it is Chicago's sustainable and premium restaurants willing to pay top dollar for The Plant's fresh, local, organic food, or local produce wholesalers, or the Chicago Public School System (though clearly the school board wouldn't be able to out-compete the other two on price), finding markets for the food will be the easy part.

In Davis's opinion, however, Edel's plan of having manufacturing tenants subsidize the food-growing spaces was a key element to turning The Plant into reality while the other more ambitious "food-only" skyscrapers are lingering on paper at this point. "We've been to almost every other urban agriculture site within 500 miles, and we noticed that almost all of them are being run on job-training grants from foundations. We thought that this was probably not a good way to run this. That's why I really jumped on to this project. It's technically interesting, but it has a commitment to creating a business model that can be replicated. The problem with social services and 40-story urban farms is that you train a bunch of people, but there are no businesses out there to hire them."[17]

When I remarked that it's somewhat surprising that the world's first vertical farm won't be nestled in among skyscrapers in uptown Manhattan, or in the anything-is-possible cities like Shanghai and Dubai; that it will happen on a very modest scale, on a very modest budget, in Chicago, Davis just smiled. "That's kind of the tension between New York and the Midwest. All the actual urban agriculture is happening within 500 miles of Chicago, and all the press is about these 40-story buildings."

"When Sam Walton [founder of Walmart] started, he didn't try to build a 400,000-square-foot superstore. He took an old Kresge's and said, 'I'm going to figure out this business model in this relatively small space. If it's successful, I'll make another one.' And at some point, you can afford to build a single-purpose building for a Walmart. I think if you get good at urban agriculture, and have a few technological breakthroughs, at some point you'll need an architect to design an 80-story urban farm. Maybe your business model will be sound to do that. It's just a bit premature right now."

I asked if the city was therefore giving The Plant any breaks or help in any way. "They're not subsidizing it," answered Davis. "But the most important thing in Chicago is that they're letting us do it."

Edel's concept of industrial reuse seems like a reasonable solution to the very sticky wicket that has so far kept urban vertical farms confined to academic presentations and scrolls of architectural plans. And, as Edel put it, "You've got to sell a lot of rutabagas to pay for a $100 million building." Edel's ability to reinvigorate unwanted commercial space, make it beautiful, and, perhaps most importantly, make it productive and profitable once again, might just be a catalyst that will serve post-industrial Chicago well. And it might be vertical farming's Sputnik moment, launching a vertical-farm race, so to speak, that will leave those ego-driven skyscrapers on the drawing board for the time being.

Notes

1. Dickson Despommier, *The Vertical Farm: Feeding the World in the 21st Century* (New York: Thomas Dunne Books, 2010).

2. Blake Kurasek's Living Skyscraper can be viewed at http://blakekurasek.com/theliving-skyscraper.html.

3. Vincent Callebaut's Dragonfly vertical farm can be viewed at http://vincent.callebaut.org/page1-img-dragonfly.html.

4. Despommier and Ellingsen's pyramidal vertical farm can be viewed at http://www.verticalfarm.com/designs?folder=b9aa20a4-9c6a-4983-b3ad-390c4f1fa562.

5. MVRDV's website is at http://www.mvrdv.nl.

6. The Plant's website is at http://www.plantchicago.com/.

7. Blake Davis (adjunct professor of urban agriculture at Illinois Institute of Technology), personal interview with the author, The Plant, Chicago, Illinois, January 29, 2011.

8. Personal interviews were conducted on-site at The Plant with John Edel (owner/developer/director, The Plant), Blake Davis (adjunct professor of urban agriculture, IIT), Alex

Poltorak (volunteer, The Plant), and Audrey Thibault (volunteer, The Plant), Chicago, Illinois, January 29, 2011.

9. I found several sources that reference the influence of the Chicago Stockyard's "disassembly line" on Henry Ford's idea for the automobile assembly line. He saw the efficiencies gained by giving one worker one specific task and then moving the carcasses on to the next worker. Ford reversed the process to put cars together, but the idea of worker specialization was born on the blood-soaked floors of stockyard slaughterhouses. One source, among many online, that states this is http://www.pbs.org/wgbh/amex/chicago/peopleevents/p_armour.html.

10. The backstory of how John Edel came to purchase the Peer Foods building and information on The Plant came from a personal interview with John Edel, January 29, 2011.

11. Bubbly Dynamics draws its nickname from nearby Bubbly Creek, a waterway named during the days of the stockyards and the attendant business that sprung up around the century-long livestock and slaughter industry in Chicago, where boiled waste and decaying matter made the creek appear to bubble.

12. John Edel, personal interview with the author, The Plant, Chicago, Illinois, January 29, 2011.

13. Ibid.

14. John Edel and Nathan Wyse in conversation with the author, The Plant, Chicago, Illinois, January 29, 2011.

15. John Edel, personal interview with the author, The Plant, Chicago, Illinois, January 29, 2011.

16. Blake Davis, in-person interview with the author, The Plant, Chicago, Illinois, January 29, 2011.

17. Ibid.

Moving Up Main: The Cottontown/ Elmwood Park Corridor Is Booming
Eva Moore

Curiosity Coffee Bar owner Greg Slattery had to leave Columbia to realize how much he loved the Capital City. He moved to Athens, Georgia in 2009, spending three and a half years there before moving back.

"At the time, I thought I was escaping to what I thought would be a more musically hip scene with more arts and culture going on. But I found out I was dead wrong. Just not right at all. Not only do I feel like the music scene's better here, but now I am a part of the renaissance in Columbia."

The new center of that renaissance, for Slattery and others, is along a stretch of Main Street between Elmwood Avenue and River Drive, an area bounded by the Cottontown and Elmwood Park neighborhoods.

That's where Slattery and his partner, Sandra Moscato, just opened a small coffee shop inside local wine shop Vino Garage.

"I was most excited about the idea of being a part of the development of this area," Slattery says. "It's just such a neat stretch. I love the industrial building sort of vibe. . . . Looking at this, it felt like I could be part of something I'd be really proud of."

Curiosity Coffee Bar isn't the only coffee shop to open here in the past month. One block away, Indah Coffee Co., a longtime Soda City Market vendor, opened its first brick-and-mortar spot in the former Dunn Electric Co. building on Sumter Street; it shares the airy, welcoming space with Circa Barber Shop.

The caffeine boom had led some to dub the area "Coffeetown."

But it's more than just coffee. Curiosity and Indah are among a slew of new businesses that have opened or are about to open in this area, including a brewery, an architecture firm, a trendy furniture store and a yet-to-be-announced project by an out-of-state restaurant group.

The boom is no accident; the City of Columbia and the surrounding neighborhoods have been laying the groundwork for years. But the new development is raising inevitable tensions—fears of gentrification, and even a quibble over what the area should be called.

With development over the last few decades focused on the Vista and downtown, it's been a long time since Columbia had a real explosion of changes in one of its urban neighborhoods. But as the city fills in and further diversifies, people are paying close attention to how this area will grow.

Boomtown

Folami Geter owns Lamb's Bread Vegan Café, which has been at the corner of Main and Franklin at least since 2005; she bought the business from her father several years back. During a recent lunch hour, Curtis Mayfield was on the stereo and Geter and her staff were spooning out collards, vegan mac-and-cheese and other specialties. The clientele at this black-owned business is a mix of black and white.

"Maybe six or seven years ago, there were only two or three thriving businesses on our stretch of Main Street," Geter says in a later email interview. "We were surrounded by empty abandoned buildings."

In some ways, they still are. One of those abandoned properties is Jim Moore Cadillac; the dealership closed in 2009. Vacant warehouses, garages and weedy parking lots dot both sides of the street. Christ Central Ministries, which serves the homeless and other disadvantaged people, owns properties both north and south of Elmwood on Main. Men sometimes gather outside a liquor store on the east side of the street.

But recently, Geter says, "The landscape has changed tremendously."

"It's interesting to see folks who would have never thought of coming this far [up] North Main, now flocking to area businesses," she says. "It's proof that our city is growing. It's absolutely different now. We don't mind the change."

Over the last several years, other businesses began to open. In 2011, David Roberts opened DER Kitchen in a building he'd bought five years earlier on the corridor. Roberts rents commercial kitchen space to food trucks, caterers and other food purveyors. Chocolate Nirvana is probably his most prominent kitchen user—and in the next few months, Roberts will be converting the front of his building into a retail space for the dessert maker.

In late 2012, Doug Aylard opened Vino Garage, bringing his beer and wine expertise to a low-key little wine shop on the west side of Main Street.

The most recent explosion began in earnest, though, with the opening of restaurant The War Mouth. Its owners chose Cottontown after an exhaustive search.

"Rhett and I creeped every street in the Metro, basically," says Porter Barron, who co-owns The War Mouth with Chef Rhett Elliott and developer Frank Cason. "We knew we wanted to be as close to the city center as possible, but we didn't want somewhere so concentrated that we couldn't have a barbecue pit. This was a commercial district that wasn't too crowded and was close."

"We also wanted to be close to the river so we could go catfishing late at night when we get off work," he adds.

The area makes a lot of sense for a restaurant, says Barron.

"We were surprised nobody beat us here, because it's been obvious that the neighborhoods surrounding this commercial district have long since surpassed the offerings of the commercial corridor," Barron says. "The residents in these areas have invested lots into these homes over the past several decades; it's only the commercial district that was still blighted. It was clear this was an underserved area."

The War Mouth opened to great reviews in December 2015, serving food inspired by hunting and fishing and Midlands barbecue joints.

Since then, developer Cason has bought several more properties in the area, including the building that now houses Indah and Circa, and one that will soon house Columbia Presbyterian Church. It's won him over, he says.

"I'm from Columbia and lived here all my life and honestly didn't know much about it," Cason says. "My impression was 'Don't go north of Elmwood.'"

He found, though, that the Elmwood Park, Earlewood and Cottontown neighborhoods are filled with people with disposable income.

"There's probably no area in Columbia that has that big of a gap between perception and reality," Cason says. "Many people perceive that area as blighted not just commercially but residentially. The commercial needs help, but the residential is very nice. Lot of millennials, empty nesters."

There are other newcomers. Architecture firm Studio 2LR recently renovated the old Wilson Furniture building at Main and Confederate, and moved in. A new furniture store, Copper Barn, is in the midst of its grand opening. Cromer's P-Nuts plans to move to a building along the corridor that it bought in February. Restaurateur Kristian Niemi announced a project called Revival, though it's not rolling yet. The area just above River is even getting a Pelican's SnoBalls, the bright pink-and-blue New Orleans frozen treat franchise.

The area's first brewery, Cotton Town Brew Lab, hopes to have its beer production up and running by the end of the summer. Owner Zack Jones says he started off looking at buildings in Charleston—"the mecca of breweries," he says—but decided to stick around Columbia instead. The warehouses and garages that dot Cottontown are ideal for light industry like a brewery—at the future Cotton Town Brew Lab, the 16-foot ceiling means plenty of space for big tanks. Once production is up and running, Jones plans to turn his attention to building a tasting room and, eventually, a canning line.

And, as Free Times reported last week, it's not just homegrown businesses eyeing the area anymore. A Tennessee-based development group called Fresh Capital has bought a property at 2203 Main St., which currently houses A&F Body Shop and a few other ramshackle buildings. Fresh Capital paid $463,000.

The group is associated with such chains as Taziki's, Jim 'N Nick's Community Bar-B-Q, Martin's Bar-B-Que Joint and I Love Juice Bar—but real estate agent JP Scurry of Colliers International says the buyer hasn't yet decided what restaurant to develop on the site.

"Obviously they liked the property; there are some neat buildings on it," Scurry says. "But they have not confirmed or finalized what they see there. They're a very flexible group. Creative. Lot of different concepts."

None of this development, it turns out, was an accident.

All About the Neighborhoods

For years, city planners and neighborhood groups have been trying to figure out how to lift up North Columbia.

You'll hear quibbles from some—including some in this story—but to many Columbians, everything north of Elmwood Avenue is North Columbia. It's a majority-black district with many proud, historic neighborhoods, and institutions like Columbia College and the Lutheran Seminary. It's also struggled with poverty, and particularly with attracting businesses like grocery stores and restaurants.

Zero in on the area just north of Elmwood, though, and you'll find something different. According to data compiled in 2014 using U.S. Census figures, the two-square-mile Earlewood/Cottontown/Elmwood Park area is more than half owner-occupied homes, with a median household income that mirrors that of the city at large. It's about 60 percent white, 36 percent black—slightly whiter than the whole city, and certainly whiter than North Columbia.

A lot of stones have been laid over the years to help North Columbia, including the Elmwood-to-River-Drive stretch of Main. A detailed City of Columbia master plan released in 2005 visualizes the North Main corridor as a series of "villages," with an "artist village" centered around Main Street and River Drive. City development corporations have built and redeveloped buildings throughout North Columbia, and given businesses reduced rents or loans to open in the area.

City leaders have also specifically targeted the area that's now developing. Federal grants helped the city streetscape Main from Elmwood to River Drive, burying the utilities underground and smoothing the road and sidewalks. The city developed a façade loan program to give businesses along the corridor money to improve their storefronts. The city also did a zoning overlay for the area, reducing the number of parking spaces required for new businesses to move in, hoping to reduce the barriers to entry.

Another probable factor in the recent redevelopment? Bull Street. Greenville developer Bob Hughes is redeveloping the former state mental hospital property; it has a city-funded baseball stadium and a lot of new infrastructure going in. And it's not far from Cottontown.

But the neighborhoods just north of Elmwood felt they had to do more. It turns out that the education Frank Cason got about the Cottontown area was probably no accident.

"Our neighborhood had always been on the defensive," says Paul Bouknight, president of the Cottontown/Bellevue Historic District Neighborhood Association. "A few years ago we decided to go on the offensive."

The Earlewood, Elmwood Park and Cottontown neighborhoods compiled some information for developers and started getting the word out.

The community also started a branding effort, according to various community members, trying to educate people about the fact that "North Main Street" doesn't start until just above River Drive. The area immediately north of Elmwood is still plain old Main Street, and it's in the same zip code—29201—as downtown Columbia.

"People refer to it as North Main, but it's Main Street," Bouknight says of the rapidly developing corridor. "Similar to what they did in Charleston with 'Upper King,' we did 'Upper Main.' All of that has seemed to help."

There've been other efforts to separate out the "Upper Main" area. David Roberts, who owns DER Kitchen and has lived in Elmwood Park since building a house there in 1997, jokes that he briefly tried to rebrand the area SNOE, for Slightly North of Elmwood.

"We're struggling for an identity," Roberts says. "Everyone knows Main Street, the Vista, Olympia. What do we call our little section of Main?"

"It's nothing against being associated with North Columbia," he adds. His business is a member of the North Columbia Business Association. But he thinks his area needs its own name and identity.

Roberts says he's seen some recent changes in the neighborhoods themselves, not just the corridor.

"Elmwood Park and Cottontown are very diversified," he says. "That's one reason we like it. We couldn't have bought our lot in Shandon."

But he notes that until recently, he and his wife were some of the few people in the neighborhood with kids—and who sent their kids to the neighborhood schools.

"When we moved in, you were either gay, single, double-income-no-kids, or retired," he says. Now, people with kids are staying.

Not everyone thinks the booming area needs its own brand.

"I've never seen a reason to not just call it North Main," says Slattery of Curiosity Coffee Bar. "I feel like the only reason you don't want to call it North Main is whatever association you might have with that name. To me it is what it is. I've always loved this area. It's affordable, it's fun. Honestly, the only vandalism or crime that's ever happened to my property while living in this area was from a drunk white college dude who went through everyone's car on our street and threw our change out in the street."

The G Word

While metrics are hard to come by this early in the boom, developers tell Free Times there's already been a spike in the cost of some commercial properties in the area, with owners feeling their lots are worth a lot more than they used to be. And there are very few residential properties for sale in the Cottontown area these days, Bouknight notes.

What's more, it's indisputable that many of the new businesses in the area are white-owned, while many of the older businesses in the area are black-owned.

With the Elmwood-to-River corridor so hot, is there a concern that the attention might harm what people love about the area, or push out people who are already there?

Sam Davis, the area's long-serving councilman, is used to getting pulled a lot of different ways, as he represents basically all of North Columbia.

"I think gentrification, as everyone knows, has positives and negatives," Davis says.

Davis says development will be good for the entire North Columbia area—"businesses follow rooftops," he notes—but that he wants to make sure the new businesses don't push out or make life harder for existing businesses or residents. He cites the façade program as an example of how the city has tried to help existing businesses prepare for the changes coming to the area. The city needs to stay focused on projects like that, he says.

"Affordability along the North Main corridor is an attraction," Davis says. "We did a good experiment in the Vista, now we need to focus our energies in the northern part of the city and eastern part of the city."

The area's newer business owners say they've tried to tread lightly.

"That's a tricky thing," says Barron, co-owner of The War Mouth, when asked whether the new development is a force for good. "In this case, we certainly aren't gentrifying this area. It's only the commercial corridor that has not kept pace. The neighborhood associations around here have been clamoring for commercial business; they were just opposed to El Cheapos and liquor stores, places that would result in a lot of calls to the precinct. When we came and introduced ourselves to the neighborhood associations first thing, we were deferential coming in, and I'm proud to say we have a very good reputation."

On the other hand, while commercial development is positive, being a hip new area could bring undesirable focus, according to Slattery.

"I do worry about gentrification," Slattery says. "I've lived in these neighborhoods since '06. My biggest concern, and what I hope doesn't happen is that the culture and the heritage of this part of town gets lost in brand new banners saying, 'Whoo, we're It.'"

Cason, the developer, also sees the boom just north of Elmwood as a potential way to boost the entire North Columbia region.

"They desperately want more services out there, more retail," he says of Eau Claire and areas further up Main. "I believe this will help them. [But] between Elmwood and Sunset, I think that has to happen first.... We need some infill development. Once people start to see that, retailers will start to take notice."

Bouknight, the Cottontown neighborhood president, is excited about the changes in the area—but he's very clear about his priorities.

"Our great concern is not to hurt the quality of life in our neighborhoods," he says. "Life is good in Cottontown, Elmwood Park and Earlewood. It's quiet, family-centric neighborhoods. We're a bunch of porch dwellers.... We don't want what happened in Five Points where it has metastasized into the neighborhoods, parking and so forth. We want the business, but we want it contained and we want to maintain the privacy of our neighborhoods."

What's New

Recently opened:

Carolina Kernels

Circa Barber Shop

Copper Barn

Curiosity Coffee Bar
(inside Vino Garage)

Indah Coffee

Studio 2LR

The War Mouth

Coming soon:

Chocolate Nirvana retail storefront (inside DER Kitchen)

Columbia Presbyterian Church

Cotton Town Brew Lab

Cromer's P-Nuts

Pelican's SnoBalls

TBA restaurant project
by Fresh Capital

Sound Off: Free Times Misses the Mark on Gentrification

Julia Dawson

I'm deeply disturbed by "Moving Up Main: The Cottontown/Elmwood Park Corridor Is Booming" (Free Times cover story, May 31). I'm a Charleston native but have lived in Elmwood Park for five years. Due to what I've learned about gentrification, I'll soon be leaving this neighborhood.

Today, our city and state enact laws and policies that create new forms of racial and class segregation. Segregation determines who benefits from rising home prices, or who is robbed of wealth through common yet sometimes sinister real estate practices with cute sounding terms like house "flipping."

My parents are retired teachers near Charleston. Partly because of racial and class segregation, their home is worth more than the exact same home in a low income neighborhood somewhere else. My parents borrowed against their house to pay for my college. This sort of asset access and building is denied communities that have been divested of their housing wealth through some of the forces you superficially allude to in this article. These laws and practices create systems that deny wealth from some groups (people of color, low income people) while pouring it into others (white, middle and upper income). This is white supremacy. It is also wealth supremacy. It is not hip. It is legalized, socially sanctioned theft and a form of violence.

Your article could have been a careful journalistic attempt to understand and courageously confront this, then provide examples of alternatives; a series with installments authored by various Eau Claire residents—people experiencing institutional theft and neglect, and also those entrepreneurs with creative visions they've already built or want to build.

Referring to gentrification as "The G-word" and offering nothing but quotes from people who have benefited or are actively seeking to benefit from this extremely unethical system is irresponsible.

Another unethical element is the fact that the mostly Black "upper North Main" residents are spoken about but never heard from in this article. Also, are any of the new businesses featured owned by people of color? When we see new business loans going almost exclusively to members of a racial category that already holds most of the city's economic assets, we must pause, identify this as white supremacy, then organize radical shifts away from it.

People like USC professor Dr. Bobby Donaldson, and the Columbia SC '63 project offer regular opportunities to learn about Columbia's neighborhoods, specifically historically Black neighborhoods. BlackLivesMatter Charleston's Muhiyidin d'Baha explains gentrification in an important YouTube video: http://bit.ly/gentrify-chas.

Journalists like Nikole Hannah-Jones have long taught about segregation in the U.S. I hope you take time to listen and meaningfully join the just housing work of groups like BlackLivesMatter and Movement for Black Lives. I hope next time you write about "development," you ask whose voices are missing, then interview them and hire them as reporters instead of talking about them. I hope you never again gloss housing segregation as positive and lighthearted.

This Is What Happens After a Neighborhood Gets Gentrified
Richard Florida

Back in 2014, Spike Lee famously expressed his disdain for the forces of gentrification in New York: "Why does it take an influx of white New Yorkers in the south Bronx, in Harlem, in Bed Stuy, in Crown Heights for the facilities to get better?" he argued. "What about the people who are renting? They can't afford it anymore!" Lee's criticisms reflect a now-familiar narrative in cities all over the U.S.: As wealthier residents flow back into once-low-income, often minority neighborhoods, longtime residents can be priced out.

But exactly how does this dynamic play out, and is displacement inevitable? A new comprehensive review of what we know about gentrification sheds much-needed light on this heated issue. The review, by researchers at the University of California Berkeley and UCLA and published by the Federal Reserve of San Francisco, takes a close look at studies of gentrification and displacement conducted over the past several decades. (I wrote about the review's insights on how public investment shapes gentrification last week). It helps us better understand several questions related to gentrification and displacement: Just how extensive is displacement, exactly what kinds of people are displaced, and how do people and groups fare after they leave gentrifying neighborhoods?

The earliest studies of displacement conducted in the 1980s generated widely varying estimates of how many people are displaced by gentrification. A 1982 study found that roughly 1 percent of all Americans, 5 percent of families, and 8.5 percent of urban families were displaced from their homes between 1970 and 1977 by either eviction, public action, sale or reoccupation, or the changing state of their neighborhood. A 1983 study of five cities (Boston, Cincinnati, Richmond, Seattle, and Denver) found that nearly a quarter (23 percent) of residents in these urban neighborhoods were displaced due to eviction, increased rent, or the fact that the house they were renting was sold between 1978 and 1980. Similarly, a 2001 study of gentrifying areas of Boston by Jacob Vigdor found evidence of heightened housing turnover in gentrifying neighborhoods.

Perhaps the foremost student of gentrification and displacement is Lance Freeman of Columbia University. His 2004 study with Frank Braconi found that poor households in gentrifying neighborhoods of New York City were less likely to move than poor households in non-gentrifying neighborhoods. This of course may have to do with the fact that there are fewer poor households in gentrifying neighborhoods to begin with. Still, the authors concluded that "a neighborhood could go from a 30% poverty population to 12% in as few as 10 years without any displacement whatsoever." In a subsequent 2005 study, Freeman found that the probability that a household would be displaced in a gentrifying neighborhood was a mere 1.3 percent. A follow-up 2007 study, again with Braconi, examined apartment turnover in New York City neighborhoods and found that the probability of displacement declined as the rate of rent inflation increased in a neighborhood.

Disadvantaged households in gentrifying neighborhoods were actually 15 percent *less* likely to move than those in non-gentrifying households.

And, in a 2009 study, Freeman found that gentrifying neighborhoods are becoming more racially diverse by tracking neighborhood change from 1970 to 2000 (although he does note that cities overall are becoming more diverse as well). Freeman also discovered that changes in educational diversity were the same for both gentrifying and non-gentrifying areas. Ultimately, while some residents were displaced from 1970 to 2000, gentrifying neighborhoods were generally more diverse when it came to income, race, and education as opposed to non-gentrifying neighborhoods.

Counterintuitively, several studies have even found that gentrification can in some cases reduce displacement. Neighborhood improvements like bars, restaurants, waterfronts, or extended transit can and sometimes do encourage less advantaged households to stay put in the face of gentrification. A 2006 study found that displacement accounted for only 6 to 10 percent of all moves in New York City due to housing expenses, landlord harassment, or displacement by private action (e.g. condo conversion) between 1989 and 2002. A 2011 study concluded that neighborhood income gains did not significantly predict household exit rates. What did predict out-migration was age, minority status, selective entry and exit, and renting as opposed to buying.

A 2010 study on "Who Gentrifies Low-Income Neighborhoods" found that the impact of gentrification on black residents varies based on level of education. By examining around 15,000 census tracts in 64 metros from 1990 to 2000, the authors found that gentrification tends to benefit highly educated black households. In fact, one-third of the increase in income among gentrifying neighborhoods during this period came from the progress of this specific demographic. This in turn causes gentrifying neighborhoods to be more attractive to middle-class black households. But gentrification can also have a negative effect on less educated black households, by pushing those who did not complete high school out of gentrifying neighborhoods.

That said, displacement can be and is a big issue in places where gentrification is occurring at a feverish pace. In her coverage of related research by the UC Berkeley Urban Displacement Project, my *CityLab* colleague Tanvi Misra points to the strong link between gentrification and displacement in a high-gentrification city like San Francisco. Over a quarter of San Francisco's neighborhoods (422 of the nearly 1,600 surveyed) are at risk of displacement. The study's lead author, Karen Chapple, writes that by 2030, San Francisco, Oakland, "and many other Bay Area communities may realize that their neighborhood has turned the corner from displacement risk to reality."

Indeed, displacement is becoming a larger issue in knowledge hubs and superstar cities, where the pressure for urban living is accelerating. These particular cities attract new businesses, highly skilled workers, major developers, and large corporations, all of which drive up both the demand for and cost of housing. As a result, local residents—and neighborhood renters in particular—may feel pressured to move to more affordable locations.

A 2013 Cleveland Fed study found that extensive gentrification is the province of a limited group of large superstar cities and knowledge hubs like New York, San Francisco, Seattle, Boston, and Washington D.C. In three-quarters of America's 55 largest cities, less than 10 percent of all neighborhoods experienced gentrification from 2000 to 2007, and gentrification affected 5 percent or less of a total of 22 neighborhoods. Not surprisingly, these cities are the ones being hit hardest by displacement. And with real estate prices in these cities surging toward all-time highs, there is reason to believe that displacement may worsen over time.

Of course, an even bigger issue is the neighborhoods that are untouched by gentrification and where concentrated poverty persists and deepens. A 2014 study found that for every gentrified neighborhood across 51 U.S. metro areas, 10 others remained poor and 12 formerly stable neighborhoods fell into concentrated disadvantage. A Harvard study of Chicago found that the gentrification process continues for neighborhoods with over 35 percent of white residents, and either slows or stops if the neighborhood is 40 percent black. The reality is that the displaced are getting pushed out of working-class neighborhoods that are "good enough" to attract people and investment, while the poorest and most vulnerable neighborhoods remain mired in persistent poverty and concentrated disadvantage.

Gentrification and displacement, then, are symptoms of the scarcity of quality urbanism. The driving force behind both is the far larger process of spiky reurbanization—itself propelled by large-scale public and private investment in everything from transit, schools, and parks to private research institutions and housing redevelopment.

All of which points to the biggest, most crucial task ahead: creating more inclusive cities and neighborhoods that can meet the needs of all urbanites.

Cultural Representation

Ready for Prime Time: After Twenty-Five Years as a Road Comic, Leslie Jones Becomes a Star
Andrew Marantz

On TV talk shows, the host introduces a guest, then music plays while the guest emerges from backstage. On podcasts, the etiquette is still being worked out. The host often launches into an introduction while the guest sits quietly in the same sound booth. A couple of years ago, the co-hosts of a podcast called "Alias Smith and LeRoi" began this way, speaking about their guest, the comedian Leslie Jones, as if she were not there.

"This is gonna be kind of a hot one," Ali LeRoi said.

"I've been waiting to sit her ass down for a minute," Owen Smith said. "One of the funniest women in the game."

"Funniest *comedian* in the game," Jones interrupted. "Not just woman. I hate that shit." End of introduction.

Comedians are combatants: they "kill," they "bomb," they "destroy." Such bluster can mask insecurity, and Jones had good reason to feel defensive. She was forty-six, and had been a standup comedian for more than a quarter century; her peers respected her, but that respect rarely translated into high-paying gigs. "I remember some nights where I was, like, 'All right, this comedy shit just ain't working out,'" she told me recently. "And not just when I was twenty-five. Like, when I was *forty*-five." She was a woman in a field dominated by men, and an African-American in an industry that remained disturbingly segregated. Although she had opened for Katt Williams and Dave Chappelle, acted in movies alongside Ice Cube and Martin Lawrence, recorded a standup special for Showtime, and made several appearances on HBO's "Def Comedy Jam" and BET's "ComicView," she worried that the gatekeepers of mainstream comedy—bookers for the "Tonight Show," casting directors of big-budget films—had never heard her name. "Every black comedian in the country knew what I could do," she said. "But that doesn't mean everyone else is paying attention." Chris Rock, who met Jones when they were both road comics in the late eighties, told me, "Black women have the hardest gig in show business. You hear Jennifer Lawrence complaining about getting paid less because she's a woman—if she was black, she'd *really* have something to complain about."

Jones spent much of her career performing in what she calls "shitty chitlin-circuit-ass rooms, where you're just hoping the promoter pays you." She told me that, around 2010, "I stopped only doing black clubs. I stopped doing what I call 'nigger nights'—the Chocolate Sundays, the Mo' Better Mondays. I knew how to relate to that audience, and I was winning where I was, but I wasn't moving forward." She lived in Los Angeles at the time, and she began asking for spots at the Comedy Store, where David Letterman and Robin Williams got their starts.

A comedian named Erik Marino, who befriended her there, said, "She felt very strongly that she was being pigeonholed as a black comic—a BET comic."

For a while, Jones performed at the Store at odd hours. Then, she said, "I went to the booker and I threw the race card at him. 'Why you won't let me go up at ten on a Friday? 'Cause I'm black?'" The booker gave her a prime-time slot. "She destroyed, obviously," Marino said. "Bookers are the ones who care about black rooms versus white rooms. To us comedians, it's, like, if you know what you're doing and you can connect with an audience, they're gonna laugh."

Rock saw Jones perform at the Store in 2012. After her set, he told her, "You were always funny, but you're at a new level now."

"You're right," she responded. "But I'm not gonna really make it unless someone like you puts me on." Rock took out his iPhone and added her name to a list labelled "Funny people."

Jones has big eyes and a round, rubbery face. She is six feet tall, and often exaggerates her stature by wearing high heels and gelling her hair upward, fright-wig style. "I know I'm fly—don't get me wrong," she told me. "But I don't look, like, standard Hollywood. As a comedian, it's something you learn to use."

Some paunchy male comics, such as Louis C.K. and Jim Gaffigan, occasionally refer to their looks; others seem oblivious of their appearance. Women don't have this luxury. Jones often begins her standup sets by "taking away their bullets"—neutralizing anything that might distract an audience, so that "they can stop looking at my outfit, stop worrying about whether I think I'm sexy, and just listen." Her Showtime special, "Problem Child," which aired in 2010, began that way:

> I know y'all already noticed that I'm a big bitch ... When I walk in a Payless, it gets quiet than a motherfucker ... I swear, men, if you can get past my big-ass feet and how tall I am, I'm a great fucking catch ... I'm fine. I can fuck. I can fight. Oh, I ain't no damsel in distress, motherfucker. You can go get the car, baby, while I handle these three thug motherfuckers.

The final line devolves into shadowboxing—Jones bobbing and weaving like a mean-mugging Buster Keaton.

One bullet that this opening takes away is speculation about Jones's sexuality. She has never been married and has no children; much of her act these days is about trying to find a man. "I speak for the lonely bitches," she said. She was born in Memphis and raised in a churchgoing family. At one point, she told me, "It's too bad I'm not gay, 'cause I'd get the flyest bitches."

The opening of her special also allows her to pivot quickly to pantomime, one of her greatest comedic skills. Roger Ailes, the chairman of Fox News, likes to say that an anchor should be interesting even with the TV on mute. Jones has similar thoughts about comedy. "People get hung up on writing smart shit," she said. "To me, it's more about performance. Lucille Ball and Moms Mabley, they had *face*. Before they even said a word, they made you crack up." Paul Feig, the director of "Bridesmaids" and other comedies, compared Jones to Will Ferrell and Chris Farley: "They all have the ability to take a larger-than-life persona and present it in a real, accessible way."

Some self-consciously hip venues foster an arch, hyperverbal style of standup that is sometimes called alt comedy. A Jones show is more like a semi-improvised concert. "She has a presence, when you see her live, that is extremely rare," the comedian Marc Maron said. "And, honestly, it has very little to do with what she's saying. The first time I saw her, I was blown away, and yet I couldn't tell you a single one of her jokes."

Michael Che, a writer and a performer on "Saturday Night Live" who also does standup, told me, "A black audience—we expect our performers to actually *perform*. And Leslie comes out of that tradition." Bernie Mac's first appearance on "Def Comedy Jam," in 1992, became canonical not because of his punch lines but because of a defiant refrain that he directed at the audience: "I ain't scared of you motherfuckers." Che continued, "It's not that Leslie yells and screams and jumps around. It's that she's brutally honest, and she knows how to sell material more convincingly than anyone I can think of. As soon as she walks onstage, you know she's the boss."

Near the end of her Showtime special, Jones takes a deep breath and wipes her face with a small towel printed with the word "Leslie." "This is my favorite part of the show," she says. Then she wades into the audience with a cordless microphone. She crouches over a black woman in the front row who is wearing a shiny headband. "Is that a goddam antenna?" Jones says. "I bet you get all the DirecTV channels." By this point, Jones is practically lying on top of the woman, whispering directly into her ear (and into the microphone). Nearby, audience members laugh so hard that they fall out of their seats. Comedians have always used personalized insults to establish dominance over a crowd; Jones literally gets in her audience's face.

A few rows back, she clambers over several audience members to get to a light-skinned black woman wearing blue contact lenses. "Yeah, I saw your pretty ass, you fuckin' pretty bitch," she says. She asks the woman many variations of the same question: "Are you sucking dick?" The woman, unfazed, shakes her head no. "Do you even like dick?" Jones asks. Again, the woman shakes her head. "Wow," Jones says, wide-eyed. First, she leans toward the woman. Then she backs away. "Don't you bitches be trying to flirt with me," she says. Under her breath, almost to herself, she adds, "I'm not going to Hell, Lord, like that."

Jones surveys her audience before picking targets. She told me, "I can look into a person's eyes for one second and go, 'Don't fuck with him—that's somebody who won't get over what you're about to say. Talk about that other guy instead.'" When I saw her perform at Carolines on Broadway, a comedy club near Times Square, she got only ninety seconds into her set before turning to a white man with a vintage vest and sculpted facial hair. "That goatee is _bull_shit," she said. "And your girl is pissed that you wore that shit." Pause. "Her family fuckin' hates you. It's cool to be in New York with your goatee and your vest. In South Dakota, that's some _bullshit!_" Mocking a goatee is not trenchant observational humor, but Jones's swagger, and the specificity of her language, made the bit feel charged, like a knife trick performed at close range.

She ended the set by singling out a young white woman in the audience and contriving a reason to bury her face in the woman's hair—less a joke than a performance of trampled social mores. As the houselights came up, the woman said, with a dazed smile, "Her sweat is all over me! What just happened?"

On the "Alias Smith and LeRoi" podcast, which was recorded in late 2013, Jones returned often to the topic of sexism. "You guys gotta support us," she said. "You have somebody like the dude from 'S.N.L.' say that black women are not funny? People listen to that shit."

LeRoi corrected her: "He didn't say 'funny.' He said 'ready.'"

They were referring to a recent *TV Guide* article noting that "S.N.L." had just hired six new cast members, five of them white men. The reporter asked Kenan Thompson, one of two black males on the show, why there hadn't been a black female cast member since 2007, when Maya Rudolph left. "In auditions, they just never find ones that are ready," he said.

Soon after the article was published, Thompson was denounced online. (In a reaction video on YouTube, a woman named Dawn Melissa said, "Seriously, get it together. Because there's no joke funnier than the one your mom made when she had you.") Around this time, Jones was at an L.A. comedy club called Inside Jokes, waiting to go onstage, when someone told her about Thompson's comment. "He should come battle me," Jones said. "Give me ten minutes and I'll ruin his life." That night, she had a strong set. After her closing joke, she said, "And they say we ain't funny, huh?," dropped the mike, and walked off to a standing ovation.

On the podcast, Jones said of Thompson's remark, "They're not 'ready'? That's bullshit. 'Cause I know I'm ready."

LeRoi, who has worked as a producer on several comedy shows, said, "'Ready' is not just the can-you-be-on-camera part. When you say 'ready,' it's, like, 'Yeah, bitch, you might have four impersonations, but can you write a fucking sketch? Yes—can you get ten sketches turned down and write an eleventh sketch?'"

Jones tried to speak.

"No, no, no—keep listening," LeRoi said.

She exhaled audibly, but let him finish mansplaining. "I have never said I would want to be on 'Saturday Night Live,'" she responded. "I don't do impressions. I don't know if I could write sketch. So, no, I would never put myself into that circle. Even if they asked me to come and audition, I'd really be, like, 'Eh, I don't know if I can do that.' But I do know women who can." Pounding a hand on the table, she added, "There's motherfuckin' three bitches I can call *right now*, goddammit, that will fill that spot…Just because you don't know them, that don't mean that they don't fucking exist. That's like saying Italy does not exist. Motherfucker, yes, it does. I've been there."

That November, before the podcast with Jones came out, Kerry Washington hosted "Saturday Night Live." During the opening sketch, an announcer apologized for "the number of black women" Washington was being asked to play, "both because Ms. Washington is an actress of considerable range and talent and also because 'S.N.L.' does not currently have a black woman in the cast." It got laughs, but it was a comedic response to a serious problem.

Meanwhile, the show was secretly planning auditions for black women. The producers looked at more than a hundred women, most of them associated with the troika of traditional "S.N.L." feeder troupes: Second City, in Chicago; the Groundlings, in L.A.; and Upright Citizens Brigade, in New York. Jones was not among them.

A dozen women were selected for callback auditions, which took place in December, on the "S.N.L." stage, at 30 Rockefeller Center. A few days before the callbacks, Chris Rock had dinner with Lorne Michaels, the creator and executive producer of "S.N.L." "You should look at Leslie Jones," Rock said. "She's the funniest woman I know." Michaels agreed to give her a chance.

An "S.N.L." audition is notoriously tough: the studio is dark and cavernous, and the producers sit silently near the back. Jones recalled, "I got onstage, took the mike out of the stand, and went, 'Nope. Y'all are gonna have to move up to where I can see you.' And Lorne got his ass up and moved."

She did not attempt impersonations or funny voices; she did her act. She opened with an autobiographical anecdote about being a gangly ten-year-old who longed to be a petite gymnast. "I wrote it in 1987," she told me. "It's the closest I've come to a perfect joke, but it took years before I was talented enough to perform it." The joke is an allegory about defying parental and societal expectations, and it includes two cartwheels. I saw her perform it at Carolines three nights in a row, and it earned an applause break every time.

After the "S.N.L." audition, Jones flew back to L.A. and waited. A week later, she heard the news: the job had gone to Sasheer Zamata, a twenty-seven-year-old improviser and sketch performer at U.C.B., who is Disney-princess pretty. Jones said, "I understood why they gave it to her—she'd been doing sketch for a long time, she's a natural fit—but at the same time I was fucking pissed." The next day, she got a call from Michaels, who asked if she would take a job as a writer. "I went, 'You know I have no fucking idea how to do that, right?'" Still, she accepted the offer and moved to Harlem.

"I'd spent a while in the real world," she told me. "I'd seen some shit." Most of the other "S.N.L." writers had graduated from élite colleges within the past decade. "But one thing I learned—they're not racist. They're just white. They don't know certain things." During her first week on staff, Drake was the host. Some of the writers wanted to do a sketch about "The Glass Menagerie." Jones told me, "Now, I know what it is. I've been to college. But I went, 'People in Compton smoking a joint, they're changing the channel when this comes on. It doesn't matter if Drake is in the sketch. They don't care what a fucking menagerie is. They think it's "The Glass Ménage à Trois."'" The sketch bombed at the dress rehearsal and was cut. "Leslie is a pretty good litmus test for what America will think is funny," Zamata told me.

When Jones met Kenan Thompson, she confronted him about his *TV Guide* interview. "I came at him, like, 'I heard what you said, motherfucker.' He said, 'Come in, close the door, let's talk.'" Thompson told me, "What I said was that the show hadn't found the right people. That was true. And at the end of the day Leslie and Sasheer both got jobs, so I'm happy." These days, Jones said, "Kenan is possibly my best friend on the show."

"S.N.L." often hires good-looking young comics—Chevy Chase, Adam Sandler, Jason Sudeikis—who go on to become leading men in Hollywood. In the eighties, Al Franken, then a producer on the show, recommended a pudgy nebbish named Jon Lovitz. Franken told Michaels, "He's everything we're not looking for in one person." Lovitz was hired, and he became a key cast member for five seasons.

"I tell Leslie all the time, 'You're everything we weren't looking for,'" Michaels said. "When someone's funny, they're funny. She was fully formed as a standup. I knew she'd have to learn the sketch thing, the technique part, but with some people you go, 'Let's just get them in the building.'" After a few months, Jones was added to the cast.

Rock said, "I mentioned her to several managers and agents over the years. Everybody passed. Lorne, because he's the best at what he does, is the one who saw it. I don't think he'd hired a cast member her age in a long time." In fact, Jones was the oldest cast member "S.N.L." had ever hired.

Despite the name, about a quarter of "Saturday Night Live" is pre-taped, usually on the Thursday or Friday before the broadcast. In April, Jones spent a misty Thursday in Bayside, Queens, shooting a "Game of Thrones"-meets-"Boyz n the Hood" sketch that required her to ride a horse for the first time. "I definitely spent the morning in bed with a sore ass," she told me. "I hope people get it. Do kids even know who John Singleton is anymore?"

Late the following night, at 30 Rock, a camera crew filmed a parody movie trailer—a venerable "S.N.L." form that allows for a parade of celebrity impressions. Jones was in costume as Missy Elliott, whose song "Work It" contains a line of rhythmic nonsense: "Ra-ta-ta-ta ta-ta-ta-ta-ta-*ta*." Because the parody trailer was about space aliens, Jones was asked to replace the last "ta" with "space." One of the sketch's writers, Alison Rich, a recent Harvard graduate with blunt-cut bangs, did her best to sell the joke, but Jones gave her a befuddled look. (Later, Colin Jost, an "S.N.L." writer and performer, told me, "When Leslie thinks something is funny, she's extremely generous. When she doesn't think something is funny, you usually know it.")

Jones performed a few takes. She made the line sound better than it was, infusing the word "space" with hip-hop bravado, but she used the wrong number of syllables. Rich stopped her and said, "I think, actually—are there maybe not enough 'ta's?"

Jones said nothing.

Rich, smiling solicitously, played the song on her phone. "You see how many 'ta's there are?" she said.

"You gon' kill me on the 'ta's, bitch?" Jones said, enunciating each word for effect. It could have been the punch line in a standup bit, except that no one seemed to know if she was joking. "Why am I even listening to a white girl on this?" she said.

Rich's smile dimmed, and she looked around anxiously. The only person to meet her eye was Natasha Rothwell, a black writer, who gave Rich a subtle, reassuring nod. The shooting continued. In the final cut of the sketch, Jones delivered a different lyric from the same song.

"I've perfected the art of busting on people," Jones told me later. "That's how comedians show each other love." "Top Five," a 2014 comedy written and directed by Chris Rock, features a long, largely ad-libbed scene in which an ensemble of comedians—including Rock, Jones, and Tracy Morgan—trade admiration-tinged insults. "That was the best scene in the movie, and Leslie was the best part of it," Rock said. "Whenever I showed the movie to other directors—Ben Stiller, P. T. Anderson, Judd Apatow—their first reaction was always pointing at Leslie and going, 'Who is *that*?'" Apatow was so impressed that he and Amy Schumer created a part for Jones in "Trainwreck." When Schumer's character finds herself on a stopped subway train, she turns to Jones for help. "Do I look like I work for M.T.A.?" Jones says, her eyes lighting up with contempt. "What, I got MetroCards in my fucking purse now?"

Jones's ability to wring laughs from almost nothing—a raised eyebrow, a drawn-out pause—allows her to transmute a screenwriter's B-minus joke into an A. But, in her standup, this gift has an unfortunate consequence: she is so reliably successful with sets that consist of crowd work and time-tested jokes that she feels little pressure to write new material, like a chef who can make a gourmet meal out of whatever happens to be in the fridge. "As Leslie gets really famous, it'll be harder for her to repeat stuff," Rock said. "Until then, you do what works."

One night, I had dinner with Jones at Buddakan, an Asian-fusion restaurant in Chelsea that looks like it could serve as a set for "The King and I." "The dan-dan noodles here are fucking insane," she said. After dinner, dessert, and a couple of rounds of Patrón, we took a cab to the Comedy Cellar, in Greenwich Village. The booker, Estee Adoram, greeted Jones with a hug and implored her to perform, but she preferred to socialize. She walked past the comedian Judah

Friedlander—he grabbed her arm and said, "Keep kicking ass"—and took a seat next to Larry Wilmore. At one point, the reactionary pundit Ann Coulter stopped by their table. Wilmore was courteous, but Jones leaned across the table and stage-whispered, "What the fuck is this frightening bitch doing here?" Coulter's face froze in a rictus, and she soon backed away from the table.

We then took a taxi to the Comic Strip, on the Upper East Side, where a friend of Jones's was hosting a standup show. On the way, she predicted, "Either he's gonna make me perform or he's gonna make me smoke weed with him." The friend, standing outside the club between sets, saw Jones getting out of the cab and immediately started ribbing her: "I've been texting you. You too famous for me now?" They slipped away and returned a few minutes later, looking more relaxed. In the lobby, someone gestured at a TV mounted near the ceiling. It was a rerun of "S.N.L." Jones was performing on the show's fake-news segment, "Weekend Update." Her mouth was an emotional roulette wheel: withering glower, self-assured sneer, toothy smile. The TV was inaudible, and a bartender scrambled for a remote, but people in the lobby were already laughing.

One Tuesday night in May, Jones sat in her "S.N.L." office, talking on the phone with her accountant. On Tuesday nights, the host walks from office to office, listening as writers and cast members propose ideas for sketches; the most promising proposals become scripts, which are performed at a table read the next day. That week's host, Louis C.K., could be heard across the hall, laughing generously behind a closed door.

Jones hung up. "I have a couple of ideas I might try on Louis," she said. "There's one called 'Jungle Fever,' where he's never had sex with a black girl and she's never had sex with a white guy, and they're asking each other questions. But Kenan said, 'You gotta stop making everything about race, because sometimes it's scary to people.' So I'm figuring out how to rewrite it."

Jay Pharoah, who became a cast member in 2010, at the age of twenty-three, stopped by Jones's office. "Remember the guy who tries to steal intangible stuff?" he said, referring to an old sketch idea.

"'Yo, let me get that confidence off you,'" Jones said.

"'Let me get your appetite, son. I like the way you be eating things,'" Pharoah said.

"That's funny, Jay," Jones said. "You should write that, and put me in it."

Pharoah continued down the hall. "He's been messing around with that all year, but he never sits down and writes it," Jones said. "I love Jay to death, but he's like a toddler, man."

Later that night, Pharoah and a writer, Mikey Day, put together a draft of the sketch. It got laughs at the table read, and the producers decided to pre-tape it. So on Friday morning C.K., Pharoah, Jones, and four other cast members gathered at a warehouse in an industrial part of Brooklyn. The sketch was set at a rooftop cookout, and the warehouse's roof was crammed with camera equipment and about fifty extras. Jones, wearing a red wig and hoop earrings, stood behind a grill, flipping burgers. Every few takes, a P.A. collected them and fed them to the crew.

Pharoah wore a red Yankees cap and a cornrow wig. "Yo, lemme get that confident smile off you," he said. The other actors, playing his neighbors, rolled their eyes.

While the crew reset the cameras, Jones went inside to rest. She was in a bad mood. "I know this is a good job, but, honestly, it's brutal sometimes," she said. She had woken up before five, to get picked up in Harlem and driven to Brooklyn. "I sometimes wonder what this would have been like if I was in my twenties," she said. "Right now, I can't wait for Sunday, so I can fall the fuck asleep."

Zamata and Bobby Moynihan, another cast member, napped on leather couches nearby; C.K. and Thompson groggily refilled their coffee cups. Only Pharoah was indefatigable. He stayed on the roof, keeping the extras entertained. (To a white couple: "Let me get that comfort with being two of the only Caucasians here off you.")

The cast ran through the sketch a few more times. Between takes, C.K. pulled Pharoah and Thompson aside and said, "My voice in this—I'm not sounding, like, too black, am I?"

"You're good," Thompson said.

"Because we're also gonna do the Sprint-store thing," C.K. said. In that sketch, he played a cell-phone salesman who switched into exaggerated street slang whenever his boss, played by Jones, was in the room. "I'm just imagining articles coming out on Sunday morning about me doing racist voices."

"Just be funny, man," Thompson said. "Don't worry about the blog stuff." This led to a riff about how various iconic comedians would have responded to online scrutiny. (Pharoah, doing a Richard Pryor impression: "The thing that be botherin' me about Bossip is . . .") When standups perform, their jokes include exposition, to keep the audience from getting lost; but comedians among their own kind are like chess players executing a quick flurry of moves.

Jones, flipping burgers, continued to sulk. Between takes, Pharoah turned to her and said, "Les, you look like you're about to slice somebody's head off with that spatula."

"I am," she said.

"Yo, let me get that ability to stay angry in front of all these people that's paying you," Pharoah said.

C.K. joined in: "Let me get that unalterable edge of anger impervious to success off you."

Pharoah and C.K. were, in their way, expressing concern, and Jones seemed appreciative. Nevertheless, she played up her frustration for laughs. "I've been standing here all day inhaling smoke from this stank-ass grill," she said. Pharoah and C.K. smiled, giving her space to keep going. "I hate the sun on my face," she continued. "I hate this horrible-ass neighborhood." She peered out over the rooftop, selecting objects for ridicule. "I hate these dingy-ass auto shops. I hate this nasty graffiti everywhere. Can't even get it together to have some nice graffiti."

Gradually, she lightened up. In the next take, C.K. slipped into a stilted locution. Jones grinned and said, "Did someone tell you this was Shakespeare?"

Like many standups, Jones generates most of her material in performance, discovering funny phrases and gestures onstage. When she became a writer for "S.N.L.," she barely knew how to use a word-processing program. "I'm old school," she said. "I wouldn't even buy a cell phone until a few years ago." Zamata told me, "I remember sitting in Leslie's office and watching her go, 'How do I get the ideas out of my head and onto the page?'"

"My sense was that, before she came here, she wasn't a regular viewer," Lorne Michaels said. Jones confirmed this. "I watched 'S.N.L.' the way most black people watched it: I watched Eddie. Then I stopped."

During her first few months as a writer, Jones submitted a variety of sketches, most of them adapted from her act, including one in which Lena Dunham played Jesus' personal assistant, and one about the types of women in a night-club posse (the designated driver, the alcoholic, the slut). None made it to air. "As a comedian, it's, like, 'I'm bombing. What am I doing wrong?'" she said. "At least they still paid me."

It was her first regular paycheck. When Jones was born, her father, an electrical engineer, worked as a studio technician at WDIA, in Memphis, which is often called "the nation's first all-black radio station." In 1979, Stevie Wonder bought KJLH, an R. & B. station with offices in Compton, and hired Jones's father. The family moved to Lynwood, which borders Compton to the north.

After a while, Jones's father left KJLH and the family moved to a rougher part of Lynwood. "I remember my brother and them always having to run home from school, so the gangsters wouldn't beat them up," Jones said. "It was easier for me. People would see me walking and be, like, 'You're going straight home, right?' I was a basketball player, and they knew I was serious about success, not getting pregnant. I didn't know what I was gonna be yet, but I knew I was gonna get the fuck out of there." Crack came to Lynwood in the eighties. "That fucked everybody up. My brother started selling, and you'd see the most unexpected people coming to the window. The dude I used to have a crush on—he's a crackhead now? My high-school teacher—it got her, too?"

She went to Chapman University, a Christian college in Orange County, on a basketball scholarship. College, she said, was her "hippie phase": "no shoes, no underwear, sex with strange people—good times." Before her sophomore year, her basketball coach got a job at Colorado State, and Jones transferred there. "They weren't really my people in Colorado," she said. "A lot of white girls with ponytails." A friend signed her up for a comedy competition, and Jones won without having prepared an act. "I went, 'Fuck college, fuck basketball, I'm funny,' and I dropped out. The next week, I was back in California." She was nineteen.

A month later, she was on a bill with Jamie Foxx, who was then a touring comic. "I was doing jokes about white churches versus black churches, and imitating my uncle's stutter. I was terrible." The audience booed her off the stage. Then Foxx performed. "It was, like, a religious feeling, watching him," Jones said. "I had never seen a real comedian before, at least not in person."

After the show, Foxx took her to a Fatburger. "You could be good, but you don't have shit to talk about yet," he told her. "You need to get your heart broken, have some bad jobs—live life for a while."

Jones took this advice so seriously that she did not perform for six years. She worked as a cook, a cashier, and a waitress; she sold perfume at a mall; she became a justice of the peace and officiated at weddings. When she started performing again, in the mid-nineties, she kept working part time; a spot on BET's "ComicView" paid only a hundred and fifty dollars. "I was the funniest waitress Roscoe's Chicken and Waffles ever had," she said. "Customers would be, like, 'Didn't I just see you on BET?' I'd be, like, 'Yep. Breast and a wing or leg and a thigh?'" She and her long-term boyfriend broke up, which renewed her drive to make money, and also inspired jokes about the single woman's plight. ("I be walking up to men in the club, like, 'Can you lend me some dick till I get on my feet?'") By her estimation, it took ten years before she found her comedic voice.

One night, after a bad date, she came home alone, smoked a joint, and turned on the TV. She told me, "A slave movie was on and, out of bitterness, this ridiculous idea popped into my head: during slave times, I never would have been single." She wrote a joke based on the premise, but felt it was too personal to perform. "It wasn't a commentary on slavery," she said. "It was about my pain—about how hard it is, as a black woman, to get black dudes to date you. The first time I told it"—to a mostly black audience in L.A.—"it massacred to the point where I went, 'There's something real here.' " She told it several more times, in clubs and on TV.

For her first appearance on "S.N.L.," she repeated the joke, almost unchanged, from behind the "Weekend Update" desk. "I do not want to be a slave," she said. "Hell, I don't like working for you white people right now, and y'all *pay* me. I'm just saying . . . I would be the No. 1 Slave Draft Pick. All of the plantations would want me. I'd be on television, like LeBron, announcing which plantation I was gonna go to. I would be, like, 'I would like to take my talents to South Carolina.'" The joke sparked outrage online—Jamilah Lemieux, in *Ebony*, called it "a grossly offensive skit about slave rape"—but it also demonstrated Jones's obvious talent as a performer. "Live from New York!," a recent documentary about "S.N.L.," devoted several minutes to the joke, the backlash, and the backlash to the backlash, including a comment from Jones: "Not only did I take something of pain and make it funny, motherfucker—it was brilliant."

The next time Jones appeared on "Weekend Update," four months later, the director Paul Feig was watching at home. "I don't normally like when actors are big and loud," he said. "But she was able to do it with this grounded, relatable sort of energy. Before her segment was over, I said to my wife, 'I think she's one of our ghostbusters.'"

Feig and I were speaking in a hangarlike space in Norwood, Massachusetts, outside Boston. It was September—the sixty-ninth day of a seventy-two-day shoot. Feig's reboot of "Ghostbusters," to be released next summer, will star Melissa McCarthy, Kristen Wiig, Kate McKinnon, and Jones. In it—unlike in "Trainwreck"—Jones will play an M.T.A. employee. The movie was still officially untitled, but on-set swag was labelled "Ghostbusters 2016."

Most of the on-location filming took place on the streets of Boston, camouflaged as New York. Interior shots were captured in the Norwood building, a former Reebok warehouse, which contained green screens and a handful of lifelike sets: a Chinese restaurant's colorful façade, a two-story Art Deco hotel lobby. Jones's character, Patty Tolan, is a station agent turned—spoiler alert—ghostbuster.

The original movie and its sequel featured four ghostbusters, but the substantive roles went to the three white stars—Dan Aykroyd, Harold Ramis, and Bill Murray. Ernie Hudson, an African-American graduate of the Yale School of Drama, played Winston Zeddemore, the Zeppo of the bunch. Hudson recently wrote in *Entertainment Weekly* that, when he first read the script, "It was a bigger part, and Winston was there all the way through the movie." In the final script, the part had eroded.

Feig said that, compared with Winston, "Patty's a bigger part. I definitely wanted four equal team members." Jones told me, "He made it completely equal. It was like a superhero team, where each one has her own skill but can't use it without the others."

Before casting Jones, Feig, who wears bespoke suits and carries a walking stick, invited her for a drink at the St. Regis Hotel, in New York. "It was pleasant at first, but sort of formal," he said. "Then I started asking her about standup. All of a sudden, her personality came through." Feig did standup in the eighties, and it did not surprise him that Jones hadn't "crossed over" earlier: "You get used to seeing that, unfortunately." Before meeting Feig, Jones had appeared in about a dozen movies, often as an unnamed character (Night Nurse; Boss Lady). Many went straight to video. Her first starring role will be in "Ghostbusters 2016," whose budget is rumored to exceed a hundred and fifty million dollars.

I hadn't seen Jones in several weeks, and when I found her in her trailer she greeted me with "You can tell I lost weight, right?" She cheerfully humble-bragged about stunts she had been asked to do: "These motherfuckers don't understand I'm a comedian. They've got me doing all this Van Damme shit." The previous day, she told me, she had used one of her "Ghostbusters" checks to pay off the last of her credit-card loans. For the first time in her adult life, she was debt-free.

She texted several times a minute with McKinnon, who had returned to New York the previous night. They knew each other from "S.N.L.," where McKinnon is also a cast member, but their friendship had deepened on the set. "She had me walking everywhere—all around Boston, looking at old-fashioned doors and shit," Jones said. "I hated it at first, but then I really got into it." Though McKinnon had a girlfriend, she and Jones referred to each other as "my movie wife," "my movie husband," or simply "my bitch." "I learned a lot from watching her timing," Jones said. "She is a beast."

When her makeup and hair were in place, Jones walked through the warehouse to a replica of a New York subway station, with working turnstiles and dirt-streaked tile walls. She entered a fake ticket booth and inspected the props on the desk, which included a paperback about the Constitutional Convention. The cover depicted several Founding Fathers in tricornes. "Paul, does this look like some shit I would read?" she said. "Do you see any black people on this cover, Paul?"

Feig chuckled, sat behind a monitor, and called, "Action!" Neil Casey, a U.C.B. alumnus who plays the movie's villain, walked up to the booth.

"Can I help you?" Jones said, impatiently.

"Leslie, keep it positive at first," Feig said. "That way, he gets crazier and crazier, and you have somewhere to go."

"Cool," Jones said. In the next take, she started out with a dimpled smile, which melted away as Casey grew more menacing.

"Cut," Feig said. "Much better."

Jones, holding up the book, said, "Actually, I did find a black dude in here."

They walked across the warehouse to shoot another scene, set at a concert. In a gag reminiscent of one in "School of Rock," Jones's character had attempted to stage-dive, but the crowd had failed to catch her. In this shot, fans helped her to her feet. The line in the script was "I can't believe you let me fall!"

"Play around," Feig said. "We'll do a few."

"What is wrong with y'all? Pick my ass up!"

"Good. Again."

"I don't know if that was a race thing or a lady thing, but I'm mad as hell."

"Nice. Give me one last one—dealer's choice."

"Oh, you ain't gonna be able to use my dealer's choice," Jones said.

"Try me," Feig said.

Action. "I can't believe you let a bitch fall like that!" she said to one of the men. "I was gonna go out with you, too."

Feig laughed. When Jones was done with all her scenes, he led her toward the middle of the warehouse, where a group formed a circle around her.

"Folks, this is a Boston wrap on the lovely Ms. Leslie Jones," he said. Everyone clapped. Someone handed her flowers. Wiig stepped into the circle, hugged Jones, and said, "You did it, girl!," while doing a self-conscious wiggle dance. It all seemed a bit forced, but as Jones walked away from the set I noticed that she was crying.

In her trailer, she sat quietly for a moment, waiting for a hairdresser to remove her wig. "I think I'm scared to leave this place," she said. It took a long time to remove the wig—it was glued to her hairline—and we kept talking as the sun went down outside her trailer window. She was in a reflective mood. Though she still has extended family in Memphis, her mother, father, and brother all died within the past few years. "When death touches you that close, you say to yourself, 'It's time to start liking who the fuck you are,'" she said. "I'm not perfect, but I'm starting to get comfortable, like a sweater you want to wear all the time."

Her head was tilted back in a washbowl, her eyes closed, but her voice still controlled the room. "I'm glad this whole success thing is happening now," she said. "I can't even imagine a twenty-three-year-old Leslie in this position. They would have kicked me off the set after two days. I would have fucked half the dudes in the crew." She sat up and wrapped a towel around her head. "I was a less confident person back then. And damn sure not as funny."

Post-Princess Models of Gender: The New Man in Disney/Pixar

Ken Gillam and Shannon R. Wooden

Lisping over the Steve McQueen allusion in Pixar's *Cars* (2006), our two-year-old son, Oscar, inadvertently directed us to the definition(s) of masculinity that might be embedded in a children's animated film about NASCAR. The film overtly praises the "good woman" proverbially behind every successful man: The champion car, voiced by Richard Petty, tells his wife, "I wouldn't be nothin' without you, honey." But gender in this twenty-first-century bildungsroman is rather more complex, and Oscar's mispronunciation held the first clue. To him, a member of the film's target audience, the character closing in on the title long held by "The King" is not "Lightning McQueen" but "Lightning the queen"; his chief rival, the always-a-bridesmaid runner-up "Chick" Hicks.

Does this nominal feminizing of male also-rans (and the simultaneous gendering of success) constitute a meaningful pattern? Piqued, we began examining the construction of masculinity in major feature films released by Disney's Pixar studios over the past thirteen years. Indeed, as we argue here, Pixar consistently promotes a new model of masculinity, one that matures into acceptance of its more traditionally "feminine" aspects.

Cultural critics have long been interested in Disney's cinematic products, but the gender critics examining the texts most enthusiastically gobbled up by the under-six set have so far generally focused on their retrograde representations of women. As Elizabeth Bell argues, the animated Disney features through *Beauty and the Beast* feature a "teenaged heroine at the idealized height of puberty's graceful promenade ... [f]emale wickedness ... rendered as middle-aged beauty at its peak of sexuality and authority ... and [f]eminine sacrifice and nurturing ... drawn in pear-shaped, old women past menopause" (108). Some have noted the models of masculinity in the classic animated films, primarily the contrast between the ubermacho Gaston and the sensitive, misunderstood Beast in *Beauty and the Beast*,[1] but the male protagonist of the animated classics, at least through *The Little Mermaid*, remains largely uninterrogated.[2] For most of the early films, this critical omission seems generally appropriate, the various versions of Prince Charming being often too two-dimensional to do more than inadvertently shape the definition of the protagonists' femininity. But if the

---

1. See Susan Jeffords, "The Curse of Masculinity: Disney's *Beauty and the Beast*" for an excellent analysis of that plot's developing the cruel Beast into a man who can love and be loved in return: "Will he be able to overcome his beastly temper and terrorizing attitude in order to learn to love?" (168). But even in this film, she argues, the Beast's development is dependent on "other people, especially women," whose job it is to tutor him into the new model of masculinity, the "New Man" (169, 170).

2. Two articles demand that we qualify this claim. Indirectly, they support the point of this essay by demonstrating a midcentury Disney model of what we call "alpha" masculinity. David Payne's "Bambi" parallels that film's coming-of-age plot, ostensibly representing a "natural" world, with the military mindset of the 1940s against which the film was drawn. Similarly, Claudia Card, in "Pinocchio," claims that the Disneyfied version of the nineteenth-century Carlo Collodi tale replaces the original's model of bravery and honesty with "a macho exercise in heroism [...and] avoid[ing] humiliation" (66–67).

feminist thought that has shaped our cultural texts for three decades now has been somewhat disappointing in its ability to actually rewrite the princess trope (the spunkiest of the "princesses," Ariel, Belle, Jasmine, and, arguably, even Mulan, remain thin, beautiful, kind, obedient or punished for disobedience, and headed for the altar), it has been surprisingly effective in rewriting the type of masculine power promoted by Disney's products.[3]

Disney's new face, Pixar studios, has released nine films—*Toy Story* (1995) and *Toy Story 2* (1999); *A Bug's Life* (1998); *Finding Nemo* (2003); *Monsters, Inc.* (2001); *The Incredibles* (2004); *Cars* (2006); *Ratatouille* (2007); and now *WALL·E* (2008)—all of which feature interesting male figures in leading positions. Unlike many of the princesses, who remain relatively static even through their own adventures, these male leads are actual protagonists; their characters develop and change over the course of the film, rendering the plot. Ultimately these various developing characters—particularly Buzz and Woody from *Toy Story*, Mr. Incredible from *The Incredibles*, and Lightning McQueen from *Cars*—experience a common narrative trajectory, culminating in a common "New Man" model:[4] they all strive for an alpha-male identity; they face emasculating failures; they find themselves, in large part, through what Eve Sedgwick refers to as "homosocial desire" and a triangulation of this desire with a feminized object (and/or a set of "feminine" values); and, finally, they achieve (and teach) a kinder, gentler understanding of what it means to be a man.

Emasculation of the Alpha Male

A working definition of *alpha male* may be unnecessary; although more traditionally associated with the animal kingdom than the Magic Kingdom, it familiarly evokes ideas of dominance, leadership, and power in human social organizations as well. The phrase "alpha male" may stand for all things stereotypically patriarchal: unquestioned authority, physical power and social dominance, competitiveness for positions of status and leadership, lack of visible or shared emotion, social isolation. An alpha male, like Vann in *Cars*, does not ask for directions; like Doc Hudson in the same film, he does not talk about his feelings. The alpha male's stresses, like Buzz Lightyear's, come from his need to save the galaxy; his strength comes from faith in his ability to do so. These models have worked in Disney for decades. The worst storm at sea is no match for *The Little Mermaid*'s uncomplicated Prince Eric—indeed, any charming prince need only

3. Outside the animated classics, critics have noted a trend toward a postfeminist masculinity—one characterized by emotional wellness, sensitivity to family, and a conscious rejection of the most alpha male values—in Disney-produced films of the 1980s and 1990s. Jeffords gives a sensible account of the changing male lead in films ranging from *Kindergarten Cop* to *Terminator 2*.

4. In Disney criticism, the phrase "New Man" seems to belong to Susan Jeffords's 1995 essay on *Beauty and the Beast*, but it is slowly coming into vogue for describing other postfeminist trends in masculine identity. In popular culture, see Richard Collier's "The New Man: Fact or Fad?" online in *Achilles Heel: The Radical Men's Magazine* 14 (Winter 1992/1993). http://www.achillesheel.freeuk.com/article14_9. html. For a literary-historical account, see *Writing Men: Literary Masculinities from Frankenstein to the New Man* by Berthold Schoene-Harwood (Columbia UP, 2000).

ride in on his steed to save his respective princess. But the postfeminist world is a different place for men, and the post-princess Pixar is a different place for male protagonists.

Newsweek recently described the alpha male's new cinematic and television rival, the "beta male": "The testosterone-pumped, muscle-bound Hollywood hero is rapidly deflating.... Taking his place is a new kind of leading man, the kind who's just as happy following as leading, or never getting off the sofa" (Yabroff 64). Indeed, as Susan Jeffords points out, at least since *Beauty and the Beast*, Disney has resisted (even ridiculed) the machismo once de rigueur for leading men (170). Disney cinema, one of the most effective teaching tools America offers its children, is not yet converting its model male protagonist all the way into a slacker, but the New Man model is quite clearly emerging.

Cars, Toy Story, and *The Incredibles* present their protagonists as unambiguously alpha in the opening moments of the films. Although Lightning McQueen may be an as-yet incompletely realized alpha when *Cars* begins, not having yet achieved the "King" status of his most successful rival, his ambition and fierce competitiveness still clearly valorize the alpha-male model: "Speed. I am speed... I eat losers for breakfast," he chants as a prerace mantra. He heroically comes from behind to tie the championship race, distinguishing himself by his physical power and ability, characteristics that catapult him toward the exclusively male culture of sports superstars. The fantasies of his life he indulges after winning the coveted Piston Cup even include flocks of female cars forming a worshipful harem around him. But the film soon diminishes the appeal of this alpha model. Within a few moments of the race's conclusion, we see some of Lightning's less positive macho traits; his inability to name any friends, for example, reveals both his isolation and attempts at emotional stoicism. Lightning McQueen is hardly an unemotional character, as can be seen when he prematurely jumps onto the stage to accept what he assumes to be his victory. For this happy emotional outburst, however, he is immediately disciplined by a snide comment from Chick. From this point until much later in the film, the only emotions he displays are those of frustration and anger.

Toy Story's Buzz Lightyear and Sheriff Woody similarly base their worth on a masculine model of competition and power, desiring not only to be the "favorite toy" of their owner, Andy, but to possess the admiration of and authority over the other toys in the playroom. Woody is a natural leader, and his position represents both paternalistic care and patriarchal dominance. In an opening scene, he calls and conducts a "staff meeting" that highlights his unambiguously dominant position in the toy community. Encouraging the toys to pair up so that no one will be lost in the family's impending move, he commands: "A moving buddy. If you don't have one, GET ONE." Buzz's alpha identity comes from a more exalted source than social governance—namely, his belief that he is the one "space ranger" with the power and knowledge needed to save the galaxy; it seems merely natural, then, that the other toys would look up to him, admire his strength, and follow his orders. But as with Lightning McQueen, these depictions of masculine power are soon undercut. Buzz's mere presence exposes Woody's strength as fragile, artificial, even arbitrary, and his "friends," apparently having been drawn to his authority rather than his character, are fair-weather at best. Buzz's authority rings hollow from the very beginning, and his refusal to believe in his own "toy-ness" is at best silly and at worst dangerous. Like Lightning, Buzz's and Woody's most commonly expressed emotions are anger and frustration, not sadness (Woody's, at having been "replaced") or fear (Buzz's, at having "crash-landed on a strange planet") or even wistful fondness (Woody's, at the loss of Slink's, Bo Peep's, and Rex's loyalty). Once again, the alpha-male position is depicted as fraudulent, precarious, lonely, and devoid of emotional depth.

An old-school superhero, Mr. Incredible opens *The Incredibles* by display-ing the tremendous physical strength that enables him to stop speeding trains, crash through buildings, and keep the city safe from criminals. But he too suffers from the emotional isolation of the alpha male. Stopping on the way to his own wedding to interrupt a crime in progress, he is very nearly late to the service, showing up only to say the "I dos." Like his car and toy counterparts, he com-municates primarily through verbal assertions of power—angrily dismissing Buddy, his meddlesome aspiring sidekick; bantering with Elastigirl over who gets the pickpocket—and limits to anger and frustration the emotions appar-ently available to men.

Fraught as it may seem, the alpha position is even more fleeting: In none of these Pixar films does the male protagonist's dominance last long. After Light-ning ties, rather than wins, the race and ignores the King's friendly advice to find and trust a good team with which to work, he browbeats his faithful semi, Mack, and ends up lost in "hillbilly hell," a small town off the beaten path of the interstate. His uncontrolled physical might destroys the road, and the resultant legal responsibility—community service—keeps him far from his Piston Cup goals. When Buzz appears as a gift for Andy's birthday, he easily unseats Woody both as Andy's favorite and as the toy community's leader. When Buzz becomes broken, failing to save himself from the clutches of the evil neighbor, Sid, he too must learn a hard lesson about his limited power, his diminished status, and his own relative insignificance in the universe. Mr. Incredible is perhaps most obviously disempowered: Despite his superheroic feats, Mr. Incredible has been unable to keep the city safe from his own clumsy brute force. After a series of lawsuits against "the Supers," who accidentally leave various types of small-time mayhem in their wake, they are all driven underground, into a sort of witness protection program. To add insult to injury, Mr. Incredible's diminutive boss fires him from his job handling insurance claims, and his wife, the former Elastigirl, assumes the "pants" of the family.

Most of these events occur within the first few minutes of the characters' respective films. Only Buzz's downfall happens in the second half. The alpha-male model is thus not only present and challenged in the films but also is, in fact, the very structure on which the plots unfold. Each of these films is about being a man, and they begin with an out dated, two-dimensional alpha prototype to expose its failings and to ridicule its logical extensions: the devastation and humiliation of being defeated in competition, the wrath generated by power unchecked, the paralyzing alienation and fear inherent in being lonely at the top. As these characters begin the film in (or seeking) the tenuous alpha position among fellow characters, each of them is also stripped of this identity—dramatically emasculated—so that he may learn, reform, and emerge again with a different, and arguably more feminine, self-concept.

"Emasculated" is not too strong a term for what happens to these male protagonists; the decline of the alpha-male model is gender coded in all the films. For his community service punishment, Lightning is chained to the giant, snorting, tarspitting "Bessie" and ordered to repair the damage he has wrought. His own "horsepower" (as Sally cheerfully points out) is used against him when literally put in the service of a nominally feminized figure valued for the more "feminine" orientation of service to the community. If being under the thumb of this humongous "woman" is not emasculating enough, Mater, who sees such subordination to Bessie as a potentially pleasurable thing, names the price, saying, "I'd give my left two lug nuts for something like that!"

Mr. Incredible's downfall is most clearly marked as gendered by his responses to it. As his wife's domestic power and enthusiasm grow increasingly unbearable, and his children's behavior more and more out of his control, he surreptitiously turns to the mysterious, gorgeous "Mirage," who gives him what he needs to feel like a man: super hero work. Overtly depicting her as the "other woman," the film requires Elastigirl to intercept a suggestive-sounding phone call, and to trap her husband in a lie, to be able to work toward healing his decimated masculinity.

In *Toy Story*, the emasculation of the alpha male is the most overt, and arguably the most comic. From the beginning, power is constructed in terms conspicuously gender coded, at least for adult viewers: As they watch the incoming birthday presents, the toys agonize at their sheer size, the longest and most phallic-shaped one striking true fear (and admiration?) into the hearts of the spectators. When Buzz threatens Woody, one toy explains to another that he has "laser envy." Buzz's moment of truth, after seeing himself on Sid's father's television, is the most clearly gendered of all. Realizing for the first time that Woody is right, he is a "toy," he defiantly attempts to fly anyway, landing sprawled on the floor with a broken arm. Sid's little sister promptly finds him, dresses him in a pink apron and hat, and installs him as "Mrs. Nesbit" at her tea party. When Woody tries to wrest him from his despair, Buzz wails, "Don't you get it? I AM MRS. NESBIT. But does the hat look good? Oh, tell me the hat looks good!" Woody's "rock bottom" moment finds him trapped under an overturned milk crate, forcing him to ask Buzz for help and to admit that he "doesn't stand a chance" against Buzz in the contest for Andy's affection, which constitutes "everything that is important to me." He is not figured into a woman, like Buzz is, or subordinated to a woman, like Lightning is, or forced to seek a woman's affirmation of his macho self, like Mr. Incredible is, but he does have to acknowledge his own feminine values, from his need for communal support to his deep, abiding (and, later, maternal) love of a boy. This "feminine" stamp is characteristic of the New Man model toward which these characters narratively journey.

Homosociality, Intimacy, and Emotion

Regarding the "love of a boy," the "mistress" tempting Mr. Incredible away from his wife and family is not Mirage at all but Buddy, the boy he jilted in the opening scenes of the film (whose last name, Pine, further conveys the unrequited nature of their relationship). Privileging his alpha-male emotional isolation, but adored by his wannabe sidekick, Mr. Incredible vehemently protects his desire to "work alone." After spending the next years nursing his rejection and refining his arsenal, Buddy eventually retaliates against Mr. Incredible for rebuffing his advances. Such a model of homosocial tutelage as Buddy proposes at the beginning of the film certainly evokes an ancient (and homosexual) model of masculine identity; Mr. Incredible's rejection quickly and decisively replaces it with a heteronormative one, further supported by Elastigirl's marrying and Mirage's attracting the macho superhero.[5] But it is equally true that the recovery of Mr. Incredible's masculine identity happens primarily through his (albeit antagonistic) relationship with Buddy, suggesting that Eve Sedgwick's notion of a homosocial continuum is more appropriate to an analysis of the film's gender attitudes than speculations about its reactionary heteronormativity, even homophobia.

Same-sex (male) bonds—to temporarily avoid the more loaded term *desire*—are obviously important to each of these films. In fact, in all three, male/male relationships emerge that move the fallen alphas forward in their journeys toward a new masculinity. In each case, the male lead's first and/or primary intimacy—his most immediate transformative relationship—is with one or more male characters. Even before discovering Buddy as his nemesis, Mr. Incredible secretly pairs up with his old pal Frozone, and the two step out on their wives to continue superheroing on the sly; Buddy and Frozone are each, in their ways, more influential on Mr. Incredible's sense of self than his wife or children are. Although Lightning falls in love with Sally and her future vision of Radiator Springs, his almost accidentally having befriended the hapless, warm Mater

---

5. Critics have described the superhero within some framework of queer theory since the 1950s, when Dr. Fredric Wertham's *Seduction of the Innocent* claimed that Batman and Robin were gay (Ameron Ltd, 1954). See Rob Lendrum's "Queering Super-Manhood: Superhero Masculinity, Camp, and Public Relations as a Textual Framework" (*International Journal of Comic Art* 7.1 [2005]: 287–303) and Valerie Palmer-Mehtan and Kellie Hay's "A Superhero for Gays? Gay Masculinity and Green Lantern" (*Journal of American Culture* 28.4 [2005]: 390–404), among myriad nonscholarly pop-cultural sources.

catalyzes more foundational lessons about the responsibilities of friendship—demanding honesty, sensitivity, and care—than the smell-the-roses lesson Sally represents. He also ends up being mentored and taught a comparable lesson about caring for others by Doc Hudson, who even more explicitly encourages him to resist the alpha path of the Piston Cup world by relating his experiences of being used and then rejected. Woody and Buzz, as rivals-cum-allies, discover the necessary truths about their masculine strength only as they discover how much they need one another. Sedgwick further describes the ways in which the homosocial bond is negotiated through a triangulation of desire; that is, the intimacy emerging "between men" is constructed through an overt and shared desire for a feminized object. Unlike homosocial relationships between women—that is, "the continuum between 'women loving women' and 'women promoting the interests of women'"—male homosocial identity is necessarily homophobic in patriarchal systems, which are structurally homophobic (3). This means the same-sex relationship demands social opportunities for a man to insist on, or prove, his heterosexuality. Citing Rene Girard's *Deceit, Desire, and the Novel*, Sedgwick argues that "in any erotic rivalry, the bond that links the two rivals is as intense and potent as the bond that links either of the rivals to the beloved" (21); women are ultimately symbolically exchangeable "for the primary purpose of cementing the bonds of men with men" (26).

This triangulation of male desire can be seen in *Cars* and *Toy Story* particularly, where the homosocial relationship rather obviously shares a desire for a feminized third. Buzz and Woody compete first, momentarily, for the affection of Bo Peep, who is surprisingly sexualized for a children's movie (purring to Woody an offer to "get someone else to watch the sheep tonight," then rapidly choosing Buzz as her "moving buddy" after his "flying" display). More importantly, they battle for the affection of Andy—a male child alternately depicted as maternal (it is his responsibility to get his baby sister out of her crib) and in need of male protection (Woody exhorts Buzz to "take care of Andy for me!").[6] *Cars* also features a sexualized romantic heroine; less coquettish than Bo Peep, Sally still fumbles over an invitation to spend the night "not with me, but . . ." in the motel she owns. One of Lightning and Mater's moments of "bonding" happens when Mater confronts Lightning, stating his affection for Sally and sharing a parallel story of heterosexual desire. The more principal objects of desire in *Cars*, however, are the (arguably) feminized "Piston Cup" and the Dinoco sponsorship. The sponsor itself is established in romantic terms: With Lightning stuck in Radiator Springs, his agent says Dinoco has had to "woo" Chick instead. Tia and Mia, Lightning's "biggest fans," who transfer their affection to Chick during his absence, offer

6. Interestingly, Andy and *Toy Story* in general are apparently without (human) male role models. The only father present in the film at all is Sid's, sleeping in front of the television in the middle of the day. Andy's is absent at a dinner out, during a move, and on the following Christmas morning. Andy himself, at play, imagines splintering a nuclear family: when he makes Sheriff Woody catch One-Eyed Black Bart in a criminal act, he says, "Say goodbye to the wife and tater tots . . . you're going to jail."

viewers an even less subtly gendered goal, and Chick uses this to taunt Lightning. It is in the pursuit of these objects, and in competition with Chick and the King, that Lightning first defines himself as a man; the Piston Cup also becomes the object around which he and Doc discover their relationship to one another.

The New Man

With the strength afforded by these homosocial intimacies, the male characters triumph over their respective plots, demonstrating the desirable modifications that Pixar makes to the alpha-male model. To emerge victorious (and in one piece) over the tyrannical neighbor boy, Sid, Buzz and Woody have to cooperate not only with each other but also with the cannibalized toys lurking in the dark places of Sid's bedroom. Incidentally learning a valuable lesson about discrimination based on physical difference (the toys are not monsters at all, despite their frightening appearance), they begin to show sympathy, rather than violence born of their fear, to the victims of Sid's experimentation. They learn how to humble themselves to ask for help from the community. Until Woody's grand plan to escape Sid unfolds, Sid could be an object lesson in the unredeemed alpha-male type: Cruelly almighty over the toy community, he wins at arcade games, bullies his sister, and, with strategically placed fireworks, exerts militaristic might over any toys he can find. Woody's newfound ability to give and receive care empowers him to teach Sid a lesson of caring and sharing that might be microcosmic to the movie as a whole. Sid, of course, screams (like a girl) when confronted with the evidence of his past cruelties, and when viewers last see him, his younger sister is chasing him up the stairs with her doll.

Even with the unceremonious exit of Sid, the adventure is not quite over for Buzz and Woody. Unable to catch up to the moving van as Sid's dog chases him, Woody achieves the pinnacle of the New Man narrative: Armed with a new masculine identity, one that expresses feelings and acknowledges community as a site of power, Woody is able to sacrifice the competition with Buzz for his object of desire. Letting go of the van strap, sacrificing himself (he thinks) to Sid's dog, he plainly expresses a caretaking, nurturing love, and a surrender to the good of the beloved: "Take care of Andy for me," he pleads. Buzz's own moment of truth comes from seizing his power as a toy: holding Woody, he glides into the family's car and back into Andy's care, correcting Woody by proudly repeating his earlier, critical words back to him: "This isn't flying; it's falling with style." Buzz has found the value of being a "toy," the self-fulfillment that comes from being owned and loved. "Being a toy is a lot better than being a space ranger," Woody explains. "You're *his toy*" (emphasis in original).

Mr. Incredible likewise must embrace his own dependence, both physical and emotional. Trapped on the island of Chronos, at the mercy of Syndrome (Buddy's new super-persona), Mr. Incredible needs women—his wife's superpowers and Mirage's guilty intervention—to escape. To overpower the monster Syndrome has unleashed on the city, and to achieve the pinnacle of the New

Man model, he must also admit to his emotional dependence on his wife and children. Initially confining them to the safety of a bus, he confesses to Elastigirl that his need to fight the monster alone is not a typically alpha ("I work alone") sort of need but a loving one: "I can't lose you again," he tells her. The robot/monster is defeated, along with any vestiges of the alpha model, as the combined forces of the Incredible family locate a new model of postfeminist strength in the family as a whole. This communal strength is not simply physical but marked by cooperation, selflessness, and intelligence. The children learn that their best contributions protect the others; Mr. Incredible figures out the robot/monster's vulnerability and cleverly uses this against it.

In a parallel motif to Mr. Incredible's inability to control his strength, Buddy/Syndrome finally cannot control his robot/monster; in the defeat, he becomes the newly emasculated alpha male. But like his robot, he learns quickly. His last attempt to injure Mr. Incredible, kidnapping his baby Jack-Jack, strikes at Mr. Incredible's new source of strength and value, his family. The strength of the cooperative family unit is even more clearly displayed in this final rescue: For the shared, parental goal of saving Jack-Jack, Mr. Incredible uses his physical strength and, with her consent, the shape-shifting body of his super-wife. He throws Elastigirl into the air, where she catches their baby and, flattening her body into a parachute, sails gently back to her husband and older children.

Through Lightning McQueen's many relationships with men, as well as his burgeoning romance with Sally, he also learns how to care about others, to focus on the well-being of the community, and to privilege nurture and kindness. It is Doc, not Sally, who explicitly challenges the race car with his selfishness ("When was the last time you cared about something except yourself, hot rod?"). His re-formed behavior begins with his generous contributions to the Radiator Springs community. Not only does he provide much-needed cash for the local economy, but he also listens to, praises, and values the residents for their unique offerings to Radiator Springs. He is the chosen auditor for Lizzy's reminiscing about her late husband, contrasting the comic relief typically offered by the senile and deaf Model T with poignancy, if not quite sadness. Repairing the town's neon, he creates a romantic dreamscape from the past, a setting for both courting Sally ("cruising") and, more importantly, winning her respect with his ability to share in her value system. For this role, he is even physically transformed: He hires the body shop proprietor, Ramone, to paint over his sponsors' stickers and his large race number, as if to remove himself almost completely from the Piston Cup world, even as he anticipates being released from his community service and thus being able to return to racing.

Perhaps even more than Buzz, Woody, and Mr. Incredible do, the New Man McQueen shuns the remaining trappings of the alpha role, actually refusing the Piston Cup. If the first three protagonists are ultimately qualified heroes—that is, they still retain their authority and accomplish their various tasks, but with new values and perspectives acquired along the way—Lightning completely and publicly refuses his former object of desire. Early in the final race, he seems to somewhat devalue racing; his daydreams of Sally distract him, tempting him to give up rather than to compete. The plot, however, needs him to dominate the race so his decision at the end will be entirely his own. His friends show up and encourage him to succeed. This is where the other films end: The values of caring, sharing, nurturing, and community being clearly present, the hero is at last able to achieve, improved by having embraced those values. But Lightning, seeing the wrecked King and remembering the words of Doc Hudson, screeches to a stop inches before the finish line. Reversing, he approaches the King, pushes him back on the track, and acknowledges the relative insignificance of the Piston Cup in comparison to his new and improved self. He then declines the Dinoco corporate offer in favor of remaining faithful to his loyal Rust-eze sponsors. Chick Hicks, the only unredeemed alpha male at the end, celebrates his ill-gotten victory and is publicly rejected at the end by both his fans, "the twins," and, in a sense, by the Piston Cup itself, which slides onto the stage and hits him rudely in the side.

Conclusion

The trend of the New Man seems neither insidious nor nefarious, nor is it out of step with the larger cultural movement. It is good, we believe, for our son to be aware of the many sides of human existence, regardless of traditional gender stereotypes. However, maintaining a critical consciousness of the many lessons taught by the cultural monolith of Disney remains imperative. These lessons—their pedagogical aims or results—become most immediately obvious to us as parents when we watch our son ingest and express them, when he misunderstands and makes his own sense of them, and when we can see ways in which his perception of reality is shaped by them, before our eyes. Without assuming that the values of the films are inherently evil or representative of an evil "conspiracy to undermine American youth" (Giroux 4), we are still compelled to critically examine the texts on which our son bases many of his attitudes, behaviors, and preferences.

Moreover, the impact of Disney, as Henry Giroux has effectively argued, is tremendously more widespread than our household. Citing Michael Eisner's 1995 "Planetized Entertainment," Giroux claims that 200 million people a year watch Disney videos or films, and in a week, 395 million watch a Disney TV show, 3.8 million subscribe to the Disney Channel, and 810,000 make a purchase at a Disney store (19). As Benjamin Barber argued in 1995, "[T]he true tutors of our children are not schoolteachers or university professors but filmmakers, advertising executives and pop culture purveyors" (qtd. in Giroux 63). Thus we perform our "pedagogical intervention[s]" of examining Disney's power to "shap[e] national identity, gender roles, and childhood values" (Giroux 10). It remains a necessary and ongoing task, not just for concerned parents, but for all conscientious cultural critics.

Works Cited

Bell, Elizabeth. "Somatexts at the Disney Shop: Constructing the Pentimentos of Women's Animated Bodies." Bell, *From Mouse to Mermaid* 107–24.

Bell, Elizabeth, Lynda Haas, and Laura Sells, eds. *From Mouse to Mermaid: the Politics of Film, Gender, and Culture.* Bloomington: Indiana UP, 1995.

Card, Claudia. "Pinocchio." Bell, *From Mouse to Mermaid* 62–71.

Cars. Dir. John Lasseter. Walt Disney Pictures/Pixar Animation Studios, 2006.

Collier, Richard. "The New Man: Fact or Fad?" *Achilles Heel: The Radical Men's Magazine* 14 (1992–93). <http://www.achillesheel.freeuk.com/article14_9.html>.

Eisner, Michael. "Planetized Entertainment." *New Perspectives Quarterly* 12.4 (1995): 8.

Giroux, Henry. *The Mouse that Roared: Disney and the End of Innocence.* Oxford, Eng.: Rowman, 1999.

The Incredibles. Dir. Brad Bird. Walt Disney Pictures/Pixar Animation Studios, 2004.

Jeffords, Susan. "The Curse of Masculinity: Disney's *Beauty and the Beast*." Bell, *From Mouse to Mermaid* 161–72.

Lendrum, Rob. "Queering Super-Manhood: Superhero Masculinity, Camp, and Public Relations as a Textual Framework." *International Journal of Comic Art* 7.1 (2005): 287–303.

Palmer-Mehtan, Valerie, and Kellie Hay. "A Superhero for Gays? Gay Masculinity and Green Lantern." *Journal of American Culture* 28.4 (2005): 390–404.

Payne, David. "Bambi." Bell, *From Mouse to Mermaid* 137–47.

Schoene-Harwood, Berthold. *Writing Men: Literary Masculinities from Frankenstein to the New Man.* Columbia: Columbia UP, 2000.

Sedgwick, Eve Kosofsky. *Between Men: English Literature and Male Homosocial Desire.* New York: Columbia UP, 1985.

Toy Story. Dir. John Lasseter. Walt Disney Pictures/Pixar Animation Studios, 1995.

Wertham, Fredric. *Seduction of the Innocent.* New York: Reinhart, 1954.

Yabroff, Jennie. "Betas Rule." *Newsweek* 4 June 2007: 64–65.

READING APPEALS

Like Unit 2, each of the readings in this unit presents more specific arguments about the debate in question; however, rather than focusing your reading on mapping the overall claims of each reading, pay closer attention to the **methods of reasoning** and **proofs** that each argument uses—are they **inductive** or **deductive**—if both methods of reasoning are used, how are they integrated? What *topoi* are invoked, and which **appeals** give the argument support? Finally, consider how these concepts are related to issues of **genre** and **design**. Do particular genres tend to use one method of reasoning over another? Does a certain design choice tend to emphasize a particular appeal; for instance, do the images, charts, and graphs in the "Hollywood Diversity Report" make ethical, logical, or pathetic appeals? What **opportunities** and **constraints** do particular genres provide?

As you think through these questions and these readings, remember to consider how they relate to the overall rhetorical situation developed in these debates. Given this knowledge, what ideas do you have for deploying specific appeals and methods in your own argumentative composition?

Border Control

The Cost of Immigration Enforcement and Border Security
American Immigration Council

Since the last major overhaul of the U.S. immigration system in 1986, the federal government has spent an estimated $263 billion on immigration enforcement.[1] As discussions with a new President and Congress start to focus on what immigration enforcement and border security should look like it is important to review how much money has already been spent on these initiatives and what outcomes have been produced.

Immigration enforcement spending largely falls into two issue areas: border security and interior enforcement. Border spending includes staffing and resources needed for U.S. Customs and Border Protection (CBP), an agency of the Department of Homeland Security (DHS) working at and between United States ports of entry. Interior enforcement is primarily focused on staffing and resources for U.S. Immigration and Customs Enforcement (ICE), also part of DHS, to apprehend noncitizens in the interior of the country, detention for those undergoing removal proceedings, and the deportation of those ordered removed.

Currently, the number of border and interior enforcement personnel stands at more than 49,000.[2] The number of U.S. Border Patrol agents nearly doubled from Fiscal Year (FY) 2003 to FY 2016.[3] Additionally, the number of ICE agents devoted to its office of Enforcement and Removal Operations (ERO) nearly tripled from FY 2003 to FY 2016.[4]

What has this spending bought? The United States currently has over 650 miles of fencing along the Southern border, record levels of staff for ICE and CBP, as well as a fleet of drones, among other resources. Some of these resources have been spent on ill-conceived projects, such as the $1 billion attempt to construct a "virtual fence" along the Southwest border, a project initiated in 2005 that was later scrapped for being ineffective and too costly.[5] Even with record level spending on enforcement, enforcement alone is not sufficient to address the challenges of undocumented migration.[6] It also has significant unintended consequences, according to U.S. Border Patrol statistics, the Southwest border witnesses approximately one death per day.[7] All of these efforts that have accumulated in the name of security, however, do not necessarily measure border security.[8] It is past time for the United States to focus on metrics that actually assess achievements and progress on security.[9] DHS lacks transparent, consistent, and stable metrics for evaluating border enforcement. Before deciding how to address border security, Congress should require clear reporting on metrics from DHS.[10] Such metrics would better allow Congress and the public to hold the immigration agencies accountable and assess whether and what additional resources are needed (or not needed) to secure our border.

The Cost in Dollars

The immigration enforcement budget has increased massively since the early 1990s, but Congress continues to call for more taxpayer dollars to be spent at the border.

■ Since 1993, when the current strategy of concentrated border enforcement was first rolled out along the U.S.-Mexico border, the annual budget of the U.S. Border Patrol has increased more than ten-fold, from $363 million to more than $3.8 billion (Figure 1).[11]

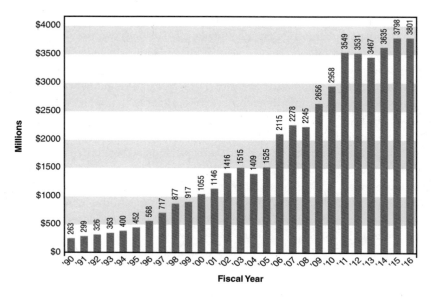

Source: U.S. Customs and Border Protection, "U.S. Border Patrol Fiscal Year Budget Statistics (FY 1990-FY 2015)," January 12, 2016.

Figure 1. U.S. Border Patrol Budget, FY 1990–2015

■ Since the creation of DHS in 2003, the budget of CBP has more than doubled from $5.9 billion to $13.2 billion per year (Figure 2).[12]

■ On top of that, ICE spending has grown 85 percent, from $3.3 billion since its inception to $6.1 billion today (Figure 2).[13]

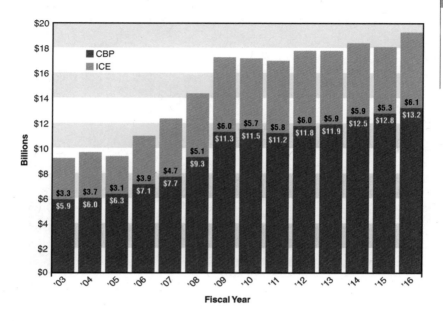

Source: U.S. Department of Homeland Security, Budget-in-Brief, FY 2005–2017.

Figure 2. CBP & ICE Annual Budgets, FY 2003–2016

Increases in Personnel

- Since 1993, the number of U.S. Border Patrol agents nearly doubled from 10,717 to a congressionally mandated 21,370 in FY 2016 (Figure 3).[14]

- The number of CBP officers staffing ports of entry (POEs) grew from 17,279 in FY 2003 to 21,423 in FY 2012 (Figure 3).[15]

- The number of ICE agents devoted to Enforcement and Removal Operations increased from 2,710 in FY 2003 to 7,995 in FY 2016 (Figure 3).[16]

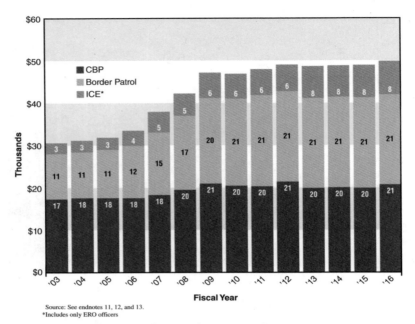

Figure 3. CBP Officers, Border Patrol Agents, and ICE Agents, FY 2003–2016

The federal government has already met the border security benchmarks laid down in earlier Senate immigration reform bills.

- As the American Immigration Lawyers Association pointed out in a January 2013 analysis, the "benchmarks" for border security specified in the bipartisan 2006, 2007, and 2010 immigration-reform legislative packages in the Senate have been largely met.[17]

- The requirements in those Senate bills for more border enforcement personnel, border fencing, surveillance technology, unmanned aerial vehicles, and detention beds have been fulfilled and in many ways surpassed.[18] As the Homeland Security Advisory Panel noted in 2016, ICE detention rose from the normal 34,000 beds to 41,000—an all-time high.[19]

Border security depends on the smart and efficient use of available resources. At the same, border enforcement cannot and should not be done in isolation. Instead, it must be examined in the larger context of reforms needed for the entire immigration system.

Endnotes

1. *See* American Immigration Council, *Giving the Facts a Fighting Chance: Addressing Common Questions on Immigration* (Washington, DC: December 2015), 16, https://www.americanimmigrationcouncil.org/research/addressing-common-questions-immigration; U.S. Department of Homeland Security, *Budget-in-Brief*, FY 2017, 17, https://www.dhs.gov/publication/fy-2017-budget-brief.

2.   See American Immigration Council, *Giving the Facts a Fighting Chance: Addressing Common Questions on Immigration* (Washington, DC: December 2015), 18, https://www.americanimmigrationcouncil.org/research/addressing-common-questions-immigration.

3.   U.S. Government Accountability Office, "U.S. Customs and Border Protection: Review of the Staffing Analysis Report under the Border Patrol Agent Reform Act of 2014," May 2016, http://www.gao.gov/assets/680/677475.pdf.

4.   U.S. Department of Homeland Security, "Congressional Budget Justification," FY 2016, https://www.dhs.gov/sites/default/files/publications/FY%202017%20Congressional%20Budget%20Justification%20-%20Volume%202_1.pdf.

5.   Julia Preston, "Homeland Security Cancels 'Virtual Fence' After $1 Billion is Spent," *New York Times*, January 2011, http://www.nytimes.com/2011/01/15/us/politics/15fence.html.

6.   Doris Meissner, Donald M. Kerwin, Muzaffar Chishti, and Claire Bergeron, Immigration Enforcement in the United States: The Rise of Formiddable Machinery, Migration Policy Institute, January 2013, http://www.migrationpolicy.org/research/immigration-enforcement-united-states-rise-formidable-machinery.

7.   United States Border Patrol, Southwest Border Sectors, https://www.cbp.gov/sites/default/files/assets/documents/2016-Oct/BP%20Southwest%20Border%20Sector%20Deaths%20FY1998%20-%20FY2016.pdf.

8.   Bipartisan Policy Center, "Measuring the Metrics: Grading the Government on Immigration Enforcement," February 2015, http://bipartisanpolicy.org/library/measuring-the-metrics-grading-the-government-on-immigration-enforcement/.

9.   Ibid.

10. Ibid.

11. U.S. Department of Homeland Security, "Department Management and Operations, Analysis and Operations, Office of the Inspector General, U.S. Customs and Border Protection," *Congressional Budget Justification FY 2017-Volume I*, 880, https://www.dhs.gov/sites/default/files/publications/FY 2017 Congressional Budget Justification - Volume 1_1.pdf.

12. U.S. Department of Homeland Security, *Budget-in-Brief*, FY 2005-2017, https://www.dhs.gov/dhs-budget.

13. Ibid.

14. U.S. Government Accountability Office, "U.S. Customs and Border Protection: Review of the Staffing Analysis Report under the Border Patrol Agent Reform Act of 2014," May 2016, http://www.gao.gov/assets/680/677475.pdf.

15. U.S. Department of Homeland Security, *Congressional Budget Justification*, FY 2003 and 2012, https://www.dhs.gov/dhs-budget.

16. U.S. Department of Homeland Security, *Congressional Budget Justification*, FY 2003-2016, https://www.dhs.gov/dhs-budget.

17. Greg Chen and Su Kim, *Border Security: Moving Beyond Past Benchmarks* (Washington, DC: American Immigration Lawyers Association, January 2013), http://www.aila.org/content/default.aspx?bc=25667|43061.

18. Ibid.

19. Homeland Security Advisory Council, "Report of the Subcommittee on Privatized Immigration Detention Facilities," *Department of Homeland Security*, December 1, 2016, https://www.dhs.gov/sites/default/files/publications/DHS%20HSAC%20PIDF%20Final%20Report.pdf; National Immigrant Justice Center, "Immigration Detention Bed Quota Timeline," January 2017, https://immigrantjustice.org/sites/default/files/content-type/commentary-item/documents/2017-01/Immigration%20Detention%20Bed%20Quota%20Timeline%202017_01_05.pdf.

The Case for Building a Wall to Keep Canadians Out
The Economist

Aaron Heitke, who heads the border patrol in Grand Forks, North Dakota, would like the federal government to send more money his way. Just over 2,000 agents patrol America's northern border, compared with 17,000 down south. Mr. Heitke wants some of them to come up and lend a hand. Heidi Heitkamp, a Democratic senator from North Dakota who co-authored the Northern Border Security Review Act, signed into law by then-President Barack Obama in December, would like more federal dollars for her state, too. The world's longest land border, running through Montana's mountains, four Great Lakes, glorious woods and wild prairies, is also one of the least patrolled and surveyed. Some see Donald Trump's election as a chance to change that.

Between 2000 and 2010 taxpayers spent an estimated $90bn on the southern border, which included paying the salaries of guards, building fences, x-ray machines that can peer into cargo trains and trucks, tower-mounted cameras, ground sensors, predator drones and drug-sniffing dogs. Expenditure on the northern border in the same period was in the millions rather than billions. Yet the northern border sees the world's largest bilateral daily flow of goods and people, on average $190m and nearly 400,000 respectively. It offers more opportunities for illegal crossings: in many places a small white obelisk somewhere in a field is the only marker of the border. Some streets and buildings are shared between Canada and America. On the north side of Canusa Street in Vermont (Rue Canusa in Québécois) lies Canada; to the south is America. The Haskell Free Library and Opera House straddles both countries.

If America is to spend even more on border security, would marginal dollars be better spent on the northern border than the southern one? If the main purpose is to nab illegal immigrants, the answer is no. In 2016 border-patrol agents caught only 2,300 illegal migrants on the northern border, compared with almost 200 times as many (408,000) on the southern one. If the purpose is to prevent drug-smuggling, the case is a bit stronger. The DEA reports that lots of marijuana and ecstasy enters from the north, though in total the quantity of drugs seized is much lower: 700lb (318kg) of cocaine and marijuana in the north versus 1.7mlb in the south.

Those who see the northern border as alarmingly porous worry about terrorists crossing it, too. About the same number of Canadians and Americans joined IS in Syria, which suggests that Canada has a bigger problem with homegrown jihadists (who might go south), points out Bruce Hoffman of Georgetown University.

For their part, Canadians are as fixated on their border with America as Americans are on theirs with Mexico, says Nik Nanos, a Canadian pollster. Ninety percent of Canada's population lives within a 90-minute drive of it. Some have started to fret about asylum-seekers crossing from America into Canada illegally to escape the immigration policies of the new administration. (If they crossed legally, at official border posts, they would be turned away under agreements between America and Canada, which say that refugees must request protection in the first safe country they arrive in.) Their numbers are small, in the hundreds perhaps, though this could change in the warmer months. Canadians continue to show their traditional generosity of spirit towards asylum-seekers, says Mr. Nanos, but they also dislike people jumping the queue. All of which shows that it is usually easier to make the argument for harder borders than for more open ones.

Privacy and Cyber-Security

The Supreme Court Just Greatly Strengthened Digital Privacy
Louise Matsakis

In a highly anticipated decision released Friday, the US Supreme Court updated Fourth Amendment protections for the digital era. In a 5–4 ruling, the court decided in *Carpenter v. United States* that the government generally needs a warrant in order to access cell site location information, which is automatically generated whenever a mobile phone connects to a cell tower and is stored by wireless carriers for years. The ruling does leave the door open for law enforcement to obtain such information *without* a warrant in some instances. Still, the court recognizes that cell phones are not voluntary but necessary for modern life, and that their technology poses some unique circumstances for the law.

"We decline to grant the state unrestricted access to a wireless carrier's database of physical location information," Chief Justice John Roberts wrote in the majority opinion. "In light of the deeply revealing nature of CSLI, its depth, breadth, and comprehensive reach, and the inescapable and automatic nature of its collection, the fact that such information is gathered by a third party does not make it any less deserving of Fourth Amendment protection."

Roberts was joined by Justices Ruth Bader Ginsburg, Stephen Breyer, Sonia Sotomayor, and Elena Kagan. Justices Anthony Kennedy, Clarence Thomas, Samuel Alito, and Neil Gorsuch dissented.

The court's ruling represents a win for digital privacy advocates, and, while narrow, it may have implications for all sorts of information held by third parties, including browsing data, text messages, emails, and bank records.

"The government can no longer claim that the mere act of using technology eliminates the Fourth Amendment's protections. Today's decision rightly recognizes the need to protect the highly sensitive location data from our cell phones, but it also provides a path forward for safeguarding other sensitive digital information in future cases—from our emails, smart-home appliances, and technology that is yet to be invented," ACLU attorney Nathan Freed Wessler, who argued the case before the court, said in a statement.

At issue was an antiquated legal principle called the third-party doctrine, which holds that information customers voluntarily provide to a third party—such as a telecom company or a bank—is outside the bounds of Fourth Amendment protections. The doctrine comes from *United States v. Miller*, a 1976 case in which the court ruled that law enforcement doesn't need a warrant in order to access bank records because "the Fourth Amendment does not prohibit the obtaining of information revealed to a third party."

Three years later, in 1979, the court ruled in *Smith v. Maryland* that the third-party doctrine also extends to call records collected by phone companies.

But on Friday, the Supreme Court said that cell site location information is a "qualitatively different category" of information. CSLI allows law enforcement to paint a nearly complete picture of Americans' movements. Last year, AT&T and Verizon jointly received nearly 125,000 requests from law enforcement for CSLI data, according to their transparency reports. Law enforcement officials will now only be able to make such requests after obtaining a warrant, which will require them to demonstrate probable cause.

The court has expressed uneasiness about the collection of vast amounts of digital data before. In the 2014 case *Riley v. California*, it ruled that police generally need a warrant to search the cell phone of a person under arrest. And in 2012, in *United States v. Jones*, the court said that it does violate a person's Fourth Amendment rights for the government to place a GPS tracker on their car without a warrant.

In *Carpenter*, Roberts left the door open for courts to obtain location information without a warrant in two circumstances. The court declined to decide on whether law enforcement seeking a smaller window of records—fewer than seven days, which is what the government requested from Sprint in the case—constitutes a Fourth Amendment search. The opinion also allows for exceptions for emergencies, like "bomb threats, active shootings, and child abductions."

"This is a huge victory not only for privacy, but also frankly for reality," says Sarah St. Vincent, a national security and surveillance researcher at Human Rights Watch. "When you share your location data via your cell phone, it's not really voluntary. What's critical is those exceptions—the lower courts are going to need to be vigilant about making sure they're not abused."

Carpenter v. United States began in December of 2010, when a series of robberies hit Michigan and neighboring Ohio. Ironically, the perpetrators were after cell phones. Over the course of a year, they robbed several Radio Shack and T-Mobile stores at gunpoint, filling plaid laundry bags with smartphones. The police arrested four men, including the petitioner, Timothy Carpenter, who was later convicted of committing several of the robberies and sentenced to 116 years in prison (thanks, in part, to mandatory minimums).

Law enforcement was able to connect Carpenter to the crimes by obtaining more than 100 days' worth of his smartphone location data records from Metro PCS and Sprint, all without a warrant. Those records placed his phone at over 12,000 different locations, revealing which Sundays he attended church, and when he didn't spend the night in his own home.

Law enforcement officials were able to get the records under the Stored Communications Act, passed in 1986, which requires prosecutors to demonstrate "specific and articulable facts showing there are reasonable grounds to believe" that electronic data being sought is relevant to an ongoing criminal investigation. But the law stops short of requiring that prosecutors demonstrate probable cause, which is necessary to obtain a warrant.

Before his trial, Carpenter argued that obtaining the records constituted a Fourth Amendment search, and therefore the police should have needed a warrant. His motion was denied, and the Sixth Circuit Court of Appeals later upheld the case. The Supreme Court agreed to hear it last year.

In one of the dissents, Justice Kennedy, joined by Justices Thomas and Alito, maintains that "Cell-site records, however, are no different from the many other kinds of business records the Government has a lawful right to obtain by compulsory process." They call the distinction between CSLI and other records like financial or telephone records made by the court "illogical."

Orin Kerr, a prominent Fourth Amendment scholar at George Washington University, filed a brief in support of the government. He argued that cell phone location data merely simulates the real world. You can't expect privacy when you walk to the store, he argued, so you aren't entitled to privacy when it comes to the cell phone location records that show you went there. A neighbor, or the store clerk, may have a memory of where you went, just as your cell phone keeps a record.

"This is a location tracking opinion case, which just happens to involve cell-site records," Kerr wrote in a tweet after the decision came out. "The facts here, and the existing technology, are less important."

Justice Roberts rejected Kerr's argument. "Sprint Corporation and its competitors are not your typical witnesses. Unlike the nosy neighbor who keeps an eye on comings and goings, they are ever alert, and their memory is nearly infallible," the majority opinion reads.

Fourteen of the largest US tech companies—including Google, Apple, Facebook, and Microsoft—filed a brief in support of updating the Fourth Amendment for the digital era. It was technically not filed in support of either party, but largely backed Carpenter's position.

The cohort even included Verizon, which cooperated with the National Security Agency as part of its broad bulk surveillance programs for years. Verizon's stance is particularly notable because the company holds the specific kind of location records that were at issue in the case.

Cyrus Farivar, a reporter at Ars Technica and the author of *Habeas Data*, a new book about privacy laws and the rise of surveillance technology, says the ruling shows that the court views cell phones differently.

"They're an entirely separate class of devices that provide a very intimate look into the most detailed elements of our life, not only where we go generally, but where we go extremely specifically," he says.

He also notes that the court was split and that it took a long time for it to come to its decision, which was unusually released on a Friday. "That suggests that this is an issue that the court came to with a great deal of thought, discussion, and deliberation. This is not an easy decision to reach."

We don't yet know how the ruling might impact other forms of government surveillance. Justice Roberts was careful to note that the ruling is intended to be narrow in its scope, writing that the court does not "call into question conventional surveillance techniques and tools, such as security cameras. Nor do we address other business records that might incidentally reveal location information. Further, our opinion does not consider other collection techniques involving foreign affairs or national security."

Ultimately, if digital privacy advocates want to limit government surveillance, the Supreme Court is likely not the best avenue to do so.

"It's important to remember that the facts of Carpenter took place eight years ago. My iPhone and your iPhone have gotten a lot better in those eight years," says Farivar. "We can't wait for the Supreme Court to get there. We need to do a lot more on the front end, we need to do a lot more ideally in Congress, otherwise in our states and our cities to decide where the limits are."

The decision might not mean much for Timothy Carpenter, due to the good faith exception, which says if law enforcement obtained evidence believing they were acting according to legal authority, it's still admissible in court, even if the law changes.

From the pages of

TIME

Revenge Porn: How Women Are Fighting Against Revenge Photos
Charlotte Alter

For years, Kara Jefts lived with a terrible secret. When she met a guy, she wouldn't reveal her last name until they had been on four or five dates. When she began a new job, she would immediately befriend the IT expert who could help her block hostile emails. When she spoke with a new boss, she would force an awkward conversation about her romantic history. Her secret was so terrible because it wasn't a secret at all: for the past five years, nude photos of Jefts have been only one email, Facebook post, or Google search away.

Jefts is a thoughtful academic in her mid-30s, an archivist and art historian at a Chicago university who never intended for images of her naked body to circulate on the internet. But in 2011, soon after Jefts ended her long-distance relationship with a boyfriend who lived in Italy, explicit screenshots from their Skype conversations began to appear online. They were emailed to her family and friends, posted on Facebook with violent threats against her, and even appeared on websites devoted to exposing people's sexually transmitted diseases, with false allegations about her sexual history.

There's a name for what Jefts has experienced, a digital sex crime that has upended thousands of lives but still mostly eludes law enforcement: nonconsensual porn, more commonly known as revenge porn. The distinction is one of motive, not effect: revenge porn is often intended to harass the victim, while any image that is circulated without the agreement of the subject is nonconsensual porn. Both can result in public degradation, social isolation, and professional humiliation for the victims.

Enabled by the technological and cultural upheaval that put a camera in every pocket and created a global audience for every social media post, nonconsensual porn has become increasingly common. Practically every day brings reports of a new case: A 19-year-old woman in Texas blackmailed into having sex with three other teens after a former partner threatened to release an explicit video of her. A 20-something in Pennsylvania had strange men coming to her door after an ex-boyfriend posted her pictures and address with an invitation to "come hook up." An Illinois school superintendent in her 50s was fired after her ex-husband allegedly sent an explicit video of her to the school board.

Some of these private photos and videos find their way to porn sites, where "revenge" is its own genre. More often, however, they're also posted on social media, where all the victim's friends can see them. Facebook received more than 51,000 reports of revenge porn in January 2017 alone, according to documents obtained by *The Guardian*, which led the site to disable more than 14,000 accounts. A 2016 survey of 3,000 internet users by the journal Data and Society found that roughly 1 in 25 Americans have either had someone post an image without permission or threaten to do so—for women under 30, that figure rose to 1 in 10. And a June Facebook survey by the anti-revenge porn advocacy group Cyber Civil Rights Initiative found that 1 in 20 social media users have posted a sexually graphic image without consent.

The problem exploded into public view earlier this year, when hundreds of active duty and veteran Marines were found to be circulating explicit images of current and former women service members. The images were posted in a secret Facebook group, passed around the way that their grandfathers might have traded copies of *Playboy*. Roughly two dozen service members have been investigated since the scandal broke in January, leading the Marines to formally ban nonconsensual porn in April. In May, the House unanimously voted to make nonconsensual porn a military crime subject to court marshal.

In some cases, the perpetrators are hackers who target famous women, searching for compromising photos to leak. Last year, Saturday Night Live star Leslie Jones was hacked and her nude pictures were spread online. In 2014, nude photos of Jennifer Lawrence and other female celebrities were hacked and leaked in one of the biggest nonconsensual porn cases to date. It's a problem nearly everywhere in the world: in May, nude photos purportedly of Rwandan presidential candidate Diane Shima Rwigara appeared online days after she announced her intention to challenge the nation's longtime leader, Paul Kagame.

This type of harassment shows how sexual violation can now be digital as well as physical. And its rapid spread has left law enforcement, tech companies and officials scrambling to catch up. When evidence lives in the cloud and many laws are stuck in the pre-smartphone era, nonconsensual porn presents a legal nightmare: it's easy to disseminate and nearly impossible to punish.

Advocates are trying to change that, in part by pushing a Congressional bill that would make nonconsensual porn a federal crime. But there are obstacles at every corner, from the technological challenges of fully removing anything from the internet, to the attitude of law enforcement, to the very real concerns over legislation that could restrict free speech. In the meantime, victims live in fear of becoming a 21st century version of Hester Prynne. "I have to accept at this point that it's going to continue to follow me," Jefts says. "It's kind of like having an incurable disease."

Why Would Anyone Share a Nude Photo?

Jefts never thought of herself as the kind of person who would send nude photos. She is circumspect and professional—and acutely aware of the power of images. But then she met a man who lived an ocean away, and quickly fell in love. Skype was critical to keeping the relationship alive, and the pair often sent each other photos and videochatted in ways that sometimes became sexual. "If it's World War II and your husband leaves, you send letters and pictures, you have this correspondence that helps maintain that emotional connection," she explains. "It's more instantaneous [today] because of the technology, but the origin of it is the same."

While some nonconsensual porn comes from pictures that are hacked or taken surreptitiously, in many cases the images were flirtatiously traded between partners as sexts. According to a 2016 study of nearly 6,000 adults by researchers at Indiana University, 16% had sent a sexual photo, and more than one in five had received one. Of those who received nude photos, 23% reported sharing them with others, and men were twice as likely as women to do so.

Boomers might be baffled by this practice, but for many under 30 sexting isn't seen as particularly transgressive. "It's embedded in modern relationships in a way that makes us feel safe," says Sherry Turkle, a professor of the social studies of science and technology at MIT. "This is a question that doesn't need an answer if you grew up with a phone in your hand."

According to Turkle, many digital natives are so comfortable on the internet that they imagine that there are rules about what can and can't happen to the content they share. "If you feel the internet is safe, you want to share everything, because it'll make you feel closer and it's a new tool," she says. "People made up a contract in their minds about the online spaces they're in."

Women sometimes circulate male nudes, but studies show the vast majority of nonconsensual images are photos of women spread by men. When accused, some men say they were hacked and the photos must be coming from another source. Others admit that they posted the photos out of anger, lashing out over a perceived slight. One Louisiana tattoo artist told police he posted a sex tape of his ex on a porn site as retribution after she damaged his car. A Minnesota man reportedly admitted he posted explicit images of his ex-wife on Facebook because he was jealous of her new boyfriend.

The dissemination of images can be as much about impressing other men as it is about humiliating the victim. Boys once presented stolen underwear as trophies from conquests—now, a nude selfie can signal the same thing. As a result, schools around the nation have dealt with what are often referred to as sexting rings. In 2014, more than 100 teens in a rural Virginia county were investigated for circulating more than 1,000 nude photos of mostly underage girls on Instagram. A Colorado District Attorney chose not to bring charges against teens who were circulating photos of high school and middle schoolers in 2015. Similar incidents have popped up recently in schools in Ohio, New York and Connecticut. The practice has become common enough that the American Academy of Pediatrics developed a guide for parents on talking to children about sexting.

"Lots of this isn't intentional," says Erica Johnstone, a San Francisco attorney with a practice dedicated to sexual privacy. "It's just part of the hypermasculine culture: sex pictures become like currency."

Why It's So Hard to Stop the Spread

On an otherwise ordinary day in 2011, Holly Jacobs decided to Google herself. When a porn site came up in her search results, Jacobs went into what she now describes as "a complete state of shock."

"I could feel the blood rushing out of my head," she says. "I was turning white as the page was buffering." She would soon learn that her photos were posted on nearly 200 porn sites. A collage of nude images had been sent to her boss and co-workers. Explicit pictures of her were shared with her father on Facebook. She says she almost lost her job at a Florida college after someone online accused her of masturbating with students there, and she eventually stopped working as a statistical consultant because "every time I met with a client I wondered if they had seen me naked."

"I never thought this kind of violation was happening to everyday people," says Jacobs, who originally sent the photos to someone she knew and trusted. "I didn't realize there was a market for naked photos of people nobody knows."

Jacobs says she was diagnosed with depression and PTSD, and became afraid to meet new people for fear that they would find the photos. "It was a living nightmare," she says. "I kept being rejected by police, the attorneys, the FBI because they kept saying there was nothing they could do."

Now in her 30s, Jacobs ended up legally changing her name to escape her online footprint. But she also decided to fight back. She started the Cyber Civil Rights Initiative (CCRI) a nonprofit devoted to helping victims of nonconsensual porn reclaim their identities. Since they launched the helpline in 2014, more than 5,000 victims have called CCRI, Jacobs says, adding that the group now gets between 150 and 200 calls a month.

"I'm a good person and I didn't do anything wrong," she says. "There's nothing wrong with sharing nude images with someone I trust, so something needs to be done about this."

Many victims think the moment they see their nude photos online is the worst part of their ordeal. Then they start having awkward conversations with bosses, fielding relatives' questions about obscene social media posts, and getting strange looks from co-workers. It becomes impossible to know who has seen your photos, and what they think of you if they have. And when these victims start trying to get the pictures taken down, they realize something even worse: this type of cyber crime can leave a lasting digital stain, one that is nearly impossible to fully erase.

"Once the images and videos have been exposed or published, the internet is permanent," says Reg Harnish, the CEO of cyber-risk assessment firm GreyCastle Security, who worked with Kara Jefts to successfully remove most of her photos.

But even if you get an image scrubbed from one site, there's no way to guarantee it hasn't been copied, screenshotted, or stored on a cache somewhere. "There are literally hundreds of things working against an individual working to remove a specific piece of content from the internet," he says. "It's almost impossible."

When victims seek help from law enforcement, they rarely get an effective response. "This is a case they put at the bottom of the stack," says Johnstone, who represents victims of revenge porn. "They think that the victim was asking for it because they created the content that got them into the situation. They think they're not as deserving of police hours as someone who was the victim of a physical assault."

Jefts says she filed six police reports in three different New York counties (where she was living at the time) and got several restraining orders against her ex, but legal remedies were futile. Police officers often didn't know how to handle digital crimes, and even if they sympathized with her predicament, they said there was nothing they could do because her ex no longer lived in the same state or even the same country. The restraining orders had "zero impact," she says, and the harassment continued until she sought help from a tech experts like Harnish who helped her get the photos taken down.

As a result of growing awareness and increased pressure from victims and advocates, the number of states with a law addressing revenge porn has jumped from 3 to 38 since 2013. But the statutes are inconsistent and riddled with blind spots, which make them particularly difficult to enforce.

"There are no state laws across the U.S. that fit perfectly together," says Elisa D'Amico, a Miami lawyer and co-founder of the Cyber Civil Rights Legal Project. "It depends on where your victim is, where your perpetrator is, where someone was when they viewed pictures."

One of biggest inconsistencies among state laws is the way they treat motive. Some states criminalize nonconsensual porn only if there is "intent to harass," a targeted campaign to debase and humiliate the victim, as with Jefts. But in many cases, like the Marine photo sharing scandal, the distribution of images isn't intended to harass, because the victims were never supposed to know that their pictures had been shared. According to the CCRI's June survey of 3,000 Facebook users, 79% of those who said they had spread a sexually explicit image of someone else said they did not intend to cause any harm.

To those who have had their most intimate moments exposed on social media, such thinking misses the point. "These were images that I took under the assumption that it was a consensual, private relationship," says Jefts, who has devoted her career to studying the power and dissemination of images. "The context in which they were shared changed their meaning. That trumps their original intention."

To address the legal patchwork, U.S. Rep. Jackie Speier is planning to reintroduce a bill this June to make nonconsensual pornography a federal crime—regardless of whether the suspect intended to harass the victim. "The intent of the perpetrator is irrelevant really," says Speier, a Democrat whose district includes San Francisco. "Whether he's doing it for jollies or money, it's destroying another person's life." Facebook and Twitter backed her bill, called the Intimate Privacy Protection Act, or IPPA, as has billionaire Trump supporter and internet privacy advocate Peter Thiel. It also has bipartisan support from seven Republican co-sponsors.

But Speier's bill, which stalled in committee last year, has vocal critics who oppose enacting new criminal laws that target speech. The American Civil Liberties Union (ACLU) objects to the very portion of the bill embraced by victim advocates: the part that criminalizes nonconsensual porn regardless of intent. "The Supreme Court has correctly said again and again that when the government criminalizes speech, intent is a crucial component," says Lee Rowland, a senior staff attorney for the ACLU's speech, privacy and technology project. "We do not put somebody in jail in this country simply because their speech offends someone else."

With the law enforcement response in flux, tech companies have begun to respond to growing pressure to help address the problem. Under the 1996 Communications Decency Act, platforms like Google and Facebook aren't liable for the content they host, which means they can't be held legally responsible for the nonconsensual porn on their networks. But in response to an outpouring of user requests, several major websites have developed new policies to help fight revenge porn. In 2015, streaming porn site Pornhub announced it would remove revenge porn from its site, and Google announced it would remove the images from its search results. Twitter and Reddit have also updated their rules to prohibit nonconsensual porn. In April, Facebook unveiled a tool that enables users to flag content they think is being shared without consent; company technicians then check if it's appeared anywhere else on the network to prevent it from spreading further. But this kind of response from tech companies requires significant manpower, since nonconsensual porn is difficult to identify. Unlike child pornography, which can often be spotted on sight, an image posted without consent doesn't necessarily look different than one posted willingly.

No matter what steps Congress and tech companies take, nonconsensual porn remains a problem without easy solutions. And as lawyers sue and lawmakers debate, millions of pictures are still out there circulating, multiplying, waiting to ruin a life.

Pearson, NJ, Spying on Social Media of Students Taking PARCC Tests

Bob Braun

Pearson, the multinational testing and publishing company, is spying on the social media posts of students—including those from New Jersey—while the children are taking their PARCC, statewide tests, this site has learned exclusively. The state education department is cooperating with this spying and has asked at least one school district to discipline students who may have said something inappropriate about the tests. This website discovered the unauthorized and hidden spying thanks to educators who informed it of the practice—a practice happening throughout the state and apparently throughout the country.

The spying—or "monitoring," to use Pearson's word—was confirmed at one school district—the Watchung Hills Regional High School district in Warren by its superintendent, Elizabeth Jewett. Jewett sent out an e-mail—posted here—to her colleagues expressing concern about the unauthorized spying on students.

She said parents are upset and added that she thought Pearson's behavior would contribute to the growing "opt out" movement. So far, thousands of parents have kept their children away from the tests—and one of the reasons is the fear that Pearson might abuse its access to student data, something it has denied it would do.

In her email, Jewett said the district's testing coordinator received a late night call from the state education department saying that Pearson had "initiated a Priority 1 Alert for an item breach within our school."

The unnamed state education department employee contended a student took a picture of a test item and tweeted it. That was not true. It turned out the student had posted—at 3:18 pm, well after testing was over—a tweet about one of the items with no picture. Jewett does not say the student revealed a question. There is no evidence of any attempt at cheating.

Jewett continues: "The student deleted the tweet and we spoke with the parent—who was obviously highly concerned as to her child's tweets being monitored by the DOE (state education department).

"The DOE informed us that Pearson is monitoring all social media during the PARCC testing."

Jewett continued: "I have to say that I find that a bit disturbing—and if our parents were concerned before about a conspiracy with all of the student data, I am sure I will be receiving more letters of refusal once this gets out."

The school superintendent also expressed concern about "the fact that the DOE wanted us to also issue discipline to the student." Clearly, if Pearson insists on claiming test security as a justification for its spying on young people, that reasoning is vitiated by its cooperation with the state education department in trying to punish students who are merely expressing their First Amendment right to comment on the tests.

I contacted Jewett by email. By that time she had discovered not one but three instances in which Pearson notified the state education department of the results of its spying. In her email to me, Jewett was vague about the role of Pearson and the education department.

She wrote: "In reference to the issue of PARCC infractions and DOE/Pearson monitoring social media, we have had three incidents over the past week. All situations have been dealt with in accordance with our Watchung Hills Regional High School code of conduct and academic integrity policy. Watchung Hills Regional High School is a relatively small district and a close-knit community; therefore, I am very concerned that whatever details your sources are providing may cause unnecessary labeling and hardship to students who are learning the consequences of their behavior."

Jewett acted professionally, I believe, but I must point out the irony of her lecturing me about protecting the identity of students when she has just dealt with both an inexcusable breach of privacy involving minors and an attempt by state government to punish dissent. I made it clear to her I have no intention of revealing names of students—but I would be more than happy to speak with their parents.

The state education department official identified as the person cooperating with Pearson is Veronica Orsi, who is in charge of assessment for grades 9–12 in the department. She refused to answer this website's questions about her involvement and passed them on to superiors who also did not answer.

Neither the state education department nor Pearson's would respond to my emails on the company's spying on students. New Jersey is paying $108 million to run its PARCC testing program, an enterprise that has engendered opposition throughout New Jersey—and that was before the spying was revealed.

One motivation is clear—the more students who take the test, the more Pearson gets paid. This explains a lot about the state's and the company's aggressiveness in ensuring as many students as possible take the test.

But what isn't explained is the willingness of the state education department to punish New Jersey children on behalf of a private company. According to sources—and not denied by Jewett—state officials tried to have the students involved suspended.

State Education Commissioner David Hespe spent hours testifying before the Legislature's Senate Education Committee Thursday but did not once mention the possibility that the London-based Pearson would be "monitoring" the social media accounts of students taking the test. Jewett's email, however, indicated the department—presumably including Hespe—were well aware of the practice.

A few days earlier, state education department officials—including Orsi—held a background briefing for some media—Bob Braun's Ledger was not invited—and none of the mainstream media accounts of the session revealed the Pearson spying program.

Testing is scheduled for this month and May. Passing or failing the test has no consequence for the students who take it. PARCC does not serve as a graduation test. It can, however, be used in the evaluation of teachers.

• • •

UPDATE: The Washington Post's Valerie Strauss picked up the story and managed to get Pearson to comment:

> "The security of a test is critical to ensure fairness for all students and teachers and to ensure that the results of any assessment are trustworthy and valid. We welcome debate and a variety of opinions. But when test questions or elements are posted publicly to the Internet, we are obligated to alert PARCC states. Any contact with students or decisions about student discipline are handled at the local level. We believe that a secure test maintains fairness for every student and the validity, integrity of the test results."

The Washington Post also posted a letter written by Jewett:

> Dear Watchung Hills Regional High School Learning Community,
>
> On Friday, March 13, 2015, Bobbraunsledger.com published a story referencing an email I had sent to other superintendents about issues regarding PARCC testing and Pearson's monitoring of social media. The email shown in his article is authentic. It was an email I sent on March 10, 2015 at approximately 10:00AM to a group of superintendents to share my concerns and to see if other schools had a similar experience. I did not authorize the release of this email nor am I aware of who did release it. I am also not aware of the motives they may have had behind the release. That said, I completely stand behind my comments as they represent not only my views and concerns; they also represent the views and concerns of our Board of Education.
>
> The article references instances involving students during PARCC testing and any related disciplinary action. For student privacy issues, we cannot comment on any of the specific students or discipline referred to in the article. What I am able to share is that all issues have been dealt with in accordance with our Code of Conduct, Academic Integrity and Acceptable Use of Technology Policies.
>
> Our main concern is, and will always remain, supporting the educational, social and emotional needs of our students. The privacy and security of student information remains the utmost priority for our district.
>
> The district will have no further comment on this matter at this time.

• • •

This site also has learned that at least one of the three students at Watchung Hills Regional was suspended. It should be kept in mind that there are no consequences to students for this test—and students everywhere are smart enough to know when there are no consequences and they act accordingly—as they do when a sub shows up.

That one or more students may have been suspended for treating PARCC like the bad joke it has become shows how sad—and maybe scary—this cooperation between government and the private testing industry has become.

Healthcare

Outcry Over EpiPen Prices Hasn't Made Them Lower
Charles Duhigg

A few weeks ago, after some particularly incompetent parenting on my part (nuts in the dessert, a rushed trip to an emergency room after my child's allergic reaction), I visited the local pharmacy to fill an EpiPen prescription.

You might recall EpiPen as last year's poster child for out-of-control drug prices. Though this simple medical device contains only about $1 of the drug epinephrine, the company that sells it, Mylan, earned the public's enmity and lawmakers' scrutiny after ratcheting up prices to $609 a box.

Outraged parents, presidential candidates and even both parties in Congress managed to unite to attack Mylan for the price increases. By August, the company, which sells thousands of drugs and says it fills one in every 13 American prescriptions, was making mea culpas and renewing its promise to "do what's right, not what's easy," as the company's mission statement goes.

So I was surprised when my pharmacist informed me, months after those floggings and apologies had faded from the headlines, that I would still need to pay $609 for a box of two EpiPens.

Didn't we solve this problem?

Not quite. What's more, Mylan is back in the news. On Wednesday, regulators said the company had most likely overcharged Medicaid by $1.27 billion for EpiPens. The same day, a group of pension funds announced that they hoped to unseat much of Mylan's board for "new lows in corporate stewardship," including paying the chairman $97 million in 2016, more than the salaries of the chief executives at Disney, General Electric and Walmart combined.

Over the last several weeks, I've spoken with 10 former high-ranking executives at Mylan who told me that they weren't surprised EpiPen prices were still high. Nor were many startled by last week's developments.

Mylan, they said, is an example of a firm that has thrived by learning to absorb, and then ignore, opprobrium. The company has an effective monopoly on a lifesaving product, which has allowed its leaders to see public outrage as a tax they must pay, and then move on.

Mylan has been called out again and again over the years—by the company's own employees, regulators, patients, politicians and the press—and hasn't changed, even as revenue has skyrocketed, hitting $11 billion last year. The firm is a case study in the limits of what consumer and employee activism, as well as government oversight, can achieve.

Which means this time, if we're hoping for a different outcome, something more needs to be done.

To understand Mylan's culture, consider a series of conversations that began inside the company in 2014. A group of midlevel executives was concerned about the soaring price of EpiPens, which had more than doubled in the previous four years; there were rumors that even more aggressive hikes were planned. (Former executives who related this and other anecdotes requested anonymity because they had nondisclosure agreements or feared retaliation. Aspects of their accounts were disputed by Mylan.)

In meetings, the executives began warning Mylan's top leaders that the price increases seemed like unethical profiteering at the expense of sick children and adults, according to people who participated in the conversations. Over the next 16 months, those internal warnings were repeatedly aired. At one gathering, executives shared their concerns with Mylan's chairman, Robert Coury.

Mr. Coury replied that he was untroubled. He raised both his middle fingers and explained, using colorful language, that anyone criticizing Mylan, including its employees, ought to go copulate with themselves. Critics in Congress and on Wall Street, he said, should do the same. And regulators at the Food and Drug Administration? They, too, deserved a round of anatomically challenging self-fulfillment.

When the executives conveyed their anxieties to other leaders, including the chief executive, Heather Bresch, these, too, were brushed off, they told me.

Those top leaders' responses are a far cry from the message on Mylan's website, which says that "we challenge every member of every team to challenge the status quo," and that "we put people and patients first, trusting that profits will follow."

But Mylan is a prime example of how easy it is for leaders to say one thing publicly and act differently in private. When we talk about consumer or employee activism, we tend to focus on firms like United Airlines, which quickly apologized and changed its policies after a video emerged of a passenger being dragged off a plane.

However, in many other cases, outrage is ineffective. Mylan's behavior persists because it is hard, and often tedious, for employees and the public to continue complaining—particularly when bosses disagree, or when some newer outrage appears on our Facebook feed.

But the costs of going silent are real. Regulators missed an opportunity to reform Mylan in 2012 when the company produced a television commercial showing a mother driving her son to a birthday party and implying that he could eat whatever he wanted, despite his nut allergy, as long as an EpiPen was nearby to counteract a reaction. The commercial also suggested that an EpiPen was a sufficient treatment on its own.

Mylan knew neither of those was true, according to executives from that period. In fact, Mylan had recently started a major lobbying effort to encourage schools to stock EpiPens by arguing that people with serious food allergies are always at risk, and that EpiPens were a necessary supplement to emergency medical treatment.

Before the birthday advertisement aired, the ad went through multiple internal review processes. Mylan executives told Ms. Bresch that the commercial was improper. One employee went so far as to send an internal email saying the advertisement would increase the frequency of allergic reactions, according to a person who saw the correspondence.

Ms. Bresch disagreed. She said it was better to act boldly, according to a former executive who participated in that conversation.

So the advertisement went on television. And a record number of consumer complaints arrived at the Food and Drug Administration. The agency ordered the commercial pulled after just a few days because it was "false and misleading," "overstates the efficacy of the drug product" and "may result in serious consequences, including death." The agency ordered Mylan to broadcast another ad, this one acknowledging that the "EpiPen cannot prevent an allergic reaction."

But regulators never investigated why Mylan's internal protocols had allowed the dangerous ad to air. And a year later, Mylan received something akin to a government endorsement. President Barack Obama signed a federal law encouraging schools to stock emergency epinephrine supplies. The White House celebrated it as the "EpiPen Law."

When I approached Mylan about these and other anecdotes, the company disputed employees' accounts. In a statement, it wrote that "any allegations of disregard for consumers who need these lifesaving drugs, government officials, regulators or any other of our valued stakeholders are patently false and wholly inconsistent with the company's culture, mission and track record of delivering access to medicine."

Mr. Coury declined to be interviewed, but Ms. Bresch sat down with me last month at Mylan's Manhattan offices. She said that Mylan was "a pretty rare and unconventional company," and that it was focused on delivering low-cost drugs. A broken health care system, she said, is responsible for the inefficiencies and high prices that plague consumers.

She added that Mylan had responded promptly when the Food and Drug Administration criticized the company's advertisement in 2012, and that the EpiPen had become more expensive because Mylan had invested in public awareness and improving the device.

"Look at what we've built, and what we deliver day-in and day-out," Ms. Bresch told me, "and at the center of all of that is the patient."

But it seems hard to reconcile those comments with allegations from employees, regulators and other companies. In December, attorneys general in 20 states accused Mylan and five other firms of conspiring to illegally keep prices high on an antibiotic and a diabetes drug. In October, Mylan returned nearly a half-billion dollars to the federal authorities in an attempt to stem the investigation into overcharging that regulators cited on Wednesday. And in April, one of Mylan's competitors, Sanofi, filed a lawsuit accusing the firm of committing antitrust violations to keep an EpiPen competitor off the market.

Then there are situations that, at other firms, might have set off firings or corporate soul-searching, but that at Mylan caused neither. In 2007, reporters discovered that Ms. Bresch had not received the M.B.A. degree she claimed on her résumé. In 2012, Mr. Coury was criticized by investors and the media for repeatedly using the company plane to fly his son to music concerts. (And then there was the time, in 2013, when Mr. Coury, at a Goldman Sachs conference, indicated his dislike for hypothetical questions by saying that "if your aunt had balls, she'd be your uncle.")

In our interview, Ms. Bresch said there was nothing in Mylan's culture she would change. The company also said it had found no evidence of price-fixing or antitrust behavior, that the government overcharges had resulted from an innocent disagreement over regulatory interpretations and that Mylan's compensation policies were appropriate.

"We are a for-profit business, and we have a commitment to shareholders," Ms. Bresch told me. "But I think if there's any company out there that has demonstrated you can do good and do well, we're one of the few." For instance, Ms. Bresch noted that Mylan had recently released a generic version of EpiPen.

When I asked my pharmacist for the generic EpiPen, he told me that I would have to wait 90 minutes, until he could get my doctor on the phone to authorize the substitution. Then, he charged me $370 for the generics.

Mylan points out there are online coupons for EpiPen customers. In fact, the company says that since it came under attack in August, nearly 90 percent of EpiPen buyers have paid less than $100 per box because of insurance, discounts or coupons.

But for parents in urgent need of an EpiPen, or for patients who are poor, are not internet savvy or have high insurance deductibles—which are increasingly common—those programs can mean little. The most vulnerable often end up paying the highest prices, which is troubling when you consider that 15 million Americans have food allergies.

But hope springs eternal. With the recent criticisms coming on the heels of last year's controversies, Mylan will have to change, right?

Perhaps. But only if people stay angry and active. Doctors need to write different prescriptions. Pharmacists need to guide patients to alternatives. Investors should examine further efforts to elect new Mylan board members.

In the meantime, I still believe—perhaps foolishly—that sustained attention might create change. And so, as long as Mylan flouts the norms of good corporate behavior, it seems worth continuing to scrutinize what the company is doing, and questioning why EpiPens cost so much.

Women Absent from Debates About Women's Health
Jenny Gold and Anna Gorman

Women have a lot at stake in the fight over the future of health care.

Not only do many depend on insurance coverage for maternity care and contraception, they are struck more often by autoimmune conditions, osteoporosis, breast cancer and depression. They are more likely to be poor and depend on Medicaid, and to live longer and depend on Medicare. And it commonly falls to them to plan health care and coverage for the whole family.

Yet in recent months, as leaders in Washington discussed the future of American health care, women were not always invited. To hammer out the Senate's initial version of a bill to replace Obamacare, Majority Leader Mitch McConnell appointed 12 colleagues, all male, to closed-door sessions—a fact that was not lost on female Senators. Some members of Congress say they don't see issues like childbirth as a male concern. Why, two GOP representatives wondered aloud during the House debate this spring, should men pay for maternity or prenatal coverage?

As the debate over health care continues, one of the challenges in addressing women's health concerns is that they have different priorities, depending on their stage in life. A 20-year-old may care more about how to get free contraception, while a 30-year-old may be more concerned about maternity coverage. Women in their 50s might be worried about access to mammograms, and those in their 60s may fear not being able to afford insurance before Medicare kicks in at 65.

To get a richer sense of women's varied viewpoints on health care, we asked several women around the country of different ages, backgrounds, and political views to share their thoughts and personal experiences.

Patricia Loftman, 68, New York City

Loftman spent 30 years as a certified nurse-midwife at Harlem Hospital Center and remembers treating women coming in after having botched abortions.

Some didn't survive.

"It was a really bad time," Loftman says. "Women should not have to die just because they don't want to have a child."

When the Supreme Court ruled that women had a constitutional right to an abortion in 1973, Loftman remembers feeling relieved. Now she's angry and scared about the prospect of stricter controls. "Those of us who lived through it just cannot imagine going back," she says.

A mother and grandmother, Loftman also recalls clearly when the birth control pill became legal in the 1960s. She was in nursing school in upstate New York and glad to have another, more convenient option for contraception. Already, women were gaining more independence, and the Pill "just added to that sense of increased freedom and choice."

To her, conservatives' attack on Planned Parenthood, which has already closed many clinics in several states, is frustrating because the organization also provides primary and reproductive health care to many poor women who wouldn't be able to get it otherwise.

Now retired, Loftman sits on the board of the American College of Nurse-Midwives and advocates for better care for minority women. "There continues to be a dramatic racial and ethnic disparity in the outcome of pregnancy and health for African-American women and women of color," she says.

Terrisa Bukovinac, 36, San Francisco

Bukovinac calls herself a passionate pro-lifer. As president of Pro-Life Future of San Francisco, she participates in marches and protests to demonstrate her opposition to abortion.

"Our preliminary goal is defunding Planned Parenthood," she says. "That is crucial to our mission."

As much as the organization touts itself as being a place where people get primary care and contraception, "abortion is their primary business model," Bukovinac says.

She said the vast majority of abortions are not justifiable and that she supports a woman's right to an abortion only in cases that threaten her life. "We are opposed to what we consider elective abortions," she says.

Bukovinac says she also tries to help women in crisis get financial assistance so they don't end their pregnancies just because they can't afford to have a baby. She supports women's access to health insurance and health care, both of which are costly for many. "Certainly, the more people who are covered, the better it is" for both the mother and baby.

Bukovinac herself is uninsured because she says the premiums cost more than she would typically pay for care. Self-employed, Bukovinac has a disorder that causes vertigo and ringing in the ear and spends about $300 per month on medication for that and for anxiety.

She doesn't know if the Affordable Care Act is to blame, but she said that before the law "I was able to afford health insurance and now I'm not."

Irma Castaneda, 49, Huntington Beach, Calif.

Castaneda is a breast cancer survivor. She's been in remission for several years but still sees her oncologist annually and undergoes mammograms, ultrasounds, and blood tests.

The married mom of three, a teacher's aide to special education students, is worried that Republicans may make insurance more expensive for people like her with pre-existing conditions. "They could make our premiums go sky high," she says.

Her family previously purchased a plan on Covered California, the state's Obamacare exchange. But there was a high deductible, so she had to come up with a lot out-of-pocket money before insurance kicked in. "I was paying medical bills up the yin yang," she says. "I felt like I was paying so much for this crappy plan."

Then, about a year ago, Castaneda's husband got injured at work and the family's income dropped by half. Now they rely on Medicaid. At least now they have fewer out-of-pocket expenses for health care.

Whatever the coverage, Castaneda says, she needs high-quality health care. "God forbid I get sick again," she says. And she worries about her daughter, who is transgender and receives specialized physical and mental health care.

"Right now she is pretty lucky because there is coverage for her," Castaneda says. "With the Trump stuff, what's going to happen then?"

Celene Wong, 39, Boston

The choice was agonizing for Wong. A few months into her pregnancy, she and her husband learned that her fetus had chromosomal abnormalities. The baby would have had severe special needs, she said.

"We always said we couldn't handle that," Wong recalls. "We had to make a tough decision, and it is not a decision that most people ever have to face."

The couple terminated the pregnancy in January 2016, when she was about 18 weeks pregnant. "At the end of the day, everybody is going to go away except for your husband and you and this little baby," she says. "We did our research. We knew what we would've been getting into."

Wong, who works to improve the experience for patients at a local hospital, says she is fortunate to have been able to make the choice that was right for her family.

"If the [abortion] law changes, what is going to happen with that next generation?" she wonders.

Lorin Ditzler, 33, Des Moines, Iowa

Ditzler is frustrated that her insurance coverage may be a deciding factor in her family planning. She quit her job last year to take care of her 2-year-old son and was able to get on her husband's plan, which doesn't cover maternity care.

"To me it seems very obvious that our system isn't set up in a way to support giving birth and raising very small children," she says.

While maternity benefits are required under the Affordable Care Act, her husband's plan is grandfathered under the old rules, which is not uncommon among employers that offer coverage. Skirting maternity coverage might become more common if Republicans in Congress pass legislation allowing states to drop maternity coverage an [sic] "essential benefit."

Ditzler looked into switching to an Obamacare plan that they could buy through the exchange, but the rates were much higher than what she pays now.

If she goes back to work, she could get on a better insurance plan that covers maternity care. But that makes little sense to her. "I would go back to a full-time job so I could have a second child, but if I do that, it will be less appealing and less feasible to have a second child because I'd be working full time."

Ashley Bennett, 34, Spartanburg, S.C.

Bennett describes herself as devoutly Christian. She is grateful that she was able to plan her family the way she wanted, with the help of birth control. She had her daughter at 22 and her son two years later.

"I felt free to make that choice, which I think is an awesome thing," she says. She's advised her 12-year-old daughter to wait for sex until marriage but has also been open with her about birth control within the context of marriage.

But she draws the line at abortion. "I just feel like we're playing God. If that conception happens, then I feel like it was meant to be."

Bennett had apprehensions about Trump but voted for him because he was the anti-abortion candidate. "That was the deciding factor for me, [more than] him yelling about how he's going to build a wall."

For her, opposition to abortion must be coupled with support for babies once they are born. She supports adoption and is planning to become a foster parent.

She also is concerned about the mental and physical well-being of young women. Bennett teaches seventh-grade math and coaches the school's cheerleading and dance teams.

She watches the girls take dozens of photos of themselves to get the perfect shot, then add filters to add makeup or slim them down.

"There's going to be an aftermath that we haven't even thought about," she says. "I worry we're going to have more and more kids suffering from depression, eating disorders and even suicide because of the effects of the social media."

Maya Guillén, 24, El Paso, Texas

When Guillén was growing up, her family spent years without health insurance. They crossed the border into Juárez, Mexico, for dental care, doctor appointments, and optometry visits.

Guillén is now on her parents' insurance plan under a provision of the Affordable Care Act that allows children to stay on until they turn 26. She's been disheartened by Republicans' proposed changes to contraception and abortion coverage, she says.

In high school, Guillén received abstinence-only sex education. She watched her friends get pregnant before they graduated.

When it came time to consider sex, she thought she'd be able to count on Planned Parenthood, but the clinic in El Paso closed, as have 20 other women's health clinics in Texas. She worries that if Republicans defund Planned Parenthood, more young girls, especially those in predominantly Hispanic communities like hers, will not be able to get contraceptives.

Jaimie Kelton, 39, New York City

When Jaimie Kelton's wife gave birth to their baby 3½ years ago, she thought the country was finally becoming more open-minded toward gays and lesbians.

"Now I am coming to realize that we are the bubble and they are the majority and that's really scary," says Kelton, now pregnant with her second child.

Kelton says it seems as though Republicans have launched a war against women in general, with reproductive rights and maternity care at risk.

"It is crazy to think that most of the people making these laws are men," she said. "Why do they feel the need to take away health care rights from women?"

Gentrification

Gentrification and the Artistic Dividend: The Role of the Arts in Neighborhood Change

Carl Grodach, Nicole Foster, and James Murdoch, III

Problem, research strategy, and findings: There is a conflict between recent creative placemaking policies intended to promote positive neighborhood development through the arts and the fact that the arts have long been cited as contributing to gentrifiation and the displacement of lower-income residents. Unfortunately, we do not have data to demonstrate widespread evidence of either outcome. We address the dearth of comprehensive research and inform neighborhood planning efforts by statistically testing how two different groups of arts activities—the fine arts and commercial arts industries—are associated with conditions indicative of revitalization and gentrification in 100 large U.S. metropolitan areas. We find that different arts activities are associated with different types and levels of neighborhood change. Commercial arts industries show the strongest association with gentrification in rapidly changing areas, while the fine arts are associated with stable, slow-growth neighborhoods.

Takeaway for practice: This research can help planners to more effectively incorporate the arts into neighborhood planning efforts and to anticipate the potential for different outcomes in their arts development strategies, including gentrification-related displacement.

Keywords: arts, cultural industries, gentrification, neighborhood planning, revitalization

The arts are widely credited with sparking neighborhood change resulting in both positive and negative outcomes. Traditionally, the arts and artists have been seen as contributing to gentrification and the displacement of lower-income residents from central city neighborhoods (Ley, 2003; Zukin, 1982). However, more recent literature argues that 1) art-based gentrification is limited to a handful of places and 2) that the arts are more likely associated with the kind of neighborhood revitalization that benefits existing residents (Markusen & Gadwa, 2010; Stern & Seifert, 2010). In fact, what we know about the impact of the arts on communities is based primarily on case study research, which makes generalization difficult. Moreover, much of the research does not explain how the presence of different types of arts activities may result in different outcomes.

How the arts relate to neighborhood change has become a particularly important question because governments now routinely support the arts explicitly to spur development in targeted areas. For example, the National Endowment for the Arts, the public–private partnership ArtPlace and other foundations, and state and local governments have recently committed significant funding toward "creative placemaking," a strategic attempt at place-based, arts-led revitalization (Coletta, 2012; Markusen & Gadwa, 2010; Nicodemus, 2013).

We address the dearth of comprehensive research and inform neighborhood planning efforts by statistically testing how two different types of arts activities—the fine arts and commercial arts industries—are associated with conditions indicative of urban revitalization and gentrification in 100 U.S. metropolitan areas with a population greater than 500,000. First, we summarize literature on the relationship of the arts to gentrification and neighborhood revitalization. Next, we provide an overview of our study's data and methods. The following sections discuss the findings and implications for planning practitioners and scholars.

Our findings show that the arts are not inextricably linked to either gentrification or revitalization. Moreover, the fine arts and commercial arts exhibit different relationships to the type and pace of neighborhood change. While fine arts activities are more likely associated with our measure of revitalization, commercial arts industries are strongly associated with gentrification. Further, while the fine arts tend to be located in stable, slow-growth neighborhoods, commercial arts industries are associated with rapidly changing areas. This research can help planners to more effectively incorporate the arts into neighborhood planning efforts and anticipate the potential for different outcomes in their arts development strategies including gentrification-related displacement.

The Relationship Between the Arts and Neighborhood Change

A sizable literature has established that the arts can play a key role in reshaping conditions in downtown areas and urban neighborhoods. However, there is debate over the type of neighborhood change most closely associated with the arts. On the one hand, a long line of research has documented the role of the arts in gentrification, a process of reinvestment in depressed central city areas marked by a demographic shift toward higher educated, more affluent, and often White residents along with rising rents (Deutsche & Ryan, 1984; Ley, 1986, 2003; Mathews, 2010; Zukin, 1982). Some argue that gentrification is a potential vehicle for bringing improvements to disadvantaged neighborhoods such as higher property values, lower crime rates, and enhanced neighborhood amenities and services (Brown-Saracino, 2010; Freeman & Braconi, 2004; Papachristos, Smith, Scherer, & Fugiero, 2011). Far more numerous, however, are those who critique gentrification for causing the displacement and outmigration of long-time residents and small businesses that are not able to remain in the neighborhood to enjoy reinvestment (Bridge, Butler, & Lees, 2011; Doucet, 2014; Newman & Wyly, 2006; Slater, 2009; Smith, 1979; Zukin, 1982, 2010). On the other hand, some claim that the arts can spur neighborhood revitalization without gentrification, creating positive, place-based change that does not result in a demographic shift and population turnover and therefore benefits existing residents (Grodach, 2011a; Markusen & Gadwa, 2010; Stern & Seifert, 2010).

Substantial case study research demonstrates that individual artists, artistic businesses, and art spaces (e.g., galleries, theaters, and music venues) collectively function as a "colonizing arm" that helps to create the initial conditions that spark gentrification (Cameron & Coaffee, 2005; Deutsche & Ryan, 1984; Ley, 2003; Lloyd, 2010; Mathews, 2010; Zukin, 1982). Decades ago, Zukin (1982) explained through the concept of an "artistic mode of production" that gentrification is accomplished through the artists' symbolic appropriation of space, which is in turn seized by investors to attract capital reinvestment in the built environment (p. 176). In other words, artists indirectly set the stage for change through their cultural capital (Ley, 2003). Using their sweat equity, artists aesthetically revalue places by transforming dilapidated, impoverished, and often ethnically segregated areas into a "neo-bohemia" filled with art studios, galleries, bars, coffee shops, and restaurants (Lloyd, 2010; Silver & Clark, 2013; Zukin, 2010). The general presence of artists paves the way for future property reinvestment by real estate developers and higher-income members of the creative class by renovating places mainstream culture considers blighted into attractive destinations.

Over time, the arts have come to play a more direct role in gentrification as an instrument of urban policy and planning as well (Cameron & Coafee, 2005; Grodach & Silver, 2013). Local governments have provided substantial funding for the opening and expansion of flagship museums, theaters, and performing arts complexes and planned new arts districts hoping that they will catalyze future development in downtowns and central city neighborhoods (Birch, Griffin, Johnson, & Stover, 2013; Grodach, 2010; Johnson, 2009; Strom, 2002). Public investments in cultural facilities have expanded significantly since the late 1990s following the highly publicized success of the Guggenheim Museum Bilbao, which is credited with transforming the Spanish city into a global destination (Evans, 2003; Grodach, 2011b). In addition, as many case studies show, city officials inspired by Richard Florida's *Rise of the Creative Class* (2002) have invested in smaller-scale arts-themed areas as amenities to attract skilled labor and engender neighborhood redevelopment (Catungal, Leslie, & Hii, 2009; Grodach, 2012, 2013; Johnson, 2009; Ponzini & Rossi, 2012). As a corollary, nonprofit arts institutions and organizations now join with coalitions of city officials, property developers, and businesses to promote downtown development (Ashley, 2014; Grodach, 2012; Strom, 2002).

Cities not only invest in museums and the performing arts, but also concentrate on commercial arts industries—film, music, and design-based sectors—in their local economic development planning programs. Abundant research demonstrates that arts industries have a greater propensity to cluster in urban areas to take advantage of and capitalize on concentrations of specialized labor and services along with related industries in media, finance, and high technology (Currid & Williams, 2010; Grodach, Currid, Foster, & Murdoch, 2014; Scott, 2006). Although less common than investing in nonprofit arts activities, urban growth coalitions also target arts industries to generate redevelopment. Toronto, for example, has invested heavily in new film studios and design industries to stimulate development in their central city areas, while Austin (TX) invests in their music industry as a component of new downtown building projects (Catungal et al., 2009; Grodach, 2012, 2013; also see Hutton, 2009).

Arts-led gentrification, both as an instrument of urban policy and through individual actions, can bring positive changes to many urban areas. For example, museums and performing arts institutions can serve as urban anchors that have a significant impact on center city redevelopment by attracting property development, jobs, and new services (Birch et al., 2013). Similarly, following Richard Florida (2002), cities have constructed new arts amenities to spur local economic growth and increase real estate values through the attraction of upwardly mobile professionals.

However, others argue that by attracting a largely White, educated, professional population to spur urban redevelopment, arts-based gentrification ultimately has negative results. Despite the many place-based improvements, incorporating arts venues into urban redevelopment schemes has created privatized bubbles that primarily serve tourists and the upwardly mobile creative class while excluding some residents and even artists themselves (Eisinger, 2000; Grodach, 2008; Peck, 2005; Shaw & Sullivan, 2011). At the same time, the influx and concentration of artistic businesses and arts industry workers in particular areas can bid rents upward and produce waves of displacement as former tenants are forced to move elsewhere (Cameron & Coaffee, 2005; Catungal et al., 2009; Grodach, 2012, 2013).

Alternatively, another stream of research concentrates more specifically on the arts as assets in neighborhood revitalization without gentrification (Grodach, 2011a; Jackson, Kabwasa-Green, & Herranz, 2006; Markusen & Gadwa, 2010; Stern & Seifert, 2010). Markusen has been one of the most active researchers to conceptualize and document the development contribution of the arts (Markusen & Schrock, 2006; Markusen & Gadwa, 2010). Her work stresses the importance of an "artistic dividend": the value added to local and regional economies through artistic work (Markusen & Schrock, 2006, p. 1661). Beyond attracting a creative class workforce, artists and art groups may generate economic gain through export of their work by supplying skills that improve the productivity of nonartistic industries, or by attracting visitors to specific neighborhoods. Because artistic networks tend to be concentrated and rooted in place, these benefits can spill over into the immediate area, leading to neighborhood improvements.

While much of this work recognizes that these benefits can create conditions for gentrification, they also argue that most places do not experience the high levels of property appreciation and demand for central city space that drives the gentrification process (Ryberg, 2012; Stern and Seifert, 2010). For example, in their study of Philadelphia, Stern and Seifert (2010) find that neighborhoods with higher levels of neighborhood arts activity are more likely than others to experience factors they considered to be indicators of revitalization, such as increased population density, higher housing values, employment growth, and declining poverty rates. Further, they and others show that places that are home to a diversity of arts offerings, including lower-income neighborhoods, remained stable rather than experiencing a dramatic upscaling (Grams & Warr, 2003; Stern & Seifert, 2007). Supporting this research, case studies provide evidence that community art spaces often work with neighborhood groups to foster change without noticeably high levels of neighborhood turnover (Grodach, 2011a; Markusen & Johnson, 2006; Stern & Seifert, 2007). Silver and Miller (2013) find a strong association between neighborhoods with an artistic presence and rising local wages and median incomes, while Noonan (2013) finds that cultural districts have a modest but positive effect on property values, employment, and income without clear evidence of gentrification.

In sum, while some consider an artistic presence as a catalyst for change that largely benefits elites and results in the displacement of established residents and businesses, others claim that the arts can spur neighborhood revitalization to their benefit. Both streams of literature, however, suffer from two problems. First, the literature is highly contextual. There are many rich case studies of neighborhoods, some of which focus on how the arts influence neighborhood change in particular cities. However, with few exceptions (Noonan, 2013; Silver & Miller, 2013), researchers have not identified the generalized patterns of how the arts are associated with neighborhood change. Second, much of the literature on the arts and gentrification does not concentrate specifically on how different types of arts activity relate to urban change. Studies tend to focus either on a single type of arts activity (e.g., a museum or the music sector) or, more common, broadly consider an artistic presence. The fact is that "the arts" encompass a very diverse set of activities. Similarly, artists work in a wide range of fields from film, design, and other commercial industries to nonprofit dance companies, symphonies, museums, and art schools. A more nuanced understanding of the relationships that different types of arts activities have with gentrification and revitalization will help planners and policymakers to more effectively incorporate the arts into their redevelopment programs.

Analytic Strategy: Modeling the Relationship of the Arts to Neighborhood Change

To determine how the arts are associated with neighborhood change, we study the relationships between arts industries and a set of variables commonly discussed in the literature as indicative of gentrification and neighborhood revitalization in the first decade of the 21st century. We focus on 100 U.S. metropolitan statistical areas (MSA) with a population of 500,000 or more in 2010. A more detailed description of the study data and methodology appears in the Technical Appendix.

All data are gathered at the zip code level, which we treat as a proxy for the neighborhood. We study neighborhoods within 10 miles of any central business district (CBD) in each metro. Our decision to use a 10-mile radius is based on the fact that the vast majority of the literature concentrates on gentrification in neighborhoods located in more established, built-out areas around the CBD. However, we recognize that regions have varied histories, phases, and character of development. Indeed, researchers are beginning to analyze inner-ring suburbs as sites of gentrification (Charles, 2011). As such, limiting the sample to zip codes immediately surrounding a CBD may exclude important areas from the analysis. Therefore, the 10-mile radius is meant to capture potential sites of gentrification in the varying geographies of U.S. MSAs.

The dependent variables in the study—gentrification and revitalization—are based on a set of 10 variables previously used in the literature (Freeman, 2005; Ley, 1986; Sands & Reese, 2013). These include the growth rate in the following variables: average household income, the proportion of the employed population, the proportion of the population not in poverty, the proportion of households not receiving public assistance, the proportion of the population 25 years of age and older with a bachelor's degree or higher, the proportion of the White population, residents in management occupations, mean housing value, and population density. We also include the proportion of homeowners that moved to the neighborhood in 2005 or later.

Gentrification and revitalization are complex processes that vary with the local context. Therefore, we do not attempt to subjectively assign the variables to specific categories. Rather, we conduct a principal component factor analysis to statistically identify groups of related variables indicative of neighborhood change. This approach attempts to deal with the challenge of operationalizing the terms "revitalization" and "gentrification" and allows for the possibility that gentrification and revitalization may exhibit some similar or overlapping features. In other words, we anticipate that the factor analysis will produce categories that reflect urban revitalization as well as indications of potential displacement.

The factor analysis produced three factors that capture different dimensions of neighborhood revitalization and gentrification discussed in the literature. We label these factors "neighborhood revitalization," "neighborhood upscaling," and "neighborhood build-out" (see Table A-1 in the Technical Appendix for factor analysis results). The primary variables that contribute to the neighborhood revitalization factor are growth in income, employment rates, housing values, and the proportion of residents not living in poverty. This factor incorporates indicators of neighborhood improvement without clear warning signs of displacement and most closely reflects the findings of Stern and Seifert (2010) in their study of the arts and revitalization.

The other factors, which we label as gentrification factors, are variables denoting neighborhood improvement alongside signs of neighborhood instability.

Neighborhood upscaling describes places where there is a growing rate of employed residents and a declining proportion of residents on public assistance along with a growing White population, highly educated residents, and residents in management occupations. Neighborhood build-out represents neighborhoods that are becoming denser, have an increasing proportion of new homeowners, and contain an increasing proportion of residents in management and those with high levels of income and education.

In short, the neighborhood revitalization factor is distinct from the other two because there are no entry signs of a gentrifying population (namely, an educated, White professional population), while the other factors include these. However, given the available data, our factors cannot directly capture an important component of gentrification: the displacement of existing, lower-income residents and their replacement by upwardly mobile professionals. What we study are variables indicative of potential displacement. Our study is therefore a better reflection of change in the status of places than changes in specific populations. To be clear, we are not able to directly identify the inflows and outflows of residents to account for displacement, which is a limitation that we hope will be addressed in future work. What we can study are factors indicative of these concepts and determine statistically how the arts are related to each of these factors.

The independent variables are two different sets of arts industries that represent the fine arts and commercial arts sectors. The commercial arts consists of people employed in film, music, and design industries. The fine arts consists of employment in sectors that tend to be a blend of for-profit and nonprofit visual and performing arts and museums, art galleries, and fine arts schools (see Table A-2). All industries are classified by the North American Industrial Classification System (NAICS) in the zip code business pattern (ZBP) dataset provided by the U.S. Census Bureau (2010). Our arts industry measures come from the year 2000 data file.

There are arguments both for and against the use of industry data to study the arts. Those who focus on artistic occupations point to two weaknesses of studying industries (Markusen, Wassall, DeNatale, & Cohen, 2008). First, industry data do not include self-employed workers, which are an important portion of the arts workforce. Second, arts industry employment data include those who do not work in the arts, so the data are not an actual count of artists. We agree with this assessment, but argue that any artistic production involves more than the artists themselves, and that the nonartistic staff that contribute to an artistic business are a necessary component for the arts to flourish (Becker, 1982). The ideal approach would be to look at arts industries and occupations simultaneously; however, industry data are the only consistent source of data on employment in the arts across all U.S. metropolitan areas over an extended period of time at the micro level. Moreover, the NAICS dataset captures both the fine and commercial arts discussed in the literature (e.g., museums, performing arts centers, art galleries, and film and design industries) as well as independent artists (NAICS 711510). Admittedly, the latter is not an ideal representation of individual artists given that they infrequently support themselves with their artwork alone (and, as a result, many are not counted in occupational data as well). The NAICS data do capture artists indirectly through their employment in arts industries. For these reasons, we feel the data adequately model different forms of artistic presence and hope to improve representation as better data become available.

Alongside the arts variables we use a range of social, economic, and housing variables taken from the 2000 census as well as per capita employment in consumer amenities (e.g., bars, coffee shops, markets, and restaurants), drawn from the ZBP, to control for potential differences in neighborhood context. In this way, we can determine the extent to which the arts are related to neighborhood change independent of differences in the status of a neighborhood at the beginning of the study period in terms of variables like average income, level of education, or average age of residents, all of which may have an influence on revitalization and gentrification (see Table A-3 for a complete list of variables).

To estimate the relationship of the arts industries to gentrification and revitalization, we specify linear regression models using the neighborhood revitalization, neighborhood upscaling, and neighborhood build-out factors as dependent variables. We first run the regression model on the entire dataset to get a sense of the relationships of the arts to neighborhood change overall. Next, because neighborhoods that experience different levels of change may have varying associations with arts activity, we use quintile regression. This approach divides our dependent variable into five levels of change from the 20% of neighborhoods exhibiting slowest rate of change to the 20% with the highest rate of change. This is in contrast to other studies of gentrification, which define neighborhoods as either gentrifying or not gentrifying regardless of the pace of change (Freeman & Braconi, 2004; Ley, 1986; Newman & Wyly, 2006). We feel that this approach better models the potential revitalization and gentrification scenarios and enables us to determine how the arts are associated with different levels of change. This approach is also useful in situations where the data are skewed, which we find in studies of gentrification.

The Fine Arts and Commercial Arts Are Associated with Different Types of Neighborhoods

We first examine the relationship of the fine arts and commercial arts to the three types of neighborhoods overall: revitalizing neighborhoods and the two representations of gentrification, neighborhood upscaling and neighborhood build-out. Our results indicate that the arts are not a homogenous group. Rather, different arts activities exhibit distinct relationships to different types of neighborhood change.

Both groups of arts industries hold up as important variables under specific conditions (see Table A-4 for regression results). The commercial arts have a significant association with both of the gentrification factors, but show no relationship to neighborhood revitalization. Conversely, the fine arts have a positive association with neighborhood revitalization, but correlate negatively with gentrifying neighborhoods. These findings lend support to claims of the power of the arts to revitalize central city neighborhoods, but also clarify their role in gentrification processes, revealing a link between the commercial arts industries and gentrification, but not with the fine arts.

The commercial arts exhibit by far the strongest association with the neighborhood build-out gentrification factor, which is defined by neighborhoods that are becoming denser, experiencing rising homeownership rates, and contain an increasing proportion of upwardly mobile residents. Looking at the control variables, it makes sense that this form of gentrification is associated with neighborhoods that have a positive association with Whites, a young adult population, low rates of public assistance, and the presence of amenities at the start of the study period. Further, this form of gentrification is negatively related to areas where an employed and highly educated population already exists. We may infer from these results that prior to the study period, gentrification processes have likely been under way to some extent and that commercial arts are not only attracted to such neighborhoods, but also may be associated with their gentrification.

Commercial arts industries also display positive but weaker associations with the other gentrification factor, neighborhood upscaling. In this case, neighborhoods experience increasing employment, an influx of educated and White residents, and a declining proportion of residents on public assistance. These neighborhoods reflect considerably different associations with the control variables. This form of gentrification is strongly associated with neighborhoods that begin the study period with major challenges in that the proportion of employed residents and those not on public assistance show a strong negative relationship, as does, to a lesser extent, the average rent variable. They do begin the study period with mixed indicators of gentrification through a negative association with amenities and young adults, but a weak positive relationship with median housing values and a White population.

In contrast, fine arts have a weak but positive association with revitalization, characterized by neighborhoods experiencing growing income levels, employment, housing values, and residents living above the poverty line. These neighborhoods resemble the neighborhood upscaling controls at the beginning of the study period with three notable exceptions: They are marked by the presence of highly educated individuals and fewer people on public assistance, yet lower home values. This mix of educated residents and signs of poverty resembles Stern and Seifert's (2010) "pov-prof" neighborhoods, where they find strong associations with artistic activity. In sum, the different types of arts activity maintain separate relationships to revitalizing and gentrifying neighborhoods and emanate from different initial neighborhood conditions.

The Fine Arts and Commercial Arts Are Associated with Different Levels of Neighborhood Change

Here, we turn to examining the relationships between the arts and the different neighborhood types based on the level of change. We break the level of change into five increments, or quintiles, organized from slowest to fastest. We continue to see that the two arts groups exhibit opposing associations with revitalization and gentrification at all five levels of change where the variables are statistically significant (see Tables A-5, A-6, and A-7, and Figure A-1 for regression results). Results for the areas with the highest rate of change (81% to 100%) in each of the gentrification models (neighborhood upscaling and neighborhood build-out) are by far the most robust and are stronger than the model in the preceding section. Further, with the exception of the slowest growth areas (0% to 20%), the other levels of neighborhood change possess virtually no relationship to each of the neighborhood types. Therefore, much of what we capture in the model here actually may be a reflection of neighborhoods undergoing the most significant change over the study period and, to a lesser extent, those that have undergone very little change.

The fine arts retain their negative association to rapidly gentrifying neighborhoods (Tables A-6 and A-7), but in contrast to the full regression model, also exhibit a negative relationship to areas with the highest rates of neighborhood revitalization (Table A-5). Rather, their modest association with this measure of neighborhood change occurs only in neighborhoods where revitalization processes are at their slowest. These neighborhoods are defined by a Hispanic population, educated residents, above-average population density, White residents, and above-average rent and tend to have fewer young adults and amenities, lower housing values, and a smaller foreign-born population.

For the commercial arts industries, the associations with the gentrification factors are strongest and significant in the areas experiencing the highest levels of change (Tables A-6 and A-7; Figure A-1). Further, in contrast to the model in the preceding section, the commercial arts also display a strong link to the revitalization factor in high-growth areas. In fact, the commercial arts maintain a strong relationship to high-growth neighborhoods across all three neighborhood change factors. The link with neighborhood upscaling dramatically increases from the full model, and there is a notable increase in the relationship with neighborhood build-out as well. With one exception (61% to 80% quintile in neighborhood build-out), there is no positive association between the commercial arts and slower levels of gentrification. The commercial arts industries also show a strong negative relationship, whereas the fine arts have a positive relationship, namely in slow growth revitalization neighborhoods (Figure A-1).

All high-growth neighborhoods where the commercial arts are common are defined by low levels of employment and low levels of highly educated residents at the start of the study period. Neighborhoods with the most pronounced levels of neighborhood upscaling, however, do show some signs of gentrification. These neighborhoods contain amenities, a higher than average White population, and above-average housing values, but also high levels of public assistance, low rent, and above-average vacancy rates, indicating further room for development. Mixed signs of gentrification similarly define neighborhoods exhibiting high rates of build-out. In addition to a strong association with commercial arts industries and the negative associations with employment and high education, these neighborhoods exhibit reasonably strong associations with amenities, housing values, White and foreign-born populations, young adults, and larger households, but also lower rent, public assistance, and vacant units. In other words, commercial arts industries are associated with areas with incipient gentrification, which rapidly develop over the study period.

Conclusions

This study tests the relationship of the fine arts and commercial arts industries to conditions indicative of neighborhood revitalization and gentrification in 100 U.S. metropolitan areas with a population greater than 500,000. Our research provides two important findings that inform the debate on how the arts are associated with neighborhood change. First, fine arts and commercial arts industries exhibit different associations with the types of neighborhood change. The fine arts, such as performing arts companies, museums, and arts schools, are more likely associated with our measure of revitalizing neighborhoods. In contrast, the commercial arts, which include film, music, and design-based industries, are aligned with our measures of gentrification. Second, the arts vary in their relationship with the level of change that occurs in a neighborhood. The fine arts are found in slow-growth neighborhoods that are experiencing gradual revitalization and not in gentrifying neighborhoods. Conversely, the commercial arts are strongly linked to neighborhoods experiencing the highest levels of change, particularly in rapidly gentrifying areas.

These findings extend the arts and neighborhood change literature and provide important knowledge for planners interested in incorporating the arts into their revitalization programs and engaging in creative placemaking. For one, our work complements the case study research by statistically testing competing theories of the relationship between the arts and neighborhood change, suggesting generalizable patterns across many metropolitan areas. We clarify that the arts are not uniformly implicated in either gentrification or revitalization processes. Rather, the commercial arts and fine arts show distinct associations to different types and levels of neighborhood change.

Extending from these findings, the results do not support claims that large cultural institutions and arts districts attract major development or the creative class because we do not find evidence that our group of fine arts activities are associated with gentrification and rapid growth areas (Birch et al., 2013; Florida, 2002). We do not doubt that flagship arts and creative class strategies have remade some urban districts, but this is more likely the exception than the rule. Indeed, the results seem to validate studies that argue museums and art centers are development catalysts only in rare instances (Grodach, 2010). Conversely, our work supports those case studies that find commercial arts industries spur gentrification (Catungal et al., 2009; Grodach, 2012; Hutton, 2009). Finally, the results provide some support, albeit weak, for the arts-based revitalization argument (Markusen & Gadwa, 2010; Stern & Seifert, 2010).

Building off of these findings, we need further research that helps to explain why these patterns occur. Are the fine arts unrelated to gentrifying areas because they cannot afford such neighborhoods, or are they displaced in the gentrification process? Or, alternatively, are these arts groups not widely attracted to such areas? Why are the commercial arts sectors attracted to rapidly gentrifying areas, and in what ways do they catalyze change there? To what extent are residents actually displaced from gentrifying arts neighborhoods, and in what ways do they benefit, if it all?

Planners can and should take account of the consequences of advancing different forms of arts-based development. This includes considering the contexts in which different interventions are likely to be successful or harmful to existing communities. At present, the most common arts development approach is to invest in flagship cultural facilities and arts-themed districts to attract upscale development. However, this study shows that commercial arts industries are more likely to serve as growth catalysts. Further, the results also imply that commercial arts industries are strongly associated with displacement. As a result, if cities turn toward arts industries in their redevelopment programs, they must also pay close attention to the availability of affordable housing and mechanisms that mitigate the displacement of long-time residents and small businesses. Alternatively, cities should not underestimate the potential stabilizing force of the fine arts, which may in fact be preferable to rapid growth and change in many communities. An understanding of how different arts activities relate to varying neighborhood contexts equips planners with knowledge to develop more informed and targeted arts development strategies.

Acknowledgments

The authors would like to thank Ann Gadwa Nicodemus, Dan Silver, and three anonymous reviewers for their helpful comments on this article.

Research Support

The research was supported by a grant from the National Endowment for the Arts.

References

Ashley, A. J. (2014). Negotiating risk in property-based arts economic development: Exploring the innovative but untimely development partnership between the Seattle Art Museum and Washington Mutual. *Cities, 37*, 92–103. doi:10.1016/j.cities.2013.11.003

Becker, H. (1982). *Art worlds*. Berkeley: University of California Press.

Birch, E., Griffin, C., Johnson, A., & Stover, J. (2013). *Arts and culture institutions as urban anchors*. Philadelphia: Penn Institute for Urban Research, University of Pennsylvania Press. Retrieved from http://penniur.upenn.edu/uploads/media/arts-and-culture-institutions-a-surban-anchors.pdf

Bridge, G., Butler, T., & Lees, L. (Eds.). (2011). *Mixed communities: gentrification by stealth?* Bristol, England: Policy.

Brown-Saracino, J. (2010). *A neighborhood that never changes: Gentrification, social preservation, and the search for authenticity*. Chicago, IL: University of Chicago Press.

Cameron, S., & Coaffe, J. (2005). Art, gentrification, and regeneration: From artist as pioneer to public arts. *European Journal of Housing Policy, 5*(1), 39–58. doi:10.1080/14616710500055687

Catungal, J. P., Leslie, D., & Hii, Y. (2009). Geographies of displacement in the creative city: The case of Liberty Village, Toronto. *Urban Studies, 46*(5–6), 1095–1114. doi: 10.1177/0042098009103856

Charles, S. L. (2011). *Suburban gentrification: Understanding the determinants of single-family residential redevelopment, a case study of the inner-ring suburbs of Chicago, IL, 2000–2010*. Cambridge, MA: Joint Center for Housing Studies of Harvard University. Retrieved from http://140.247.195.238/sites/jchs.harvard.edu/files/w11-1_charles.pdf

Coletta, C. (2012). *Building a better understanding of creative placemaking*. Washington, DC: ArtPlace America. Retrieved from http://www.artplaceamerica.org/under standing-creative-placemaking

Currid, E., & Williams, S. (2010). Two cities, five industries: Similarities and differences within and between cultural industries in New York and Los Angeles. *Journal of Planning Education and Literature, 29*(3), 322–335. doi:10.1177/0739456X09358559

Deutsche, R., & Ryan, C. G. (1984). The fine art of gentrification. *October, 31*, 91–111. Retrieved from http://www.mitpressjournals.org/october

Doucet, B. (2014). A process of change and a changing process: Introduction to the special issue on contemporary gentrification. *Tijdschrift Voor Economische En Sociale Geografie, 105*(2), 125–139. doi:10.1111/tesg.12075

Eisinger, P. (2000). The politics of bread and circuses: Building the city for the visitor class. *Urban Affairs Review, 35*(3), 316–333. doi:10.1177/107808740003500302

Evans, G. (2003). Hard branding the culture city: from Prado to Prada. *International Journal of Urban and Regional Research, 27*(2), 417–440. doi:10.1111/1468-2427.00455

Florida, R. (2002). *The rise of the creative class*. New York, NY: Basic Books.

Freeman, L. (2005). Displacement or succession? Residential mobility in gentrifying neighborhoods. *Urban Affairs Review, 40*(4), 463–491. doi:10.1177/1078087404273341

Freeman, L., & Braconi, F. (2004). Gentrification and displacement: New York City in the 1990s. *Journal of the American Planning Association,* 70(1), 39–52. doi:10.1080/01944360408976337

Grams, D., & Warr, M. (2003). *Leveraging assets: How small budget arts activities benefit neighborhoods*. Chicago, IL: Richard Driehaus Foundation and John D. and Catherine T. MacArthur Foundation.

Grodach, C. (2008). Looking beyond image and tourism: The role of flagship cultural projects in local arts development. *Planning Practice & Research, 23*(4), 495–516. doi:10.1080/02697450802522806

Grodach, C. (2010). Beyond Bilbao: Rethinking flagship cultural development and planning in three California cities. *Journal of Planning Education and Research, 29*(3), 353–366. doi:10.1177/0739456X09354452

Grodach, C. (2011a). Art spaces in community and economic development: Connections to neighborhoods, artists, and the cultural economy. *Journal of Planning Education and Research, 31*(1), 74–85. doi:10.1177/0739456X10391668

Grodach, C. (2011b). Cultural institutions: The role of urban design. In T. Banerjee & A. Loukaitou-Sideris (Eds.), *Companion to Urban Design* (pp. 405–418). New York, NY: Routledge.

Grodach, C. (2012). Before and after the creative city: The politics of urban cultural policy in Austin, Texas. *Journal of Urban Affairs, 34*(1), 81–97. doi:10.1111/j.1467-9906.2011.00574.x

Grodach, C. (2013). Cultural economy planning in creative cities: Discourse and practice. *International Journal of Urban and Regional Research, 37*(5), 1747–1765. doi:10.1111/j.1468-2427.2012.01165.x

Grodach, C., Currid, E., Foster, N., & Murdoch, J. III. (2014). The location patterns of artistic clusters: A metro and neighborhood level analysis. *Urban Studies*. Advanced online publication. doi:10.1177/0042098013516523

Grodach, C., & Silver, D. (2013). *The politics of urban cultural policy: Global perspectives.* New York: Routledge.

Hutton, T. A. (2009). *The New economy of the inner city: Restructuring, regeneration and dislocation in the 21st century metropolis.* Abingdon, England: Routledge.

Jackson, M. R., Kabwasa-Green, F., & Herranz, J. (2006). *Cultural vitality in communities: Interpretation and indicators.* Washington, DC: The Urban Institute.

Johnson, A. (2009, October). *Chasing smokestacks and artists: The evolving relationship between local economic development and the arts.* Paper presented at the Society for American City and Regional Planning History Conference, Oakland, CA.

Ley, D. (1986). Alternative explanations for inner-city gentrification: A Canadian assessment. *Annals of the Association of American Geographers, 76*(4), 521–535. doi:10.1111/j.1467-8306.1986.tb00134.x

Ley, D. (2003). Artists, aestheticisation and the field of gentrification. *Urban Studies, 40*(12), 2527–2544. doi:10.1080/0042098032000136192

Lloyd, R. (2010). *Neo-bohemia: Art and commerce in the postindustrial city* (2nd ed.). New York, NY: Routledge.

Markusen, A., & Gadwa, A. (2010). Arts and culture in urban or regional planning: A review and research agenda. *Journal of Planning Education and Research, 29*(3), 379–391. doi:10.1177/0739456X09354380

Markusen, A., & Johnson, A. (2006). *Artists' centers: Evolution and impact on careers, neighborhoods and economies.* Minneapolis: Project on Regional and Industrial Economics, University of Minnesota.

Markusen, A., & Schrock, G. (2006). The artistic dividend: Urban specialization and economic development implications. *Urban Studies, 43*(10), 1661–1686. doi:10.1080/00420980600888478

Markusen, A., Wassall, G., DeNatale, D., & Cohen, R. (2008). Defining the creative economy: Industry and occupational approaches. *Economic Development Quarterly, 22*(1), 24–45. doi:10.1177/0891242407311862

Mathews, V. (2010). Aestheticizing space: Art, gentrification and the city. *Geography Compass, 4*(6), 660–675. doi:10.1111/j.1749-8198.2010.00331.x

Newman, K., & Wyly, E. K. (2006). The right to stay put, revisited: Gentrification and resistance to displacement in New York City. *Urban Studies, 43*(1), 23–57. doi:10.1080/00420980500388710

Nicodemus, A. G. (2013). Fuzzy vibrancy: Creative placemaking as ascendant U.S. cultural policy. *Cultural Trends, 22*(3–4), 213–222. doi:10.1080/09548963.2013.817653

Noonan, D. (2013). How US cultural districts reshape neighborhoods. *Cultural Trends*, *22*(3–4), 203–212. doi:10.1080/09548963.2013.817652

Papachristos, A., Smith, C., Scherer, M., & Fugiero, M. (2011). More coffee, less crime? The relationship between gentrification and neighborhood crime rates in Chicago, 1991 to 2005. *City and Community*, *10*(3), 215–240. doi:10.1111/j.1540-6040.2011.01371.x

Peck, J. (2005). Struggling with the creative class. *International Journal of Urban and Regional Research*, *29*(4), 740–770. doi:10.1111/j.1468-2427.2005.00620.x

Ponzini, D., & Rossi, U. (2010). Becoming a creative city: The entrepreneurial mayor, network politics and the promise of an urban renaissance. *Urban Studies*, *47*(5), 1037–1057. doi:10.1177/0042098009353073

Ryberg, S. (2012). Putting artists on the map: The geography of artists in Cuyahoga County, Ohio. *Journal of Urban Affairs*, *35*(2), 219–245. doi:10.1111/j.1467-9906.2012.00623.x

Sands, G., & Reese, R. (2013). Fair weather friends? The impact of the creative class on the economic health of mid-sized US metropolitan areas, 1990–2009. *Cambridge Journal of Regions, Economy and Society*, *6*(1), 71–91. doi:10.1093/cjres/rss013

Scott, A. (2006). Creative cities: Conceptual issues and policy questions. *Journal of Urban Affairs*, *28*(1), 1–17. doi:10.1111/j.0735-2166.2006.00256.x

Shaw, S., & Sullivan, D. M. (2011). "White Night": Gentrification, racial exclusion, and perceptions and participation in the arts. *City & Community*, *10*(3), 241–264. doi:10.1111/j.1540-6040.2011.01373.x

Silver, D., & Clark, T. 2013. *Scenes: Culture and place*. Chicago, IL: University of Chicago Press.

Silver, D., & Miller, D. (2013). Contextualizing the artistic dividend. *Journal of Urban Affairs*, *35*(5), 591–606. doi:10.1111/j.1467-9906.2012.00642.x

Slater, T. (2009). Missing Marcuse: On gentrification and displacement. *City 13*(2), 292–311. doi:10.1080/13604810902982250.

Smith, N. (1979). Toward a theory of gentrification: A back to the city movement by capital not people. *Journal of the American Planning Association*, *45*(4), 538–548. doi:10.1080/01944367908977002

Stern, M., & Seifert, S. (2007). *Culture and urban revitalization: A harvest document*. Philadelphia: University of Pennsylvania.

Stern, M., & Seifert, S. (2010). Cultural clusters: The implications of cultural assets agglomeration for neighborhood revitalization. *Journal of Planning Education and Research*, *29*(3), 262–279. doi:10.1177/0739456X09358555

Strom, E. (2002). Converting pork into porcelain: Cultural institutions and downtown development. *Urban Affairs Review*, *38*(1), 3–21. doi:10.1177/107808702401097763

U.S. Census Bureau. (2010). *ZCTA Gazetteer file*. Retrieved from http://www.census.gov/geo/maps-data/data/gazetteer2010.html

Zukin, S. (1982). *Loft living: Culture and capital in urban change*. Baltimore, MD: Johns Hopkins University Press.

Zukin, S. (2010). *Naked city: The death and life of authentic urban places*. Oxford, England: Oxford University Press.

Technical Appendix

Defining the Unit of Analysis

To approximate neighborhoods, we rely on the zip code as the unit of analysis.[1] While not a perfect means of capturing neighborhoods, zip codes are the most consistent geography at which the U.S. Census reports business patterns data at the micro level and so give us an approximation of neighborhood-level change. We study neighborhoods within a 10-mile radius of the central business district (CBD) in each metro. To define CBD locations, we use the 1980 Census of the Population Master Area Reference File 2 (MARF 2) available from the Inter-University Consortium for Political and Social Research (ICPSR). Although 1980 precedes the study period, we rely on this data because it is the most recent release that contains CBD coordinates. Our sample of 4,266 zip codes contains 100 of the 101 metropolitan statistical areas (MSAs) with a population of 500,000 or more that existed in 2010.[2] Once we obtained the CBD coordinates, we identified coordinates (internal points) for all 2010 zip codes from the 2010 Zip Code Tabulation Area (ZCTA) Gazetteer file. We then used the vincenty STATA program to calculate the distance between each zip code and each CBD.

Zip code boundaries are not constant through time, but change along with the neighborhoods they represent. To ensure that all data we use approximates the same geographic area over time, we adjusted all data from 2000 to match 2010 ZCTA geographic boundaries. To do so, we first obtained the TIGER/ Line shape files of 2010 and 2000 ZCTAs from the Census Bureau. Next, we intersected these two files using ArcGIS and weighted 2000 data based on the land area overlap with the 2010 ZCTAs.[3] In instances where more than one 2000 ZCTA overlaps with a single 2010 ZCTA, the sum of the weighted 2000 ZCTA data was calculated and used to approximate the neighborhood captured by the 2010 ZCTA. Finally, cases where data from 2000 are zero and data from 2010 are nonzero, or data from 2010 are 0 and data from 2000 are nonzero, are not included in our final sample. This avoids the occurrence of potentially invalid calculations in the growth variables described below.

Table A-1. Factor analysis results.

Variables	Neighborhood Revitalization	Neighborhood Upscaling	Neighborhood Build-Out
Employment growth	0.3709	0.4106	
Household income growth	0.7191		0.4145
Above poverty growth	0.7423		
Not receiving public assistance growth		0.7268	
Bachelor's degree or higher growth		0.5726	0.3628
White growth		0.6529	
Manager growth		0.4257	0.5175
Housing value growth	0.6842		
New homeowners since 2005			0.7092
Density growth			0.6353
Variance explained	19%	18%	16%

Dependent Variables. To measure the dependent variables of neighborhood change (gentrification and neighborhood revitalization), we collected zip code data on a set of 10 variables from the 2000 Census and the 2007–2011 American

Communities Survey (ACS).[4] Using these data, we conducted a principal component factor analysis with a normalized varimax rotation to identify groups of related variables or factors. This results in the three dimensions of neighborhood change (Table A-1).

Independent and Control Variables. We define the independent variables—fine arts and commercial arts—based on prior empirical research as well as theoretical considerations. Each of the independent variables is a composite of arts industry employment per capita because we specifically want to model the concentration of neighborhood employment in the arts. To control for potential differences in neighborhood context, we employ a range of census and industry variables. Table A-2 shows the complete list of arts industries in each category, and Table A-3 shows the list of control variables.[5]

Table A-2. Arts industries.

Commercial Arts		Fine Arts	
NAICS	Industry	NAICS	Industry
512110	Motion picture and video production	453920	Art dealers
512191	Teleproduction and postproduction services	611610	Fine arts schools
512199	Other motion picture and video industries	711110	Theater companies and dinner theaters
512210	Record production	711120	Dance companies
512220	Integrated record production/ distribution	711130	Musical groups and artists
512230	Music publishers	711190	Other performing arts companies
512240	Sound recording studios	711510	Independent artists, writers, and performers
541310	Architectural services	712110	Museums
541320	Landscape architectural services		
541410	Interior design services		
541420	Industrial design services		
541430	Graphic design services		
541490	Other specialized design services		
541922	Commercial photography		

Table A-3. Regression control variables.

Census Variables[a]		Amenities Composite Variables[b]	
Variable	Description	NAICS	Industry
20 to 34 years old	Percentage of residents 20–34 years old	311811	Retail bakeries
White	Percentage of White residents	445110	Supermarkets
Population density	Persons per square mile	445120	Convenience stores
Employment	Percentage of residents in civilian workforce	445210	Meat markets
Avg HH income[c]	Average household income	445220	Fish and seafood markets
Bachelor's degree or higher	Percentage of residents with Bachelor's or higher degrees	445230	Fruit and vegetable markets
Manager[c]	Percentage of residents with management occupation	445291	Baked goods stores
Mean housing value	Mean housing value	445292	Confectionary and nut stores
Not receiving public assistance	Percentage of residents not receiving public assistance	448110	Men's clothing stores
Not in poverty[c]	Percentage of residents not in poverty	448120	Women's clothing stores
Black[c]	Percentage of Black residents	448130	Children's and infants' clothing stores
Hispanic	Percentage of Hispanic residents	448140	Family clothing stores
Foreign	Percentage of foreign-born residents	448150	Clothing accessory stores
Average household size	Average household size	448190	Other clothing stores
Average rent	Average rent	448210	Shoe stores
Vacant units	Percentage of vacant housing units	448310	Jewelry stores
Walk to work	Percentage of employed residents who walk to work	448320	Luggage and leather goods stores
Fixed effects	Absorbs metro-level effects	451211	Book stores
		451212	News dealers
		452110	Department stores
		453110	Florists
		722210	Full-service restaurants
		722213	Snack and nonalcoholic beverage bars
		722410	Drinking places (alcoholic beverages)
		812191	Diet and weight reducing centers
		812199	Other personal care services

[a] Source: 2000 U.S. Census Bureau.

[b] Source: 2000 U.S. Census Bureau, North American Industrial Classification System.

[c] Variable dropped from final regression models because VIF score is less than 5.0.

Regression Models. Each regression model takes the form:

$$y = \mathbf{X}\beta + \mathbf{D}\gamma + \varepsilon$$

where $\mathbf{y}$ is a vector $(n \times 1)$ of observations of the dependent variable (revitalization or the gentrification factors); $\mathbf{X}$ is a matrix $(n \times p)$ of observations of the independent variables (the arts industries groups and control variables); β is a vector $(p \times 1)$ of regression coefficients; $\mathbf{D}$ is a matrix $(n \times j)$ of MSA dummy variables taking on a value of 1 when the zip code is nested in the MSA and 0 otherwise; γ is a vector $(j \times 1)$ of regression coefficients for each of the MSA dummy variables; and ε is a vector $(n \times 1)$ of random error terms. The MSA fixed effects are not reported in the results, but are rather meant to absorb any contextual effects that may affect results. Our sample includes MSAs in multiple regions of the country that have likely experienced growth and gentrification differently. An example is the massive growth Sun Belt MSAs have experienced in contrast with many metropolitan areas in the Rust Belt. The MSA fixed effects account for differences in MSA context by controlling for the effect of being in any given MSA in the sample. An f test of the significance of the MSA fixed effects as a group is provided in all regression output. All results are obtained using ordinary least squares (OLS).

Table A-4. OLS regression results: the relationship between the arts and neighborhood change.

Variables	Revitalization	Upscaling	Build-Out
Commercial arts	0.014	0.092***	0.404***
Fine arts	0.050***	−0.024*	−0.055***
Amenities	−0.036***	−0.109***	0.167***
20 to 34 years old	−0.073***	−0.106***	0.184***
White	0.116***	0.194***	0.133***
Population density	0.092***	0.024	−0.048***
Employment	−0.230***	−0.368***	−0.090***
Bachelor's degree or higher	0.292***	0.025	−0.090***
Mean housing value	−0.210***	0.110***	0.092***
Not receiving public assistance	0.157***	−0.440***	0.188***
Hispanic	0.151***	−0.050**	−0.099***
Foreign	−0.073***	0.097***	0.084***
Average household size	−0.096***	0.049**	0.026
Average rent	−0.070***	−0.130***	−0.022
Vacant units	0.009	0.008	0.104***
Walk to work	0.002	0.075***	0.082***
Fixed effects $F(99, 4168)$	16.263***	3.971***	3.423***
R^2	0.380	0.480	0.440
Adjusted R^2	0.360	0.460	0.430
N	4,284	4,284	4,284

$^*p < .1; \,^{**}p < .05; \,^{***}p < .01.$

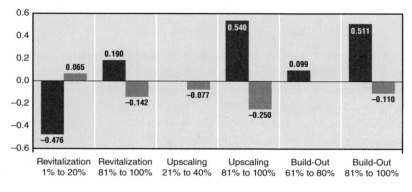

■ Commercial Arts
■ Fine Arts

Figure A-1. Significant arts industries regression coefficients in quintile regressions.

Table A-5. Quintile regression results: neighborhood revitalization.

Variables	1% to 20%	21% to 40%	41% to 60%	61% to 80%	81% to 100%
Commercial arts	−0.476***	0.009	0.013	−0.011	0.190*
Fine arts	0.065**	0.018	−0.068	0.050	−0.142***
Amenities	−0.088***	−0.009	0.033	−0.020	0.074
20 to 34 years old	−0.216***	0.024	0.021	0.053	−0.005
White	0.108**	0.199***	0.115	0.146**	0.005
Population density	0.123***	−0.023	−0.066	0.067	−0.040
Employment	−0.089	−0.082	−0.139*	−0.093	−0.436***
Bachelor's degree or higher	0.196**	0.292***	0.124*	−0.015	−0.121**
Mean housing value	−0.168***	−0.177**	−0.031	0.026	−0.012
Not receiving public assistance	0.095	−0.057	0.132*	−0.013	0.050
Hispanic	0.225***	−0.101	−0.033	−0.061	0.021
Foreign	−0.166***	0.040	0.044	0.127*	0.038
Average household size	−0.098**	0.178***	0.035	−0.017	−0.172***
Average rent	0.114*	−0.035	−0.108	−0.039	0.137***
Vacant units	−0.068*	0.044	0.058	0.046	0.041
Walk to work	−0.070*	0.007	0.005	−0.054	0.104**
Fixed effects	6.393*** $F_{(89, 751)}$	1.465*** $F_{(91, 749)}$	1.778*** $F_{(90, 750)}$	1.177 $F_{(81, 759)}$	2.006*** $F_{(80, 759)}$
R^2	0.650	0.170	0.200	0.130	0.470
Adjusted R^2	0.600	0.050	0.090	0.020	0.400
N	857	857	857	857	856

*$p < .1$; **$p < .05$; ***$p < .01$.

Table A-6. Quintile regression results: neighborhood upscaling.

Variables	1% to 20%	21% to 40%	41% to 60%	61% to 80%	81% to 100%
Commercial arts	−0.103	0.068	0.072	−0.035	0.540***
Fine arts	−0.034	−0.077*	−0.020	−0.058	−0.250***
Amenities	−0.173***	−0.039	−0.015	0.085*	0.085***
20 to 34 years old	−0.148***	−0.069	0.010	−0.004	−0.061*
White	0.168***	0.106	−0.032	−0.070	0.084**
Population density	0.041	−0.067	0.000	0.060	0.032
Employment	−0.195***	0.040	−0.061	−0.022	−0.192***
Bachelor's degree or higher	0.001	−0.130*	−0.023	−0.052	−0.036
Mean housing value	0.040	0.209**	0.099	0.142*	0.175***
Not receiving public assistance	0.002	−0.117	0.069	−0.121*	−0.369***
Hispanic	0.022	0.091	−0.068	0.085	−0.156***
Foreign	0.023	0.013	0.060	0.102	0.065
Average household size	−0.251***	−0.120**	0.061	0.064	0.174***
Average rent	0.058	0.050	−0.219***	−0.080	−0.195***
Vacant units	−0.251***	−0.026	0.036	0.123***	0.113***
Walk to work	−0.044	0.057	0.002	0.045	0.030
Fixed effects	1.764*** $F_{(93, 747)}$	1.224* $F_{(98, 742)}$	1.053 $F_{(95, 745)}$	0.895 $F_{(96, 744)}$	2.441*** $F_{(87, 752)}$
R^2	0.310	0.160	0.140	0.240	0.640
Adjusted R^2	0.210	0.030	0.010	0.130	0.590
N	857	857	857	857	856

*$p < .1$; **$p < .05$; ***$p < .01$.

Table A-7. Quintile regression results: neighborhood build-out.

Variables	1% to 20%	21% to 40%	41% to 60%	61% to 80%	81% to 100%
Commercial arts	0.000	0.069	−0.020	0.099**	0.511***
Fine arts	−0.061	−0.060	0.010	−0.040	−0.110***
Amenities	−0.096**	−0.055	0.047	0.021	0.196***
20 to 34 years old	0.148***	0.085	0.138***	0.130**	0.151***
White	0.041	0.008	0.091	0.078	0.158***
Population density	0.087*	0.078	0.059	−0.024	−0.136***
Employment	0.131*	0.207***	−0.10	0.053	−0.078**
Bachelor's degree or higher	0.035	0.040	−0.002	0.035	−0.134**
Mean housing value	−0.120*	−0.060	−0.059	0.063	0.200***
Not receiving public assistance	0.425***	−0.039	0.013	−0.105	−0.115**
Hispanic	0.170**	0.104	0.040	0.014	−0.279***
Foreign	0.016	−0.061	−0.112	−0.019	0.282***
Average household size	−0.235***	−0.125**	−0.023	0.040	0.280***
Average rent	0.183***	0.107	0.179**	−0.103	−0.139***
Vacant units	−0.015	−0.026	−0.021	−0.012	0.216***
Walk to work	−0.059	0.006	0.002	0.015	0.102**
Fixed effects	1.653*** $F_{(78, 762)}$	1.158 $F_{(89, 751)}$	1.085 $F_{(93, 747)}$	1.126 $F_{(98, 742)}$	2.151*** $F_{(95, 744)}$
R^2	0.440	0.170	0.150	0.160	0.590
Adjusted R^2	0.380	0.050	0.020	0.040	0.530
N	857	857	857	857	856

*$p < .1$; **$p < .05$; ***$p < .01$.

Prior to running regression models, we first examine the relationship of the dependent variables to the arts industries with scatter plots. This gives us a first cut of the relationships we are modeling (excluding controls) and helps to identify any significant outliers that may disproportionately influence results. We are especially concerned with outliers in this analysis because we know from abundant research that gentrifying neighborhoods comprise a small proportion of all neighborhoods in a region and that the arts are highly concentrated. In other words, we anticipate that both dependent and experimental variables may be unevenly distributed. To address this, we reproduce all scatter plots with and without outliers and examine the differences.[6] In each case, the removal of outliers causes the slope of the fitted line to increase. Moreover, the slope of the fitted line remains statistically significant at the 99% confidence level with the exception of the scatter plot depicting commercial arts and neighborhood upscaling without outliers, which is significant at the 95% confidence level. The evidence suggests that extreme outliers affect results by reducing the power of the relationships. Outliers, therefore, are not driving the relationships or causing a relationship to appear when it does not otherwise exist.

We also check for the potential of multicollinearity among our exogenous variables by examining each variable's variance inflation factor (VIF) as well as the VIF overall. Based on this, we remove some of our initial control variables (see Table A-3). However, the VIFs indicate the effects of these variables are well represented by the other controls in the model. In our final model, none of the exogenous controls have a VIF greater than 5, and the overall VIF is 2.8.[7]

Notes

1. The term "neighborhood" has both social and geographic connotations. We use the term in this study simply to mean a small geographic area that is larger than a block and exists within a city or region. Like most neighborhood studies and planning efforts, we define the neighborhood based on the available census data geography. However, the reality is that neighborhoods are extremely difficult to accurately define because individual residents often have different perceptions of what constitutes the defining features and geographic boundaries of their neighborhood.

2. Two issues pertain to the sample. First, we excluded the McAllen–Edinburg–Mission (TX) MSA from the study due to missing coordinate data for its CBD. Second, given the available data, it is possible that we do not capture arts activity that could have emerged around newer CBDs in our sample. However, given that gentrification tends to occur in older urban areas, we feel that we capture the vast majority of arts activity.

3. We used two different weights. For absolute numbers (e.g., population), we calculated weights using the formula $w = a_{int}/a_{2000}$, where a_{int} is the land area from the 2000 ZCTA that overlaps with the 2010 ZCTA area and a_{2000} is the total area of the 2000 ZCTA. For ratios (e.g., the percentage that walked to work), we calculated weights using the formula $w = a_{int}/a_{2010}$, where a_{int} is the same as above and a_{2010} is the total area of the 2010 ZCTA.

4. The 2007–2011 ACS data is a collection of data over a five-year time period and therefore does not capture one point in time. It is, however, the most reliable and best available source of SES data at the micro level and has been used by others in time-series analysis.

5. Unfortunately, given data availability, we were not able to study potentially important variables related to land use and property characteristics, although we recognize that they may have an effect on the relationship between arts industries and neighborhood change.

6. To identify outliers, we calculate the z score for each variable included in the scatter plot. If a zip code has a z score of 3 or higher (or -3 or lower), we consider it an outlier.

7. While we have made an effort to control for a wide range of variables, as in any time series model, changes can occur over the time period that we do not control for that may affect results.

There Goes the Neighborhood School
Jennifer C. Berkshire

When the city of Chicago shuttered some fifty neighborhood schools last year, officials used antiseptic-sounding words like "underperformance" and "underutilization." But visit neighborhoods that bore the brunt of the closings, as I did recently, and you'll hear that the battle over the city's schools is about something much larger: the future of the city itself and who gets to live here.

Parents, teachers and community leaders told me that the replacement of neighborhood schools serving the city's poorest children with privately run charters that don't, can't be separated from the relentless gentrification that's rapidly transforming Chicago into a wealthier, whiter city. Think urban renewal but without the bulldozers.

Take the El down from O'Hare and Chicago's remaking is hard to ignore. Cranes dot the skyline, and as the train snakes its way through Bucktown, a formerly Polish working-class neighborhood turned trendy and expensive, you pass close enough to see what looks to be the very last tenement, being demolished brick by brick. Farther down the Blue Line, what Mayor Rahm Emanuel is fond of calling the "New Chicago" really comes into view. We're on the Near North Side now, formerly the site of the notorious Cabrini-Green housing project that, at its peak, housed 15,000 residents, most in vast towers. The neighborhood now boasts a Whole Foods, complete with a wine bar, as well as an exclusive private school: the British School of Chicago, a modern structure graced with images of smiling white students gazing toward where Cabrini's towers once loomed. And had community opposition not ruled the day, this site would also have been home to Chicago's newest selective enrollment high school, Barack Obama College Prep.

As for the Cabrini residents who called this neighborhood home until 2011, their whereabouts constitutes one of the great mysteries of New Chicago. What is beyond dispute is this: According to census data, Chicago has lost 200,000 of its African American residents over the past decade.

"The city is squeezing us out," says South Side education organizer Jitu Brown. And like so many activists I spoke to, Brown views the closure of schools as an effort to replace Chicago's poor, minority residents with wealthier inhabitants. "When you shut down a neighborhood school, you send a powerful signal to the people who've been living there: 'This neighborhood isn't for you.'"

While the pace of Chicago's gentrification is unmistakable on the Near North Side, it can be harder to discern in the west side neighborhood of North Lawndale. Once the headquarters of no fewer than five corporations, including Sears Roebuck, Zenith, and Sunbeam, North Lawndale has been hemorrhaging jobs—and residents—for decades. Down from a population of more than 100,000 in the 1960s, the community claims just 38,000 residents today. Still, for all of the abandoned buildings and boarded up storefronts, we're just fifteen minutes from the Loop, and an easy twenty-minute ride down the Eisenhower expressway from wealthy Oak Park. According to real estate tracking sites, property here is selling swiftly as buyers anticipate future development.

When Chicago public school officials announced plans to close two schools in North Lawndale, they cited dwindling student enrollment. But local activist Valerie Leonard, who grew up in North Lawndale and whose father was a principal at the recently closed Paderewski Elementary School, believes that the school system's own policy of opening so-called schools of choice here exacerbated the student shortage. And before that, says Leonard, the community had been losing students to a housing crisis that dates back even before the 2010 foreclosure crisis that ravaged this area.

When the Department of Housing and Urban Development condemned a mile-long stretch of multi-unit housing in the heart of North Lawndale, the city lost more than 10 percent of its housing stock overnight.

"Those were kids who attended neighborhood schools and suddenly they're gone," says Leonard. "At the same time, you have this push for all of these new schools even as our student population is shrinking."

Two-thirds of North Lawndale's schools are now charters, including a KIPP (one of the national charter chains) school that's just down the street from where Martin Luther King lived briefly in 1967. The area bordering scenic Douglas Park, which is at the center of an ambitious plan to redevelop North Lawndale, has no traditional public schools left. Leonard believes that the city's growing roster of college-prep-style charters is no replacement for schools like Paderewski that served as community anchors.

"The charters are harder for kids to stay in, and getting kicked out makes it harder to do well at your next school," says Leonard. "Those kids end up back in the few remaining neighborhood schools, which are now the schools of last resort."

Leonard also offers the clearest explanation I've heard as to how the remaking of the city and its schools go hand in hand. "Economic development and education reform in Chicago are being driven by the same people," she says. She's referring to the powerful Civic Committee of the Commercial Club of Chicago, a veritable who's who of local captains of industry. The group's executive committee is chaired by former banker Harrison Steans, whose Steans Family Foundation has been a driving force behind efforts to redevelop North Lawndale and expand charter schools in the community.

In fact, the Civic Committee seems to view charters as the cure for all that ails Chicago's poor neighborhoods. Visit the website for the committee's education initiative and you'll be greeted by smiling minority students in KIPP uniforms and the bald claim that the city's neighborhood schools have failed.

But nearly two decades into Chicago's charter experiment, the sales pitch may be wearing thin. A recent study by the University of Minnesota Law School found that Chicago's charters have weakened the larger school system and heightened segregation in the city's schools.

"You keep thinking you've reached a place beyond which nothing can be worse, and yet the charters have managed to expand the threshold of segregation, expand the threshold of low performance in Chicago," study author Myron Orfield says. Orfield's study is the latest in a series of studies to demonstrate that the city's charters have been no match for the endemic poverty and segregation that blunt the prospects of so many of the city's students.

A *Chicago Tribune* poll taken this summer found that 77 percent of voters disapproved of Emanuel's policy of expanding charter schools at the expense of neighborhood schools. Among African Americans, disapproval was even higher. A full 83 percent of black voters gave Emanuel's charter policy a thumbs down.

Then there's the taint of corruption that clings to some of the city's most prominent charter networks.

UNO charter, which operates sixteen charter schools serving nearly 8,000 Latino students, is currently under investigation by the IRS and the SEC for a long list of shady dealings, the exposure of which forced the ouster of its politically connected CEO, Juan Rangel.

And don't forget Concept Schools, Inc., the pet charter network of Illinois's powerful Speaker of the House, Mike Madigan, which was recently raided by the FBI for what agents described as "an ongoing white-collar crime matter."

Troy LaRaviere, the principal of Blaine Elementary School in the Lakeview neighborhood on the Northside, keeps a running tally of stories like these, not to mention a stack of studies, including one he recently conducted, on charter school performance.

"The data that is emerging paints a very clear picture that [charters] are doing far worse than neighborhood public schools at growing student academic skills," says LaRaviere, who leads a group of principals critical of the direction of education reform in Chicago, including the expansion of charter schools. "The students in those schools are losing out and the private management companies that benefit from the public dollars that flow into charter schools are benefiting from those students' loss."

In Bronzeville on Chicago's South Side, students and education activists are fighting to save Dyett High School, the last open-enrollment high school in the neighborhood. Back in 2012, the mayoral-appointed Chicago Board of Education voted to close Dyett after its senior class, down to just thirteen students, graduates at the end of this school year. The Coalition to Revitalize Dyett High School has been pushing hard to turn Dyett into what they call a "global leadership and green technology" high school open to any neighborhood student. When Chicago public school officials recently announced plans to hire a private operator to run the school, local activists like Jitu Brown were having none of it.

"Why can't we have public schools? Why do low-income minority students need to have their schools run by private contractors?" asks Brown, who is the education organizer for the Kenwood-Oakland Community Organization. "Why aren't these students entitled to the same kind of schools and the same kind of programs as students on the North Side?

"We want this school to anchor the community for the next seventy-five years," Brown adds. "We're not interested in a short-term contract that can be broken."

Brown also questions just how fair the Chicago public school search for an outside contractor to run the school is likely to be. This is an allegation I hear again and again during my travels. The same neighborhoods that bore the brunt of the 2013 school closures have seen many of their remaining public schools taken over by the Academy for Urban School Leadership. Now essentially a district within the district, the organization currently runs thirty-two Chicago schools, attended by 18,000 mostly poor, minority students. When it takes over a school, all of the staff and teachers are replaced, the latter by a Teach For America-like corps of teacher trainees from Chicago's National Louis University. Brown and other education activists charge that the relationship between the academy and the board of education is rife with conflicts of interest. "The people who benefit from these deals are insiders," says Brown.

Beyond the technical questions of who will run Dyett High, or even the kind of programs and curriculum the school's students will have, looms a far larger question: Who gets to live in a neighborhood like Bronzeville? Brown sees the fight over Dyett as one for the very existence of Chicago's poorest residents.

That Chicago has no answer for this question is apparent in the tortured tale of Bronzeville's public schools. When the city tore down public housing high rises more than a decade ago, nearby schools went, too. Students at the newly closed schools were then shuffled between the neighborhood schools that remained until these too were shut, or turned around, due to low test scores. In the past decade, Bronzeville has lost twenty-five of its neighborhood schools. The "schools of choice" that have replaced them—an academically selective high school, an endless array of college prep charters—are more restrictive in how they admit students.

Brown and the other members of the Coalition to Revitalize Dyett High are planning more civil disobedience as they press their case to make Dyett a genuine community anchor. "This is not a done deal," says Brown.

Brown sees the fight over Dyett as a litmus test, not just for Bronzeville, but for a city that seems intent on making life harder for its low-income residents. His message to the Chicago public schools is starkly simple: "Treat all students like they're precious."

Charleston's Landscape of Memory:
The Gentrification of History
Robert R. Macdonald

The Charleston History Commission's effort to formulate wording for a plaque intended to place the monument to John C. Calhoun on Marion Square in historical context is comparable to placing a band-aid on a cancerous lesion. The wound here is the landscape of memory presenting a mythical Charleston past almost totally bereft of African Americans. If your knowledge of Charleston's history came solely from what you heard on guided tours or saw preserved and honored in the City's cultural landscape, you would not know that Africans and African Americans had a central role in the city's history. What one does see and learn about are totems of wealth and privilege detached from those who made them possible, the enslaved Africans and African Americans who worked and died in the Lowcountry's rice and cotton slave labor camps euphemistically called plantations. Black sweat and blood made antebellum Charleston one of the richest communities in the world. The absence of African Americans in Charleston's memory recalls the words of Hector St. John de Crevecoeur, the French American writer who was an early observer of the new nation born of the American Revolution. In his 1782 Letters from an American Farmer he wrote,

While all is joy, festivity, and happiness in Charles-Town, would you imagine that scenes of misery overspread in the country? Their ears by habit are become deaf, their hearts are hardened; they neither see, her, nor feel for the woes of their poor slaves, from whose painful labors all their wealth proceeds. Here the horrors of slavery, the hardship of incessant toils, are unseen; and no one thinks with compassion of those showers of sweat and of tears which from the bodies of Africans, daily drop, and moisten the ground they till. The cracks of the whip urging these miserable beings to excessive labour, are far too distant from the gay Capital to be heard.

The absence of African Americans in Charleston's landscape of memory did not occur by happenstance.

In 1924 the then Charleston Mayor Thomas P. Stoney coined the phrase, **Charleston: America's Most Historic City**. It was part of an effort to help the struggling Charleston economy, that had yet to recover from the Civil War, develop a tourist industry. The slogan later appeared on a billboard that greeted visitors as they entered the city from the north on the old Cooper River Bridge. Fortuitously, the post-Civil War economic stagnation prevented Charleston from tearing down the old, run-down mansions South of Broad and redeveloping the city's historic neighborhoods. Efforts by such groups as The Preservation Society and the Historic Charleston Foundation fostered the restoration of antebellum mansions and other historic houses. Neighborhoods were rehabilitated, gardens and plantations prettied up, and carriage and walking tours created to tell a romanticized tale of a simpler time. New hotels sprung up; restaurants opened, historic houses turned into Bed & Breakfasts. Charleston's "revival" was accompanied by a dramatic shift in the city's demographics. Wealthy absentee owners and young, white urban professionals replaced African Americans who could no longer afford the increased taxes. The displaced moved to the Charleston's suburbs where they found affordable housing and lower taxes.

Charleston's transformation continues today as African American neighborhoods north of Calhoun Street become the site of new restaurants, bars, hotels, and upscale apartments, and condominiums. Gentrification has resulted in the African American population, once a majority of the town's citizens, becoming a minority. As recently as 1980 two thirds of Charleston's population was African American. In 2016 the percentage of blacks in Charleston had declined to 22.4 percent of the population.

Gentrification of the [sic] Charleston's history accompanied the physical and demographic transformation. Since Mayor Stoney made his pronouncement in 1924, a fabricated landscape of memory fashioned a romantic "Gone with the Wind" tableau of an idyllic, genteel town where "the living was easy." Historian Stephanie E. Yuhl describes the result as *A Golden Haze of Memory*. Reinforcing the miasmas are the Jim Crow era monuments erected in the late nineteenth and early twentieth centuries affirming the "redemption" of Charleston and South Carolina and the implicit restoration of white supremacy.

The most famous of these Jim Crow monuments is Marion Square's memorial to John C. Calhoun. But Calhoun is only one among many. Marion Square is also the site of an obelisk to Wade Hampton, the Confederate General elected South Carolina Governor in 1876 with the help of the "Red Shirts," South Carolina's version of the Ku Klux Klan. The Red Shirts terrorized South Carolina blacks and murdered more than one hundred suppressing the black vote that led to Hampton's election. It was Governor Hampton, "The Redeemer," that initiated the restitution of white supremacy culminating in the 1895 South Carolina Constitution disenfranchising blacks and opening the gates to segregation and Jim Crow.

Between 1879 and 1932 nine monuments were erected in Charleston to honor the Confederacy and its heroes. Besides Marion Square, these shrines are found in White Point Garden, Magnolia Cemetery, and Washington Square Park adjacent to Charleston's City Hall. Not limited to erecting monuments, in 1904 the City Council renamed the Washington Race Course, which had served as a Confederate prison for Union POWs, Hampton Park. The most recent monument to the Confederacy was erected in 1932 when the United Daughters of the Confederacy placed a shrine to the "Confederate Defenders of Charleston" in White Point Garden. Then there is the *H.L. Hunley*, the Confederate submarine that sank the Union blockade ship, the *Housatonic*, in 1864. The Hunley, which also sank in its attack, was resurrected from Charleston Harbor in 1995 and is being preserved as a Confederate icon by the State of South Carolina at the cost of millions of dollars.

Except for the monument to Denmark Vesey, who planned a slave revolt in 1822, there are few substantial memorials in Charleston recognizing African Americans and their role in the city's history. Ironically the Vesey monument, which took twenty years to accomplish, was placed in a hidden grove in Hampton Park after being rejected for placement in Marion Square.

So, how should Charleston redress the skewed memory of its past that has for the most part excluded African Americans? It will take more than a band-aid of plaques or even a virtual walking tour. It will require the creation of new monuments and renaming opportunities that will acknowledge overlooked and essential parts of Charleston's history.

As a consultant to the International African American Museum, I recommended a *Monument to African Ancestors* for Gadsden's Wharf, the last and most important entrepot for the arrival and sale of enslaved Africans in North America. There should also be a monument to the famed Massachusetts 54 Regiment of Colored Troops many of whom died attacking the Confederate Ft. Wagner on the Harbor and who formed a major contingent of the Union Army that occupied Charleston following the Confederate surrender of the city on February 18, 1865. What about a monument to the workers of the Cigar Factory who created the Civil Rights anthem, *We Shall Overcome* when they struck for better wages in 1946? The courageous black women of the infamous 1969 Hospital Workers Strike deserve a monument as do the Civil Rights leaders Septima Clark and Esau Jenkins. The City should also return Hampton Park to its original name, Washington Race Course Park or Washington Park.

In my December 14, 2017, Post & Courier Op-Ed, I proposed what could be one of the most meaningful monuments in the United States, a memorial to the victims of white supremacy standing on Marion Square adjacent to the Calhoun Monument and Holocaust Memorial. There is possibly no place in America that has more emotional and physical links to how the ideology of white supremacy that Calhoun endorsed has plagued the country's soul for more than three hundred years. The memorial would recognize and honor the thousands of African and African American men, women, and children who have suffered and died because of an ideology that views them as inferior to whites. The victims include those brought here in slave ships to work and die in slave labor camps that were engines of the young nation's economy, the more than 4,000 African Americans lynched during the Jim Crow era, and the Emanuel Nine gunned down only a block from Marion Square.

Charleston has an opportunity to face the burden of history and the cancer of white supremacy by creating monuments that respond to a skewed fabricated history promoted for too long. The monuments I propose would be a source of learning for generations and encourage understanding and reconciliation that will advance American values. They would also be a model for the country as it continues to confront its past and heal old wounds.

Cultural Representation

Nobody Mean More to Me Than You and the Future Life of Willie Jordan
June Jordan

Black English is not exactly a linguistic buffalo; as children, most of the thirty-five million Afro-Americans living here depend on this language for our discovery of the world. But then we approach our maturity inside a larger social body that will not support our efforts to become anything other than the clones of those who are neither our mothers nor our fathers. We begin to grow up in a house where every true mirror shows us the face of somebody who does not belong there, whose walk and whose talk will never look or sound "right," because that house was meant to shelter a family that is alien and hostile to us. As we learn our way around this environment, either we hide our original word habits, or we completely surrender our own voice, hoping to please those who will never respect anyone different from themselves: Black English is not exactly a linguistic buffalo, but we should understand its status as an endangered species, as a perishing, irreplaceable system of community intelligence, or we should expect its extinction, and, along with that, the extinguishing of much that constitutes our own proud, and singular, identity.

What we casually call "English," less and less defers to England and its "gentlemen." "English" is no longer a specific matter of geography or an element of class privilege; more than thirty-three countries use this tool as a means of "intranational communication."[1] Countries as disparate as Zimbabwe and Malaysia, or Israel and Uganda, use it as their non-native currency of convenience. Obviously, this tool, this "English," cannot function inside thirty-three discrete societies on the basis of rules and values absolutely determined somewhere else, in a thirty-fourth other country, for example.

In addition to that staggering congeries of non-native users of English, there are five countries, or 333,746,000 people, for whom this thing called "English" serves as a native tongue.[2] Approximately 10 percent of these native speakers of "English" are Afro-American citizens of the U.S.A. I cite these numbers and varieties of human beings dependent on "English" in order, quickly, to suggest how strange and how tenuous is any concept of "Standard English." Obviously, numerous forms of English now operate inside a natural, an uncontrollable, continuum of development. I would suppose "the standard" for English in Malaysia is not the same as "the standard" in Zimbabwe. I know that standard forms of English for Black people in this country do not copy that of Whites. And, in fact, the structural differences between these two kinds of English have intensified, becoming more Black, or less White, despite the expected homogenizing effects of television[3] and other mass media.

Nonetheless, White standards of English persist, supreme and unquestioned, in these United States. Despite our multi-lingual population, and despite the deepening Black and White cleavage within that conglomerate, White standards control our official and popular judgments of verbal proficiency and correct, or incorrect, language skills, including speech. In contrast to India, where at least fourteen languages co-exist as legitimate Indian languages, in contrast to Nicaragua, where all citizens are legally entitled to formal school instruction in their regional or tribal languages, compulsory education in America compels accommodation to exclusively White forms of "English." White English, in America, is "Standard English."

This story begins two years ago. I was teaching a new course, "In Search of the Invisible Black Woman," and my rather large class seemed evenly divided among young Black women and men. Five or six White students also sat in attendance. With unexpected speed and enthusiasm we had moved through historical narration of the 19th century to literature by and about Black women, in the 20th. I then assigned the first forty pages of Alice Walker's *The Color Purple*, and I came, eagerly, to class that morning:

"So!" I exclaimed, aloud. "What did you think? How did you like it?"

The students studied their hands, or the floor. There was no response. The tense, resistant feeling in the room fairly astounded me.

At last, one student, a young woman still not meeting my eyes, muttered something in my direction:

"What did you say?" I prompted her.

"Why she have them talk so funny. It don't sound right."

"You mean the language?"

Another student lifted his head: "It don't look right, neither. I couldn't hardly read it."

At this, several students dumped on the book. Just about unanimously, their criticisms targeted the language. I listened to what they wanted to say and silently marvelled at the similarities between their casual speech patterns and Alice Walker's written version of Black English.

But I decided against pointing to these identical traits of syntax, I wanted not to make them self-conscious about their own spoken language—not while they clearly felt it was "wrong." Instead I decided to swallow my astonishment. Here was a negative Black reaction to a prize-winning accomplishment of Black literature that White readers across the country had selected as a best seller. Black rejection was aimed at the one irreducibly Black element of Walker's work: the language—Celie's Black English. I wrote the opening lines of *The Color Purple* on the blackboard and asked the students to help me translate these sentences into Standard English:

You better not never tell nobody but God. It'd kill your mommy.

Dear God,

I am fourteen years old. I have always been a good girl. Maybe you can give me a sign letting me know what is happening to me.

Last spring after Little Lucious come I heard them fussing. He was pulling on her arm. She say it too soon, Fonso. I aint well. Finally he leave her alone. A week go by, he pulling on her arm again. She say, Naw, I ain't gonna. Can't you see I'm already half dead, an all of the children.[4]

Our process of translation exploded with hilarity and even hysterical, shocked laughter: The Black writer, Alice Walker, knew what she was doing! If rudimentary criteria for good fiction include the manipulation of language so that the syntax and diction of sentences will tell you the identity of speakers, the probable age and sex and class of speakers, and even the locale—urban/rural/ southern/western—then Walker had written, perfectly. This is the translation into Standard English that our class produced:

Absolutely, one should never confide in anybody besides God. Your secrets could prove devastating to your mother.

Dear God,

I am fourteen years old. I have always been good. But now, could you help me to understand what is happening to me?

Last spring, after my little brother, Lucious, was born, I heard my parents fighting. My father kept pulling at my mother's arm. But she told him, "It's too soon for sex, Alfonso. I am still not feeling well." Finally, my father left her alone. A week went by, and then he began bothering my mother, again: pulling her arm. She told him, "No, I won't! Can't you see I'm already exhausted from all of these children?"

(Our favorite line was "It's too soon for sex, Alfonso.")

Once we could stop laughing, once we could stop our exponentially wild improvisations on the theme of Translated Black English, the students pushed to explain their own negative first reactions to their spoken language on the printed page. I thought it was probably akin to the shock of seeing yourself in a photograph for the first time. Most of the students had never before seen a written facsimile of the way they talk. None of the students had ever learned how to read and write their own verbal system of communication: Black English. Alternatively, this fact began to baffle or else bemuse and then infuriate my students. Why not? Was it too late? Could they learn how to do it, now? And, ultimately, the final test question, the one testing my sincerity: Could I teach them? Because I had never taught anyone Black English and, as far as I knew, no one, anywhere in the United States, had ever offered such a course, the best I could say was "'I'll try.'"

He looked like a wrestler.

He sat dead center in the packed room and, every time our eyes met, he quickly nodded his head as though anxious to reassure, and encourage me.

Short, with strikingly broad shoulders and long arms, he spoke with a surprisingly high, soft voice that matched the soft bright movement of his eyes. His name was Willie Jordan. He would have seemed even more unlikely in the context of Contemporary Women's Poetry, except that ten or twelve other Black men were taking the course, as well. Still, Willie was conspicuous. His extreme fitness, the muscular density of his presence underscored the riveted, gentle attention that he gave to anything anyone said. Generally, he did not join the loud and rowdy dialogue flying back and forth, but there could be no doubt about his interest in our discussions. And, when he stood to present an argument he'd prepared, overnight, that nervous smile of his vanished and an irregular stammering replaced it, as he spoke with visceral sincerity, word by word.

That was how I met Willie Jordan. It was in between "In Search of the Invisible Black Women" and "The Art of Black English." I was waiting for departmental approval and I supposed that Willie might be, so to speak, killing time until he, too, could study Black English. But Willie really did want to explore contemporary women's poetry and, to that end, volunteered for extra research and never missed a class.

Towards the end of that semester, Willie approached me for an independent study project on South Africa. It would commence the next semester. I thought Willie's writing needed the kind of improvement only intense practice will yield. I knew his intelligence was outstanding. But he'd wholeheartedly opted for "Standard English" at a rather late age, and the results were stilted and frequently polysyllabic, simply for the sake of having more syllables. Willie's unnatural formality of language seemed to me consistent with the formality of his research into South African apartheid. As he projected his studies, he would have little time, indeed, for newspapers. Instead, more than 90 percent of his research would mean saturation in strictly historical, if not archival, material. I was certainly interested. It would be tricky to guide him into a more confident and spontaneous relationship both with language and apartheid. It was going to be wonderful to see what happened when he could catch up with himself, entirely, and talk back to the world.

September, 1984: Breezy fall weather and much excitement! My class, "The Art of Black English," was full to the limit of the fire laws. And in Independent Study, Willie Jordan showed up weekly, fifteen minutes early for each of our sessions. I was pretty happy to be teaching, altogether!

I remember an early class when a young brother, replete with his ever-present porkpie hat, raised his hand and then told us that most of what he'd heard was "all right" except it was "too clean." "The brothers on the street," he continued, "they mix it up more. Like 'fuck' and 'motherfuck.' Or like 'shit.'" He waited. I waited.

Then all of us laughed a good while, and we got into a brawl about "correct" and "realistic" Black English that led to Rule 1.

Rule 1: *Black English is about a whole lot more than mothafuckin.*

As a criterion, we decided, "realistic" could take you anywhere you want to go. Artful places. Angry places. Eloquent and sweetalkin places. Polemical places. Church. And the local Bar & Grill. We were checking out a language, not a mood or a scene or one guy's forgettable mouthing off.

It was hard. For most of the students, learning Black English required a fallback to patterns and rhythms of speech that many of their parents had beaten out of them. I mean beaten. And, in a majority of cases, correct Black English could be achieved only by striving for incorrect Standard English, something they were still pushing at, quite uncertainly. This state of affairs led to Rule 2.

Rule 2: *If it's wrong in Standard English it's probably right in Black English, or, at least, you're hot.*

It was hard. Roommates and family members ridiculed their studies, or remained incredulous, "You studying that shit? At school?" But we were beginning to feel the companionship of pioneers. And we decided that we needed another rule that would establish each one of us as equally important to our success. This was Rule 3.

Rule 3: *If it don't sound like something that come out somebody mouth then it don't sound right. If it don't sound right then it ain't hardly right. Period.*

This rule produced two weeks of compositions in which the students agonizingly tried to spell the sound of the Black English sentence they wanted to convey. But Black English is, preeminently, an oral/spoken means of communication. And spelling don't talk. So we needed Rule 4.

Rule 4: *Forget about the spelling. Let the syntax carry you.*

Once we arrived at Rule 4 we started to fly, because syntax, the structure of an idea, leads you to the world view of the speaker and reveals her values. The syntax of a sentence equals the structure of your consciousness. If we insisted that the language of Black English adheres to a distinctive Black syntax, then we were postulating a profound difference between White and Black people, per se. Was it a difference to prize or to obliterate?

There are three qualities of Black English—the presence of life, voice, and clarity—that intensify to a distinctive Black value system that we became excited about and self-consciously tried to maintain.

1. *Black English has been produced by a pre-technocratic, if not anti-technological, culture:* More, our culture has been constantly threatened by annihilation or, at least, the swallowed blurring of assimilation. Therefore, our language is a system constructed by people constantly needing to insist that we exist, that we are present. Our language devolves from a culture that abhors all abstraction, or anything tending to obscure or delete the fact of the human being who is here and now/the truth of the person who is speaking or listening.

Consequently, there is no passive voice construction possible in Black English. For example, you cannot say, "Black English is being eliminated." You must say, instead, "White people eliminating Black English." The assumption of the presence of life governs all of Black English. Therefore, overwhelmingly, all action takes place in the language of the present indicative. And every sentence assumes the living and active participation of at least two human beings, the speaker and the listener.

2. *A primary consequence of the person-centered values of Black English is the delivery of voice:* If you speak or write Black English, your ideas will necessarily possess that otherwise elusive attribute, voice.

3. *One main benefit following from the person-centered values of Black English is that of clarity:* If your idea, your sentence, assumes the presence of at least two living and active people, you will make it understandable, because the motivation behind every sentence is the wish to say something real to somebody real.

As the weeks piled up, translation from Standard English into Black English or vice versa occupied a hefty part of our course work.

Standard English (hereafter S.E.): "In considering the idea of studying Black English those questioned suggested—"

(What's the subject? Where's the person? Is anybody alive in here, in that idea?)

Black English (hereafter B.E.): "I been asking people what you think about somebody studying Black English and they answer me like this:"

But there were interesting limits. You cannot "translate" instances of Standard English preoccupied with abstraction or with nothing/nobody evidently alive, into Black English. That would warp the language into uses antithetical to the guiding perspective of its community of users. Rather you must first change those Standard English sentences, themselves, into ideas consistent with the person-centered assumptions of Black English.

Guidelines for Black English

1. *Minimal number of words for every idea:* This is the source for the aphoristic and/or poetic force of the language; eliminate every possible word.

2. *Clarity:* If the sentence is not clear it's not Black English.

3. *Eliminate use of the verb* to be *whenever possible:* This leads to the deployment of more descriptive and, therefore, more precise verbs.

4. *Use* be *or* been *only when you want to describe a chronic, ongoing state of things.*

He *be* at the office, by 9: (He is always at the office by 9.)

He *been* with her since forever.

5. *Zero copula:* Always eliminate the verb *to be* whenever it would combine with another verb, in Standard English.

    S.E.: She is going out with him.

    B.E.: She going out with him.

6. *Eliminate* do *as in:*

    S.E.: What do you think? What do you want?

    B.E.: What you think? What you want?

7. Rules number 3, 4, 5, and 6 provide for the use of the minimal number of verbs per idea and, therefore, greater accuracy in the choice of verb.

8. *In general, if you wish to say something really positive, try to formulate the idea using emphatic negative structure.*

    S.E.: He's fabulous.

    B.E.: He bad.

9. *Use double or triple negatives for dramatic emphasis.*

    S.E.: Tina Turner sings out of this world.

    B.E.: Ain nobody sing like Tina.

10. *Never use the* ed *suffix to indicate the past tense of a verb.*

    S.E.: She closed the door.

    B.E.: She close the door. Or, she have close the door.

11. *Regardless of intentional verb time, only use the third person singular, present indicative, for use of the verb* to have, *as an auxiliary.*

    S.E.: He had his wallet then he lost it.

    B.E.: He have him wallet then he lose it.

    S.E.: We had seen that movie.

    B.E.: We seen that movie. Or, we have see that movie.

12. *Observe a minimal inflection of verbs:* Particularly, never change from the first person singular forms to the third person singular.

    S.E.: Present Tense Forms: He goes to the store.

    B.E.: He go to the store.

    S.E.: Past Tense Forms: He went to the store.

    B.E.: He go to the store. Or, he gone to the store. Or, he been to the store.

13. *The possessive case scarcely ever appears in Black English:* Never use an apostrophe ('s) construction. If you wander into a possessive case component

of an idea, then keep logically consistent: ours, his, theirs, mines. But, most likely, if you bump into such a component, you have wandered outside the underlying world view of Black English.

S.E.: He will take their car tomorrow.

B.E.: He taking they car tomorrow.

14. *Plurality:* Logical consistency, continued: If the modifier indicates plurality then the noun remains in the singular case.

S.E.: He ate twelve doughnuts.

B.E.: He eat twelve doughnut.

S.E.: She has many books.

B.E.: She have many book.

15. *Listen for, or invent, special Black English forms of the past tense, such as:* "He losted it. That what she felted." If they are clear and readily understood, then use them.

16. *Do not hesitate to play with words, sometimes inventing them:* e.g. "astropoto-mous" means huge like a hippo plus astronomical and, therefore, signifies real big.

17. *In Black English, unless you keenly want to underscore the past tense nature of an action, stay in the present tense and rely on the overall context of your ideas for the conveyance of time and sequence.*

18. *Never use the suffix -ly form of an adverb in Black English.*

S.E.: The rain came down rather quickly.

B.E.: The rain come down pretty quick.

19. *Never use the indefinite article* an *in Black English.*

S.E.: He wanted to ride an elephant.

B.E.: He wanted to ride him a elephant.

20. *Invariant syntax:* in correct Black English it is possible to formulate an imperative, an interrogative, and a simple declarative idea with the same syntax:

B.E.: You going to the store?

You going to the store.

You going to the store!

Where was Willie Jordan? We'd reached the mid-term of the semester. Students had formulated Black English guidelines, by consensus, and they were now writing with remarkable beauty, purpose, and enjoyment:

I ain hardly speakin for everybody but myself so understan that.

Kim Parks

Samples from student writings:

Janie have a great big ole hole inside her. Tea Cake the only thing that fit that hole....

That pear tree beautiful to Janie, especial when bees fiddlin with the blossomin pear there growin large and lovely. But personal speakin, the love she get from starin at that tree ain the love what starin back at her in them relationship. (Monica Morris)

Love a big theme in, *They Eye Was Watching God*. Love show people new corners inside theyself. It pull out good stuff and stuff back bad stuff.... Joe worship the doing uh his own hand and need other people to worship him too. But he ain't think about Janie that she a person and ought to live like anybody common do. Queen life not for Janie. (Monica Morris)

In both life and writin, Black womens have varietous experience of love that be cold like a iceberg or fiery like a inferno. Passion got for the other partner involve, man or women, seem as shallow, ankle-deep water or the most profoundest abyss. (Constance Evans)

Family love another bond that ain't never break under no pressure. (Constance Evans)

You know it really cold/When the friend you/Always get out the fire/ Act like they don't know you/When you in the heat. (Constance Evans)

Big classroom discussion bout love at this time. I never take no class where us have any long arguin for and against for two or three day. New to me and great. I find the class time talkin a million time more interestin than detail bout the book. (Kathy Esseks)

As these examples suggest, Black English no longer limited the students, in any way. In fact, one of them, Philip Garfield, would shortly "translate" a pivotal scene from Ibsen's *A Doll's House*, as his final term paper.

Nora: I didn't gived no shit. I thinked you a asshole back then, too, you make it so hard for me save mines husband life.

Krogstad: Girl, it clear you ain't any idea what you done. You done exact what I once done, and I losed my reputation over it.

Nora: You asks me believe you once act brave save you wife life?

Krogstad: Law care less why you done it.

Nora: Law must suck.

Krogstad: Suck or no, if I wants, judge screw you wid dis paper.

Nora: No way, man. (Philip Garfield)

But where was Willie? Compulsively punctual, and always thoroughly prepared with neat typed compositions, he had disappeared. He failed to show up for our regularly scheduled conference, and I received neither a note nor a phone call of explanation. A whole week went by. I wondered if Willie had finally been captured by the extremely current happenings in South Africa: passage of a new constitution that did not enfranchise the Black majority, and militant Black South African reaction to that affront. I wondered if he'd been hurt, somewhere. I wondered if the serious workload of weekly readings and writings had overwhelmed him and changed his mind about independent study. Where was Willie Jordan?

One week after the first conference that Willie missed, he called: "Hello, Professor Jordan? This is Willie. I'm sorry I wasn't there last week. But something has come up and I'm pretty upset. I'm sorry but I really can't deal right now."

I asked Willie to drop by my office and just let me see that he was okay. He agreed to do that. When I saw him I knew something hideous had happened. Something had hurt him and scared him to the marrow. He was all agitated and stammering and terse and incoherent. At last, his sadly jumbled account let me surmise, as follows: Brooklyn police had murdered his unarmed, twenty-five-year-old brother, Reggie Jordan. Neither Willie nor his elderly parents knew what to do about it. Nobody from the press was interested. His folks had no money. Police ran his family around and around, to no point. And Reggie was really dead. And Willie wanted to fight, but he felt helpless.

With Willie's permission I began to try to secure legal counsel for the Jordan family. Unfortunately, Black victims of police violence are truly numerous, while the resources available to prosecute their killers are truly scarce. A friend of mine at the Center for Constitutional Rights estimated that just the preparatory costs for bringing the cops into court normally approaches $180,000. Unless the execution of Reggie Jordan became a major community cause for organizing and protest, his murder would simply become a statistical item.

Again, with Willie's permission, I contacted every newspaper and media person I could think of. But the Bastone feature article in *The Village Voice* was the only result from that canvassing.

Again, with Willie's permission, I presented the case to my class in Black English. We had talked about the politics of language. We had talked about love and sex and child abuse and men and women. But the murder of Reggie Jordan broke like a hurricane across the room.

There are few "issues" as endemic to Black life as police violence. Most of the students knew and respected and liked Jordan. Many of them came from the very neighborhood where the murder had occurred. All of the students had known somebody close to them who had been killed by police, or had known frightening moments of gratuitous confrontation with the cops. They wanted to do everything at once to avenge death. Number One: They decided to compose a personal statement of condolence to Willie Jordan and his family, written in Black English. Number Two: They decided to compose individual messages to the police, in Black English. These should be prefaced by an explanatory paragraph composed by the entire group. Number Three: These individual messages, with their lead paragraph, should be sent to *Newsday*.

The morning after we agreed on these objectives, one of the young women students appeared with an unidentified visitor, who sat through the class, smiling in a peculiar, comfortable way.

Now we had to make more tactical decisions. Because we wanted the messages published, and because we thought it imperative that our outrage be known by the police, the tactical question was this: Should the opening, group paragraph be written in Black English or Standard English?

I have seldom been privy to a discussion with so much heart at the dead beat of it. I will never forget the eloquence, the sudden haltings of speech, the fierce struggle against tears, the furious throwaway, and useless explosions that this question elicited.

That one question contained several others, each of them extraordinarily painful to even contemplate. How best to serve the memory of Reggie Jordan? Should we use the language of the killer—Standard English—in order to make our ideas acceptable to those controlling the killers? But wouldn't what we had to say be rejected, summarily, if we said it in our own language, the language of the victim, Reggie Jordan? But if we sought to express ourselves by abandoning our language wouldn't that mean our suicide on top of Reggie's murder? But if we expressed ourselves in our own language wouldn't that be suicidal to the wish to communicate with those who, evidently, did not give a damn about us/Reggie/ police violence in the Black community?

At the end of one of the longest, most difficult hours of my own life, the students voted, unanimously, to preface their individual messages with a paragraph composed in the language of Reggie Jordan. *"At least we don't give up nothing else. At least we stick to the truth: Be who we been. And stay all the way with Reggie."*

It was heartbreaking to proceed, from that point. Everyone in the room realized that our decision in favor of Black English had doomed our writings, even as the distinctive reality of our Black lives always has doomed our efforts to "be who we been" in this country.

I went to the blackboard and took down this paragraph dictated by the class:

You Cops!

We the brother and sister of Willie Jordan, a fellow Stony Brook student who the brother of the dead Reggie Jordan. Reggie, like many brother and sister, he a victim of brutal racist police, October 25, 1984. Us appall, fed up, because that another senseless death what occur in our community. This what we feel, this, from our heart, for we ain't stayin' silent no more.

With the completion of this introduction, nobody said anything. I asked for comments. At this invitation, the unidentified visitor, a young Black man, ceaselessly smiling, raised his hand. He was, it so happens, a rookie cop. He had just joined the force in September and, he said, he thought he should clarify a few things. So he came forward and sprawled easily into a posture of barroom, or fire-side, nostalgia:

"See," Officer Charles enlightened us, "most times when you out on the street and something come down you do one of two things. Over-react or under-react. Now, if you under-react then you can get yourself kilt. And if you over-react then maybe you kill somebody. Fortunately it's about nine times out of ten and you will over-react. So the brother got kilt. And I'm sorry about that, believe me. But what you have to understand is what kilt him: Over-reaction. That's all. Now you talk about Black people and White police but see, now, I'm a cop myself. And (big smile) I'm Black. And just a couple months ago I was on the other side. But it's the same for me. You a cop, you the ultimate authority: the Ultimate Authority. And you on the street, most of the time you can only do one of two things: over-react or under-react. That's all it is with the brother. Over-reaction. Didn't have nothing to do with race."

That morning Officer Charles had the good fortune to escape without being boiled alive. But barely. And I remember the pride of his smile when I read about the fate of Black policemen and other collaborators in South Africa. I remember him, and I remember the shock and palpable feeling of shame that filled the room. It was as though that foolish, and deadly, young man had just relieved himself of his foolish, and deadly, explanation, face to face with the grief of Reggie Jordan's father and Reggie Jordan's mother. Class ended quietly. I copied the paragraph from the blackboard, collected the individual messages and left to type them up.

Newsday rejected the piece.

The Village Voice could not find room in their "Letters" section to print the individual messages from the students to the police.

None of the TV news reporters picked up the story.

Nobody raised $180,000 to prosecute the murder of Reggie Jordan.

Reggie Jordan is really dead.

I asked Willie Jordan to write an essay pulling together everything important to him from that semester. He was still deeply beside himself with frustration and amazement and loss. This is what he wrote, unedited, and in its entirety:

> Throughout the course of this semester I have been researching the effects of oppression and exploitation along racial lines in South Africa and its neighboring countries. I have become aware of South African police brutalization of native Africans beyond the extent of the law,

even though the laws themselves are catalyst affliction upon Black men, women and children. Many Africans die each year as a result of the deliberate use of police force to protect the white power structure.

Social control agents in South Africa, such as policemen, are also used to force compliance among citizens through both overt and covert tactics. It is not uncommon to find bold-faced coercion and cold-blooded killings of Blacks by South African police for undetermined and/or inadequate reasons. Perhaps the truth is that the only reasons for this heinous treatment of Blacks rests in racial differences. We should also understand that what is conveyed through the media is not always accurate and may sometimes be construed as the tip of the iceberg at best.

I recently received a painful reminder that racism, poverty, and the abuse of power are global problems which are by no means unique to South Africa. On October 25, 1984 at approximately 3:00 p.m. my brother, Mr. Reginald Jordan, was shot and killed by two New York City policemen from the 75th precinct in the East New York section of Brooklyn. His life ended at the age of twenty-five. Even up to this current point in time the Police Department has failed to provide my family, which consists of five brothers, eight sisters, and two parents, with a plausible reason for Reggie's death. Out of the many stories that were given to my family by the Police Department, not one of them seems to hold water. In fact, I honestly believe that the Police Department's assessment of my brother's murder is nothing short of ABSOLUTE BULLSHIT, and thus far no evidence had been produced to alter perception of the situation.

Furthermore, I believe that one of three cases may have occurred in this incident. First, Reggie's death may have been the desired outcome of the police officer's action, in which case the killing was premeditated. Or, it was a case of mistaken identity, which clarifies the fact that the two officers who killed my brother and their commanding parties are all grossly incompetent. Or, both of the above cases are correct, i.e., Reggie's murderers intended to kill him and the Police Department behaved insubordinately.

Part of the argument of the officers who shot Reggie was that he had attacked one of them and took his gun. This was their major claim. They also said that only one of them had actually shot Reggie. The facts, however, speak for themselves. According to the Death Certificate and autopsy report, Reggie was shot eight times from point-blank range. The Doctor who performed the autopsy told me himself that two bullets entered the side of my brother's head, four bullets were sprayed into his back, and two bullets struck him in the back of his legs. It is obvious that unnecessary force was used by the police and that it is extremely difficult to shoot someone in his back when he is attacking or approaching you.

After experiencing a situation like this and researching South Africa I believe that to a large degree, justice may only exist as rhetoric. I find it difficult to talk of true justice when the oppression of my people both at home and abroad attests to the fact that inequality and injustice are serious problems whereby Blacks and Third World people are perpetually shortchanged by society. Something has to be done about the way in which this world is set up. Although it is a difficult task, we do have the power to make a change.

Willie J. Jordan Jr.

EGL 487, Section 58, November 14, 1984

It is my privilege to dedicate this book to the future life of Willie J. Jordan Jr., August 8, 1985.

Notes

1. *English Is Spreading, But What Is English?* A presentation by Prof. S. N. Sridhar, Department of Linguistics, SUNY, Stony Brook, April 9, 1985: Dean's Convocation Among the Disciplines.

2. Ibid.

3. *New York Times*, March 15, 1985, Section One, p. 14: Report on Study by Linguists at the University of Pennsylvania.

4. Alice Walker, *The Color Purple* (New York: Harcourt Brace Jovanovich, 1982), p. 11.

Either/Or: Sports, Sex, and the Case of Caster Semenya
Ariel Levy

When people in South Africa say "Limpopo," they mean the middle of no-where. They are referring to the northernmost province of the country, along the border with Botswana, Zimbabwe, and Mozambique, where few people have cars or running water or opportunities for greatness. The members of the Moletjie Athletics Club, who live throughout the area in villages of small brick houses and mud-and-dung huts, have high hopes nonetheless.

One day in late September, twenty teenage athletes gathered for practice on a dirt road in front of Rametlwana Lower Primary School, after walking half an hour through yellow cornfields from their homes, to meet their coach, Jeremiah Mokaba. The school's track is not graded, and donkeys and goats kept walking across it to graze on the new grass that was sprouting as the South African winter gave way to spring. "During the rainy season, we can't train," said Mokaba, a short man wearing a brown corduroy jacket with a golden Zion Christian Church pin on the lapel. "We have nowhere to go inside."

For cross-country, Mokaba and his co-coach, Phineas Sako, train their run-ners in the miles of bush that spread out behind the track, toward the mountains in the distance. The land is webbed with brambles, and the thorns are a serious problem for the athletes, who train barefoot. "They run on loose stones, scrap-ing them, making a wound, making a scar," Sako, a tall, bald man with rheumy eyes and a big gap between his two front teeth, said. "We can't stop and say we don't have running shoes, because we don't have money. The parents don't have money. So what must we do? We just go on."

The athletes and their coaches apologized for not having a clubhouse in which to serve tea. They didn't like talking out in the wind and the dust. There was music playing down the road at a brick-front bar, and chickens squawking in people's front yards, where they are kept in enclosures made out of tree branches. "The most disadvantaged rural area," Sako said, laughing a little and stretching his arms out wide. "That is where you are."

The fastest runner in the club now is a seventeen-year-old named Andrew who recently became the district champion in the fifteen-hundred-metre event. The average monthly income for black Africans in Limpopo—more than ninety-seven per cent of the local population—is less than a thousand rand per month, roughly a hundred and thirty-five dollars. (For white residents, who make up two per cent of the population, it is more than four times that amount.) "I think I will go to the Olympics," Andrew said, with conviction.

Joyce, a tiny girl in a pink sweater who is eighteen but looked much younger, was similarly optimistic. "I want to be the world champion," she said, her voice so soft it was almost a whisper. "I *will* be the world champion. I want to participate in athletics and have a scholarship. Caster is making me proud. She won. She put our club on the map."

Caster Semenya, the current world champion in the eight hundred metres, was a member of the Moletjie Athletics Club until a year ago. She was born in Ga-Masehlong, a village about fifteen miles from the track, and she was, Coach Sako said, "a natural." Even before Semenya left Limpopo for college, in Pretoria, she had won a gold medal in her event at the 2008 Commonwealth Youth Games, in Pune, India, with a time of 2:04, eleven seconds behind the senior world record set by the Czech runner Jarmila Kratochvílová in 1983. "I used to tell Caster that she must try her level best," Sako said. "By performing the best, maybe good guys with big stomachs full of money will see her and then help her with schooling and the likes. That is the motivation." He added, "And she always tried her level best." Semenya won another gold medal in July, in Mauritius, at the African Junior Athletics Championships, lowering her time by a remarkable seven and a half seconds, to come in at 1:56.72. This beat the South African record for that event, held by Zola Budd, and qualified Semenya for her first senior competition, the 2009 World Championships, in Berlin.

Semenya won the eight-hundred-metre title by nearly two and a half seconds, finishing in 1:55.45. After the first lap of the race, she cruised past her competitors like a machine. She has a powerful stride and remarkable efficiency of movement: in footage of the World Championships, you can see the other runners thrashing behind her, but her trunk stays still, even as she is pumping her muscle-bound arms up and down. Her win looks effortless, inevitable. "Even when we were training, I used to pair her with the males," Sako told me. "I feel like she was too powerful for ladies." It was a stunning victory for Semenya, for the Moletjie Athletics Club, and for South Africa.

After the race, Semenya told reporters, "Oh, man, I don't know what to say. It's pretty good to win a gold medal and bring it home." (Her voice is surprising. As Semenya's father, Jacob, has put it, "If you speak to her on the telephone, you might mistake her for a man.") She continued, "I didn't know I could win that race, but for the first time in my life the experience, the World Championships ..." She broke into a grin. "I couldn't believe it, man."

Since the day Semenya broke Zola Budd's record, people in South Africa had been talking about her. Semenya does not look like most female athletes. People questioned whether she was really a woman. Some even e-mailed the International Association of Athletics Federations, the worldwide governing body for track and field, with their doubts. Before Semenya was awarded her gold medal in Berlin, on August 20th, a reporter asked about a story that had been circulating at the Championships, that Semenya's sex was unclear and that she had been required to undergo gender-verification testing before the race. The I.A.A.F. confirmed the rumor, arguably in violation of its confidentiality policies. ("The choice is that you lie, which we don't like to do," Nick Davies, the communications director, told the *New York Times*.) The story ripped around the world. Several of Semenya's competitors in the race were incensed that she had been allowed to participate.

"These kind of people should not run with us," Elisa Cusma, of Italy, who came in sixth, said. "For me, she is not a woman. She is a man."

"Just look at her," Mariya Savinova, of Russia, who finished fifth, said.

Semenya is breathtakingly butch. Her torso is like the chest plate on a suit of armor. She has a strong jawline, and a build that slides straight from her ribs to her hips. "What I knew is that wherever we go, whenever she made her first appearance, people were somehow gossiping, saying, 'No, no, she is not a girl,'" Phineas Sako said, rubbing the gray stubble on his chin. "'It looks like a boy'—that's the right words—they used to say, 'It looks like a boy.' Some even asked me as a coach, and I would confirm: it's a girl. At times, she'd get upset. But, eventually, she was just used to such things." Semenya became accustomed to visiting the bathroom with a member of a competing team so that they could look at her private parts and then get on with the race. "They are doubting me," she would explain to her coaches, as she headed off the field toward the lavatory.

South Africa has eleven official languages. The majority of people in Limpopo speak the Pedi language, and many also speak English and Afrikaans, which schoolchildren were required to learn under apartheid. Sako's English was fluent but rough, and he frequently referred to Semenya as "he." "Caster was very free when he is in the male company," Sako said. "I remember one day I asked her, 'Why are you always in the company of men?' He said, 'No, man, I don't have something to say to girls, they talks nonsense. They are always out of order.'"

On September 11th, Australia's *Daily Telegraph*, a tabloid owned by Rupert Murdoch, reported that Semenya's test results had been leaked, and that they showed that Semenya, though she was brought up as a girl and had external female genitalia, did not have ovaries or a uterus. Semenya was born with undescended testes, the report said, which provided her with three times the amount of testosterone present in an average female—and so a potential advantage over competitors.

"I know what Caster has got," her aunt Johanna Lamola told the *Times*. "I've changed her nappies." Semenya's father said, "I don't even know how they do this gender testing. I don't know what a chromosome is. This is all very painful for us—we live by simple rules." Semenya did not cheat. She has not been evasive. It is very common for élite female athletes, who exert themselves to their physical limits as a matter of course, not to menstruate. There's no reason that Semenya or her coaches would have been alarmed if she were amenorrheic. "Maybe it's because we come from a disadvantaged area," Jeremiah Mokaba said. "They couldn't believe in us."

The I.A.A.F. has yet to inform Semenya whether she can continue running in international female competitions. I asked Sako what he thought would happen. "Caster," he said firmly, "will remain Caster."

Sports have played an important role in modern South African history. A crucial part of the African National Congress's strategy to end apartheid during "the struggle," as everyone calls it, was to secure international condemnation of South Africa's government through boycotts and the banning of South African athletes from all international competitions. Conversely, during the 1995 rugby World Cup Nelson Mandela managed to unite the entire country behind the Springboks, the South African team, which had been a hated symbol of Afrikaner white supremacism. It was pivotal to his success in avoiding civil war and in establishing a new sense of national solidarity. Sports are "more powerful than governments in breaking down racial barriers," Mandela said. "Sport has the power to change the world. It has the power to inspire, the power to unite people that little else has." Sometimes it can unite people against other people. The South African Minister of Sport and Recreation, Makhenkesi Stofile, has warned, "If the I.A.A.F. expels or excludes Semenya from competition or withdraws the medal, I think it would be the Third World War."

In August, when Semenya returned from Germany, thousands of cheering supporters waited to welcome her at O. R. Tambo Airport, outside Johannesburg. President Jacob Zuma met with her to offer his congratulations, as did Nelson Mandela.

Phat Joe, one of the most famous radio d.j.s in the country, was fired by Kaya FM for suggesting on his show that Semenya might have testicles. Lolly Jackson, the owner of a chain of strip clubs called Teazers, put up an enormous billboard in a suburb of Johannesburg picturing a naked woman lying flat on her back above the words "No Need for Gender Testing!" Jackson subsequently claimed that the billboard had nothing to do with Semenya, but he sent her lawyers, at the firm of Dewey & LeBoeuf, a check for twenty thousand rand.

"I think it is the responsibility of South Africa to rally behind this child and tell the rest of the world she remains the hero she is and no one will take that away from her," Winnie Madikizela-Mandela, an ex-wife of Mandela's and a recently elected Member of Parliament, was quoted as saying in the London *Telegraph*. "There is nothing wrong with being a hermaphrodite. It is God's creation. She is God's child." By contrast, the African National Congress Youth League, a division of the African National Congress, issued a statement saying that it "will never accept the categorization of Caster Semenya as a hermaphrodite, because in South Africa and the entire world of sanity, such does not exist."

The African National Congress is part of the Tripartite Alliance, with the South African Communist Party and the Congress of South African Trade Unions. This year's meeting of the Congress happened to coincide with Heritage Day, and many of the hundreds of delegates who assembled at a conference center outside Johannesburg were in traditional tribal dress. Winnie Madikizela-Mandela wore a Xhosa turban and cape. A representative from the police and prison workers' union, wearing nothing but a loincloth made from springbok pelts and a Swazi necklace of red pompoms, mingled with fellow union members at the back of an enormous auditorium, where delegates were debating the items of the day: whether to support the legalization of prostitution in time for the soccer World Cup, which South Africa will host in 2010, and whether to pass a resolution in support of Caster Semenya.

The sessions are meant to evoke the African tradition of villagers gathering to share opinions on local matters. Everyone gets to speak, though men speak much more than women. The prostitution question was examined from every angle: some were concerned about "the downgrading of our women by capitalism"; others felt that every source of income was desperately needed and that sex workers, like everybody else, deserved the protection of a union. After several hours, the delegates decided that what was needed was more discussion.

The South African Minister of Women, Children, and Persons with Disabilities, Noluthando Mayende-Sibiya, went to the lectern dressed in red Xhosa regalia to speak about "the issue of our young star, Caster Semenya." Everyone applauded. "She is our own," Mayende-Sibiya said. "She comes from the working class." The crowd blew horns in support, and some people ululated. "You cannot be silent! The human rights of Caster have been violated," she concluded. The resolution passed with unusual alacrity.

South Africans have been appalled by the idea of a person who thinks she is one thing suddenly being told that she is something else. The classification and reclassification of human beings has a haunted history in this country. Starting with the Population Registration Act of 1950, teams of white people were engaged as census-takers. They usually had no training, but they had the power to decide a person's race, and race determined where and with whom you could live, whether you could get a decent education, whether you had political representation, whether you were even free to walk in certain areas at certain hours. The categories were fickle. In 1985, according to the census, more than a thousand people somehow changed race: nineteen whites turned Colored (as South Africans call people of mixed heritage); seven hundred and two Coloreds turned white, fifty Indians turned Colored, eleven Colored turned Chinese, and so on. (No blacks turned white, or vice versa.)

Taxonomy is an acutely sensitive subject, and its history is probably one of the reasons that South Africans—particularly black South Africans—have rallied behind their runner with such fervor. The government has decreed that Semenya can continue running with women in her own country, regardless of what the I.A.A.F. decides.

South Africans have compared the worldwide fascination with Semenya's gender to the dubious fame of another South African woman whose body captivated Europeans: Saartjie Baartman, the Hottentot Venus. Baartman, an orphan born on the rural Eastern Cape, was the servant of Dutch farmers near Cape Town. In 1810, they sent her to Europe to be exhibited in front of painters, naturalists, and oglers, who were fascinated by her unusually large buttocks and had heard rumors of her long labia. She supposedly became a prostitute and an alcoholic, and she died in France in her mid-twenties. Until 1974, her skeleton and preserved genitals were displayed at the Musée de l'Homme, in Paris. Many South Africans feel that white foreigners are yet again scrutinizing a black female body as though it did not contain a human being.

Mayende-Sibiya has asked that the United Nations get involved in Semenya's case, and I asked her what she thought it could do. "I would like to see it getting more information from the I.A.A.F.," she said over lunch at the Congress. "We wrote to the I.A.A.F. to ask a number of questions, including what precedents informed the action that it took on Caster. Why pick up on her? What were the reasons? The I.A.A.F. has not responded, and that to me raises questions on how it conducts business." Mayende-Sibiya is a big, warm woman, a grandmother and a former nurse, who hugs everyone she meets. She sighed. "There is a lot that has gone wrong in this process."

The I.A.A.F. has behaved erratically on the issue. On November 19th, the South African Ministry of Sport and Recreation announced that the I.A.A.F. had said that Semenya could keep her medal, but the I.A.A.F. refused to confirm this. Its president, Lamine Diack, was scheduled to visit South Africa several weeks ago to talk to Semenya and to representatives of the government, but he cancelled his trip at the last minute. In late October, I got in touch with the I.A.A.F., with questions about Semenya, and received a form-letter reply (dated September 11th) that it would not comment on the case until after its council meeting, at the end of November. Then, a few hours later, Nick Davies, the director of communications, wrote back by e-mail:

> Two things triggered the investigation. Firstly, the incredible improvement in this athlete's performance...and more bluntly, the fact that SOUTH AFRICAN sport Web sites were alleging that she was a hermaphrodite athlete. One such blog (from sport24.co.za) stated, "Caster Semenya is an interesting revelation because the 18 year old was born a hermaphrodite and, through a series of tests, has been classified as female." With this blatant allegation, and bearing in mind the almost supernatural improvement, the I.A.A.F. believed that it was sensible to make sure, with help of A.S.A., that the athlete was negative in terms of doping test results, and also that there was no gender ambiguity which may have allowed her to have the benefits of male hormone levels, whilst competing against other women.

A.S.A. is the abbreviation for Athletics South Africa, the national governing body in charge of track and field. The group's president, Leonard Chuene, who was also on the board of the I.A.A.F., and had been in Berlin for the Championships, told reporters when he returned, "We are not going to allow Europeans to define and describe our children." South Africa would have no part in tests conducted by "some stupid university somewhere," Chuene, who also happens to be from Limpopo, said. "The only scientists I believe in are the parents of this child." He claimed to be shocked by the way that the I.A.A.F. had treated Semenya, and he resigned from the board in protest before he left Berlin. (A week later, Chuene wrote the I.A.A.F. a letter saying that his resignation had been hasty, and asked to be reinstated.)

In fact, Chuene was not only aware of the Berlin tests; he had authorized them, and, at the urging of the I.A.A.F., he had also had Semenya tested before she left Pretoria. On August 3rd, the I.A.A.F.'s anti-doping administrator, Dr. Gabriel Dollé, had sent an e-mail to Harold Adams, A.S.A.'s team doctor, citing the Web-site posting that Nick Davies mentioned to me, which alleged that Semenya is a "hermaphrodite…classified as female." Dollé asked Adams if sex verification had been conducted—or ought to be. (Debora Patta, the host of a South African investigative program called "3rd Degree," obtained the e-mail exchange and forwarded it to me.) Adams then sent the following e-mail to Leonard Chuene and A.S.A.'s general manager, Molatelo Malehopo:

> After thinking about the current confidential matter I would suggest we make the following decisions.
>
> 1. We get a gynae opinion and take it to Berlin.
>
> 2. We do nothing and I will handle these issues if they come up in Berlin.
>
> Please think and get back to me A.S.A.P.

Malehopo replied the same day, agreeing to the exam. Semenya was taken to the Medforum Medi-Clinic, in Pretoria, for tests by a gynecologist.

"They did not even consult us as parents," Semenya's mother, Dorcus, told the *Star*, a South African daily. "They acted like thieves. They did whatever they wanted to do with our child without informing us."

On August 8th, Adams and Semenya flew to Germany to join the rest of the South African team and the A.S.A. staff at the training camp. Adams, who is also one of President Zuma's personal physicians, told Chuene that the Pretoria test results were "not good." He recommended that they withdraw Semenya from the competition, rather than subject her to further testing.

"The reason for my advice was that the tests might prove too traumatic for Ms. Semenya to handle, especially without the necessary support of family and friends around her," Harold Adams wrote in a subsequent report to Parliament. "The other reason was that being tested at the World Championships would not give her enough time to consult extensively and perhaps arrive at a decision to refuse the testing."

Leonard Chuene did not take Adams's advice. Instead, Semenya ran in a qualifying heat on August 16th and then in the semifinals, the next day. After her success in the semifinals, a television reporter outside the stadium blurted out, "With that comes rumors. I heard one that you were born a man?" The video is very hard to watch. As the reporter speaks, Semenya's breathing quickens, and she appears to be on the verge of panic. Then she looks at the ground and says, "I have no idea about that thing....I don't give a damn about it," and walks away from the cameras. August 18th was supposed to be a rest day before the finals. Semenya spent it undergoing a second round of tests. The next day, after two weeks of confusion and scrutiny, Semenya won the gold medal.

In September, the Johannesburg weekly *Mail & Guardian* exposed Chuene's dishonesty about authorizing the tests in Pretoria and Berlin. Chuene contends that he was simply following I.A.A.F. procedure, and that his deceit was a well-intentioned attempt to maintain confidentiality. After the story broke, he held a press conference to apologize for lying to the nation, but the apology was not unconditional. "Tell me someone," he said, "who has not lied to protect a child."

Semenya is back at the University of Pretoria now, training with her coach, Michael Seme. I asked Seme how he thought she was doing. "Sometimes you can look at somebody thinking he is O.K.," Seme said. "But you find out in his heart, maybe it is complaining. I can't see what's happening in her heart."

At a meeting of the British Gynaecological Society on April 25, 1888, Dr. Fancourt Barnes declared that he had "in the next room a living specimen of a hermaphrodite." The person was nineteen years old, and had always believed that she was female. Barnes thought otherwise. He cited "1) the appearance of the head, 2) the *timbre* of the voice, 3) the non-development of the breasts," and "the utter absence of anything like a uterus or ovaries," as evidence of the subject's insufficient femininity.

Other members of the society who examined the patient disagreed. Dr. James Aveling asserted that "the face was feminine, the throat was decidedly that of a woman." Dr. Charles Henry Felix Routh argued that Barnes's diagnosis was "guess work," and claimed that "the mere fact" that this patient might not have a uterus was "no argument against its being a woman." (Routh was not entirely convinced that the patient lacked a uterus and suggested that unless Barnes tried to "pass his entire hand into her rectum" they could not be sure.) Dr. Heywood Smith finally "suggested that the Society should divide on the question of sex," and so it did. Before the doctors sent their patient home with her mother, they took a photograph. In the foreground, a "medical man" holds the "living specimen" 's genitals with his thumb and forefinger for the camera, between her spread legs. In the background is the blurred image of the subject's head, not quite obscured by the blanket that covers her torso. The subject's face is grainy, but it is set in an unmistakable expression of powerless panic.

The society's inability to reach consensus was due, in part, to its failure to locate either testicles or ovaries in the patient. Until 1915, that was the generally accepted determining factor for sex. In "Hermaphrodites and the Medical Invention of Sex," Alice Domurat Dreger calls the period from 1870 to 1915 "the Age of Gonads."

The way doctors, scientists, and sports officials have determined sex has changed radically over the years. Before 1968, the International Olympic Committee verified the sex of female athletes by looking between their legs. Athletes complained about these humiliating inspections—which weren't always conclusive—and, for the 1968 Olympics, in Mexico City, the I.O.C. decided to implement chromosomal testing. (There were rumors that some men from Eastern Bloc nations had plans to masquerade as women.) These assessments proved problematic, too.

In normal human development, when a zygote has XY, or male, chromosomes, the SRY—sex-determining region Y—gene on the Y chromosome "instructs" the zygote's protogonads to develop as testes, rather than as ovaries. The testes then produce testosterone, which issues a second set of developmental instructions: for a scrotal sac to develop and for the testes to descend into it, for a penis to grow, and so on. But the process can get derailed. A person can be born with one ovary and one testicle. The SRY gene can end up on an X chromosome. A person with a penis who thinks he is male can one day find out that he has a uterus and ovaries. "Then, there is chromosomal variability that is invisible," Anne Fausto-Sterling, the author of "Sexing the Body," told me. "You could go your whole life and never know."

All sorts of things can happen, and do. An embryo that is chromosomally male but suffers from an enzyme deficiency that partially prevents it from "reading" testosterone can develop into a baby who appears female. Then, at puberty, the person's testes will produce a rush of hormones and this time the body won't need the enzyme (called 5-alpha-reductase) to successfully read the testosterone. The little girl will start to become hairier and more muscular. Her voice may deepen, and her testes may descend into what she thought were her labia. Her clitoris will grow into something like a penis. Is she still a girl? Was she ever?

If a chromosomally male embryo has androgen-insensitivity syndrome, or A.I.S., the cells' receptors for testosterone, an androgen, are deaf to the testosterone's instructions, and will thus develop the default external sexual characteristics of a female. An individual with androgen-insensitivity syndrome has XY chromosomes, a vagina, and undescended testes, but her body develops without the ability to respond to the testosterone it produces. In fact, people with complete A.I.S. are less able to process testosterone than average women. Consequently, they tend to have exceptionally "smooth-skinned bodies with rounded hips and breasts and long limbs," Dreger writes in "Hermaphrodites."

People with incomplete A.I.S., on the other hand, could end up looking and sounding like Caster Semenya. Their bodies hear *some* of the instructions that the testosterone inside them is issuing. But that does not necessarily mean that they would have an athletic advantage.

For example, the Spanish hurdler Maria Patiño, who had A.I.S., went to the World University Games in Kobe, Japan, in 1985, and forgot to bring a letter from her doctor verifying that she was female. Until 1999, gender verification was compulsory for all female athletes. Officials scraped some cells from the inside of her cheek for chromatin testing. If visual inspection had still been the standard, Patiño's gender never would have been questioned. Her genitals, and the rest of her, looked female, but according to the test she was male. The story got out, and she was stripped of her past titles. Her boyfriend left her. Her scholarship was revoked, and she was evicted from the national athletic residence.

In 1991, the International Association of Athletics Federations abandoned this method as unreliable, and, nine years later, so did the International Olympic Committee. Patiño was requalified in 1988, when she was able to prove that her body could not make use of its testosterone, and that she had developed as a woman. "I knew I was a woman," Patiño said, "in the eyes of medicine, God, and most of all in my own eyes."

The approach that the I.A.A.F. appears to be taking in its review of Semenya's test results from Berlin is not unlike the British Gynaecological Society's muddled attempt to determine the sex of its living specimen. The I.A.A.F.'s gender policy states that an athlete "can be asked to attend a medical evaluation before a panel comprising gynecologist, endocrinologist, psychologist, internal medicine specialist, expert on gender/transgender issues." It has not come up with a single litmus test for sex; its goal, like that of the I.O.C. in such situations, is to reach consensus. The federation does not define the criteria that its group of experts must use to reach their determination, however. "It seems to be working with a kind of 'I know it when I see it' policy," Dreger, a professor of clinical medical humanities and bioethics at Northwestern University's Feinberg School of Medicine, told me. The policy does not indicate who should be tested and on what grounds. An athlete will be examined if "there is any 'suspicion' or if there is a 'challenge'" to her sex. Evidently, a blog post qualifies as a challenge.

In conjunction with other sports bodies, the I.A.A.F. will hold a special conference, in January, 2010, to review the policy. On November 18th, it sent out a press release stating that there would be "no discussion of Caster Semenya's case" at the November council meeting, despite its earlier promise to resolve the issue there.

Unfortunately for I.A.A.F. officials, they are faced with a question that no one has ever been able to answer: what is the ultimate difference between a man and a woman? "This is not a solvable problem," Alice Dreger said. "People always press me: 'Isn't there one marker we can use?' No. We couldn't then and we can't now, and science is making it more difficult and not less, because it ends up showing us how much blending there is and how many nuances, and it becomes impossible to point to one thing, or even a set of things, and say that's what it means to be male.

In 2000, Anne Fausto-Sterling, a professor of biology at Brown University, conducted what remains the study of record on the frequency of intersexuality, and concluded that 1.7 per cent of the population develops in a way that deviates from the standard definition of male or female. (Some scholars have argued that Fausto-Sterling's categories are too broad, because they include individuals who show no noticeable expression of their chromosomal irregularity.) Based on this figure, intersexuality is much more common than Down syndrome or albinism, though it can be harder to keep track of: every baby born in the United States is registered as "male" or "female."

The word "hermaphrodite" is as outdated and offensive to the people it once described as the word "mulatto." In one Greek myth, Hermes, the son of Zeus, and Aphrodite, the goddess of love, have a child endowed with all the attributes of both of them. "Hermaphrodite" implies a double-sexed creature, fully male and fully female, which is a physical impossibility for human beings. (You can be half and half, but you can't be all and all.)

In the nineteen-nineties, a movement spearheaded by an activist who used to call herself Cheryl Chase, and now goes by the name Bo Laurent, insisted that what was needed was a new identity. Chase founded the Intersex Society of North America (now defunct) to draw attention to the frequently tragic consequences of doctors' performing irreversible surgery on newborns to enforce a sex—one that the baby might just as easily as not grow up to reject. The society advocated assigning intersex children a gender at birth but leaving their bodies intact, so that upon adulthood they could make their own choices about whether they wished to undergo surgical modification.

Then something unexpected happened. "The intersex identity started getting inhabited by people who weren't really intersex," Dreger said. "The people who accumulated around the intersex identity tended to be queer and out and comfortable with this identity outside the gender binary." They felt that refraining from interfering with infants' ambiguous genitalia was the first step on a desirable path to dissolving gender altogether. To them, this idea was "as politically inspiring as it is utterly disconnected from the actual experience of intersex people or the heart-wrenching decisions their parents have to make when an intersex child is born," as Vernon A. Rosario, a professor of psychiatry at U.C.L.A., put it in a recent issue of *The Gay and Lesbian Review*.

Semenya, whether she wants to be or not, has become a hero to many people who "don't fit the sex and gender boxes," as Jarvis, from Winnipeg, posted on the Web site casterrunsforme.com. A person named Megan Ewart wrote, "I'll bet you've got a lot more transgendered allies than just me that are feeling your pain."

Now there is an even newer term of art for people born with ambiguously sexed bodies who do not wish to be connected with the "L.G.B.T.Q.I."—lesbian, gay, bisexual, transgender, queer, intersex—camp: "disorders of sex development," or D.S.D. By naming the condition a medical "disorder," advocates of the D.S.D. label hope to make the people it describes seem less aberrant. "Oddly enough, it does normalize it in a certain way," Fausto-Sterling said. "It's putting it on the same plane as other anomalous development—like congenital anomalies of the heart." Advocates of the D.S.D. label are not seeking to create a third sex. Rather, they want disorders of sex development to be treated like any other physical abnormality: something for doctors to monitor but not to operate on, unless the patient is in physical discomfort or danger.

In science and medicine, categories are imperative, but they are also inflected by social concerns. "Mammals," for example, were so named by Linnaeus, in the eighteenth century, because their females produce milk to suckle their young. Was it irrelevant that scientists like Linnaeus sought to encourage mothers to breast-feed their own children, and to do away with the "unnatural" custom of wet-nursing? "There are philosophers of science who argue that when scientists make categories in the natural world—shapes, species—they are simply making a list of things that exist: natural kinds," Fausto-Sterling said. "It's scientist as discoverer. The phrase that people use is 'cutting nature at its joint.' There are other people, myself included, who think that, almost always, what we're doing in biology is creating categories that work pretty well for certain things that we want to do with them. But there is no joint."

If sex is not precisely definable, how else might sports be organized? Theoretically, athletes could be categorized by size, as they are in wrestling and boxing. But then women would usually lose to men. Or athletes could be categorized by skill level. Almost always, this would mean that the strongest élite female athletes would compete against the weakest élite male athletes, which would be pretty demoralizing all the way around.

Another option would be to divide athletes biochemically. Testosterone is, for an athlete, truly important stuff. Developmentally, testosterone spurs linear bone growth in adolescents. Fully grown people use testosterone in doping because it helps create muscle mass and increases red-blood-cell production, which, in turn, increases cellular oxygen-carrying capacity. The more oxygen an athlete has in her cells, the more efficiently her muscles operate and the longer it takes for her body to start producing lactic acid, the substance that causes cramps and pain. Testosterone makes a faster, better athlete, and enables a body to recover more quickly from exhaustion. Hypothetically, according to Eric Vilain, a professor of human genetics and pediatrics at U.C.L.A., those with a certain level of functional testosterone (testosterone that the body can actually make use of) could be in one group, and those below it could be in another. Although the first group would be almost all male and the second group would be almost all female, the division would be determined not by gender but by actual physical advantages that gender supposedly, yet unreliably, supplies.

But, setting aside the issue of gender, there is still no such thing as a level playing field in sports. Different bodies have physical attributes, even abnormalities, that may provide a distinct advantage in one sport or another. The N.B.A., for instance, has had several players with acromegaly—the overproduction of growth hormone. Michael Phelps, who has won fourteen Olympic gold medals, has unusually long arms and is said to have double-jointed elbows, knees, and ankles. Is Caster Semenya's alleged extra testosterone really so different?

There is much more at stake in organizing sports by gender than just making things fair. If we were to admit that at some level we don't know the difference between men and women, we might start to wonder about the way we've organized our entire world. Who gets to use what bathroom? Who is allowed to get married? (Currently, the United States government recognizes the marriage of a woman to a female-to-male transsexual who has had a double mastectomy and takes testosterone tablets but still has a vagina, but not to a woman who hasn't done those things.) We depend on gender to make sense of sexuality, society, and ourselves. We do not wish to see it dissolve.

What the I.A.A.F. concludes about Caster Semenya could have ramifications for sports in general and for South Africa in particular. This is true not only because it is Semenya's place of origin. South Africa has an unusually high level of intersex births. Nobody knows why.

During apartheid, for every white town there was a black township. Only the white towns appeared on maps, though the townships were nearly always more populous. John Carlin, in his account of the 1995 rugby World Cup, "Playing the Enemy: Nelson Mandela and the Game That Made a Nation," describes townships as "the black shadows of the towns." Khayelitsha is the black shadow of Cape Town. According to the most recent census, half a million people live there, but in reality the number is probably much higher. Many of their parents and grandparents settled in the Cape Flats, outside of Cape Town, after the Group Areas Acts of the nineteen-fifties made it illegal for them to live in the city. "Khayelitsha" is Xhosa for "New Home." Shacks made of corrugated tin, cardboard, and scrap wood, many without electricity or running water, sprawl for miles along mostly unmarked dirt roads, punctuated by beauty parlors and fruit stands in structures no bigger than British telephone booths.

By Khayelitsha standards, Funeka Soldaat's small home, with its solid brick walls and tiled floor, is very fine. Soldaat is an L.G.B.Q.T.I. activist. Both she and a cousin—whom Soldaat, following local custom, referred to as her sister—were born with anomalous genitalia, and both underwent "corrective" partial clitoridectomies when they were young, which they now regret. This is the standard "treatment" for babies born with a clitoris longer than one centimetre but smaller than 2.5 centimetres, at which point it becomes a medically acceptable penis. The scar tissue that forms after such a procedure can impede sensation for the rest of a person's life.

"My sister, she look just like Caster," Soldaat said, smiling. "She don't have the breasts. She never get a period. Everybody thinks she's a guy, just like Caster. We call them, in Xhosa, *italasi*. It is not a new thing—everybody has a word for it." That there is a name for intersex does not mean it is a condition that is ever spoken about. "One thing that is so difficult for African people: there's no way that you can discuss about something that's happened below the belt," Soldaat said. "All the time you don't know what's happening in your body, and there's nobody that try to explain to you. *Then* it becomes a problem. If my mom would know that I'm intersex and there's nothing wrong about it, then there was nothing going to make me panic."

Particularly in remote areas, where babies tend to be born in the presence of a mother, a grandmother, and maybe a midwife, it is easy to keep a baby's genitalia a secret. People want to insulate their children from the shame of being different, so they simply pretend that they are not. "Limpopo and Eastern Cape are the high incidence of intersex people," Soldaat said. "And when you grow up in the rural areas it's a mess, because people don't even go to doctors." The determination of gender is made very simply. "It depends what they do when they go to the loo," Soldaat said. "That's what makes their children to be women. If they go to the loo and they sit, that's it."

On her coffee table, Soldaat had a photocopy of the South African magazine *You*, which featured a photo spread showing Caster Semenya dressed in high heels and a short skirt, her hair fluffed out and her face made up. Her expression was painfully uncomfortable, and the pictures were garish.

"My sister was crying when she saw this whole thing on paper," Soldaat said, flipping through the pages. "It's a disaster. She look like a drag queen! I can just imagine her at night when she's alone, looking at these pictures."

Soldaat tossed the papers on the floor. "When we are really, really poor sometimes, and we really, really want to protect ourselves, people take an advantage," she said. "That's why it was easy for people to force her to do this, for A.S.A. to do this." Athletics South Africa received a payment from *You* in exchange for Semenya's appearance in its pages. "To say that she enjoyed doing this, that's a lie! There is no way. There is no way!"

Soldaat has a shaved head and was wearing big jeans and a baseball cap with the words "Mama Cash," the name of a Dutch women's-rights organization, on it. She is a lesbian, and she said that she suspected Semenya is, too.

"Everyone! Everyone who is like this likes women," Soldaat said, laughing. "Everyone!" ("Caster has never cared about men other than as friends," her father told a reporter. "Her sisters were always after boys in the way that I, too, was always after girls when I was younger. But Caster has never been interested in any of that.") If Soldaat is right, then Semenya's life may well get more difficult. Soldaat was going to court later that day to listen to the proceedings against several men accused of raping and murdering a lesbian in Khayelitsha. "They are raping lesbians to correct them," she said. "In order they can be a proper woman."

Soldaat said that Semenya should run with women. "It will never be like intersex women have their own Olympic Games—that's ridiculous!" she said. Soldaat has a big, raucous laugh, and the idea of that imaginary competition absolutely killed her. Soldaat was a runner herself when she was young. "If she can't run in the Olympics, Caster has to continue running with other girls in South Africa. Because, really, that's what she wants, that's what she is, that's what keeps her alive: that's running."

The only thing more slippery than the science in the Semenya case is the agendas of the men who have involved themselves in it. There is a bounty of political gain for whoever spins the story most successfully.

Julius Malema, the president of the A.N.C. Youth League, has said that he does not believe in the existence of intersex people, and has tried to frame the concept as a suspect and unwelcome import from abroad. "Hermaphrodite, what is that?" Malema asked at a press conference in October. "Somebody tell me, what is 'hermaphrodite' in Pedi? There's no such thing. So don't impose your hermaphrodite concepts on us." (The word is *tarasi*, according to a professor of South African languages at Yale.) The Youth League issued a press release decrying a "racist attack on Semenya" orchestrated by the media in "Australia, which is the most lucrative destination for South Africa's racists and fascists who refused to live under a black democratic government."

Julius Malema is not known for being levelheaded. He won the presidency of the Youth League in a highly contested election in 2008. Just a few months later, while Jacob Zuma was fending off charges of racketeering and fraud (the charges have since been dropped), Malema became notorious for vowing, "We are prepared to die for Zuma. Not only that, we are prepared to take up arms and kill for Zuma." (Zuma also beat a rape charge, in 2006.) Zuma has called Malema "a leader in the making," worthy of "inheriting the A.N.C." one day. Malema has demonstrated an ability to mobilize people and an almost reckless willingness to use charges of racism to do so. He has been Leonard Chuene's most steadfast defender.

Chuene has, since the revelation of his deceit, become almost as controversial a figure in South Africa as Caster Semenya. Countless editorials have accused Chuene of sacrificing her in his quest for a gold medal and have demanded his ouster. In Dr. Harold Adams's report to Parliament, he calls Chuene's decision "short-sighted and grossly irresponsible." Though Chuene received a vote of confidence from Athletics South Africa's board after his admission, the A.N.C. asked him to apologize; its rival party, the Democratic Alliance, demanded his resignation, and the Deputy Minister of Sport called him a liar. Minister Mayende-Sibiya told me that Chuene's behavior was "totally unacceptable."

Julius Malema has continued to paint any criticism of Chuene as racist. In early October, one of A.S.A.'s biggest sponsors, Nedbank, announced that it would withdraw its support pending a change in A.S.A.'s leadership. Malema retaliated by calling for a boycott of the bank. "We will teach them a lesson about the power of the masses," Malema said. "They may have money, but we can defeat them because we have the masses."

On three occasions, Leonard Chuene's personal assistant made an appointment for me to interview "the president," as she calls her boss. She always called or e-mailed at the last minute to cancel. We had several calls scheduled, but Chuene never picked up his phone at the appointed time. Then, one day, I got on an airplane going to Polokwane, a small northern city. Sitting in an empty row, in a navy blazer and pressed jeans, was Leonard Chuene.

Chuene wanted to know how I recognized him. Only minutes before, I had been looking at his photograph in a newspaper, alongside a story about Nedbank's withdrawal of funds from A.S.A. and A.S.A.'s failing finances. "I have become more famous than Caster," he said, and chuckled. Chuene has a shiny bald head and a little gut. He was once a serious runner and has completed more than a hundred marathons, he told me. He said he had no choice but to get Semenya tested. "You cannot just argue like a fool and say no. This is not the law of the jungle!" He speaks very quickly. He explained why he had not heeded Adams's advice to withdraw Semenya from the race.

"I don't have the results in my hand!" he said. "How did you expect me to take an informed decision?"

Indeed, Adams had had word from the Pretoria clinic but no actual documentation of the test results. "Where is the evidence?" Chuene said. "Now I come back home and they will say, 'When this black child from the rural be No. 1, why do you deprive her?' "

Chuene shrugged. "They say I lied. That's what they are saying. I said no. There is confidentiality! I.A.A.F. is in trouble for breaching that. Who was going to be Leonard to say that?" The engines started roaring as the small plane took off. "It was 22-Catch situation!" Chuene shouted over the noise. "If I will do this, it's 'Why did you withdraw her?' If I did not, 'Why did you allow her to run?' Whatever way you look at it, I'm judged. I'm judged!"

There were around twenty people on the plane. We were airborne, and the engines quieted. Chuene did not. "The stupid leader is the one who says, 'I'm not sure; I don't know.' I had to take a decision! She must run. If Chuene didn't allow her, it meant she was going to stay in South Africa. This thing has given her more opportunity! Everybody knows her. The world is out there to say, 'Your problems are our problems.' Imagine if I had not let her win!" As we touched down in Polokwane, he said, "If there is to be help, it is because of the opportunity created by Leonard Chuene."

Recently, Semenya told the *Guardian*, "It's not so easy. The university is O.K. but there is not many other places I can go. People want to stare at me now. They want to touch me. I'm supposed to be famous." She added, "I don't think I like it so much."

The law firm Dewey & LeBoeuf announced in September that it was taking on Caster Semenya as a client. It is still sorting through what happened and deciding whom to sue. One afternoon, I drove with Benedict Phiri, an associate in the firm's Johannesburg office, across the Blood River from Polokwane to Ga-Masehlong to meet Semenya's mother. Ga-Masehlong is a small village dotted with jacaranda trees; goats graze on the garbage and the grass on the roadsides. The houses have tin roofs, and people put rocks on top of them to keep them from blowing away. There are satellite dishes in several yards, but most people have dug their own wells and collect firewood from the bush for cooking. Everyone knows everyone else in Ga-Masehlong, and it was easy to get directions to the house of the champion.

At the Semenya home, there was a flyer tacked to the front door promoting a lecture that Julius Malema was giving at the local elementary school. Phiri knocked. We heard shuffling and then the sound of locks turning and bolts sliding. Phiri called out that he was Caster's lawyer, but nobody came to the door.

A few minutes later, a pretty girl wearing an orange fleece jacket walked into the yard and introduced herself as Maphela. She said she was fourteen. "Do you want my story?" she asked in English. "I am Caster's sister! But I am not like her. I am different from Caster." I asked her what she meant, and Maphela replied emphatically, "I am not that way."

Maphela looked toward the window where her mother, Dorcus, was hiding her face behind the curtain and motioning vigorously for her daughter to stop speaking with us. We asked Maphela if she would tell her mother that Phiri was Caster's lawyer. Maphela ran off toward the back door.

We sat on the stoop of a cooking hut in the Semenyas' front yard, and waited with the chickens and the goats. An elderly neighbor named Ike came into the yard. "Caster has done a wonderful thing," he said. "This has brought to mind when the Philistines were persecuting the Israelites." Ike told us that he just wanted to check on the family and see how their visit from Julius Malema the previous evening had gone. This made Phiri nervous.

After a few minutes, Maphela returned. She told us that her mother would not meet with Phiri, because she did not agree that Caster should have a lawyer.

As we drove away through the bush, Phiri called his boss in Johannesburg, a white former rugby player named Greg Nott. I could hear Nott yelling through the phone. "We knew this would happen all along," Phiri said, trying to calm him. "Julius Malema is Chuene's ally, and Julius is giving Caster money."

On the occasion of the A.N.C. Youth League's sixty-fifth anniversary, in October, Julius Malema presented Caster Semenya with a hundred and twenty thousand rand (about sixteen thousand dollars) at a gala dinner in Johannesburg. "I can even see it," Phiri said on the phone. "They probably told the mom, 'People will come and say they're her lawyer. Don't believe it.' " Phiri was afraid that Malema would step in and persuade the family to side with Chuene, who comes from the same region, and whose interests might not be served by lawyers poking around. One of the first things that Dewey & LeBoeuf did when the firm took the case was to ask both A.S.A. and the I.A.A.F. to provide documentation of the tests and any other pertinent paperwork; neither organization has fully complied.

The firm is representing Semenya pro bono, so good publicity will be its only reward. "And that," Phiri said, "could blow up in our faces."

Nobody wants Chuene out of office more than an old friend and colleague named Wilfred Daniels, who started at A.S.A. with him, sixteen years ago. "From day one we connected, in the struggle days, you know?" Daniels said. "We were like, we *belong* together." Both Daniels, fifty-eight, and Chuene, fifty-seven, grew up as promising athletes who could never compete internationally because of apartheid. They understood each other then, but not anymore.

Daniels—whom everyone calls Wilfie—is the unofficial mayor of Stellenbosch, a leafy college town in the wine country. He likes to hold court at the Jan Cats restaurant, in front of the elegant Stellenbosch Hotel. As he sat at his street-front table on a sunny afternoon in a green Izod jacket and track pants, drinking a bottle of Chenin blanc, every other person who passed by stopped to pay his respects, or at least waved at him driving by. Daniels was a famous athlete in his youth, and he is even more famous now. In early September, he resigned from A.S.A. in protest over its handling of Caster Semenya, and had since been in the papers constantly. "We allowed it," he said. "If we as management were on our game, we would've objected. We accompanied her to the slaughter. And that is my dilemma."

Daniels was not directly involved in the testing or the coverup. During the first training session in Berlin, "while she was warming up and stretching, putting on her spikes, she told me they had done tests on her. I said, 'What tests?'" Semenya told him that she didn't know what they were for, but she described what had happened. "They put her feet in straps and 'they work down there,' she said. They told her it was dope tests." Semenya had undergone routine doping tests many times before. She knew that this was something very different.

"If you and me who come from the big cities, if we find it repulsive, I mean, what about a rural girl," Daniels said. "She doesn't know what's happening around her. She's seven, eight months in the city now, in Pretoria, a new life altogether, and nobody takes the time to explain to her?" He shook his head in disgust. "It was unprovoked talk, and she's not somebody who talks, normally. And she spoke to me as a Colored guy, as a man, about intimate, female things. That to me was like a cry for help."

The sins of A.S.A., as Daniels sees it, are, first, not giving Semenya adequate information about the Pretoria tests—including her right to refuse them—and, second, not pulling her out of the competition in Berlin.

"It's the day before the championships," Daniels said. "Eighteen years old, your first World Championships, the greatest race of your life. You can't focus, because you have to go for gender testing. And you come back and you have to watch on TV: they are explaining the possibilities. I found her in her room, sitting in front of the TV like this," Daniels put his hand up to his face to show how close she was to the screen. "And they're talking about her and she's trying to understand what they're saying. Because nobody has spoken to her, to tell her, Look, this is what these tests might mean. I felt so ashamed."

Daniels has worked in various capacities at A.S.A. over the years, first in management, then as a coach, and, most recently, as A.S.A.'s coördinator with the High Performance Centre, the program at the University of Pretoria where Semenya is now. Daniels does not agree with the I.A.A.F.'s assessment that Semenya's seven-and-a-half-second improvement was "supernatural." She went from training on the dirt roads of Limpopo to a world-class facility. She is also an extraordinarily hard worker. "Understand: Maria Mutola is her hero," Daniels said. "So she had wonderful goals and ideals for herself; she was really trying to emulate her hero one day." Maria Mutola is a runner from Mozambique whose event, like Semenya's, was the eight hundred metres. Mutola also happened to have a strikingly masculine appearance.

Daniels believes that the best that can happen for Semenya at this point is to have a career like his. He has travelled the world and met many of his heroes. He has a cellar with more than two thousand bottles of red wine. He eats his grilled springbok at Jan Cats and clearly enjoys being a local eminence. But it is probably not the life he would have led if apartheid hadn't prevented him from competing internationally; and it is not the life that was in front of Caster Semenya before she went to Germany. "I understand that her running days are over," Daniels said.

There's another scenario, in which Semenya's story could become one of against-all-odds victory. The I.A.A.F. could apologize and decree Semenya female. Kobus van der Walt, the director of sport at the High Performance Centre, pointed out that though Semenya has beaten the South African record for her event, she hasn't come anywhere near Kratochvílová's world record, which means that there are plenty of women with a chance of besting Semenya. Conceivably, one day we will see Caster Semenya at the Olympics with a medal hanging from her neck. She could be the poster child for triumphant transgression.

But that is not what Daniels thinks will happen. "Now her life is over," he said. "Not only as an athlete but as a human being. Even if the I.A.A.F. says there's nothing wrong with her, people will always look at her twice. There should be hell to pay for those responsible." He pounded his fist on the table. "I've got a daughter. If that was my daughter, what would I have done as a father? Somebody might have been dead by now."

On November 5th, Chuene and the entire board of A.S.A. were suspended by the South African Sports Confederation and Olympic Committee, pending an investigation into how they handled Caster Semenya.

One afternoon at the High Performance Centre, I sat up in the bleachers, killing time before a meeting with Kobus Van der Walt. I was surrounded by a spread of neatly partitioned fields, like a Brueghel painting: there are twenty-four cricket nets, six rugby fields, twenty-two outdoor tennis courts, nine soccer fields, seven squash courts, and a track surrounded by a three-thousand-seat stadium, all kept in impeccable condition. Runners in little packs zoomed around the fields and into the distance. Spring sunlight flicked along the blue of the swimming pool.

A figure in a black sweatshirt with the hood up walked along the path about thirty yards in front of me. There was something about this person's build and movements that drew my attention. I got up and followed along the path, until I caught up to the person where he or she was stopped behind the cafeteria, talking to a waiter and a cook, both of whom were much shorter than she was. It was Caster Semenya.

She wore sandals and track pants and kept her hood up. When she shook my hand, I noticed that she had long nails. She didn't look like an eighteen-year-old girl, or an eighteen-year-old boy. She looked like something else, something magnificent.

I told her I had come from New York City to write about her, and she asked me why.

"Because you're the champion," I said.

She snorted and said, "You make me laugh."

I asked her if she would talk to me, not about the tests or Chuene but about her evolution as an athlete, her progression from Limpopo to the world stage. She shook her head vigorously. "No," she said. "I can't talk to you. I can't talk to anyone. I can't say to anyone how I feel or what's in my mind."

I said I thought that must suck.

"No," she said, very firmly. Her voice was strong and low. "That doesn't suck. It sucks when I was running and they were writing those things. That sucked. That is when it sucks. Now I just have to walk away. That's all I can do." She smiled a small, bemused smile. "Walk away from all of this, maybe forever. Now I just walk away." Then she took a few steps backward, turned around, and did.

Excerpt from 2017 Hollywood Diversity Report: Setting the Record Straight

The Ralph J. Bunche Center for African American Studies at UCLA[1]

Diversity and the Bottom Line: Casting, Box Office, and Ratings

"I was determined the lead [for a film] would be a black woman, and I remember the executive saying, 'Why does she have to be black?' And me saying: 'She doesn't have to be; I want her to be black. Why would you not consider it?'"

—John Ridley

In the previous three reports in this series, a consideration of overall cast diversity in theatrical releases and television shows has consistently revealed a curious disconnect between Hollywood industry production choices and market realities. That is, the industry produces an inordinate number of low-performing films and television shows year in and year out that are not very diverse, while the films and television shows that actually perform best, on average, better reflect the diversity of America.

The current report extends the analysis of the relationships between overall cast diversity and bottom-line performance an additional year in order to consider the top 200 theatrical films released in 2015 and the television shows airing during the 2014–15 television season. Do previous findings linking cast diversity to bottom-line performance hold up in the face of a fourth year of data and analysis?

The following headlines address this question.

Film

1. Films with Relatively Diverse Casts Continue to Excel at Box Office

Figure 85 presents an analysis of median global box office by cast diversity interval for the top 168 films released in 2015. As a benchmark for comparison, it includes analyses presented in earlier reports in this series for films released between 2011 and 2014. Several findings emerge from the chart. First, median global box office peaked in 2015 for the 25 films with casts that were from 21 percent to 30 percent minority ($105 million). Films that occupied this cast diversity interval in 2015 included: *Spectre, Ant-Man, San Andreas, Terminator: Genisys*, and *Fantastic Four*.

---

1. This report was authored by Dr. Darnell Hunt, Dr. Ana-Christina Ramón, Michael Tran, Amberia Sargent, and Vanessa Díaz. Michelle Berman, Brittany Botts, Funmilola Fagbamila, Briana McKoy, Carmella Stoddard, and Michael Tran contributed to data collection for analysis.

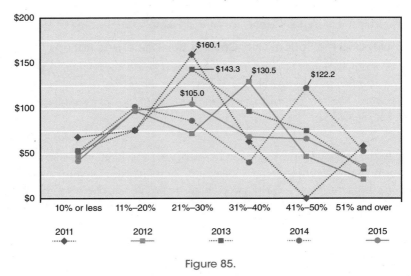

Global Box Office (000,000s) by Minority Cast Share,
Theatrical Films, 2011–2015 (n = 172, 164, 163, 162, 168)

Figure 85.

By contrast, median worldwide box office was only $41.9 million for the 64 films with casts that were 10 percent minority or less in 2015. Interestingly, though films in this cast diversity interval were the poorest performers, on average, they were by far the most numerous. Indeed, the relatively large number of low-performing films that lack cast diversity has been a consistent finding throughout this report series. By contrast, median box office peaked for films that were from 41 percent to 50 percent minority in 2014 ($122.2 million), those that were from 21 percent to 30 percent minority in 2011 and 2013 ($160.1 million and $143.3 million, respectively) and those that were from 31 percent to 40 percent minority in 2012 ($130.5 million).

2. Films with Relatively Diverse Casts Continue to Excel in Terms of Return on Investment

If we consider return on investment,[1] which factors a film's budget into the analysis, we see a similar pattern, which echoes findings from the previous reports. As **Figure 86** illustrates, the 25 films that fell into the 21 percent to 30 percent minority interval in 2015 also posted the highest median return on investment (2.5). This was also the diversity interval associated with the highest return on investment in 2011 and 2013, while 41 percent to 50 percent minority was the peak interval for 2014 and 2012. As was the case with global box office (see above), less diverse films, on average, were relatively poorer performers in terms of return on investment across the years examined in this report series.

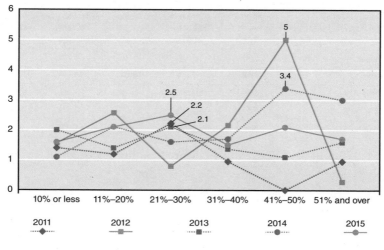

Return on Investment by Minority Cast Share,
Theatrical Films, 2011–2015 (n = 160, 147, 153, 162, 168)

Figure 86.

3. Minorities Continue to Drive Relationship between Cast Diversity and Box Office

Table 4 compares median box office and audience demographics for the films in each cast diversity interval in 2015. It demonstrates that minorities account for a disproportionate share of box office at every cast diversity interval—except for the interval containing the 64 least-diverse and worse performing films (i.e., 10 percent minority or less). Indeed, at 38.4 percent of the population in 2015, minorities constituted 46.9 percent of the audience (14 percent black, 18.7 percent Latino, 12 percent Asian American, and 2.2 percent other) for the 25 films falling in the 21 percent to 30 percent minority cast diversity interval that year.

The films in this interval, you will recall, had the highest median global box office ($105 million) and return on investment (2.5) in 2015. Meanwhile, minorities constituted the majority of the audience for films with casts that were from 41 to 50 percent minority (50.1 percent share) and over 50 percent minority (57.2 percent share).

Similarly, an analysis of the top 10 theatrical releases in 2015 (ranked by global box office), reveals that minorities accounted for the majority of the box office for five of the films (see **Table 5**), up from four of the top 10 films in 2014. These films include: *Furious 7*, which earned $1.5 billion (61 percent share); *Avengers: Age of Ultron*, which earned $1.4 billion (51 percent share); *Minions*, which earned $1.2 billion (52 percent share); *Inside Out*, which earned $857.4 million (51 percent share); and *Mission Impossible: Rogue Nation*, which earned $682.3 million (54 percent share).

Table 4. Median Box Office and Audience Demographics, by Overall Cast Diversity (2015)

Percent Minority	N Films	Global Box Office (000,000s)	White Share	Black Share	Latino Share	Asian Share
10% or less	64	$41.4	59.6%	11.2%	16.0%	10.4%
11%–20%	39	$98.5	51.8%	16.3%	18.2%	11.6%
21%–30%	25	$105.0	53.1%	14.0%	18.7%	12.0%
31%–40%	18	$68.7	51.3%	14.4	21.7%	10.2%
41%–50%	10	$65.8	49.9%	13.2%	23.7%	10.7%
Over 50%	12	$35.3	42.8%	30.4%	21.6%	8.2%

Table 5. Top 10 Box Office Films' Audience Minority Share (2015)

Rank	Title	Box Office (000,000s)	Return	Audience Minority Share
1	Star Wars: The Force Awakens	$2,068.2	7.44	39%
2	Jurassic World	$1,670.4	10.10	49%
3	Furious 7	$1,516.0	7.00	61%
4	Avengers: Age of Ultron	$1,405.4	4.62	51%
5	Minions	$1,159.4	14.67	52%
6	Spectre	$880.7	2.59	41%
7	Inside Out	$857.4	3.90	51%
8	Mission Impossible: Rogue Nation	$682.3	3.55	54%
9	The Hunger Games: Mockingjay–Part 2	$653.4	3.08	41%
10	The Martian	$630.2	4.84	34%

4. Diversity Sells Regardless of Film Genre

Skeptics of the notion that diversity is a plus factor for the bottom line have questioned whether the outsized performance of minority-led films like *Furious 7*, for example, may be more an artifact of genre than audience demand for a diverse cast. Action films sell regardless of the diversity of the actors on the screen, the argument goes.

Table 6 presents peak median box office, by genre and overall cast diversity for 805 top films (ranked by global box office), pooled across the years 2011 to 2015. It reveals that, regardless of genre, median box office peaked for films with casts that were *at least* 21 to 30 percent minority—the cast diversity interval, you will recall, in which median global box office peaked for films of *all* genres in 2015.

Table 6. Peak Median Box Office, by Genre and Overall Cast Diversity, 2011–2015 Films (n = 850)

Percent Minority	Action	Animation	Comedy	Drama	Family	Horror	Sci-fi	Thriller
10% or less	$161.8 (n = 41)	$147.4 (n = 11)	$39.2 (n = 81)	$37.9 (n = 101)	$190.7 (n = 16)	$52.3 (n = 31)	$174.4 (n = 6)	$34.6 (n = 10)
11%–20%	$176.8 (n = 44)	$198.7 (n = 12)	$44.0 (n = 46)	$35.5 (n = 47)	$158.4 (n = 7)	$85.4 (n = 17)	$226.0 (n = 10)	$62.7 (n = 15)
21%–30%	**$219.9** (n = 45)	$290.6 (n = 8)	**$78.8** (n = 28)	$34.5 (n = 25)	**$506.2** (n = 7)	$47.2 (n = 3)	**$269.7** (n = 8)	$22.0 (n = 6)
31%–40%	$131.9 (n = 15)	$295.9 (n = 4)	$52.4 (n = 17)	$36.5 (n = 6)	$44.0 (n = 1)	$87.9 (n = 1)	$208.3 (n = 6)	$32.3 (n = 8)
41%–50%	$133.6 (n = 6)	**$500.2** (n = 5)	$52.1 (n = 10)	**$48.1** (n = 7)	— (n = 0)	$7.2 (n = 1)	$184.7 (n = 4)	**$90.8** (n = 2)
Over 50%	$55.7 (n = 14)	$84.2 (n = 2)	$32.3 (n = 19)	$31.9 (n = 23)	$63.4 (n = 4)	**$90.9** (n = 1)	$67.1 (n = 2)	$57.3 (n = 4)

Television[2]

1. Broadcast Scripted Shows with Diverse Casts Continue to Excel in Ratings

Figure 87 presents an analysis of median ratings (18–49, white households, black households, Latino households, and Asian American households) by minority cast share for broadcast scripted shows from the 2014–15 season. The general upward trajectory of the lines, as in the previous reports in this series, suggests that cast diversity has a meaningful, positive relationship to the ratings bottom line. For white households (4.98 ratings points), black households (6.24 ratings points), and Latino households (2.77 ratings points), median ratings peaked for shows featuring casts that were majority minority. Eleven shows fell into to this cast diversity interval during the 2014–15 season, including *Empire* (Fox), *Black-ish* (ABC), *Law and Order: Special Victims Unit* (NBC), *Hawaii Five-O* (CBS), and *The Carmichael Show* (NBC).

Meanwhile, for viewers 18–49 (2.37 ratings points) and Asian American households (2.96 ratings points), median ratings peaked for shows with casts that were from 41 to 50 percent minority. Examples of these shows include *Brooklyn Nine-Nine* (Fox), *Elementary* (CBS), *New Girl* (Fox), and *Sleepy Hollow* (Fox).

Despite the obvious popularity of more diverse shows across the various audience segments, it is worth noting that the majority of broadcast scripted shows examined in 2015—as in previous years—had casts that were only 20 percent minority or less (67 of 123 shows).

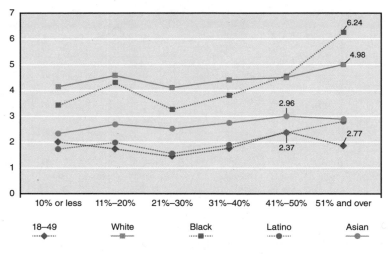

Median Ratings by Minority Cast Share, 18–49 and HH Race,
Broadcast Scripted, 2014–2015 Season (n = 127)

Figure 87.

2. Audience Engagement with Social Media Peaks for Broadcast Scripted Shows with Casts that Reflect America

Figure 88 charts the median volume of tweets and unique authors for broadcast scripted shows by cast diversity interval for the 2014–15 season. It shows that the median volume of tweets (9,400) peaked for shows with casts that were from 31 to 40 percent minority—the cast diversity interval that contained the minority share of the population in 2014–15. The median number of unique Twitter authors also peaked in this interval (2,800), though the differences across intervals were less pronounced than with the volume of tweets. Twenty-seven shows fell into this cast diversity interval, including *Grey's Anatomy* (ABC), *Parks and Recreation* (NBC), *The Flash* (CW), and *The 100* (CW).

By contrast, social engagement for shows which had casts that were less than 20 percent minority (i.e., the majority of shows) was significantly lower. That is, the median volume of tweets for both shows with casts between 11 and 20 percent minority and for those with casts 10 percent or less minority was just 5,100.

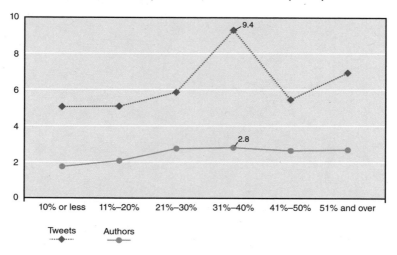

Median Tweets and Authors (000s) by Minority Cast Share,
Broadcast Scripted Shows, 2014–2015 Season (n = 122)

Figure 88.

3. Ratings Continue to Peak among Cable Scripted Shows with Diverse Casts

Figure 89 applies the ratings analyses presented above for broadcast scripted shows to the case of cable scripted shows from the 2014–15 season. Though the trajectory of the lines reveal that relatively diverse cable scripted shows excel with most audience segments, the picture for cable is considerably more complex than the one depicted above for broadcast. As noted in earlier reports in this series, this is largely due to the niche marketing strategy adopted by key cable networks that almost exclusively target specific ethnic and/or racial groups (e.g., BET, TVONE, El Rey, etc.).

Indeed, median ratings peaked among black households (3.08 ratings points) for cable scripted shows that had majority-minority casts. Twenty shows fell into this diversity interval during the 2014–15 season, including black-themed sitcoms and dramas like *Being Mary Jane* (BET), *The Game* (BET), *Survivor's Remorse* (Starz), *Power* (Starz), *The Haves and the Have Nots* (OWN), and *Love Thy Neighbor* (OWN).

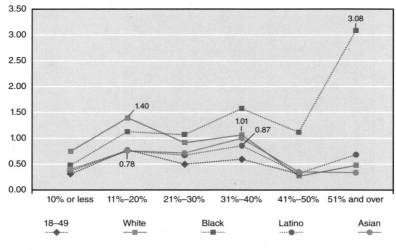

Median Ratings by Minority Cast Share, 18–49 and HH Race,
Cable Scripted Shows, 2014–2015 Season (n = 198)

Figure 89.

Meanwhile, among Asian American households (1.01 ratings points) and Latino households (.87 ratings points), median ratings peaked for cable scripted shows featuring casts that were from 31 to 40 percent minority—the cast diversity interval encompassing the minority share of the U.S. population in 2015 (i.e., 38.4 percent). This interval contained 19 shows during the 2014–15 season, including *Fear the Walking Dead* (AMC), *Major Crimes* (TNT), *Suits* (USA), and *Jessie* (Disney).

By contrast, median ratings for white households (1.40 ratings points) and viewers 18–49 (.78 ratings points) peaked for cable scripted shows with casts that were from 11 to 20 percent minority during the 2014–15 season. Examples of the 36 shows falling into this cast diversity interval include the following: *American Horror Story* (FX), *Salem* (WGN), *Sons of Anarchy* (FX), and *The Librarians* (TNT).

4. Audience Engagement with Social Media Peaks for Cable Scripted Shows with Casts from 21 to 30 Percent Minority

Figure 90 charts the median volume of tweets for cable scripted shows by cast diversity interval for the 2014–15 season. It shows that the median volume of tweets (3,400) peaked for cable scripted shows with casts that were from 21 to 30 percent minority. Twenty-three shows fell into this cast diversity interval that season, including *The Walking Dead* (AMC), *The Fosters* (Freeform), and *Pretty Little Liars* (Freeform). Majority-minority cast shows and those with casts that were from 11 to 20 percent minority followed closely behind, both with median volume of tweets of 3,200. Meanwhile, the median number of unique Twitter authors (1,500) peaked for cable scripted shows with majority-minority casts.

Median Tweets and Authors (000s) by Minority Cast Share, Cable Scripted Shows, 2014–2015 Season (n = 187)

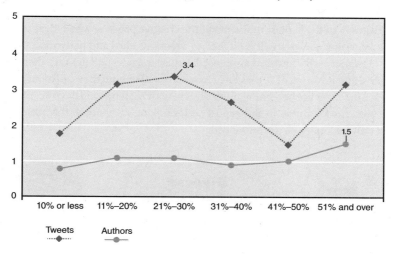

Figure 90.

Conclusion: Setting the Record Straight

"It's always a weird conversation when you're trying to explain how a film about kids from Inglewood can be mainstream, but you don't have the same conversation about a very specific set of kids in suburban Chicago or South Boston."

—*Rick Famuyiwa*

"Networks say, 'We're on board with diversity,' and they'll develop it, but they seldom program it."

—*Eva Longoria*

The goal of the Hollywood Diversity Report series is to the set the record straight with respect to the myths, half-truths, and excuses industry decision makers have used to justify business-as-usual on the diversity front. Since the last report, the good news is that minorities and women have made some progress, particularly in television, which is currently engaged in what might be characterized as a "golden age."

The bad news is that despite these gains, minorities and women remained underrepresented on every measure in television during the 2014–15 season. Meanwhile, because underrepresentation was much more severe for minorities and women in film in 2015, both groups had much further to go in this sector before they approached anything resembling proportionate representation.

Still, the most important takeaway from this report—and the three before it—is, yes, diversity does indeed sell in film and television. This is not to say that it is enough to hastily append a few actors of color or women to a cast that is at its core white and male. No, the appeal of diversity for today's audiences has everything to do with the storytelling, which extends beyond who's in front of the camera to the earliest moments of the creative process, when ideas for films and television shows are first pitched to agents, studios and networks.

Diversity sells, first and foremost, because today's audiences are themselves diverse and in search of stories and characters with whom they can identify. And these audiences are becoming more diverse with each passing day, meaning that the patterns identified in this report series linking diversity to the bottom line will only become more pronounced.

Indeed, the combined buying power of people of color in America approached $3.5 trillion in 2015,[3] and these growing, diverse audience segments purchased more movie tickets and watched more television on a per capita basis than their white counterparts. For the Hollywood industry to continue to produce as many low-performing films and television shows as it does, which are not very diverse, simply does not make good business sense in light of these facts.

Telling It Like It Is

The problem, as we have pointed out in earlier reports, is that the Hollywood industry is not currently structured to make the most of today's market realities. The studios, networks, talent agencies, and academies are demographically and culturally out of step with the diverse audiences on which their collective future will increasingly depend.

Pipeline initiatives are useful interventions but no panacea for Hollywood's diversity problems. In the final analysis, it's not about the availability of diverse talent. There's more than enough of that to go around. It's more about the failure of Hollywood organizations, at their own peril, to find ways to include this talent beyond just the margins.

Hollywood's diversity problems begin at the very top of the studios and networks, in the executive suites, where decisions are made about what gets made and with what size production and marketing budgets. Unfortunately, the individuals in these decision-making positions (typically white men) are not motivated to share their power with diverse women and men whose reservoirs of experience equip them with the perspectives necessary to connect more effectively with today's audiences.

Despite false claims to the contrary, there is no tradeoff in Hollywood today between diversity and profitability. Diversity is clearly a plus factor for the bottom line. Nor is there a tradeoff between diversity and quality. Quality storytelling *plus* rich, diverse performances *equals* box office and ratings success. Year after year, the evidence supporting this equation continues to mount.

Endnotes

1. For these analyses, simple return on investment is computed as follows: (Revenue – Budget)/Budget. That is, the higher the ratio, the higher the rate of return.

2. Only dramas and comedies are considered in these analyses.

3. "2015 Multicultural Economy Report," Selig Center for Economic Growth, University of Georgia, Athens, GA.

Acknowledgements *(continued from copyright page)*

Banaji, Mahzarin R. and Anthony G. Greenwald, "On Stereotypes." Excerpt from *Blindspot: Hidden Biases of Good People* by Mahzarin R. Banaji and Anthony G. Greenwald, copyright © 2013 by Mahzarin R. Banaji and Anthony G. Greenwald. Used by permission of Bantam Books, an imprint of Random House, a division of Penguin Random House LLC. All rights reserved.

Banks, William C., "Cyber Espionage and Electronic Surveillance: Beyond the Media Coverage," *Emory Law Journal*, Vol. 66:513 (2017). Reprinted by permission of the author.

Bendix, Jeffrey, et al., "Top 2018 Challenges," republished with permission of Advanstar Communications, Inc., from *Medical Economics*, December 25, 2017; permission conveyed through Copyright Clearance Center, Inc.

Berkshire, Jennifer C., "There Goes the Neighborhood School," *The Progressive*, December 29, 2014. Reprinted by permission of the publisher.

Braun, Bob, "Pearson, NJ, Spying on Social Media of Students Taking PARCC Tests" from Bob Braun's Ledger, March 13, 2015. http://www.bobbraunsledger.com/breaking-pearson-nj-spying-on-social-media-of-students-taking-parcc-tests/. Reprinted by permission of the author.

Butler, Judith, excerpt from *Gender Trouble*. Republished with permission of Routledge/Taylor & Francis Books, Inc., from Judith Butler, *Gender Trouble: Feminism and the Subversion of Identity*, copyright © 1990 Routledge/Taylor & Francis Books, Inc.; permission conveyed through Copyright Clearance Center, Inc.

Childish Gambino, "This Is America." Words and Music by DONALD GLOVER, JEFFREY WILLIAMS and LUDWIG GORANSSON. Copyright © 2018 WARNER-TAMERLANE PUBLISHING CORP., SONGS OF ROCK NATION, LUDOVIN MUSIC, ARTIST 101 PUBLISHING GROUP, 300 RAINWATER MUSIC, ATLANTIC SONGS, YOUNG STONER LIFE PUBLISHING LLC, CHILDISH INDUSTRIES and SONGS OF UNIVERSAL INC. All Rights on behalf of itself, SONGS OF ROCK NATION, LUDOVIN MUSIC, ARTIST 101 PUBLIHING GROUP and 300 RAINWATER MUSIC administered by WARNER-TAMERLANE PUBLISHING CORP. All Rights Reserved. Used by permission of ALFRED MUSIC and Hal Leonard Corporation.

Cisneros, Henry and Carlos Gutierrez, "Working with Mexico is the Key to Strong American Border Security," first published in *The Hill*, July 2, 2018. Copyright © 2018 Capitol Hill Publishing. Reprinted by permission of Featurewell.com, Inc.

Cockrall-King, Jennifer, "Chicago: The Vertical Farm." Reprinted from Jennifer Cockrall-King, *Food and the City: Urban Agriculture and the New Food Revolution* (Amherst, NY: Prometheus Books, 2012), pp. 263–282. Copyright © 2012 by Jennifer Cockrall-King. All rights reserved. Used with permission of the publisher; www.prometheusbooks.com

Dawson, Julia, "Sound Off: Free Times Misses the Mark on Gentrification," *Free Times*, June 14, 2017. Reprinted by permission of the publisher.

Duhigg, Charles, "Outcry Over EpiPen Prices Hasn't Made Them Lower," From *The New York Times*, June 5, 2017, copyright © 2017 The New York Times. All rights reserved. Used by permission and protected by the Copyright Laws of the United States. The printing, copying, redistribution, or retransmission of this Content without express written permission is prohibited.

Fayyed, Abdallah, "The Criminalization of Gentrifying Neighborhoods," *The Atlantic*, December 20, 2017. Copyright © 2017 The Atlantic Media Co., as first published in The Atlantic Magazine. All rights reserved. Distributed by Tribune Content Agency, LLC.

Lamott, Anne, "Shitty first Drafts" from *Bird by Bird: Some Instructions on Writing* by Anne Lamott, copyright © 1994 by Anne Lamott. Used by permission of Pantheon Books, an imprint of Knopf Doubleday Publishing Group, a division of Penguin Random House LLC. All rights reserved.

Larocca, Amy, "The Wellness Epidemic," *New York Magazine*, June 26, 2017. Reprinted by permission of New York Media, LLC.

Levy, Ariel, "Either/Or: Sports, Sex, and the Case of Caster Semenya," *The New Yorker*, November 30, 2009. Reprinted by permission of the author.

Love, Tirhakah, "Marvel Ain't Foolin' Nobody," Inverse.com, May 4, 2017. Reprinted by permission.

Macdonald, Robert R., "Charleston's Landscape of Memory: The Gentrification of History," *The Charleston Chronicle*, February 23, 2018. Reprinted by permission of the author and The Charleston Chronicle.

Marantz, Andrew, "Ready for Prime Time: After Twenty-Five Years as a Road Comic, Leslie Jones Becomes a Star," *The New Yorker*, January 4, 2016. Copyright © 2016 Conde Nast. Reprinted by permission.

Matsakis, Louise, "The Supreme Court Just Greatly Strengthened Digital Privacy," *Wired*, June 22, 2018. Copyright © 2018. Conde Nast. Reprinted by permission.

Moore, Eva, "Moving up Main: The Cottontown/Elmwood Park Corridor Is Booming," *Free Times*, May 31, 2017. Reprinted by permission of the publisher.

Pan, Yuqing, "The U.S. Cities That Are Gentrifying the Fastest—You'll Never Guess No. 1," Realtor.com, January 23, 2017. Reprinted by permission.

Ralph J. Bunche Center for African American Studies at UCLA, from *2017 Hollywood Diversity Report: Setting the Record Straight* pages 61–74. Ralph J. Bunche Center for African American Studies at UCLA, February 2017. Reprinted with permission.

Sage, William M., "Minding Ps and Qs: The Political and Policy Questions Framing Health Care Spending." Republished with permission from Sage Publications, from *The Journal of Law, Medicine & Ethics*, 44 (2016): 559–568; permission conveyed through Copyright Clearance Center, Inc.

Sellers, Frances Stead, "British Health Care: Free for Citizens, Low-Priced for Visitors. Is That the Whole Story?" From *The Washington Post*, March 24, 2014. Copyright © 2014 The Washington Post. All rights reserved. Used by permission and protected by the Copyright Laws of the United States. The printing, copying, redistribution, or retransmission of this Content without express written permission is prohibited.

Sisson, Paul, "Why Our Health Care Costs So Much—and Why Fixes Aren't Likely." *The San Diego Union-Tribune*, March 18, 2017. Reprinted with permission of The San Diego Union-Tribune.

Steinkuehler, Constance and Sean Duncan, "Scientific Habits of Mind in Virtual Worlds." Republished with permission of SPRINGER-VERLAG DORDRECHT, from *Journal of Science Education and Technology* 17, 2008. Copyright © Springer Science + Business Media. Permission conveyed via Copyright Clearance Center, Inc.

Suárez-Orozco, Marcelo M. and Carola Suárez-Orozco, "How Immigrants Become 'Other.'" Republished with permission of Rowman & Littlefield Publishing Group, from *Arizona Firestorm*, ed. by Otto Santa Ana (2012); permission conveyed through Copyright Clearance Center, Inc.

The Economist, "The Case for Building a Wall to Keep Canadians Out." Republished with permission of The Economist Newspaper Ltd., from *The Economist*, June 3, 2017; permission conveyed through Copyright Clearance Center, Inc.